Revolting New York

Revolting New York

HOW 400 YEARS OF RIOT, REBELLION, UPRISING,
AND REVOLUTION SHAPED A CITY

GENERAL EDITORS

NEIL SMITH
DON MITCHELL

EDITORS

ERIN SIODMAK

JENJOY ROYBAL

MARNIE BRADY

BRENDAN P. O'MALLEY

THE UNIVERSITY OF GEORGIA PRESS
Athens

© 2018 by the University of Georgia Press
Athens, Georgia 30602
www.ugapress.org
All rights reserved
Set in 10/12.5 Minion Pro Regular by Kaelin Chappell Broaddus
Printed and bound by Thomson-Shore, Inc.
The paper in this book meets the guidelines for permanence
and durability of the Committee on Production Guidelines for
Book Longevity of the Council on Library Resources.

Most University of Georgia Press titles are
available from popular e-book vendors.

Printed in the United States of America
22 21 20 19 18 P 5 4 3 2 1

Library of Congress Cataloging-in-Publication Data pending
ISBN 9780820352817 (hardcover : alk. paper)
ISBN 9780820352824 (paperback: alk. paper)
ISBN 9780820352800 (ebook)

CONTENTS

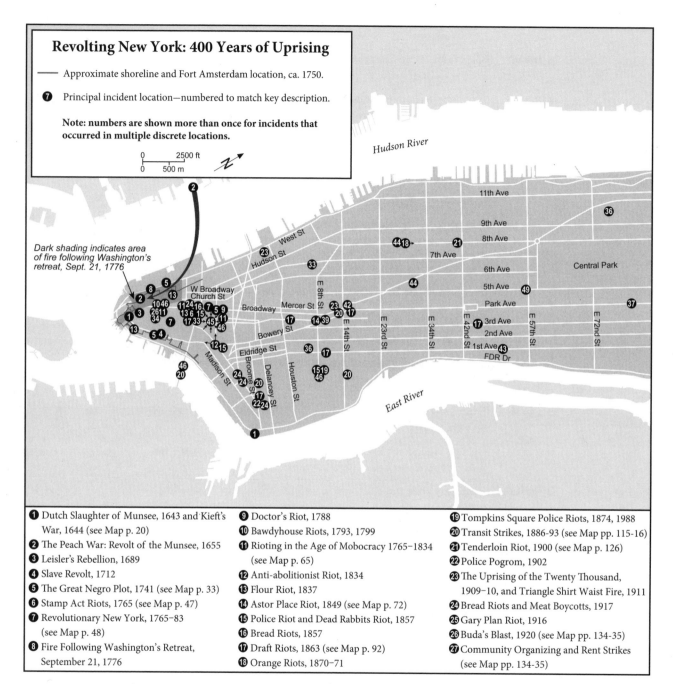

Revolting New York: 400 Years of Uprising

—— Approximate shoreline and Fort Amsterdam location, ca. 1750.

❼ Principal incident location—numbered to match key description.

Note: numbers are shown more than once for incidents that occurred in multiple discrete locations.

0 — 2500 ft
0 — 500 m

Dark shading indicates area of fire following Washington's retreat, Sept. 21, 1776

Hudson River

East River

Central Park

11th Ave · 9th Ave · 8th Ave · 7th Ave · 6th Ave · 5th Ave · Park Ave · 3rd Ave · 2nd Ave · 1st Ave · FDR Dr

West St · Hudson St · W Broadway · Church St · Broadway · Mercer St · E 8th St · E 14th St · E 23rd St · E 34th St · E 42nd St · E 57th St · E 72nd St · Madison St · Broome St · Delancey St · Houston St · Bowery · Eldridge St · Bowery St

❶ Dutch Slaughter of Munsee, 1643 and Kieft's War, 1644 (see Map p. 20)
❷ The Peach War: Revolt of the Munsee, 1655
❸ Leisler's Rebellion, 1689
❹ Slave Revolt, 1712
❺ The Great Negro Plot, 1741 (see Map p. 33)
❻ Stamp Act Riots, 1765 (see Map p. 47)
❼ Revolutionary New York, 1765–83 (see Map p. 48)
❽ Fire Following Washington's Retreat, September 21, 1776

❾ Doctor's Riot, 1788
❿ Bawdyhouse Riots, 1793, 1799
⓫ Rioting in the Age of Mobocracy 1765–1834 (see Map p. 65)
⓬ Anti-abolitionist Riot, 1834
⓭ Flour Riot, 1837
⓮ Astor Place Riot, 1849 (see Map p. 72)
⓯ Police Riot and Dead Rabbits Riot, 1857
⓰ Bread Riots, 1857
⓱ Draft Riots, 1863 (see Map p. 92)
⓲ Orange Riots, 1870–71

⓳ Tompkins Square Police Riots, 1874, 1988
⓴ Transit Strikes, 1886–93 (see Map pp. 115–16)
㉑ Tenderloin Riot, 1900 (see Map p. 126)
㉒ Police Pogrom, 1902
㉓ The Uprising of the Twenty Thousand, 1909–10, and Triangle Shirt Waist Fire, 1911
㉔ Bread Riots and Meat Boycotts, 1917
㉕ Gary Plan Riot, 1916
㉖ Buda's Blast, 1920 (see Map pp. 134–35)
㉗ Community Organizing and Rent Strikes (see Map pp. 134–35)

Revolting New York: 400 Years of Uprising.
Cartography: Joe Stoll, Syracuse University Cartography Lab and Map Shop.

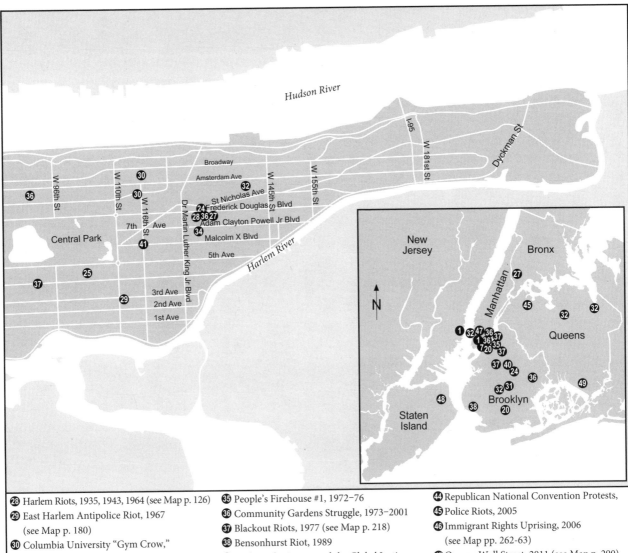

Revolting New York

The Lightning Flash of Revolt

DON MITCHELL

There are many ways to tell the story of New York. It can be told through its architecture or its infrastructure, through the lives of its immigrants or those of its elite. It can be told as a history of progressive betterment (with however many reversals) or perpetual decline (with however many moments of unexpected triumph). The landscape can be revealed as seen from the summits of finance (one clever financial instrument after another, one multibillion-dollar deal after another) or as seen from the troughs of racism (one lost job after another, one brutal murder after another, one struggle for justice after another). The story of New York could be titled *City of Disorder* or *Triumph of Order*, or, as is the case, both.[1] The landscape—the built form of the city—can be seen as the product of a few outsized figures (Jacob Astor, Frederick Law Olmsted, Robert Moses, Michael Bloomberg) or of millions of anonymous slaves, hod carriers, stone crushers, ironworkers, glaziers, electricians, and roofers who actually put in the labor required to make it rise, and the store clerks, cooks, waitresses, housecleaners, building superintendents, and street cleaners who keep it ticking. It could be told from the perspective of immigrant girl workers in the garment factories or the "club" and "society" women set on aiding and reforming those girls. Or the story of New York could be told through its culture: the artists and musicians nurtured or pushed away, the shifting literary scenes, the Broadway plays and musicals. It can be

told as a story of changed political fortunes as the Dutch give way to the British, the British to the Americans, the Whigs to the Republicans, the Republicans to the Tammany Democrats, Tammany to the Progressives and back to Tammany, the New Deal Democrats to the law-and-order Republicans and millionaire businessmen, and on to progressive Democrats. Or it could be told, simply, as a story of real estate.

Another way to tell the story of New York is as a story of revolt—a many-headed, deeply contradictory history of riots, rebellions, uprisings, and revolutions. Riots, rebellions, uprisings, and revolutions expose the social geography of a city—the Harlem Renaissance writer Alain Locke described the 1935 Harlem Riot as "a revealing flash of lightning"— even as they force the remaking (or the reinforcement) of that geography. Revolts arise out of the very social and physical structure of the city, and when they do, they suddenly illuminate it. The reaction to revolt is just as illuminating. *Revolting New York* tells the story of New York's evolution— exposes and examines its historical geography—as a story of near-continuous popular (and sometimes not-so-popular) uprising. In doing so it brings to light how social struggle over the city's architecture and infrastructure, its progressive development and regressive decline, its flows of capital and racist practices, its immigrant neighborhoods and policing strategies, the rights of its workers and the demands of its elites, its culture, and its real estate has shaped and continues to shape the urban landscape. A close focus on revolt exposes the geography of *power* that undergirds the city.

❏ ❏ ❏

Surveying the history of riots, revolts, and revolutions in New York from the first Dutch settlement to the present makes one thing clear: just how remarkably continuous urban uprisings are. No era passes—rarely a decade passes—without being marked by violent revolt (and counterrevolt): slave uprisings, police riots, militant strikes, bombings and arson, ritual overturnings of the social order, spontaneous outbursts, organized assaults, highly localized tumults and citywide boycotts, shady conspiracies and out-in-the-open grabs at power. It is almost as if social peace is the exception, a small island of calm in an always-churning sea. There is some validity to this sense. Certainly contestation and social struggle (conflict over relations of class, race, ethnicity, sexuality, and gender, as well as over political and economic power and who wields it) are always present. But, of course, sometimes, indeed much of the time, struggle takes the form not of violent uprising but of steady organizing and behind-the-scenes positioning, as powerful interests—New York's shifting class of elites and the institutions they control—exercise a good degree of hegemony over everyday urban life. Focusing the story of New York on its historical geography of riots, rebellions, uprisings, and revolutions, then, provides something of a distorted picture that tends to underplay both the steady work of organizing and the ways in which power squelches upheaval, making rebellion all but unthinkable. But if the story told in these pages is a distortion, it is a helpful distortion. By training our sights on moments of violent upheaval we can better see how the very substance of the city—its class, race, and ethnic geography—is made and remade, or is preserved and protected. We can see in whose interest the landscape is built and what happens to those who must necessarily be part of it (slaves, working people,

The Folly of England and the Ruin of America: **The Stamp Act Riots in New York (drawn in 1886).**
Courtesy, Art and Picture Collection, New York Public Library.

immigrants, many women) but who are excluded from its formal mechanisms of power.

The long history of riots, rebellions, uprisings, and revolutions in New York City shows not only that the New York landscape is violent but that violence is often productive. That is, it is an engine of change, both in the built form of the city and in how it operates socially. Violent upheaval influences investment decisions—how capital circulates in or flees from the urban landscape—and thus where and how New Yorkers can live, work, and play. Urban violence, whether organized or disorganized, shapes laws, leads to new strategies of policing, and influences the development of institutions (like the police department itself).

Violence is not only the property of rioters, revolutionaries, and others seeking to upset the existing order. It is also a tool of those in power who seek to maintain that order or to enhance their position within it. Military and police violence is neither new nor exceptional in the streets of the city. From the earliest days—the great slave revolts of 1712 and 1741 (chapter 2), for example—authorities have used violent force to quell disorder, teach lessons, and impose their rule. What constitutes "violence" and how it should be understood within the ongoing life of a city is thus itself a matter of controversy.[2] When exercised by authorities, "force" is often not considered to be the same as violence, even when that force is deadly and seemingly out of control. Yet in its origins, the word "violence" implies "vehemence." Vehemence is a quite apt descriptor of how the force of authority has been exercised in New York, from white officials stringing up and burning at the stake rebellious slaves and their supporters, to police opening fire on unruly crowds, to militiamen driving into a mob with their bayonets lowered (chapters 5 and 6), to city officials prosecuting agitators who are seen to be fomenting rebellion (chapter 12), to cops and bulldozers ripping into the Occupy Wall Street encampment (chapter 19). And it is not too much of a stretch to see

Otto Boetticher, *Seventh Regiment on Review, Washington Square, New York* (1851).
The Edward W. C. Arnold Collection of New York Prints, Maps, and Pictures, Bequest of Edward W. C. Arnold, 1954, The Metropolitan Museum of Art.

the withholding of force by authorities as itself sometimes an act of violence. For example, during the Tenderloin Race Riot of 1900 (chapter 9), not only did policemen beat and seriously injure African Americans who came to them for protection (an outright act of violence), but they refused to restrain white mobs when they set upon black citizens (an act of omission that promoted the violent reassertion of the racist social order).

However, the word "violence" also implies "impetuosity." In this sense, violence implies unruly behavior, and, as Raymond Williams long ago noted, with this sense a consequential slippage occurs. Unruliness threatens law and order, that is, the existing social order: it is a kind of violence that serves to *violate* "some custom or some dignity." But if violence is physical assault or the use of physical force, then only by a twist of language can all unruliness be deemed violent. As Williams put it, "It is within the assumption of 'unruly,' and not, despite the transfer of the word, of physical force, that loud or vehement (or even strong and persistent) verbal criticism has been commonly described as violent, and the two steps beyond that—threat to some existing arrangement, threat to some actual force—sometimes become a moving staircase to the strong meanings of violence" in the sense of physical assault and the use of force.[3] Because it was vehement, and because it seemed always to threaten to become unruly, picketing by striking workers (and other activists) was understood by courts in the early twentieth century as *necessarily* violent; courts therefore hampered workers' use of the streets to press economic and political claims, as was apparent in the Uprising of the Twenty Thousand and other labor disputes of the era (chapter 8).[4] Even before that, the vehemence with which orators in Tompkins Square criticized city authorities and the capitalist class in 1874 led officials to determine that the unruly crowd had to be put down—that it portended violence—even though it was in fact quite peaceful (chapter 7).

And yet, as they are in any social history, matters are complex. From medieval times to the early nineteenth century, ritualized unruliness—including rioting—was part of the social order itself in European and American societies. Revolution—an *overturning*—was ritualized, particularly on feast days or during festival times (All Hallows' Eve and later Guy Fawkes Day, or Pope Day, in the fall, midsummer, and midwinter, including Christmas, followed by Mardi Gras and similar days in the spring).* The social order was suspended or upended as servants became royalty and elites took on the role of paupers. Marauding bands of the poor demanded that the wealthy hand over bread, meat, and strong drink or risk having their homes or barns torched or their effigies hanged on the common: *treat* or *trick*. The ruled became the unruly, at least for a time, and they claimed what they saw as being rightfully theirs. Rioting was a means of redistribution. Ritualized revolt thus overturned and reinforced the social order even as it often threatened to break its bounds and truly revolutionize the social world. Elites tried hard to shape, control, direct, and deploy the mob violence that was an essential part of ritualized unruliness, to put it to particular, often factional ends, not always with total success (chapters 2, 3, and 4). If ritualized mob violence has, since the nineteenth century, been shorn of much of its political force, it has not entirely disappeared, as the highly ritualized rioting after Super Bowl, World Series, or NCAA championship victories or the generalized debauchery of spring break or Saint Patrick's Day in Manhattan make clear.[5] It also echoes in the looting that often accompanies rioting. As a mayor's commission reported after the 1935 Harlem Riot, the people of Harlem saw looting as a chance "to seize what rightfully belonged to them but had long been withheld" (chapter 12).[6]

Ritualized rioting is not rebellious; that is, it is not necessarily directly aimed at challenging the authority of the social order. Nonetheless, it can have revolutionary effects,

---

* During the nineteenth century, the Fourth of July took on something of the traditional midsummer festivities in New York. Beer was rolled out early in the morning, and fireworks and pistol shots split the air all day amidst all manner of carousing.

By the end of the 1990s, the carnivalesque had returned to protest. Here the Rude Mechanical Orchestra performs at the Free University, May 1, 2012.

Photo by Manissa M. Maharawal, used by permission.

if revolution is understood not only as an overturning but as an alteration.[7] Rioting, whether directly rebellious or not, induces change. The Astor Place Riot in 1849 (chapter 5) not only exposed a tense class geography (Astor Place was where elite neighborhoods butted up against plebeian districts) but also induced a broad shift in that geography as elites moved north in reaction. Similarly, the Tenderloin Race Riot in 1900 (chapter 9) was crucial in inducing African American migration into Harlem, while in the aftermath of the Occupy Wall Street encampment, not only were the global class politics of contemporary capitalism exposed and contested, so too was the landscape of the Wall Street neighborhood altered as "defensible spaces"—already prominent since the 1995 terrorist attack on the World Trade Center—were even further hardened, public spaces closed off, and the laws and rules governing publicly accessible but privately owned space reconsidered.* Each of these alterations were in and of themselves small, but they add up. The long historical geography of revolt and riot in New York City is revolutionary in the sense that popular uprisings, and the reactions to them, have constantly remade—altered, revolutionized—the cityscape. This has been (to borrow another phrase from Raymond Williams) a "long revolution," not just an instantaneous overturning but a steady accretion of change, progressive and regressive, that has made the contemporary urban world what it is.[8] By focusing on the sharp moments of upheaval that have marked the city from the beginning, *Revolting New York* charts this long revolution.

❑ ❑ ❑

New York was born out of the flames of revolt (chapter 1). The Munsee uprising against the Dutch colony on Manhattan helped convince the authorities in Holland to sell out to the English. As the British took over, New York quickly became the largest slaveholding city outside the South. The city was second only to Charleston in the importance of slavery to its economy, a fact that persisted well into the nineteenth century. Slave revolts were a constant threat and deeply consequential. In 1712 and especially in 1741, slave uprisings not only led to massive moral panics but also truly threatened both the stability and the economy of the colony, even as some aspects of each uprising (again especially in 1741) traded in precisely the forms of ritualized unruliness that had long been part of the social order. But this was a serious upheaval in 1741. The "Great Negro Conspiracy" seemed to portend not a preservation of the social order but its radical overturning, especially since the rebellion also seemed to be upending the *racial* order. The response was furious, as chapter 2 details, with hundreds of slaves being hanged, im-

---

* Partially in reaction to an earlier, 1920 terrorist bombing on Wall Street, city elites formulated plans for the city's deindustrialization, laying the groundwork for the mass dislocation of production from the city after World War II. See the vignette "Bombs and Boatmen."

prisoned, or transported out of the colony. From its earliest days, New York's racial order, including its racial geography, has been an uneasy one and has regularly exploded in riot and rebellion.

Slavery was the most prominent form of servitude in New York, but it was not the only one. Indenture was common, as was the impressment of young men into the navy (and later their drafting into the army). Resistance to impressment also turned riotous, even as it was caught up in popular dissent over British colonial policies, including tariffs and taxation. Perhaps the high point of ritualistic rioting in the colonial era came with the passage and attempted enforcement of the Stamp Act in 1765, an important prelude to the Revolution (chapter 3). But the rituals were shifting. On the one hand, rioting and revolt were understood to be, and used as, political tools to contest colonial rulers and thus represented a broad-based discontent. If white mechanics and artisans were the men in the street, they gave force to a set of complaints also articulated by elites in other venues (legislative chambers, courts of law, and so forth). On the other hand, class relations in the city were shifting: mechanics and artisans were also working for themselves, pursuing their own interests. Elites had to wonder how much control they had over the tumult of the Stamp Act Riots. The lightning bolt of riot, in this instance, seemed to illuminate a new class landscape. Even more, it seemed to light a way for slaves and women to grasp the reins of power, a prospect that frightened city elites.

The British Parliament responded by stepping up impressment and increasing penalties for mutiny (and the colonies were by now in a near-constant state of mutiny). The largely plebeian Sons of Liberty encouraged children "to nightly trampouze the Streets" and made a show of burning the colonial governor in effigy, lighting massive bonfires, and erecting Liberty Poles, pushing New Yorkers toward revolution (chapter 4). New York became a crucible of revolt, but during the war it was captured by the British and became one of their most important redoubts. Many slaves and free blacks sided with the British, since it was clear that the rev-

olutionaries had little interest in abolishing slavery or promoting equality. When, after the war, the British evacuated the city, many black people fled too. New York remained a slave town, but its black population was now quite diminished (the proportion of black people in the city population would not recover its pre–Revolutionary War level until the Great Migration around World War I). Radical control of the city government after the war meant that a vicious anti-Toryism prevailed even as a new foundation for the city as a financial center was laid.

Race and class struggle defined the city during the nineteenth century, and each of the major, and most of the minor, riots of the century were directly related either to racist practices in the city or to its shifting class geography as New York became at once a financial and industrial center (chapters 5–9). Ritualistic, *communal* violence faded as a social force as new divisions emerged in society. Partially as a result, the police force—long tied to political factions—was reformed and reformed again, though it never lost its role as the police for elite classes. The police became a means of enforcing—that is, *forcing*—social order, though as the struggles among policing agencies in the 1850s showed, this was hardly a simple or straightforward matter.

Unrest in the city was tightly linked to the vagaries of first an increasingly national and then an increasingly global capitalist economy. Hard times led to discontent among artisans and laborers, disgust with bankers and other elites, and efforts to organize the working classes into a political force. Such efforts were intertwined with ethnic or sectarian struggles (such as between Irish Catholic and Irish Protestant immigrants) and also, especially still, with race. The intense racism of the 1863 Draft Riots—the deadliest riots in American history to that point—was extraordinary primarily in its scope. Earlier riots against African Americans and abolitionists had already reshaped the racial geography of the city, and the Tenderloin Race Riot of 1900 in many ways replicated the virulent attacks on black people in 1863. But the Draft Riots (chapter 6) *were* extraordinary in other ways. They began as an out-and-out insurrection against civilian

***Charge of the Police at the
Tribune Office, 1863 Draft Riot.***
*Harper's Pictorial History of
the Civil War* (1894).
Library of Congress, Pictures
and Photographs Division.

and military authorities. Only later did they transmogrify into vicious attacks on African Americans, who were perceived by many whites to be undeserving beneficiaries of a hopeless war. Soon rioting spread to other cities. The North, not the South, now seemed to be in a state of rebellion. Troops were rushed back from the front and bivouacked in parks all around the city.

Property destruction was widespread during the Draft Riots, and as the city rebuilt—amid working-class demands for rent control—the state legislature passed a new tenement law in hopes of creating safer, more sanitary homes for the city's immigrants and workers. The law did not achieve its goals, but it did significantly shape the city's landscape, as a postwar building boom, which lasted until the economic crisis of 1873, rapidly expanded the city's footprint (chapter 7). The 1873 economic crisis was severe: nearly a hundred thousand people lost their homes, as unemployment soared. As workers organized (especially immigrants, many of whom were radicals who had fled Europe after the 1848 revolutions), the city government, especially the police commissioner, did all it could to thwart them, banning or disrupting meetings. In January 1874 the police rioted against workers and their families in a mass meeting at Tompkins Square, then the heart of Manhattan's Little Germany. Elite New Yorkers gloried over how the police "broke and drove the crowd" and prevented the formation of the "American Commune." If there had ever been any doubt in whose interests the police policed, it was permanently laid to rest in Tompkins Square. So too was Tompkins Square itself presumably permanently laid to rest as a center for radical organizing, as, in the wake of the police riot, the square was transformed into a leafy park.*

Throughout the nineteenth century, city authorities rarely hesitated to call out the military to put down rioting. By 1893, in the midst of another economic depression, that willingness was extended to Brooklyn, as the New York State militia was called out to support the streetcar companies in their efforts to break the transit unions (chapter 8). Both Manhattan and Brooklyn grew rapidly in the decades after the Civil War. Immigration from Europe was the driving

---

* Permanence is relative: in 1988 Tompkins Square Park once again became the site of a violent police riot (chapter 16).

force, but the deepening of the Industrial Revolution drove formerly rural people into the city as agriculture was restructured across the United States and as new opportunities for work opened up in the major cities. Like Chicago and Manchester, England, New York was a "shock city" of the era, experiencing explosive growth.[9] With the completion of the Brooklyn Bridge in 1883, Manhattan and Brooklyn were knitted together as never before. The new streetcar line across the bridge—together with the extension of horsecar and streetcar lines, as well as elevated railways up and down Manhattan and across Brooklyn—radically transformed the scale at which everyday life was lived for New Yorkers. These advances in transportation also reworked the industrial geography of the city as working-class (and, for that matter, middle-class and elite) neighborhoods could now be built farther from centers of production. The streetcars became the arteries of the city, and if they clogged, it could spell severe economic sickness, if not death. Streetcar workers thus possessed a good degree of power. They also received a great deal of sympathy from city residents—as well as city merchants—who despised the streetcar companies just as, nationally, Americans despised the railroad barons and their monopolies. The transit strike in Brooklyn was intense, and it was only broken through the combined might of 7,500 militiamen and 1,700 policemen deployed to protect and assert the interests of the trolley companies. Class lines were once again starkly drawn across the cityscape.

As the twentieth century dawned, these lines deepened. Communal, racist violence never disappeared—as evidenced by the 1900 Tenderloin Race Riot (chapter 9) and the "police pogrom" on the Lower East Side two years later—but class struggle became the defining feature of urban unrest in the decades before World War II. New York was a hotbed of radicalism: socialists, anarchists, Wobblies, communists, and more all worked the streets and meeting halls, agitating against the capitalist bosses and the Wall Street financiers. Anarchists detonated bombs on Wall Street and elsewhere even as syndicalists sought to gain control of the shop floor. One result was that bankers, city planners, and various elite factions began planning the deindustrialization of the city as early as the early 1920s.[10]

Women could be particularly militant, organizing both on the factory floor and in their apartment buildings, striking for better wages, boycotting gouging butchers and bakers, and fighting for control over their children's schooling (chapter 10). By the outset of the Depression, the Communist Party had become perhaps the dominant radical force, organizing councils of the unemployed, striking workers, and rent strikes all around the city (chapter 11). Rent strikers and work strikers were not infrequently met by police violence—or the violence of thugs hired by landlords and bosses—as the Depression-era streets of working-class and minority neighborhoods, especially black Harlem and the Jewish neighborhoods of the Bronx and Brooklyn, became class battlegrounds. Communists worked hard to overcome racial divides among the working classes and racist attitudes and practices among its white members, though not with complete success.

By this time, ritualistic, carnivalesque aspects of protest seemed to have totally faded. There was little carnivalesque, or even necessarily ritualized, when Harlem's streets exploded into six days of rioting in 1935 in the wake of rumors that police had seriously hurt or even killed a teenager who had been caught shoplifting at the Kress store on 125th Street (chapter 12).* This 1935 riot—and two that followed in 1943 and 1964—also marked a significant shift in the nature of racialized violence in the city. The 1900 Tenderloin Riot had been an attack by white people and the police on black people. It was racist violence aimed directly at the bodies of African Americans (even if it also featured a good deal of property destruction). It was a ra*cist* riot. The 1935 and later Harlem riots were different. While police were injured in these riots (and a number of African Americans lost their lives), black people in Harlem did not target whites, even if they saw the white power structure as deeply culpable in their oppression. Rather, they targeted *property* owned by

---

* Though, as noted, the looting that accompanied the rioting did in fact reenact some of the redistributive aspects of earlier communal rioting.

whites.* These riots may have been "race riots" (as we often think of them), but in temper and object, and, of course, in terms of which racial group took the offensive, they were not at all "race riots" of the same type as the Tenderloin Riot, the Draft Riots, or the Anti-abolitionist Riots.†

Race and racism remained a central site of struggle when students grew militant in the 1960s. The struggle over open admissions in the City University of New York (CUNY, chapter 13) was launched by black and Puerto Rican students demanding greater access for nonwhite students at City College, as well as greater representation of blacks and Puerto Ricans in the curriculum. Pointing to the long history of discrimination and racism in New York's universities and drawing on ideologies and tactics of an insurgent Black Power movement, students at City College, Queens College, Brooklyn College, and elsewhere shut down CUNY for more than a month, convulsing not only the university's administration but the city government. In part by occupying buildings, insisting on black and Puerto Rican prerogatives in running their own strike (by kicking whites out of their occupied buildings and encouraging them to find their own place to protest), City College students were taking the lead from the Columbia University / Morningside Heights student occupation of the year before. At Columbia militant black demands for change at the university and for an end to Columbia's colonialist relationship to Harlem (as exemplified by a Columbia plan to build an essentially segregated gym in Morningside Heights) intersected with militant white students' demands that Columbia sever its ties with the United States' war machine, but black activists were insistent that they remain in full control of their own building occupation, forc-

* Including, significantly, property owned by Jews. If, during the Depression, class solidarity together with a deep radicalism possessed by many immigrant working-class Jews opened up pathways to solidarity between Jews and blacks, it was also the case that the Jewish population itself was class divided. Attacks on Jewish shopkeepers were frequently tinged with anti-Semitism.

† There is evidence in 1935 and 1964 that the rioting drew in radicals and agitators from across the racial spectrum, even as members of the black bourgeoisie worked hard to quell the violence.

ing white protesters to take over other buildings. With the National Guard killing of students at Kent State in 1970, the student movements—for open access, radically transformed curriculum, and an end to war—fused, but not before catalyzing a furious reaction, coordinated in part by the "dirty tricks" office in President Richard Nixon's White House that saw several well-organized riots by "hard hats" in New York's Financial District.

The student strikes, as well as the "hard hat riots," were symptomatic of a remarkable remaking of the American social order that occurred in the 1960s and 1970s. The civil rights movement, the women's movement, radicalized students, and a whole raft of revolutionary organizations pushed hard against the established order, often upsetting it. The battles were often bloody, but the carnivalesque also started to creep back in. Uprisings *overturned* the status quo; uprisings were sometimes revolutionary. This is certainly the case with the Stonewall Riots (chapter 14). Outraged over constantly being harassed and exploited, when queers finally fought back in June 1969, they were met by impressive police violence. But, in turn, they met that violence not only with red-hot rage but also with cleverness and humor, mocking the authorities and at the same time liberating themselves. The result was electrifying. Here was a lightning bolt that struck hard and started a wildfire of social change in what sexuality *is* in New York, in the United States, and around the world—a wildfire we are still living through. Wedding militant resistance to high camp, queers at the end of the 1960s opened up whole new worlds.

But if metaphorical wildfire was rapidly spreading across the arid prairies of bourgeois sexuality, actual fire was literally remaking—or, rather, destroying—the urban landscape itself. By the end of the 1960s, disinvestment, abandonment, and straitened urban finances were combining to make what historian David Nye calls an "antilandscape," a landscape fairly unfit for human habitation.[11] This was no accident. Prominent officials like Daniel Moynihan (Richard Nixon's advisor on urban issues and future New York senator) and Roger Starr (the New York City housing administrator) were

Gay Liberation Front Marches on Times Square, 1969.
Photo by Diana Davies, Manuscript and Archives Division, New York Public Library; used by permission.

publicly calling for the emptying out of "pathological" neighborhoods—"planned shrinkage," Starr called it—so that one day they could be refilled with middle- and upper-class residents, while landlords went on an arson spree, happy to collect insurance payouts. The city government aided the remaking of the city into an antilandscape by withdrawing services—fire and police protection in particular—from disinvested or about-to-be-disinvested neighborhoods (except when residents organized to keep them, as with People's Firehouse #1 in Williamsburg). It was a harrowing time in New York, and it all erupted on July 13, 1977, when the lights went out and the streets in every borough exploded in an orgy of rioting and looting (chapter 15). Poor neighborhoods were particularly hard hit, but few places were totally spared. This was an instantaneous but significantly inchoate uprising. The social order was certainly overturned for a time (echoes of the plebeian riots of the eighteenth and nineteenth centuries are not hard to discern), but the object of rioters', looters',

and arsonists' outrage was not directly obvious. To a degree, people took the blackout as an opportunity to redistribute wealth (or perhaps to just get some needed commodities like diapers and canned food that they could not otherwise regularly afford), but to an even larger degree they seemed to take the blackout as a chance simply to rage—to rage against the inequities, oppressions, and studied disinvestment that had defined their lives over the previous decade.

No one can live in an antilandscape, but they have to live in it anyway. Even before the blackout, residents in disinvested neighborhoods around the city had started taking over empty lots, clearing them out, planting them with vegetables and flowers, and building casitas. Others squatted in abandoned buildings. In the wake of the fiscal crisis, as City Hall lavished its attention on the financial sector and pinned its hopes on the newly built World Trade Center (and yet-to-be-built Battery Park City), people in the neighborhoods planted over the rough edges of abandonment, rewired the

Harvey Wang, *The Garden of Eden 1979*, picturing Adam Purple's amazing garden on the Lower East Side, developed in part as a counter to the concerted disinvestment— the making of an antilandscape— in New York in the 1970s. Photo courtesy of Harvey Wang; used by permission.

tenements, and, ironically, prepared the ground for gentrification by doing the hard work of showing disinvested neighborhoods to in fact be livable, maybe even desirable. Decades of abandonment and decay and a dozen years of arson had opened up a yawning "rent gap" into which the relatively new forces of gentrification now stepped.* Abandonment, on the one hand, and now gentrification, on the other, together with a rapidly eroding commitment to affordable housing in the city, led to an explosion of homelessness in New York (and everywhere else in the United States). By the mid-1980s, Tompkins Square Park was ground zero for those evicted from the New York economy and housing market.[12] It was also the heart of organized resistance against gentrification and thus intolerable to development interests and Mayor Ed Koch alike. In 1988 the cops were sent in to retake the park (chapter 16), and, as they had back in 1874,

the police performed their duties with relish, bludgeoning protesters with their nightsticks, chasing them down on their horses, and, in the words of eyewitnesses, "levitating with . . . hatred." Police riots indeed happen here, in Tompkins Square Park.

Or, as the *New York Times* put it, "class war" had "erupt[ed] on Avenue B." The reconquest of Tompkins Square Park signaled a remarkable class reorientation of the urban landscape, as Manhattan in particular but soon Brooklyn, Queens, and now the Bronx gentrified. Remaking the class landscape has entailed resorting the racial and ethnic landscape, and this process has been fraught, with "intercommunal" struggles not infrequently erupting in Graves End, Howard Beach, Bensonhurst, and Crown Heights, to name the most prominent examples. The first three of these were sparked by racist attacks by whites on black men perceived to be "out of place." The last was sparked by a car crash that killed a small boy—a body guard for the Lubavitcher Rebbe

* A "rent gap" is the difference between actual capitalized land values and potential values if land is put to its "highest and best use."

Menachem Mendel Schneerson ran a red light, was hit by another car, and careened into six-year-old Gavin Cato, killing him and severely injuring his cousin—and brought to the surface all the simmering tensions between the majority Afro-Caribbean population of Crown Heights and the politically powerful Chabad Lubavitch Hasidim who lived there too. The rioting that ensued drove a wedge between a long-standing black-Jewish civil rights coalition in New York, a perhaps fateful split, as police violence against black people in the city has continued unabated.

By the 1990s police brutality against and murder of African Americans in the city had been given a name, "Giuliani Time," in honor of the hard-line mayor whose contempt for radicals, people of color, homeless people, and the poor in general was rarely disguised. The story leading to the name "Giuliani Time"—a cop claiming he could do what he wanted because it was Giuliani Time as he sodomized a black immigrant, Abner Louima, with a broom handle—was apocryphal, but the tag stuck because it seemed to describe the nature of police-citizen relations, organized through the aggressive "zero tolerance" and "quality of life" policing of the era. Giuliani Time extended into the community gardens that had sprung up in the rubble of the 1970s. Rudolph Giuliani wanted to reclaim many of them and hand the land over to developers, and his administration was not averse to using brute force in the effort. This called up a vibrant—and colorful—opposition that linked activists across the boroughs in their attempts to save the spaces they had made, leading to a struggle that not only drew in a wide array of activists, celebrities, and politicians but also seemed set to determine the tenor of urban neighborhoods beset by gentrification for decades to come. The "win" by the gardening activists, however limited, was nonetheless important for showing how concerted resistance—strong revolt against authority—could still shape the urban social geography.

The community gardens were both something struggled over and spaces from which struggles were launched. Closely aligned with the community gardens movement in the 1990s—sometimes even organizing actions from within the gardens—was the burgeoning Global Justice Movement (chapter 17), a multifaceted uprising geared toward showing that "another world is possible," a world not defined by the neoliberal capitalism that had evolved out of the 1970s global economic crisis in general and New York's fiscal crisis more specifically. Global justice organizations like Reclaim the Streets and Critical Mass consciously sought to revive the festive, carnivalesque modes of revolt that had marked earlier centuries (and were pretty adept at doing so) while also taking aim at very specific targets: the corporate privatization of public space; the dominance of the car on city streets; and, more broadly, the institutions governing the global, capitalist, political economy, like the World Trade Organization and the International Monetary Fund, as well as "free trade" agreements like NAFTA and the proposed Free Trade Agreement of the Americas. Global justice activists sought to promote a "carnival against capitalism"; they also sought to invent new modes of organization—horizontal and consensual rather than vertical and directive—that would prefigure a postcapitalist world to come.

But if the Global Justice Movement was remarkably inventive, so were the police as they developed new methods for disrupting social movements and corralling protesters. The end of the 1990s and the first half of the 2000s thus saw in New York a running battle between protesters bent on protesting (against the World Economic Forum, which relocated to New York in an act of "solidarity" after the September 11, 2001, terrorist attacks in 2002, against the planned War on Iraq in 2003, and against the Republican National Convention in 2004, which likewise came to town in a show of "solidarity") and police bent on stopping them. Protest permits were denied, spies and provocateurs were planted, mass arrests were effected, and the right to rebel was all but eviscerated. New Yorkers were still revolting, but they were more and more being confronted with policing that was, to give the most charitable description possible, "heavy-handed."

Heavy-handedness was justified in part by the terrorist attacks on 9/11 and the perceived need for stringent new rules of public order and social control. But that need had been shown to be false, at least to a fair extent, by the remarkable popular transformation of Union Square in the days immediately following the attack. Here was an uprising—maybe "upwelling" is a better word—of a very different sort. Thousands of people, in all their differences, descended on the square to mourn, to debate, to organize (e.g., to support Muslim New Yorkers during the official and vigilante backlash that was sure to come), or just to be with others. Union Square became a remarkable place, bringing to life the dream of "prefiguring" a world to come. It was spontaneous but ordered at the same time, at once agonistic and solidaristic. The Giuliani administration did not know what to do with it, so it shut it down. Claiming a need to preserve the homemade memorials that had sprouted all over the park from an impending rainstorm and citing concerns about "security," the city fenced off what had become New York's best public space, intolerable because it existed mostly outside the structures of authority.

The terrorist attacks on 9/11 helped deepen the power of the national security state and provided cover for many antidemocratic practices of local police, and it also launched a panic over immigration and presumably "unsecured" borders. By the beginning of 2006, the U.S. House of Representatives had passed, and the Senate was considering, a draconian immigration reform measure that would have turned teachers and doctors into snitches, undocumented workers into felons, and local police forces into direct arms of the border patrol. Immigrants around the country quickly mobilized, leading to a remarkable uprising that spring, with immigrant rights marches and protests in innumerable cities and of striking militancy. In New York, which came to the immigrant rights struggle a bit slowly, the eventual response was a series of mass actions, peaking in a rally of more than one hundred thousand people on Monday, April 10, demanding amnesty for undocumented immigrants and a path to citizenship for children brought across the border illegally but mostly making the point that the whole social and economic world within which we live is one significantly made

March for immigrant rights, April 30, 2006, Knickerbocker Avenue, Bushwick, Brooklyn.
Photograph courtesy of Make the Road New York.

by, and continually made possible by, immigrants (chapter 18). This was a revolt of the directly oppressed and exploited and, by May Day, both a *strike* and a claim for visibility. If, a generation after Stonewall, queer activists could adopt the slogan "We're queer, we're here, get used to it" as they made a bid to be seen as part of the public, immigrants seemed to be saying "Take a look: we're here, and who cares if you get used to it or not, you can't live without us." There was, of course, a significant backlash to this uprising in New York and across the country, but the spring 2006 immigrant uprising sparked a new militancy that was both a militancy of immigrants and a militancy of workers. The legacy of, for example, the Uprising of the Twenty Thousand continues to live on.

Revolt returned to its roots on September 17, 2011 (chapter 19). After being chased around the Financial District by the cops for much of the day, a ragtag bunch of activists, seeking to "occupy Wall Street," regrouped on the steps of the Museum of the American Indian on Bowling Green. The museum is in the old U.S. Custom House, which was built on the site of Fort George, which before that was Fort James, and before that, when the Dutch still held Manhattan, Fort Amsterdam, from which Dutch settlers tried to defend themselves against the revolt of the Munsee. The first fire of the Great Negro Plot of 1741 engulfed a house in Fort George. Fort George was a frequent target of popular discontent in the years leading to the Revolution. Activists who were gathered at the site 235 years later learned that nearby Zuccotti Park was undefended by the police and relatively open. Thus was born one of the most remarkable, sustained uprisings in New York's long, continuous history of revolt. For two months, Zuccotti Park—redubbed Liberty Square—became a center of agitation, an inspiration for movements around the world, an experiment in horizontal democracy, and a thorn in the side of the Wall Street plutocrats who thought they had come out of the recent economic crisis (the very crisis they had caused) relatively unscathed. At such a short remove from Occupy Wall Street and its later offshoots, like Occupy Sandy, it is hard to know just how it has changed New York's urban fabric, but it is clear that it has shifted the city's (and the nation's) political fabric significantly. Inequality is now a central political concern and a site of significant ongoing struggle. And the heavy-handed policing of the movement—never absent from New York's landscape of revolt—made police brutality plain for all to see.

Perhaps some of that police brutality seemed shocking because it was exercised against white people. People of color have, of course, always been subject to unremitting police violence. The histories of police (and extrapolice) violence against black New Yorkers detailed in the pages that follow make that abundantly clear. On occasion, such as in the wake of the three Harlem riots or the smaller but still significant East Harlem uprising of 1969, which gave birth to the Young Lords, such violence has occasioned strong social movements to contest it. We are in the midst of another such moment. Police killings across the country, including the killing of Eric Garner on Staten Island as he was being arrested for selling unlicensed cigarettes, have sparked the vitally important Black Lives Matter movement. It is an uprising still unfolding, both of a piece with the never-ending history that is revolting New York and a product of its own dynamics. It is a national (and increasingly global) movement and a local one, like so many of the other uprisings chronicled here. How it will evolve and what its lasting effects will be are hardly predictable.* What can be said is that it is part of, and now it is shaping, a remarkable history of revolt, rebellion, uprising, and revolution in New York City that is not just a way to tell the story of New York but a history without which the story of New York cannot be told.

❏ ❏ ❏

The pages that follow fill out this story. The focus is on the city's tumultuous events themselves. The analysis of their

* As *Revolting New York* went to press, Donald J. Trump's Electoral College victory in the 2016 presidential election unleashed a new round of furious protest on the streets of New York. It is a reasonable assumption that, given Trump's tight connection to New York, opposition to his rule will continue to be especially strong in the city as—signaled by his first-round cabinet picks—he heightens racial tensions so as to better enact policies that further demonize immigrants and Muslims, quicken the upward redistribution of wealth, hand over control of the environment to the world's biggest polluters, and destroy what remains of the environment and social safety net (as the president himself cozies up to autocrats, reaps huge profits from various interests seeking favor through his businesses, and helps the current government of Israel to destroy any chance for Palestinian sovereignty).

significance for shaping and reshaping the city emerges from within the moments of uprising (rather than in the act of abstract theorizing), for, we think, it is precisely in seeing how struggle has unfolded on the streets (and in the tenement houses, factories, meeting halls, and public parks) that one can glimpse just *how* riot, rebellion, uprising, and revolution have been central to the city's history and geography. Words, maps, engravings, photographs: together these paint a vivid picture of New York in revolt—and New York responding to revolt. The pages of *Revolting New York* illuminate a remarkable social—and spatial—history. *Revolting New York* shows a city and cityscape being made, unmade, and remade over and over again.

For a generation now, geographers have been showing how spaces—the actual physical spaces of the world, as well as the social spaces that intersect with them—are *produced*. They are not just there, like some kind of a void waiting to be filled. Rather, the spaces within which we live are made—structured and restructured—through social relations and social struggles.[13] The structuring power of capitalism—the circulation of capital, the production of value—has, at least since the mid-nineteenth century, been the dominant force in producing New York City space, but intense social interaction and struggle has been the *decisive* force, the one that determines just what kinds of spaces (what landscapes) will be produced where and to whose benefit and whose detriment.* In turn, the produced spaces shape the social order. The urban landscape is, thus, dialectical or recursive: a moment of unrest or upheaval rearranges social relations and produces new spaces (a newly fortified Fort George or a remade Tompkins Square Park, a rebuilt schoolhouse or a relocated asylum for black orphans) and new spatial relationships (a separation of workplace and living space, a citywide linked-up gardening movement, or neighborhood-specific

"broken windows" policing).† In turn, these new spaces and spatial relationships both solidify a social order and transform it, setting the stage for the next moment of upheaval. Geographical space is in this sense a solidification or concretization, however temporary or permanent, of relations of power among its users, owners, designers, and managers (including the police).[14]

Such a sense of the city—of the production of the urban landscape—is better shown than abstractly explained, and that is what *Revolting New York* sets out to do. We are not the first to have attempted to tell the history of New York's riots. In 1873 the journalist, reformer, and Know-Nothing politician Joel Tyler Headley published a wonderfully sensationalist (and often condescending) history titled *The Great Riots of New York*, and historians have drawn on—and corrected—his work ever since.[15] It remains exciting reading (though it ends right at a moment of change in the nature of New York rioting, as the last vestiges of populist, communal, sometimes-order-affirming unruliness fade out, to be replaced by a new, sharper class politics). And of course just about every one of the events chronicled here has attracted a clutch of contemporary commentators and later social and historical analysts—and we rely heavily on them.‡ We rely most heavily of all (at least until the dawn of the twentieth century) on Edwin G. Burrows and Mike Wallace's stupendous *Gotham: A History of New York City to 1898*. This remarkable book places New York City's moments of upheaval

---

* Even an actor as powerful as Robert Moses did not build in a vacuum. His interventions too reflected and were shaped by the state of class, race, and ethnic relations at different moments in the mid-twentieth century. He was, as Robert Caro showed, a power *broker*.

† Geographers (following the lead of French spatial philosopher Henri Lefebvre) often explain the dialectical or recursive production of space in this way: (1) planners, politicians, engineers, architects, and the like *conceive* (or plan) the remaking of the landscape (e.g., the 1811 street grid, the Brooklyn streetcar network, and the Lincoln Center redevelopment of San Juan Hill in the 1960s and again in the early 2000s), often destroying or totally reworking lived landscape, people's *places*, in the process; (2) other folks—residents, visitors, users, tourists, passersby—*perceive* the space sometimes in accordance with the planners' conceptions, but quite often not; (3) they thus use it in ways both intended and not intended, engaging in a suite of *spatial practices* that give the urban form meaning. Spatial practices are often habitual, but they are also mutable, and, of course, they can be subject to violent upheaval, as in moments of rebellion or unrest.

‡ This is a work of synthesis, not so much of original research.

within a vivid political and social context, and all we can do is hope that we somehow have been able to come close to replicating the excitement and importance of the events that Burrows and Wallace portray. *Gotham* is a book that likely cannot be surpassed, but it is also twelve hundred pages long and only takes us to 1898, the moment modern New York City was created by the merger of Manhattan, Brooklyn, the Bronx, Queens, and Staten Island. By condensing New York's history into a history of riots, rebellions, uprisings, and revolutions and by extending that history into the present, we think we have been able to show more sharply just what role social upheaval has played in the making of the city.[16]

Through this focus on unrest, *Revolting New York* shows the city being made and remade, but it also provides glimpses into the rise and reform of policing, the shifting fortunes of political factions, the role economic crisis plays in social life and social struggle, the significance of popular (and sometimes not at all popular) organizing in forcing progressive (and sometimes quite regressive) change. The lightning strike of revolt illuminates the social structure at a particular, precise moment, but, like time-lapse photography, the succession of lightning strikes shows how some structural forces persist, while others rise and just as quickly disappear. Racism does not go away, but it does shift in form—and locale. Police brutality persists, but it does at times get damped down. Class struggle remains a constant, but it always takes on a new form.* The struggle of oppressed or marginalized groups to make a place for themselves in the city never ends, but it gets pushed about. Sometimes it gets driven underground, sometimes—as with Stonewall, the Uprising of the

* Not always to the liking of radicals and progressives, as the Hard Hat Riot in 1970 made plain.

Twenty Thousand, or the Great Negro Plot of 1741—it bursts incandescently into view (and then, not infrequently, is snuffed out).

The story *Revolting New York* tells is thus not a romantic or a heroic one. It is simply wrong to assume that rioters and revolutionaries always achieve their aims (or even, sometimes, know what those aims are). It might be true, as the Reverend Martin Luther King Jr. claimed, that the "arc of the moral universe . . . bends toward justice," but if so, the arc of history does not do so in any clear or simple way. The arc is exceedingly sinuous, defined as much by its reversals as by its forward momentum, and to assume otherwise is to assume an ahistorical progressivism that does not square with reality. Rather, riot, rebellion, uprising, and revolution shape a city as much through their failure or their crushing—the reassertion of an existing order—as they do through their victories, which are themselves inevitably incomplete and sometimes only temporary. If the sinuous arc of history bends toward justice anyway, it is only because social struggle, which never ends, has, over a long revolution, made it do so not only because of its victories but despite its defeats. Which is all to say that the lightning bolt of revolt illuminates the structure and exercise of power, even as, by producing new spaces and spatial relationships, it reworks the geography of that power—though not necessarily in the ways intended.

Revolting New York shows New York in revolt. It shows why riot, rebellion, uprising, and revolution have been and continue to be so important to the social history and historical geography of the city. It shows why New York—now the capital of capitalism—is, in all the senses of the term, *revolutionary*.

AN INVITATION TO READERS

Just as there are many ways to tell the story of New York, there are many ways you can read *Revolting New York*. We have written the book chronologically—as a history—because the sequence of events is important: each round of revolt (by revolutionizing social relations, calling up the forces of reaction, or both) sets the stage for the next round of revolt. How the city responded to the extreme violence of the 1863 Draft Riots, for example, in part determined how worker unrest in 1874 was policed. Much can be gained by reading *Revolting New York* in order, since, by doing so, a whole historical geography—a city being successively shaped by round after round of upheaval—comes into view.

Yet we have also written *Revolting New York* as a reference book. While there is no way we have adequately explained—much less even uncovered—all the moments of unrest that have made the city, we do provide the most complete guide available to New York's revolting history. Thus, with its mix of full chapters marked by considerable detail and sustained analysis and its shorter—lightning flash–like—vignettes, and relying on the full index we have provided, you could fairly easily read the book thematically rather than chronologically.

You could, for example, trace a history of policing, police reform, and the use of militias to quell rioting, beginning with the Slave Revolt of 1712 and continuing through the Astor Place Riots, the feuding police forces of the 1850s,

the Draft Riots and the Tompkins Square Riot, the transit strikes, the "police pogrom" of 1902, and on to the innumerable police riots of the late twentieth century (beginning again in Tompkins Square Park) and ending—for now—with the police killing of Eric Garner in 2014. Or you could draw a line through different kinds of revolt: for example, popular, carnivalesque protest (and rioting) was important in early New York history and then faded as a mode of dissent in the industrial era, only to return in the post-industrial era, revived by global justice activists contesting the new neoliberal forms capitalism was taking around the world and in the city. A similar line could be drawn through commodity riots, or labor unrest, or struggles to open up exclusive institutions, or class-based struggles. Or you could trace a history of race and racism in the city, since race is so often at the heart of rebellion and uprising. Race riots have persisted, but they have also shifted form, from early slave uprisings that attacked white people as well as whites' property to white attacks on the bodies of black people (most prominently in the Draft Riots and the Tenderloin Race Riot of 1900, but also in Bensonhurst in the 1980s) to black attacks almost exclusively on property during the Harlem Riots of 1935, 1943, and 1964 and then back to a mix of attacks on persons and property in Crown Heights a generation later. Or, finally, you might want to pick a place—Fort Amsterdam–Fort James–Fort George–the customhouse on

Bowling Green; or Union or Tompkins Squares; or where the Great Negro Plotters were hanged in 1741, which is right near Foley Square and surrounded by courthouses (a space of "justice" then and a space of "justice" now)—and trace its appearance and role across the centuries.

In reading *Revolting New York* thematically you will find that few of the lines you draw can be disentangled from the others: race riots are also class riots, the politics of policing and the politics of class can never be separated (any more than either can be separated from race), the carnivalesque is frequently drawn on to mock class pretensions (or the mores of established society, as with Stonewall), and so forth. You will then be forced to confront, perhaps in a way that is different from how we have presented it, how a complex *historical geography* both gives rise to and shapes unrest in the city. You will also find that the terminology we use—riot, rebellion, uprising, and revolution—also cannot be disentangled: revolts against authority are often violent and unruly,

that is, riotous; riots quickly turn into uprisings; revolutions simmer and explode in any number of unpredictable ways. "Riot" is not necessarily a pejorative term, and riots take many forms (from Stamp Act patriots burning effigies to police rampaging against peaceful protesters), while "uprising" is not always a positive one (the 1863 Draft Riots were also an uprising). Reading thematically, then, you might then start drawing some incredibly interesting conclusions about the nature and efficacy of revolt in New York City, conclusions that we ourselves only barely apprehend or have not even thought of. That's what we hope, anyway.

Either way—by reading from beginning to end or by dipping in and out (or, maybe best of all, both)—we trust that *Revolting New York* will illuminate the city for you in new ways, showing just how alive (as well as deadly) its historical geography of riot, rebellion, uprising, and revolution is and always has been.

CHAPTER 1

The Revolt of the Munsee

The Destruction of New Amsterdam and the Creation of New York, 1629–1664

AMANDA HURON AND RAYMOND PETTIT

New York City was born out of the ashes of revolt.

Early in the morning of September 15, 1655, a fleet of sixty-four canoes filled with nearly two thousand Munsee warriors set off from the shores of what is now New Jersey, heading east across the Hudson River toward the island of Manhattan. The Munsee and other Lenape bands had for decades been engaged in a low-grade war with Dutch settlers, and relations were once again reaching a breaking point. When the Munsee landed on the beaches of Manhattan that late summer day, they began an all-out assault against the Dutch. Over the course of three days, the Munsee burned farms, destroyed buildings and cattle, and killed settlers. Known as the Peach War, it was the most terrifying attack during the period of Dutch rule, paving the way for the English seizure of the territory just a few years later in 1664. Without the Munsee revolt, New York might never have become New York.

The Dutch, the Munsee, and Manhattan

At the time of European contact, the Munsee were loosely affiliated indigenous groups living in a region from roughly what is now New Jersey to Connecticut—an area called Lenapehoking, the Land of the Lenape. "Munsee" refers to a language group, a dialect of the larger Delaware language, but it is also used to refer to many of the "bands" of Lenape.

"Lenape" itself is a Munsee word meaning "People" (or "Men").[1] The Munsee of the Manhattan area were respected by surrounding groups (many of them also Munsee)—the Raritans, Hackensacks, Tappans, Wiechquasgecks, Sinawoys (or Siwanoys), Matinecocks, Rockaways, and others—with whom they sometimes formed alliances and sometimes skirmished. While not politically centralized, something like these groups' sovereignty over Lenapehoking was well established when the first European contact was made by explorer Giovanni de Verrazano (or Verrazzano) on behalf of the French in 1524.

When the Munsee set out to attack Manhattan on that September morning in 1655, they had their sights set on New Amsterdam, the small Dutch town at the very southern tip of the island that was the capital of the larger Dutch territory of New Netherland, itself established as part of the Dutch effort to create a vigorous overseas mercantile empire.* The Dutch first visited the area in 1609 under Henry Hudson, an English explorer hired for the voyage. Hudson had been contracted by the Dutch East India Company to find a northwest passage to the Pacific, but he stumbled upon Manhattan and its surrounds instead. The Dutch laid claim

---

* The Dutch Republic itself had gained independence from the Spanish monarchy only a few decades earlier. Formal independence was finally recognized in 1648 with the Peace of Münster, which was part of the larger Treaty of Westphalia, which established the modern state system.

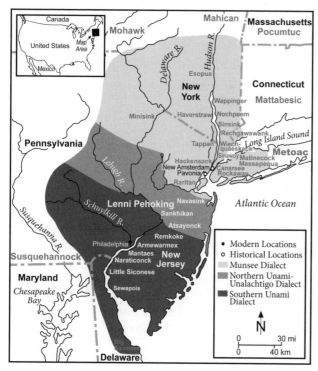

Native American Geography at the Time of Dutch Colonization.
Cartography: Joe Stoll, Syracuse University Cartography Lab and Map Shop, redrawn from a map by Nikator.

to the land Hudson found and called it New Netherland. The land seemed unusually abundant in resources, and its estuarine ecosystem was especially rich. Indeed, the whole area seemed rich in potential for profit. As an entry from Hudson's ship's log noted, Manhattan "is as pleasant a land as one can tread upon, very abundant in all kinds of timber suitable for ship-building, and for making large casks. The people have copper pipes, from which I inferred that copper must exist there; and iron likewise according to the testimony of the natives, who, however, do not understand preparing it for use."[2]

New Netherland was not originally a proper colony but a Dutch "sphere of interest." The Dutch claimed to possess

legal authority only onboard their boats—the "law of the ship"—while the Munsee were sovereign on the land. Dutch crews wintered in New Netherland, but not with an eye to settling. There was thus no fixed Dutch governmental administration planted on the land and charged with overseeing a colony. In the first years of the Dutch claim, New Netherland comprised a heterogeneous mass of sovereign Munsee bands near the mouth of the Hudson, each of which had to be negotiated and traded with by individual naval representatives of Dutch power. There was no standard policy of objectives for Dutch and Munsee interactions, other than to generate a profit in the trade of beaver furs. Neither the Dutch nor the Munsee dominated, and legal and commercial relations and boundaries were quite fluid. Early New Netherland was a classic "middle ground" of European and Native American contact.[3]

The fur trade that dominated Dutch commercial activity in New Netherland in the early years did not require a permanent European population. Furs were collected by Munsee and then traded at various points along the coast for European goods, hence New Netherland's status as merely a sphere of interest. But the States-General—the Dutch parliamentary chamber—as well as some Dutch mercantile interests thought New Netherland needed to be populated to act as a bulwark against encroaching English colonists. The States-General therefore granted the Dutch West India Company (a quasi-commercial, quasi-governmental organization) a monopoly over New Netherland trade in 1621 and encouraged the establishment of a permanent colony. Some in the company directorate argued against settling colonists, fearing that fur-trade profits were insufficient to support a permanent colony. Some even turned the bulwark argument on its head, contending that if a hostile takeover by English settlers or others was possible, then a *lack* of colonial investment was no bad thing. The colonizing faction countered that a Dutch colony could be self-sufficient in two or three years and would not unduly burden the company. A compromise was effected between the two factions in 1624. The company would encourage colonists to settle

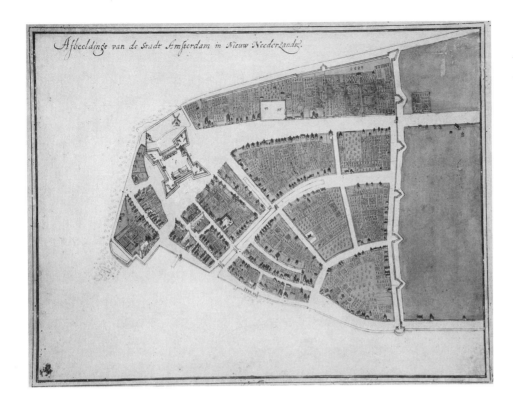

Afbeeldinge van de Stadt Amsterdam in Nieuw Neederland.

A ca. 1665 copy of Jacques Courtelyou's 1660 map of New Amsterdam, *Afbeeldinge can de Stadt Amsterdam in Nieuw Neederland*.
The Miriam and Ira D. Wallach Division of Art, Prints, and Photographs, New York Public Library.

in New Netherland, but it would maintain a monopoly on commerce, and all colonists would technically be company employees.

As a result, the Dutch needed to set up a local government in New Netherland. The company ordered its colonial director, Peter Minuit, to purchase land from the Munsee. He bought Manhattan in January 1626.* As Domine Michaëlius informed company heads in Amsterdam, "This island is the key and principal stronghold of the country,

* The purchase of Manhattan and other Native lands during the colonial period has generated an ongoing debate about indigenous perspectives concerning property—whether they considered these transactions to indicate exclusive ownership or only a right to share the land. The only available document referencing the purchase of Manhattan is a brief report from Peter Schaghen, a merchant, to the Dutch government in 1626, so it is difficult to determine how the Munsee viewed the purchase.

and needs to be settled first."[4] With the purchase came a new administrative policy. No longer did the Dutch understand the Munsee to be completely sovereign peoples. Instead they were ambiguously independent Dutch subjects: the Dutch made it clear that the Munsee were still largely autonomous, but they claimed authority to regulate Dutch and Munsee trade. Whereas previously the Dutch claimed sovereignty only aboard their own boats, now the Dutch extended this sovereignty onto land and made moves to regulate Dutch-Munsee interactions even beyond trade. The Munsee maintained their independent status and rights, but those were now contingent on Dutch consent. And as Minuit's purchase had made plain, Munsee land could now be bought and sold.

Claiming control is not the same as exercising it. At the

Nieu Amsterdam, date unknown. The figures in the foreground were stock characters in Dutch engravings of the early colonial era.
The Miriam and Ira D. Wallach Division of Art, Prints, and Photographs, New York Public Library.

very southern tip of Manhattan, the Dutch West India Company quickly established Fort Amsterdam and New Amsterdam as the center of Dutch administration, but outside the fort and the town's walled enclosures it was hard for the Dutch to enforce what they now saw as their exclusive right to the land. After they sold the island to Minuit, Munsee bands continued to live and hunt on Manhattan well into the 1630s.

Low rates of European immigration to New Amsterdam and New Netherland forced the West India Company to change its settlement policy in 1629, opening the colony to nonemployees under a patroonship system. Under this system, the company made land grants (meaning the right to negotiate a purchase from the Munsee) to anyone willing to sponsor and settle fifty individuals in New Netherland. Such

"privatization of colonization" may have brought settlers to the colony, but it also lessened governmental supervision.[5] Dutch administrators in New Amsterdam viewed both sets of rural subjects—Munsee and Dutch patrooners—suspiciously, because, away from New Amsterdam, they tended to intermix and because, distant from the central market of New Amsterdam, much of their trade went untaxed. As the colonial secretary, Cornelius van Tienhoven, saw it, these remote settlements "produced altogether too much familiarity with the Indians . . . [rural Dutch colonists] not being satisfied with taking them into their houses in the customary manner, but attracting them by extraordinary attention, such as admitting them to table, laying napkins before them, presenting wine to them and more of that kind of thing."[6] Such unruliness undermined the arguments that New Netherland would serve as an effective bulwark against the English.

Colonial Administration, Munsee-Dutch Interdependence, and Munsee Subjugation

Back in the home country, Dutch elites viewed New Netherland distrustfully, its viability increasingly suspect. The colony seemed to be marked by high rates of alcohol consumption and low rates of Sabbath observance. As the first Dutch minister sent to the colony wrote of the settlers in a 1628 letter home, "The people for the most part are rather rough and unrestrained."[7] When Willem Kieft, the colony's fifth director general, arrived in New Amsterdam in 1638, he found rotting ships, two of the company's three windmills broken, a corrupt colonial administration, and the company's five farms untenanted, their land having been "thrown into the commons."[8] Kieft set about attempting to restore discipline by implementing new rules and threatening lawbreakers with penalties and fines. In 1643, for instance, the council of New Amsterdam outlawed the sale of alcohol to Native peoples, concerned by the violence they thought accompanied Munsee drinking. But settlers who lived in outlying parts of the colony, farther from New Amsterdam, continued to trade secretly with Natives in order to avoid paying taxes to the colonial administration. Because guns fetched such high prices, settlers also traded them to Natives, even though Kieft had strictly forbidden such activity. It was only "in the neighborhood of Manhattan, where a more rigid police was maintained," wrote one early historian, that "the supply of arms [to Natives] was prevented."[9]

European market demands soon began to shape the daily lives of the Munsee. As contact between the Munsee and the Dutch increased, the Munsee became dependent not only on European guns and alcohol but also on goods like duffel cloth (a heavy woolen cloth that the Munsee came to prefer to skins for clothing), sewing needles, cooking pots, and more. The Munsee therefore had increasing incentive to trade with the Dutch, while the Dutch desire for beaver furs and land made them eager to trade with the Munsee. But unfortunately for the Munsee, they were quickly losing access to the beaver trade. Beavers had been hunted nearly to extinction in areas closest to colonial trading posts, leaving the fur trade to powerful rivals to the north and south. In the upper Hudson River valley and farther west in present-day New York State, Mohawks and Mahicans had easier access to beavers, and the Susquehannocks similarly dominated the hunting and trapping regions to the southwest in present-day New Jersey and Pennsylvania.

With reduced access to beaver, many Munsee turned to wampum production as a way to trade for the European goods on which they had increasingly come to rely. Wampum, small tubular beads made from marine shells such as clams and quahogs, had long served as sacred goods for Native peoples. The Europeans, minimally interested in the social complexities of wampum, understood it as mere currency. Dutch money was in short supply in the colony, so the Dutch incorporated wampum into their economic system, using it to trade for furs, land, and other goods. In New Amsterdam, settlers used wampum for all kinds of transactions, including paying for mortgages and ferry rides and for making tithes to the church. Wampum became the common currency of the North American colonies, with Dutch, English, and many indigenous groups using it. For many Munsee bands, wampum production and continued Dutch demand for it became a primary means for securing sustenance. This pushed the Munsee into a dependent role in the colonial economy, opening an opportunity for the Dutch under Kieft to use their dominant position to deepen Munsee colonial subjugation in New Netherland. The Dutch began to replace mere claims to colonial control with an active exercise of it.

Beginning in 1639, Kieft imposed taxes on the Munsee living in and around the New Netherland colony, demanding payment in fathoms (six feet) of wampum. The tax was necessary, Kieft argued, to recompense the Dutch for their protection of the Munsee against their Native enemies. But the Munsee resisted payment of the tax, or tribute, primarily because they did not feel adequately protected by the Dutch.

According to one interpretation, however, the Munsee were upset by taxation for another reason: taxation cemented Munsee status as subjects of the Dutch.[10]

Kieft's War

The question of tribute appears to be a primary cause of the violence that broke out between Munsee and Dutch in 1640—what came to be known as Kieft's War. That year, a group of Raritans who lived on the mainland west of Staten Island threatened a Dutch ship that had come to trade with them and probably also to exact tribute. Later, when a number of hogs were killed on Staten Island, the Dutch blamed the Raritans.* Dutch soldiers then attacked the Raritans to exact vengeance, killing several individuals and destroying property, even though the soldiers had been ordered only to cut down the Raritans' corn and to arrest the alleged offenders. In response, a year later, Raritans attacked Staten Island, killing four Dutch farmers. Kieft induced other bands, themselves eager to maintain good relations with the Dutch, to attack the Raritans.

The roiling conflict boiled over in 1641 when a man from the Munsee band Weckquaesgeek killed a Dutch settler, Claes Smits,† to avenge the murder of his uncle during the construction of Fort Amsterdam.[11] Smits had run a public house on Manhattan (outside New Amsterdam) frequented by both Dutch and Munsee. Kieft attempted to use Smits's murder to mobilize Dutch settlers against their Munsee neighbors, but he was largely unsuccessful, despite increased tensions.

Meanwhile, most Munsee were still feeling pressure from rival tribes in the area, and two years later, in 1643, bands of Weckquaesgeeks and Tappans found themselves fleeing toward the coast from conflict with Mahican enemies to the north. They took refuge near Dutch settlements in Pavonia, across the river from New Amsterdam in present-day New

Jersey, and also near a fort at Corlear's Hook, on Manhattan, just north of New Amsterdam. Kieft took this opportunity to order an attack on the hastily encamped Munsee at Pavonia, supposedly in retribution for Smits's death. His men killed eighty Munsee in a single night, making no distinction between victims. Contemporary Dutch witness David de Vries gave a harrowing account of the massacre: "Infants were torn from their mother's breasts, and hacked to pieces in the presence of their parents, and the pieces were thrown into the fire and in the water, and other sucklings, being bound to small boards, were cut, stuck and pierced, and miserably massacred in a manner to move a heart of stone." Other children "were thrown into the river, and when the fathers and mothers endeavored to save them, the soldiers would not let them come on land but made both parents and children drown—children from five to six years of age, and also some old and decrepit persons."[12]

In response to the slaughter, eleven bands of Munsee, including the Weckquaesgeeks and the Raritans, came together to fight the Dutch, and later that year, a force of fifteen hundred Munsee warriors attacked the colony of New Netherland. De Vries once again described what happened: "As soon as the savages understood that the Swannekens [white men] had so treated them, all the men whom they could surprise on the farm-lands, they killed; but we have never heard that they have permitted women or children to be killed. They burned all the houses, farms, barns, grain, haystacks, and destroyed everything they could get hold of. So there was an open destructive war begun."[13]

The year 1643 became known among colonists as "the year of blood."[14] Accounts from this time make clear how terrified colonists were by Native attacks and what a devastating effect these continual attacks had on the colony. Roger Williams, a witness to the Munsee attacks in response to the Pavonia massacre, wrote: "But before we weighed Anchor their Boweries were in flames[.]‡ Dutch & Eng[lish] were slaine; mine Eyes saw . . . flames at their Townes . . . &

---

* As it turned out, the hogs had in fact been killed by disgruntled Dutch servants.

† The settler also appears in the record as Claes Swits and Claes Rademaker.

‡ Bouwery or Bowery translates roughly as "farm."

Flights & Hurries of Men, Women & Children, the present Remoovall of all yt could for Holland."[15] Drawing on contemporaneous reports, a later historian described the revolt of the Munsee as a "devastating tide" that "rolled over the island of Manhattan itself": "From [Manhattan's] northern extremity to the Kolck [southern tip], there were now no more than five or six bouweries left; and these were 'threatened by the Indians every night with fire, and by day with the slaughter of people and cattle.' No other place remained, where the trembling population could find protection, than 'around and adjoining Ft. Amsterdam.' The women and children lay 'concealed in straw huts,' while their husbands and fathers mounted guard on the crumbling ramparts above. For the fort itself was almost defenseless."[16] Many colonists blamed Kieft. In October 1644 a group of colonial civic leaders wrote a long letter to the Dutch government in Amsterdam, complaining of Kieft's administration and especially its conduct of the war. The Munsee, they wrote, "continually rove around in parties, night and day, on the Island of Manhattans, killing our people not a thousand paces from the Fort; and things have now arrived at such a pass, that no one dare move a foot to fetch a stick of fire wood without an escort."[17] A French visitor noted in 1643 that the "natives . . . while I was there, actually killed some two score Hollanders, and burnt many houses and farms full of wheat."[18] Constant rumors circulated among settlers about imminent Munsee attacks, and one early historian wrote, "The wildest stories were circulated among the fireside gossips at Manhattan. . . . Anxiety and terror . . . pervaded the defenseless hamlets around Fort Amsterdam."[19] Fear ruled the day.

The Peach War: The Final Revolt of the Munsee

Kieft and Munsee leaders signed a peace treaty in 1645, officially ending Kieft's War. But hostilities between the groups persisted, even after the replacement of Kieft as director general by Peter Stuyvesant in 1647. Much of this conflict was made up of ongoing small-scale violence taken up by young Munsee warriors intent on avenging the deaths of family members. Then in 1655 these mostly minor skirmishes erupted once again into a full-scale Munsee revolt. Tensions were already high. A Dutch sortie had seized New Sweden (along the Delaware River to the southwest), a colony that had been allied with the Susquehannocks, a powerful group among the Lenape who now found themselves at a disadvantage. Meanwhile, on Manhattan, a Dutch colonist killed a Munsee woman for picking peaches from his garden. Susquehannocks and Munsee, wanting revenge for the death of the woman, banded together to attack New Amsterdam, sparking the so-called Peach War. Fighting was fierce when the group of nearly two thousand warriors landed on Manhattan early that September morning. On the first day of the war, three Dutch and three Munsee were killed, and a number of farms were burned. The Munsee then crossed back over the Hudson to Pavonia and on to Staten Island and over three days destroyed farms, buildings, and cattle. They killed between fifty and one hundred settlers and imprisoned scores more. They held their prisoners hostage, releasing them only after receiving an ample supply of ammunition in exchange. Once again "terror seized the land."[20] The colony, a local official lamented after the fighting subsided, "has gone backward so much, that it will not be in the same flourishing state for several years, that it was six weeks ago."[21] During peace negotiations, Stuyvesant was even forced to repurchase resettlement rights to the land on the west bank of the North (Hudson) River. New Netherland was considerably weakened.

Over the course of Dutch colonial rule, Munsee raids and sorties were largely tit-for-tat retaliation for murder. Avenging murder by killing a member of the rival group, as with the murder of Claes Smits, was common practice among the Munsee. But it seems that this 1655 coordinated attack went beyond the attempt to avenge a particular death (even if that death was a spark). The Peach War was also about territory (hence the Susquehannock involvement) and property rights—about who had usufruct on the land that used to be the Munsee's. As Dutch control became surer and European notions of property more certain, the Munsee seemed to be losing control over their own livelihoods. The Munsee-Dutch encounter had begun with Munsee still sovereign on their land and Dutch sovereignty confined to their ships, but by now European hegemony on the land was, while by no means total, at least strong, and the Munsee had been increasingly reduced to a kind of second-class citizenship. In directly attacking New Amsterdam, the Munsee (and their Susquehannock allies) were making one last attempt to reject Dutch control.

The Coming of New York

Despite seeming to win the Peach War, the Munsee were eventually driven from their lands, their population devastated by conflict and disease. Some settled in Canada at Christian missions in the eighteenth century, while in the nineteenth, others ended up living in Kansas near their Delaware brethren. But if they were pushed out, their re-volt nonetheless had long-lasting geopolitical consequences: there is a fairly straight line from the near-constant Munsee-Dutch skirmishing to the surrender of New Netherland to the English in 1664. In a 1665 letter to his masters in Holland, Peter Stuyvesant gave as his cause of surrender, first, the "troublesome neighbors of new England," but second, "the exceedingly detrimental, land-destroying and people-expelling wars with the cruel barbarians, which endured two years before my arrival there, whereby many subjects who possessed means were necessitated to depart, others to retreat under the crumbling fortress of New Amsterdam."[22] The ongoing revolt of the Munsee against the Dutch was a terror-inducing, debilitating affair that finally resulted, as David de Vries had years earlier feared it would, in the "murder [of] our own [Dutch] nation."[23] The rebellions of the Munsee, it turns out, helped destroy New Amsterdam and clear the way for the rise of New York.

LEISLER'S REBELLION, 1689–1691

New Amsterdam became New York, but the Dutch imprint on the city was still strong, even as English officials tried to mute it by passing laws offensive to the Dutch (e.g., barring wives from purchasing land or conducting business in their own names) and even as New York became a remarkably diverse and thus unruly place. Among its earliest acts, the New York Assembly passed laws governing slaves, laborers, and apprentices. Workers pushed back. In 1684 cartmen (primarily Dutch) went on strike—"the first transport strike in the city's history"—in response to a range of restrictions on their activities and new demands for uncompensated labor. Farmers and merchants were growing restless as trade faltered and huge tracks of land up and down the Hudson and on Staten and Long Islands were granted as feudal manors to members of the Anglo-Dutch elite.[1]

But much of the unrest of the last two decades of the seventeenth century was intimately connected to the Catholic/anti-Catholic monarchal struggles that led to England's "Glorious Revolution" and Restoration. New York itself was heavily populated not with Catholics or Anglicans, who were relatively few in number, but sect upon sect of dissenters (Quakers of various sorts, Anabaptists, independents, Sabbatarians, Huguenots, etc.) and some Jews. Most were "antipopish," and militias and masses alike repeatedly took to the streets in 1689 to prevent what they feared would be a papist uprising. In June, when New York's lieutenant governor, Francis Nicholson, and its mayor, Stephanus Van Cortlandt, hesitated to recognize King James II's abdication and proclaim the reign of William and Mary, massed crowds forced them and their council out of office and stormed the courts and customhouse (Van Cortlandt went into hiding). The antipapists quickly established the Committee of Safety to govern New York and spent the summer reopening the courts, collecting taxes, and shoring up the city's defenses. The committee appointed Jacob Leisler, a German-born militia officer and wealthy landowner, to command Fort James (as it was still called). Leisler took the opportunity to name himself lieutenant governor.[2]

Leisler organized a crew of disparate insurgents to hold New York against the "Popish Doggs and Divells" who continued to threaten it. Second-generation Dutch settlers, Dutch and English merchants, "Stuart-hating" Long Island villagers, and masses of sailors, shopkeepers, cartmen, laborers, and women threatened what Van Cortlandt feared would be "people's Revolucions."[3] In the autumn, the Committee of Safety called for elections, including, for the first time, the election of militia captains and justices of the peace. A social earthquake ensued: workingmen gained the majority on the Board of Aldermen; a carpenter became sheriff; a bricklayer became marshal; a Huguenot was elected mayor. "Scenes of class conflict became commonplace in the city," and arrest warrants were issued for the old elite. Anti-Leislerian merchants tried to blow up the fort and seize Leisler and kill him. A cartman, John Langstaet, waded in, allowing Leisler to escape.[4] In 1690 new elections for the provincial assembly led to the abolition of monopolies, new trade restrictions, and the demand that anti-Leislerians who had fled the city be returned and impressed into military or civilian service. In the midst of the turmoil, legislators turned their attention to the question of rights and liberties, and Leisler—who had ruled in part through the arbitrary arrest of dissidents and who was increasingly seen as ineffectual against the French and Indian threat to the north—saw his power begin to slip away.[5]

New York's old elite meanwhile had the ear of King William and convinced him to disavow Leisler and replace his council. The new governor, Col. Henry Sloughter, pledged to sweep Leisler and the "rabble" out of the city. Leisler refused to go and, with his supporters, held the fort while they awaited Sloughter's arrival. Once he arrived, Leisler and his band yielded and were sentenced to hang. Sloughter called new elections for the Common Council and the assembly, which both immediately began to legislate against workingmen and the Dutch: new rules for apprenticeship were written; the privileges of freemanship became harder to obtain; cartmen were faced with new licensing requirements. Anyone who now disturbed "the peace good and quiet of this their Majestyes Government" would be guilty of high treason. The assembly reformed the courts in accordance with English common law (bringing them firmly under the authority of the Crown) and created a new supreme court with significant powers. Sheriffs and justices of the peace were newly empowered to prosecute "moral crimes." The template for the intense factionalism that would mark the city and colony for the next hundred years was set.[6]

On May 16, 1691, the others having been pardoned, Leisler and his son-in-law and confidant, Jacob Milborne, were hanged at the eastern edge of the Commons. Their heads were chopped off when they were brought down, their heads were sewed back on, and their bodies were buried on Leisler's nearby property on what is now Park Row at the foot of the Brooklyn Bridge.

THE SLAVE REVOLT, 1712

New York in the eighteenth century was a slave city, second only to Charleston in number of slaves. Colonial governor Edmund Andros prohibited the enslaving of local Indians in 1679, but no restrictions were placed on the importation of slaves from Africa or the West Indies. By the beginning of the century, 14.2 percent of the city's population was black. In 1711 the Common Council designated the Meal (Grain) Market at the foot of Wall Street as the city's primary slave market.[1] In early April 1712 the slaves revolted.

A dozen or so slaves, many newly arrived from the Gold Coast of Africa and sworn to secrecy, hid away muskets, swords, and other weapons. In the very early hours of April 7, they armed themselves and set fire to buildings near the house of Peter van Tillburgh on Maiden Lane, which was then near the northern end of town. When white neighbors rushed to the scene, the slaves stabbed and shot them, killing nine people, among them some of the most prominent men of the city. Another dozen were seriously injured.

The governor ordered the firing of the fort's cannon to rouse the citizenry, and the slaves fled north, slashing and hacking at whites heading toward the conflagration. Six fleeing blacks (including one couple) killed themselves before they were apprehended; militiamen rounded up nineteen more the next morning.[2]

Two early twentieth-century depictions of the New York slave market at the foot of Wall Street in the first half of the 1700s.
Art and Picture Collection, New York Public Library.

The fear of a general uprising did not abate. News soon reached New York of a similar uprising in Jamaica, and more slaves were rounded up. Within a week, seventy Africans were in custody. Twenty-three slaves were quickly convicted of murder by a hastily convened court; two others were convicted of attempted murder. Twenty Africans were hanged; three were burned at the stake. Tom, owned by Nicholas Roosevelt, was sentenced to burn "in Torment for Eight or ten hours & Continue burning in the said fire untill he be dead and Consumed to Ashes." The slave Clause was to be "broke alive upon a wheel." And Robin was hung up alive in chains and made to starve to death. The governor found these to be "the most exemplary punishments that could possibly be thought of."[3]

New laws were quickly passed. The assembly passed a new slave code, making manumission prohibitively expensive for owners and barring freed slaves from owning land. The assembly's Act for Preventing Suppressing and Punishing Conspiracy and Insurrection of Negroes and Other Slaves allowed slave owners to punish slaves up to the point of loss of life or limb "at Discretion" and to penalize slaves with "such manner" of death "as the aggravation or enormity of their Crimes" merited, if they were found guilty of murder, rape, arson, or assault. The Common Council banned slaves from traveling in the city after dark without a lantern. Other provisions banning slaves from possessing weapons and barring the meeting together of three or more slaves (except in "servile Imployment for the Master or Mistress") were strengthened. Slaves were now whipped, transported, hanged, and burned to death with startling frequency not only for assault or insubordination but for "Vile Expressions against the White People."[4]

Conspiracy was in the air, and slave revolt seemed an ever-present threat in eighteenth-century New York. Whites' fears were not necessarily misplaced.

CHAPTER 2

The Great Negro Plot, 1741

KATHLEEN DUNN

Fires again tore through New York in the spring of 1741. Many of those who witnessed these fires had also been witness to the Slave Revolt of 1712. History seemed to be repeating itself, only now even more sinisterly: this seemed to be not just a slave revolt but a plot to make New York a black city under the protection of Catholic Spain. Buildings in Fort George at the Battery, the seat of colonial government, burned to the ground the day after Saint Patrick's Day, and fifteen other residences and commercial properties went up in flames over the next several weeks.[1] Panic gripped the city. Could it be that slaves and lower-class whites were rising together in revolt? A mass inquisition of the city's black population and suspected white sympathizers was set to find out.[2]

The proceedings quickly took on the tenor of a witch hunt.* One hundred and fifty-two black people and twenty whites were arrested and interrogated in connection with the fires, though nobody could be found who claimed to have seen who started them. By the end of the summer, sixty-seven confessions had been extracted through torture and threat of death. Following a series of contentious trials led by prosecutor (and judge of the New York Supreme Court of Judicature) Daniel Horsmanden, thirty-one black people,

The Negroes Sentenced, an early nineteenth-century depiction of the conspiracy trials.
Art and Picture Collection, New York Public Library.

* Contemporaneous observers readily saw parallels with the Salem Witch Trials of 1692, and the sense that some sort of hysteria gripped the city has persisted down the years.

both slave and free, and four whites were executed—hanged or burned at the stake. The presumed leaders of the plot, a white cobbler and tavern owner named John Hughson, who (so the conspiracy theory went) would be king, and a slave named Caesar, who would be elected governor, were hung up in chains and their bodies left to rot in public. Eighty-two of those accused were sold and transported to the West Indies.[3]

A Time of Unrest

The 1730s were a decade of rapid change in New York. Economic depression had ushered out the 1720s, and a smallpox epidemic in 1731 cost the city 6 percent of its population. The black population expanded, reaching about 16 percent of New York's total population of eleven thousand in 1737. Four years later—the year of the fires—one in seven residents of New York colony was black; in the city nearly one in five was.[4] Enslaved blacks lived with their masters; the few free black folks in the city lived in the Fields, an outlying, largely rural area north of the Negroes Burial Ground, itself well outside the built-up area of New York.[5] The unstable economy meant that artisans, free blacks, rented-out slaves, and newly arrived foreign workers (particularly Irish, many of whom were criminals recently transported to the New World) often fought for the same jobs. Slaves were especially important workers on the docks.[6]

Political power was held in tenuous balance. Among elites a bitter factional fight occurred throughout the 1730s between the relatively cosmopolitan Court Party, headed by Governor William Cosby, and the more provincially based Country Party, peaking most famously in the trial of John Peter Zenger in 1735. Zenger was a printer who published the opposition *New-York Weekly Journal*, which was relentless in its attacks on Governor Cosby. Zenger's acquittal set a massive precedent for free press in America, but it did not quell the fires of factionalism, or what was then known as party politics. When Cosby died, opponents sought to set up a rival government, nearly unleashing civil war. War was averted by the timely arrival of news that the king had appointed John West, First Earl De La Warr, as governor and George Clarke as his lieutenant. De La Warr never arrived in New York, and Clarke—aligned with the Court Party—

served as de facto governor until 1743, even as oppositional members of the Country Party sniped at him in the pages of the *Weekly Journal*.[7]

By the end of the decade, war was brewing with Spain (and maybe also France), further pressuring the ruling elite and weakening the defense of the New York colony. The faraway War of Jenkins' Ear, as it was later known, had decidedly local consequences.* Imperial authorities required New York to cough up six hundred white recruits—almost one in six of the able-bodied white men in the city—and imposed a stringent draft on food. Defenses against the French and Iroquois pressing in from the north, Spanish privateers pushing from the south, and whatever dissenters there were at home were all weakened. And from late 1739 to early 1740, many dissenters, especially low-class laborers and apprentices, the city's poor and its enslaved, were finding a new outlet for expression in the preaching of the Methodist revivalist, Englishman George Whitfield. Whitfield called for the humane treatment of slaves, which some interpreted as a call to question authority more broadly. A "spirit of confusion is blazing up more and more," worried one Dutch Reformed Church minister.[8]

But that spirit did not quite blaze up into a conflagration—not quite yet. First the winter of 1740–41 had to be got through. It was the coldest anyone could remember. More than ten feet of snow fell over Christmas. The North (Hudson) and East Rivers, as well as Long Island Sound, were frozen for weeks on end. Boats and ships were crushed in the shifting ice or else pushed out to sea, unable to free them-

---

* Britain and Spain fought a series of deadly skirmishes between 1739 and 1748 for control of key trading and slavery sites in the Caribbean, extending to Florida and north into Georgia as Britain sought to assert its hegemony over trade in the region. Eventually, the War of Jenkins' Ear (so later named because the British used the severing of merchant vessel captain Robert Jenkins's ear by the Spanish Coast Guard in a 1731 dispute that later historians traced as the root of the conflict) merged with the large War of Austrian Succession, which did little to immediately resolve dispute over control of the Caribbean. That was not finally determined, largely in Britain's favor, until the 1760s.

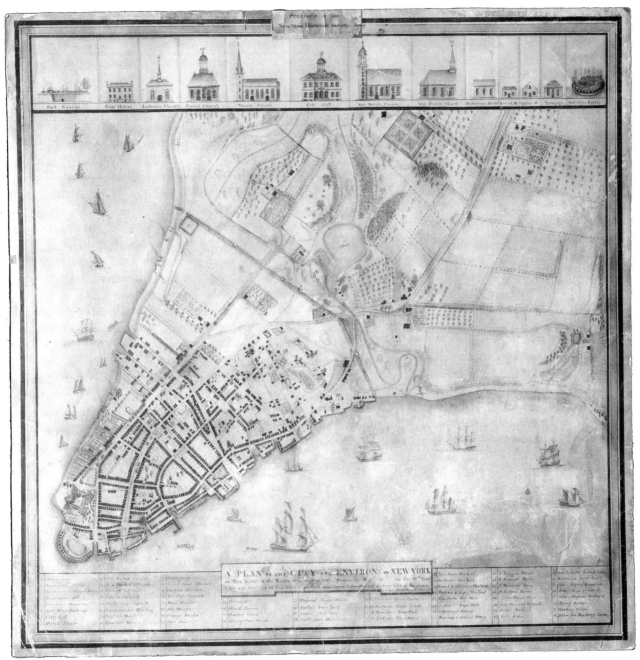

David Grimm, *A Plan of the City of and Environs of New York as They Were in the Years 1742, 1743 & 1744*.
Presented to the New York Historical Society by David Grim; 1813; black and color ink, black and color pencil,
and black and color wash on paper; 57 x 57 cm; #M2.1.1; image #3046. Used with permission.

selves. Slaves and the poor went hungry and suffered frostbite: a "Spanish Negro" was unable to walk for months.* One slave mother reportedly left her suckling child to freeze in the snow. Prices spiked; so did burglaries. As food supplies dried up except for people with plenty of cash, the "merciless contrast between rich and poor" became unavoidable, and some in the city took it upon themselves to even things out. Even with charities promising coal, clothing, and food to those "in Real Need of Relief," discontent ran deep. And so did rumors: in November, Charleston had burned in a great suspicious fire, and only a year before, the Stono Rebellion had left a wake of damage in South Carolina as slaves made their way to Spanish St. Augustine. Slave rebellions and Maroon wars persisted across the Caribbean, and each ship arriving in New York brought news not only of them but often also of rebellious slaves being transported north.[9]

Conspiracy?

As the snows fell, a great Christmas feast took place at John Hughson's tavern near Gerardus Comfort's house and dock on the North River.† Or at least so reported Mary Burton, John and Sarah Hughson's sixteen-year-old indentured Irish serving girl, when she testified against Hughson and the slave Caesar in connection with a robbery. The feast was elaborated on later by a quartet of slaves when confessions were wrung out of them: forty or fifty people (slaves; a few free blacks; Spanish Negroes; Hughson and his wife and daughter; the Irish woman Peggy Kerry, pregnant with Caesar's child) sat down to plates heaped with veal, duck, mutton, goose, and pork and pots of punch. Revelers swore themselves to a plot to "take the Country"—to burn the city, kill the white men, and take their wives for their own. The world was turned on its head. Black men feasted, swore oaths, and plotted while being waited upon by white women.

* A dark-skinned Spanish-speaking sailor, sold into slavery by English privateers.
† Hughson's tavern and Comfort's house and dock were just south of what is now the World Trade Center site.

Perhaps. The feast may never have happened; the confessions are suspect, and Burton's accusations shifted, evolved, and contradicted themselves as the trials and executions of the conspirators wore on. Arrested slaves confessed to all kinds of fantastical things.[10]

But there is little doubt that Hughson's tavern, like Comfort's house and the well outside it, where slaves fetched tea water, were meeting places. Slaves and servants, dockworkers and newly transported Irish, a "motley proletariat" and "the outcasts of the nations of the earth" gathered together to drink, talk, gamble, watch cocks fight, get warm—and fence stolen goods. Hughson's tavern was a great clearinghouse of ill-gotten goods. It was a vital node in a vibrant underground economy. Tavern keepers often extended credit to sailors and slaves, servants and apprentices, debts that could be paid with stolen loot. Sailors, meanwhile, were often also the buyers of stolen goods to be used by themselves or sold on at their next port of call. Colonial legislators tried vainly to halt such doings. Hughson's tavern itself was so notorious a market that it gained the nickname "Oswego" after the Lake Ontario port and trading post where the English and Iroquois swapped goods: jewelry, clothes, silverware, coins, and especially guns. Hughson was a fence, and a particularly important one for John Gwin, also known as Caesar. Gwin and his friend Prince were well known as daring thieves, and brash ones: they commemorated an early heist gone bad—of a big barrel of Geneva gin, or jenever, for which they were paraded around town and whipped—by forming the Geneva Club, complete with Freemason-like rites and dedicated to profitable thievery. At the beginning of March, Caesar was jailed, suspected of relieving a "bulge" in the cash drawer in a shop on Bond Street and fencing the coins and other stolen goods at Hughson's.[11]

At places like Hughson's and Comfort's, "the outcasts of the nations" exchanged more than goods. They also swapped information: about where goods could be purloined; about who was treated harshly by their masters; about rebellions, uprisings, and fires up and down the Atlantic coast and throughout the Caribbean. That the tavern might have played host to some kind of plot is not hard to imagine. But what kind of plot? Was it a Negro plot—a great uprising of slaves? Or was it a Spanish plot to claim the colony from the English, as was intimated as the summer of fires and trials wore on? Or was it a popish, priestly plot, as the prosecutor Horsmanden came to believe as summer waned? Or was it all a big joke, a prank, as the historian Jill Lepore somewhat implausibly claims?[12]

The Fires

Whatever the plot was, it scared the wealthy white residents of New York.* The Fort George fire on Wednesday, March 18, which destroyed the home of Governor George Clarke and the office of the secretary, was the biggest. While it burned, the slave Cuffee danced a jig and upended fire buckets passed his way.† Two other slaves, Dundee and Patrick, watched the fire from a hill, with Patrick stating that he "wished the Governor had been burnt in the middle of it."[13] The fire looked to be an accident—the result of a careless welder mending a leaky gutter on a windy afternoon. Such fires were commonplace in eighteenth-century cities. Cities were firetraps, and life, heated by coal and wood and illuminated by candles, was shaped by fire. Fire was a weapon of revolt, but it was also simply a daily hazard. Cuffee may have danced, and Patrick may have wished, but they might very well have been celebrating their good fortune: nature was doing what they had perhaps only dreamed of doing.

Then another fire erupted on Wednesday, March 25, at the home of Capt. Peter Warren. It seemed to be a chimney fire—a common occurrence—and it was quickly extinguished. The next Wednesday, April 1, Winant Van Zandt's house burned to the ground, the fire probably started by a resident smoking a pipe near hay stored inside. Three fires on three Wednesdays: suspicions mounted. The next fires broke the pattern. On Saturday, April 4, a haystack in the Fly Market burst into flames.‡ Patrick told Dundee that "the Fires in Town were not half done yet." Soon another fire erupted at Ben Thomas's house, this one clearly set. The next morning, smoldering coals were found under a haystack near Joseph Murphy's house, casting suspicion on one of his slaves. Later that day, a housewife overheard John Walter's slave Quack (or Quaco) laugh and shout to two companions "*Fire, Fire, Scorch, Scorch*, A LITTLE, *Damn it*, BY-AND-BY."§ Monday morning, April 6, brought four more fires, including one at the home of the slave trader and privateer Capt. Jacob Sarly. Suspicion focused on Sarly's slave, the Spanish Negro Juan de la Silva, who had been captured from a ship by fellow privateer Capt. John Lush. A rumor rapidly spread that Spanish Negroes had damned Sarly and threatened to ruin the town if they were not set free and sent to "their own Country." Vigilantes rounded up de la Silva and four other Spanish Negroes and threw them into the jail in the basement of City Hall. As interrogations began, Frederick Philipse's New Street warehouse caught fire, and one of those fighting the flames saw Adolph Philipse's slave Cuffee lurking nearby. Cuffee took flight, chased by a mob, who caught him at Adolph's house. The cry went up: "The Negroes are rising."[14]

But then that was it. Just as suddenly as the rash of fires hit the city, they stopped. Perhaps the conspiracy had been broken; perhaps there was no conspiracy. Or perhaps there was. Mobs had rounded up nearly a hundred blacks and Spanish Negroes, mostly from the East, Montgomerie, and

---

* Who constituted white New Yorkers in 1741 was not who we might think constitutes them now: "To those who gathered at Hughson's the 'white people' were, in code or cant, the rich, the people with money, not simply the ones with a particular . . . skin color." Thus white-skinned David Johnson could pledge at Hughson's "to burn the town, and kill as many white people as he could," according to Horsmanden (Linebaugh and Rediker, *Many-Headed Hydra*, 209).

† Cuffee was probably a variation on Kofí (or similar), the Akan name for a boy born on Friday; the slave name Quack (or Quaco) was derived from Kwakú (Wednesday); Joe and Cudjoe from Kwadwó (Monday); and so on. Other slaves were named for places (e.g., Dundee, Cuba, London) or their masters. Still other slave names were biblical, classical, or literary references (Jacob, Neptune, Othello).

‡ Fly is from the old Dutch *vly*, meaning "valley."

§ Under interrogation, Quack claimed he was actually praising English admiral Edward Vernon's defeat of the Spanish at Jamaica's Porto Bello.

West Wards, where both fires and slaves were thickest. Daniel Horsmanden, the colony's recorder and the junior justice on the supreme court, convinced the city council to raise a reward for information leading to the "discovery of the incendiaries, their confederates and accomplices, as that they should be convicted thereof." A reward of £100 was offered to any white person providing information; free blacks, mulattoes, and Indians were offered £45; slaves were offered £20 and manumission (their owners to be compensated £25). These were huge sums: £45 was four or five years' wages for a free black or mulatto; £100 was more than the city typically received in revenue from franchises and properties in a year. Horsmanden also engineered a plan to search all houses and businesses in the city where information regarding stolen goods and "suspicious persons" might be found. The council agreed to try this first before making the rewards public. The search got under way on Monday, April 13, with troops blocking the streets. All persons were subject to search. Little was turned up (though one enslaved couple, Robin and Cuba, owned by the city clerk, were jailed because Robin possessed "some things unbecoming the condition of slaves").[15]

Rumors continued to swirl—slaves rising, the Spanish on their way—but no more fires broke out. On April 17, a month after the first fire, Governor Clarke proclaimed the rewards, and a grand jury of seventeen men, including some who had seen their buildings burn, was impaneled four days later. Mary Burton was an early and, at first, reluctant witness. She refused to be summoned, then she refused to be sworn, then she refused to answer questions. The clerk read her the reward proclamation. Burton said nothing, and she was ordered to jail for contempt. Fearing being locked up with John and Sarah Hughson, Caesar, and Peggy Kerry, all of whom she had accused of burglary and fencing (both capital offenses), Burton said she would tell the grand jury what she knew of the burglaries, "but I'll say nothing about the fires."

Eventually Burton did testify to knowledge of the "uprising," saying Caesar, Prince, and Cuffee met often at Hugh-son's and talked "frequently of burning the fort and that they'd go down to the Fly and burn the whole town." Sarah and John Hughson pledged to assist them. John Hughson would become king, Burton told the jurors, and Caesar would become governor. Cuffee gave the motive: "A great many people have too much and others too little," Burton said Cuffee had declared at the big party at Hughson's. "My old master has a great deal of money," Cuffee went on, "but in a short time, he should have less and I should have more."* Burton detailed a conspiracy just like the one in 1712: fires would be set at night, and when white people came to put them out, the conspirators would "kill and destroy them." Sometimes the three slave plotters were joined by twenty or thirty others at Hughson's. Sarah Hughson told Mary Burton that if she ever breathed a word of the burglaries or the fire plot Sarah would burn *her*.[16]

New Yorkers Burning—and Hanging

Mary Burton's testimony set the court in action. All the lawyers eligible to practice before the supreme court were called to a meeting to plan out the prosecutions. Despite there being no legal need for a jury trial for slaves accused of arson, burglary, or conspiracy, the lawyers decided to have jury trials anyway, with the supreme court justices serving as lead prosecutors. Caesar and Prince, in jail since March 2 (weeks before the first fire), were tried on May 1 and found guilty of burglary and sentenced to hang. The Hughsons and Peggy Kerry would be next, charged with receiving stolen goods. First, though, Arthur Price, a petty thief, a white man, in jail with Peggy, claimed Peggy told him that fourteen conspirators had sworn a bond of blood and planned to set the town alight. Peggy, knowing of the plot, was sworn to secrecy. Peggy Kerry and the Hughsons were tried on May 6 and found guilty of burglary. Cuffee was moved to Arthur Price's cell and given alcoholic punch to loosen his tongue; Cuffee

---

* Plotters believed, according to Horsmanden, that in New York "there should be a motley government as well as motley subjects" (Linebaugh and Rediker, *Many-Headed Hydra*, 176).

An **1860 depiction of a slave being hanged during the Negro Revolt, by George Hayward, printmaker.** Art and Picture Collection, New York Public Library.

detailed the conspiracy (according to Price) and fingered John Roosevelt's Quack as the one who set the fort on fire. Quack was soon arrested.[17]

Caesar and Prince were hanged on May 11, not far from the Negroes Burial Ground, denying conspiracy to the end. Caesar's lifeless body was gibbeted and hung up in chains at Little Collect Pond nearby, left to rot in hopes that the example of his "Punishment might break the Rest." Mary Burton added to her story. More slaves were arrested, and evidence was wrung from them. A slave named Sandy told prosecutors that Quack had told him he planned to set fire to the fort and boasted afterward, "The Business is done." A slave named Fortune named Cuffee as the arsonist at Philipse's storehouse. Quack and Cuffee were both found guilty and sentenced to burn at the stake. On the afternoon of May 30, they were led to the edge of the Negroes Burial Ground and chained to tall stakes. A huge crowd—a mob some called it—gathered to watch. Lied to by their exe-

cutioners, promised hanging instead of burning, the two slaves confessed, each owning up to setting the fires they'd been accused of and naming almost thirty others as conspirators. Both named John Hughson as the leader of the plot. Afraid of the mob that had come to see a burning, the sheriff refused to commute Quack's and Cuffee's sentences to hanging. The fires were lit.[18]

On the basis of Quack's and Cuffee's confessions, John and Sarah Hughson, their daughter Sarah, and Peggy Kerry were rearraigned on charges of conspiracy and tried on June 4. The jury quickly found them guilty, and on June 8 they were sentenced to die by hanging. They could not be burned because they had not committed "petty treason," as had Quack and Cuffee. But maybe what they were guilty of was worse. Judge Frederick Philipse, victim of a fire, laid it out with all the disgust he could muster: "For People, who have been brought up, and always lived in a Christian Country, and also called themselves Christians, to be guilty not only of

A Mob Demanding the Quack Be Burnt, an early nineteenth-century depiction of the Negro Revolt.
Art and Picture Collection, New York Public Library.

making Negro Slaves their Equals, but even their Superiors, by waiting upon, keeping with, and entertaining them, with Meat, Drink, and Lodging; and what is much more amazing, to plot, conspire, consult, abet and encourage these black *Seeds of Cain*, to burn the City, and to kill and destroy us all.—GOOD GOD!"[19] John Hughson and his wife, Sarah, together with Peggy Kerry, were hanged on June 12, confessing nothing. The Hughsons' daughter Sarah was spared for a few days in hopes that seeing her parents die would loosen her tongue. Once dead, John Hughson was taken off the gallows and hung up in chains to rot next to Caesar.

More black men and women were rounded up. As fast as slaves (and a few others) were arrested and tried, they were dispatched. In one trial, on June 8, six male slaves were tried and convicted of conspiracy. All were sentenced to death, five by burning at the stake. One named names and was spared the flames. More were arrested. Prosecutors learned that Hughson had kept a list of conspirators, which, they

were told, was now held by the slave Ben. Ben denied it but was found guilty and sentenced to burn. More were arrested. Amnesty was offered to anyone, free or slave, who fingered others by July 1. More were arrested. By the end of June more than a hundred slaves were in jail. Nearly two hundred in all were named or accused. The cost to slaveholders was steep, and soon talk turned to pardons and transportation out of the colony. It turned also to the question of whether it was neither a slave revolt nor a Spanish plot but maybe a papist one. A new ringleader was soon named: John Ury, presumed to be a priest in disguise. Black men recanted their confessions. On July 10 a slave named Othello belonging to Chief Judge James De Lancey (who had been away in New England until late June) was sentenced to burn at the stake (even though he had yet to be tried). Othello quickly confessed to having been at the conspiratorial meetings at Hughson's tavern, where he saw many soldiers and maybe a priest. Othello was hanged rather than burned.[20]

A final batch of slaves were brought to trial on July 15, eight black men who had refused to plead guilty. Witnesses placed them at Hughson's, and they were found guilty. Two were given a reprieve and transported; five were hanged; one went up in flames.

A New York Underworld

Fires returned to New York beginning in February 1742. Once again, rumors of revolt in Charleston were making the rounds. And the first fire seemed a clear case of arson. But as hard as Horsmanden pushed, New Yorkers this year seemed to have less stomach for grand conspiracy than they had the previous year. Horsmanden's credibility was already waning.* Even before the final trials were conducted the previous summer, some had begun to question whether there

---

* So was Mary Burton's. With Horsmanden's help she tried all year to get her £100 reward. In March 1742 the council discharged her indenture and awarded her £3 for clothing and necessities. It was reluctant to do more. Months of more wrangling finally led to Mary being awarded £81, with which she fled the colony.

Fulton Ferry in 1750, from the Brooklyn Shore (from an Old Print), **1801.**
The Miriam and Ira D. Wallach Division of Art, Prints, and Photographs, New York Public Library.

had really been a plot after all—a Negro one, a Spanish one, or a papist one. Horsmanden had taken the extraordinary step (and the assembly's money, which had been dedicated for another purpose) to allay such talk by writing up and publishing the proceedings of the year before, an effort that eventually became *A Journal in the Proceedings in the Detection of the Conspiracy Formed by Some* White *People in Conjunction with* Negro *and Other* Slaves *for the Burning of the City of New-York in America and Murdering the Inhabitants* (1744), "one of the most startling and vexing documents in early American history."[21] It is the primary source upon which all histories of the Great Negro Plot rely. Historians have interpreted it (and the scant other surviving evidence) in remarkably different ways: as proof of "a revolutionary conspiracy, Atlantic in scope . . . a conspiracy by a motley proletariat to incite urban insurrection";[22] as a more local plot to do "damage to the society enslaving them";[23] as a confused and confusing moment in New York history wrapped up in extreme party politics, maybe just a ruse or a joke, or quite possibly something to do with "revolution";[24] or as a not very "well-organized coup—by slaves against their masters, by the poor against the rich, or a combination of the both," or perhaps just a plan "to cover up multiple burglaries."[25]

Whatever Horsmanden's *Journal* is, and whatever the real nature of the plot, together they give an invaluable glimpse into the underworld of colonial New York, a glimpse at the city's class and race geography. It was a handsome city, with tree-lined streets and elegant clubs. Already, buildings were reaching skyward, some as high as four or five stories. The great Broad Way boasted fine civic buildings and a market and was a place for the well-heeled to promenade. Meanwhile, slaves also walked the streets and alleys, gathering on the docks, at the water pumps, and in the taverns. They met up with sailors and petty thieves and fences. Husband and wife slaves were forced to live apart, so they broke the law and sneaked out at night, walking the streets without lanterns to visit each other. Quack's wife lived at the fort, and his being barred from visiting her may have led him to set the first fire of 1741.[26] Slaves like Caesar climbed through second-story windows not only to steal things but also to visit their lovers, like the "Irish Newfoundland beauty" Peggy Kerry.* Gangs formed—the Smith Fly Boys, the Long Bridge Club, and the Geneva Club. Slaves and sailors traded rumors and maintained ties with sailors and slaves in distant places.† They reinvented Akan and other West African rites. And they danced. They danced in the Fields in great "frol-

---

* Peggy Kerry was also known as "Negro Peg," and, depending on interpretation, her blackness was either a reflection on whom she consorted with or a comment on what she did: she was known as a "notorious prostitute," and she complained that Mary Burton's accusations had made her "as black as the rest."

† Many of the slaves involved in the 1712 rebellion were newly arrived from West Africa; after that uprising direct importation from Africa slowed, and more arrived instead from the Caribbean, many of whom were being transported from there for rebelling or for crimes. The New York slave world was a rebellious slave world.

icks," proof to Horsmanden of the "Excess of Liberty" slaves in New York lived by.[27]

Sometimes, slaves turned the world upside down. Christmas itself was a time of turning. Across the city (as across Europe), Christmas was a carnival during which men dressed as women, women dressed as men, and masters served their servants. The poor wandered the streets, expecting coins and food from the rich. Mobs in the streets, black and white, turned riotous. In the taverns, great upside-down feasts were held. The big revel at Hughson's tavern—where the plot to burn New York may have been hatched—was a Christmas feast. Eventually, the New York elite (and the newly emerging middle class) would seek to impose a new kind of public order on Christmas and on the mob, but not before learning to use revelry and the mob to its own revolutionary purposes. And not before, in a final turning, John Hughson's corpse would turn black and Caesar's white.[28]

CHAPTER 3

The Stamp Act Revolt, 1765

JENJOY ROYBAL

The Stamp Act was to take effect on November 1, 1765, and as the date approached, colonial authorities in New York became increasingly anxious. Back in August anti–Stamp Act protests in Boston and Newport had erupted into violence and the destruction of property. In Boston an angry mob had attacked the tax office, then proceeded to ransack the house of Andrew Oliver (Boston's official stamp administrator) and burn him in effigy. Several days later, a mob destroyed the house of Lieutenant Governor Thomas Hutchinson. Soon after word reached him of the Boston uprising, James McEvers, the wealthy merchant appointed as New York's stamp distributor, resigned in fear.[1] Tensions remained high throughout the fall.

On October 23 the *Edward*, the ship carrying the stamps (which served as evidence that a new duty on all manner of printed material had been paid in valid British currency and not colonial paper money) sailed into New York Harbor escorted by two warships. Sailors on nearby ships lowered their flags to half-mast to demonstrate disapproval. As the ship neared Lower Manhattan, the shouts of an angry crowd gathered on the Battery could be heard across the water. The ship anchored under the protection of a rebuilt Fort George, just northwest of the Battery. Governor Cadwallader Colden, who had publicly sworn to enforce the Stamp Act, ordered a detachment of marines to wait until nightfall to whisk the stamps into the relatively safe confines of Fort George. Colden had already heightened tensions in the previous weeks by making it known he would employ military force to carry out his duty. He had received reinforcements for Fort George from Gen. Thomas Gage and had ordered the commander, Maj. Thomas James, to position his guns so that they could fire on mobs gathered on Broadway.

On the evening of October 31—the night before the act was to take effect—a throng of tradesmen, artisans, shopkeepers, mechanics, farmers, and sailors amassed to conduct a mock funeral for "Liberty." A rumor arose among them that on the next day there would be an attempt to bury alive Major James, Fort George's artillery commander. James had bragged in public that he would force the stamps down the throats of New Yorkers on the tip of his sword. While the faux funerary procession was under way, a group of the city's most prominent merchants met at the City Arms Tavern to organize an embargo of British goods. On hearing that the merchants had failed to endorse more radical measures, a contingent of the mock mourners broke away from the procession and raced through the streets in a "mobbish manner," breaking windows and streetlamps.

The Stamp Act and the People's Unrest

The tension had been building since spring. The Stamp Act had been passed by Parliament on March 22, 1765, with word of it reaching the colonies several weeks later. It required a tax on all legal documents, permits, commercial contracts, newspapers, wills, pamphlets, and even playing cards sold in the colonies. Almost all business transactions were subject to the tax. The act was an attempt to recover some of the enormous debt Britain had incurred during the Seven Years' War and to defray the cost of maintaining a strong military presence in the colonies. The colonists perceived it as obnoxious from the moment they heard about it, equating it with enslavement. Never before had colonists been forced to pay a tax that impinged on nearly every aspect of daily life. Intense opposition helped form bonds among the individual colonies where they had never existed before. The Sons of Liberty and many other less famous ad hoc protest groups spontaneously emerged in almost every colony in the wake of the passage of the act. Along with fomenting protests and riots in their own towns and cities, these groups corresponded with each other in an attempt to coordinate a boycott of British imports and efforts to destroy the stamps themselves.

Alongside the organized boycott, a legal argument against the Stamp Act began to take shape. In June James Otis of Massachusetts proposed the idea of a Stamp Act Congress meeting in New York to consider action against the hated tax.[2] The congress convened at City Hall from October 7 to 24, with twenty-seven men representing nine of the thirteen colonies. The group drafted a legal document suggesting the act subverted the rights of the colonists by taxing them without representation in Parliament and issued the "Declaration of Rights and Liberties" on October 19. The declaration was propagated far and wide and influenced the thinking of people from the lowest to the highest ranks of colonial society.* While men organized the formal political protests and legal arguments, women played a vital role in organizing the boycott and pushing public opinion against the Stamp Act. They popularized the ban on British goods by reviving skills like spinning and weaving cloth and by wearing homemade garments rather than imported ones. Children were caught

---

* The British North American colonies had one of the highest literacy rates in the world at the time.

up in the excitement too, chanting "Liberty, Property, and No Stamps"—the Sons of Liberty's slogan—as they played on the streets.[3]

The Sons of Liberty were the prime movers of the New York protests, especially merchant and sailor Isaac Sears, who was one of the group's most respected leaders. By October 31 the Sons had posted a placard on the door of every public office and in all the streets that gave the name "Voice of the People" to their movement:

> Pro Patria.
> *The first man that either distributes or makes use of the stamped paper, let him take care of his house, person, and effects.*
> vox Populi
> "We Dare"

The Sons also circulated a public letter that said they would not submit to the Stamp Act on any account and would not rest until it was done away with entirely. While these efforts, along with the threatened boycott, helped exert considerable pressure on colonial authorities, Sears and the Sons knew these measures alone might not be enough to bring about the desired end.[4]

Rioting in the Eighteenth Century

The Anti-impressment Riot of 1764 was only the most recent demonstration of public protest, and it offered a template for what the city might face when the Stamp Act came into effect. Anti-impressment riots had been a staple of colonial unrest for much of the century. Colonists reacted violently to impressment—forced enlistment in the Royal Navy. In 1747, for example, rioters forced the Massachusetts governor to flee in the midst of a three-day uprising in Boston. In New York two separate anti-impressment riots had taken place in 1760, and the end of the Seven Years' War in 1763 only heightened volatility in the city as unemployment among sailors and maritime workers soared.

Across the colonies some twenty thousand sailors were released from duty and unable to find work. With war over, the lucrative practice of privateering had dried up, cutting

Howard Pyle, *At the Sign of the Griffin*, 1879, depicting an eighteenth-century anti-impressment riot.
Yale University Art Gallery.

off a major supply of income for sailors and a staple of New York City's economy. New regulations, customs laws, and stricter enforcement of older laws killed off much of New York's trade with the West Indies, further depressing the maritime economy. The navy also stepped up its efforts against smuggling, a common source of income for colonial sailors and a staple of the local economy. New Yorkers thought the war's completion would bring an end to impressment, but the navy's expansion of its enforcement activities actually increased its demand for labor, so the practice of forcing sailors into service continued unabated.[5]

New York's 1764 riot was a response to the impressment of several fishermen. A naval officer who came ashore was surrounded by a mob, and although he was not harmed, he was forced to declare publicly his opposition to impressment and sign an affidavit to that effect. Meanwhile, the long boat in which the officer had been rowed ashore was dragged to

the Commons—now City Hall Park—and burned in a great bonfire.[6] A year later the Sons were fully aware that they could use the menace of the mob as political leverage in their fight against the Stamp Act.

Theatrical gestures, like the burning of the longboat, backed with the threat of real violence, were a common part of eighteenth-century political culture in the colonies—a continuation of practices and traditions imported from the old countries where participating in a mob had long been a form of entertainment as well as a form of popular politics.[7] The royal authorities would produce great public events to celebrate the arrival of dignitaries and royal members of the court, the king's birthday, military victories, and even executions and would encourage excited participation with drink and food. Running around, behaving badly, drinking, and smashing up a limited amount of property were accepted to a degree during both formal and informal public events.

Young sailors and artisans especially were given leeway to act in this manner. For plebeians, public rowdiness was a means of expressing political concerns and of scorning individuals who transgressed community norms. When a person did something against the moral convictions of the community, a public parade of ridicule, ending at that person's doorstep, might ensue. Such practices helped maintain a common moral order, uniting a community through public spectacle. The idea of corporatism—that society was an organic whole—gave legitimacy to the rowdy mob actions, which were generally tolerated by royal authorities.[8]

As in Europe, public protest in the colonies involved mock role reversal with elites. Plebeians would construct effigies that mimicked officials, religious leaders, or characters in stories and parade them through the streets, accompanied by much dancing, drinking, and general carnival-like behavior. Charivari or shivaree, the banging of pots and wooden barrels with sticks, was a frequent part of the ritual. Through such antics, people acted out fantasies, told moral stories, and played out preferred political outcomes. Sometimes they would run around demanding tribute or unofficial taxes.* The public merriment would sometimes end in breaking windows or ripping up fences. Rioters built symbolic structures—a carriage representing the elite or a boat representing the Royal Navy—and set them alight in huge bonfires. Rarely were people hurt (though they might be menaced); eighteenth-century street theater had rules usually followed by both rioters and those in power. Authorities tolerated a degree of destruction, but once it reached a certain point, the mob was read the riot act and given an hour or so to disperse before authorities used force.† Such rules of rioting maintained the bonds of society. The plebeians were able to vent their anger, while elites maintained their power. Rioting was a safety valve.[9]

* The lyrics of the English carol "We Wish You a Merry Christmas" give some sense of these ribald goings-on.
† In 1715 Parliament passed the Riot Act in the midst of much tumult and the Jacobite uprising (see p. 45); from that year, reading the Riot Act was literally what happened.

Guy Fawkes Day was a favorite public celebration among plebeians in both England and the colonies. Every November 5 mobs would gather to remember Guy Fawkes's attempt to blow up the Houses of Parliament in 1605. Amid much drinking, noise making, and huge bonfires, revelers would sneer at the authority of the religious establishment, government, and social hierarchy. In the colonies, the festivities usually involved the burning of a grotesque effigy of the Roman Catholic pope, who was accompanied by a devil and the Catholic pretender to the throne, both poised as if whispering in the pope's ear. By the 1740s the celebrations had begun to incorporate protests against local conditions and authorities, setting precedent for revolutionary era uprisings.

On both sides of the Atlantic, the early eighteenth-century writings of the English coffeehouse radicals known as the True Whigs or Commonwealthmen formed an important ideological foundation for public protest.[10] The writings excoriated the corrupt convergence of money and political power in King George I's London, holding it as a serious threat to English liberty. Commonwealthmen advocated action in the streets as a means of checking the power of the court. Many in the colonies had read True Whig pamphlets, and the arguments they propounded had captured colonial imaginations long before the Stamp Act Revolts. Liberty for the elite and plebeians was defined differently, but they both agreed on its desirability.[11] The elites in the colonies coupled liberty with paternal responsibility for the lower ranks of society. The elites felt it was their duty to protect the lower orders and thus maintained a certain tolerance for public riots, since the elites viewed riots as legitimate means for plebeians to articulate problems that concerned the whole society.[12]

But the perception and meaning of rioting had begun to change in New York as a result of the city's rapidly growing population and stagnant economy immediately following the Seven Years' War. The growing complexity of the social order made it difficult for elites to feel confident that the mobs were truly expressing interests of concern to the whole community. In fact, the plebeians themselves had varied reasons for rioting. Older traditions that embraced shared values within an entrenched social hierarchy clashed with new egalitarian ideals of individualism increasingly favored by sailors and artisans. Imperial regulations imposed from abroad, like the Stamp Act (which was as regressive as any tax), furthered the corrosion of communal feelings. New York society was increasingly a class society.

The Stamp Act Riots

November 1, 1765, was eerily calm; New York's usually bustling waterfront was quiet, and little traffic passed on the streets.[13] But as the sun set, a throng of laborers, sailors, youths, and artisans gathered on the Commons. The crowd hoisted two effigies on a gallows, one representing Governor Cadwallader Colden, the other the devil. Colden's effigy held a boot and a stamped paper in one hand and had a drum on its back. The boot represented the Earl of Bute, the king's main advisor on taxes and a main architect of the Stamp Act. The drum represented the widespread rumor that in 1715, while in Scotland to marry his wife, Colden served as a drummer in a Jacobite army that failed to restore a Catholic king, James III and VIII, to the thrones of England and Scotland. The devil effigy was posed whispering into the ear of Colden. Given the Protestant bent of the crowd, these signifiers struck a chord with the people, especially since farmers and villagers from throughout the region (many recent immigrants from Scotland, Ireland, and England familiar with its recent, turbulent history) were pouring into the city in anticipation of the annual celebration of Pope Day—Guy Fawkes Day's other name. Moreover, similar effigies had been used in Boston's Stamp Act protests in August, accounts of which were well known to New Yorkers.

A second mob marched to the Commons with another effigy of Colden—borne atop Colden's own coach, which the mob had seized. This crowd merged with the first, and the effigies and coach led a parade of thousands down Broadway toward Fort George. If mobs of the time typically numbered fifty or a hundred people, this one exceeded two thousand.

The torch-lit parade to the fort, where Colden and the military waited, must have been an impressive sight—and an intimidating one. The protesters threw bricks and stones, smashing windows and knocking down fences, gathering up their pieces for kindling for a bonfire. At the fort they taunted the soldiers, challenging them to fire on the crowd. The protesters demanded that the gates to the fort be open. Inside, Colden and Major James, who had been guarding the fort since the arrival of the *Edward*, knew the growing mob could overwhelm it if incited. And since many of the soldiers in the fort had themselves been impressed into service, it was not clear just where their loyalties lay. Colden and James gave strict orders not to fire. A standoff ensued. Tensions remained high.

Some of the rioters moved on to Bowling Green, where they built a large bonfire out of the green's fencing and anything else they could get their hands on. Others paraded the effigies and Colden's cart back to the Commons, where they were fed into another massive bonfire while the mob chanted threats to Stamp Act supporters. A third group of rioters marched to the house of Major James at Vauxhall and gutted it, breaking every piece of furniture and destroying everything of value, from books to artwork.* His wine cellar was plundered and his garden ripped up. After James's house was destroyed, the rioting ebbed, and the mobs had dispersed by 4:00 a.m. Later that morning, authorities hung a large banner on Fort George stating that stamps would no longer be kept there.[14]

Aftermath

The Sons of Liberty wanted the stamps, but Colden negotiated a compromise with them. The stamps would be handed over to municipal officials, who would place them in City Hall. There matters rested. On November 13 a new governor arrived to replace Colden, a switch that cooled the city's fervor. Henry Moore had been governor of Jamaica and had

---

* Vauxhall is now West Broadway.

gained royal favor by crushing a slave revolt, but he showed no inclination to resort to violence in New York. His strategy was to let the protesters' embargo play out, assuming the resulting economic damage to the city would eventually bring compliance to the act. But, contrary to expectations, the boycott held. On March 16, 1766, Parliament repealed the Stamp Act.[15]

In the wake of the Stamp Act Revolt, John Adams wrote, "The people, even to the lowest ranks, have become more attentive to their liberties, more inquisitive about them and more determined to defend them than they were ever before known or had occasion to be."[16] The Stamp Act agitation politicized New Yorkers across society. Merchants, lawyers, and shipbuilders united with sailors, laborers, and artisans in a common cause. The sailors would have an important role in the decade that led up to the American Revolution, pushing a revolutionary ideology and taking again and again to the streets.[17] They encouraged egalitarianism and freedom against the tyranny of impressment, which came to stand for the injustice of colonial rule.

Almost everyone in New York was deeply affected by the Stamp Act Riots. No doubt the twenty-six hundred slaves in the city saw a promise of freedom in the uprising—more than just the "rumor of revolt" that was the Great Negro Plot of 1741.[18] Women tasted political empowerment as they took a central role in organizing the boycott. The wealthy saw the threat of mob action as useful leverage against the British, even as they feared they might lose control of it: perhaps the power of the mob was a newly dangerous force. The moral order that governed public misrule in the preceding decades seemed to be breaking down, and a new order was yet to be born. The Sons of Liberty had capitalized on Guy Fawkes Day—Pope Day—traditions to threaten British authority. But when Cadwallader Colden and Major James trained their guns on the mob, an implicit social contract was broken. Not only did the angered mobs in New York and around the colonies together with the Stamp Act Congress force the repeal of the Stamp Act, they also showed the newly political purpose to which mob action (street theater, we would now call it) could be put. They set the stage for the Boston Tea Party, other acts of resistance, and the armed revolt that would follow.

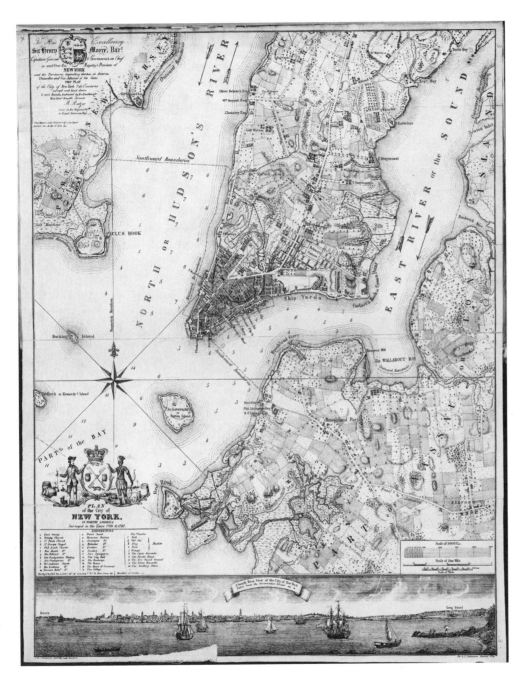

Plan of the City of New York, 1766 and 1767.
Courtesy the Lionel Picus and Princess Firyal Map Division, New York Public Library.

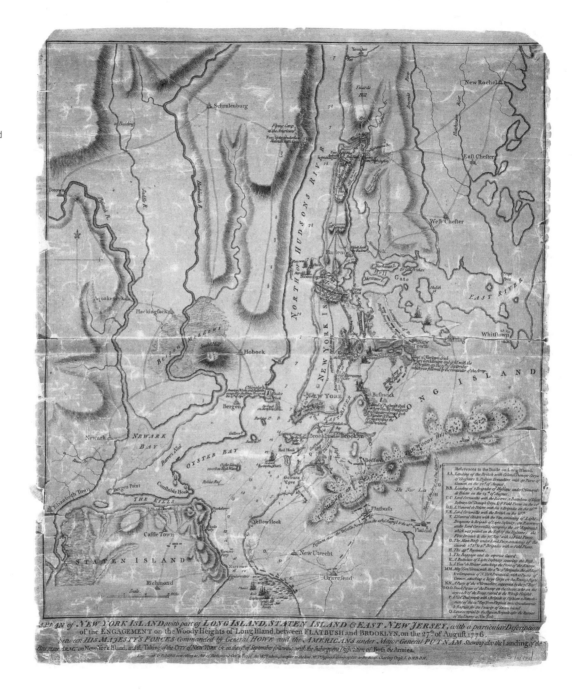

Plan of New York with Parts of Long Island Showing General Howe's Attack, August 27, 1776.
Courtesy the Lionel Picus and Princess Firyal Map Division, New York Public Library.

CHAPTER 4

Revolution

New York in Revolt, 1765–1783

NEIL SMITH

The Stamp Act Riots were only the beginning. At the same time Parliament passed the Stamp Act in 1765, it also passed a Mutiny Act, as it had every year since 1688. Annual renewal of the Mutiny Act was necessary because Britain had no legal standing army during peacetime. Of course, Britain had a standing army anyway, and so there needed to be a law to punish—with death—soldiers and officers for desertion, sedition, and mutiny. But the 1765 Mutiny Act was different. It was accompanied by the Quartering Act, which required colonists to billet soldiers in inns, alehouses, barns, outbuildings, unoccupied houses, "and other buildings"—and to shoulder the costs. Like the Stamp Act, colonists saw the Quartering Act as an onerous taxation in which they had had no say. When fifteen hundred troops arrived in New York City in 1766, the New York Assembly refused to comply with the Quartering Act.

"Liberty," 1765–1766

The pressure on the assembly from below was intense. The Sons of Liberty, led by seaman-privateers, the son of a transported burglar, and a cabinetmaker, repeatedly took to the streets in the winter of 1766, leading riotous crowds carrying effigies of Cadwallader Colden and other officials and encouraging "Children [to] nightly trampouze the Streets with lanthorns upon Poles & hallowing," as Governor Moore

wrote.* In May they disrupted a theater performance, declaring it was "highly improper that such Entertainments should be exhibited at this Time of public distress, when great numbers of poor people can scarce find substance," and driving the audience out with brickbats, relieving many of them of "their Caps, Hats, Wigs, Cardinals, and Cloak Tails" as they fled. Even more spectacularly, the mob then dismantled the theater itself, dragged the pieces to the Commons and lighting a huge bonfire. The radicalism of New York's Sons paled, however, in comparison with that of upriver farmers who were in rebellion against their landlords and threatened to invade the city and pull down their townhouses, hoping to rally the city's poor to the farmers' cause. But the city's radicals did not respond as the farmers hoped. Governor Moore called out the militia, and the farmers were pushed back upstate.[1]

More cautious than the farmers, the Sons of Liberty were nonetheless a power, and they frightened New York's elite. Wild rumors circulated that the Sons were clandestinely led by city gentlemen—"inferior People" were incapable of

---

* Seamen Alexander McDougall and Isaac Sears worked their way from below decks to captaincies and made small fortunes (not entirely legitimately); John Lamb, the son of the burglar, made optical instruments; cabinetmaker Marinus Willitt was swept up by the leveling forces of evangelicalism and was a regular presence at Pope Day festivals. Sears's father-in-law owned an alehouse, and Willitt's father operated a tavern, both popular gathering places for the city's workers.

Defence of the Liberty Pole in New York, **1765**, **by Felix O. C. Darley, engraved by Albert Bobbett, 1879.**
Art and Picture Collection, New York Public Library.

hatching a "Plan of Riot," according to Gen. Thomas Gage, the commander of the British forces in the city—but this was hardly the case: the Sons were not gentlemen, and they were indeed perfectly capable of hatching not just riotous plans but revolutionary ones. Even before Christmas in 1765, the Sons had formed a Committee of Correspondence charged with creating a union or at least a military alliance with other colonies. By spring the committee had drawn up a plan for a Union of the Colonies that quickly gathered support up and down the seaboard.

When word of the Stamp Act's repeal finally reached New York on May 20, 1766, the city erupted in celebration. On the king's official birthday (June 4), the city held a giant party on the Commons and erected a liberty pole. Buckets of tar were attached to the top and blazed through the night. With the British soldiers' barracks and parade grounds nearby, this was a provocation. Over the months, soldiers pulled or chopped down the liberty pole four times, and New Yorkers put it back up five. The last time, in 1770, it was a spectacular ship's mast of sixty-eight feet, surmounted by a smaller pole of twenty-two feet, capped by a weather vane reading LIBERTY, sunk into a hole twelve feet deep (in midwinter), and girded at its base with iron bars and hoops. A remarkable feat of labor—shipwrights, teamsters, gravediggers, and ironworkers were all involved—this fifth liberty pole stood until the British army occupation of the city in 1776, symbolizing not only colonists' resistance against Britain but also ordinary people's demands that the existing class order be upended. The pole and the Commons were rallying points, as General Gage noted: "It is now common here to Assemble on all Occasions of Public Concern at the Liberty Pole and Coffee House, as for the Ancient Romans to repair to the Forum. And Orators harangue on all sides." Mass meetings became commonplace. Political power was shifting.[2]

In the meantime, though, more Royal Navy transports ferrying three or four thousand troops had arrived in mid-June 1766, and General Gage quickly dispatched a regiment of them north to wipe out the tenant farmers' insurgency. They arrested scores, dispersed others at gunpoint, and freely ransacked property. Seventy farmers were brought to trial in special court (overseen by now chief justice Daniel Horsmanden) and sentenced to jail and steep fines for riotous assault; one was sentenced to death for high treason (though eventually pardoned by the king). The Sons of Liberty decided to disband but stood ready to re-form should Americans' rights and liberties again be threatened. In London, despite the repeal of the Stamp Tax, Parliament reaffirmed its right to tax colonists "in all cases whatsoever."[3]

A Fight in the Streets, 1767–1773

Across the colonies people seethed. Boston was a simmering cauldron of radicalism; Philadelphia, the largest port, was a little less so, but passions were certainly heated. In June 1767 they all boiled over when Parliament imposed new taxes—the so-called Townsend taxes (named after the chancellor of the exchequer)—on paper, ink, paint, glass, and tea exported to the colonies. Streets filled with protesters, and the legislative halls were in an uproar. The Massachusetts legislature attempted to organize a colonies-wide refusal of the taxes and was summarily disbanded by Parliament, and troops were sent to Boston. In New York and Philadelphia merchants organized a Chamber of Commerce and endorsed the nonimportation of British goods; by August 1768 "nearly all the Merchants and Traders in town" had signed on and set a starting date of November 1. With a revivified Sons of Liberty vowing enforcement, New York commerce ground to a halt. When the New York General Assembly objected to the Townsend taxes, Governor Moore dissolved it, then dissolved it again when it voted its support of the Massachusetts boycott. New elections were called. Alexander McDougall, a Sons of Liberty leader, called on the people to

"assemble in the fields" and to "go in a body to your members" of the assembly and force them to act on quartering and the taxes.[4] When the new assembly issued the "Declaration of Rights," Moore dissolved it yet again, and yet more elections were called for March 1769. The faction that the Sons of Liberty threw their support behind—headed by the landowning James De Lancey—swept to power.[5] In the city, more artisans were elected to the Common Council, and as constables, assessors, and collectors. In a deal to put the now eighty-one-year-old Cadwallader Colden back in the governor's seat, De Lancey's faction soon betrayed the Sons and agreed to abide by the Quartering Act and provision the garrisoned British troops.[6]

"A Son of Liberty" published a broadside accusing the assembly and Colden of abetting British tyranny and linked the Sons' struggle to that of smallholders and workers in London trying to seat the radical John Wilkes in Parliament.* London seemed on the verge of revolution.[7] In New York crowds gathered at the liberty pole to denounce the assembly. Quartering the troops traduced rights, protesters argued, but it also made life harder for working people faced with a stiff new tax. The night of January 13, 1770, soldiers tried to blow up the pole; it held fast, and so the soldiers ransacked Montayne's tavern on the west side instead. The tavern was a gathering place for cartmen and had become a headquarters for the Sons. Two nights later soldiers tried again to topple the pole, again failing. Finally, the soldiers succeeded at felling the pole (for the last time) on January 16 and deposited the pieces on Montayne's doorstep. Then, on Friday, January 19, a big fight erupted on Golden Hill (John Street near William) between bayonet-armed soldiers and

---

* Alexander McDougall was eventually identified as the writer of the broadside and arrested for seditious libel. Horsmanden set bail at £2,000. McDougall hardly languished in jail. The number 45 was a symbolically significant number to Wilkes in London. On the forty-fifth day of the year, February 14, forty-five men dined with McDougall in his cell, eating forty-five pounds of beef from a forty-five-month-old cow; forty-five virgins paraded to the jail and read out the forty-fifth psalm. The dinner ended with forty-five toasts in McDougall's honor.

cutlass- and club-wielding workingmen and sailors. Many were injured, and one sailor died, stabbed with a bayonet. Numerous fights broke out across the city the next day. Sailors blamed the soldiers not only for the death of their comrade but also for taking their jobs with their moonlighting.* Eventually, the mayor and the Common Council intervened, and passions cooled. Two weeks later a new liberty pole—the tall, fortified one—went up.[8]

The coast-wide embargo on imported British goods had held strong all through 1769: in New York imports were cut by 85 percent over the previous year. Together with the street fights in New York (and the horrors of the Boston Massacre), the embargo made the Townsend taxes untenable. In April 1770 Parliament repealed them all—except the one on tea. Should the embargo be maintained? A few rich merchants were doing alright, but most traders were suffering, and privation was digging deep into the working classes. In 1768 and 1769 stevedores, tailors, carpenters, and bricklayers struck for higher wages. The city peeled back sick benefits and funeral services, and new workingmen's organizations arose to try to fill the void. People were restive. The Sons of Liberty, along with associated artisans (who had been the embargo's enforcers), pushed to keep it; merchants and traders wanted to undo it. Both camps went door-to-door canvassing support, calling on the opinions and commitments of all residents (except slaves, of course), whether enfranchised or not. In June and July the factions turned on each other and brawled in the streets. The embargo collapsed, and the deepening class divisions of the city—landowners, merchants, and traders on the one side; artisans, mechanics, and day laborers on the other—stood newly exposed.[9]

When a British credit bubble burst and the colonial economy collapsed again in 1772, suffering deepened. The winter of 1772–73 was nearly as bad as 1740–41, and the city grew desperate. The municipal poorhouse overflowed, and the Common Council appropriated and appropriated again funds to transport vagrants out of the city, many of them

newly arrived and embittered Scots and Irish peasants removed from their smallholdings by engrossing landlords. Even so, expenditures for "outdoor relief" of the poor soared to four times what had been spent in 1760. People became sick, and a new hospital had to be built on the outskirts of the town (at Broadway and Duane), further draining the city's coffers. Crime grew too, and the city shelled out for a new jail at the north end of the Commons to house a growing number of criminals. (Not all criminals could be dealt the same fate as the pickpockets Mary Daily and Margaret Siggens, who were simply hanged in 1771.) The new jail was the second new jail constructed in a dozen years. New York was a class-riven city, and this was the result. Nonetheless, General Gage declared the city to be entering an era of "domestic tranquility."[10]

If tranquility ever existed, it didn't last. Parliament passed a new Tea Act aimed to shore up the flagging fortunes of the British East India Company by allowing it to directly import tea into the colonies. Besides sidelining colonial merchants, this was also a means to collect the remaining Townsend tax on tea. The whole idea of the Townsend taxes was to get colonists to accept the authority of Parliament to impose taxes in the colonies. Colonists were not going to stand for this. Sons of Liberty leaders William Smith, Isaac Sears, and Alexander McDougall leaped back into action, forming the Committee of Vigilance. The committee called a mass protest outside the Coffee House for Guy Fawkes Day—that traditional day of carnival and protest. A local merchant who supported the East India Company was hanged in effigy. Later, the committee created an association to enforce the nonimportation of British tea, declaring that any who opposed them was "an enemy to the liberties of America," a declaration supported by even "the better sort of the Inhabitants," the governor reported. Agents for the East India Company resigned, fearing retribution. Sears and McDougall began to organize a blockade of the port, and McDougall even wondered aloud whether they might want to "kill [the] Gov[ernor] and all the Council." A crowd of more than three thousand gathered at City Hall on December 17, 1773,

---

* When British soldiers garrisoned in Boston learned of the skirmishes in New York, they went on a rampage: the Boston Massacre.

to protest the Tea Act.* Word was that two tea ships were on their way to the city, but another harsh winter meant they did not arrive until April 1774. One captain quickly turned his ship around. The other, who had brought the stamps to New York in 1765, tried to bluff his way in and was forced to publicly apologize at Fraunces Tavern. Emulating protesters in Boston, a party of "Mohawks" dumped the tea and other cargo in the harbor. The captain beat a hasty retreat.[11]

As New York "Mohawks" were dumping tea in the harbor in April 1774, Parliament in London, incensed by the earlier Boston outrages, passed a series of Coercive Acts—the Intolerable Acts, as they were known in the colonies—shutting down the port of Boston, reorganizing courts throughout the land to better prosecute rebels, and restricting town meetings and legislatures. The king named General Gage the new governor of New York and sent yet more troops to support him.[12]

Crucible of Revolt, 1774–1776

Gouverneur Morris, a young New York gentleman, thought the mobs that had formed and re-formed in New York streets over the past decade and who were now agitating against the Intolerable Acts were "Poor reptiles" coming out of their winter slumber. He feared that the "mob [was] begin[ning] to think and reason" and were now poised "to bite." They had learned to "correspond with the other colonies, call and dismiss popular assemblies, make resolves and bind consciences of the rest of mankind, bully poor printers, and exert with full force all their other tribunitial powers."[13] The gentry felt the threat of the growing power of ordinary people—including women. No less central in the success of the Townsend embargo than they were in the Stamp Act boycott half a decade before, the Daughters of Liberty fashioned clothes from local materials, stretched scant provi-

sions of food across seemingly endless winters, and began to see themselves as "persons of consequence" instead of merely "poor females." "Though this body is not clad with silken garments," wrote one New Yorker, "these limbs are armed with strength, the Soul is fortified by Virtue, and the Love of Liberty is cherished within this bosom." She hoped one day to be part of "a fighting army of amazons . . . armed with spinning wheels."[14]

Rallies, meetings, street fights: the summer was a hot one. The assembly had lost its legitimacy, and the more radical among the artisans were losing faith in the Sons too. They soon formed the Committee of Mechanics. When the more conservative, merchant-dominated Committee of Fifty-One produced a slate of representatives to a Philadelphia meeting of representatives of twelve colonies—the Continental Congress—the Mechanics drew up their own slate and called a big public meeting in the Fields on July 6, 1774, to ratify it. Eventually, the Mechanics agreed to the Fifty-One's slate, just so long as it promised to support and enforce a colonies-wide nonimportation agreement. The delegates left for Philadelphia on September 1, where they and the other representatives quickly authorized a new government in Massachusetts and encouraged its citizens to take up arms. It also backed up the nonimportation accord and created Committees of Inspection to enforce it in every city, town, and county. The Congress had essentially declared war.[15]

Despite the turmoil of the preceding decade, New York had always been the most British—the most loyal—of colonial cities. As resistance against the Intolerable Acts and against redcoat occupation grew throughout the colonies, and as war became inevitable, New York gentlemen—"die-hard conservatives" who refused to countenance reform, according to one historian—abandoned the city in droves. In August 1775 a Loyalist clergyman described the city streets looking "plague-stricken, so many houses [of the gentry] are closed." The Committee of Mechanics—plebeians to the core—continued to outradicalize the radical Sons of Liberty, putting severe pressure on the second Continental Congress in Philadelphia, demanding popular ratification of any new

---

* As they talked, wondered, and organized, radicals in Boston celebrated the success of their great "Party" the night before, when, dressed as Mohawk Indians, they dumped several chests of British East India tea into the harbor. In Philadelphia a tea ship was turned back.

constitution that might be written and the same popular ability to alter it once it had been accepted.[16]

As the authority of the assembly collapsed, the new Provincial Convention, with representatives from every county in the province, was called to select new representatives to the Continental Congress. The Provincial Convention met on April 20, 1775, and three days later New Yorkers learned of the rout of the redcoats in Lexington and Concord on April 19. The Sons paraded to the docks and expropriated provisions intended for British forces from two ships. Other militants raided the City Hall arsenal and grabbed six hundred muskets, cartridge boxes, and bayonets to distribute to rebel patriots. On April 24 a third of New York's population—eight thousand people—turned out at City Hall, where the Committee of Sixty, which had essentially been running the city, proposed that the Provincial Convention become the Provincial Congress and assume the authority of government and that the Sixty be expanded to a Hundred to govern and defend the city. Militias were formed, organized by city ward. At a mass meeting on April 29, the Hundred (dominated by moderates but pushed by radicals) presented the people with Articles of Association and pledged "never to become Slaves." The Sons' Isaac Sears, leading 360 armed men, seized the keys to the customhouse and declared the port to be closed. His house served as the militia headquarters and de facto seat of government. A Loyalist complained that the city was ruled "by Isaac Sears & a parcel of the meanest people, Children & Negroes." Business in the city ground to a halt as men and women gathered in taverns and on the streets, trying to discern the future that might await them. This was, according to one New York Tory, "total revolution."[17]

The militias practiced in the Fields while workers built up barricades and breastworks and dug trenches. Britain ordered the withdrawal of its last regiment of soldiers on June 6, but the Sons of Liberty cut them off and relieved them of their weapons and baggage. Other Sons raided a royal storehouse but gave back what they had commandeered when ordered to do so by the Hundred. George Washington passed through town in June en route to Massachusetts and was hailed as a hero by the masses lining the streets. More Loyalists fled north. On August 23 a company of Liberty Boys raided the Grand Battery and made off with two dozen cannon, exchanging fire with British troops from the ship *Asia*. The commander of the *Asia* ordered the bombarding of the city. Little damage was done, but this first military assault on New York sent the townspeople into a panic. The city further emptied out, including this time the royal governor of New York. Population declined from twenty-five thousand before the upheaval to fifteen thousand by the end of 1775 to only five thousand or so by the summer of 1776. One departing Loyalist observed that "women and children are scarcely to be seen," their places, and their homes, taken over by thousands of incoming soldiers.[18]

When King George III formally declared the colonies in open rebellion and sent a punitive force to put it down in early 1776, talk turned to independence, egged on by Tom Paine's newly published *Common Sense*.[19]

War, 1776

In early 1776 the radical, experienced, and respected Gen. Charles Lee brought two New England regiments to New York. He immediately set up headquarters at Montayne's tavern, the radicals' redoubt near the Fields. The Continental Congress wanted him to hold New York against what everyone assumed was coming: a British assault on the city. With its deep harbor and access up the Hudson, New York was a prize. Without a navy, it was unlikely the rebels could hold it, but they could extract a high price. Thirteen forts and batteries were constructed on both sides of the East River to prevent British penetration. Barricades and earthworks were built up and down Manhattan to slow if not stop a land invasion; Brooklyn Heights, a strategically important vantage point, was protected by a string of slave-built forts, trenches, and redoubts stretching from Gowanus Creek to Wallabout

Pulling Down the Statue of George III by the "Sons of Freedom," at Bowling Green, City of New York, July 1776, painted by Johannes A. Oertel, engraved by John C. McRea, ca. **1875**.

Library of Congress, Prints and Photographs Online Catalog, LC-DIG-pga-02158.

Bay. Isaac Sears and a troop of Liberty Boys were sent to Long Island to encourage proper behavior by the remaining Tories there.[20]

Lee moved on to similarly secure Charleston, but New Yorkers continued to prepare. More batteries were built on both the East and Hudson Rivers. Twin forts were constructed on the Hudson—Fort Washington in Manhattan and Fort Lee in New Jersey—and the city itself came to resemble an armed encampment. Prices rose, the red-light district near the new jail flourished, and the stately street trees that had given the city its character were chopped down for firewood. Finally, on June 29 the British arrived in a huge fleet of ships from Halifax, anchoring off Staten Island. It looked like "a wood of pine trees," like "all London was afloat," said a Continental soldier. The redcoats set to fortifying the island. In New York to defend the city, General Washington geared up for a fight, exhorting his troops to fight to the last.[21]

In Philadelphia, meanwhile, the Continental Congress voted for independence on July 2 and ratified Thomas Jefferson's Declaration on July 4. Five days later New York's Provincial Congress approved it, and the Declaration was read to Washington's troops and a multitude of others gathered on the Commons. A mob marched down Broadway and toppled a statue of King George III that had been erected when he repealed the Stamp Act. George's head was spiked and displayed at the Blue Bell Tavern near Fort Washington.* His lead body, all four thousand pounds of it, was hauled off to Connecticut to be made into musket balls. All royal symbols were quickly stripped from the city. But out in the bay, still more British troops arrived, joined by Hessian mercenaries, eventually numbering some fifteen thousand.[22]

On August 22 the British moved, landing on Long Island near where the Verrazano Bridge now touches down

* About where Broadway and 181st Street now intersect.

in Brooklyn. Joined by several hundred cheering Loyalists, they marched northward, heading for Flatbush, where they were joined by Loyalist militiamen. Eight hundred slaves fled to the British side too and were put to work building fortifications. The long, heavily wooded glacial moraine that ran down the center of Long Island—the Heights of Guan, as it was then known—formed a natural defense, and the Americans held it. There were only four roads across the Heights of Guan, but the Americans neglected to defend one: the Jamaica Pass. A Tory spy soon brought word to the British commanders that there was an easy way through. On August 26, just after sundown, the British troops stole out of their camps (leaving their fires burning) and headed north to Jamaica Pass. At about 3:00 a.m. they made it through, encountering no resistance. By 8:30 they had made it to the village of Bedford, where they shot off two rounds to signal other troops to attack elsewhere along the Heights of Guan.* Trapped on three sides, the Americans were slaughtered— twelve hundred killed, another fifteen hundred wounded, captured, or missing.[23] The rest retreated to Brooklyn Heights while Britain's Gen. William Howe prepared for a siege. He had lost only sixty men in the rout but thought that the price would be too high to capture Brooklyn Heights itself. Washington and his ninety-five hundred troops soon slipped out of Brooklyn Heights and across the river to Manhattan.[24]

In the weeks that followed, American troops deserted or just went home. The Continental Congress decided the city should be abandoned to the enemy. Washington retreated north, leaving five thousand troops behind to cover his rear, and set up headquarters in Harlem Heights at the home of Roger Morris.† In mid-October the redcoats invaded Manhattan across the East River, covered by a barrage from nearby warships. The American militia and remaining members of the Committee of Mechanics retreated in fear and confusion, and General Howe soon held Murray Hill,

where he dallied (legend has it) over wine and cake with Mrs. Murray, giving the American army time to reach Harlem Heights and regroup. The next day Washington led a face-saving skirmish against the British in a wheat field at what is now 120th Street.[25]

When the Continental Congress first resolved to abandon New York, it contemplated setting it ablaze in retreat but decided against it. A week after the Harlem skirmish, however, the Fighting Cock tavern near Whitehall Slip went up in flames. Evidence pointed to arson, though it was hardly conclusive.[26] As rebels cheered from across the Hudson in New Jersey, the wind shifted, and the fire spread across Broadway and up to Trinity Church, which was quickly consumed. Before it burned itself out in some empty lots northwest of St. Paul's Chapel,‡ the fire burned a swath a mile long and several blocks wide. More than five hundred buildings—a quarter of the city's total—were destroyed. Even as the fire was blazing, angry mobs set on suspected rebel arsonists, killing several. A military dragnet rounded up two hundred men and women, including Nathan Hale, who confessed to being a rebel spy. Before Hale was hoisted on the gallows the next day he famously declared, "I only regret that I have but one life to lose for my country." Up in Harlem Heights, Washington was sanguine: "Providence, or some good honest fellow, has done more for us than we were disposed to do for ourselves."[27]

Occupation and Independence, 1777–1783

Another fire swept through the city in August 1778, destroying fifty buildings. By then, British authorities had declared martial law in the city, and for the city's working people, it was a miserable existence. Between a quarter and a third of New York's housing was destroyed in the two fires, even as returning Loyalists, innumerable free or escaped black people (joining hundreds of New York slaves who had been manumitted in 1775 and 1776), military men of many stripes

---

* This took place at what is now the intersection of Fulton Street and Nostrand Avenue in Bedford-Stuyvesant.
† Preserved today as the Morris-Jumel Mansion on 162nd Street.

‡ On Broadway between Fulton and Vesey, just south of the Commons.

(Hessians, Highlanders, Waldeckers), and their camp followers streamed into the city. Even with the commandeering of rebel-owned buildings and the commissioning of churches as barracks, the housing shortage was acute. Rents rose 400 percent in the first year of the occupation; food prices jumped 800 percent. Fights broke out as soldiers and civilians claimed partially burned houses as their own. A giant tent city housing hundreds or thousands grew in the burned-out lots at the foot of Broad Street. Food shortages were extreme, and quartermasters and "army foragers" expropriated what they could. The air turned foul. Smallpox, yellow fever, and cholera took their toll. Starving and racked by illness, the thousands of prisoners held around the city and on the ships in Wallabout Bay died en masse: by the end of the war 11,500 were dead.[28]

Simultaneously, the city boomed. The importation ban disappeared, and a few merchants made great fortunes. A giant fleet of privateers was commissioned to interrupt American shipping, creating work for shipwrights and eventually great wealth for the ships' captains. Officers and their families sought out luxuries. The theaters reopened; foxhunts were organized; billiards, cricket, and horse races provided diversion; great parties were thrown. Corruption was rife. Hessian and redcoat troops pillaged, raped, and murdered their way through Long Island.[29]

But the new gaiety of New York for the revived Tory ruling classes and their hangers-on proved to be short-lived. Gen. Charles Cornwallis's surrender in the British defeat at Yorktown in late 1781 signaled the end. By August 1782 Britain had accepted American independence; by November Articles of Peace had been agreed; in February 1783 the king declared the end of hostilities. When news reached New York in April, soldiers deserted in droves, and Loyalists began plotting their escape. Some forty thousand departed the city in 1782 and 1783, many of whom had only recently moved into its relatively safe confines from rebel-held territory upriver or in New Jersey and Connecticut. The New York State Assembly passed laws protecting patriots from Tory creditors and allowing them to sue Tory occupiers for damage done to their properties. On November 21, 1783, the governor, George Clinton, triumphantly returned to New York City on the promise that the British troops would soon be evacuated; by November 25 they were all gone, and patriots poured back in.[30]

Most of the departing Tories went to Canada, including eight thousand or so who established the town of Shelburne on the coast of Nova Scotia, where they were joined by some three thousand former slaves and free blacks, many of whom had allied themselves against their American slaveholders.* That slavery was going to continue was unquestioned: New York State did not finally abolish slavery until 1827.† Even before the final peace was signed, southern slave owners poured into the city looking for escaped slaves—people they regarded as their property. General Washington tried hard, without success, to get the British to return runaways. Those who had settled in Shelburne were soon driven out by white veterans; after settling nearby for a few years, many—a thousand or so—left again for Sierra Leone.[31]

Back in New York, commercial interests regrouped (the Bank of New York, the city's first, was organized in 1784), even as the party of radicals, the cream of the motley crew without whom even George Washington admitted the Revolutionary War would have been lost, took control of the government.[32] Candidates from both the Committee of Mechanics and the Sons of Liberty swept to power in both regional elections and elections for Common Council. Anti-Tory zeal reigned, taxation was overhauled, city government was remade (from a private corporation into a public one), and there was even talk of universal male suffrage. But so too did the radicals bring with them a high degree of "Whiggish" moralism: in March 1784 the New York Common Council enacted highly restrictive Sabbath laws; petitions were soon

---

* The black population in New York City rose to perhaps ten thousand during the war years; some four thousand blacks managed to get out of the city before the Americans retook control.

† In 1781 the assembly voted to manumit slaves who fought on the American side; in 1799 it had passed a law mandating gradual abolition; children born to slaves after July 4, 1799, were to be free—after serving terms of indenture of twenty-five years for women and twenty-eight years for men.

circulating seeking to abolish taverns and coffeehouses; and licenses were denied to returning theater companies. Alexander Hamilton, the central force behind the Bank of New York, published a forceful pamphlet reminding workers that whatever their importance in the direct action that helped launch the Revolution, their time had passed. Now was the time for responsible government, as well as laissez-faire economic policies, at least at the city scale. It was time for the classes to return to their appropriate, natural levels.[33] Women, of course, remained disenfranchised.

THE DOCTORS' RIOT, 1788

Riots and rebellions expose the contours of race and class in the city. These contours persist even unto death, or so the Doctors' Riot of 1788 seems to suggest.

The revolutionary era was a period of near-constant black rebellion, and New York was its heart. Escaped slaves poured into the city and the surrounding "neutral zone," where the British and Loyalists stoked resistance against the rebels and what would surely be the continuance of slavery if America won its independence. Patriots feared a black revolution (even as some black men joined the Americans' side and some slaves were forced to take their masters' places in the Continental army). A complex, protean, shifting geography of race marked the city and countryside.[1] In the wake of British, Loyalist, and black evacuation of the city in 1783, lines and boundaries—race and class geographies— had to be remade, set back in stone, even as the city's population exploded, doubling to twenty-four thousand by 1785. Free blacks organized, creating, for example, the Africa Free School on Cliff Street in 1788; meanwhile, in anticipation of restrictions on slaveholding (if not outright abolition), New Yorkers furiously sold their slaves to agents who sold them on south. They need not have worried: by 1790 New York had adopted a new comprehensive slave code and refused to close the port to slave-trading ships; the absolute number of slaves in the city grew, even as the black percentage of the population fell to 10 percent.[2]

In the midst of all this, on February 3, 1788, a group of free black men petitioned the Common Council, requesting an end to medical students poaching bodies from the Negroes Burial Ground and other black cemeteries.

> Most humbly sirs, we declare that it has lately been the practice of a number of young gentlemen in this city who call themselves students of the physic to repair to the burying ground, assigned for the use of your petitioners. Under the cover of the night, in the most wanton sallies of excess, they dig up the bodies of our deceased friends and relatives of your petitioners, carrying them away without respect for age or sex. Your petitioners are well aware of the necessity of physicians and surgeons consulting dead subjects for the benefit of mankind. Your petitioners do not presuppose it as an injury to the deceased and would not be adverse [*sic*] to dissection in particular circumstances, that is, if it is conducted with the decency and propriety which the solemnity of such occasion requires. Your petitioners do not wish to impede the work of these students of the physic but most humbly pray your honors to take our case into consideration and adopt such measure as may seem meet to prevent similar abuses in the future.[3]

The petition was roundly ignored. The Negroes Burial Ground and the nearby white paupers' cemetery continued to be pilfered.

The "doctors" made little effort to cover their tracks, and they grew bolder, stealing bodies from churchyards, as well as from the paupers' and black cemeteries.[4] Popular discontent mounted. Blacks and whites alike stood overnight guard at cemeteries and churchyards. Free blacks continued to protest in print, complaining that "few blacks are buried whose bodies are permitted to remain in the grave" and bemoaning the "merchandize of human bones."[5]

Then on Sunday, April 13, 1788, a group of boys playing outside the city hospital near the paupers' cemetery annoyed an anatomist working inside. He brandished a severed arm at them. One boy, thinking it was the arm of his recently deceased

Where the Doctor's Riot Began.
Joel Tyler Headley, *Pen and Pencil Sketches of the Great Riots:*
An Illustrated History of the Railroad and Other Great Riots (1882).

mother, ran home to tell his father. The father and some friends rushed to the grave of the mother, dug up the coffin, and found it empty. Word spread, and workers marched on the hospital, where they found several partially dissected bodies, which they displayed to the growing, angry crowd. When the crowd stormed the building, the sheriff hustled doctors and "students of physic" off to jail for their own safety. The crowd dispersed, but the anger did not subside. The next morning an even larger crowd gathered at the hospital; a delegation, including the mayor and governor, sought to convince them to disperse, promising a full inquiry. Instead, the crowd headed for Columbia College to inspect the rooms there; then they moved on to various physicians' houses; finally, they went to the

jail, where they demanded the doctors be turned over to them. The military was called out, but only to make a show of force. This had no effect. A bit later came a second military band—of only twelve men—but it was quickly overwhelmed by rock-throwing rioters, and the soldiers retreated (John Jay was among those injured in the melee). The crowd returned to the jail and broke in; the inmates defended themselves with stones and sticks. As the sun set, another militia was organized, which the crowd quickly turned on; a commander ordered the soldiers to fire; at least three people and maybe as many as twenty were killed. Discord simmered for days after, kept in check by an even larger militia called in from the countryside.[6]

Using fairly conservative estimates, one

in fifteen or one in twenty New Yorkers directly participated in the Doctors' Riot— "a surprisingly high rate of participation," as one historian put it. The mob was composed almost entirely of artisans and workers and, of course, free and enslaved black people. Rioters were "essentially plebeian," and at least one of those killed was black.[7] The motives of those in the mob clearly differed. For free blacks, the sanctity of the body was at stake and thus their status as free persons. Dissection of black bodies was justified by whites on religious grounds. Black people were, in whites' interpretation of scripture, no different from executed criminals. For free blacks, dissection looked like dismemberment, a traditional punishment for rebellious slaves. The "students of the physic" were, at least symbolically, exacting punishment on black people for winning their freedom.[8] For white artisans, grave robbing was an affront to their class status, and as robbery had moved from the paupers' cemetery to churchyards, it violated "the hierarchical spatial arrangements which circumscribed late eighteenth-century death"—and life.[9] Against such violation, "the people in the street retained a firm belief that they continued to have a right to riot": rioting was popular democracy in a world where, now that the Revolution was over, classes were meant to keep to their proper level, their proper place.[10] Rioting was a means to expose the wrongs of the city and to rectify them.

Churches built or reinforced fences around their burial grounds. Black New Yorkers struggled (against a hostile or uninterested white elite) to create con-secrated burial grounds to replace the Negroes Burial Ground and supplement private cemeteries. In early 1789 the New York legislature passed a law to "prevent the odious practice of digging up and removing for the purpose of dissection, dead bodies interned in cemeteries" and providing instead for the dissection of executed felons (murderers, burglars, arsonists, and debtors), the first codification of a law in America regulating the delivery of corpses for medical research.[11]

MOBOCRACY, 1792–1799

If New York City in the last decade of the eighteenth century was a phoenix rising where each class kept to its level, as Alexander Hamilton hoped, it was nonetheless a city where mob action still mattered. Indeed, sometimes it mattered so much that it could seem like New York was ruled by the mob—a mobocracy.

In March 1792 a speculative bubble that had spectacularly inflated in the first months of the year just as spectacularly burst when one of the biggest speculators, William Deur, defaulted on his debts, ruining a large number of investors, big and small alike. Maybe as much as $3 million was lost in the ensuing panic—lost "from the richest merchants to even the poorest women and the little shopkeepers," as a judge put it. Commerce came to a halt; ships full of goods found no buyers. On April 18 a mob of three to five hundred people formed and marched to the debtors' prison to demand access to Deur, who was languishing there. They threw stones and broke streetlamps before dispersing; over the next few nights the mob—which included all ranks of society, including slaves—gathered and gathered again, pressuring Deur and his accomplices to make the people financially right.[1]

A year and a half later, on October 14, 1793, a big crowd formed and attacked Mother Carey's bawdy house in the Fields, the poor neighborhood centered on Warren and Murray Streets that had long served as a red-light district. They hurled stones at the building, and though someone in Mother Carey's house tried to scare them off with a pistol shot, they soon invaded it, chasing out denizens and ripping apart beds and other furniture; they climbed the roof and "soon unshingled" it. All night the crowd worked to dismantle the house—that old form of protest. The next evening they set at several other bawdy houses in the district. On the third night the mayor sent a troop of horsemen to keep the peace and protect property from further damage.[2]

The crowd rioting at the bawdy houses—mostly artisans and lower-class workers—had been incensed by the acquittal of Harry Bedlow, "a well-known rake," in the rape of seventeen-year-old Lanah Sawyer. Bedlow had come to Sawyer's aid when she was being hassled on the street by another man and escorted her home. He introduced himself as "lawyer Smith." Sawyer was smitten with the older man. Even when his true identity was revealed, she reveled

in the attention of a higher-born, affluent gentleman, eventually agreeing to go on a date with him. He took her for ice cream and promenaded her around the Battery. As he walked her home late that night, he steered her to Mother Carey's, where, she said, he raped her. Bedlow countered that he merely seduced her. Sawyer pressed charges. At the trial, it was Sawyer's character that was put under examination; Bedlow's attorneys impugned not only her but also all girls of her class—the city's mechanic and working class—suggesting that it was their coarse behavior that drew the attention of well-born men like Bedlow. An attorney called Sawyer and her friends who testified on her behalf "an obscure set of people, perhaps of no character themselves." Bedlow's defense called tenants of Mother Carey's house—prostitutes—to testify against Sawyer, further enraging common people of the city. It took a few days for the rage to boil over, and when it did, it was Mother Carey and the other bawdy houses that came under attack. The mob's attack was not an attack on Bedlow for rape but rather a defense of the reputation of common girls and women, who, as historian Christine Stansell shows, were afforded a bit of freedom to roam the streets and maybe even to flirt but who were also easily associated with imprudence and vice.[3]

Six years later, rioting erupted again in the same neighborhood. On July 4, 1799, a man's body was found floating in the Hudson. He'd last been seen alive in a bawdy house at Murray and Greenwich Streets. For four nights, beginning July 17, crowds of eight hundred or a thousand threw stones at the bawdy house and threatened to destroy it. The militia was called but never opened fire. Forty-five rioters were hauled into custody. The arrested included craftsmen, artisans, grocers, and small boys; the crowd probably also included sailors, day laborers, transients, and minors of all sorts. Both this riot and the 1793 one seemed to have broad support among workers from across the city. After the 1793 riot a woman writing in the *Diary*, a city newspaper, under the name Justicia seemed to be speaking for many when she suggested that the magistrates put down the rioters with expediency, protecting many of the houses of ill repute, because men of the magistrates' class were not averse to spending time at Mother Carey's and places like it, spending many "comfortable hours . . . far from the complaints of a neglectful wife, or the very vexatious cries of hungry children." Given the complicity of the magistrates in Bedlow's acquittal and in protecting the bawdy houses, Justicia argued, the mob was right to riot. For her pains, Justicia was charged with libel.[4]

RIOTING IN THE AGE OF MOBOCRACY

Crowds and mobs remained a political force in New York City into the nineteenth century. Federalist and anti-Federalist demonstrations, parades, and riots were common, and, as had long been the case, factional political forces used public disturbances to their own ends. Customs of carnivalesque tumult persisted.*

But such "outdoor politics" were increasingly met by antimob rhetoric, stricter policing, and stiffer fines and prison sentences for those arrested. Parties and factions on the receiving end of mob action denounced mobs as threats to "life, liberty and property" and as akin to the worst excesses of the French Revolution—until, that is, they saw it in their own interest to call up a crowd.

By the second decade of the new century, city authorities had begun to exercise a heavy hand against all mob action, including political action. For authorities, the streets were no longer the legitimate locus of politics they once were. In part, the crackdown on political rioting was a reaction to the concomitant rise of ethnic rioting: sailors against Hispanics (Spanish and Portuguese); Protestant Americans against Irish immigrants; Orangemen against Irish Catholics; Irish Democrats against Whigs (the last indicating the formation of lasting political-ethnic associations).

* This explanation and the data on the map are drawn from Paul A. Gilje, *The Road to Mobocracy: Public Disorder in New York City, 1763–1834* (Chapel Hill: University of North Carolina Press, 1987).

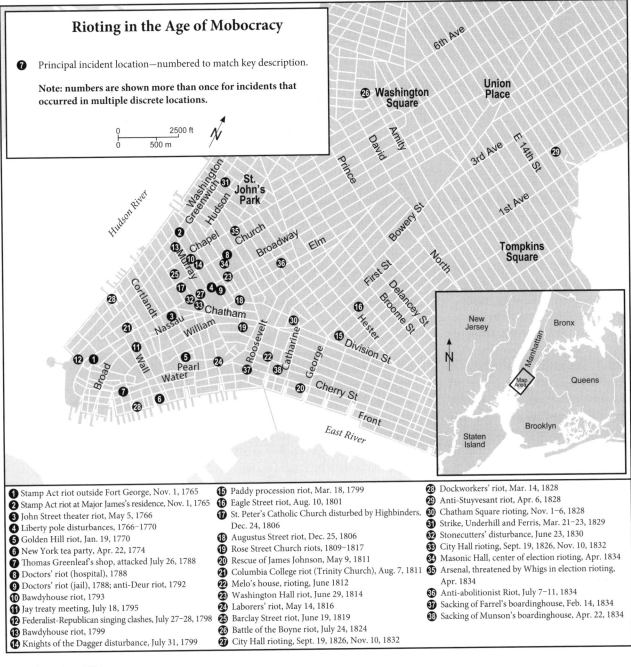

Rioting in the Age of Mobocracy

7 Principal incident location—numbered to match key description.

Note: numbers are shown more than once for incidents that occurred in multiple discrete locations.

0 ——— 2500 ft
0 ——— 500 m

N

Rioting in the Age of Mobocracy.

Cartography: Joe Stoll, Syracuse University Cartography Lab and Map Shop; redrawn from Paul A. Gilje, *The Road to Mobocracy* (1987), various pages.

1 Stamp Act riot outside Fort George, Nov. 1, 1765
2 Stamp Act riot at Major James's residence, Nov. 1, 1765
3 John Street theater riot, May 5, 1766
4 Liberty pole disturbances, 1766–1770
5 Golden Hill riot, Jan. 19, 1770
6 New York tea party, Apr. 22, 1774
7 Thomas Greenleaf's shop, attacked July 26, 1788
8 Doctors' riot (hospital), 1788
9 Doctors' riot (jail), 1788; anti-Deur riot, 1792
10 Bawdyhouse riot, 1793
11 Jay treaty meeting, July 18, 1795
12 Federalist-Republican singing clashes, July 27–28, 1798
13 Bawdyhouse riot, 1799
14 Knights of the Dagger disturbance, July 31, 1799

15 Paddy procession riot, Mar. 18, 1799
16 Eagle Street riot, Aug. 10, 1801
17 St. Peter's Catholic Church disturbed by Highbinders, Dec. 24, 1806
18 Augustus Street riot, Dec. 25, 1806
19 Rose Street Church riots, 1809–1817
20 Rescue of James Johnson, May 9, 1811
21 Columbia College riot (Trinity Church), Aug. 7, 1811
22 Melo's house, rioting, June 1812
23 Washington Hall riot, June 29, 1814
24 Laborers' riot, May 14, 1816
25 Barclay Street riot, June 19, 1819
26 Battle of the Boyne riot, July 24, 1824
27 City Hall rioting, Sept. 19, 1826, Nov. 10, 1832

28 Dockworkers' riot, Mar. 14, 1828
29 Anti-Stuyvesant riot, Apr. 6, 1828
30 Chatham Square rioting, Nov. 1–6, 1828
31 Strike, Underhill and Ferris, Mar. 21–23, 1829
32 Stonecutters' disturbance, June 23, 1830
33 City Hall rioting, Sept. 19, 1826, Nov. 10, 1832
34 Masonic Hall, center of election rioting, Apr. 1834
35 Arsenal, threatened by Whigs in election rioting, Apr. 1834
36 Anti-abolitionist Riot, July 7–11, 1834
37 Sacking of Farrel's boardinghouse, Feb. 14, 1834
38 Sacking of Munson's boardinghouse, Apr. 22, 1834

THE ANTI-ABOLITIONIST RIOTS, 1834

Though never of the scale of the slave uprisings of 1712 or 1741, black rioting in early nineteenth-century New York was a fairly regular occurrence. Significant riots occurred in 1801, 1819, 1826, and 1832, usually in connection with attempts to reenslave runaways resident in the city. Antislavery riots were vigorously denounced by the white establishment, even by New York's Manumission Society, which, though seeking the freeing of slaves through legal means, also feared that too many freed black people in New York would increase urban disorder. Penalties for blacks arrested for rioting were always more severe than for their white counterparts.[1]

Yet white attacks on black institutions were common. As black New Yorkers developed their own churches (frustrated by the increasing segregation they faced in the established churches), theaters, businesses, and schools, they were beset by mobs—laborers and tradesmen resentful of black people's growing independence, tacitly (and sometimes explicitly) supported by the city's elite—and if they sought to defend their places of worship or other institutions, they received little help from the authorities. White harassment of black people on the streets was a daily affair. In the wake of New York slaves' final emancipation (July 4, 1827), segregation hardened. Public transportation on the streets and rivers excluded black people, banning them from cabins on river steamers and barring them altogether from the omnibuses. Though growing in absolute numbers, the black population in New York declined as a percentage of the total population in the first decades of the nineteenth century. Even so, black people were seen by many as a threat. White workers insisted on segregated work sites, even if neighborhoods were not yet segregated: the Five Points neighborhood, for example, was highly integrated, and sexual mixing among the races was as much a fact of life as was conflict. (Places of racial mixing—brothels and taverns—were frequent sites of mobbery.)[2]

Amid this tense, shifting racial geography of the city, where races mixed even as elites and plebeians frequently sought to define or enforce color lines, abolitionism was a lightning rod. Many Irish workers perceived abolition as a threat to their tenuous economic hold in America, especially as elites—and popular sentiment—termed black people "smoked Irish" and Irish "niggers turned inside out."[3] Arthur Tappan, a prominent and outspoken abolitionist, was particularly despised, especially because he called for the integration not just of churches but of the seating in them. In June 1834 he came under attack for suggesting that Christ had likely been a dark-skinned Syrian. Rumors against the abolitionists exploded across the city. Abolitionists were charged with encouraging black "dandies" to seek white wives and promoting interracial marriage, among other depredations against nature.

Lightning struck in early July 1834.[4] On July 4 a mob attacked and broke up an interracial meeting at the Chatham Street Chapel marking the seventh anniversary of emancipation in New York. Three days later the group tried again to hold their commemorative meeting. They'd been given the large hall in the Chatham Street Chapel, displacing the New York Sacred Music Society, which normally met there at that time. Though the leaders of the music society had agreed to move to a smaller room, the members were outraged at being usurped by an interracial group, with a black choir taking their places in the choir stalls. A brawl erupted, but the white musicians were outnumbered. When the police arrived and arrested six black men,

Five Points, 1827.
*Manual of the Corporation
of the City of New York* (1842),
General Research Division,
New York Public Library.

they were joined by a large white mob that threatened the remaining black congregants and forced them out.

Two nights later the racial storm erupted again. An antislavery meeting had been planned for the Chatham Street Chapel. Instead, a couple thousand whites converged on the chapel; the abolitionists failed to show, and the whites broke in and passed resolutions demanding black deportation. Around the same time a large mob of day laborers and butcher boys descended on the Rose Street home of Lewis Tappan, Arthur's brother (Lewis and his family had already fled to Harlem). Egged on by merchants, the mob broke in and ransacked the place, pulling out furniture and artwork and setting it all ablaze. When the police responded, they were sent running from a barrage of brickbats. The mob, joined by a number of people from Chatham Street and now reaching perhaps four thousand in all, next headed toward the Bowery Theatre, where a play whose English stage manager was perceived to be anti-American was in progress. The mob broke in and chased the actors from the stage. They were only placated when a performer led a rousing rendition of "Yankee Doodle."

Over the next two days the unrest mounted. Handbills advertised battle plans, and crowds formed and re-formed to attack the houses and businesses of abolitionists. At Arthur Tappan's store, the mob was repelled only by a regiment of musket-wielding employees. At the Laight Street Church, where Tappan worshiped, rioters smashed windows. On Spring Street they attacked the church of Henry Ludlow, another prominent abolitionist, ripped out the organ and pews, and built barricades with the refuse (together with chained-together carts) to stop an impending cavalry charge. The National Guard eventually hacked their way through the barricade with axes and sent the crowd scurrying away, only to regroup at Ludlow's house, which they destroyed.

The virulence of the mob as it attacked the property of white abolitionists was nothing compared to when it set its sights on black abolitionists and the black community in Five Points. White families identified their houses with candles lit in the windows. Rioters attacked the darkened houses, tearing down or burning dozens. Black folks found on the streets were attacked and beaten, though none were killed. Hundreds fled.

As the rioting continued to spread and threatened to overwhelm the city, merchants and other elites—no friends of the abolitionists—grew concerned for the safety of their own property and implored the mayor to intervene. Eventually, a thousand volunteers—many of them Irish laborers opposed to the clearly nativist mobs—were sworn in to assist the National Guard. The National Guard and the volunteers were joined by the New York First Army Division, which paraded through the streets in a show of force and stood guard at the arsenal. Slowly the rioting abated, and by July 14, ten days after the first mob attack, it had ended entirely.

Most of the rioters appeared to have come from the mechanic and journeyman classes, classes that were slipping in status under the early stirring of the Industrial Revolution. White workers' fears of labor competition, which were intricately bound with racism, found an outlet in violence. The riots thus divulged not just animosity toward black people *as workers* (and the abolitionists who supported them) but also, historians have concluded, a real desire to rid New York of black people altogether. And compared to the riots of the previous century, the 1834 riot was different, not so much a communal, ritual letting off of steam but something broader and more violent. Class now mattered in a different way: calls for military intervention, interpretations of the riot, condemnation of or support for the rioters all now cleaved more clearly along class lines than they had before, in part because some factions of merchant and industrial capital understood black workers to be vital in keeping the lower rungs of the working class lower: rioters were to be condemned not because they attacked blacks but because they attacked an economic order in which African Americans could be hyperexploited. By now, rioting mobs were less to be tolerated and still less to be deployed in factional politics; they were to be condemned.[5]

THE FLOUR RIOT, 1837

By the middle of the 1830s New York was a union town—at least for white workers. By 1836 two-thirds of the workingmen in New York belonged to a union, most affiliated with the General Trades Union, an umbrella organization that itself was the center of the National Trades Union. Union newspapers flourished within a broader working-class culture of songs, stories, banners, and meetings. Workers struck for higher wages and a ten-hour day and against the use of prison labor, for example, in the cutting of stone for New York University's first buildings. They organized against runaway inflation. A massive strike on the waterfront in February that year led to the Twenty-Seventh Regiment being called out: the first use of the military to break a strike in New York. Simultaneously, employers across the city cut wages and pledged to not hire union workers. By June a compliant judge had charged unions with being illegal combinations and "foreign" institutions. Workers burned the judge in effigy at City Hall Park. The growing concentration of capital—monopoly—was a particular focus of workers' ire, or at least of their leaders'.[1]

New York, like much of the nation, was in the grip of a speculative bubble, and whatever the workers' efforts, inflation continued to spiral out of control. The price of flour had nearly tripled between 1834 and the beginning of 1837, almost doubling since September 1836 alone, exacerbated by a poor harvest. The price of other staples nearly kept pace. Though coal was abundant, its price skyrocketed too. The possibility of a rent strike was aired. A mass meeting was called for City Hall Park on Monday, February 13. Placards plastered around town declared: "BREAD, MEAT, RENT, FUEL! THEIR PRICES MUST COME DOWN!" Thousands came to the rally, despite it being the coldest day of the year so far. Speakers linked the inflation to the easy printing of paper money, and the meeting passed a resolution demanding specie. Monopolies were denounced. Special ire was reserved for the landlords and for the flour merchants, who were perceived to be holding flour off the market to keep the prices high. The final speaker declared that the flour merchant Hart and Company was particularly egregious, stockpiling fifty-three thousand barrels of flour. He urged the crowd to descend on the store and offer eight dollars a barrel, and he was about to suggest what the crowd should do if the offer was not accepted. But perhaps fearing arrest for incitement, he ended instead by saying, or "we shall depart in peace." The crowd streamed toward Hart's (on Washington between Dey and Courtland). The building was barricaded, but neither the barricades nor the entreaties of the mayor stopped the assault. Rioters poured into the counting room, destroyed desks, and sent papers flying. Barrels of flour were thrown out of upstairs windows and smashed on the streets. Women and children gathered up the flour in buckets and aprons and made off with what they could. The rioters moved on, sparing a merchant who claimed to have sold off his flour at a low price, and broke into another store on Coenties Slip, but they desisted when the merchant agreed to give all his flour to the poor. By then the militia had been called out. By nine in the evening, the riot was over.[2]

If the riot harked back to the tradition of violent petition of the colonial era, by now a new market orthodoxy among the elites meant that such communal claims for redress made no sense. A bad wheat harvest and a new speculative market in paper money had inflated prices, and they continued to do so after the riot. About this there was nothing to be done: markets were markets. Then on March 17 the bubble burst. A decline in cotton prices caused a New Orleans merchant to default on loans given by a Manhattan brokerage house; soon businesses across the city were going under as bills to southern enterprises were returned unpaid. By the end of April some 250 New York businesses had gone belly-up, and a general deflation had set in. Arthur Tappan, the wealthy abolitionist at the center of the unrest three years before and one of New York's most successful businessmen, was himself a victim, unable to pay more than a million dollars in debt. The real estate market collapsed; development ceased. Overcrowding in working-class districts worsened. The new railroads stopped laying track and stopped running. Manufacturing came to a halt. There was a run on the banks as paper money seemed increasingly worthless. On May 10 all of Manhattan's banks announced they would no longer give specie in exchange for paper. An incensed crowd massed in Wall Street. But the Twenty-Seventh Regiment was quickly called up, and the crowd was becalmed.[3]

The state government in Albany soon excused the banks from redeeming paper money, which allowed them to print more at will, and a whole economy of alternative moneys developed, saving many merchants from ruin but further impoverishing workers. For them, as the panic subsided and grinding depression deepened, the Common Council had already passed a new law providing for the expansion of the police force by 192 new watchmen.

CHAPTER 5

The Astor Place Riot, 1849

BRENDAN P. O'MALLEY

Only two blocks in length, Astor Place in the 1840s was a passageway between two different worlds: one of the fashionable, respectable, wealthy, and powerful, who paraded between palatial emporiums, opulent hotels, and grand theaters on Broadway; and another of working men and women, recent immigrants, and "sporting men" who frequented boisterous saloons and beer gardens, chaotic short-order restaurants, and cheap amusements on the Bowery. On May 10, 1849, these two worlds collided violently, ushering in a new and harsher phase of class conflict in New York City. The Astor Place Riot sharpened the lines of the city's new class geography and shattered the old republican dream that all New Yorkers could share a singular vision of a common good.[1]

Astor and Astor Place

When he died a little more than a year before the 1849 riot that erupted on the street named for him, John Jacob Astor was the richest man in the United States. Born in 1763—two years before the Stamp Act Riots—he made his initial fortune in animal skins, with his American Fur Company dominating the commercial trade of pelts. By the 1830s, however, he had stepped away from that business to devote himself to real estate and finance. Shrewdly buying up foreclosed properties during the 1837 Panic, he watched the value of his Manhattan properties skyrocket in the 1840s.[2]

Well before 1837, however, Astor had dabbled in New York real estate. In 1804 he bought a plot from the Swiss physician Jacob Sperry bordered on the west by Broadway, on the east by the Bowery, on the north by 8th Street, and on the south by 4th Street.* Sperry had cultivated a botanical garden on the land. Astor leased the land to a Frenchman named Joseph Delacroix, who opened a new Vauxhall Gardens there (New York had had two previous Vauxhall Gardens, named to evoke the grander London original). The garden became a fashionable summer resort at the then northern outskirts of the city, frequented by city dwellers from across the social spectrum. The garden featured musical and theatrical performances, fireworks, and refreshments.[3]

When Delacroix's lease was up in 1825, Astor decided to develop half of the land, bisecting the plot with an avenue he named Lafayette Place.† The city's elites were migrating north as their old turf south of City Hall was increasingly devoted to mercantile activity and warehousing, and Astor sought to capitalize on their flight. Legend has it that Lafayette himself, visiting the United States to commemorate the fiftieth anniversary of the start of the American Revolution, dedicated the new street, but there is little evidence to support this claim. The eastern half of the plot became a

---

* The plot is now home to the Cooper Union, the Astor Place Theatre, and the Public Theater. The beaver plaques in the Astor Place subway station refer to the initial source of Astor's wealth.

† Now part of Lafayette Street.

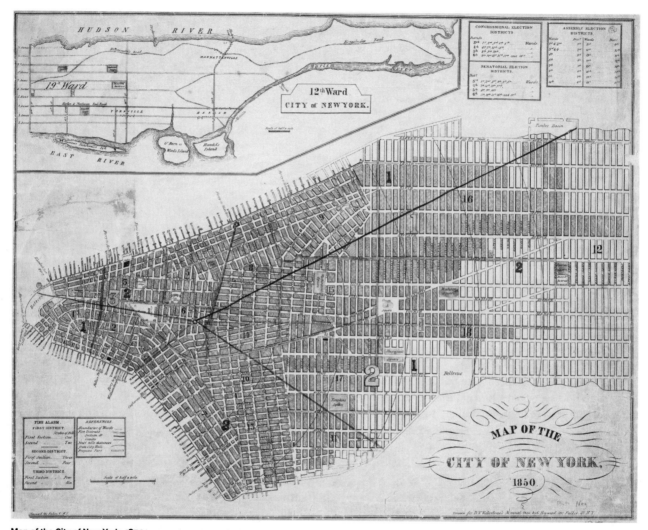

Map of the City of New York, 1850.

Astor Place is east of Washington Square and south of Union Square,
cutting diagonally across the grid from Broadway to the Bowery.

Courtesy the Lionel Picus and Princess Firyal Map Division, New York Public Library.

reduced Vauxhall Gardens, but by the early 1830s the western half featured palatial row houses designed for the city's mercantile elites.* Astor called the development LaGrange Terrace after Lafayette's country seat in France.[4]

As the elites settled into fashionable streets north of Houston Street, the rollicking working-class life of the Bowery encroached from the east. Vauxhall Gardens itself was growing more rowdy, especially after P. T. Barnum gained control of its entertainment and booked a variety of acts for short runs (a direct antecedent for vaudeville), rather than engaging expensive dramatic companies for lengthy engagements. Fashionable society stopped frequenting Vauxhall. By 1847 the garden catered exclusively to Bowery tastes, engaging blackface minstrelsy acts like Campbell's Ethiopian Serenaders, who specialized in portraying both "Northern dandy darkies" and "real Simon pure plantation negroes." By the 1840s blackface minstrelsy had become a highly popular entertainment among the city's white working classes.[5]

Astor Place itself predated Astor's division of the land. Called Art Street before 1840 and originating in Greenwich Village to the west, it cut diagonally against the gridded street plan the city had established in 1811. With the 1811 plan, much of the street was incorporated into the grid, with only Art Street and what is now Stuyvesant Street retaining their original configuration.† A proposal to rename Art Street's last remaining stretch for Astor was brought before the city's Board of Aldermen in 1840 by Alderman Graham, who had heard that the real estate mogul was considering bequeathing a library to the city on Lafayette Place (on a plot in what was still Vauxhall Gardens).[6] Graham reasoned the gesture might induce Astor to follow through, which he eventually did.‡ Before the library would even be completed, however, Astor Place would come to resonate in a way that Graham never intended and that would have horrified Astor had he been alive.

Class Acts

While Astor's library was still on the drawing board, several wealthy men formed a company to build a new theater on Astor Place near Broadway.§ Niblo's Garden at Prince and Broadway—the most prominent theatrical venue in the upper part of the city—burned down in 1846, and the need for a new, permanent home for Italian opera was acute. It was the rage in New York in the 1840s and 1850s, even though a permanent opera house did not exist for most of the period. The audience for opera ranged from artisans and mechanics to the wealthiest merchants and lawyers; theatrical performance was one of the few remaining communal experiences in a city of growing extremes of wealth and poverty. Even after the riot, the conservative lawyer and famed diarist George Templeton Strong attended a portion of Bellini's opera *La sonnambula* at the Castle Garden Theater on the Battery and observed, "The opera has created quite a furor. Everybody goes, and nob and snob, Fifth Avenue and Chatham Street, sit side by side fraternally on the hard benches."[7]

In the 1840s most theaters in New York catered to a varied audience, with expensive boxes close to the stage and cheap seats in the pit. Opera was popular art. Performances of opera singers were dissected and discussed in the next day's papers, elite and plebeian alike. But the new theater on Astor Place was different. When it opened on November 22,

---

* Four of the mansions still stand on Lafayette Street between 4th Street and Astor Place; they are often referred to as Colonnade Row.

† It has long been asserted that city authorities created Art Street, along with Reason Street (now Barrow Street), Science Street (now Waverly Place), and Commerce Street (still extant), in the 1790s in the Enlightenment spirit of French revolutionaries who renamed Parisian streets that had been associated with the ancien régime, yet there is little historical evidence to back this claim. Still, it might be indicative of the nature of New York that only Commerce Street still exists.

‡ The library opened in 1854—six years after Astor's death—in the building that now houses the Public Theater. The noncirculating library closed in 1911 when its collection was merged with that of the main branch of the New York Public Library on Fifth Avenue.

§ The site is currently occupied by an eleven-story 1891 brown-and-tan stone structure that houses a glassed-in Starbucks on the ground level. The building formerly housed the New York Mercantile Library.

Interior of the Astor Place Opera House.
Art and Picture Collection, New York Public Library.

1847, with a performance of Verdi's *Ernani* (which had premiered in Venice only three years before), it was clear that the proprietors of the sleek, temple-like, Greek Revival edifice were aiming at social exclusivity. The bulk of the seating sold at the prohibitive sum of one dollar, and even the cheaper seats were lavishly upholstered in red damask. Men in the one-dollar seats were required to wear white kid gloves, a badge of upper-class gentility. "Pompey's Rambles," a popular song written for blackface minstrels, satirized the theater's enforced gentility:

> De Astor Opera is anoder nice place.
> If *you* go thar, jest wash your face!
>
> Put on your "kids," an fix up neat,
> For dis am de spot of de *eliteet*![8]

The small, fifty-cent admission section was in the dark recesses of the third tier and not down on the floor, as had been the case in previous New York theaters. It had poor sight lines, hard and uncomfortable seats, and only one narrow exit, which would mean disaster in a fire.

In the first season, the majority of the Astor Opera House's seats were sold to seasonal subscribers, and the management had a policy of not allowing subscribers to transfer their seats. Thus each performance was a cliquish gathering of the city's elites, who attended religiously throughout the first year despite the general opinion that the company was mediocre at best, especially compared to those of Paris, London, and Venice. In late January 1848 the *New York Herald* noted, "Between the acts there is probably as much electioneering, stock-jobbing, and gossiping done, as there is in any place on Wall Street."[9] The new theater had quickly become the social headquarters for the city's mercantile elite, who in the 1840s were diversifying into finance, insurance, and, especially, like Astor, real estate.

Astor and other wealthy New Yorkers' ownership of large swaths of Manhattan was becoming an increasingly sensitive political issue. Upstate, the antirent movement had reached its peak influence and had many downstate sympathizers. Antirenters militated against the massive feudal-style, colonial-era landholdings (called "patroonships") of old Dutch families like the Van Rensselaers, which, among other things, required tenants to perform a day of labor a year for the manor. Such feudal holdovers were denounced as antithetical to a republican way of life.[10] Antirenters were joined by a growing number of adherents to Fourierism and other ideologies that cast land speculators as economic parasites living off the sweat of the brow of artisans and mechanics.* Mike Walsh, editor of the workingmen's paper, the *Subterranean*, called Astor's real estate empire a legalized system of plunder and demanded that the vast holdings of Trinity Church in Manhattan be confiscated for public use. In February 1848 radical organizers established a tenants' league to try to limit the profits of landlords, but they were unable to make much of a political impact. On the occasion of Astor's death a month later, Horace Greeley, editor of the *New York Tribune* and an advocate of a mild form of Fourierism called Associationalism, proposed an individual ownership limit of a thousand acres within city borders, noting that the inheritance of Astor's lands by his family constituted an antirepub-

lican dynasty. In the eyes of "true republican" artisans and laborers, Astor's name was synonymous with a parasitical elite feeding off artisans and laborers, who created real value, as well as with a desire to re-create a British-style aristocracy in the United States.[11]

Indeed, anti-British sentiment was burning hot in the city, especially among the city's growing Irish-born population because of the famine (which many linked to land engrossment by English landlords) and the violent suppression of the Young Irelander Rebellion in 1848. Within this context, the Astor Opera House's aristocratic pretensions and Anglophilic longings could not have been more repugnant to a large portion of the city's population.

Drama Onstage—and in the Seats

By the time it was announced that the renowned English Shakespearean actor William Charles Macready was to perform at the Astor Opera House in the late spring of 1849, the theater was already an object of contempt for a great many New Yorkers. Macready's forthcoming performance merely added insult to injury. To the popular imagination, there could not have been a more apt symbol of overly refined Britishness than Macready. He was the epitome of a cerebral and subtle style of acting that had taken hold of London's theater establishment; he himself had done much to promulgate this style during his stints as manager of the prominent Drury Lane and Covent Garden Theatres. He had undertaken tours of the United States in 1826 and 1827 and again in 1843 and 1844 and was embarking on a third and final tour in 1849. He was booked to appear at the Astor on May 7 to perform *Macbeth*.[12]

Leading up to the performance, the press made much of Macready's rivalry with the American actor Edwin Forrest, who was to play Macbeth at the more conventional Broadway Theatre about a mile farther downtown on the same night (in addition, the less well remembered but equally prominent Thomas Hamblin was to perform the same play at the Bowery Theatre). Forrest had toured the United King-

---

* An increasing number of European radicals were seeking refuge in New York in the 1840s, including prominent members of the Communist Bund der Gerechten (which would publish *The Communist Manifesto* in 1848); many such radicals joined the land reform movement, providing it with a good deal of ideological ferment.

dom in the 1830s to much acclaim and had even been hosted by Macready while there. Yet Forrest's style could not have been more different from that of the scholarly Macready. The powerfully built Forrest performed with a physicality that made him beloved by Bowery theatergoers, who viewed his forceful and melodramatic style as truly American, not a mere second-rate imitation of British acting.[13]

Part of Forrest's reputation had its origins in the fact that he had honed his craft in a troupe that toured the crude frontier "Western Circuit" of western Pennsylvania, Ohio, and Kentucky in the 1820s. He also had not shied away from the blackface minstrelsy that Bowery denizens adored but that more refined actors shunned. He gained fame playing pugnacious characters like the rebel Roman slave Spartacus and the Indian chief Metamora, who fought a bloody war against early colonists in New England. Politically, Forrest was an outspoken Democrat at a time when the majority of the city's elites were Whigs. Philip Hone, a wealthy Whig former mayor, referred to Forrest as "a vulgar, arrogant loafer, with a kindred pack of rowdies at his heels."[14]

The feud with Macready had commenced during Forrest's 1845 stay in London, where he played several roles with acclaim but was booed, hissed, and savaged in the press when he attempted Macbeth, mostly because the role was seen as inappropriate for someone of his physical style of acting. Forrest was led to believe that Macready was somehow responsible for orchestrating the attacks, so in Edinburgh a few weeks later, Forrest hissed Macready's performance of *Hamlet* during a scene in which Macready pranced around the stage, waving a handkerchief in a manner Forrest regarded as effete; the American derisively labeled this entrance a *pas de mouchoir* (dance of the handkerchief). The press on both sides of the Atlantic was soon aflame with the incident, just as jingoistic Democrats were beginning to call for war with Britain over the boundary dispute in Oregon (a dispute that would eventually lead to the current border between the United States and Canada, but not before navies were mobilized and at least a few rounds fired). The hype

subsided—the crisis was resolved in 1848—but the press was happy to use the simultaneous rival performances in New York in May 1849 to reignite it.[15]

Before Macready's May 7 performances, two notable Bowery characters, "Captain" Isaiah Rynders and Edward Z. C. Judson—the latter better known by the pen name Ned Buntline, which adorned hundreds of dime novels—set about orchestrating a protest against Macready's performance. A saloon owner, avid horse fancier, prizefighting aficionado, Tammany ward boss, and former riverboat gambler, Rynders was a leader of New York's "sporting men" in the 1840s. Politically, he had made his reputation by forming the Empire Club, which specialized in voter intimidation, its membership consisting of professional "shoulder hitters": prizefighters, volunteer firemen, and barroom brawlers. Rynders liked to claim that his club was instrumental in delivering the slim majority of votes in New York City that Democrat James K. Polk needed to carry the state and thereby the national 1844 presidential election. Even if the Empire Club's role in the election was not quite so decisive, Polk rewarded Rynders with a lucrative no-show patronage job in New York's customhouse.[16]

Rynders was an operator for the nascent Democratic Tammany Hall machine, but in the 1840s, Tammany had not yet fully embraced its later role as protector of immigrants; it was still courting alternately nativists and immigrants when politically expedient. Even future Tammany "Boss" William M. Tweed dabbled in nativist politics in the late 1840s.[17] Thus no one looked askance at the partnership—indeed, close friendship—of Rynders and Judson, the latter being an absurdly fierce nativist who published slander against all foreign groups in his weekly paper, *Ned Buntline's Own*. Judson became a leading member of the not-so-secret nativist organization, the Order of the United Americans, and a prime mover in the Know-Nothing movement of the 1850s.[18]

In the 1840s, though, American nativists and recent Irish immigrants found common ground in a hatred of the English, an animosity that Rynders and Judson, well aware of the powder-keg potential of Macready's performance, were happy to exploit. They set about ensuring an explosion. Judson published inflammatory pieces about Macready in his weekly scandal sheet from the moment the engagement was announced. Rynders used his own money and collected additional funds to buy about fifty tickets for Macready's performance and distributed them among Boweryites who had agreed to do their best to harass the English actor.[19]

On the evening of Monday, May 7, the theater filled with mostly male patrons, with only about fifty or sixty women in a theater said to hold eighteen hundred. The curtain rose and the play commenced uneventfully. But in the second scene, the actor portraying Malcolm was greeted with three loud cheers. From this point on, hisses and groans created an almost-constant roar. When Macbeth and Banquo entered in the third scene, the din escalated into a thunderous cacophony. Macready's supporters cheered, clapped, and waved handkerchiefs in counterprotest. From the gallery, a large quantity of the foul-smelling medicinal herb asafetida was released into the air, producing an ungodly stench throughout the theater. Banners were unfurled with hostile messages for Macready; a rotten egg, copper coins, and an old shoe were also tossed at him. Cheers for Forrest and competing ones for Macready sallied back and forth.[20] Leading the anti-Macready cheers was Tammany orator Edward Strahan, while Rynders calmly observed the chaos from the second tier. "Three cheers for Macready, Nigger Douglass, and Pete Williams" was a frequent cry, derisively conflating Bowery men's hatred of the English, abolitionism, and race mixing. Frederick Douglass was, of course, the prominent black abolitionist and intellectual (Rynders's Empire Club had made a habit of breaking up meetings of the Antislavery Society, where he was a frequent speaker), and Pete Williams was the African American proprietor of a notorious Five Points dance hall in which men and women of different races mingled, much to the horror of the city's "respectable" people.[21]

Police Chief George W. Matsell was present with about six of his men, but they could do little to control the chaos, or they were not inclined to do anything. Exhortations, verbal abuse, thrown objects from the audience, and even small-scale riots were not an uncommon feature of New York theater life. It was considered a right of the theatergoer to interrupt the proceedings if the performance offended in some way.* But the uproar on May 7 seemed unprecedented in scale and scope. Nonetheless, all the while, Macready soldiered on in these ridiculous circumstances, faithfully going through the motions, mouthing the words with the rest of the cast in a dumb show. At one point, he picked up a copper coin that had been thrown onstage and clutched it to his chest in a mocking gesture. Soon after the opening of the curtain for the third act, several chairs rained down from the gallery into the orchestra and onto the stage, and the crowd began to scatter. Although Macready continued, these actions finally brought the curtain down.[22]

"Burn the Damn Den of the Aristocracy!"

The show was over, but the stage was merely set. Macready was determined to leave for Britain on the next departing steamship, but a group of forty-seven wealthy and prominent citizens signed a petition pleading with Macready to stay and continue his engagement, promising that "good sense and respect for order" would protect him. Signatories included powerful Whig merchants and lawyers like shipping magnate Moses H. Grinnell and attorney and real estate developer Samuel B. Ruggles, Shakespeare scholar Richard Grant White, writer Washington Irving, and, surprisingly, twenty-nine-year-old Herman Melville, who was most associated with the Democrats. The petition was published in the city papers on Wednesday, May 9. His ego soothed, Macready agreed to give it one more go on Thursday. As plac-

---

* For example, in 1831 a series of riots broke out at the Park Theatre when the British actor Joshua Anderson was engaged there; newspapers reported that he had maligned the character of Americans and the United States during his stay in New York (see Nevis, *The Diary of Philip Hone*, 1:49–51).

ards announcing this show went up, so did ones for Forrest's performance as Spartacus in Robert Montgomery Bird's *The Gladiator* on the same night at the Broadway Theatre.[23]

Amid all the uproar surrounding Macready's performance, the Whig Caleb Smith Woodhull had been sworn in that same Wednesday as New York's seventeenth mayor, replacing William F. Havemeyer, a Democrat from a wealthy sugar-refining family who had lost favor with Tammany because he favored efficient governance over patronage. Woodhull was a principal in one of the city's most lucrative law practices and also a member of an old and influential New York family. For several years he had been among the Whig leaders in the city council and traveled in the same circles as many of the Macready petition signatories. His assumption of the mayoralty gave the petitioners hope that their promise to Macready would be kept.

On Thursday, May 10, New Yorkers awoke to find strategic crossroads of the city plastered with posters featuring the bold headline, "SHALL AMERICANS OR ENGLISH RULE THIS CITY?" The crew of an English steamer, the posters declared, had dared anyone to express their opinions about Macready's performance. While advocating "no violence," the posters urged "a free expression of opinion of all public men," concluding that workingmen and freemen should "STAND BY YOUR LAWFUL RIGHTS!" The posters were signed by "The American Committee."[24] In fact, their printing and posting had been paid for by Rynders and were attributed by many to Judson; the claim about the British steamship apparently had no basis in reality.[25] The handbills alarmed the new mayor, who called together a meeting in his office that morning that included Police Chief George Matsell, Sheriff Jacob Westervelt, theatrical producers William Niblo and James H. Hackett, city recorder Frederick A. Tallmadge, and several other city officials. With the Macready show already announced, Niblo and Hackett refused to cancel it. Woodhull stated that he had no right to force them to close, though he privately wished that they would. Matsell argued that his force could not handle the full-blown riot that might ensue on its own, his men being armed only

with wooden clubs.* Woodhull then summoned Maj. Gen. Charles W. Sandford, commander of the New York State militia forces in the city, which had put down the Flour Riot of 1837. Sandford was ordered to make ready a sufficient military presence to intervene if the civilian forces could not maintain order. It was decided that a large contingent of Matsell's men would take control of the Astor Opera House itself and that Sheriff Westervelt would deputize additional constables to make more manpower available.[26]

Sandford set the militia into motion, mustering the elite Seventh Regiment (formerly the Twenty-Seventh Regiment, which had been active in the Anti-abolitionist and Flour Riots), some other infantry and artillery units, and a cavalry squadron. Altogether the force should have totaled about 350 men, all citizen-soldiers, but since they were mustered on such short notice, only 201 reported. One corporal in the Seventh, John W. Ripley, himself a "Bowery B'hoy" (the slang term for young working-class men of Lower Manhattan), had been in the rowdy gallery of the opera house on Monday night but donned his uniform and mustered with his regiment when called to duty late Thursday afternoon (he would have to go into hiding after the night was over).[27] Some units gathered in Washington Square about 5:00 p.m. and drilled, while others did the same at the Centre Street Market between Grand and Broome Streets, which had a large drill room. An hour earlier, roughly 325 of Matsell's men had arrived at the Astor Opera House, the windows of which were being boarded up by stagehands. About a third of the police were positioned at the entrances and around the perimeter of the theater, while the rest were stationed inside. Meanwhile, Rynders, Judson, and their lieutenants were rousing all of the bodies that they could muster along the Bowery. Most were native-born, but a good number

---

* Even though the archaic policing system of the night watch, constables, sheriffs, and a limited number of municipal officers had been abandoned in 1845, the newly constituted force of twelve hundred policemen still resisted the centralized control and military discipline of later eras. For example, policemen thought it was antirepublican to wear a uniform, as policemen did in London, and insisted on wearing plainclothes well into the 1850s.

were Irish immigrants, workers tied together in their animosity toward the English and upper classes.[28]

By the time the doors opened at 7:00 p.m., Astor Place was a sea of bodies—thousands strong—that stretched up Broadway around to Eighth, down Lafayette, and along the Bowery. It appeared that the proprietors had purposefully oversold the house so that they could be selective about whom they would admit. Macready supporters had been supplied with tickets that had a special mark on the back, and these were favored for admission. As ticket holders were refused entry, the crowd became incensed. A contingent of men—some proudly wearing their volunteer firemen's uniforms—rushed the entrance to get in but were beaten back by club-wielding police. More and more people gathered, many bystanders drawn by the commotion, including a good number from the swank Sixteenth Ward. By 8:00 p.m. the crowd had swelled to at least ten thousand. Later, many wondered why Mayor Woodhull had not issued a proclamation telling New Yorkers to stay away.[29]

Inside the theater the play commenced at 7:30 p.m., and the troupe got through the first two scenes without disturbance. But when Macready made his entrance, the small contingent of Boweryites who had slipped past the police and ticket takers made an enormous racket, so much so that the actors went into dumb show mode, as they had on Monday. Macready and his supporters, now in the majority, began yelling for the arrest of the noise makers. After a consultation with other police officials on the site, Chief Matsell ordered his men to wade through the audience and seize the worst offenders, who were arrested and thrown into a storage room below the boxes. The first four young men locked up there fed some wood shavings into a gas lamp, setting a fire, but the police noticed and quickly extinguished it; the would-be arsonists were put in irons.[30]

As the second act began, the actors and audience were startled by periodic crashing thuds and the sound of shattering glass coming from the lobby. The mob outside, egged on by Judson, was heaving heavy stones against the boarded-up windows. A ready supply of paving stones had been found nearby on Broadway where the street had been torn up so sewer pipes could be laid (the mayor's request that the cobblestones be removed had been ignored). The policemen, the doors, and the boarded-up lower windows were the primary targets, but a few stones sailed through the upper windows, smashing the grand chandelier and causing the audience to take refuge under protected areas. As the crowd outside threw stones and chanted slogans—"Burn the damn den of the aristocracy!"—and despite being in obvious danger, Macready stubbornly soldiered on, though in an accelerated manner.[31]

The hail of stones continued, taking its toll on the police, as did the wave upon wave of charges by the Boweryites. Someone leaning out of an unboarded window inside the building turned a water hose on the rioters, but this only enraged them more. A little before 9:00 p.m. it became evident that the police could not hold out much longer, and many retreated into the shelter of the building. Sheriff Westervelt sent word to General Sandford that the militia was needed. As rumor spread quickly that the troops were on their way, Judson assured the crowd that the militiamen had only been issued blank cartridges. The regrouped police managed to make several forays into the crowd to arrest the most prominent instigators. In one of these sweeps, they managed to grab Judson—Ned Buntline himself—who was thrown into a makeshift holding cell in the opera house's basement.[32]

Around 9:00 p.m. the first contingent of militia—about forty mounted hussars armed with cutlasses—wheeled around Broadway and into Astor Place, electrifying the crowd. The rioters had smashed the streetlamps, but in the dark, the riders on white horses made easy targets. A deluge of stones pelted the first row, and as the crowd swarmed around them, several riders were pulled to the ground and beaten or fell as their horses threw them off. General Sandford, who rode with the hussars, was still in his black business clothes and thus was able to dismount and make his way back to the infantry, the Seventh Regiment of the state militia, marching behind the hussars. He commanded the soldiers to form a column, which then pushed its way from

Currier and Ives, *Great Riot at the Astor Place Opera House, New York: on Thursday Evening, May 10, 1849.*
Library of Congress, Prints and Photographs Online Catalog, LC-USZ2-2532.

Broadway to the rear of the opera house on 8th Street without much trouble, creating a corridor that Macready's audience would later use to exit. The police took over this position, and the troops moved back to Broadway and pushed into the thick mass of humanity on Astor Place, which did not yield so readily.[33]

Pummeled by a torrent of stones, the troops managed to create a buffer between the theater and the mob. Macready finished his performance but did not stay for an encore. Instead, friends convinced him to don a disguise; they spirited him back to his hotel (as the audience trickled out the back into the militia's corridor on 8th Street) and later out of the city like a fugitive slave. Eventually, he made his way to the relatively friendly confines of Boston.

Out front, the mob intensified its attack, pushing the troops back up onto the sidewalk. General Sandford, his immediate subordinate, Brigadier General Hall, and a Captain Shumway were all struck by stones. Shumway also discov-

ered a bullet wound in his leg; he had been shot by someone in the crowd with a pistol. Sandford ordered a bayonet charge, but it failed because the tight confines of Astor Place and the size of the crowd made it impossible for the troops to gain momentum. Mayor Woodhull, who had arrived a bit earlier, was conferring with Sheriff Westervelt, recorder Tallmadge, and Chief Matsell, when Brigadier General Hall, bleeding from his head, came to him and told the mayor that Hall's troops would not stand and be stoned to death with weapons in their hands. He begged the mayor to give the order to fire. Woodhull refused, telling Hall to wait.* The mayor soon departed to meet with the governor a couple of blocks away at the New York Hotel on Broadway between Washington and Waverly Places.[34]

The crowd continued its hail of stones. Hall told the sheriff that the troops could not hold their positions with-

* In a later inquiry, Woodhull claimed not to have had sufficient information to make the decision.

Astor Place Riot, 1849.
George W. Walling, *Recollections of a New York Chief of Police* (1887). Art and Picture Collection, New York Public Library.

out firing. Sandford, Westervelt, and Tallmadge all shouted that if the rioters would not disperse, they would be fired upon. Sandford, knocked off his feet by the mob swelling against the troops, yelled to the sheriff that the situation was untenable, so Westervelt at last gave the order to fire. General Hall instructed the troops to aim high, at "Mrs. Langdon's house," the granddaughter of the late John Jacob Astor who lived in a large mansion directly across from the opera house.[35] The muskets rang out, but the crowd kept bearing down, with several cries repeating Judson's earlier claim that the troops only had blanks. Hall ordered his men to fire again, and this time to aim low, to which a multitude of leg wounds attested. This volley at last had the desired effect of causing the rioters to fall back, and the troops were finally able to push forward to the corner of Lafayette

Place, at which point the rioters rallied one last time, only to incur yet another volley of musket fire. As rioters fell, two light artillery pieces Sandford had earlier requested arrived and were put into position. This time when the crowd was warned, it began to disperse.[36]

For the first time, the militia had opened fire on a rioting mob, and the results were catastrophic. Eighteen lay dead, all of them bystanders, none of them the Bowery B'hoys Rynders had mustered. Within a few days four more died of their wounds. More than 150 were injured. That night and over the next several days, 117 were arrested, nearly all from the city's working classes: bakers, brass finishers, butchers, chair makers, coopers, gardeners, machinists, marble cutters, masons, pianoforte makers, plumbers, printers, porters, sailmakers, and shoemakers.[37]

The Astor Opera House did not fare much better. In the wake of the riot, it was savagely satirized as the Massacre Opera House on DisAster Place and quickly declined. Five years later, a new, bigger house was built at 14th Street and Irving Place in the new elite redoubt of Union Square, protected both by distance from the heart of the Bowery and by management's prudent decision to provide plenty of cheap seats.

"To Please the Aristocracy of This City"

The day after the riot a big rally was held at City Hall Park to protest the firing on the rioters by the militia. Rynders addressed the crowd:

> Why was this murder perpetrated? Was it done for the sake of justice and for the object of preserving order? (Loud cries of "No, No.") I think not. For what, then, was it done? To please the aristocracy of this city, at the expense of the lives of the inoffending citizens—to please an aristocratic Englishman backed by a few sycophantic Americans (Loud cries of indignation). They would shoot down their brethren and fellow-citizens rather than be deprived of the pleasure of seeing him perform.[38]

Mike Walsh, editor of the *Subterranean* and a fiery orator, called for a murder prosecution and said it was only his respect for the law that kept him from calling for the crowd to mount the barricades and rekindle the revolution that had been snuffed out in Europe only a year before. Taking his hint, thousands surged out of City Hall Park and marched up to Astor Place, ready to face down the troops from behind quickly built barricades. But this time, a full charge by the militia, bayonets fixed, encouraged the crowd to disperse.[39]

The 1848 revolutions in Europe seemed to be on a lot of people's minds. In the aftermath of the riot, Whigs made the link explicit. With the decisive action of the troops, said James Watson Webb, publisher of the conservative *Courier and Enquirer*, New York had made "an excellent advertisement to the Capitalists of the old world, that they might send their property to New York and rely upon the certainty that it would be safe from the clutches of red republicanism, or chartists, or communionists [*sic*] of any description." The magistrate Charles Parker Daly assured convictions and stiff penalties for those arrested during the riot to make it clear that the old republican tolerance of mob action—the older sense that riots served a communal function of letting off steam—no longer would be tolerated.* Now, the riot showed, it was *class*—not community—that mattered in the city. In New York and across the country, a Philadelphia reporter noted, what "every patriot has hitherto felt it his duty to deny"—the existence of "a *high* class and a *low* class"—could no longer be repudiated.[40]

Class antagonism now became a defining quality of life in New York City. Astor Place, situated between Broadway and the Bowery, was where these two worlds first collided with an unprecedented violence. The riot exposed the increasingly insurmountable social distance between the city's classes. Its aftermath drove the city's elites to expand the geographical and psychic distance between these worlds, although their efforts could not insulate them from or prevent an even greater class explosion: the Draft Riots that broke out some fourteen years later.

---

* Judson got a year and was hailed as a hero when he was released. Rynders, with a good lawyer (the son of former president Martin Van Buren) provided by Tammany, got off.

DIVIDED POLICE, DEAD RABBITS, AND THE PANIC OF 1857

New York was a class-riven city, but that doesn't tell the half of it. Political and ethnic rivalry, nativism, abolitionism and anti-abolitionism, militant temperance, and the deepening divides of race crosscut the city, shaping and reshaping the urban social geography. Gangs in the working-class and immigrant neighborhoods skirmished in the streets: the nativist Bowery Boys fought the Irish Dead Rabbits; the Irish Plug Uglies took on the nativist American Guards; and the Roach Guards, Forty Thieves, and Shirt Tails (in the Irish Sixth Ward) and the O'Connell Guards, True Blue Americans, and Atlantic Guards (in the Bowery), each with a distinctive uniform, all fought among themselves. Election days and holidays like the Fourth of July were particularly rowdy, with gangs, fueled by much drink, patrolling the streets, looking for action, enforcing the wishes of ward bosses, and guarding the precincts of their territory. African Americans also banded together.[1]

By the middle of the 1850s, "ultrareformers" from the upper classes—mostly associated with the new Republican Party—were consolidating their power in the statehouse in Albany and sought to diminish, if not eliminate, Democratic control in the city. All through the nineteenth century New York City's status as a special kind of public corporation with rights against the central authority of the state had been eroding. By 1857 a series of court rulings and legislative maneuvers had succeeded in reducing the city to a subjugated creature of the state, able to exercise only those powers granted to it by the assembly, which showed little reluctance to interfere in the affairs of the municipality. On April 16 of that year Albany passed the Liquor Excise Law, which outlawed the sale of liquor on Sundays, holidays, and election days and required saloon keepers to obtain a license. The restrictions on licenses were such that local papers predicted that thirteen of every fourteen saloons in the city would have to close, and perhaps as many as ninety-nine out of a hundred in the working-class wards would be shuttered. For the reformers, the new law was a great victory after total prohibition had failed to pass two years earlier.

But the new law would be a limited victory if its enforcement was left to the city. The next day, therefore, the assembly passed the Metropolitan Police Act, which shifted control over the police from the Democratic municipal administration to the new Republican-controlled Metropolitan Police Commission, whose jurisdiction spread not only over Manhattan but also over Kings, Richmond, and Westchester Counties and whose powers included control not only over liquor-law enforcement but also over elections. Outraged city residents rallied in City Hall Park in May, the mayor urged the standing police to reject the reorganization, and the Common Council created the Municipal Police Force, consisting of existing officers, under the direct control of the mayor. Policemen chose up sides, cleaving largely along nativist-foreigner lines. About eight hundred stayed with the mostly foreign-born Municipal force, and three hundred joined the state-controlled and largely native-born Metropolitan force. Both recruited more cops from their own communities. Then they fought for control of the station houses while thieves exploited the chaos.

In June, when the reformers sought to arrest the mayor for inciting a riot, the Municipal police protecting him fought off the Metropolitans seeking his capture. The Metropolitans regrouped with a larger force and tried again, but the Municipals had recruited help from among the Irish gangs and others, and together they pushed back the Metropolitans with a rain of clubs and brickbats. It was not until the Seventh

Municipal and Metropolitan police fighting at City Hall, 1857.
George W. Walling, *Recollections of a New York Chief of Police* (1887). Art and Picture Collection, New York Public Library.

Regiment was called out that order was restored and the arrest warrant was served. Two weeks later, on July 2, the court of appeals held that the assembly had been within its rights in establishing the Metropolitan Police Commission, and the next day, the mayor disbanded the Municipal Police Force.

But the Metropolitan force refused to hire the disbanded Municipal cops and so went into the Fourth of July—traditionally a day of heavy drinking, street fighting, and rowdy celebration—as an inexperienced force. Even before the sun rose, they were under attack by gangs of young Irish men and boys in Chatham Square. The nativist Bowery Boys came to the cops' rescue. The Dead Rabbits gang, in their uniform of red-striped pants, sprang into action,

attacking a small band of Metropolitan police on Bayard Street (between Elizabeth and Mulberry). Some two hundred Bowery Boys rushed to the scene and secured a safe route out for the police. Now the street fighting between gangs erupted in earnest. Barricades were built; women gathered stones and took them to men on the roofs or behind the barricades; soon there was gunfire. When the warfare subsided—largely from sheer exhaustion rather than effective policing—twelve were dead, and another thirty-seven were injured. The next day, a Sunday, trouble again threatened, but the National Guard was mobilized. It kept the peace and assured the enforcement of the new liquor laws.

Rallies and protests against the new police and state usurpation of city power

were held all through the next week, and on the following Sunday violence erupted again as the Metropolitans tried to close saloons in Little Germany (on Avenue A at 4th Street). Before order was restored another man had died—a German blacksmith. On Monday a ten-thousand-person funeral procession for the blacksmith marched up Broadway behind a large banner declaring him to be a victim of the Metropolitan police.

And then a month later the economy collapsed. A combination of collapsing wheat prices, unwise stock speculation, and internal looting had led the Ohio Life Insurance and Trust Company to go belly-up. Other New York banks were also overextended, and soon faith that debts would be repaid evaporated; panic set in. Banks refused

"View from the 'Dead Rabbit' Barricade in Bayard Street, taken at the height of the battle by our own artist, who, as spectator, was present at the fight," *Frank Leslie's Illustrated Newspaper*, July 18, 1857. Library of Congress, Prints and Photographs Online Catalog, LC-USZ62-1222057.

to make loans and, to save themselves, forced merchants into bankruptcy. A run on the banks ensued as depositors tried to get their money back in gold. Gold reserves fell (the sinking in a hurricane of a steamer carrying $1.6 million in gold from California hardly helped matters). On October 13 eighteen New York banks failed (the carnage was worse in other parts of the country), and soon the crisis went global. In London, Marx and Engels thought they heard the death knell of capitalism, but instead, by refusing to give out metal, New York banks bolstered their reserves and began to recover by December, figuring out how to make others—merchants, industrialists, workers—pay the price of the depression

that was just settling in. Building in New York came to a halt; perhaps a hundred thousand workers in Manhattan and Brooklyn were thrown into unemployment—and frequently out of their houses. Food prices, meanwhile, stayed high. Led by the Association for the Improvement of the Condition of the Poor—which believed that almsgiving should be private, Christian charity, and even then only sparingly and sternly given—private relief to the indigent in October declined by 25 percent compared to the previous boom-time year. The rich and their newspapers fought vigorously against any sort of municipal relief or make-work programs, pushing instead for either "manly" forbearance or emigration.

Against this, Germans (associated in the Kummunisten Klub), Irish workers, and American craftsmen banded together to organize the unemployed, claiming a right to state assistance. The American Workers League called a rally for Tompkins Square on November 5 (the old Guy Fawkes Day) to demand "work and bread." Four thousand workers marched to City Hall and pre-

View in Central Park, Promenade, June, 1858, depicting crews at work in the wake of the 1857 crash. George Hayward, lithographer, 1859.
Art and Picture Collection, New York Public Library.

sented a petition to the mayor denouncing charity and claiming rights to work and life. They demanded a public works program and the municipal construction of cheap housing. The Common Council began to stir.

The following day a crowd—this time of five thousand—marched to Wall Street to demand that bankers make loans to businesses that would hire the poor. Three days later, on November 9, as demonstrators packed into City Hall (and a crowd that was larger than ever milled outside), the council approved a bond to begin work on Central Park, but nothing else. The mayor, whose power rested largely on the base of the masses outside, nonetheless deployed guards at government buildings and the flour stores (memories of the 1837 Flour Riot had not faded). Mass rallies in Tompkins Square the next two days culminated in a bread riot. Massed police and vicious calls by the media to "perforate" the bodies of rioters notwithstanding, hungry rioters attacked food merchants' wagons and shops before they were quieted.

As work began on Central Park, the unemployed descended en masse on Superintendent Frederick Law Olmsted, demanding work. Through a fairly well-oiled patronage system, a thousand were employed by January, sapping the strength of the crowds that had been gathering daily in Tompkins Square. Double that number were hired by October 1858, and nearly double again a year later.

CHAPTER 6

America's Deadliest Riot

The 1863 Draft Riots

RACHEL GOFFE AND ESTEBAN KELLY

America's deadliest riots were not simple, straightforward struggles between two opposing sides. The conditions that sparked them arose from a complex layering of New York's political factions, classes, races, ethnicities, and investments amid the country's brutal civil war. As the economic crisis of 1857 abated, a political crisis over slavery and secessionism grew. As abolitionist and anti-abolitionist divides deepened through the city, growing class and race resentments smoldered and finally burst into flames when authorities tried to implement a federally mandated draft. Manhattan burned for days, only to emerge with its geography forever restructured.

But first there was an election. New York was a unionist city during the Revolution (chapter 4), but it was a Union city during the 1860 election. A fusionist, Democratic, Union ticket (i.e., favoring the interests of the southern states) prevailed in the city on Election Day as its residents, egged on by "the Mercantile and Capitalist classes" (as the Republican *Tribune* put it), voted overwhelmingly against Lincoln. They were, however, outvoted by Republicans upstate, and Lincoln won the state and, with it, the presidency.[1]

Merchants and bankers, fearing war and the loss of their southern markets, soon met in large numbers to consolidate their interests. Specifically, they passed resolutions of solidarity with the South, including affirmation of the "superiority" of the white race and support of the rights of slaveholders, preferably within the Union but as a separate Confederacy if necessary. Within six weeks of the election, South Carolina had seceded; less than two months later, the breakaway Confederate States of America had been declared, and war was inevitable. So too, perhaps, was another economic crisis in the city, as the Confederacy quickly repudiated its northern debts and expressed its venom against New York capitalists' creaming of excessive profits off the cotton sent to Europe.

Meanwhile, realizing how dependent New York's economy was on southern commerce, Mayor Fernando Wood publicly broached the idea of the city's own secession and emergence as a "free state" that would continue to trade with the Confederacy and whose receipt of import duties would be so great that New Yorkers could be freed from paying taxes altogether. Though taken seriously in many quarters, Wood's plan went nowhere, in part because of fears that New York's secession would lead to the secession of regions elsewhere in the North and thus serve to isolate the city from its western markets, even as it was increasingly becoming isolated from the South as the Confederacy redirected trade through southern ports and toyed with joining the British Empire. Friendly as New York capitalists often were to slaveholders in the South, and deep as their sense of white racial solidarity may have been, southern moves to bypass the city turned New York opinion quickly in favor of war.[2]

After the April 12, 1861, Confederate attack on Fort Sumter in Charleston, Lincoln declared the South to be in a state of insurrection. When the president called for seventy-five thousand volunteers to put that insurrection down, New Yorkers responded enthusiastically. Within a week, the famed Seventh Regiment—composed largely of men of the professional classes—had boarded ferries to cross to Jersey City and march to Washington to defend the capital city. On April 20 a mass meeting—perhaps the largest ever held in North America to that date—was held in Union Square to rally for the Union. Lincoln authorized the secret transfer of $2 million to New York's Union Defense Committee (comprising city grandees from both parties) to buy armaments, build ships, and recruit volunteers. Mayor Wood, having jettisoned his secessionist plans, talked the Board of Aldermen into securing a $1.5 million loan from New York banks to pay volunteers and support families left behind in the city. Before the year was out, the Union Defense Committee had mustered and dispatched sixty-six regiments and provided aid to twelve thousand dependents.[3]

While support and organizing for the war by local elites was impressive, ethnic working-class support was even more so—at least at first. Germans, Swiss, Italian, and especially Irish working people enthusiastically embraced the war effort. Men mostly volunteered to be soldiers, while women served as cooks, nurses, laundresses, confidantes, and companions. For the Irish, support for the Union seemed to be a means to silence the nativists who had harassed and harried them all through the 1840s and 1850s, but it was also a means to stick it to their English colonial overlords who allied with the South. Efforts by blacks to enlist were initially rebuffed, however.[4]

War Economy in a Wartime City

The enthusiasm did not last. Agents of northern capital were harassed and threatened as they tried to ply their trade in the South, and most gave up trying and headed north. It was not long before New York's manufacturing economy collapsed. By the summer of 1861, thirty thousand New Yorkers found themselves unemployed; the homeless filled the streets and makeshift shelters in the police stations. Fortunes soon reversed, however, especially as demand for American wheat surged following a European crop failure, which in turn spurred a boom in railroad building. War contracts for ships, munitions, clothing—and now the new high technology of refined oil—assured that excesses of both skilled and unskilled labor were soon absorbed by increased production. Patrolling Confederate ships plus high tariffs on foreign goods also did their part to spur demand for New York City–made commodities.[5]

But this economic growth remained vulnerable to panic, or at least to deep uncertainty. With the Union out of money, New York and other northern banks arranged a loan of $150 million in July 1861—the depths of the summer depression. By law, the banks could not draw on their depositors' funds and had to provide gold. There was not enough. To avert bankruptcy, the federal government started printing money—the first uniform national currency. Yet, state and bank moneys continued to circulate and compete with the new greenbacks. It would take until 1865 for the new national money to win out. To back the new currency the Union government instituted new taxes on the wealthy and on commodities and services. Soon it was issuing bonds sold by armies of agents fanning out across the land, thus funding the war until its last year, when New York banks were called upon again to provide loans.

The stock market swung back and forth. Many men made fortunes, and not a few lost them. The general trend through the war, though, was up, and the stock market drew thousands of new entrants, who often made purchases with cash loaned by the banks at 10 percent interest. Commissions from the stock transactions allowed the New York Stock Exchange to buy up land and build its palace of speculation on Wall Street, while the number of millionaires in the city grew at least tenfold. By 1863 the top 1 percent was raking in 61 percent of the city's wealth. New luxury stores marched up Broadway. Fetes and charity balls ruled the night for nine months of the year before the city's wealthy decamped for the summer to Saratoga Springs and other resorts.[6]

For the working classes, the war was a far more horrible experience. Though manufacturing quickly rebounded after the 1861 summer slump, providing work and even rising wages, gains were quickly undercut by inflation. In the first two years of the war, the price of beef almost doubled, rents climbed by more than 15 percent, and wages increased by only 12 percent. Meanwhile, with all the new money being printed, currency was devalued by 43 percent. Funds appropriated to support the wives—an increasing proportion of them widows—and families of volunteers were rerouted to directly support the troops. Little new housing was being built, even as newly invigorated industry expanded its footprint into formerly residential districts. Those kicked out of their housing were pushed north into the Fourth Ward, creating the most densely populated place in the world; shantytowns sprang up north of 50th Street, and the homeless once again filled the police stations.[7]

As the war intensified in 1862—long after the three months Lincoln had promised it would take to put down the insurrection—working-class New Yorkers died by the thousands. Walt Whitman, who volunteered in noncombat roles at the front, reported that the battlefield was "a great slaughter-house & the men are butchering each other." By 1863 the Irish and Italian brigades from New York had been wiped out. Those who escaped with their lives, but perhaps not with all their limbs, filled the city streets, their numbers bolstered by large numbers of deserters who knew they were better off in the big city than back in their small hometowns, where they would quickly be fingered. In the city, returning fighters told tales of low and sometimes nonexistent pay; tyrannical, incompetent, and corrupt officers who held rank only by dint of patronage; and a good deal of nativism. Hospitals overflowed. The flush of volunteerism that marked the beginning of the war gave way, and enlistments quickly sagged.[8]

Carnage and Conscription

As Union ranks were depleted through death, injury, and desertion, agitation among the political classes for a draft gained momentum. In early 1863 Congress acted, passing the Enrollment Act on March 3. The act required all male citizens (i.e., white Americans) and immigrants applying for citizenship to enroll with a local board. Draft lotteries would begin in July. Officials hoped the threat of being drafted would induce men to volunteer, since by volunteering they could pick up an enlistment bonus of $100 or more. But the combination of Union defeats and racist agitation that welled up in the wake of the Emancipation Proclamation (January 1, 1863) discouraged enlistment. Free black people were seen by many white workers as direct competitors and a threat to their own standing as (relatively) privileged laborers. Many white workers began to question the purpose of the war. Had it become a crusade to undermine their own status as free laborers? While emancipation would free black people to serve in the army, many whites shared the anxiety published in the white nationalist paper, the *Weekly Caucasian*, that "equality as a soldier means equality at the ballot-box, equality everywhere."[9]

Racial tensions were already high. New York industrialists had begun a program of labor recruitment in Europe to fill the labor ranks depleted by men heading off to war and to keep wages down while countering the threat of strikes. Industrial magnate Peter Cooper, founder of the Cooper Institute (now Cooper Union), urged the Lincoln administration to send freed and captured black people north for work. Others directly recruited black workers as strikebreakers. The same month the Enrollment Act was passed, the Erie Railroad hired scores of black workers to replace striking whites on its Hudson piers, though they were soon driven off by a white mob of more than a thousand. The previous August a crowd of two or three thousand mostly Irish workers threatened to burn down the Watson and Lorillard tobacco factory in Brooklyn unless the black workers were dismissed. The company refused, and the mob threatened

Resumption of the Draft—inside the Provost Marshal's Office, Sixth District—the Wheel Goes Round. Note the blindfold on the man drawing numbers.
Library of Congress, Prints and Photographs Division, LC-USZ62-88856.

to "roast the niggers alive." The police prevented them from doing so, but the tensions remained.[10]

White workers were skeptical of being conscripted into a cause about which they were increasingly suspicious, and a provision of the Enrollment Act further stirred their dissatisfaction. It allowed anyone drafted to buy themselves out of the duty for the sum of $300. Supporters of the Enrollment Act defended the provision on pure class terms: since the draft was universal, it would necessarily ensnare the productive members of the capitalist and middle classes, whom the economy (presumably) could not spare. Even more, the fee was purportedly set to cap the price of a substitute on the informal market within the reach of an average American. Yet $300 nearly equaled a year's wages for most workers. Opponents of the act complained that it made it inevitable that it would be the poor who fought what was increasingly seen as a rich man's war. As Fernando Wood's brother Benjamin, the publisher of the *Daily News*, argued, "The fact that the Conscription virtually exempts the rich and fastens its iron hand upon the poor alone, is sufficient demonstration of its

injustice." Peace Democrats set to organizing white working people's discontent.[11]

Democratic governor Horatio Seymour was a "Peace Democrat" who argued for ending the war by acceding to the South's demands to continue slavery. He opposed emancipation because he felt it substituted "niggerism for nationality," and he used his pulpit as governor to vow to have the Enrollment Act overturned in court. Other Democrats militated against Lincoln's suspension of habeas corpus and the arrest of antiwar activists. Nonetheless, conscription enrollment—in which specially sworn government agents went house to house and signed up all white men between the ages of twenty and thirty-five (and all unmarried men up to age forty-five)—proceeded relatively peacefully in May and June.*

* There were sporadic acts of resistance, for example, in May men at one boardinghouse refused to be enrolled until an armed force of twenty-eight men persuaded them otherwise, and in June nine men were arrested for obstructing enrollment, but these protests were relatively muted, especially given the new power the law gave to provost marshals in every congressional district to arrest draft resisters.

But then the Confederates stormed into the North. Lee's army pushed through Virginia's Shenandoah Valley and into Pennsylvania, nearly reaching Harrisburg by June 29. New York troops mobilized and headed west, leaving only about 550 soldiers in the city to defend it against Confederate warships—or internal unrest. By July 1 the New York troops had met up with Gen. George Meade's Union army at Gettysburg and prepared for what would become the bloodiest battle in American history. The Union victory at Gettysburg marked a turning point in the war, but it did so at enormous cost.[12]

As news of the July 4 Gettysburg victory—and the scale of the carnage—was still making its way back to New York, Governor Seymour mounted an Independence Day stage at the Academy of Music and implored the crowd: "Remember this—that the bloody and treasonable and revolutionary doctrine of public necessity can be proclaimed by a mob as well as by a government."* In the antiwar papers, calls for armed resistance to the draft were not unknown. Though they were largely muted by a wait-and-see attitude, these calls were often fueled by white supremacist rhetoric, which editors and agitators used in their arguments that the draft was in service of an elite determined to making "the negro . . . as good as the white man."[13]

The waiting ended when the draft lottery got under way a week later (Saturday, July 11). Both the Republican mayor, George Opdyke, and the Democratic governor, Horatio Seymour, professed ignorance that the draft would begin that day, and it might be that federal authorities purposely kept them in the dark. Federal officials certainly hoped to contain resistance by beginning the lottery at the edges of the city—in the Ninth District on Third Avenue at 46th Street, only a block from what was then the edge of the formal city (beyond which remained less formal districts of shanties and the like). Though a large crowd gathered to watch names being pulled out of a barrel, it seemed content to merely witness

the spectacle. The provost marshal drew 1,236 names without incident before closing up for the day; the remainder of the district's 2,000-man quota was to be drawn the following Monday. Newspapers published the names of draftees on Sunday, fueling innumerable barroom discussion across the city as the fact that the draft had started—that Governor Seymour had failed to halt it—became generally known. By Sunday evening plans for concerted resistance were being laid.[14]

The Draft Riots

What became riots began as a strike. Early on the morning of Monday, July 13, hundreds of workers on the city's West Side laid down their tools and streamed north—calling others out of their workplaces as they went—to join a mass meeting in a vacant lot (on 59th Street between Fifth Avenue and Madison) near the still-uncompleted Central Park. From there they headed back south to the Ninth District draft headquarters at Third Avenue and 46th Street, where they met up with more workers—men and women alike—heading north from the downtown industrial districts and the East Side waterfront. The crowd was massive, filling the broad avenues and taking more than twenty minutes to pass a single point. As it converged on the provost marshal's office, the crowd was joined by members of volunteer fire companies, upset at losing their traditional exemption from conscription.† On Saturday a member of the Black Joke Fire Company—stationed at Eighth Avenue and 58th Street—had been drafted, and his comrades were determined not only to stop the draft but also to destroy the records of Saturday's lottery. Only a small squadron of policemen had been stationed at the office. They were no match for the burgeoning crowd as the Monday lottery got under way at 10:00 a.m.[15]

It was not long before someone launched a stone through one of the windows, and the crowd surged forward. As draft officials escaped out of the back of the building, the crowd

---

* Something like this sentiment may have been behind perhaps the deadliest antiblack riot before the Draft Riots—when white stevedores rioted in Buffalo, killing at least three black workers and injuring twelve others who had been imported as strikebreakers (Schecter, *The Devil's Own Work*, 113).

† Firemen had long been exempted from conscription into state militias.

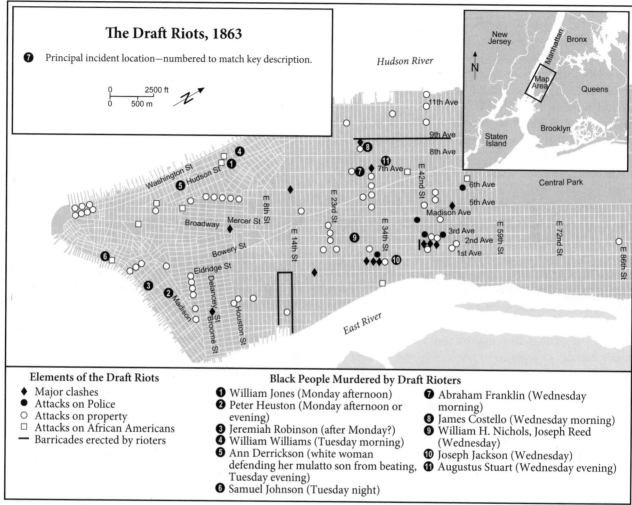

The Draft Riots, 1863

❼ Principal incident location—numbered to match key description.

0 —— 2500 ft
0 —— 500 m

Hudson River

11th Ave
9th Ave
8th Ave
7th Ave
6th Ave
5th Ave
Madison Ave
3rd Ave
2nd Ave
1st Ave
E 42nd St
E 23rd St
E 34th St
E 14th St
E 8th St
E 59th St
E 72nd St
E 86th St

Washington St
Hudson St
Broadway
Mercer St
Bowery St
Eldridge St
Delancey St
Broome St
Houston St
Madison

East River

New Jersey
Manhattan
Bronx
Queens
Brooklyn
Staten Island
Central Park
Map Area
N

Elements of the Draft Riots

◆ Major clashes
● Attacks on Police
○ Attacks on property
▢ Attacks on African Americans
— Barricades erected by rioters

Black People Murdered by Draft Rioters

❶ William Jones (Monday afternoon)
❷ Peter Heuston (Monday afternoon or evening)
❸ Jeremiah Robinson (after Monday?)
❹ William Williams (Tuesday morning)
❺ Ann Derrickson (white woman defending her mulatto son from beating, Tuesday evening)
❻ Samuel Johnson (Tuesday night)
❼ Abraham Franklin (Wednesday morning)
❽ James Costello (Wednesday morning)
❾ William H. Nichols, Joseph Reed (Wednesday)
❿ Joseph Jackson (Wednesday)
⓫ Augustus Stuart (Wednesday evening)

The Draft Riots, 1863.
Cartography: Joe Stoll, Syracuse University Cartography Lab and Map Shop; redrawn from Edwin G. Burrows and Mike Wallace, *Gotham: A History of New York City to 1898* (2000).

poured in, found the lottery wheel, and smashed it to pieces. Black Joke firemen poured turpentine all around and set the offices ablaze. As the fire spread to an adjoining building, Black Joke men prevented other fire companies from responding. More people rushed toward the scene, threatening soldiers from the city's Invalid Corps (wounded veterans on light duty), which had been sent north from the

The Rioters Burning the Colored Orphan Asylum . . . 5th Ave. & 46th St.
Harper's Pictorial History of the Civil War (1894). Library of Congress, Pictures and Photographs Division.

provost marshal's general headquarters downtown. Met by a hail of paving stones, the corps quickly retreated. The next target was Police Superintendent John Kennedy—the leader of the Republican state-authorized Metropolitans—who was beaten to a bloody pulp.

The riot began to look like an insurrection. As the crowd burgeoned, mobs of rioters spread across the city, halting streetcars and commuter trains (and ripping up tracks), felling telegraph poles linking police stations with the police headquarters, destroying picket fences to make weapons, and attacking police officers. Republican establishments were especially targeted, including the homes of the president of Columbia College (at Fifth Avenue and 49th Street) and Mayor Opdyke. Though in both cases a ransacking was prevented, the throng was hardly dissuaded. Mobs attacked mansions up and down Fifth Avenue, burning and looting them. Other crowds fought head-to-head with police, moving up Third Avenue and holding the cops at bay

until more rioters filled in behind them. The Metropolitans were routed. By now the mob stretched some thirty blocks along Third Avenue—all the way down to the Cooper Institute at Union Square—as buildings went up in flames on both sides. A large mob laid siege to the "armory" at Third Avenue and 21st Street (which was, in fact, a rifle factory owned by Mayor Opdyke's son-in-law). By late afternoon the crowd had fought its way in and seized the large mass of guns stored there. They then set fire to the building, trapping dozens of rioters on the upper floors and killing ten (three others also died at the armory).

Remarkably, already planned draft lotteries continued for much of the morning in other precincts before officials ordered all draft records be secured and transferred to Governors Island. But the rioting did not abate. Instead, focus shifted. If rich Republicans were the original targets of the mobs' wrath, by afternoon it had turned on poor black people. A crowd led by the Irish cellar digger Patrick Merry first torched the recently evacuated Eighth District provost marshal's office at Broadway and 29th Street and then headed west, torching homes of black New Yorkers as they went.[16] As afternoon turned to evening, mobs of Irish workers attacked black people found on the streets and streetcars. Black boardinghouses were set aflame. This murderous rage was not only directed at adults. The rioters turned their rage even to black children, attacking the Colored Orphan Asylum at 43rd Street and Fifth Avenue as 237 children fled for their lives. A large group was ushered to safety in the 20th Precinct police station by young Irish officer Paddy Mc-Caffrey, who found himself threatened by the mob for his efforts. Others hid out in the basements of nearby homes. Soon the children in the precinct house were joined by black adults seeking refuge. The Colored Orphan Asylum was torched and its grounds destroyed.*

Attacks on black people intensified as the night wore on. At Varick and Charlton Streets, a mob attacked a group of black men, who fought back. The Irish leader of the mob was shot, and the crowd retaliated by capturing a black man, lynching him, and setting his corpse on fire. Along the waterfront, tenements, bars, brothels, and dance halls were torched. Incensed crowds reacted with extra ferocity anywhere there seemed to be race mixing. Little seemed to be able to be done to stanch the riot. Gettysburg had siphoned off most of the city's able-bodied troops. There were only five hundred or so left in the garrisons. Many in the city and elsewhere in the North began to fear that the Confederacy—allied with European powers—might see the roiling insurrection as an opportunity to resume its push north and hive off the city from the Union.

As the race riot intensified, the insurrection against the Republicans also gathered steam. Crowds marched toward Newspaper Row, across from City Hall Park, aiming for Republican papers like the *Times* and the *Tribune*. *Times* pub-

lisher Henry Raymond had already set up a battery of Gatling guns in the upper windows, so the crowd turned toward the *Tribune* but were driven off by police reinforcements brought in from Brooklyn. The police action discouraged the crowd from continuing on to the heavily guarded Financial District. But this merely diverted it back toward the rooming house districts along the waterfront. Meanwhile, city elite pleaded with Gen. John Wool, in charge of the city's troops, to declare martial law. He refused, claiming he did not have the authority to do so. Neither would the mayor declare martial law.† In any event, a drenching thunderstorm soon doused the flames of discontent—for the night, anyway.

As the storm raged, police telegraphers set out and climbed poles to restore the communications network. Fire companies—including the Black Jokers—fought the flames the storm did not quench. And police spies—about fifteen of them—developed plans to go undercover to infiltrate the mobs should they re-form the next day. They did. As dawn broke on Tuesday, July 14, crowds, egged on by editorials in anti-abolition papers like the *World*, gathered around the city, broke into gun shops, and armed themselves. Black people were targeted early. A suite of black-owned businesses on Sullivan and Roosevelt Streets were set on fire. While large numbers of black men, women, and children headed to the ferries to try to escape the city, others were chased off the ends of piers to either swim to the safety of an anchored ship or drown. Still other black people headed north on foot even as white mobs threatened to destroy the bridge over Spuyten Duyvil both to stop the exodus and to keep troops from reaching Manhattan.

By a little after nine in the morning a full battle had broken out between a crowd of perhaps ten thousand and about three hundred policemen who had been dispatched to the scene of a fire at Second Avenue and 34th Street. As police opened fire and stormed some of the buildings, rioters in the upper floors and on the roofs fell or jumped to their deaths.

---

* Elsewhere in the city, crowds attacked other symbols of moral reform—associated with the Republicans and upper classes—like the Five Points Mission and the Magdalene Asylum, neither of which were associated with black people.

† Tammany Hall Democrats, including William "Boss" Tweed, argued against martial law, fearing it would incense the rioters even more. Republican mayor Opdyke seemed to accept this argument.

New York—the Riot in Lexington Avenue.
Joel Tyler Headley, *Pen and Pencil Sketches of the Great Riots:
An Illustrated History of the Railroad and Other Great Riots* (1882).
Art and Picture Collection, New York Public Library.

More were clubbed senseless on the streets. About 150 soldiers and an artillery unit, led by an Irishman unsympathetic to and unliked by the Irish rioters, arrived. Loud blanks were fired from the cannons, and the soldiers opened fire over the heads of the mob, killing two children and five adults watching from upper-floor windows. Rioters stampeded and fled the scene. The police and military had spared the mob but killed bystanders. As word of the debacle spread, tempers were inflamed even more.

In the Corlears Hook neighborhood (Lower East Side), 130 soldiers engaged a crowd of 5,000 on Pitt Street, opening fire and charging with their bayonets. Fourteen were killed. The next crowd the soldiers encountered quickly dispersed when threatened with the same treatment. But skirmishes continued throughout the day in the industrial districts along the East River. Northwest, at the site of the smoldering armory, another crowd stormed the nearby Union Steam Works, which held a cache of four thousand carbines. When two hundred Metropolitan police arrived at 2:00 p.m. to reclaim the building and guns, first a hand-to-hand struggle in the streets and then an intense firefight broke out. Dozens died, and still the battles continued.* Mayor Opdyke's house was attacked again on Tuesday afternoon. Across the city, buildings and stores were occupied, ransacked, or burned; black men, women, and children continued to be attacked. Some of those who had rioted on Monday—opposed to the inequities of the draft—now worked to quell the violence. In Kleindeutschland, centered on Tompkins Square (called Weisse Garten by Germans), members of the socialist Turnverein patrolled the streets, protecting buildings from the mobs. Elsewhere some Irish and native workers also joined antiriot patrols or forces.[17]

If the city's workers and immigrants were divided as the rioting wore on, its elites were even more so. Not only were there the divisions between abolitionist and anti-abolitionist, war and antiwar, Republican and Democratic, and the tribunes of a rising capitalist class and patrons of the workers, there was also a divide between those who saw the rioting as a perhaps extreme expression of popular, customary uprisings in which plebeians called their "betters" to account and those who saw it as a direct assault on the social order. As debates on how to handle and quell the violence unfolded, alliances shifted, meaning that rarely was there a coordinated, cohesive plan to restore order in the city, only hap-

* The number is unknown, in part because authorities quickly cleared the streets of bodies and disposed of them, often before identifying them. Joel Tyler Headley reported that a single physician alone "dressed the wounds of twenty-one desperately wounded men" (*Great Riots of New York*, 151).

hazard sorties as police and soldiers were dispatched from one outbreak of violence or arson to another.* Governor Seymour—unaware that the draft would begin—had left the city on July 10 to visit relatives in New Jersey. Though summoned back on Monday the 13th, he did not return until Tuesday morning. Along with Boss Tweed, Seymour made the rounds of the city, addressing crowds as "my friends" and calling for calm while promising that he would seek to have the draft repealed. Republicans accused him of more than tacitly supporting the rioters. Violence continued. Mayor Opdyke petitioned the secretary of war in Washington to send troops. Though General Lee's troops had continued to harry Union soldiers for a week after Gettysburg (as Union general Meade hesitated as to what steps to take next), by July 13 they were in retreat across the Potomac. Secretary of War Edwin Stanton felt safe in sending five regiments to New York, including the hometown Seventh.

But they did not arrive until Wednesday evening. In the meantime, the rioting continued. Tuesday evening, barricades made of telegraph poles, furniture looted from mansions, carts, stagecoaches, crates, and barrels were established in several neighborhoods, including a long one along Ninth Avenue that stretched from the Twenties to the Forties and another that sealed off a dozen blocks north of Tompkins Square. Military officials on the ground feared that the riots were turning into something like the European revolutions of 1848. When police tried to dismantle the barricades they were met by a hail of bullets shot by snipers on the rooftops and gunmen on the streets. Mobs terrorized black families in Greenwich Village and along Roosevelt Street, where they torched two black tenements. Attacks on black people were vicious. Seeking to lynch a Mr. Derrickson, a white mob paused to beat his young son and wife senseless. Mrs. Derrickson did all she could to shield her boy. He survived,

New York—Hanging and Burning a Negro in Clarkson Street.
Joel Tyler Headley, *Pen and Pencil Sketches of the Great Riots:
An Illustrated History of the Railroad and Other Great Riots* (1882).
Art and Picture Collection, New York Public Library.

saved in part by a (white) neighbor who threatened the mob with a gun, but she later died of her wounds.

Riots were spreading across the North: Boston, Hartford, Albany, Troy, Newark, Jersey City, Tarrytown, New Rochelle, Rye, Jamaica, and Staten Island all saw antidraft, antiblack violence on Tuesday. By Wednesday violence in New York—the epicenter—was showing few signs of abating. Many thought the city would be completely destroyed. Refugees—black and white alike—filled the roads and waterways. Others would have no chance. At 6:00 a.m., as rain fell heavily, James Costello, a black shoemaker, was chased by white shoemaker and fireman William Mealy. Costello turned and shot Mealy in the head. A mob quickly formed, caught Costello, beat him, stoned him, hanged him, chopped off his toes and fingers, and gashed and sliced at

---

* City, state, and military officials had established a headquarters at the St. Nicholas Hotel on Broadway near Spring Street, where they hashed out plans and generally failed to coordinate responses. The St. Nicholas was later torched by Confederate arsonists, but portions of the original building remain to this day.

New York—the Fight between Rioters and Militia.
Joel Tyler Headley, *Pen and Pencil Sketches of the Great Riots: An Illustrated History of the Railroad and Other Great Riots* (1882). Art and Picture Collection, New York Public Library.

his body with knives. They set fire to the house they thought was his and several tenements nearby. They looted other black homes. Some members of the mob, like James Cassidy, threatened and warned his black neighbors, hoping to push them forever out of the city. As they had the day before, skirmishes developed and faded, and police and soldiers rushed from scene to scene. But this day, attacks seemed redoubled against black people. Black men were beaten and hanged. Black women escaped burning buildings with nothing more than what they were wearing. The *Christian Recorder*, a black newspaper, later reported that "Many [black] men were killed and thrown into the rivers, a great number hung to trees and lampposts; numbers shot down; no black person could show their heads but what they were hunted like wolves."[18]

Rumors circulated that rioters were preparing to sab-otage the Croton water mains and that mobs would soon turn their attention back to the wealthy. Sectarian divisions between Irish Catholics and Protestants emerged (Sunday had been the anniversary of William of Orange's defeat of Catholics in the 1690 Battle of the Boyne). Some Republicans called for President Lincoln not only to declare martial law but also to suspend the city and state administrations, send in an occupying force, and enforce the draft. Meanwhile, the city's Common Council debated a bill to establish a $2.5 million fund to pay the commutation fees for any drafted New Yorker who could not afford them. Republicans and Democrats skirmished through their papers as to who was to blame for the rioting. Democrats laid blame at the feet of Republicans for attempting to elevate black people above their station in life (in which effort the war was only a piece). Republicans blamed the Democrats for condoning

The Draft Riots in New York—the Battle in Second Avenue.
Art and Picture Collection, New York Public Library.

and encouraging plebeian and racist violence. Rioters on the Lower East Side reinforced barricades, established street patrols, and conducted house-to-house searches for wounded policemen and soldiers.

And then, nearing 4:00 p.m., the military in the city finally decided to take offensive rather than merely defensive action—which is to say, it became much more aggressive about shooting into crowds. At Tenth Avenue and 42nd Street, fifty soldiers arriving in support of police battling a crowd of two thousand opened fire, sending at least five volleys into the crowd. They stormed buildings where snipers were presumed to be stationed. And then they fired more volleys into the crowd. Lieutenant Ryan, who led the charge, proudly reported that his men killed at least fifty rioters, including a number of women and children. When a Tammany judge sought to arrest Ryan, his superior, General Sandford, protected him.

When a new crowd began to form at First Avenue and 18th Street, Sandford sent 150 citizen-volunteers and two howitzers to the scene under the command of two colonels. Poorly trained, the volunteers were quickly beset and trapped by the crowd. The artillerymen sent round after round of "canister" (fragmentation bombs) from the howitzers into the crowd, killing thirty. Enraged rioters fought back, killing ten soldiers. Eventually, the governor ordered some 150 professional troops to the neighborhood to rescue the besieged volunteers. As the troops retreated, rioters claimed control of the streets and conducted house-to-house searches for injured military men, searching in particular for the colonel who had ordered the howitzers to be fired. When they found him, he barely escaped with his life, and then only because he professed to be a Catholic. Across the river in Brooklyn—which only saw light rioting—a mob set fire to two big grain elevators in retaliation for earlier use of black workers to break strikes.

Even if the volunteers were routed at First Avenue and 18th Street, the tide seemed to be turning as regiments from the Pennsylvania battlefields began arriving. By early Thursday morning, some four thousand troops had entered the city. The Seventh Regiment, long used to quelling riots in the city, landed at Canal Street and began a steady march north. But the riot was not yet over. Mobs continued to attack black people, who sought refuge in overcrowded police stations. Even as the mayor urged people to return to work and as troops guarded the city's gasworks, mobs stopped streetcars on the reopened lines, robbing passengers or just turning them back. Soldiers once again directly confronted—and shot at—menacing crowds. At midday on First Avenue near 20th Street, a company of New York militia dispatched to guard a foundry making war munition found itself surrounded by a growing crowd. They opened fire—once again with the support of howitzers—and cleared a path up the avenue. Eventually, they reached the foundry and took up positions inside, threatening the crowd (which was braying for four Metropolitan policemen holed up inside) with their rifles if it did not disperse. Every time the mob regrouped it was met with more gunfire.

Much of the city remained under the control of the crowds, and debate raged—in newspapers and among politicians—about how best to handle them: negotiation or force. On the streets, the answer to the question seemed to be pitched battles as crowds ambushed troops and troops fought back. The fighting was particularly intense near Gramercy Park on Thursday night. As troops captured snipers they shot them on the spot. Streets were cleared by canister shot, killing more than a dozen. The violence of the Gramercy skirmish—no doubt aided by sheer exhaustion—had its effect: crowds began to disperse. Taking them on one or two at a time, the Seventh Regiment cleared rioters and snipers from the barricades and took control of a large swath of the East Side, from 14th to 35th Streets. By the early hours of Friday morning the uprising had all but ended.

A Metropolis Reoriented

Some who were there claimed that a thousand people died during the week of rioting. Officials were only ever able to verify 119. The number was surely higher than that.[19] Initial claims of property damage totaled $1.5 million but soon reached $2.5 million (equaling the funds the Common Council had voted to set aside in the middle of the riots to buy New Yorkers out of the draft).* Of that, only $17,000 was claimed by black people, even though, according to the *Christian Reporter*, some three thousand black people were made homeless by the rioting. Other sources put the number of black people living in temporary encampments, police stations, or the barns and cellars of sympathetic farmers in Upstate New York and in Brooklyn and New Jersey at five thousand. More permanently, in the wake of the rioting, black residential patterns shifted significantly. Traditional enclaves like Five Points were all but abandoned, while the black neighborhood at the southeastern edge of Greenwich Village—"Little Africa"—quickly became the largest black enclave in the city. Other black people migrated uptown, abandoning districts where they had long lived. Still more abandoned the city or were pushed out of it as white workers, emboldened by the uprising, blocked their return to the docks and factories. Conductors and passengers on the streetcars refused to let black people on both because of prejudice and because of fear of sparking violence from outraged white mobs.[20] By 1865 the black population in the city had declined by 20 percent compared to 1860.†

Greenwich Village was a Republican bastion, and it was there that the draft was resumed on August 19, this time

---

* The actual cost of the riot—in damaged property alone—was higher than these figures suggest; it may have been between $3 and $5 million, or around $100 million in today's currency.

† At least a small amount of that decline can be accounted for by black volunteers who were recruited into two city Republican-sponsored battalions at the end of 1863. They departed for the war after a march through the city streets and a large rally at Union Square on March 5, 1864. While Republican papers celebrated the march of the black troops through streets on which they had not long ago been hunted down, Democratic and racist papers warned of "miscegenation" and asserted it would not be long before black troops were used to put down white workers. Once at war, African American soldiers suffered lower pay, received less support for their families, served in segregated regiments, rarely were promoted to officer, were mostly assigned menial labor—and still saw 37 percent of their ranks perish.

protected by a force of ten thousand troops, including two artillery battalions brought in from the war front in Virginia. New York looked like a city under siege. Washington Square and Madison Square were turned into encampments, and all through the month troops made a show of marching up and down the streets. At the same time, though, Lincoln refused to declare martial law and instead worked closely with War Democrats and William Tweed to assure order short of that step. Tweed and his machine assured that few rioters would be prosecuted. There were no mass trials. And while Tammany prosecutors indicted numerous individuals (some 450 rioters were arrested, and half of those were charged), most got off in trials held all through August and September. Only sixty-seven were convicted; very few received significant prison sentences. The combination of a strong military presence and a show of indictments by politicians at least partially aligned with the rioting classes seemed to assure that peace would reign—an outcome no doubt assisted by the Common Council's large fund (retained over the veto of Mayor Opdyke and closely overseen by the rising Boss Tweed) to buy out conscriptions. The draft resumed without a hitch, maybe because the stakes were now very low for most white men in New York City.[21]

Republicans, War Democrats, and (now largely discredited) Peace Democrats continued to feud as to who was responsible for the massive unrest—the largest, deadliest, costliest riot in U.S. history (it remains the deadliest).* If at times it seemed in form to echo earlier popular uprisings, it quickly exceeded and transgressed those bounds. Irish workers were nearly uniformly blamed, and they were perhaps the majority of the rioters across the five days of unrest. But there were more than two hundred thousand Irish Americans and Irish immigrants in the city—out of a total population of less than a million—and only a small percentage were out on the streets. Indeed, many Irish residents quickly aligned with the forces of order, and not a few went out of their way to protect African American neighbors. Even Republican, anti-Catholic commentators like *Harper's Weekly* praised the peacefulness of most Irish residents and the courage of Catholic priests who intervened in efforts to quell the rioting. *Harper's* saw the riot as part of a larger working-class uprising but also thought Irish rioters had been whipped into a frenzy by the combination of the decade-long assault on their own status by anti-immigrant Know-Nothing politicians, fearmongering by Peace Democrats, and others who inveighed against what they saw as Republican plans to promote black over white workers. Tammany politicians, seeing an opportunity in the aftermath of the riot, would seek through patronage to channel Irish and other working-class dissent into even greater political power, and they would largely succeed.[22]

In the wake of the riot, a mix of conservative Republicans and War Democrats founded the Citizens' Association, stocked with a broad assortment of industrialists, merchants, and other members of the elite and presided over by Peter Cooper. The association advocated large-scale urban redevelopment in the wake of the riot, noting that the rioting had been most intense in, and the rioters mostly came from, the overcrowded tenement districts. But first they turned their attention back to making money off the war effort. Incredibly violent and clearly expensive in terms of lives lost, bodies injured, and buildings and goods destroyed or looted, the week of rioting was only a small interregnum in New York's wartime boom. As they had before the riot, New York businessmen continued to coordinate (and skim the profits from) the frenzied land speculation that followed the passage of the Homestead Act (1862) and vast land grants to the railroads; stock speculation reached even more dizzying heights; and merchants found new ways to trade with the enemy Confederacy.

But while financiers, merchants, and manufacturers returned to what they did best during the war (making a kill-

---

* Many Republicans remained convinced that the riots had been part of a Confederate plot to foment unrest in key centers in the North, set back only temporarily by the Union's victory at Gettysburg. In fact, while overblown, such theories were not entirely wrong, as Confederate spies and provocateurs were at work throughout the North, and federal agents discovered any number of plots.

ing, in the colloquial sense), killing on the battlefields continued for another year, and the social wounds that gave rise to, were exposed by, or were newly inflicted in the Draft Riots festered, only some of them salved by Tammany patronage or elite calls to remake the working-class districts of the city. Racial segregation increased. The Colored Orphan Asylum, destroyed in the rioting, was forced to move first to 51st Street and then by 1870 to a distant parcel on 143rd Street in what would become the heart of Harlem. "New York rioters," in the assessment of historian Barnet Schecter, "prevailed in their attack on racial equality" in the city (even if the prospect of actual equality was highly inflated by racist whites seeking to stir up white working-class antipathy); "their demand for justice as exploited workers in an urban, industrial environment," he continued, "met with considerably less relief and sympathy from the managerial classes." Inflation continued apace, wages continued to stagnate, and employers remained adept at pitting one working-class faction against another.[23]

◻ ◻ ◻

As the war came to an end, the memory of the riots remained fresh among New Yorkers. Germans and others around Tompkins Square grew increasingly restive in their demands for rent control. Reformers in the city thus turned their attention toward remaking the urban environment. Spurred on by a cholera epidemic that hit the city at the tail end of 1865, elites sought to address threats to both public health and public order.

Many argued that overcrowded and unsanitary conditions in the tenement districts had been a significant factor in the Draft Riots. Reformers felt compelled to respond to this perception, as well as to the demands of demobbed soldiers returning from war. And so in 1867 the state legislature passed the Tenement House Act. The new law mandated fire escapes, windows in every room (a proviso builders met by inserting windows between interior rooms!), and privy stalls (one for every twenty residents). It also encouraged the replacement of wooden structures with brick ones. Fire services were reformed and—for the first time—professionalized. Apparently, the role of the feuding volunteer companies in the riots was not forgotten.

The factional torque that rent New York's motley communities in the Draft Riots configured a new social order that would last a generation. Business and property owners, immigrants, black workers, white nationalist laborers, and antiracist Republicans each pushed, pulled, or were deputized in building institutions, reconfiguring neighborhoods, and stifling or enabling progress. Boosters turned their attention toward completing Central Park and pushing open the Upper West Side for development. Democrats furiously resisted radical Republican efforts to eliminate a $250 property requirement for black male voters, which would have created universal male suffrage. This Republican reform was unsuccessful, and the Democrats' victory united European immigrants with white New Yorkers to cement the power of Tammany Hall in both the state legislature and the city.[24] A tangible legacy of the 1863 Draft Riots was thus not merely the recruitment of white soldiers for the Union army. Rather, the riots proved to be the first step in a large, contentious, putative project: the conscription of New York's ethnic Europeans into an expanded white identity—a project that would consume the city for the next hundred years.

THE ORANGE RIOTS, 1871

Boss Tweed's Tammany Hall dominance of city (and to a lesser extent state) politics lasted until 1871, when it was knocked out by a one-two punch: the Orange Riots of that year and the exposure of Tammany's own manifest fraud, which followed quickly on the riot's heels.

Times were tense. As winter turned to spring, New Yorkers followed the rise and slaughter of the Paris Commune with passionate interest. Marx's *The Civil War in France* was quickly published in the city as radical workers and German socialists rallied in support—and then in memory—of the Communards. Red flags flew high in the working-class and immigrant districts (if not so much of Kleindeutschland, where pro-Bismarck sentiment was strong among the German bourgeoisie). New York elites were worried, egging on from afar the nationalist army of Adolphe Thiers as it attacked the Communards' barricades and launched a vicious bloodletting. The elites were also fearful that a communist uprising could easily be sparked among the workers of New York: the Draft Riots seemed to have been proof of that.[1]

It wasn't long before observers thought they saw an intimation of the Commune made all the more frightening because it was cut through with a violent Catholic radicalism. On July 12, 1871, a small number of Orangemen—Protestant Irish Americans— and some of their family members gathered in a fourth-floor room in Lamartine Hall on Eighth Avenue and 29th Street to prepare for a march in commemoration of William, Prince of Orange's victory over the forces of Catholic King James II in the Battle of the Boyne (1690). Outside, a much larger crowd of Catholic Irishmen and onlookers gathered in the street.

It was not certain the march would take place. The year before the Orange had marched peacefully up Eighth Avenue, nearly reaching their destination—Elm Park at 90th Street—before getting in a brawl with Irish Catholic workers repairing the street and a following crowd of Irish Ribbonmen (an Irish secret society whose members wore green ribbons to differentiate themselves from the orange Protestants). Gunfire was exchanged, and eight people were killed.[2]

Fearing a repeat of the violence, Tammany officials announced on July 10 that the 1871 parade would be banned (the city's Tammany mayor, A. O. Hall, was a flamboyant supporter of the Irish cause, sometimes claiming his initials really stood for Ancient Order of Hibernians). Worried that rising Catholic power was giving succor to left-wing Irish nationalists, Protestants across the city objected, with Wall Street businessmen leading the way. For their part, newspapers like the *Herald* claimed that rising Irish Catholic working-class power—evidenced by its ability to stop the Orangemen's parade—expressed "the same spirit which prompted the Paris Commune." The perceived powers of the Commune and the pope, as well as fears of Irish nationalism, became completely confused, at least in the minds of many editorialists and cartoonists like the famous Thomas Nast. Protestant Orangemen were a bulwark against all three. Enormous pressure was put on city officials to let the march go forward.[3]

And so at 2:00 p.m. it did, but under the protection of five army regiments (five thousand soldiers, led once again by the Seventh Regiment, veteran of so many past uprisings), who marched alongside the Orangemen, and of fifteen hundred police officers, who stood ready. For two days rumors had been circulating that Ribbonmen had stockpiled weapons and were going to attack. Eighth Avenue was packed, and the marchers were roundly jeered. Stones were thrown while a woman pushed

NEW YORK CITY—THE ORANGE RIOT OF JULY 12th—VIEW ON EIGHTH AVENUE LOOKING FROM TWENTY-FIFTH STREET TOWARD THE GRAND OPERA HOUSE—DISPERSAL OF THE MOB BY THE NINTH, EIGHTY-FOURTH AND OTHER REGIMENTS.

her way through the soldiers and stripped an Orangeman of his regalia. Police waded into the crowd with batons raised, smashing heads as they went, seeking to clear a path for the marchers. The mob pushed back. Then, without warning, soldiers opened fire point-blank into the crowd at Eighth Avenue and 24th Street. Sixty people died immediately or later from their wounds. Scores of others were injured. One Orangeman also died. Most of the dead and injured were Irish Catholics, but some were Americans and Germans; three military men were killed, and nearly two dozen were injured (at least some by "friendly fire"); twenty policemen were injured. But now police and military men were determined that the march should go forward,

"New York City—the Orange Riot of July 12th— view on Eighth Avenue looking from Twenty-Fifth Street," *Frank Leslie's Illustrated News Paper*, **July 29, 1871.**
Library of Congress, Prints and Photographs Division, LC-USZ62-120337.

so police charged again and opened a path for the marchers down 23rd Street, where they headed to Fifth Avenue, turned south through more jeering crowds, and made their way to Cooper Union, where they disbanded.[4]

Tweed and his Tammany associates were roundly condemned by leading businessmen and establishment newspapers for their failure to control the Catholic mob—whose actions outdid even "the worst religious outrage of the Commune"— even as the police commissioner, Henry Smith (who was also a banker), lamented that "there were not a larger number killed," since "in any large city such a lesson was needed every few years." Upper-class Protestants vowed to retake control of the city.[5]

The Orange Riots brought to a boil what had been a simmering campaign against Tammany. Before the month was over the *New York Times* had published a series of exposés of Tammany corruption. Documents proving bribery, kickbacks, and padded bills were published in the paper, leading to international concerns over the fiscal stability of the city. When the Berlin stock market stopped trading New York City bonds, bankers in the city were galvanized into action, demanding the municipal government be brought down (the *Nation*'s E. L. Godkin called for Tweed to be lynched). City officials both deep inside and loosely connected to the Tammany machine turned coat and provided further evidence of malfeasance. In November the machine was routed at the ballot box. Feverish worries of the Commune—or of Irish nationalism—subsided, at least for a moment.[6]

CHAPTER 7

"A Riot Is Now in Progress in Tompkins Square Park," 1874

NEIL SMITH

Crisis, Again

After the Draft Riots and after the war New York City was a place of feverish development. The Tenement House Act of 1867, together with pent-up demand from the war, helped unleash a rash of new construction, including in some of the districts hit hardest by the riots, like the Lower East Side. But development came to a sudden halt in September 1873, when New York and the United States plunged into its deepest economic crisis to date. Bankers meeting in the New York offices of Philadelphia-based Jay Cooke and Company refused to provide that firm—heretofore understood to be a paragon of financial rectitude—with an immediate cash infusion to stave off bankruptcy. Cooke and Company was overextended in railway bonds, now coming due. The firm immediately collapsed. When word reached the New York Stock Exchange, traders panicked. With little market regulation and hardly any oversight of banks, the crisis spread rapidly, rocking the entire national banking system and forcing the whole economy into freefall. The New York Stock Exchange closed for ten days, and a quarter of the country's railroads went out of business. Workers were laid off by the thousands, and those who retained their jobs suffered drastically lower pay. In New York City, wages in the building trades fell 20–40 percent; in textiles they fell an estimated 45 percent to as little as ninety-nine cents for a ten-hour day;

for railroad workers the pay cut was 30–40 percent. Ninety thousand homeless people, 40 percent of them women, headed to the police stations for shelter, but most were barred from spending more than one or two nights a month there and consequently became known as "revolvers." Many workers scavenged for food scraps in garbage dumps, earning them the name "dumpies." "Go West" was the heartless, dismissive, and patently unrealistic shrugged response from the city's comfortable classes. (Those who did go west mostly succeeded in setting off the first of what would be a generation of "tramp scares.") The depression lasted until 1878.[1]

As with past economic crises, workers in the major industrial cities loudly demanded public relief. In New York, German workers set up an unemployed council, but their demands fell on deaf ears among the ruling classes and political functionaries. In fact, the city's working classes were already in a weakened state even before the crisis hit. The previous year, after much agitation, including by workers organized through Marx's International Workingmen's Association, laborers around the city threw down their tools in strike action after strike action, creating in effect a near-general strike—a hundred thousand workers left their jobs in May 1872—to demand an eight-hour day. Furniture workers and piano makers were particularly militant. When Steinway and Sons tried in early June to pick off a chunk of the striking labor force with a promise of higher pay if workers kept the ten-hour day, strikers called a mass rally. Steinway got the city administration, eager to flex its probusiness muscles, to send in the cops. Faced with flailing police batons, and no doubt with the memory of the Draft Riots and Orangeman bloodlettings fresh in their minds, the piano workers put up little resistance, and the overall strike seemed on the edge of being broken. But fortunes were reversed—so it seemed—when some fifteen thousand members of the Iron and Metal Workers' League quit work and joined the struggle. Seeing "the specter of Communism" and vowing "to take it by the throat and say it has no business here" (in the words of the owner of a steam pump factory), bosses resolved to break the strike. And they did. As the city deployed battalion after battalion of police officers, now firmly on the side of capital (in the form of the newly organized Employers' Central Executive Committee, with representation from merchants, manufacturers, and industrialists), to bash heads and make way for scabs to be brought into the factories, the strike crumbled, one trade at a time. It was all over by July. The ten-hour day was the rule, even in industries where it had not been before; labor was left to lick its wounds.[2]

Now, as the current crisis deepened, any liberal empathy for the unemployed and their families was drowned out by moralistic rebukes about laziness tinged with an equal foreboding about violence and unrest in the streets. For, despite its losses in 1872, labor remained a potent force. Before 1873 ended, those hit hard by the crisis had created the Committee of Safety, comprising socialists, antimonopoly organizers, unemployed people, white workers from many unions, and sections of the International Workingmen's Association. But the committee's demands on City Hall—for relief and for work—were met by a deafening silence. In response, and following an overflowing mid-December meeting at the Cooper Institute, the committee announced a January gathering "for all those in sympathy . . . with the suffering poor." Demanding the instigation of public works and jobs, food for families, and a cessation of evictions of the unemployed, the Cooper meeting resolved to march from Tompkins Square to City Hall on January 13, 1874, and immediately

set to organizing for the event by distributing handbills in German and English and by calling a series of preparatory meetings and demonstrations.[3]

In the first days of January, these events, including a small demonstration in Tompkins Square, were met by widespread incendiary hostility in the press, which, still nervous about the Commune (after all, the Committee of Safety had taken its name from the Commune's own provisional government) and the Orange Riots, inveighed against "enemies of society" and "European socialists" and those who would abuse the "liberty of speech." The city government promised to arrest any workers using "inflammatory language." Amid rising tension, Police Board commissioner Oliver Gardner, who doubled as chair of the Central Committee of the Republican Party, barred the march on City Hall (and a parade that was to follow), instead opting to have the police stockpile weapons and ammunition in a nearby armory. With the police commissioner set on frustrating the Tompkins Square meeting, the Committee of Safety appealed to the governor to permit a march, but the appeal was refused. The police upped the ante, demanding the city's Parks Department also deny a permit to meet at all in Tompkins Square. A young carpenter, socialist, and Committee of Safety leader named Peter McGuire demanded to know from the Police Board: "Is the Square private, police, or public property? Has martial law been proclaimed?" "Never mind the law," replied the police commissioner. But with the organizers promising to present their "demands for work" and then "quietly disperse," the Department of Parks issued the permit for the Tompkins Square meeting.[4]

Constructed in 1834 following the drainage of swampland donated to the city by fur trader and capitalist John Jacob Astor, Tompkins Square was one of several parks intended for "military and civic parades, and for parties, and what is perhaps of more importance, to serve as ventilators to a densely populated city"—a safety valve, as urban planners of the time liked to say. Covering ten acres, it was an obvious location for the march of the unemployed. Not only did it sit amid the working-class immigrant neighborhood of the city's "East Side," as the area was then known, but it had been the site of prior union organizing and militant protests during earlier economic crises. During the 1857 Panic, mass rallies in Tompkins Square had been critical in encouraging the Common Council to create public works programs to provide jobs for the unemployed. During the Civil War, the square, like others in the city, was given over to the Union army as a parade ground. After the war, it was a favorite locale for International Workingmen's Association street agitation. It was the militant heart of Little Germany.[5]

The Police Riot

Wednesday, January 13, was freezing cold. Still, by 11:00 a.m., seven thousand men, women, and children (many, if not most, foreign-born) had converged on Tompkins Square, even though the night before the Police Board—composed of city elites—had forced the Department of Parks to withdraw its permit. More were streaming in from the other working-class districts of the city. The crowd swelled into perhaps the largest labor demonstration the city had ever seen. The gathering crowd was expecting to present their demands and to hear Mayor William Havemeyer address the city's workers, as he had agreed to do, presumably offering something of a program of relief (though Havemeyer, the son of a wealthy sugar merchant, was no fan of public relief, thinking workers should instead become better savers). Instead, Police Commissioner Gardner, at the head of the massed forces of the city police—almost two-thirds of the total police force had been called in for riot duty—waded into the large milling crowd and announced: "Now, you all go home, right away!" With that, what (according to the *New York Herald*) had "hitherto [been a] peaceful and monotonous" demonstration "suddenly changed." Without waiting for a response by the crowd, the police, "on horseback and on foot, immediately launched into the crowd and began a terrifying assault, blocking the square's exits."

Perhaps this was a riot preordained, given New York's

"The red flag in New York—riotous Communist working men driven from Tompkins Square by the mounted police, Tuesday, January 13," *Frank Leslie's Illustrated News Paper*, January 31, 1874. Library of Congress, Prints and Photographs Division, LC-USZ62-111180.

nineteenth-century history of rebellion and class violence, given the free use police had put to batons and rifles after the Civil War, and given the incendiary headlines in the establishment newspapers for the preceding month. It was certainly a riot predicted: even as the very first billy clubs were finding their targets, the entrepreneurial *New York Graphic*, a recently established tabloid rag, rushed onto the streets a special edition announcing "A RIOT IS NOW IN PROGRESS IN TOMPKINS SQUARE." Later papers provided the descriptions: "Police clubs rose and fell"; "Women and children ran screaming in all directions. Many of them were trampled underfoot in the stampede for the gates. In the streets bystanders were ridden down and mercilessly clubbed by mounted officers"; "The horsemen beat the air with their batons and many persons were laid low"; "One policeman actually rode into a grocery store and scattered the terrified inmates." Quickly petitioned to bring the police force to heel, the mayor refused to meet with a "body of crazy men" and callously referred workers seeking protection from police violence back to the police themselves. The protracted onslaught lasted several hours, and it fanned outward from the park as escaping workers fled the swinging truncheons.* When angry crowds gathered on Fifth Avenue outside a police station to demand the release of arrested workers, they were attacked again. It was as if the police were "seized with a fit of St. Vitus' dance," reported one journalist.† "It was only a question of luck who was clubbed and who was not."[6]

Among those scrambling for cover in and around the square was a young worker in the cigarmakers' union, Samuel Gompers, who in the 1880s would become a founding member and longtime president of the American Federation of Labor. Gompers later recounted that he survived the police riot only by jumping into a cellarway, where he cowered as policemen rampaged by, batons swinging. For Gompers, what the police unleashed in and around Tompkins Square that day was nothing less than "an orgy of brutality."

Results and Prospects

Compared to the other riots of recent decades—Astor Place, the Dead Rabbits, the Draft Riots, the Orange Riots—the orgy of brutality was, in fact, comparatively mild. No one died. Several scores were injured, and forty-six workers were arrested.‡ But the effects were lasting. Class divides were deepened, and there was no longer any doubt about whose side the police were on (if there had been after the police's role in breaking the eight-hour movement). And the riot would prove to have lasting effects on the city's social geography and built landscape.[7]

Those arrested were slapped with an unaffordable and punitive $1,000 bail, most charged merely with disorderly conduct. Their defense—that they were entitled to defend themselves against illegal and unnecessary police force—

---

* One fairly large contingent of German workers held fast and fought back in the northeast corner of the square under the banner of the Tenth Ward Workingman's Association, but they too were soon routed.

† Saint Vitus' dance was a term applied to a range of ailments with epilepsy-like symptoms.

‡ Twenty-four of the arrested were German-born, ten were native-born, and the rest were a hodgepodge of immigrants from France, Poland, Ireland, Italy, Sweden, and more.

---

proved unsuccessful in court. One worker, Justus Schwab, a socialist and anarchist, was indicted for inciting a riot. His offense: waving a red flag. Christian Meyer was charged with assault and battery on a police officer after coming to the aid of another worker, who was also jailed for assault. Meyer's defense charged the police with brutal assault "without the authority of law," but the judge was unsympathetic, sentenced Meyer to six months, and took the opportunity to warn "members of his class that there are certain laws in this country which they must respect."[8]

If the orgy of brutality was mild by contemporary standards, the orgy of triumphant glee among the politicians and press that followed the police riot was not. For one member of the Police Board, "the way the police broke and drove the crowd" was a "glorious sight." For others, in obvious reference to Paris, the "American Commune" was tamed in Tompkins Square, and the threat was gloatingly reiterated, by a clergyman no less, that whosoever stood "against law, order, and good government" would be "mowed down like grass before a scythe." The legitimacy of organized violence in defense of private property was a central theme: only "force," wrote the *Herald* in the days that followed, would teach workers to "respect the rights of those who have plenty when [they] have nothing." Some muted voices in the establishment press did condemn the clubbing of peaceful demonstrators and even supported their right to free speech and the right of assembly, most notably the *New York Sun* and the *New York Graphic* (possibly somewhat embarrassed by its role in the riot's early moments). Perhaps the most notable journalistic voice in support of the workers was the Scottish American abolitionist John Swinton, then writing for the *New York Sun*, later an American interlocutor of Karl Marx and founder of his own muckraking broadsheet, *John Swinton's Paper*. Swinton had been invited to speak at the Tompkins Square protest and barely escaped getting caught up in the melee.[9]

But it was left to the city's labor papers to condemn what the *New York Irish World* aptly called a "brutal contempt for the law" by the police. In the weeks that followed, the *Irish*

World's sentiment was echoed by union leaders in New York and around the country who joined the Committee of Safety in assailing the brutal behavior of the police and the paucity of public works and relief for workers. At the end of January a large meeting at the Cooper Union—infiltrated and shadowed by a deputation of New York's finest—called for relief. But the city government was obdurate. In March, Swinton and two German workers petitioned the assembly in Albany, providing an affidavit of police brutality. Swinton insisted that the police had been wrongly used: "*Riot*," Swinton declared, "should consist only in *rioting*—in actual resistance to authority. It should not be considered riot when some man of a multitude threatens to become *riotous*. . . . If we so consider it, we thereby give a power to our rulers dangerous to public liberties which may be wantonly used to surpass the popular right of meeting or of speech." Swinton and his colleagues insisted that the Police Board be disbanded.[10]

If this rearguard action did not succeed in ousting the corrupt Police Board, it did have a salutary effect, as even some of the more conservative press exposed the trumped-up threats of dangerous and secret conspiracy conjured up by police and retroactively began to entertain the possibility that this indeed had been a police riot. Former mayor Fernando Wood even joined the indictment, arguing that the "police authorities have no right to break up a meeting called for any purpose by the people," echoing an earlier iron molders' union complaint that "every protest, petition, or demand of labor is met with the cry of 'Commune'" and the threat of violence. The complaints had some effect. Early in the summer a concerted campaign by working men and women had secured Christian Meyer's release from prison, and at the end of the summer, on August 31, the city's first political demonstration since the January police riot was held in Tompkins Square to noisily celebrate his release. The mood was quite different from the one at the beginning of the year. This time both the Police Board and the Department of Parks authorized a permit, with the latter declaring: "The people have a right to gather at any park set aside for meetings and to pass resolutions and make speeches to their

heart's content." The Committee of Safety established a two-hundred-strong Police Committee to maintain order during the demonstration, and the Metropolitan police kept their distance, admonished by city papers to not replicate their "clumsy knavery and trickery" of January, in the words of the *New York Evening Tribune*. Meyer was also quietly pardoned by New York governor John Adams Dix, who in doing so implicitly conceded the popular injustice of the police riot.[11]

But the quiet admission of police culpability for the riot did not translate into a major victory for workers. Despite several large demonstrations against police brutality, and even as unemployment worsened and the depression deepened, the movement found it increasingly difficult to expand, and it never fully regained the momentum it had started to build in the months before Tompkins Square. A revived Tammany Hall found ways to co-opt the movement leadership in some city wards, sacrificing mass action for machine building. When a new Tammany city administration took office in January 1875, it tried to jumpstart a program of public works, but landowning, insurance, and banking interests—working through non-Tammany allies who controlled the Comptroller's Office—managed to block these efforts. Simultaneously, employers took advantage of reactionary anti-immigrant sentiment (the *Times* inaccurately reported that all those arrested in the riot were foreign-born) to tighten the noose on union demands and by breaking a five-week stevedore strike in October 1874 not only reduced wages to twenty-five cents an hour but also shattered the union's power on the docks (wages would not recover until the eve of World War I).[12]

Disputes among different factions of the workers also frustrated the prospects of any unified working-class response to the riot and the depression more generally. Even prior to the demonstration, and much to the delight of the city's newspaper owners, the bricklayers' union leader, Patrick Dunn, berated the Committee of Safety, denounced its leaders as communists, and collaborated instead with the police. Both before and after the police riot, emerging differences between Marxist and Lassallian socialists added to the difficulties.* In a difference that was more than tactical, Lassallians argued for the establishment of a U.S. labor party as an electoral alternative, while Marxists leaned more toward building the labor unions as a sine qua non of sustainable political power.† The Lassallian-Marxist divide was intensified by German immigrants seeking refuge from the Franco-Prussian War and Parisian workers escaping the wrath of the French state, only to meet up on the streets of New York. Meanwhile, in the Lower East Side, the police sent spies, including a number of women, to infiltrate workers' and socialist meetings as part of a wider clampdown. Rumors of imminent sedition and anarchy quickly followed and were widely broadcast. Soon the police were putting pressure on neighborhood landlords to evict suspect organizations, like the French immigrant group the Société de la Commune.

Indeed, the protests that engulfed the working-class and immigrant districts of the city—leading up to and after the Tompkins Square police riot—produced what might be considered the first American "Red Scare," even though that descriptor did not become current until after World War I. A feverish antisocialist hysteria gripped the ruling classes. Already in the days leading up to the riot, the *New York Times* denounced a meeting as "decidedly communistic," and a similarly dismissive verbiage took hold over the rest of the decade. More broadly, militant workers and unionists were subject to blanket vilification as foreign in the extreme—

communists and revolutionists, socialists and anarchists, labels that many wore proudly.[13]

Whatever the warnings of New York and national elites, such radical workers moved to the front of the labor movement—or at least a part of it—and through a series of strikes around the country (resulting more often in defeat than victory), U.S. labor lurched toward an erratic and often defensive unity, embodied in the fledgling Workingmen's Party, founded in 1876. The growing class struggle came to a head in 1877 with the momentous railroad strike, when the railroad companies, seen as a cause of the depression (alongside the banks) and hated by small business owners, farmers, and even larger capitalists for their extortionate rates and regional monopolies, moved against workers, firing many while cutting wages and increasing work demands on those they retained. The strike began in mid-July among firemen and brakemen in Martinsburg, West Virginia; moved quickly to the Baltimore and Ohio railyards in Baltimore and Camden; and then spread furiously along the tracks, jumping from railroad to railroad and state to state. Within just a few days it was essentially nationwide. Trackmen, switchmen, blacksmiths, sectionmen, black and white, all joined the strike. The workers claimed broad sympathy. Militias fraternized with the strikers, and in an unprecedented move, except during wartime, federal troops were mobilized against the strikers. The conflict abruptly escalated in Pittsburgh after imported Philadelphia troops shot twenty workers, only to be besieged and beaten out of town. Troops later cut down twelve workers in Chicago. In several cities, the strike spilled into other sectors, briefly threatening a general strike, leading an alarmed St. Louis newspaper to call it not a strike but a "labor revolution."[14]

Even before the strike reached the Empire State, it was clear that the militia here would also refuse any orders against the strikers, and William Vanderbilt, president of the New York Central Railroad, was forced to rescind wage cuts and even promise wage increases in Buffalo and other upstate cities, while the governor declared martial law, ringing Albany with troops. But little of this applied to New

---

* Lassalian socialists followed the ideas of Ferdinand Lassalle, one of the founders of the Allgemeiner Deutscher Arbeiterverein, (General German Workers' Association, the first German socialist party), who advocated a form of "state socialism" wherein the state granted, or perhaps was forced to grant, various programs and concessions to organized labor, cooperatives, and so forth. This "socialism from above" was quite at odds with the Marxian conception of *independent* cooperatives and producers leading a transformation of society from below.

† This difference in where to invest political energies—on where the real sources of power lay within capitalist democracies—would bedevil the socialist and labor movement well into the twentieth century, and not just in New York. For example, it led to early splits in the Industrial Workers of the World, founded in Chicago in 1905 but powerful in its early years in the eastern mills, including in New York.

"New York City—the Railroad Strike Excitement—Workingmen's Mass Meeting in Tompkins Square, Wednesday Evening, July 25th," *Frank Leslie's Illustrated Newspaper.*

York City. While a union town, it was not especially a railroad town as some secondary regional centers were, and in the sharply divided city, its middle class bucked the national trend of sympathy with the railroad strikers. Still, the howl against communism, anarchism, and the specter of an American Commune was again raised in New York as the *Times* proclaimed, "The City in Possession of Communists." Other newspapers, smug rather than alarmed, were less restrained. The *Tribune* unceremoniously recommended shooting any striking New Yorkers, while the Congregationalist *Independent* asserted that Napoleon was right when he said the one way to deal with a mob was to exterminate it.[15]

Tompkins Square did not miss out on the 1877 action. The newly formed national Workingmen's Party, of which Peter McGuire was now a leader, organized a strike support meeting for the square on July 25. New York Central president Vanderbilt failed to get the mayor to ban the meeting, but against the supposed threat of open revolt, a

"phenomenal mobilization of military might" was effected, including the vaunted Seventh Regiment (called back from vacation), the First and Second Divisions of the New York National Guard, a thousand specially requisitioned sailors and marines, and the whole police force (all leaves were canceled). Gatling guns guarded Wall Street, Frederick Law Olmsted secured Central Park headquarters with howitzers, and the U.S. Navy and the Treasury Department sent troops and a warship to protect the gold bullion stored in the U.S. Custom House at the tip of Manhattan. Back uptown on a speakers' platform waved over by an American flag in a well-lit Tompkins Square, labor leaders and others, including John Swinton, addressed a crowd of twenty thousand—their speeches repeated in German, French, and other languages from another platform—offering support to the railroad workers and demanding assistance for workers forced into abject poverty by the depression. Entirely calm and orderly, and reaching a high point of sedition with a call for "political revolution through the ballot box," the meeting closed after two hours, whereupon the police immediately charged and clubbed the crowd, which had offered no provocation. Heartily approving of these actions, a Seventh Regiment officer observed that the "large and dangerous assemblage in Tompkins Square was inspired with a wholesome terror." Fearing that such a large and quickly assembled show of official force would not always be possible under current conditions, the War Department followed New York's lead and began establishing permanent armories in all major cities.* Not all approved. Labor papers inveighed against the establishment of permanent armies in the cities, and the *New York Sun* complained that doing so would lead to "a radical revolution in our whole republican system of government."[16]

Other responses to the deep depression of the 1870s were less spectacular but perhaps more consequential for the city's landscape. At the start of the depression, nearly 65 percent of Manhattan's residents lived in tenements (a remarkable figure, given that the percentage was not far from zero as recently as 1850).† Already by 1873, the 1867 Tenement House Act had been deemed a failure. So in 1879, just as post-depression urban development was recommencing, New York State significantly revised its tenement law. Where before the law had only required windows in each room, now it required actual ventilation: all rooms had to open to the street, to a backyard, or onto an airshaft, resulting in the so-called dumbbell tenements that still mark much of the city—though not as much the Lower East Side, since so many tenement houses had already been built under the earlier law

or before. Dumbbell tenements—wide front and back and narrow in the middle to accommodate the airshaft—would define the city until 1901, when the law was overhauled once again.

Tompkins Square Park

Tompkins Square in 1874 taught the city's workers what many already knew, namely, that the police represented not so much a neutral body devoted to keeping the peace as an armed arm of the state devoted to protecting class interests already written into law. Where the law contravened these interests, the law was more likely to be jettisoned than the class interests. The police were the means but not the cause of repression. The 1874 event was also formative for Samuel Gompers, teaching him a different lesson. By his own admission, his future inspiration for the American Federation of Labor was learned while cowering in the sunken cellarway, escaping the police truncheons above. The lesson he

Popular concert in Tompkins Square, 1891.
Art and Picture Collection, New York Public Library.

---

* In New York, the Seventh Regiment had been agitating for a new and permanent base since 1873; by 1874 a plot of land between Park and Lexington and 66th and 67th Streets had been identified. When the city comptroller vetoed city expenditures on the armory, the Seventh undertook a fund-raising campaign, raising more than half a million dollars. The new, lavish, highly defendable armory opened in 1879. It was not until after the 1877 strike that the War Department sought to generalize the armory movement.
† Depending on the definition of the word "tenement," the first tenement was built in the city in either the late 1820s or 1838. Numbers grew in the 1840s and exploded after 1850.

learned was that revolutionary organization was dangerous and futile and that militancy had to lead nowhere else than to the ballot box.[17]

As for Tompkins Square, 1874—and 1877—cemented its deep symbolic resonance as a space of class struggle. For authorities, this, plus the square's physical openness, which allowed for assemblies of tens of thousands, had to be addressed. In a case of classic design flattery-cum-optimism, whereby the reorganization of physical space is attempted in order to change its social and political resonance, Tompkins Square was reconfigured after 1878 with the explicit purpose of creating a more easily controlled space. The city planted 450 elm trees as the square was turned into a park. At its center a temperance fountain was erected. Nearby a children's playground was built. Tompkins Square Park was to become a place of leisure and recreation, no longer a space for dissent.[18]

Be that as it may, 1874 was not the first police riot in the area, nor would it be the last. More than a century later, following another such riot in the park that followed a strangely parallel script (chapter 16), a graffiti artist tagged the sidewalks all around the park with a reminder of the histories congealed therein: POLICE RIOTS HAPPEN HERE.

CHAPTER 8

A New Urban Order

Transit Strikes, 1886–1895

DON MITCHELL

Working-Class New York—and Brooklyn

On March 20, 1883, the year-old Central Labor Union (CLU) of New York, Brooklyn, and Jersey City sponsored a mass meeting at Cooper Union to memorialize the recently deceased Karl Marx and to honor the still very much alive Henry George, the famous American radical and advocate of a "single tax" on land that would radically leaven inequalities of wealth. The polyglot thousands who attended represented dozens of nationalities and even more trades. Socialists, anarchists, Lassallians, Marxists, old Communards, men, women, young girls working in the sweatshops, and old grandees of labor were all there. New York was an industrial powerhouse—the largest industrial agglomeration in the world—and a diverse one in terms of both things made and trades pursued and in the composition of its working class. That class was now huge. Manhattan's population grew by 77 percent between 1860 and 1890; by 1900 it had grown by 127 percent (to 1,850,000). Across the river, Brooklyn's growth had been even more spectacular. Between 1860 and 1890 the population grew by 196 percent; by 1900 its 1,167,000 residents represented a 318 percent increase over 1860. In 1900 nearly 43 percent of Manhattan's population was foreign-born. In Brooklyn the figure was 30.5 percent.

The thousands meeting at Cooper Union may not have been a representative cross section of the population, but they were certainly indicative of its extensive, ethnically complex, still-militant, industrial working class. The CLU had already shown its skills in organizing and to a good degree in unifying large sections of the working class—for example, organizing the first Labor Day demonstration and parade on September 5, 1882, in Union Square—in defiance of both the bosses and Samuel Gompers's growing federation of "business" unions, which admitted workers in skilled crafts only. The Marx-George mass meeting made the bosses, the craft unions, and the newspapers nervous: the memories of 1874 and 1877 had hardly faded. And the growing working class seemed restive.

Street Car Struggles

Organizing extended into the ethnic, working-class neighborhoods—the districts of old tenements and the new ones thrown up to house the rapidly growing population on both sides of the river. There was a general understanding that successful organizing in the workplace required concomitant organizing on the streets and in the tenements. Home and work, neighborhoods and downtown were all linked by an expanding horsecar, streetcar, and elevated rail network. Mobility at an urban scale was a reality—and a necessity—for people of all classes. To meet this need, horsecars had been operating since 1832 and would remain on some

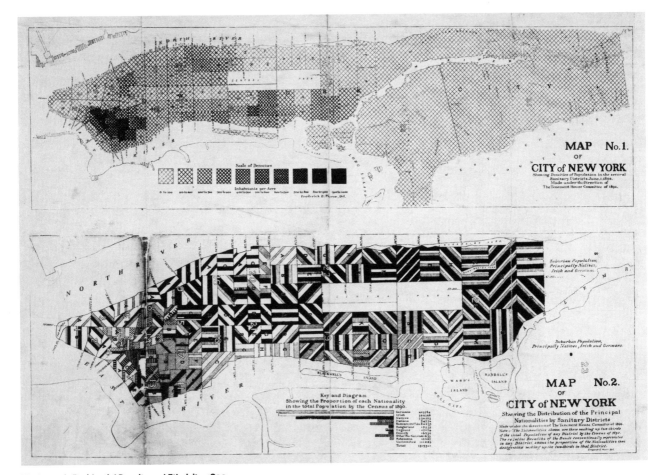

Manhattan's Residential Density and Ethnicity, 1890.

The top map shows residential density in 1890, with denser hatching representing denser populations. The lightest hatching (appearing in the Upper West Side, Harlem, and all of the Bronx) indicates densities of 0–100 inhabitants per acre. The darkest hatching (on the Lower East Side) respresents densities of 800–900 people per acre, while the one solid box (around Tompkins Square) indicates a density of 900–1,000 residents per acre.

The lower map shows ethnic concentrations in 1890. The light hatching represents Germans (27 percent of the total population), solid white represents Irish (26 percent), and solid black represents native-born whites (22 percent); various other symbols represent other ethnic groups (7 percent of the population is unclassified and thus not mapped). African Americans comprised less than 2 percent of Manhattan's population at the time and are shown only near Greenwich Village and in a small part of the Tenderloin.

Drawn by F. E. Pierce for the Tenement House Committee, 1894.

Courtesy the Lionel Picus and Princess Firyal Map Division, New York Public Library.

***Brooklyn's Transportation
Problem Solved.***

Following the 1894 Trolley Strike,
transit companies embarked on an
ambitious expansion of elevated
railroads and underground
subways, as well as continuing
to electrify street car lines.

Courtesy the Lionel Picus and Princess
Firyal Map Division, New York Public
Library.

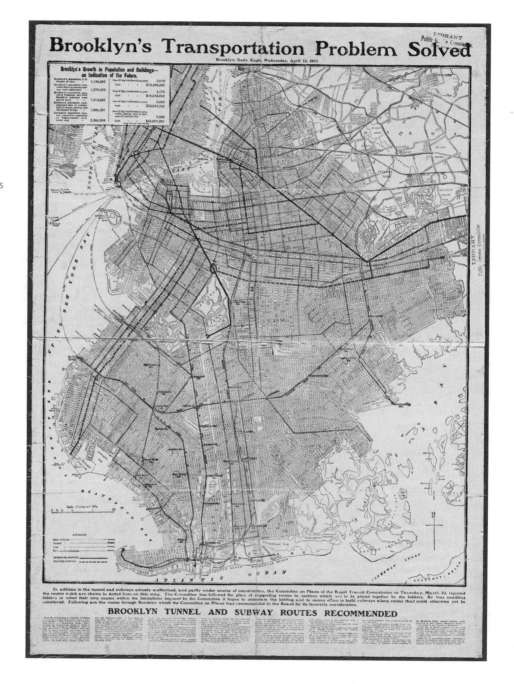

Blockading the trolley lines was a common occurrence in transit disputes. This instance is from 1871, *Car Blockade in the Bowery, from a Sketch by Stanley Fox.* Art and Picture Collection, New York Public Library.

city streets until World War I. By 1880 elevated trains were operating on Third and Ninth Avenues, and a line was under construction above Second Avenue. In late May 1883, two months after the Marx memorial at Cooper Union, the city's first cable car opened, linking Manhattan with Brooklyn across the just-completed Brooklyn Bridge. And by 1887 streetcars, powered by overhead cables, began to replace the horsecars on the surface rails.[1]

The struggle for the eight-hour day had not faded—it was a central plank of the CLU's platform—but on the horsecar lines, workdays typically stretched to sixteen or seventeen hours, with no time off for meals. Following a month of minor strikes on various city horsecar lines, workers on the Dry Dock line (Grand Street) had enough and struck on March 2, 1886. The company quickly hired scabs, and on March 3 and 4 the city deployed police to escort them to work and the horsecars along the tracks. But residents in the neighborhoods along the line threw up barricades to halt the cars. The superintendent of police responded on the 4th by deploying 750 policemen, a quarter of the total force: 500 along Grand Street and 250 to escort a car out of the stables. A growing crowd of thousands pelted the police with rocks, eggs, and rotting vegetables and smothered the tracks at intervals with piles of cobblestones and coal. Police responded with truncheons, beating back the mob and eventually escorting a lonely horsecar down the length of the line. That night the CLU voted to call a citywide horsecar strike. Sixteen thousand workers stayed off the job the next day. The city ground to a halt: the streets were at a standstill, and the overhead rail lines were quickly overburdened. By the end of the day, the Dry Dock Company capitulated, sparking jubilant parades and celebrations. The celebrations did not last.

A week later, workers on the 34th, 23rd, and Bleeker Street lines struck. They were out for a week, but the strike ended inconclusively. A month after that, drivers and conductors on the Third Avenue line struck to protest the hiring of non-union workers. By now, though, the employers were organized. Despite revelations of corruption among the bosses of the Third Avenue line (they had bribed their way to the concession and had been getting away without paying taxes), and despite a series of citywide transit strikes in support of the Third Avenue workers, they were defeated in June by the combined forces of the police and company goons, but not before horsecar workers in Brooklyn managed to unionize under the auspices of the Knights of Labor and win a contract with one of the companies that reduced the working day to twelve hours while nearly doubling wages.[2]

The Panic of 1893 and the Great Brooklyn Trolley Strike

Even as strikes continued to roil the city for the remainder of the decade, the city—like the country as a whole—boomed. Immigrants continued to pour in. New industries opened up. Horsecar lines across the city and in Brooklyn were electrified. More elevated trains were completed. Capitalists made fortunes from production and speculation alike.

Until they didn't. The global economic crisis of 1893 had been building for some time before it finally broke on American shores. But when it did, it was deep and especially damaging to workers and the poor. It would last for five years. Like every time before, the homeless population surged. Breadlines quickly formed. This time, though, labor was militant. Anarchists had long been at work in the city. Emma Goldman was something of a celebrity (and was quickly targeted by New York's elite and jailed for inciting a riot after telling the hungry that they ought to just "go get" the bread they needed). Distress was deep. Socialists and communists set to work organizing the unemployed, even as city elites debated just how much charity was too much. The Knights of Labor, the heart of the CLU, continued organizing, with considerable success.

On the streetcar lines, electrification meant changed work patterns, more difficult labor, and for the companies—squeezed by the depression—what they saw as an opportunity to increase flexibility in scheduling, decrease their wage bill, and recoup investments and prosper despite straitened economic times.[3] When the Brooklyn streetcar contracts came up for renewal at the end of 1894, the companies saw their chance. The Knights of Labor represented workers on all of Brooklyn's lines and figured they could win a twenty-five-cent-a-day raise. Workers also wanted to have to run fewer trips each day so their schedules would accord with a new state law limiting streetcar work to ten hours. They also wanted more all-day routes and thus fewer rush-hour-only runs (whose operators endured a split workday). In negotiations, the Knights expected they would have to yield on one or two of their demands. But the companies stonewalled on all of them, refused arbitration, and forced a strike. Workers took up the challenge gladly: on January 11, 1895, they voted 97 percent in favor of striking. On January 14 the streetcars of Brooklyn stopped.

The companies were prepared. They had already begun recruiting scabs from across the region and around the country. Men suffering the effects of the depression and desperate for work flooded the trolley offices. (Theodore Dreiser's George Hurstwood in *Sister Carrie* was one.) Within four days, eight lines were running (of the forty-eight in Brooklyn), though even these were plagued with stoppages and missed runs, sometimes the result of the overhead wires being sabotaged (there were sixteen thousand miles of electric trolley lines in Brooklyn). Hundreds of thousands of workers had to find other means of transport—bicycles, feet, the more expensive and now very crowded elevated trains—or not show up. Business fell off; theaters stayed empty. But mostly, among the working classes at least, sympathy lay with the strikers, and as the companies tried to get the lines going with scabs, large crowds turned out to stop them. Within a week, crowds began to reach five or six thousand strong. Standoffs were tense. Violence flared. Arrests were made. In the first week or so, though, things were fairly calm, especially by New York mob standards. Members of the Knights moved through the crowds militating against violence, engaging instead in what they referred to as "missionary work"—teams of two deployed all along the lines to cajole scabs to leave their jobs and join the union and strike.

Despite the threat the strike posed to their bottom lines, many Brooklyn businesses, antagonistic to the trolley companies, supported the strike. Restaurants and grocery stores refused to serve police imported to escort the streetcars or break up the crowds. Others sued the streetcar companies for loss of business. Political clubs in Brooklyn and beyond called for their charters to be revoked. Benefit shows and rallies were held around the city. Yet the strikers, sympathetic businesses, political clubs, and crowds were up against the considerable police—and military—power of the elite political machines. At the behest of the trolley companies, the mayor vetoed any attempts to revoke charters, ordered police to escort every car, and, as it became clear that many policemen sympathized with the strikers, called out the militia. On Saturday, January 19, despite the so far peaceful nature of the strike, the Second Brigade of the New York State National Guard—Brooklyn's militia—was activated in its entirety: the first total call-out in the city's history and the first time the National Guard had been used for strike duty in Brooklyn.

This show of force on behalf of the trolley company bosses incensed the working people of Brooklyn. The trolleys, like the railroads more broadly, were generally hated, their owners seen as being connivers always willing to use monopoly to their advantage, cook the books, and screw over small merchants and workers alike. Work and trip schedules required trolleymen to consistently break the ten-mile-per-hour speed limit (by two or three times) if they were to make their runs on time. Pedestrian collisions and deaths were not uncommon, even as "trolley dodging" quickly became a sport among the youth of Brooklyn. It's no surprise, then, that a militia perceived to be protecting the companies was met with crowds hurling abuse. The first evening the militia was out, a large crowd formed near an

"Scenes in Brooklyn during the Trolley Strike, January, 1895," *Frank Leslie's Weekly.*
Art and Picture Collection, New York Public Library, Astor, Lenox and Tilden Foundations.

East New York trolley barn and taunted the soldiers guarding it. The soldiers charged, bayonets first, wounding dozens and further inflaming strikers and sympathizers. Panicking, the mayor requested the activation of the First Brigade from Manhattan, which arrived on Brooklyn's streets two days

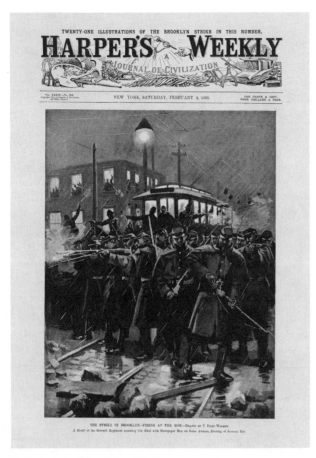

The Strike in Brooklyn—Firing at the Mob, *Harper's Weekly*, February 2, 1895.
Used by permission.

later, swelling the number of military men to 7,500 (there were 1,700 police officers on strike duty). Innumerable skirmishes followed. In one, a man heading toward a streetcar refused to stop when ordered to by soldiers and was shot dead. In another, guardsmen peppered the upper windows of a tenement to encourage hecklers to stop; a man repairing the roof was killed by a stray bullet. Brooklynites complained of the city being turned into an armed encampment (even as militiamen complained of rotten conditions, as they were provided poor or no housing, and merchants refused to serve them).

Nonetheless, the mobilization of military might worked. With the guns on their side and with scab recruits willing to brave the crowds for a paycheck, the trolley bosses were able to wait the strikers out. Striking workers, suffering the loss of pay, began to drift back to work (when the companies would have them), and the strike fizzled. Eleven days after first being activated, militia companies began to stand down. The Knights called an end to the strike on February 16, just over a month after it started, winning none of their demands. Sheer force and raw power had won the day. Flush with victory, the trolley companies refused to hire back most of the striking workers, until a streetcar boycott forced them to in August. The Knights of Labor—the driving force of the American labor movement since the 1870s—was all but destroyed. Samuel Gompers saw further proof that his elite, craft-based, business unionism was the only way to go.

The Triumph of Order?

Historian Lisa Keller argues that the defeat of the Brooklyn Trolley Strike was a key moment in "the triumph of order" in New York City. The deployment of the military against the Brooklyn strikers (and their sympathizers) was certainly an act of raw class power to assure the trolley bosses would prevail, but it was presented as an exercise merely in maintaining order. The effect, Keller suggests, was to redefine what behaviors were and were not acceptable in public space, as well as to cement into place the idea that "order" was a good in and of itself in the modern city.[4] The last vestiges of premodern patterns and practices of popular revolt that had so defined the city into the early nineteenth century were driven back, as it were, at the point of the militia's bayonets.

Such an argument is surely right, as New York's and Brooklyn's upper and middle classes—the reformers and the rising class of "progressives"—worked to shape and reshape the city in their image, a task to which they not infrequently brought the virtues of militarism. Elites of a number of stripes had been organizing for some years to clear out resurgent Tammany, with its roots in the working-class neighborhoods.* Republicans surged to victory both in the cities and in the state in November 1894, with the Republican New York mayor, millionaire William L. Strong, taking office on January 1, 1895, just as Brooklyn's streetcar workers were preparing to strike. Strong promised "efficiency and economy" and a cleaner, more orderly city. He would start by cleaning the streets.

Strong hired Civil War veteran Col. George Waring Jr. for the task. Colonel Waring took the Department of Street Cleaning—heretofore a nest of patronage and inefficiency—and whipped it into military shape. Department workers were required to purchase sharp white uniforms out of their wages—wages that Waring immediately cut from $700 to $600 a year (he got away with this by threatening to fire the lot and replace them with $350-a-year Italians). He banned strikes (but implemented a management-labor arbitration board). And he set crews to work mucking out the 2.5 million pounds of manure deposited each day on New York streets, the heaps of garbage, and the snow when it fell. He had unharnessed vehicles cleared away and ticketed and towed the carts of the city's truckers if they left them too long. He created a recycling system and taught—through the deployment of uniformed police—residents to sort their trash.[5]

If the streets were going to be cleaned, then the police had to be cleaned up too. Mayor Strong appointed Theodore Roosevelt to the task. First, though, after heartily and publicly approving the violent "clubbing right and left" by the police during the transit strike, Roosevelt set about clearing the homeless out of their lodgings in the police stations, sending thousands of unemployed men, women, and children into the cold in the midst of a depression.† The newly

established Municipal Lodging House only sopped up a small percentage. The rest were chased from corner to alley to riverbank by newly created "tramp and beggar squads." With the stations thus cleansed he began work on the police themselves. As the chair of the four-person Police Commission (composed of two Democrats and two Republicans), Roosevelt's powers were limited, but he managed to wield them effectively—clearing out scandal-tainted superintendents and inspectors, creating a merit-based appointment and promotion system, hiring a whole raft of new officers (some two thousand, and many of them not from the old Irish police strongholds), sacking cops for drinking on the job, and developing bicycle squads for rapid deployment—before botching an attempt to ban Sunday drinking and leaving for a position as assistant secretary of the navy in 1897 just before he could be booted from the Police Commission.[6]

As Roosevelt departed, first for Washington, then for San Juan Hill, city officials were engineering the great merger of New York, Brooklyn, the Bronx, Queens, and Staten Island—the creation of a whole new urban order. The Brooklyn Bridge had helped usher in a new era of connection and a new scale of urban life.

Yet it is not accurate to say that there was a *triumph* of order against the multifarious uprisings, rebellions, and riots that had thus far been so crucial in making the city. There was certainly a new order, a modern, industrial, and financial order, a progressive order of governance and policing, but this order was every bit as fragile as the ones that had preceded it. Whatever the new mores governing public space, whatever the social purposes of its redesign—as with the remaking of Tompkins Square Park after 1874—city-shifting riots did not abate as now–Greater New York entered the twentieth century. Indeed, only eight months into the 1900s, New York would be racked by a race riot, smaller in scope than the Draft Riots a generation earlier, but just as important for reordering the racial geography of the city. And in its wake, the reformed police would not come out shining.

---

* Tammany was reeling from exposure of police patronage, corruption, and lawlessness by the muckraking Lexow Commission, funded by the Chamber of Commerce (following an appropriation veto by the Tammany-affiliated governor).

† Roosevelt had earlier cheered on violent policing during the Draft Riots, saying that the "over 1,200 rioters . . . slain [was] an admirable object lesson to the remainder." While the death toll was an exaggeration, his point was clear enough.

CHAPTER 9

"I Did Nothing Whatever to Justify This Brutal Assault upon Me"

Manhattan's Tenderloin Race Riot, August 1900

BRENDAN P. O'MALLEY

August heat waves are far from uncommon in New York City, but the one that gripped the metropolitan area in 1900 was unusually lengthy and punishing, the worst in the short span since such records were kept. City newspapers over the weekend of August 11 and 12 featured finely rendered line drawings of tenement dwellers taking refuge on stoops and fire escapes, sleeping on roofs, and playing in the spray of opened fire hydrants. The Tenderloin district of Manhattan usually bustled until the early morning hours, but the streets, stoops, and saloons were particularly crowded late at night as people sought relief from the heat.

Late Saturday, a twenty-two-year-old black man, Arthur J. Harris, left his rented room at 241 West 41st Street and headed for McBride's Saloon near the corner of Eighth Avenue. Born in Richmond, Virginia, Harris had come to New York first by way of Washington, D.C., where he lived with his mother, and then New Jersey, where he joined his father, who had separated from his mother many years earlier. In 1899 Harris lived in Jersey City and worked a series of odd jobs: cook, baker, carpenter, and pool room attendant. He now lived with his common-law wife, twenty-year-old May Enoch, with whom he took the 41st Street room at the beginning of August 1900. Enoch came to McBride's to fetch Harris sometime after midnight, telling him, "Kid come up on home." Harris would not leave right away, so Enoch waited patiently for him outside the saloon.[1]

Emerging on the street around 2:00 a.m. (Sunday), Harris discovered Enoch being accosted by an unfamiliar white man. When Harris tried to stop the man from forcibly handling Enoch, the white man produced a club and knocked Harris to the ground. The fracas began to attract a small crowd of bystanders. Harris later testified that he thought the man meant to beat him to death and thus responded by cutting his attacker near the shoulder with a cheap penknife with a two- or three-inch blade (several newspaper accounts had Harris thrusting it three times into the man's stomach).

The stabbed man, Robert J. Thorpe, was a patrolman in plainclothes arresting Enoch for solicitation. The arrest was not surprising, given the neighborhood's reputation, and Thorpe's probable assumptions about a black woman standing alone on a street corner in the early hours.* Harris, who had no previous criminal record, fled the scene and was reported to have taken the Cortlandt Street Ferry to Jersey City. From there he took a streetcar to Newark and caught a train to Washington, D.C.[2] Police found Harris at his moth-

---

* And given also that the series of reforms Theodore Roosevelt launched in an effort to curb Sunday drinking had, perversely, led to an increase in prostitution linked to bars throughout the city, as a new state law allowed only hotels with ten or more rooms to serve on that day. Bars all around town quickly remodeled to meet the letter of the law and then recouped costs by renting rooms by the hour to prostitutes. In turn, the police force responded with one of its periodic—often undercover—campaigns against vice.

er's Washington home a few days later. Thorpe was taken to nearby Roosevelt Hospital to be treated for his wounds. Enoch also fled the scene but was picked up by the police at her home the following day.

New York in Black and White

Later that Sunday, a violent thunderstorm brought brief respite from the heat but also reports of deaths from lightning strikes. "Wild Storm Bursts in Fury over City; Death in Its Train," screamed a headline in Monday's *New York World*. In retrospect, the storm may have been viewed by some as a harbinger of the coming week's violence and the headline as prescient. The day before, the *World* had published what also could have later been read as a sign in its Funny-Side section. The lead comic strip, *Four Comical Coons* by Syd B. Griffin depicted racist caricatures of four obviously rural, southern, child-like blacks with leering simian visages. In the strip, the four hatched a scheme to get to New York: they cut open giant watermelons and hid within them to be shipped north in a boxcar. They later burst forth from the watermelons at a picnic of well-to-do whites, who look on with mildly shocked, bemused expressions. Though meant to be humorous, the strip expressed growing white anxiety over recent, substantial migration of southern black folks into New York. Indeed, between 1890 and 1910, the black population of New York nearly quadrupled, increasing from 23,601 to 91,709. By 1910 the majority of African Americans in the city had been born in the South.[3]

On Monday, August 13, Officer Thorpe died at the hospital from his wounds. Thorpe, probably of English descent, both lived and worked in the Tenderloin neighborhood and was well liked by his mostly Irish fellow officers. He had recently converted to Catholicism for the sake of his newly declared fiancée, Elizabeth Murray, who also lived in the neighborhood.[*] Thorpe's death palpably increased tension in the Tenderloin and on the West Side more generally. The area was marked by a patchwork ethnic geography of islands of African Americans in a sea of first- and second-generation Irish and Germans. Blacks and whites almost never lived in the same building. Rather, several consecutive buildings of African Americans would give way to Irish or German residences, sometimes at midblock. While black and white areas could be identified street by street, blacks and whites lived in close proximity on the tightly packed grid of the West Side. When a building "went black," it usually stayed that way, as the landlord could charge higher rents and get away with spending less on upkeep.

In 1900 the 60,666 blacks counted in the census for New York represented only 1.8 percent of the total population. But most of them lived on the West Side of Manhattan, from about 23rd Street north to around 60th, and bordered on the east and west by Fifth and Ninth Avenues.[†] At the heart of this swath was the Tenderloin, centered on Sixth Avenue and extending from 23rd Street to 42nd Street. The Tenderloin's reputation for prostitution and police graft was well deserved. The story most frequently told to explain the name may be apocryphal, but it does give a sense of the district's place in the popular imagination. A young police captain, Alexander "Clubber" Williams, upon being told of his transfer to the graft-ridden West 13th Street police station in 1876, supposedly remarked, "I've lived on chuck steak long enough—from now on it's tenderloin."[4] Police profited from collecting protection money from brothels, gambling dens, and illegal liquor sales. In 1894 the Lexow Committee—which paved the way for the election of Governor Strong and Teddy Roosevelt's police reforms—exposed the graft of Clubber Williams and his cronies (as well as wider corruption throughout the city), and in 1899 the Mazet Committee went after Tammany Hall again. While both led to some

---

[*] Several historians, including Gilbert Osofsky, claim that Thorpe was to be the son-in-law of the acting captain of the 37th Street precinct house, but that man's name was Cooney rather than Murray.

[†] The African American exodus north to Harlem had only just begun. In 1907 it was greatly accelerated by the start of construction on the new Pennsylvania Station and the trans-Hudson network of tunnels and yards. The huge project led to the destruction of five hundred buildings and the dislocation of about five thousand residents, both black and white.

reforms, neither eliminated police-led graft or the police-tolerated underworld that defined the Tenderloin.

The city's primary red-light district, the Tenderloin was one of the few places black families of modest means could find housing. For both white and black New Yorkers who sought to maintain an appearance of respectability, the neighborhood was fraught with peril (though less so for wealthy white males who frequented its lobster palaces and brothels). As Jervis Anderson, *New Yorker* writer and chronicler of black New York, later wrote, "Negros of all classes lived together in tenement ghettos. Almost every contemporary observer remarked upon this fact." Anderson quotes a contemporary white reporter, G. L. Collins, who noted that "college graduates and cutthroats huddled in the same neighborhood." In 1902 Paul Lawrence Dunbar's novel *The Sport of the Gods* reinforced this sense of class mixing (and its attendant dangers) as it chronicled a respectable but naive southern black family's gradual slide into moral dissolution and tragedy over the course of five years living in the Tenderloin. Respectability was dangerously difficult to discern and maintain in the Tenderloin, and many whites did not care to expend the effort necessary to make such distinctions among black people.[5]

The Tenderloin had not yet taken on the completely racialized spatial definition that Harlem would later assume, but many whites perceived the black presence as one and the same with the district's vice and corruption (despite the fact that most vice enterprises were run by whites and protected by an all-white police force).* Further exacerbating this perception of the neighborhood was the almost manic white fear of race mixing.† White newspapers singled out the Tenderloin's "black and tan" saloons (where blacks and whites of varying social classes and sexual orientations mixed freely) as the most debauched establishments in the city. Both white and black prostitution flourished in the district, although in different sections, with blacks usually farther west. "By the early 1900s," historian Timothy Gilfoyle notes, "West Thirty-sixth to Forty-first Streets between Eighth and Ninth Avenues was filled with black women 'soliciting in the streets and any hour of the day or night,'" as a contemporaneous account complained. Two Progressive Era studies of prostitutes in the city indicated that African American women were disproportionately represented in the population studied. In 1910 black people were less than 2 percent of the population, but in one study of 647 prostitutes, 13 percent were black; in the other study, of 2,363 prostitutes, 4.78 percent were black. The lack of economic opportunity pushed many black men and women into prostitution and other illicit activities associated with the neighborhood.[6]

The New York Negro Hunt

On Wednesday, August 15, Thorpe's body was taken to 481 Ninth Avenue, between 36th and 37th Streets, where Thorpe had lived on the top floor with his two brothers and two sisters.‡ That evening, a wake was held over the policeman's body. Hundreds of friends, colleagues, and relatives gathered, patronizing the saloons at each end of the block and filling the avenue with an unusually large crowd. The *New York Sun*, *New York Times*, and *World* tell similar stories as to what incited the ensuing violence. As two white women passed the house where Thorpe's body lay around 8:30 p.m., one lamented his fate aloud. Her comments supposedly infuriated an intoxicated black passerby, Spencer Walters. Walters yelled at the women and brandished a revolver while the two women ran away screaming. The saloons quickly emptied. Thomas J. Healy, a white resident at 401 West 38th Street, grabbed Walters and disarmed him, and then the mob set upon Walters, kicking and beating him. Officer

---

* Historian Thomas Sugrue's discussion of spatialized racial definition in post–World War II Detroit is equally apposite to early twentieth-century New York. In Detroit Sugrue found a process in which "whiteness and blackness assumed a spatial definition. . . . White perceptions of black neighborhoods provided seemingly irrefutable confirmation of African American inferiority."

† This fear of race mixing has, of course, deep (if tangled) roots in New York, as the panic surrounding the 1741 "Great Negro Plot" made clear (chapter 2).

‡ The address no longer exists. Buildings on the west side of this stretch of Ninth Avenue were destroyed to make way for the Lincoln Tunnel approach.

Tenderloin rioting, depicted in the *New York World*, August 16, 1900.

Kelley of the 37th Street police station managed to extract Walters and take him down to the station house. The mob followed the pair, throwing missiles at them. The *Brooklyn Daily Eagle* offers an alternate version of the riot's genesis, in which a drunken white woman leaving the wake stirred up the passions of the white crowd, egging them on to attack the first black to walk by. Black witnesses later claimed that an intoxicated Healy had attacked Walters without any provocation.[7]

The *World* headline of the next day, while perhaps exaggerating the number of participants, left no doubt as to the wide-scale eruption of violence—and its nature—that ensued: "Negro Hunt by 10,000 Persons on Broadway—Excited Crowds on West Side Streets Savagely Attack All the Colored Men and Women in Sight to Avenge the Murder of Policeman Thorpe—Dragged from Street Cars and Beaten—Police Reserves from Six Precincts Called Out, but Are Unable to Suppress Disorder—Drunken Negro with Revolver Incited Mob to Fury." The *World* reported: "The rough element took instant advantage of the situation, and mobs walked up and down the streets inhabited by negroes and

drove them into their houses." The *Brooklyn Eagle* reported that "the infection of riot and destruction extended to certain gangs of white loafers, who infest the neighborhood, notably known as the 'Hell's Kitchen gang,' and they readily joined in the assaults against the negroes. 'Kill the niggers' was the slogan for the lower west side for blocks around."[8]

In the early moments, though, it was not clear that such a big race riot was inevitable. After policemen of the 37th Street police station moved in and dispersed the main mob in the original altercation, they retreated to the station house, perhaps because they thought they had quelled the disturbance (though it is plausible they decided to let events take their course). Reinforcements were not called in. Once the police retreated, the mobs re-formed almost immediately, and the violence was in full swing by midnight. Most black residents, at once realizing the nature and extent of the violence, barricaded themselves inside their tenements, occasionally retaliating by throwing objects from the roofs and windows of their buildings. Most did not dare venture into the street, and those who did were attacked if found. Many other black people on the streets were unaware of the situation, returning home from work or evening appointments in other parts of the city or simply passing through the riot area on streetcars or on foot.

Several black people who looked for refuge in the police stations that first night of rioting were rudely surprised when policemen clubbed them without provocation or did nothing as the mob set upon them. The case of Howard Lytle, a black office employee of the New York Central Railroad, was typical:

I was coming up Thirty-fourth street on Wednesday night and met the mob. I ran into Thirty-fifth street through Seventh avenue. I met a policeman running towards me, striking his nightstick on the ground. I stopped short and said "Take me and protect me." He answered, "Like hell I will," and knocked me down with his club.

He pulled me to my feet and two more policemen began striking me. The blood was in my eyes and I only remember

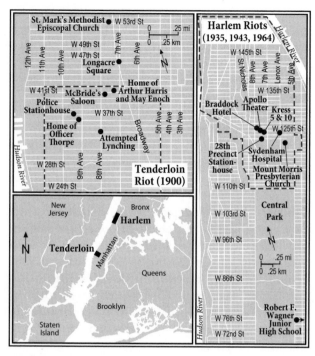

Race Riots: Tenderloin and Harlem.
Cartography: Joe Stoll, Syracuse University Cartography Lab and Map Shop.

blows falling on me. The next I remember I was in a cell and a young man was dressing my wounds.[9]

Almost immediately, testimony emerged of black men and women being beaten by police even within precinct houses during the riots, especially those who had been arrested carrying weapons. Local police stations and hospitals began to fill with the wounded. "The Bellevue physicians said the West Thirty-seventh Street Station resembled a battle-field hospital," reported the *World*. Ambulances worked all night ferrying the most badly injured there, as well as to New York and Roosevelt Hospitals.[10] Black church and political leaders immediately complained to newspaper reporters and city and police officials that it appeared as if more black people had been hurt by police than by the mobs.

The mobs were not entirely discriminating in their choice of victims: a Chinese man was set upon, although the beating was halted once the perpetrators realized he was not black. He was then lifted up into the air and carried for a block, the object of taunts. Youth did not shield individuals from the mob either, as two young newsboys were beaten in Longacre Square.* Nor did fame prove a deterrent, as a mob gathered outside of the New York Theater near Herald Square, where the renowned black vaudeville duo Williams and Walker were performing in the roof garden. The crowd tried to enter but were repulsed by police. The waves of violence ebbed and flowed through Wednesday night into the early morning hours of Thursday. Once again a powerful thunderstorm, sweeping into town at 2:00 a.m., dampened the mayhem, at least temporarily. Soon, though, white gangs were back on the streets looking for victims; however, they found few black people.

Magistrate Cornell, who sat at the West Side Police Court on Thursday, August 16, when many of those arrested on Wednesday night were arraigned, complained that too few whites had been brought before him. "The white people who caused the most of this trouble acted like wild beasts. They were a lot of loafers—poor white trash. There have been but one or two white prisoners brought before me in connection with this riot. I should like to see a few more of these white persons who caused this trouble." Cornell continued: "There was one bad negro who started it by killing a policeman, but that is no reason why all the other negroes should be beaten." Police Chief William Devery responded, "The police are sworn to protect everybody alike, and notwithstanding what their personal feelings may have been on account of the murder of Thorpe, they did their duty last night. They did not join with the rioters in attacking negroes."[11]

Whatever the exhortations of Magistrate Cornell and the protestations of Police Chief Devery, the rioting resumed on Thursday. The front page of the *World* featured a sketch of a gigantic brawl at 5:15 p.m. on Thursday involving whites,

* Renamed Times Square in 1904.

blacks, and policemen at Eighth Avenue and 35th Street. Three hours later, a mob grabbed a young black man and nearly succeeded in stringing him up on a lamppost at 34th Street and Eighth Avenue before police rescued him. Still, though, police in the Tenderloin tended to act reluctantly. But this incident finally forced Devery's hand, and he ordered the cops to be much more aggressive. At 10:30 he banned whites from other areas of the city from entering the Tenderloin and called in police regiments from around the city. The last major outbreaks of violence were quelled by midnight.

The Citizens' Protective League and the Struggle for Justice

Before the race riots, most black people in the city—while certainly feeling the constraints of social and economic discrimination—did not view local authorities as complicit in systematic repression of their claims on citizenship, as was the case in the Jim Crow South. They enjoyed aspects of citizenship denied in the South, including the vote (for men), access to public education, jury duty, and the ability to turn to the courts to assert certain rights.* But the two nights of rioting forced black people of all backgrounds to reassess—once again—their place within the social and political fabric of the city. While the mob violence could be dismissed as the work of hooligans and "poor white trash," police brutality combined with police inaction could not so easily be discounted. Even white establishment papers like the *Herald* called the riot a "police riot." The *Tribune* asserted that the rioting lasted as long as it did because "a police mob in uniform incited a mob without uniform to break the laws."[12]

Black leaders felt strongly that letting the police brutality evident in the riots pass unpunished would not only be unjust but also deepen antagonism and mistrust between the black community and city authorities. And it was clear

---

* Jim Crow was legally consolidated in the South in the two decades around 1900 as jurisdiction after jurisdiction passed laws making de facto segregation de jure or inventing new segregations altogether.

to them that punishment would never happen without the exertion of considerable political pressure. This was driven home when grand jury proceedings in late August failed to indict a single police officer. William Henry Brooks, the pastor of St. Mark's Methodist Episcopal Church (then on West 53rd Street and the largest black congregation in the city), demanded redress. Born on a Maryland plantation, Reverend Brooks possessed a doctorate in divinity and would later become a founding member of both the NAACP and the National Urban League. "We must be calm and law-abiding and we will win," Brooks declaimed on August 30.[13]

With other prominent black leaders in the city, Brooks created the Citizens' Protective League, which was formally organized at St. Mark's on September 3. Aside from Brooks, who served as president, the officers and executive committee consisted of twelve prominent ministers; T. Thomas Fortune, the publisher of the *New Age*, a black newspaper; D. Macon Webster, a lawyer; and other community leaders. At the initial meeting, some advocated arming black people to defend their homes, but ultimately more moderate strategies won out. The league resolved, in Webster's words, to demand redress for the city's "humblest citizens." "One might think we [were] aliens," given their treatment by the police, he declared.[14]

The members of the league had reason to believe that their calls for justice would be heeded. White middle-class and elite opinion seemed outraged by the police conduct, and recent legislation, like the New York State Civil Rights Act of 1895 (also known as the Malby Law), had reinforced black claims on citizenship. The legislation had expanded the federal Civil Rights Act of 1875, giving all people equal access to "inns, restaurants, hotels, eating houses, barber shops, theatres, music halls, public conveyances on land and water, and all other places of public accommodation or amusement." The 1875 federal act had been struck down as unconstitutional in a series of Supreme Court decisions in 1882, forcing the issue back into the states. And while New York took its time remedying the Supreme Court's action, in the era of *Plessy v. Ferguson* (1896), which upheld state segregation laws, the Malby Law was relatively progressive. Indeed, in 1900—the year of the riot—New York State *also* passed a law forbidding segregation in schools.[15]

The league hired two white lawyers to seek redress for the police violence: Frank Moss and Israel Ludlow. Moss, a follower of the prominent anti-Tammany reformer Dr. Charles Pankhurst, was himself one of the leading reformers of the city. He first made his name when (with Pankhurst) he took on the gambling dens of Chinatown. Later he served as a counsel to the Lexow Committee (1894) and then as the state's chief counsel during the Mazet Committee hearings in 1899, which together significantly cleared out Tammany corruption. In between the two committees, he served as Theodore Roosevelt's successor as police commissioner in Mayor William Strong's administration. Moss and an army of notaries fanned out across the city to collect testimony, which was added to that collected by Ludlow. Soon after the riots, Ludlow—later a doomed pioneer aviationist (the *New York Times* called him "the inventor of the aeroplane" when he died in 1906 after falling from the sky in one of his prototypes in Florida)—started taking depositions to pursue a suit on behalf of several African Americans injured during the mayhem. After the league formed, it asked him to join forces with Moss and broaden the scope of his work; Ludlow eventually brought civil suits against the police totaling more than $250,000. The collected depositions were soon published by the league as *The Story of the Riot*.[16]

As public pressure mounted, Mayor Robert A. Van Wyck charged the Board of Police commissioners with conducting hearings to investigate allegations of police abuse. The first hearing took place on September 7 to examine the allegations of William J. Elliot, a hall boy employed at the Imperial Hotel who claimed to have been severely beaten at the 37th Street police station. Elliot had been arrested for carrying a revolver. Ludlow and Moss both attended the hearing, Ludlow as Elliot's counsel and Moss as a representative of the Citizens' Protective League and two white civic organizations. The president of the Police Board, Bernard York, informed Ludlow and Moss that they could not cross-examine witnesses or elicit evidence that had not been submitted to the board for prior review. He stated that he would not allow outside lawyers to run the proceedings, and while Moss argued that he was qualified to cross-examine officers since he had once occupied York's position and was more familiar with the case than anyone else, York held firm. He argued that the board could not provide fresh evidence for those who might press legal charges against the city. A heated exchange followed in which Ludlow shouted, "I knew beforehand this would be a whitewash." York threatened, "And I will have you know, that unless you talk more carefully you will be ejected from this room."[17] Ludlow's words were prophetic: after a month of hearings, York declared all allegations of police brutality unwarranted, as anyone present during the riots got what they deserved.

In the meantime, the league organized a mass meeting on September 12 at Carnegie Hall, reportedly attended by thirty-five hundred people. In "An Appeal to the Mayor," dated that same day, Reverend Brooks, writing in his capacity as president of the league, made the following pleas:

> We ask for the conviction, and removal from the force of those officers whom we are able to prove guilty.
>
> We appeal to you, sir, as the chief magistrate of this city, to give this matter special personal attention.
>
> If the guilty are shielded it will encourage the mob to repeat the same offense, the officers to commit the same deed, and our people to prepare for self-defense in spite of law or gospel. This can have no other termination than bloodshed and butchery.[18]

Despite pressure from the league and white good government groups for the mayor to take up the investigation personally—an act well within his official capacities—he refused to do so and referred the matter back to the commissioners of the Police Board.* Ultimately, the only officer to get into

---

* Brooks's appeal to the mayor was itself quite personal while also meant to speak for his whole race: "The color of a man's skin must not be made the index of his character or ability. From the many ugly threatening letters I have received I feel my own life is not safe, but I am unwilling to purchase it by silence at the expense of my unfortunate race. We feel keenly our position, and again appeal to you for common justice."

legal trouble during the riots was one William Powers, who, off-duty and thoroughly intoxicated, flourished a revolver at another police officer.

Republican reformers and newspapers seized upon the riots and the police brutality that accompanied them, as well as the ensuing failure to obtain justice, as symptomatic of the corruption and mismanagement of Tammany rule. The *New York Daily Tribune*, for example, published a cartoon of an oversized Tammany tiger in a police uniform swinging a club at a bloody black man huddled below with the caption, "He's On the Police Force Now."[19] Even with the support of progressive Republican elites, however, it is hardly surprising that the black community—politically weak and divided—found little redress after the riots. Only a few years earlier the much more powerful Lexow and Mazet Committees had only very limited success in weeding out the lucrative corruption emanating from the Tenderloin. Moreover,

whatever their sympathies, Republican reformers' attention on Tammany allowed them to sidestep the more substantial and politically knottier facets of economic, social, and racial discrimination that marked the city. In the clashes between Tammany and the reformers, concerns of the black community were drowned out. With the outrages of 1900 still fresh, the black community did help elect the reformist Seth Low—the fusion candidate of both the Republican and Citizens Union Parties—to the mayoralty in 1901 but received little in return.

A New Century?

To many, the New York riots negated northerners' claims to the moral high ground on race. A big race riot in Akron, Ohio, a little more than a week after the New York riots reinforced this sense. The North was no paragon of racial justice as the country entered a new century. Perhaps the racist social, economic, and indeed geographic structure of New York—and the North more generally—was little changed from the era of the bloody Draft Riots almost forty years before. A series of telegrams from white southern newspaper editors to the *New York World*, published just two days after the start of the violence, gleefully drew connections between the New York rioting and racist violence in the South. As the editor of the *Columbia State* of South Carolina noted, "A sardonic smile spreads over the South at finding so exact a parallel in New York to the disgraceful anti-negro riots in New Orleans. The moral seems to be that since we all live in glass houses we should be slow in throwing stones."[20]

The type of economic and social discrimination African Americans experienced in New York City may have been less systematic and overtly linked to the political structure than in most locales in the Jim Crow South. But it nonetheless provoked a singular kind of frustration. The state of New York had held out tantalizing advances in civil rights,

and the city seemingly offered greater economic opportunities for black people than almost anywhere else in the United States. Yet as the riots proved, official ability—much less desire—to protect these rights and improve the precarious position of most of the city's black people just was not there when it really counted.

For those African Americans who could, the response was to get out of the Tenderloin. Especially as the new subway pushed north (it opened along Lenox Avenue in 1904), Harlem held new attraction for members of the black bourgeoisie—and increasingly the black working class—as a district with comparatively better housing and comparatively less violence. Up around 135th Street, Harlem seemed to hold promise as a place where, unlike in the Tenderloin, African Americans could exercise a degree of self-determination in the new century. Within twenty years, of course, Harlem would be the heart of black culture in America, even if any dream of a space free from the violence of race in America would soon thereafter be shattered once again (chapter 12).[21]

THE "POLICE POGROM," 1902

Whatever the goals of police reformers, and whatever shame (if any) the city administration and police department felt over police rioting in the Tenderloin race riots in 1900, these seemed to have little effect on police enthusiasm for smashing heads, especially ethnic ones.

The Lower East Side—heart of radical labor organizing in the 1870s—remained a seething cauldron of radical political experimentation and struggles for socialism or anarchism, and by 1900 such struggles were continually injected with new energy as the area became the first home to wave upon wave of Jewish immigrants from central and eastern Europe. Between 1900 and 1902 more than 176,000 Jews arrived in New York, three-quarters of them settling in the Lower East Side, joining hundreds of thousands already there.

Relations between the new Jewish immigrants and longer-standing communities of Irish and Irish Americans were tense, to say the least. One hot spot was Robert Hoe and Company—a printer—on the corner of Grand and Sheriff Streets (now essentially where East Broadway meets Grand).[1] Irish apprentices of the company made a habit of assaulting passing Jews, and the Irish-dominated police in the district made

little—often no—effort to intervene. Jewish complaints to authorities were met with silence.

On July 28, 1902, Chief Rabbi Jacob Joseph passed away. He had come to New York in 1888 as part of an effort to unify the eastern European Jews of the city (an effort sponsored by a number of Orthodox Ashkenazi congregations but opposed by Reform, Liberal, and secular Jews). Though his tenure had been marked by considerable internal strife (his sponsors stopped paying his salary in 1895; it was picked up by a consortium of kosher butchers), more than fifty thousand spectators lined the streets on June 30 when his body was processed through them to the Grand Street Ferry (whence it would be transported to a Brooklyn cemetery). There was to be only a light police escort (the department had ignored requests for more police when the size of the crowd became apparent). Even before the parade began there were scuffles outside the rabbi's house as police tried to clear a path through the massive crowd. Witnesses described a near police riot as desperate officers shoved men and women about and dragged them off the street and walks. The rough handling angered many in the crowd, and the police

finally called in reinforcements. The one hundred arriving officers created a force that—later investigations determined—was about a quarter the size needed to effectively handle such a large crowd.

Once the procession got under way, however, all seemed calm—at least until 1:00 p.m., when it reached Hoe and Company, where employees on the roof showered the hearse and marchers with buckets of water and debris. Two delegations of Jewish marchers entered the Hoe building to protest to management, the second more upset and yelling in Yiddish; they were forcibly ejected, but not without a struggle. As the crowd outside surged forward in response, Hoe employees repulsed them with fire hoses while management called for more police. Jews fought back, but with the arrival of police, calm was restored by about 1:20 p.m. But then about two hundred more policemen arrived and tore into the remaining crowd, clubs swinging. Few were spared as the police—joined by employees of Hoe and Company—lashed out at men, women, and children alike. Jews seeking to escape the melee were chased down by police and clubbed; two claimed they were choked by officers while they were being detained in a paddy wagon. The police rampage continued for half an hour. More than a hundred Jews required medical attention from doctors who rushed to the scene and worked for two hours before the last person was attended to. Nine Jews were arrested and fined five or ten dollars for disorderly conduct. Two were charged with inciting a riot and held on $1,000 bail. One Hoe employee was arrested after he fire-hosed a cop.

The police claimed they had only used force to restrain a disorderly crowd. Robert Hoe asserted that the Jewish marchers had been creating a disturbance as they got close to his establishment. Inspector Adam Cross, who had led the charge into the crowd that injured scores, conducted his own investigation. He interviewed a few policemen who had been involved, as well as some Hoe employees, and then announced that Jewish marchers had been carrying paving stones and iron bolts as they neared the factory: they had all along

planned to attack the company. Outrage at these findings was not confined to the Jewish community. Police Commissioner John Partridge found them to be absurd and transferred Inspector Cross out of the Lower East Side. But that was not enough for many in the neighborhood. Protest meetings were held, and new organizations, like the East Side Vigilance League, were founded, making anti-Semitic violence a political issue. Pogroms, it seemed, had followed Jews to America—only, as many pointed out, even the Russian police would refrain from attacking a funeral procession—and now it was, as the Yiddish press regularly averred, a "police pogrom."[2]

Feeling a good deal of political pressure in the wake of the Cross report, Mayor Seth Low established a citizens' investigatory committee. The committee's final report made it clear that the Jewish marchers were not to blame; Hoe workers were. Moreover, it documented decades of

abuse by police of Jewish residents and focused attention on police brutality and police racism. While the report was thin on recommendations for specific reforms, it was widely hailed at the time for shining a light on the ethnic and racial dimensions of police corruption. It led the mayor to order the police commissioner to bring charges against a number of police officers involved in the riot (including Cross). A few months later, however, the commissioner dropped all the charges, claiming insufficient evidence. As *Forward* now complained, "The police can now, as always, beat up Jews and no one will punish them."[3]

Yet as historian Marilynn S. Johnson shows, the history of police abuse that blacks and Jews shared in New York was vital to the formation of a long-lasting African American–Jewish civil rights alliance in the middle part of the century, one that worked diligently to monitor and expose racist police abuse in the city.

LABOR, COMMUNIST, ANARCHIST, AND SOCIALIST STRUGGLE, 1886–1941

Just as in the era of "Mobocracy," the years leading up to the turn of the twentieth century (and extending until World War II) were a time of considerable political fermentation—and political violence. Marxists and Lassallians, anarchists and syndicalists, Bolsheviks and any number of other kinds of communists, to say nothing of conservative and radical labor unionists, suffragists, birth control advocates, and radical antiracists, all put forward, and sometimes fought in the streets over, how (in a slogan of the Industrial Workers of the World) to create a new world out of the shell of the old.

Such radical struggle changed the city, as it always does. Maybe "Buda's blast" did this most spectacularly, helping to hasten Manhattan's deindustrialization (see the vignette "Bombs and Boatmen"), but the city was changed in countless other ways too. As this map shows, all kinds of new places—labor union headquarters,

socialist newspaper offices, Communist and Socialist Party meeting places, meeting houses for black and women activists, and more—became entrenched in New York's urban landscape. Meanwhile, traditional gathering places like Union and Tompkins Squares and City Hall Park remained sites of significant organizing and unrest.

Organizing and unrest were of a quite diverse character up until World War I, as women workers struggled over conditions in the sweatshops, schoolkids resisted "progressive" education reforms, militant streetcar drivers sought more control over their working conditions, and working-class and ethnic women fought—quite literally— to put bread on their tables. In the Depression years, however, the Communist Party and other left-wing union activists tended to dominate. As shown in chapter 11, the work of the Communist Party was impressively broad and, despite significant shifts

in ideology and organizing strategy that sometimes undermined its own campaigns, quite effective in fighting for the rights and needs of the unemployed and of tenants facing eviction or contesting rent gouging, winning workplace concessions from the bosses, and addressing the "race question."

Which is not to say that racist violence and interethnic strife disappeared: the Tenderloin Riot, the police pogrom, and the 1935 Harlem Riot all make it clear that race and racism remained central forces in shaping the city. Even so, as the accompanying map makes plain, the period from 1886 to 1941 was one of remarkable agitation and tumult. It wasn't until the Keynesian reforms of the New Deal began to take hold and full employment became something of a reality as the World War II economy heated up that the militancy that marked the turn of the century began to subside.

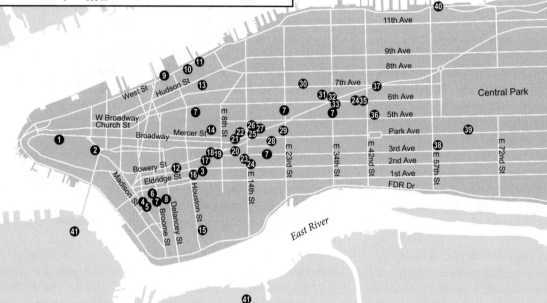

Labor, Anarchist, Communist, and Socialist Struggle, 1886–1941

7 Principal incident location—numbered to match key description.

Note: numbers are shown more than once for incidents that occurred in multiple discrete locations.

1 Buda's Blast
2 *The Daily People* Offices, Socialist Labor Party
3 Transfiguration Cath. Church, Chinese Hand-Laundry Alliance
4 *The Jewish Daily Forward* Offices
5 United Hebrew Trades
6 The Daily Shape-up
7 1886 Street Car Strike
8 Irving Hall, Newsboy Strike
9 The Holland Tunnel, International Union of Operating Engineers and The Sandhogs
10 Casa del Popolo, Socialist Party meetings
11 New York Piers, Longshoremen Strike

12 El Centro Español, Communist Party Activities, Hispanic Branch Hotel Workers Union
13 Chumley's, Industrial Workers of the World Meetings
14 Triangle Shirtwaist Company Fire
15 Lower East Side Kosher Meat Boycott
16 *The Catholic Worker* Offices
17 The Labor Lyceum
18 Cooper Union
19 The Shirtwaist Makers Strike, Uprising of Twenty Thousand, ILGWU
20 Webster Hall

21 Labor Research Association Offices
22 The Workers' Lab Theater (Theater of Action)
23 Emma Goldman Residence
24 Labor Temple
25 Union Square & First May Day
26 The Rand School
27 The International Ladies Garment Workers' Union
28 *Il Martello* Offices
29 Women's Trade Union League Headquarters
30 The Fur District Strike
31 Jewish Labor Committee Headquarters

Labor, Communist, Anarchist, and Socialist Struggle, 1886–1941.

Cartography: Joe Stoll, Syracuse University Cartography Lab and Map Shop.

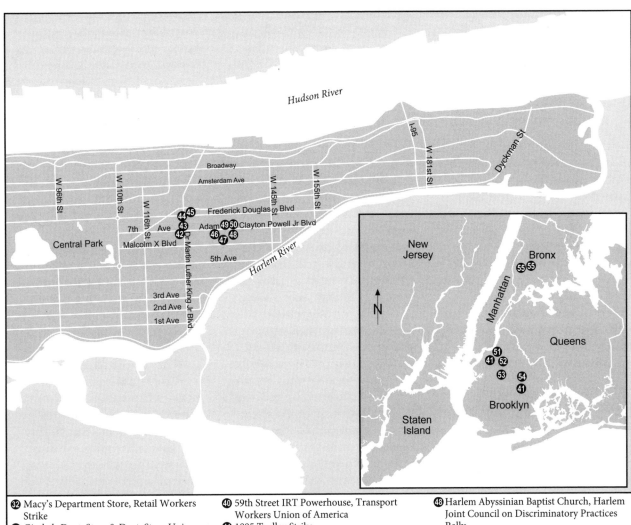

32 Macy's Department Store, Retail Workers Strike

33 Gimbels Dept. Store & Dept. Store Union Strike

34 Labor Stage Theater, Pins and Needles

35 Elizabeth Gurley Flynn Residence

36 General Society of Mechanics & Tradesmen Headquarters

37 American Labor Party Headquarters, Non-Partisan League

38 Lexington Ave. Opera House, Actors' Equity Assoc. Strike

39 Eleanor Roosevelt's Apartment

40 59th Street IRT Powerhouse, Transport Workers Union of America

41 1895 Trolley Strike

42 Harlem Labor Union, Rally for Jobs

43 Blumstein's Department Store, Jobs-for-Negroes Boycott

44 Harlem Unemployed Council, Unemployment Rally

45 Negro Labor Committee, Harlem Labor Center

46 Brotherhood of Sleeping Car Porters Headquarters

47 *The Messenger* Offices

48 Harlem Abyssinian Baptist Church, Harlem Joint Council on Discriminatory Practices Rally

49 *The Amsterdam News* Offices

50 African Blood Brotherhood Headquarters

51 Brooklyn Navy Yard, International Brotherhood of Electrical Workers Strike

52 Brooklyn Labor Lyceum

53 Malbone Street Subway Station

54 Margaret Sanger Birth Control Clinic

55 1932 Rent Strikes

THE UPRISING OF THE TWENTY THOUSAND, 1909–1911

In the black of winter in nineteen-nine
When we froze and bled on the picket line
We showed the world that women could fight
And we rose and won with women's might

"The Uprising of the 20,000"

Workers in New York's shirtwaist (blouse) industry—mostly women, mostly immigrants, mostly Jewish—had been striking on and off since late summer, and now, on November 22, 1909, they had gathered in their thousands at the Cooper Union to decide whether to make their strike general. Girls and young women, and a smaller number of men, had been arriving all day—so many that it was necessary to find rooms in nearby halls to accommodate the overflow. The stage at the Cooper Union was crowded with men: Samuel Gompers from the American Federation of Labor; officials with the International Ladies' Garment Workers' Union (ILGWU, founded in 1900) and its Local 25, covering the shirtwaist industry (founded in 1905); socialist lawyers; and one woman, Mary Dreier, the president of the Women's Trade Union League (WTUL, founded in 1903).[1]

The women in the audience grew restless as the men onstage droned on, counseling moderation, until twenty-one-year-old Clara Lemlich rose from the audience and demanded the floor. Lemlich had immigrated to America from Russia in 1903 and soon found work in the shirtwaist industry. She was smart and defiant—she had taught herself to read over the objections of her Orthodox father—and had been one of the founders of Local 25 to look after the interests of the mostly female shirtwaist workers. Lemlich was employed at Leiserson's, a large employer, where she quickly proved her mettle in 1908, convincing the male employees that their strategy of striking alone was foolish and assuring the whole factory struck together. Leiserson's was out for eleven weeks in the 1908 dispute. In one altercation with scabs and police, several of Lemlich's ribs were broken.[2]

Workers at Leiserson's in 1909, like their counterparts at other shirtwaist companies such as the Triangle Waist Company, were disgruntled over the exploitative subcontracting system through which work was organized, the endless work hours, the outsourcing of work to cheaper factories elsewhere in the city, and the way employers tried to pit new lower-waged Italian immigrant girls against the more established Jewish workers. When the workers at Leiserson's walked out, the company immediately advertised for scabs. The cops were on the company's side. By legal definition, picketing was "violence" in America. At best, strikers could get away with one or two emissaries pacing near a shop entrance, just as long as they did not "dog"

scab employees. Indeed, whenever a striking girl sought to speak with a scab, police would arrest her and then bribe the scab to testify against her in court. The company also hired gangsters to intimidate the strikers. Such tactics backfired, however: non-striking Italian girls, outraged, soon joined the strike. The workers at Triangle also walked out, but here management did not just hire scabs and gangsters, it also hired prostitutes and their pimps in an attempt to smear the striking girls by association.[3]

For their part, the police engaged in outright intimidation, in one notable instance raiding a union hall and staring at the strikers who were meeting there so as to remember their faces on the picket line. Such actions drew the involvement of the WTUL, whose members served as witnesses to police intimidation, as well as other upper-class progressive women. Their effect was limited: by the time of the November 22 meeting, Clara Lemlich had been arrested seventeen times. And she was in no mood to listen to the men onstage counsel moderation. "I am tired of listening to speakers," she told the crowd massed at Cooper when she gained the floor. "What we are here for is to decide whether we shall or shall not strike. I offer

(L) Clara Lemlich; (R) women shirtwaist strikers. Photographers unknown.
Courtesy, Kheel Center, Cornell University.

a resolution that a general strike shall be declared—now." The crowd erupted in cheers and shouts that lasted more than five minutes before the chairman could restore order and ask for a second. When he did the whole crowd rose to second the motion.[4]

At first it was not clear how many workers would join the strike. The next morning many girls—many, if not most, workers were still in their teens—hesitated by their machines, waiting to see if others would go. But soon the floodgates opened. By noon, fifteen thousand workers had walked out; as night fell, more than twenty-five thousand had quit work and joined the strike. Within days, 75 percent of the city's shirtwaist workforce was on strike. Most were not yet members of the union. The early days of the strike were chaotic as

Local 25 scrambled to hire halls where women could gather and join up. The men of the union were overwhelmed, and soon it was the women who took charge—mostly women workers, but also supporters from the WTUL and the Socialist Party.[5]

The primary aim of the ILGWU and Local 25 was union recognition and a closed shop. Both were essential, they felt, to gaining control over the iniquitous subcontracting system, wildly varying piece-rate schedules, and unreasonable seasonality of the work. They also wanted better and safer work conditions. This was a sweatshop industry, and the factories—filled with the detritus of cotton and thread—were firetraps. Finally, they wanted an end to the practice of charging the workers for needles, thread, and electricity. The strikers were fierce in their determination to

win, despite little or no strike pay, constant intimidation on the picket lines, and judges who sentenced them to the workhouse or jail on the flimsiest of pretexts or charged them with prostitution for having the temerity to be on the streets—all in increasingly bitter weather.[6]

It wasn't long before some of the smaller companies, feeling a quick pinch to their profits, settled (a third of the striking workers returned to work within a week). But the bigger companies, like Triangle and Leiserson's, organized into the Association of Waist and Dress Manufacturers (AWDM), remained intransigent, especially about

(L) Shirtwaist strikers march to City Hall;
(R) striking garment workers rally in Union
Square. Photographers unknown.
Courtesy, Kheel Center, Cornell University.

union recognition. In response, striker solidarity grew: divisions between Russian Jewish workers, newer lower-paid Italian immigrants, and usually higher-paid native-born Americans were, at least partially, overcome (the few black women in the trade were ignored by all sides). Support from socialist and progressive women and men also increased, though this was no unalloyed good, as upper-class supporters also sought to gain control over the strike and moderate its militancy. When officials from the AWDM, the ILGWU, and arbitrators reached a compromise at the end of December, reducing the workweek to fifty-two hours, ending employee charges for materials and equipment, creating a

system to share work during slack periods, negotiating shop-wide wages, and refusing to discriminate against union members, the rank and file refused to vote on it because it did not include union recognition and a closed shop. Elite support for the strike began to fracture. Socialists and WTUL members stood fast, but some of the society women who had made the strike a cause célèbre retreated—much to the delight of the establishment press—declaring the strike too radical.[7]

As the strike dragged on through January, the union began settling piecemeal with the large firms, winning on some demands, losing on others. By early February the strike was all but over, and on February 15, 1910, the ILGWU declared its end. In many of the smaller firms, the ILGWU gained union recognition, but it failed in this demand in the big companies. Even so, over the course of the strike, membership in Local 25 grew from around five

hundred to more than twenty thousand. The ILGWU became a force on the New York labor scene, though hardly a radical one: as industrial relations scholar Richard Greenwald makes clear, the ILGWU quickly became a means for moderating and channeling worker demands into a bureaucratic process that closely resembled the "business unionism" Gompers advocated.[8]

The militancy of the striking young women gained the city's and the nation's attention. Their growing political radicalism frightened both, especially since it seemed (to some) to be so foreign, even as it seemed of a piece with the rise of radicalism more generally. Anarchists had been scaring the bourgeoisie for a generation now (a fear only intensified with the assassination of William McKinley in 1901), the founding of the Industrial Workers of the World (IWW) in 1905 seemed to portend a new phase of militant worker- and class-centered struggle, and socialists seemed to be making political inroads in a number of cities across the land. And now women and girls were taking to the streets to demand better work conditions and more control over their work lives, and they were garnering the support of suffragists, society women, and many more besides. Low-paid, highly exploited women and girls were discovering their power. As Clara Lemlich declared after the strike, "They used to say that you couldn't even organize women. They wouldn't come to union meetings. They were 'temporary' workers. Well, we showed them!"[9]

But soon the Uprising of the Twenty Thousand—or thirty thousand, if the actual number of strikers is considered—would be overshadowed. One of the demands the union did not win was that the Triangle Waist Company unlock the doors and provide safe fire escapes for its upper-floor factory. On March 25, 1911, just over a year after the strike ended, a fire broke out there and quickly engulfed the building. Unable to escape through the fire doors, many women jumped to their deaths from tenth-floor windows. Others who managed to gain the fire escape had to jump the final dozen feet, where an iron fence waited below to impale them. Still others were roasted alive. In all, 146 girls and women (out of 500) died, the worst factory disaster to date. The Triangle owners were tried for negligence but got off. Instead, they rented new quarters for their factory in a condemned building not far away.

The Triangle Shirtwaist fire, 1911. Photographer unknown.
Courtesy, Kheel Center, Cornell University.

BOMBS AND BOATMEN
THE ANARCHIST THREAT, 1910–1920

The shirtwaist strike and the Triangle deaths were highly visible reminders of the state of class relations—of class struggle—in New York in the first two decades of the twentieth century. But city officials, the New York police, state-level politicians, and the federal government were far more concerned with a hidden, even secretive, threat to class order, one that seemed just as nefarious, just as threatening, just as confusing, and just as shot through with potential foreign intrigue as did the Great Negro Plot back in 1741. Instead of torches, though, now the conspirators had bombs.

Bombs and other acts of sabotage had long been part of the American radicals' toolkit, and their efficacy was often and openly debated. As debates raged, bombs went off, from the Haymarket bombing in Chicago in 1886 to the dynamiting of the *Los Angeles Times* building in 1910 and the San Francisco Preparedness Day bombing in 1916. New York was far from immune, and by 1914—another year of economic depression in the city and nation—there seemed to be an epidemic of bombing in the city. On July 4, 1914, a big bomb exploded prematurely in a model tenement building at 1626 Lexington Avenue near 103rd Street, killing four people and

destroying most of the house. It was less than a week after Archduke Franz Ferdinand had been assassinated in Sarajevo, and some in the city quickly made a link to European tensions. But the intended victim was John D. Rockefeller, responsible for the Ludlow Massacre of striking coalminers in Colorado a few months earlier. The bomb was intended more as retribution than geopolitics.[1]

The Lexington Avenue explosion was just one of a flurry of blasts to rock the city that year. St. Patrick's Cathedral was targeted in October, and St. Alphonsus Church was hit twice the same month; the Bronx County Courthouse and the Tombs Police Court were targeted the following month. As a result, the Police Commission created an undercover bomb squad charged with infiltrating the city's radical underground—the first public squad of its type in the United States. Directed by Thomas Tunney, the undercover squad set to work ferreting out IWW conspirators and anarchists—as well as a shadowy cast of boatmen who seemed central to the moving of dynamite into and around the city. In February 1915 the squad announced its first triumph, the arrest of two "Bresci Circle" anarchists in the act of planting yet another bomb at St.

The July 4, 1914, premature Lexington Avenue explosion of a bomb meant for John D. Rockefeller.
George Grantham Bain Collection, Library of Congress, Prints and Photographs Division, LC-DIG-ggbain-16476.

Patrick's. (The Bresci Circle was named for a Patterson, New Jersey, anarchist who successfully assassinated King Humbert in Italy in 1900.) As the police trumpeted their catch, famed anarchist Emma Goldman worried that the whole affair smacked of agent provocateur strategies.[2]

Perhaps. But bombs continued to go off: on May 3, 1915, the Bronx Borough Hall, and on July 5, a year and a day after it all suddenly started, at the doors of the Brooklyn police headquarters on Court Street. Then, just as suddenly, the bombings stopped. Tunney and his men did not rest, though. Tunney was particularly concerned with what he called "Chenangoes." The derivation is unclear: it could refer to boatmen on the long-since-closed Chenango canal in Upstate New York, or it could refer to the USS *Chenango*, a steam paddlewheel warship that blew up in New York Harbor during the Civil War, but it was the name Tunney gave to a shadowy network of boatmen, longshoremen, anarchists and revolutionaries, and German agents and saboteurs who plied the waterways and wharves of the city, manufacturing and transporting dynamite. As Tunney's agents tailed the Chenangoes, they seemed always on the verge of uncovering a radical plot—or maybe a German one—that was global in scope. Indian revolutionaries were busy in New York buying weapons and matériel with which to overthrow the Raj. Marxists were preaching revolution (Trotsky spoke to an overflow crowd at Beethoven Hall in 1915). Anarchists like Goldman and Alexander Berkman were stirring up discontent. Mostly, though, there seemed to be a mass

of secretive, invisible operatives—many living in whole floating villages of moored house- and canal-boats along the rivers and inlets—who ferried explosives and other illicit goods into, out of, and around the city.[3]

A series of fires and small explosions on ships in New York Harbor in 1915 turned Tunney's attention toward sugar, which many of the ships seemed to be transporting. Tunney became convinced that explosives were being slipped into sugar bags in the city's refineries and then transported around the rivers and harbor by "lighters"— small boats that transferred the sugar from the refinery to oceangoing boats. In turn, after following the lighters and their boatmen—the Chenangoes—the bomb squad discovered a vast portside market of illicit goods: dynamite, TNT, potash, coal tar, and more. Tracing these led the men to dynamite stores in Perth Amboy, paint factories in Manhattan, and a particular clockmaker who seemed to regularly be purchasing nitroglycerine—plus what seemed to be a nest of German spies. Eventually, the bomb squad got a hit: sailors on the *Kirkosvald* found bombs before they could detonate. When the bomb squad retraced how the bombs got there, they found that the bombs began in the lab of a German chemist in Manhattan who packed the explosives into a bag of sawdust and delivered them to the Labor Lyceum in Brooklyn. From there someone else took them to a saloon on Manhattan's West Side, where Chenangoes were contracted to take them to and load them on the *Kirkosvald*. One of the German conspirators exposed through the

Kirkosvald investigation claimed that a similar plot had been effected for the *Lusitania* but that German torpedoes had destroyed the ship before the bombs could.[4]

Then, in the very early morning of July 30, 1916, massive explosions tore through Black Tom, an island munitions store in the New York Harbor hard by the Statue of Liberty. Damage in Lower Manhattan was vast, and windows were blown out as far north as 42nd Street. The Brooklyn Bridge swayed in the shockwave, and the Hudson River train tunnels shuddered. The telephones went down. Four people were killed. In the shocked panic that followed, police officials quickly declared the explosions to be an accident, even as they suspected they might have been the work of anarchist IWW saboteurs exacting revenge for the arrest of some of their own the day before. The explosions had, in fact, been the work of German agents seeking to disrupt the exportation of munitions to the European Allies, perhaps employing a fire on one of the Chenangoes' lighters to spark the blast.[5]

Distinctions between German saboteurs, Wobbly syndicalists, and anarchists did not matter much to New York's undercover cops, not in the wake of this blast or that of the San Francisco Preparedness Day parade bombing a week earlier, which officials claimed to be the work of radical labor organizers—anarchists—closely affiliated to New York's Berkman and Goldman. In February 1917 Congress passed a new immigration law that ordered the deportation of anyone advocating the destruction of property or the assassination

The aftermath of Buda's Wall Street blast, September 16, 1920.
George Grantham Bain Collection, Library of Congress, Prints and Photographs Division, LC-DIG-ggbain-31304.

of public officials, and in April the United States finally entered the war. Perhaps recalling the Draft Riots of 1863, Congress included provisions in the Selective Service Act, passed in May, outlawing making statements against the draft. Berkman and Goldman were arrested, along with hundreds of others. By September nationwide raids had likewise detained hundreds of Wobblies and other political radicals, many under the provisions of the Espionage Act, passed in July. The postmaster soon started confiscating publications that complained about plutocrats or speculated about wartime profiteering. By May 1918 the new federal Sedition Act made it a crime to utter "disloyal" comments about the government or the Constitution. Wartime dissent had been thoroughly criminalized. Socialists, anarchists, syndicalists, pacifists, more

Wobblies, Bolsheviks, and Germans were all soon caught up in the dragnet, and not just because they were seditious. As the great socialist Eugene Debs (himself jailed for sedition) remarked, "Wall Street mortally fears the I.W.W. and its growing menace to capitalist autocracy and misrule."[6]

Wartime hysteria outlasted the war. In 1919 New York joined a growing list of American states in passing antisyndicalism laws, and nationally, at the end of 1919, U.S. Attorney General A. Mitchell Palmer launched America's first official "Red scare," leading to the deportation of more than five hundred radicals, many of them involved in a wave of labor struggles that followed hot on the heels of the war's end. Bombings had resumed too, with bombs mailed to three dozen prominent citizens, including John D. Rockefeller and Palmer

himself in April (most of these bombs failed to reach their intended targets because of insufficient postage), and then in June there were eight simultaneous blasts in cities across the United States, including in New York, where a watchman was killed.

But the big one went off a bit more than a year later, on September 16, 1920. Mario Buda, an Italian immigrant anarchist, follower of Luigi Galliani (whose circle was likely responsible for the San Francisco Preparedness Day bombing, not the labor organizers framed for it, and for the 1919 mail bombs), and friend of the Boston martyrs Sacco and Vanzetti, drove his horse-drawn wagon to the corner of Wall and Broad Streets, parked it across from J. P. Morgan and Company, and walked away into the crowd. As Trinity Church's bells pealed noon, the wagon exploded in a ferocious blast. J. P. "Jack" Morgan was the likely target (he had also been targeted in the earlier mail bombs, as well as shot by an unsuccessful assassin on July 3, 1915), but he was not in the office. His son was, though, and he was injured in the blast. Out on the street, the bomb created a huge crater, broke windows, mangled building facades, and sent shrapnel flying. Thirty-eight people were killed; hundreds were injured. Trading was halted on the New York Stock Exchange. It was the deadliest act of terrorism in the United States until the Oklahoma City bombings in 1995.[7]

Buda was never found—much less even identified—by either the New York bomb squad or the Department of Justice's Bureau of Investigation. Anarchists were suspected, and the bureau, hoping to suss out the bomber's identity, soon emulated the New York bomb squad by placing undercover agents on New York's wharfs and on the lighter boats that plied the harbor, but the culprit remained a mystery (he was identified—circumstantially, at least—long after the fact by historian Paul Avrich).[8]

The results of Buda's bomb, and the long decade of anarchist agitation and sabotage that led up to it, were tragic and ironic, in turn. Tragically, even before the bomb, police, operating at the behest of a state legislature committee investigating seditious activity, raided the Socialist Party's Rand School of Social Science, and five elected socialist members of the New York Assembly (from the Lower East Side, Harlem, and the South Bronx) were expelled from the legislature after their colleagues determined their socialist politics to be treasonous. With the bombing, repression of dissent—even exercised through the ballot box—reached a new height. Ironically, after the bomb, Wall Street boomed.[9]

Then the irony turned geographic. Reflecting concerns about the shadowy underworld of Chenangoes and anarchists, syndicalists and floating villages, city elites, working under the auspices of the Russell Sage Foundation, began plotting the deindustrialization of Manhattan and the transformation of the industrial and freight-moving infrastructure into office towers, ocean liner terminals, and luxury apartments. Finance, design, telecommunications, and the media were to be the future of the city, according to the architects of the famous *Regional Plan,* published in 1929 but begun in 1922. Chemical manufacture in particular needed to be pushed out, and the lighter-boat system of transshipment needed to be eliminated. The decade of bombs and boatmen had the ironic effect of tightening Wall Street's hold on the city.[10]

"WOMEN IN BREAD RIOT AT DOORS OF CITY HALL," 1917

While undercover agents were scouring the city for bomb-throwing anarchists, women from the poor districts of the city were up in arms about a different kind of criminal element: war profiteers. The economic crisis of 1913–14 had hit hard, and when war in Europe began to pull the urban economy out of the doldrums, working people and their families hardly benefited. Wages didn't budge much—but prices did. American farmers and manufacturers found they could make a killing by exporting to Europe rather than providing for domestic markets. By November 1916 flour was selling in the city at prices higher than any time since the Civil War, potatoes and cheese had doubled in price in less than a year, and butter was quickly moving out of reach of most households in the city. Calls for export or price controls had gone nowhere. Prices continued to rise in the New Year.[1]

In mid-February food prices leaped even farther upward. Angry that she could not afford even the most basic foods, a woman on Belmont Avenue in Brownsville overturned a pushcart. When the vendor chased her down the street, hundreds of women set upon him and then turned their attention to the other peddlers and their pushcarts, chasing off the former and setting the latter alight. At least a thousand women rioted for more than two hours before police quelled the uprising. At 4:00 the next morning, rioting erupted again, now in Williamsburg as women overturned carts and set them afire, sometimes first hauling off bags and pails of onions and potatoes as peddlers fled in fear. Remarkably, given their history, the police merely stood by. As one officer explained, "I just didn't have the heart [to arrest the women rioters]. They were just crazy with hunger, and I don't see how I could blame them."[2]

The peddlers blamed the wholesale markets and the middlemen and claimed they were hurting just as much. But this did not mollify the women. The next day four hundred women gathered at Rutgers Square (now Strauss Square) on East Broadway in the Lower East Side. From there they marched to City Hall to demand a meeting with the mayor. The mayor was away at a meeting with the Merchants' Association, but the women persisted, rushing the locked gates of the building and demanding in Yiddish, "Give us bread!" and "We want food!" They demanded that the mayor lower prices. Five emissaries from the crowd—Mrs. Ida Harris of the Mothers' Vigilance Committee, the highly regarded anarchist Sweet Marie Ganz, and three others—gained admission to City Hall and registered for a meeting with the mayor. When they came back out, Ganz addressed the crowd. As she did, the police grabbed her, dragged her back into the building, and arrested her for disorderly conduct. The reaction was swift. Women set upon the police, ripping their uniforms and scratching their faces, before they were dispersed by a mounted force. "Women in Bread Riot at Doors of City Hall," shouted the *New York Times*.

Outraged, ten thousand people met at Forward Hall (175 East Broadway), an important radical meeting site, and denounced capitalism and war profiteering. "It was not a reasoning crowd," tutted the *New York Times*. Plans were made to demonstrate in front of J. P. Morgan's offices, and demands were made on the city to appropriate a million dollars so food could be distributed at cost. A delegation of women was finally allowed to meet Mayor John Purroy Mitchel the next day. He expressed sympathy but told them the city had no authority to appropriate food. By then, rioting had begun to spread, first to Philadelphia, then to Boston, then across the South.

A food protest on East Broadway, February 20, 1917.
George Grantham Bain Collection, Library of Congress, Prints and Photographs Division, LC-DIG-ggbain-23742.

Privation was real. City health authorities were mapping increased infant mortality on the East Side; dysentery and malnutrition spiked as children's milk was diluted to the point of nothingness or substituted with tea, as leaves could be soaked and soaked and soaked again. The riots in New York did not abate—women rioted against a sharp uptick in chicken prices on Friday, February 22, as merchants sought to profit ahead of the coming Sabbath, and they rioted again two days later when a crowd of five thousand marched from Madison Square to the Waldorf Astoria to demand food—but direct action was supplemented by coordinated boycotts of selected produce, onions and chickens primarily. On March 1 rioting broke out citywide—from the Lower East Side to the Bronx and across to Brooklyn—as the newly formed Anti–High Price League enforced the boycotts. The Hebrew Grocers League warned the mayor that the Lower East Side was in a "state of rebellion."

City elites, federal officials, and police immediately suspected the riots were the work of German agents, of course. At best, they suggested hungry residents should switch from potatoes to rice and from chicken to smelt. Socialist congressman Meyer London (from the East Side) instead condemned capitalist profiteers, arguing that America was in the midst of a "prosperity crisis," and called for the nationalization of the food supply. In New York, socialists and others called for city-owned markets. By March 19 poultry retailers on the East Side and in Harlem had joined the protests, boycotting the wholesalers who were rapidly jacking up prices in advance of Passover. The effect was immediate: three days later thirty poultry slaughterhouses in the city shut down.

Prices never really fell, but the rioting slowly abated. As the United States entered the war, the government pinned its hopes on voluntary, patriotic efforts by food producers to keep prices down. This was unavailing, and within months Food Administrator Herbert Hoover was seeking authority to implement price controls. Congress obliged with some watered-down controls that, Meyer London charged, would do little but favor rich farmers over poor ones and assure that the nation's poor, while perhaps not starving, would remain little more than wage slaves.

CHAPTER 10

The Children's Crusade

The Gary Plan Riots, October 1917

PETER WALDMAN

Not long after the food riots receded, rioting erupted again in New York. This time it began with schoolkids throwing rocks and bottles and smashing windows at Public School 171 on 103rd Street near Madison Avenue.[1] More than five hundred students had gathered on the evening of October 15, 1917, to protest the piloted implementation of the Gary plan, an educational initiative that ultimately promised citywide progressive change to school layout, curricula, and pedagogical traditions. Over the next four nights rioting spread across East Harlem, the Bronx, and Brooklyn as thousands of (mostly) Jewish immigrant elementary and high school students (aided by some parents and other adults) expressed their disgruntlement. No one was seriously injured, but the riots—which erupted less than three weeks before the 1917 municipal elections—toppled the administration of progressive Republican mayor John Purroy Mitchel and returned power to a Tammany administration headed by Brooklyn judge John F. Hylan. As a result, control over the schools remained firmly in Tammany, and therefore local, hands. Tammany would control City Hall and the schools until Mayor Fiorello La Guardia took office in 1934.

The Gary plan had been imported into New York City by Mayor Mitchel in 1915 from the industrial city of Gary, Indiana, in an effort to modernize education, but especially as a means to wrest control of the schools from the Tammany-dominated Board of Education. Part of the plan was to slash the size of the board and centralize administrative and curricular authority over the schools in City Hall. Mitchel controlled the board's purse strings (through his control over the Board of Estimate) and had the support of a slew of progressive educators who saw the Gary plan as a means of bringing to New York a Deweyan brand of progressive, democratic education, even as it cut costs.* He did not reckon on a sustained—in fact, highly organized—and effective season of rioting by schoolkids to upset his plans.

The Gary Plan

The Gary plan was a "platoon system" of schooling that aimed to maximize efficiency by providing the greatest amount of schooling for the largest number of learners for the greatest amount of time.[2] The plan was sold to New York City by its Gary architect, William Wirt, and by a number of progressive educators. It promised reform for the city's troubled school system on two fronts: the plan was pledged to pedagogical progressivism—John Dewey endorsed it—and to administrative progressivism, which would apply scien-

---

* John Dewey advocated a deeply democratic mode of education that emphasized highly active modes of learning over the one-way transmission of knowledge from teacher to pupil. He also advocated that learning be rooted in the acquisition of practical skills relevant to students' lives through which they would then develop more abstract knowledge.

tific management strategies of efficiency as an antidote to the public profligacy of Tammany.[3] Under the Gary plan, the loosely configured and localized forms of public schooling that had developed under Tammany (which allowed for a good deal of teacher autonomy and control over curriculum and assessment) were to be overhauled in favor of a citywide system. The public schools were to be taken out of the hands of ward bosses and put into the hands of pedagogical and administrative "experts."

The Gary plan created what Wirt called "work-study-play" schools in which students were divided into two platoons, X and Y. While one group used academic classrooms, the other would be divided between shops, nature study, auditorium, gymnasium, and outdoor recreational equipment. All the facilities would thus be used all the time. In other words, one school could operate at 200 percent capacity. The Gary plan imagined an intermingling and cooperative interplay among the city's institutions, including "libraries, churches and playgrounds," resulting in a "new type of municipal institution that will make the city a fit place for the rearing of children." But Wirt had dreams beyond organizational economy and the prevention of waste: it was his intention to bring "the virtues of country life" to the teeming precincts of New York City.[4]

Wirt did not much care for cities, despite the fact that he was to spend most of his life in them, and he certainly found them to be inferior environs in which to raise children. He believed that "city children associated with people who look upon work as an evil" and that they learned "the ideals of the loafers and the outcasts of society in the streets." Wirt was devoted to providing children with "the old value system . . . [in] the environment of the old time home and shops." By contrast, city street life was "a real school working at maximum efficiency educating children in the wrong direction."[5]

Writing a year before the riots, Dewey acolyte Randolph Bourne described the progressive pedagogical character of the Gary schools: "This plant carries out a belief in educating the whole child, physically, artistically, manually, scientifically, as well as intellectually.* . . . This can be done only in a school which provides, besides the ordinary classrooms, also playgrounds and gardens, gymnasiums and swimming pools, special drawing and music studios, science laboratories, machine shops, and intimate and constant contact with supplementary community activities outside the school." The Gary-style plant had a double advantage: "The ideal Wirt school contains in one school plant the complete school, with all the classes from kindergarten through the common school and high school. By this plan both economic and educational advantages are realized."[6]

Contested Reform

Mayor Mitchel staked much on school reform when he took office on January 1, 1914, announcing that he "firmly believed that better education could be had for less money." But to many New Yorkers used to overcrowded and inefficient schools, the Gary plan seemed too good to be true. And the Mitchel administration underestimated the power of Tammany to use the plan to mobilize its largely immigrant constituency.

The inefficiency of New York's schools was notorious, especially as expansion of the system had failed to keep up with the enormous wave of immigrants from eastern and southern Europe who flooded the city toward the end of the nineteenth century. The schools were bursting at the seams: twenty thousand teachers served eight hundred thousand children, and twenty thousand of them only received part-time schooling because of overcrowding.† Half the student body left school after the sixth grade, and only 10 percent graduated from high school. Those who did not graduate were pushed into low-wage jobs in sweatshops and factories. The school budget stood at $44 million when Mitchel took

---

* Just as people referred to the Gary steel mills as a "plant," Bourne referred to the school buildings as a "plant," in essence, equating schooling with factory production.

† By comparison, some eighty thousand teachers serve 1.1 million students today.

A New York school on opening day, 1913.
George Grantham Bain Collection, Library of Congress, Prints and Photographs Division, LC-DIG-ggbain-14329.

office—the largest allocation of the city budget. Mitchel saw the Gary plan as a way to replace New York's overcrowded, expensive, and inefficient school system with a more "productive" one that had larger classes, lower teacher salaries, and extended an school day and year. Besides worrying parents and students, Mitchel's plans immediately alienated the city's twenty-thousand-strong teaching corps.[7]

Still the mayor pressed ahead. He enlisted Wirt to refurbish two elementary schools, PS 89 in Brooklyn and PS 45 in the Bronx, "a badly overcrowded school." Even before he completed the schools' physical transformation into "Gary" schools—gymnasiums had yet to be installed, and swimming pools, libraries, and workshops were still in the planning stages—Wirt announced plans for the platoon system to be extended to eleven elementary schools in the Bronx.

Mayor Mitchel, meanwhile, made it clear he planned to extend the platoon system to all the city's elementary schools in 1915.[8]

Besides alienating teachers, the rapid introduction of the Gary plan also alienated religious authorities. The New York City Archdiocese complained that the hectic schedule of the Gary plan left no time for religious instruction. City officials soon negotiated a "religious option" for students of PS 45, which allowed for "released time for religious instruction" when students were not involved in schoolwork.

While the religious option had been used without incident in Gary, it became a lightning rod in New York. In October, for example, the Reverend Dr. William Hess told his Trinity Congregational Church worshipers that "religious instruction by an outsider should come after school hours."

"Beware the enemies of the public school system," he continued. "The Gary plan gives them a chance to put in an entering wedge. Long live the public school system, we say. It is the very foundation of our free government." His target was not only the Gary plan itself but also the door it left open to the Roman Catholic Church. Other Protestant denominations clearly felt that the way to counteract the Catholic Church was not protestation but usurpation: within a month the Episcopal Church was organizing to include its own religious instruction in the Gary plan schools. For their part, Catholic leaders denied they were conspiring to use the Gary plan to wedge open the schools for religious indoctrination.[9]

Jewish parents were less disturbed with religious instruction in the Gary schools than with the vocational aspects of the new curriculum and with its lack of academic robustness. As one Jewish parent demanded in the midst of the riots, "We want our kinder to learn mit der book, der paper und der pensil und not mit der sewing and der shop." For Jewish immigrant parents, "paper and pencil" education was the proper education for their children. Despite the socialist tendencies of many Jewish immigrant parents, school was useful only when it helped their children to assimilate and to compete for the class prerogatives of mainstream (WASP) culture and society.[10]

The complaints of parents mounted. They were concerned about the Gary plan's requirement that students move from room to room for their classes, which they feared would be an easy way to spread contagion. They were concerned that discontinuance of the one-teacher/one-classroom model in the early grades would mean an end to motherly nurturance. Class sizes were too big; disorder in the hallways between classes would mean chaos; there was too little supervision in the auditoriums and playgrounds; workshops were inadequately equipped, leaving many students idle. In short, for many parents, the Gary plan in New York created a program of schooling with "too much freedom."[11]

Nonetheless, the plan had its supporters, especially among pedagogical progressives. Alice Barrows, an advisor on vocational education to the Progressive Education Association (PEA) of New York, had heard Wirt speak at a teachers' conference in 1912 and became a vocal and effective advocate for the city's adoption of the Gary plan. One historian describes Barrows as Wirt's propaganda minister in New York. Along with PEA members Randolph Bourne and Howard Nudd, Barrows formed something of a public relations unit for the Gary plan in New York. PEA itself effectively served as the educational advisor to the Mitchel administration. Ties between PEA and the administration were tight. Just as the 1917 municipal elections were gathering steam, PEA, under Barrows's direction, charged the Gary School League, an influential and elite parents' group advocating Gary in New York, with getting the word out on the plan. The Gary School League was enormously effective on this front: 110,000 people viewed films boosting the Gary plan at neighborhood theaters around the city, and another 200,000 people were reached by pro-Gary speakers in the street and at organized meetings.[12]

Riots, Elections, Agitators . . . and Tammany Again

Education reform—the Gary plan—was a central plank in Mayor Mitchel's 1917 reelection platform. He positioned Gary plan schooling as both progressive and a democratizing force. Against him stood Judge John F. Hylan of Brooklyn, a Tammany stalwart, and the prominent socialist Morris Hillquit, who had been a central figure in the Uprising of the Twenty Thousand eight years earlier. Hylan campaigned in pure class terms, arguing that the Gary plan was little more than a conspiracy to turn out "wage slaves . . . only for the mill and the factory." Hillquit did not exactly disagree but argued rather for a more complete plan of school reform that included new school construction, higher salaries for teachers and a voice for them in school governance, and other social democratic reforms, including free medical and dental care for students and free food and clothing for students in need. He would fund his plan through a steeper tax on the "possessing class."[13]

On the evening of October 15, adults were holding a Liberty Loan meeting inside PS 171 when about five hundred of the school's students arrived to protest their conscription into the Gary plan.* When the students' shouts and taunts did not disrupt the meeting, they took aim at the school's windows with rocks and bottles. More than a hundred windows were smashed. The *New York Times* described the melee as a student strike; indeed, the next morning the students called for a general strike. All day long on October 16, the *Times* reported, "Police reserves from the East 104th Street Station were busy bringing truants to the schools . . . breaking up the demonstrations and protecting the public school properties from bands of children who tried to throw stones through the windows." Students—all under fifteen years old, according to press reports—established pickets around school entrances and tried to prevent other kids from entering. At PS 72 (Lexington Avenue and 105th Street) about two hundred students blocked entrances, but police gave chase, catching seventy-five and returning them to their schools. After lunch more disturbances broke out around PS 72 as schoolkids massed again, this time aided by "groups of mothers" shouting "their derision of the police and the schools" and attempting to keep the police from hauling their children off to the police station. That night, about five thousand students demonstrated in the streets, shouting anti-Gary slogans and carrying signs and banners reading "Down with the Gary System" and "Can the Gary System and Mitchel." The PS 72 principal blamed the disturbances on "soapbox agitators."[14]

The next morning rioting spread to the Bronx as a thousand students at PS 54 (Intervale Avenue and Freeman Street) "stoned" the police. Then it spread some more: to PS 50 (Bryant Avenue and 172nd Street), PS 44 (Prospect Avenue and 146th Street), PS 120 (at the intersection of Fox, Simpson, and 167th Streets), and PS 55 (on St. Paul's Place

between Washington and Park Avenues). Then on the third day, the rioting spread to Brooklyn, where in Williamsburg and Brownsville the most violent episodes of the several days of rioting took place. The rioters—"mainly foreigners," according to the *Times*—stoned the police and slashed the tires and battery wires of the police patrol wagon.[15]

Though decreasing in intensity, rioting continued for two more days. Newspapers and the mayor's campaign first blamed socialists and IWW agitators but eventually turned their fire on Hylan and Tammany, accusing them of turning the campaign into a "class war" and "capitalizing on the ignorance of great alien populations in New York City." Mitchel accused Hylan of "aiding and abetting pro-German propaganda in this country."† Alice Barrows took to following Hylan around on the campaign trail and challenging him with questions about the Gary plan, but to no avail. Hylan prevailed in a landslide, bringing Tammany back into the mayor's office.[16]

Public disillusionment with the Gary plan was central to Mitchel's defeat—a disillusionment deepened by Mitchel's "elitist personality and lifestyle," as one history puts it, as well as the top-down manner in which the plan was proposed. Progressive school reform in New York was not nearly democratic enough school reform, as progressive educator John Dewey suggested when he pointed out that New York's Gary plan was "fundamentally compromised in the way in which it was formulated from above."[17]

Shortly after taking office, Mayor Hylan dismantled the Gary plan. Although it survived in some schools through the 1920s, Gary-style pedagogical progressivism "had come to an ignominious end in New York City." As prominent education historian Diane Ravitch concludes: "In 1915, the Gary school system was a favorite of progressive reformers, and the platoon system was adopted in many cities. However, it eventually came to be seen as a system that valued scientific

---

* To fund the war effort, Congress had passed the second Liberty Loan Act on October 1, 1917. Subscriptions to the first round of Liberty Bonds had been lackluster, and so this time around patriotic citizens and officials organized community meetings to promote bond sales.

† New York State had recently passed a law mandating military training in high schools. Mitchel supported the law. Hylan did not, hence Mitchel's charge. Though not the central focus of student unrest, mandatory military training was a focus of at least some picketing at the schools.

management and economy over good education."[18] Whatever the role of Tammany—or, for that matter, IWW agitators and socialists—in sparking the demonstrations that led to the riots or in helping to sustain them, schoolkids in Harlem, the Bronx, and Brooklyn had a sense of the limits and purpose of the Gary plan. And through their rioting they exposed the inherent tensions between progressive scientific management and progressive social reform, centralization and local control, the religious and the secular, the vocations and academics. Tammany was able to then manipulate these tensions to wrest control over City Hall and the Board of Education from Mayor Mitchel and his more elitist, reformist bloc.

CHAPTER 11

"Fight, Don't Starve!"

The Communist Party and Mass Organizing during the Great Depression

HARMONY GOLDBERG

Wall Street boomed after Mario Buda's blast in 1920—until it imploded on October 29, 1929. The decade that followed was one of intense struggle in New York City. Workers and the unemployed around the world quickly mobilized after the stock market crash and declared March 6, 1930, to be International Unemployment Day. In New York, at least thirty-five thousand unemployed people (and maybe many more than that) gathered in Union Square, holding banners that read "Fight, Don't Starve!" When they tried to march to City Hall, they were met by a thousand baton-wielding cops. The street fighting that ensued set the tone for the decade to follow. In the next several years, unemployed people across the city mobilized in large numbers to "unevict" tenants who had been thrown out of their apartments, fighting off the police and moving furniture back into apartments. Black Harlem residents broke down doors of the local relief bureau and occupied its offices until they received city aid. And working-class tenants organized rent strikes in hundreds of buildings across the city during the Great Rent Strike War of 1932, withholding rent, occupying their buildings, and fighting off police until they won significant rent reductions. Three years later, working-class women shut down more than forty-five hundred butcher shops to protest the rising price of meat at a time of economic hardship, winning price reductions of up to 2 percent. In the face of hardship, New York City's poor and exploited came alive and fought back.

At the heart of it all was the Communist Party U.S.A. (CPUSA). When the market crashed, the CPUSA was ready to spring into action, rapidly adapting its long-standing political work in the city to channel growing working-class anger into outright resistance, including direct action. Almost immediately, the party initiated a massive drive to organize the unemployed to fight for jobs and for government relief. It organized tenants who were being thrown out of their homes because they could not afford to pay rent. It organized working-class women to fight the rising cost of meat and bread. It put racism at the front and center of its struggles, fighting against segregation and the heightened impact of the Depression on the black community. In each of these struggles, the CPUSA combined practical fights to win real changes in people's lives with an explicit analysis of the capitalist system and a call for socialist revolution. By recognizing the political possibilities of the historic moment and by building a strong and militant base in working-class communities, the Communist Party became an important player in city and national politics during the Depression decade.

The CPUSA

The CPUSA was a force in New York. It had been founded in 1919 in the wake of the Russian Revolution and quickly filled the void left by the repression of the Industrial Workers of the World in the United States. It was the official affiliate of the Comintern—the international federation of Communist Parties led by the Soviet Union. New York City became home to the central office of the CPUSA in 1927. By 1932 it had 2,350 official members in the city, 20 percent of its national membership. By 1939 it counted more than 25,000 members in New York, 50 percent of its total membership. Well into the 1930s, CPUSA membership consisted overwhelmingly of immigrant workers. Indeed, by some accounts 90 percent of the party's members were immigrants—Finns, Slavs, eastern European Jews, Lithuanians, Ukrainians, Hungarians, and others. The party also worked hard to recruit black workers, though their representation remained low (about 2 percent before the 1930s and never surpassing 7 percent of the total membership).[1]

In 1928 the Comintern passed two crucial measures that would shape the politics of the CPUSA in the coming years: the institution of the Third Period and a resolution entitled "The Black National Question in the United States." The Third Period was supposed to be a new phase of the class struggle. The First Period was the time immediately following the Russian Revolution, when the main priority of communists was to encourage the spread of revolutionary activity around the world. The Second Period followed the end of World War I, when capitalism reconsolidated itself. Global revolution no longer seemed possible, and so communists' main political priority was to defend the Soviet Union. During the Third Period, capitalism was predicted to enter an ultimate crisis, and so revolutionary activity was back on the agenda of communists worldwide. Party members were pulled out of any joint work with liberals and other socialists. They instead were supposed to initiate direct organizing of working-class people into militant unions and mass organizations. "Dual unionism" became the rule in the United States (at least ideologically) as communist unions competed directly for workers with more mainstream unions such as those affiliated with the American Federation of Labor. Third Period independence

meant that the CPUSA was able to respond quickly when the market crashed, devoting enormous effort to organizing and building a mass movement of poor people. This new effort did not eliminate the party's focus on the shop floor; instead, it also focused new energy on communities and neighborhoods where the party strove to organize African Americans (who were particularly hard hit by the Depression) and working-class women (who were now struggling harder than ever to keep their families together). At the same time, the party engaged in bitter denunciations of almost every other force on the liberal-left side of the political spectrum, attacking union leaders, civil rights activists, religious leaders, socialists, and many more. Third Period divisiveness often proved disastrous and isolated the party from broader political forces, limiting its effectiveness.[2]

The Comintern resolution on the black national question reflected years of political struggle by black leaders inside the CPUSA. As historian Robin Kelley has shown, black leaders argued that "the Negro stood at the fulcrum of class struggle: there could be no successful working-class movement without black workers at the center." The Comintern's 1928 resolution (as with another one passed in 1930) was based on the assessment that black people in the United States constituted an oppressed "nation within a nation" that had the right to national self-determination, placing the struggle against racism at the heart of CPUSA strategy. Communists were expected to actively struggle for the right to black self-determination in the South and for social, political, and economic equality in the North. This meant that the party had to prioritize both the direct organizing of black communities and the work of educating and organizing white workers to fight against racial oppression. The two black national question resolutions, together with the Third Period dictats, framed the work of the Communist Party in New York City during the early years of the Great Depression. Inspiring militancy was interwoven with destructive sectarianism as Communist organizers strove to instigate a revolutionary class struggle that had the fight against racism at its core.[3]

Mass Struggle in Third-Period New York

Nationally, the advent of the Third Period shifted the Communist Party's labor-organizing strategy. Where previously it had been CPUSA policy to "bore from within" AFL unions, shifting Comintern strategy, together with intense opposition from AFL unions to the boring-from-within strategy, led to the evolution of the "dual union" strategy: the creation of separate, militant unions that operated alongside and against the conservative AFL unions, seeking to organize the same industries while also organizing industries the AFL had ignored. In 1929 the CPUSA created the Trade Union Unity League (TUUL) as an umbrella organization of communist unions. Party organizers stressed "bottom-up," rank-and-file participation as an alternative to the AFL approach, which centered responsibility in the hands of union officials.[4]

TUUL-affiliated unions were particularly active and somewhat successful in New York City, particularly in the garment industry. Even before the TUUL was formed, the communist-led National Textile Workers' Union (NTWU) and the Needle Trades Workers' Industrial Union (NTWIU) were making inroads against the International Ladies' Garment Workers' Union and various craft-based unions in the city. And while dual unionism was the official policy of TUUL and Third Period communism, leaders in the United States, as well as in the Comintern, understood—especially after bosses set out to destroy the NTWU after a big win in the Lawrence, Massachusetts, mills—that TUUL unions would be successful only if militants also actively worked to organize from within and from "below" in the established unions. They thus fostered "united-front-from-below tactics" in the AFL and independent unions. With this dual strategy, the NTWIU won a number of early strikes in New York City in 1931. Unlike elsewhere in the country, where TUUL unions languished in the early years of the Depression, in New York they grew, with membership increasing from 8,500 to 17,000 in the four months between October 1931 and February 1932. Organizers estimated that through various means, the TUUL had "direct organizing contact" with 115,000 New York workers in this period and that its "ideological influence" was even greater still. Between August 1931 and February 1932 TUUL-affiliated unions led around 11,000 New York workers out on strike both to stop wage cuts and to win wage increases. They won 65 percent of the time.[5]

New York's communist unions had their greatest effects in the needle trades and among smaller companies. They were less successful in organizing the basic industries and big industry-leading firms. Outside of the needle trades, they also had little success, and concentrated little effort, on organizing women workers and African Americans. With the passage of the National Industrial Recovery Act in 1933, union membership boomed across the United States, and strike activity blossomed, with perhaps a million workers walking out on strike in the first ten months of the year. TUUL union membership grew to 125,000 nationally, compared to the AFL's 2.8 million. Still, TUUL unions led nearly half as many strikes as did the AFL. New York City accounted for 45,000 of the TUUL's 125,000 members, with NTWIU boasting more than 18,000 workers and the Shoe Leather Workers' Industrial Union (SLWIU) accounting for another 8,500. In the city, these two unions and other TUUL affiliates took more than 65,000 workers out on strike during the first ten months of 1933, winning union recognition, pay increases, and shared work agreements for slack times. In one case (bathrobe workers), they won a thirty-five-hour workweek. The SLWIU and the NTWIU attributed their success to both the militancy of their own unions and their ability to create a "united front from below." Indeed, the NTWIU had a good deal of success on this front among clothing workers: after a fur workers' strike, just about the whole of the International Fur Workers' New York branch defected to the NTWIU (leading to a similar defection in Philadelphia); the NTWIU also succeeded in forming significant oppositional cadres within the Cloth Hat, Cap, and Millinery Workers' and the Tailors' Unions. More broadly, Red organizers gained control over independent Hod Car-

An estimated ten thousand people gathered at a Communist rally at Union Square, August 1, 1932, part of a worldwide protest against war. Signs also demand the Scottsboro Boys be released.
AP Photo.

riers' and Alteration Painters' Unions. When the Hat Workers' Union struck in late 1933, TUUL organizing from below led members to reject a "sellout settlement" made by union leadership and win a further 15 percent wage increase.[6] By mid-1934, however, worker militancy had begun to be re-directed, as the Comintern brought the Third Period to a close and began to focus instead on a united popular front against fascism.[7]

The CPUSA did not concentrate only on organizing at the point of production: its conception of the "working class" was much broader than that. As the Depression deepened and unemployment skyrocketed, the party determined that the struggle of the unemployed was "the tactical key to the present state of the class struggle." It threw many of its resources into building a movement of the unemployed. Communist Party organizers worked in poor and working-class neighborhoods throughout American cities to build a move-ment of Unemployed Councils. The movement was strongest in New York.[8]

Like Communist Party organizing in the trade unions, Communist Party organizing of the unemployed predated the Wall Street crash, but the formal initiation of the Unemployed Council movement took place in 1930. In March the party-organized International Unemployment Day saw demonstrations across the country and around the world. The police riot against the demonstrators in New York's Union Square—"Hundreds of policemen and detectives swinging nightsticks, blackjacks and bare fists, rushed into the crowd, hitting out at all with whom they came in contact," according to the *New York Times*—garnered a great deal of popular sympathy for the unemployed and brought more militants into the fold. This and other mass demonstrations in New York, together with the appearance of shanties in Central Park and empty lots, tent cities along the riverbanks, and (once again) large numbers of the poor descending on police stations for shelter, eventually pressured the New York City Board of Estimate to appropriate a million dollars for unemployment relief.[9]

The party assigned dozens of members, many of whom were themselves unemployed workers, to serve as organizers to build the Unemployed Councils. Organizers fanned out into the neighborhoods and among the shanties to reach unemployed people, to stage demonstrations, and to build local councils. Council organizers seemed indefatigable—and everywhere. They went to relief centers where people were trying to get benefits. They went to factories where unemployed workers were demanding jobs. They went to soup kitchens, shelters, and street corners, listening to people's frustrations and encouraging them to join the struggle.[10]

As the Unemployed Council movement grew, the organizing method shifted from mass demonstrations to localized actions targeting relief agencies that were denying benefits to unemployed people. Many people had a hard time getting the bureaucracies to move on their own, and they turned to the Unemployed Councils for help. In response, the councils organized groups of unemployed people to go to the nearest relief office and demand benefits. If they were refused, they would stage sit-ins until their demands were met or they were arrested. When threatened with arrest, protesters often fought back. In June 1932, for example, council members stormed a Harlem relief office, broke down its door, and "overturned desks and chairs" before they were arrested. Across the city, demonstrations frequently "ended in pitched battles between police and Council activists that resulted in bloodied heads and numerous arrests."[11] Communist organizations believed not only that confrontational tactics were central to winning concrete benefits but also that they would serve to expose the violent nature of the capitalist system. Violent confrontation became commonplace in the city. All New York's relief agencies reported regular engagement with the communist-led unemployment organizations. In one mid-1930s study of five of the city's forty-two relief agencies, social workers reported that unemployed organizations made 196 demands over the course of thirty days and were granted 107 of them.[12]

The Harlem Unemployed Council was one of New York's strongest. Unemployment in that part of the city stretched to 80 percent at times, making clear just how class was shaped by racism (and vice versa). The party thus invested heavily in organizing the unemployed in Harlem, seeing it as vital to the party's efforts to fight racism—in the wake of the black national question resolutions—even as the party struggled against unemployment. By 1935 the Harlem chapter was the largest in the city, reporting a membership of three thousand.[13]

Unemployed Council militancy proved effective. Besides winning increased relief from the city's Board of Estimate, the councils won $20 million in relief from the state in 1931.

Police arresting rent strikers, Bronx, 1932.
Sueddeutsche Zeitung Photo / Alamy Stock Photo.

Grassroots unemployed workers' struggles also laid the groundwork for New Deal policies like the Works Progress Administration and Social Security.[14]

Besides fighting for relief, the Unemployed Councils also set to work organizing tenants. High rates of unemployment meant many in the working class could not meet their rent and therefore faced eviction. During the Great Depression, eviction rates doubled and then tripled.[15]

Eviction resistance was the Communist Party's first strategy. When tenants were being thrown out of their homes, party organizers would pick up their furniture and move it back in. Sometimes the police would intervene, but in most cases, the communists were able to "unevict" people peacefully. Whenever necessary, organizers would call on community members for support, pulling together spontaneous demonstrations of hundreds of people. Though only a short-term solution in most cases, "uneviction" bought struggling

tenants time in which to scare up their rent. There were hundreds of such eviction resistance actions in the early 1930s in the neighborhoods hit hardest by the Depression: Harlem, the Lower East Side, Hell's Kitchen, the South Bronx, Brownsville, and Coney Island.[16]

In 1931 the Unemployed Councils initiated a second strategy: rent strikes. In addition to putting working-class people back in their homes, Communist Party organizers now worked to get rents reduced. If workers were being paid less, they reasoned, they should not have to pay as much for housing. Rent strikes spread slowly at first, but when they finally caught on they spread like wildfire, leading to the Great Rent Strike War of 1932. The "war" began in January in a group of three large apartment buildings in the mostly eastern European Jewish neighborhood of Bronx Park East, organized by the Upper Bronx Unemployed Council. Tenants in the buildings went on strike, demanding a 15 percent reduction in rent and a moratorium on evictions. When marshals and landlords tried to evict seventeen striking families from the building at 2302 Olinville Avenue, they fought back. More than four thousand people joined the "rent riot," throwing bottles and brickbats or urging the combatants on from the sidelines. Before squadrons of police reinforcements could quell the uprising, strikers barricaded themselves in the buildings and managed to negotiate reduced rent and the return of evicted families to their apartments.

The action moved on to 665 Allerton Avenue, where a riot nearly as big erupted as marshals tried to remove three families from their homes. Women led the charge. But this time the police, in the form of more than fifty foot and mounted officers, together with an army of marshals and moving men, succeeded in evicting the families. Hoping to break the strikes, landlords, including at 665 Allerton, pushed for arbitration (even as they organized and raised funds to break the strikes and provide legal assistance to all landlords who needed it). Strikers resisted, though not always successfully. Even so, strikes spread, particularly to other militant, mostly Jewish neighborhoods across the Bronx (Crotona Park East, Morrisania, and Melrose) and Brooklyn (Brownsville,

Williamsburg, and Boro Park). The war lasted too: more than two hundred buildings went on strike in the Bronx in 1933. Over and over in January and February 1932, then again in December and on into January 1933, pitched battles erupted. The battles could be fierce, with skirmishes involving thousands of strikers and their supporters and hundreds of police and lasting hours at a time. Arrests reached into the hundreds and then the thousands. The strike spread to tenements and artists' colonies in the Lower East Side. The movement went citywide.[17]

The landlords' counterthrust was strong. They won injunctions against picketing. They rallied the cops and the marshals to their side. In the heat of a strike, the streets could seem like a war zone. During a strike in Brownsville, according to the *Daily Worker*, "the police have set up a temporary police station outside one of the buildings. Cops patrol the street all day. The entire territory is under semi-martial law. People are driven around the streets, off the corners, and away from the houses." Landlords convinced prosecutors to prepare indictments for "criminal conspiracy" against strike leaders. They drew up "red lists" of banned tenants, and demanded that the mayor take the lead in suppressing the strike. The city corporation counsel responded by declaring the picketing of apartment houses to be illegal and authorizing the police to arrest any and all picketers, no matter how peaceful. The counsel's ruling had an effect: the number of strikes quickly dwindled; the strike epidemic faded.*

The Unemployed Councils shifted tactics once again.

---

* Rent strikes were rekindled in the summer of 1934, but not under CPUSA leadership. One developed among middle-class black residents in Sugar Hill, Harlem, to protest high rents and deteriorating conditions as the neighborhood switched from white to black. Not only was the strike a success (in part because La Guardia refused to enforce his predecessor's no-picketing ruling), it also led to the formation of the Consolidated Tenants' League, which proved to be an especially effective organization in protecting tenant rights. Another strike in the middle-class and professional Knickerbocker Village on the Manhattan side of the Brooklyn Bridge won most of its demands while creating a large cadre of newly radicalized political activists.

While continuing to block evictions, Unemployed Council–organized tenants began a series of sit-ins at relief bureaus, refusing to leave until they were given funds to pay rent. The city responded more progressively this time, instituting a policy preventing evictions until the "rent consultant of the home relief bureau" had been informed and given an opportunity to provide aid. Evictions slowed; government involvement in the rental market became acceptable. The new La Guardia mayoral administration, pressured by reformist housing activists, themselves pressured by the communists on their left, lobbied for a program of mass low-rent public housing (in part to replace the millions of dilapidated Old Law tenement units that were at the heart of many of the strikes).† The foundation for a lasting tenants' movement—and for public housing—in New York had been laid.[18]

Organizing Women

The CPUSA's dual organizing focus—factories and shop floors through the unions, and neighborhoods through the Unemployed Councils—suggested an understanding that working-class struggles extended across all phases of life, from economic production to social reproduction. Moreover, throughout the Depression decade, women were on the front lines of many of the rent strikes; women and girl workers proved to be some of the most militant among the factory strikers. The party thus understood that organizing work among working-class women—in the factory, in the home, and on the streets—was vital to the class struggle. This signaled a significant (if temporary) shift in analysis and strategic orientation, one that laid the groundwork for party members' future contributions to the women's liberation movement.[19]

On the front lines, women were militant. During the

---

† Old Law tenements were those built after the Tenement House Act of 1879 (see chapter 7) and the New York State Tenement House Act of 1901. They required better ventilation, outward-facing windows for all rooms, indoor toilets, and other improvements.

"rent riots," when the police would charge a crowd, women would rush in to try to shield the men who were likely to be targeted by the police. They also defended the home space. As one woman activist described it, "On the day of evictions, we would tell all the men to leave the building. We knew the police were rough and would beat them up. It was the women who remained in the apartments, in order to resist. We went out onto the fire escapes and spoke through bullhorns to the crowd gathered below." The women would also boil pots of water and threaten to dump them onto the heads of any police officers or marshals who attempted to enter the buildings.[20]

Beyond their work in the Unemployed Councils, women party members came together in the United Council of Working Class Women (UCWCW), a national party-affiliated women's organization that organized around tenant rights, relief, and the rising cost of food.* The UCWCW came together to fight on issues that impacted women's traditional roles as wives and mothers: rent, food prices, schools, and clothing for their children. One Communist Party organizer said, "Work among these women is not difficult. . . . [A]ll working class mothers would fight with their very lives to obtain a better life for their babies." By 1931 the UCWCW had established forty-eight branches in New York City alone.[21]

The UCWCW organized meat and bread boycotts across the city, beginning in Jewish neighborhoods but rapidly spreading to other communities. In addition to Jewish women, black women in Harlem were particularly active in the boycotts. The largest of the meat boycotts took place

in 1935.† Beginning on May 22, women set up pickets outside butcher shops around the city, demanding a reduction in prices. As usual, police responded with arrests. For his part, Mayor La Guardia called on the federal government to reduce meat prices while fielding intense pressure from the New York State Retail Meat Dealers' Association, which made it be known that it would call in "gangsters" to put an end to the strike. The UCWCW decided to call off the boycott, but not before organizing mass protests in front of wholesale meat distribution centers. The effect was electrifying. Instead of winding down, women intensified their boycott in New York, and the movement quickly spread across the country (with strikes in Los Angeles, Philadelphia, Boston, St. Louis, Kansas City, and elsewhere, including a near-general strike in Detroit). In New York, pickets lasted for more than four weeks, shutting down more than forty-five hundred businesses in a militant protest against what Clara Lemlich Shavelson called the "meat packer millionaires."[22]

The *Daily Worker* described the meat boycott in Harlem: "More than a thousand customers formed a flying squad and moved down Lenox Avenue holding meetings in front of all the open stores. All stores between 129th Street and 145th Street . . . have reduced prices by 25%. So great was the sense of power of the workers that when butchers agreed to lower prices, housewives jumped up on the tables in front of the stores and tore down the old price signs and put up new ones. . . . No store held out for more than five minutes after the pickets arrived."[23]

Fighting for the Black Nation

While such scenes were common across the city, they were particularly intense in Harlem, where the CPUSA focused particular attention. The Depression bit deeply into black

---

* The UCWCW was an outgrowth of the earlier United Council of Working Class House Wives, of which Clara Lemlich Shavelson, the heroine of the 1909 garment workers' strike—the Uprising of the Twenty Thousand—was the founder. "Lemlich" was still a famous name in New York in the 1920s, and so Clara, blacklisted from the garment industry, used her married name, Shavelson, almost exclusively as she became an important Communist Party organizer in the city. In the wake of the meat boycott, she ran for the New York State Assembly on the party ticket, failing to win, but doing quite well for a third-party candidate.

† The boycott movement began in Chicago as a series of mass women-led protests at the stockyards. By early summer meat boycotts were being organized in a number of cities across the United States.

Harlem protest against the Scottsboro Boys' conviction.
Everett Collection Historical / Alamy Stock Photo.

communities, exposing and exacerbating the racially stratified nature of the class system in the United States. The unemployment rate for black workers was more than twice that of white workers, and eviction rates in Harlem were nearly triple those in white neighborhoods. The CPUSA responded quickly. It had been active in Harlem before the stock market crash. Black communist Richard Moore formed the militant Harlem Tenants League in mid-1929 to fight the expiration of rent control laws and to expose the complicity of black landlords and churches in profiting from segregation. Moore wrote, "The capitalist caste system, which segregates Negro workers into Jim Crow districts makes these doubly exploited Black workers the special prey of rent gougers. Black and white landlords and real estate agents take advantage of this segregation to squeeze the last nickel out of the Negro working class who are penned in the Black ghetto. Rents in Negro Harlem are already double and sometimes

triple those in other sections of the city." The league sponsored marches and organized tenants in buildings, preparing the ground for the rent strikes to follow a few years later.[24]

Besides its work in Harlem on rent (through the Harlem Tenants League and the Unemployed Councils), beginning in 1931, the CPUSA was centrally involved in agitation around and support for the Scottsboro Boys, nine young black Alabama boys facing the death penalty on charges of raping a white woman. Civil rights organizations like the National Association for the Advancement of Colored People (NAACP) at first thought the case was too controversial to touch. The CPUSA jumped in, providing legal support through its International Labor Defense Fund (ILD). By June 1933 the Harlem ILD had nine chapters, each named after a different Scottsboro Boy, and claimed a membership of seventeen hundred. The party organized demonstrations, raised money, and promoted the case of the Scottsboro Nine wherever it could. Party-organized demonstrations in Harlem drew thousands of participants—and not infrequently a violent response from the police. At a March 1934 demonstration, for example, the cops drew their batons and guns and beat several demonstrators, including a young girl.* The Communist Party's work on the Scottsboro defense—which succeeded in saving the young men from the death penalty—earned it a great deal of respect from many in Harlem.[25]

The Communist Party also organized around a range of other issues of concern to the black community. It fought police brutality and job discrimination in Harlem, organized against lynching in the South, and promoted solidarity with Ethiopia against the Italian invasion. The party's work against racism attracted the support of a number of prominent Harlem intellectuals and artists, some of whom became members of the party, while others were "fellow travelers" (allies), including Claude McKay, Ralph Ellison, Langston Hughes, and Richard Wright.[26]

The party's work against racism was not restricted to its black members; white party members were expected to participate actively in campaigns against racism. They were expected to challenge interpersonal racist practices, termed "white chauvinism" by the party. The CPUSA's internal work against white chauvinism entailed extensive political education for its white members and reprimands (including public trials and expulsions) for members who continued to be white chauvinists.†[27]

The Popular Front

Communist Party strategies began to shift in 1933 for both international reasons (the need for a united front to fight fascism) and internal ones (the success of united-front-from-below tactics, a shifting union and housing landscape with the election of Roosevelt's New Deal government, etc.).‡ Third Period purism had shown its limitations: a purist commitment to militant struggle did not always reflect the needs or culture of the working-class communities the communists were trying to organize, and party members realized they needed to shift strategy, as well as ideology. Divisive denunciations of other political actors did not advance party members' work to build effective campaigns, nor did it help the party legitimize itself in working-class communities. Local organizers began extending united front tactics to include building relationships with other leftist organizations (not just boring from within) and liberals more generally. The need for a broader-based, more collaborative struggle became even clearer as New Deal policies began to have their effect. Make-work projects through the Works Progress Administration, pension and income security through the Social Security Act, and forms of immediate relief sapped the Unemployed Councils as mass organizations as members drifted away, now that their immediate needs were being better met.§ The party's fiery rhetoric had less purchase now that working people could see hope on the horizon.[28]

In 1935 President Roosevelt signed into law the National Labor Relations Act, further encouraging the boom in unionization that the National Industrial Recovery Act had unleashed. It enshrined into law the right to unionize, strike,

---

* Although the chief police inspector found that officers had used excessive force, the police commissioner exonerated the officers involved.

† The CPUSA's work to challenge white chauvinism extended even to the point of providing dance classes to its white male members so they would not be intimidated to ask black women to dance at interracial party functions.

‡ With Hitler's rise to power in 1933, the Comintern questioned its previous assumption that the international communist revolution was imminent, and now with the German invasion of the Soviet Union possible, maybe even likely, the Comintern called on its forces around the world to enter into alliances to counteract the spread of fascism both within the capitalist democracies and geopolitically. The Comintern thus called on its parties to develop broad united or "popular" fronts.

§ In 1936 the CPUSA resolved to ally with the New Deal Democratic Party, becoming at first critical supporters of the New Deal and then active advocates for it. Many party activists took positions in New Deal agencies like the Works Progress Administration and fought for progressive change from within. In doing so, the party gained a good deal of public legitimacy and attracted new members, but it also toned down its revolutionary critique of capitalism.

and bargain collectively. Industrial unionism (organizing across whole industries, rather than in crafts), which had been the hallmark of the Industrial Workers of the World and then TUUL unions, took off with the founding of the Congress of Industrial Organizations (CIO) the same year. As grassroots strikes and industrial union drives took off in basic industries, the CIO quickly became the major vehicle for the expression of working-class power in the United States. The CPUSA responded by dismantling the TUUL and redeploying party organizers into CIO unions, abandoning the Unemployed Councils and UCWCW along the way.[29]

Communists came to play a central role in the CIO. Drawing on a cadre of organizers who had gained valuable organizing experience over the past five years, the party provided many of the CIO's most experienced and dedicated front-line organizers. As party members gained more influence within the CIO, however, they risked losing touch with the foundations of the labor movement. Over time, the party also toned down its advocacy of worker militancy and its challenges to racism in the unions. Many of the black community leaders, artists, and intellectuals who had gravitated to the party in the early 1930s were disillusioned by these actions.[30]

But then events on the streets of New York began to overtake the communists and their Popular Front allies, especially in Harlem.

CHAPTER 12

The Harlem Riots, 1935, 1943, and 1964

NICOLE WATSON

"A Ghetto Mutiny," 1935

Tuesday, March 19, 1935, 2:30 p.m., the Kress 5–10–25¢ store on 125th Street. Sixteen-year-old Lino Rivera—variously described in the papers and later reports as a "dusky little Puerto Rican," "colored," and a "young Negro boy"—slipped a ten-cent penknife into his pocket. He was spotted by the store manager, Jackson Smith, and his assistant, Charles Hurley, and grabbed on his way out the door. Smith and Hurley threatened the boy (depending on the source, either with slicing him with the knife he was stealing or with being taken "down in the basement [to] beat the hell out of him"). In fear, Rivera frantically bit his captors' hands. As the commotion escalated, a sales girl fainted, and black customers—*Time* magazine claimed some five hundred of them—began yelling and overturning counters.[1]

Matters quickly grew confused. According to *Time*'s sensational account, as an overwhelmed police officer, Donahue, rushed to the scene and attempted to quell the melee, Rivera escaped from the store. Not convinced he was free, the crowd insisted on learning of his whereabouts only to be told by backup police arriving on the scene that it was none of their business. In hopes of gaining control of the situation, the cops began pushing patrons toward the door, infuriating the shoppers and heightening suspicions that something had happened to Rivera. In other versions, thinking the shoplift-

ing was a "relatively unimportant case of juvenile pilfering," Smith instructed Donahue to let the would-be thief go without arrest. In order to avoid the curious and excited crowd, Donahue decided to escort Rivera out of the store through the basement rear entrance on 124th Street. Seeing Rivera taken to the basement, a "hysterical Negro woman" cried out that Rivera was being taken away to be beaten.[2]

Confusion mounted inside the store and out on the sidewalk on 125th Street. With no sign of Rivera, rumors flew. An ambulance arrived but soon left empty. Then a hearse arrived. Normally it was garaged on 124th, but its driver pulled up in front of Kress to visit his brother-in-law. The departure of the empty ambulance and the arrival of the hearse fueled speculation that Rivera had been killed. Many out on the streets were newly arrived in Harlem from the South—part of the post–World War I Great Migration—and memories of lynching and police connivance with vigilantism were fresh. As the Mayor's Commission on Conditions in Harlem later suggested, Rivera's disappearance "awakened the deep-seated sense of wrongs and denials and even memories of injustice in the South," as well as "the smoldering resentments of the people of Harlem against racial discrimination and poverty in the midst of plenty."[3]

The police ordered a group of men assembling at a nearby street corner to disperse. Instead, the men moved to the front of the store and set up a speakers' stand. As speak-

In hopes of saving his store, a proprietor proclaims its colored ownership during the 1935. AP Photo.

ers rose to address the people, cops pulled them down and charged them with "unlawful assemblage," further incensing the crowd. Rumors of Rivera being beaten and possibly dying spread rapidly, making their way to the headquarters of the Young Liberators, a predominantly black organization with some communist members. When the group's president, Joseph Taylor, was turned away from a nearby police station where he was attempting to verify the rumors, the Young Liberators printed and circulated a leaflet announcing that a child had been brutally beaten and was near death. The leaflet called for black and white workers to protest "this Lynch attack," boycott Kress, and stop police brutality. The Young Communist League quickly got out its own version of the leaflet.[4]

But by the time these leaflets hit the street at around 7:30 p.m., the rioting was already in full swing. In the unsympathetic words of *Time*, "Harlem gave itself over to riot, pillage, and bloodshed." First targeted was the Kress store itself, which was pelted with debris. As the crowd swelled—to as many as three thousand—rioting spread along 125th from Seventh Avenue to Lenox. Windows were smashed and stores were looted. Clusters of rioters sprang up spontaneously as rumors spread. The crowds were dispersed by police and quickly re-formed. The sounds of screaming sirens, pistol shots, and breaking glass filled the air. The mood of looters seemed both resentful and playful, as if (the mayor's commission reported) looting was an opportunity for the people of Harlem "to seize what rightfully belonged to them but had long been withheld."[5]

Black shopkeepers quickly put up signs in their windows:

Police making arrests during the 1935 Harlem Riot.
Bettmann / Getty Images.

descended on Harlem in squad cars, on horses, and by foot. The battle was pitched. Cops waded into crowds with nightsticks swinging and pistols raised. Before the night was over, two African Americans were killed. Between thirty and sixty more were injured, including a handful the police described as "robbers," whom the police shot. At least three officers were hospitalized after being hit by stones and bottles. Black rioters were blamed for beating a white man to death. The first black man killed was a "robber," gunned down by the police. The second was Lloyd Hobbs, a sixteen-year-old on his way home from the movies after midnight with his brother, Russell. On their way home, the brothers were attracted to a crowd gathered on Seventh Avenue near 128th Street. When police approached with guns drawn, the crowd ran. But instead of following others northward, Lloyd crossed 129th Street diagonally. Without warning, patrolman John Heineray fired a fatal shot. The mayor's commission was unsparing in its condemnation of Hobbs's killing: "The shooting of Lloyd Hobbs . . . on the night of the riot was inexcusable and brutal on the part of the police." The commission dismissed as fabrications police reports that Lloyd had participated in the looting and was carrying stolen goods.[7]

The Harlem Renaissance Boiling Over

Contemporaries variously diagnosed the riot as "a depression spasm, a Ghetto mutiny, a radical plot and a dress rehearsal of proletarian revolution," as the African American writer and "Dean of the Harlem Renaissance," Alain Locke, put it not long after the events.[8] Many outside Harlem blamed communists (who had been active in Harlem all during the Depression), especially the Young Communist League and the Young Liberators. *Time* claimed that "the affair would probably have ended had not a mischiefmaking band of youthful Harlem Reds calling themselves the Young Liberators seized upon the incident as material for a demonstration." Picking up the theme, the district attorney of New York County, William C. Dodge, "attributed the whole affair to a communist plot" and indicted sixteen so-called ring-

"COLORED STORE." Some white merchants followed suit: "COLORED HELP EMPLOYED HERE." A Chinese laundryman announced in his window: "ME COLORED TOO." The Harlem Merchants Association telegraphed Governor Herbert Lehman in Albany, calling for the National Guard to be dispatched (the request went unheeded).[6]

As merchants boarded up their stores, a Fifth Avenue bus was stoned, and so was a squadron of white police officers when they arrived on the scene. Swarms of police

leaders, including "a bumptious young white radical from nearby College of the City of New York."[9]

New York was, of course, no stranger to riotous violence—by both mobs and police. And racial violence had been part of the landscape from the beginning. But earlier skirmishes between rent strikers and the police notwithstanding, this was the first full-scale riot in Harlem. Harlem was a recent center of black residence and black cultural life, only really developing after the Tenderloin Riot of 1900 and the extension of the Lenox Avenue subway in 1904 and through the inducement of realtors and developers who had overbuilt and, in the midst of the 1904–5 recession, saw migrating black residents as a possible solution to their economic predicament. As black New Yorkers pushed north out of the Tenderloin and San Juan Hill, they were joined by thousands of southern blacks who had arrived as part of the Great Migration, looking for new opportunities in New York's burgeoning World War I industries.* By 1920 New York's black population had reached nearly a quarter million, and Harlem had become the cultural capital of black life in America, home to pioneering black intellectuals, poets, musicians, and artists such as Langston Hughes and Zora Neale Hurston, Billie Holiday and Duke Ellington. Harlem was not just a place but a cultural and intellectual movement.

But beneath this shiny facade lurked a Harlem where discrimination and poor housing were commonplace—the Harlem that the CPUSA, the Harlem Tenants League, the Unemployed Councils, and other communists like the Young Liberators and the Young Communist League worked hard to organize.† The poor population grew fast. Between 1910 and 1935 the black population in Harlem increased 600 percent, resulting in population densities 75 percent greater than the average for Manhattan. The block bounded by 138th and 139th Streets and Lenox and Seventh Avenues was the densest in the city by the mid-1930s, with 630 persons per acre.[10]

Rents for black households were steep—15 to 20 percent higher than in immigrant French, German, Italian, and Jewish quarters, according to the Urban League. Many black households paid more than 50 percent of their income in rent. Residents made do by doubling up and taking in lodgers. One of the worst blocks in Harlem, the block bounded by 133rd and 134th Streets and Lenox and Seventh Avenues housed no fewer than 301 families in twenty-one houses, nine of which were condemned. Conditions in general were bad. Much of Harlem's housing was characterized as "unsanitary," "dilapidated," and even "totally unfit for human habitation," as the Harlem Renaissance gave way to the Depression.[11]

And it was not as if Harlem residents could easily escape these conditions. Barriers to housing mobility were everywhere evident. Harlem's growing black population was both implicitly and explicitly barred from free movement within the city. Signs announcing lodging "for whites only" or for "respectable people only" were not uncommon across the city. That segregation was the natural order seemed like common sense to many. As the concentration of black families grew in Harlem, whites who remained were routinely described as "marooned" (if not simply stubborn). Racially restrictive covenants were common in white neighborhoods.‡ One association of property owners and residents successfully forced black families to move east of Convent Avenue between 135th and 168th Streets, where landlords charged exorbitantly for dilapidated units largely abandoned by immigrant whites.[12]

The labor market mimicked the exclusion and isolation that black people felt in the city's neighborhoods. As the Mayor's Commission on Conditions in Harlem noted after the riot, the same excuses "used for nearly a century to prevent the Negro from competing on an equal basis with

---

* San Juan Hill is now occupied by Lincoln Center.

† Reporting on the riot, *Time* declared that what many saw as a "Nigger Heaven" had by the Depression become a "Nigger Hell."

‡ Racially restrictive covenants proliferated in tandem with the Great Migration as a means of creating and enforcing neighborhood-scale segregation. Such covenants were not declared "unenforceable" by the Supreme Court until 1948 (in *Shelley v. Kraemer*, 344 U.S. 1 [1948]), and even then they remained a part of many property deeds.

whites" perpetuated entrenched patterns of employment discrimination. For example, the Fifth Avenue Coach Company "maintained a caste system in regard to employment of Negroes." Black workers were often excluded from unions (except Communist Party–affiliated ones) and confined to menial work with menial pay. According to sociologists of the time, economic discrimination against New York's black residents led to "a tragic train of unemployment, undernourishment, bad housing, disease, vice, [and] unrest." High food prices in Harlem contributed to high rates of malnutrition. Boycotts of white merchants who refused to hire black employees achieved few results (even as CPUSA boycotts of bakers and butchers did lead to lower prices).* By 1935 only a few light-skinned black clerks had been hired in white-owned stores (whatever the signs hastily posted in stores during the riot may have implied). Relations with police were always tense, as the heavy-handed response to the Scottsboro Boys demonstrations attested.[13]

The riot that followed Lino Rivera's disappearance was "like a revealing flash of lightning" (as Alain Locke put it) that suddenly illuminated for a broad public the Harlem already familiar to social workers, street-corner orators, an emerging radical press, and, of course, its residents. It exposed a dark reality that was every bit as much a part of Harlem as was its renaissance and its earlier speakeasies for slumming whites. But as with a lightning flash, it is sometimes hard to understand just what has been so fleetingly revealed.[14]

Mayor La Guardia quickly appointed the Commission on Conditions in Harlem to investigate the social and economic circumstances underlying the explosion that ignited on March 19. The commission was chaired by Dr. Charles H. Roberts, a respected black reformer who had long been dedicated to social, economic, and cultural advancement in Harlem, and was composed of a mix of esteemed black and white academics and community leaders. Beginning on March 30, the commission held twenty-one public hearings

and four closed hearings at the Seventh District Municipal Building on 131st Street. In addition, it commissioned Howard University sociologist E. Franklin Frazier to lead an eight-month investigation of social and economic issues in Harlem with the assistance of a staff of thirty men and women from the Home Relief Bureau. The resulting 127-page report, *The Negro in Harlem: A Report on Social and Economic Conditions Responsible for the Outbreak of March 19, 1935*, dug deeply into issues of employment, education, health, housing, and crime and was highly critical of the city government in allowing conditions in Harlem to fester.† The commission ultimately attributed the riot to a host of social and economic conditions, including indifference or racism among public officials, economic deprivation, and racial discrimination. Everything that had bubbled below the surface of the Harlem Renaissance and the slide into the Depression had boiled over.

The report also debunked the political agitator / communist plot conspiracy theories that had gained much currency among segments of New York society, noting that the Young Liberators and Young Communist League leaflets were not distributed until after the disorder and attacks against property were well under way. Moreover, the commission concluded that the activities of both black and white radical leaders may have had some influence in pushing the crowd to target property rather than people during the riot. After initially being indicted as the riot's primary cause, communist groups were eventually touted as deserving "more credit than any other element in Harlem for preventing physical conflict between whites and blacks." This distinction between persons and property marked a shift in the nature of "race riots." Instead of riots being characterized by white mobs attacking black victims (as with the 1900 Tenderloin Riot), the riot of 1935 was distinguished by black destruction of white property. It thereby highlighted the inextricable link between race and class in the black Harlem experience.[15]

Once the commission's findings became public, La Guar-

---

* The "Don't Buy Where You Can't Work" boycott campaign collapsed in 1934, a year before the riot.

† Mayor La Guardia was reluctant to release the report, sitting on it for several months until it was leaked to the *Amsterdam News* in July 1936.

dia made efforts to appoint black people to city offices and to speak to black audiences in Harlem, but little was done to improve economic conditions. Segregation remained embedded in official policy, with the Public Works Administration and later housing authorities continuing to build housing projects that reflected the racial composition of neighborhoods—that is, that perpetuated segregation. Other departments that operated with relative autonomy, like the police department, were insulated from political challenges to racist practices. Thus, although the 1935 riot triggered a public response that documented (though did not voluntarily publicize) evidence of racism, discrimination, and isolation, buttressing black people's complaints, conditions in Harlem were slow to change.[16]

Wartime Riots, 1943

Conditions were slow to change, but they did change, at least a bit. Black activism in particular and the New Deal more generally led to improved access to health care, education, and political participation in Harlem as the Depression decade wore on. The Harlem Renaissance continued to echo, reinforcing the belief that for African Americans there were few places better than New York, despite the persistence of poor housing, inadequate educational and recreational facilities, and unequal opportunities for work. And though his government balked at the sort of structural changes necessary for it to happen, Mayor La Guardia's public political commitment to racial fairness was attractive to many.[17]

As war in Europe heated up and American involvement seemed inevitable, the economy picked up as new defense industries developed and older manufacturing plants were retooled to meet growing demands for armaments. Gains for African American workers were sluggish and muted compared to those for their white counterparts, however. In response to discrimination against black job seekers in war industries, union activist A. Philip Randolph threatened a mass march on Washington in 1941. Widespread grassroots support for the demonstration led President Franklin D.

Roosevelt to issue Executive Order 8802 (June 25, 1941), which prohibited racial discrimination in defense industries. Symbolically important, the order did not in fact end discrimination.* Racial tensions were rarely far below the surface in the industrial regions of the United States, and on June 20, 1943, violence erupted in Detroit in a massive race riot that was calmed only after federal troops were dispatched to the city.[18]

In Harlem, matters were just as uneasy. Overcrowding in the district persisted, with three hundred thousand people living in housing better suited for seventy-five thousand, according to press reports. Laws prohibiting discrimination in housing and hiring were frequently ignored. All summer long tensions mounted, until the storm broke on Sunday, August 1. The day began typically enough, with Harlemites strolling down sidewalks in their Sunday best—bright print dresses for women, uniforms for servicemen, and zoot suits for young sharps. Mrs. Florine Roberts, an African American maid from Middletown, Connecticut, had traveled to the city for the weekend to visit her son, Private Robert Bandy, and his fiancée. Like many others enjoying that warm summer day in Harlem, Mrs. Roberts and her son had come north as part of the Great Migration. Robert had been born in Alabama, but the two had made their way north to Connecticut, where Robert was raised. Robert, now twenty-six and a member of the Army's Military Police Battalion stationed in Jersey City, was on leave from his post across the Hudson. As a domestic worker, Mrs. Roberts was likely of limited means and was staying at the seedy Braddock Hotel on the southeast corner of 126th Street at Eighth Avenue during her visit. The hotel had developed a reputation for prostitution and hosted an imposing police presence that was especially unfriendly to mixed-race couples. A policeman had been stationed in the lobby since a string of brawls earlier in the summer. But Mrs. Roberts didn't let the un-

---

* The continuing segregation of the military made it clear that the government still officially sanctioned discrimination. That segregation led to a great deal of resentment among black troops, who found themselves fighting for liberties they did not enjoy.

The start of the 1943 Harlem Riot.
Photo by Weegee (Arthur Fellig,
International Center of Photography /
Getty Images).

savory surroundings keep her from enjoying breakfast at the hotel with her dapper, uniformed son and future daughter-in-law on the last day of her trip.[19]

After leaving Mrs. Roberts's luggage at the hotel desk, the trio attended church and then spent the afternoon visiting with friends and going to the movies. When Robert Bandy escorted his mother back to the hotel to get her luggage at around 7:30 that evening, the pleasant weekend activities came to an abrupt end. An argument was raging in the lobby between rookie patrolman James Collins and Marjorie "Margie" Polite, an area resident.* Polite screamed profan-

* The reason the argument began is unclear. Polite lived a couple of blocks from the hotel. The best speculation is that the argument began as Polite was leaving a raucous party at the hotel.

ities at the cop and pleaded with other patrons to "protect me from this white man!" When Collins grabbed Polite in an attempt to arrest her for disturbing the peace, Bandy protested. Collins brandished his nightstick and told Bandy to mind his own business.[20]

Bandy tussled with Collins—either out of a sense of chivalry (some accounts suggest that Bandy's mother was the first to demand Polite's release) or because he was incensed by an act of perceived injustice. According to official police reports, Mrs. Roberts joined her son in the struggle, and Bandy was able to grab the patrolman's baton. He struck Collins in the head with it and made a run for the door. Though knocked to the floor, Collins was able to unholster his revolver; he shot Bandy in the back at his left shoulder.

The shot stopped Bandy in his tracks, but the wound was not serious.

Bandy's story was different. According to Bandy's account, he protested when Collins pushed Polite. Collins threw his nightstick, and Bandy caught it. In his version, Collins shot Bandy when he refused to return the stick. As a small crowd in the lobby looked on, Collins and Bandy then exited the hotel together and headed toward the Sydenham Hospital on the next block.[21]

Just like eight years before, when rumors of young Rivera's fate fanned the flames of suspicion and anger, the sound of gunfire drew a crowd in front of the hotel, and inflammatory stories spread through the streets. The story of Bandy's scuffle with Collins and his resulting shoulder wound was repackaged and retold with growing intensity as crowds as large as three thousand gathered at the hotel, hospital, and 28th Precinct headquarters on West 123rd Street. Truth mixed with exaggeration: a white policeman shot a black soldier; a black soldier was shot in the back in front of his mother; the soldier was seriously wounded, even dying.[22]

As the rumor spread that a cop had shot and maybe killed Bandy, tensions on the streets mounted, and at 10:30 rioting erupted. As James Baldwin later described the scene, African Americans "pour[ed] out of their rabbit-warren houses" and jammed the streets. While men and teenage boys were in the majority, women, teenage girls, and children joined in—and so did members of the middle classes, no matter how much contemporary commentators attributed the rioting to "hoodlums." What united the crowd was race, and since there were few white civilians around, the primary target of the crowd's animus was the police.[23]

As in 1935, businesses owned by whites (and by Jews) were the primary targets. Destruction was swift and widespread. Rioters swept up both sides of 125th Street smashing windows before continuing up and down Seventh and Eighth Avenues, where stores were gutted and entire blocks were plunged into darkness after streetlamps were smashed. The sound of sirens filled the air as the rioting spread in all directions: east to Lenox Avenue, west to St. Nicholas Avenue, north to 145th Street, and south to 110th—Central Park's northern border. Dozens of fires were set. Nearly fifteen hundred stores were damaged and looted, including grocery stores, pawn shops, and liquor stores. Thousands of windows were broken. As the night wore on, "Harlem looked like a battlefield"—quite literally. The police response was swift and large. With memories of 1935 not entirely faded, and hoping to avoid a fate similar to Detroit's a few weeks earlier, where rioting lasted for days, thousands of city police officers, state guardsmen, and civilian volunteers—including many African Americans—rushed to Harlem. Because the riot had been started by the shooting of a black soldier, scores of military police were also deployed, rolling through Harlem in jeeps and trucks in an effort to clear the streets of black servicemen.[24]

Mayor La Guardia, now in the ninth year of his tenure, enlisted a broad spectrum of Harlem's community leaders to appeal to rioters to rein in the violence. But the pleas largely went unheeded, so at 1:05 a.m., La Guardia took to the radio himself, making the first of five radio broadcasts aimed at quelling the unrest. He announced a curfew. The Braddock Hotel and all bars were closed. Efforts to dispel rumors and bring order to the streets of Harlem continued all night. The next morning, La Guardia outlined plans to replenish Harlem's food supply, which was seriously depleted by looting and store closures. A host of black volunteers joined city patrol units, military police, and air raid wardens in efforts to secure the riot area. Thousands of National Guard troops were placed on standby at metropolitan armories. Nonetheless, outbreaks of rioting continued through August 2 and 3, even as city workers fixed streetlamps and boarded up windows. By Wednesday, August 4, though, order had been restored enough for La Guardia to relax curfews and begin scaling back the police presence in the area. But by then, the damage was severe. Millions of dollars' worth of property had been damaged, six African Americans had been killed, and as many as seven hundred others had been injured. Between five hundred and a thousand people had been arrested. Dozens of law enforcement officers had been injured.[25]

Despite the extent of the destruction, the press hailed La Guardia's response to the riots. "The tinder blazed," wrote the *New York Times*, "but it did not set the city on fire. For this reassuring outcome we can thank Mayor La Guardia." In particular, the *Times* lauded the haste with which La Guardia responded and noted that, unlike in Detroit, federal troops did not have to be called in to quell the unrest.* Black leaders also praised La Guardia, along with Police Commissioner Lewis J. Valentine and U.S. Army colonel John McNulty for their work. Some black leaders, together with La Guardia, also worked hard to position the riot as *not* race based, largely in an effort to avoid condemning Harlem as a whole. As the *Times* wrote, "The rioters fought the police, among them some Negro policemen, but there were no attacks by Negro civilians on white people or by white civilians on Negroes." Edward S. Lewis, the executive secretary of the Urban League, averred that "this outbreak was not a race riot in the usual sense of the term." Similarly, Reverend Adam Clayton Powell Jr., American Labor Party city councilman and editor of the *People's Voice*, opined that the riot was "in no way racial."† For Lewis, the denial of race as foundational to the riot was important to preserving unity in a time of war, saying, "Now is not the time to fix the blame or engage in recrimination."‡[26]

If in 1935 politicians and commentators in the press were quick to blame communists for stoking unrest, by 1943, with the Soviet Union and the United States now allies, such scapegoating was more difficult. Instead, many blamed the riots on "hoodlumism," and in doing so, they were able to minimize the role of race in the riot. "Hoodlumism," the *New York Times* declared, "is not racial." Indeed, "New York City has had a shocking outbreak of hoodlumism, . . . but we have not had a race riot." Walter White, the secretary of the NAACP, condemned looters for seizing "the occasion to pillage and destroy, just as irresponsible persons always use such occasions."[27]

Yet both the *Times* and black leaders called out the underlying grievances that, while they did not justify the rioting, certainly contributed to it. There was no denying that social and economic conditions in Harlem remained dismal: "Some of the ultimate causes have been explored again and again. Bad and costly housing, lack of recreational facilities, the failure to give equal economic opportunities— these things corrupt the weak and unstable among the Negro population just as they do among other varieties of the population."[28] Like the earlier riot, the 1943 uprising gave black leaders—in this instance, Powell and the NAACP's White—a platform to address the consequences of Jim Crow proscription, job discrimination, and the high cost of housing in Harlem. Powell's People's Committee (connected to the *People's Voice* and an important vehicle of community power) advocated for Harlem rents to be "rolled back to Jan. 1, 1942 levels" and for the "appointment of Negroes to Harlem rationing boards" as a response to the underlying causes of the riot. Likewise, the City-Wide Citizens' Committee on Harlem recommended "the immediate enforcement of price ceilings," as well as additional playgrounds, recreational facilities, and summer schools.[29]

The denial of race as a causative factor in the rioting rang hollow. Race was a simmering national problem. In 1944 250 race riots erupted across forty-seven U.S. cities and towns, and black servicemen and servicewomen continued their agitation against segregation and discrimination—the perpetuation of Jim Crow—in the military. In New York, as pa-

---

* Not everyone was quite so sanguine. Conservatives complained that the La Guardia administration overrestrained the police, and Westbrook Pegler, the right-wing columnist for the *World-Telegram*, blamed La Guardia for coddling black criminals and for ignoring communist involvement in the riots.

† An activist pastor and the first African American elected to the New York City Council, Powell had participated in the "Don't Buy Where You Cannot Work" campaign and led a 1941 bus boycott in Harlem in an effort to get more black drivers and mechanics hired. He went on to have a long and distinguished career as a U.S. representative (1945–71). The American Labor Party was a left-wing alternative to the Tammany-controlled Democratic Party.

‡ For his part, Walter White, the secretary of the NAACP, linked the severity of the rioting to the fact that it had been a black soldier who had been shot, arguing that the shooting of a black civilian, no matter of what class, would not have similarly stirred the rioters' passions.

pers like the *People's Voice* publicized numerous instances of police brutality against black residents, Mayor La Guardia announced in March 1944 the formation of the Committee on Unity to "promote understanding and mutual respect among all the racial and religious groups in our city." The committee advised La Guardia and Police Commissioner Valentine to hire more black police officers. In 1943 only 155 of 16,000 officers were black, and there were only ten black detectives in Harlem. Valentine complied, but recruiting was difficult, given the historical racism of the force. He thus worked with the Urban League and the Harlem YMCA to set up training courses. Over the next decade another five hundred black officers were recruited.* More generally, the findings of the committee became a blueprint for the findings of the first President's Committee on Civil Rights, established by President Truman in 1946. The war, and the nationwide race riots that accompanied it, including in Harlem, launched the new struggle for civil rights that marked the postwar era.[30]

Civil Rights, Police Wrongs, 1964

Even as conditions of overcrowding, high rents, and job discrimination persisted in Harlem, as the civil rights movement of the 1950s gained force, the district remained a beacon, the heart of African American life and culture. But tension and unrest never disappeared. Communist activists remained active. Police brutality against black citizens remained common. The left-wing Civil Rights Congress, established in 1946, submitted a 240-page petition to the new United Nations in 1951 entitled *We Charge Genocide*, which argued that police killings were replacing lynching in America and that "the killing of Negroes has become the policy in the United States." It detailed hundreds of cases of racial assault in New York City in the five preceding years, as well as more than forty cases of police brutality and eleven police

killings of African Americans. A year later, a consultant appointed by the mayor confirmed the congress's findings and indicted the New York Police Department for lax punishment of transgressing officers. Despite reforms following a police brutality scandal in 1953, relations between New York police and the city's African American residents hardly improved.† Nonetheless, for liberal whites, such as those affiliated with the New York Civil Liberties Union, the lack of overt unrest in the streets indicated that problems of police brutality had been muted in the city.[31]

Such was not the case, and as civil rights organizations broadened their scope of concern to include northern cities, activists returned their attention to the problem of racist policing in New York City. For New York Congress on Racial Equality (CORE) chapters, police brutality was closely linked to other racist practices. In the summer of 1963, therefore, New York CORE opened a season of direct action, reviving rent strikes and school boycotts and demanding equal access to jobs, targeting the building trades in particular in a series of striking protests in which African Americans lay down in front of bulldozers and chained themselves to gates of construction sites and cranes. More than eight hundred protesters were arrested during the summer. While the protests were generally nonviolent in at least two instances, police drew their clubs and beat demonstrators. When CORE and other groups staged a sit-in at the ABC studios to protest an appearance by Alabama governor George Wallace, they were met by police violence, leading to a large picket in front of the police commissioner's office. Further protests against the police resulted from police inaction after a black man in the Bronx came to a police station to report that his car had been stolen only to be viciously beaten and scalded with hot coffee by precinct cops.[32]

In Harlem itself, distress at ongoing police brutality continued to grow. In April 1964 a small riot broke out on Lennox Avenue when police responded with swinging clubs to

---

* Historian Marilynn Johnson shows that on the whole, the midcentury NYPD understood black officers more to be "riot insurance" than officers of equal standing.

† The most significant reform was the creation of the Civilian Complaint Review Board, which in fact had no civilian members but was staffed by three police officers, who reported directly to the commissioner.

a disturbance at a fruit stand. Three teenage boys, claiming they wanted to protect smaller children from police blows, intervened. They were arrested and subsequently beaten during interrogation at the precinct station. Ten days later two of the teens were detained again—this time charged with killing two white women—and beaten once again.* Police claimed the boys were followers of Malcolm X and part of an "antiwhite gang," a claim local residents thought was incredible. Farther east, in Puerto Rican East Harlem, tensions over police brutality were just as high. While the Patrolmen's Benevolent Association, supported by the John Birch Society and other right-wing groups, dismissed claims of racial bias and brutality, black activists and white supporters demonstrated in favor of an independent police review board, eventually getting a bill before the City Council. In June 1964 the City Council's City Affairs Committee indefinitely shelved the bill, claiming more study was needed. Its timing could not have been worse.[33]

On the morning of Thursday, July 16, 1964, students attending summer school gathered in front of Senator Robert F. Wagner Junior High School in the Yorkville neighborhood of Manhattan's Upper East Side, among them fifteen-year-old James Powell from the Bronx. Powell, like many of the students waiting for school to start, was black. The superintendent of an apartment building located across the street at 215 East 76th Street, thirty-four-year-old Patrick Lynch, was washing down the sidewalk with a hose. As fourteen-year-old black student Shirley Robinson later recounted, the superintendent "didn't want anybody standing on that side of the street, . . . so he began spraying the water on everybody." She heard Lynch make racialized comments like "I'm going to wash all the black off you." The teens who had been sprayed exchanged "heated words" with the superintendent, and a physical altercation ensued—though precisely how it unfolded remains in dispute. What is not in dispute is that James Powell ended up dead.[34]

As the police told it, an off-duty police lieutenant, Thomas

* The central Harlem police precinct station was locally known as "the meat grinder."

Gilligan of Brooklyn's 14th Division, was in a television repair shop at the time and went to investigate the commotion. Three teenagers, including Powell, had pursued Lynch when he ran into the apartment building, and Gilligan "saw the boys banging on an apartment door with a garbage can lid." According to Gilligan, he ordered the teenagers to stop and flashed his police shield. But Powell came after Gilligan with a knife and failed to heed several warnings as he continued to advance. In self-defense, according to the police version, Gilligan fired his service revolver. In this account, the first shot struck Powell in the hand but did not stop him. Gilligan maintained that Powell got so close that the officer was cut on the finger, purportedly by a pocketknife the police later found in the street. Gilligan again shot at Powell and killed him.[35]

Student witnesses told a different story. Antagonized by Lynch, some students responded by throwing bottles and ash can lids at him. When Lynch fled into the apartment building, Powell followed him, without a knife, and soon emerged laughing and running. To the dismay of young onlookers, it was at this point that Gilligan shot Powell three times without warning and then turned Powell's body over with his foot. This account was supported by Beulah Barnes, an African American housewife and nurse who was at the scene that morning:

> I saw the superintendent spraying a bunch of colored kids . . . and as the kids moved back, he went after them with more water. Then someone threw an empty soda bottle, and then another bottle. Then the man went into the building and then a colored boy ran after him. The boy didn't stay two minutes. Then this tall man with black hair came out of the radio shop and he had a little black revolver. I saw that. As the boy came out, he shot him twice and then the boy fell to the sidewalk, and this man stood there for maybe 10 minutes just staring at the body. The boy never had any words with the man.[36]

Whatever the exact sequence of events, students surged into the street in response to the shooting. Policemen tried to push the crowd back to the school, and teachers worked to keep students calm. But the students' sense of outrage only escalated. "This is worse than Mississippi," girls yelled. Others cried, "Come on, shoot another nigger!" Seventy-five patrolmen in riot gear—wearing steel helmets and carrying truncheons—quickly deployed to the scene to disperse the crowd. Three screaming girls were apprehended but reportedly released after they calmed down. Transit police at the subway station at Lexington Avenue and 77th Street detained several students who had jumped the turnstile and were creating a disturbance.[37]

Yet outrage at Powell's death had not been stamped out. Much as the president of the Young Liberators had done in 1935, members of several civil rights groups made their way to the neighborhood police station at East 67th Street, seeking facts about Powell's shooting. CORE and the New York branch of the NAACP demanded an investigation. On Saturday, July 18, two days after Powell was killed, CORE shifted the focus of a rally at 125th Street and Seventh Avenue, previously planned to protest the recent disappearance of three Mississippi civil rights workers, to address Powell's death and police brutality. Members of CORE, the United African Movement, and the Harlem Progressive Labor Party (PLP) made stirring speeches, taking turns standing atop a kitchen chair. The Reverend Nelson C. Dukes of the Fountain Spring Baptist Church at 158 West 126th Street was one of the last to speak, calling for a march on the same West 123rd Street police station that had been a focal point of rioters in 1943. The rally broke up about 8:45 that evening, and Reverend Dukes led the 250-person crowd down Seventh Avenue toward the station house to demand Officer Gilligan's arrest for murder.[38]

But the protesters were stopped at the front door of the station by officers standing with their arms locked. As police pushed the crowd across the street, spectators continued to gather. Bottles and ash can covers were thrown from rooftops. The crowd chanted against killer cops, police brutality, and Police Commissioner Michael J. Murphy. Police in riot helmets barricaded streets and roamed rooftops. Sometime after 10:00 p.m., the police cleared the block in front of the

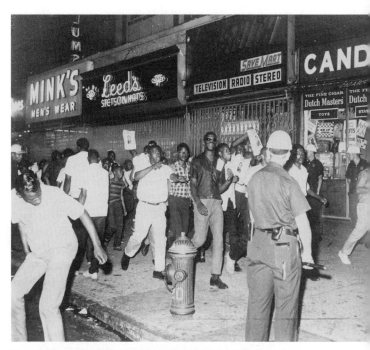

Protesters march through the streets of Harlem with a photograph of Lieutenant Gilligan at the start of the 1964 Harlem riot.
New York World-Telegram and Sun staff photo by Dick De Marsico, Library of Congress, Prints and Photographs Online Catalog, LC-USZ62-136895.

station and fired shots into the air to disperse the crowds that had been pushed back to surrounding avenues. The tactic backfired, and the scene quickly escalated.* Shop windows and patrol car windshields were smashed. Trash cans were set on fire, and Molotov cocktails were thrown into the streets. A motorcycle detail and tactical force teams were sent to the area, to mixed reactions from roving crowds. Some ran, but others held their ground. Bullhorn demands for rioters to go home proved ineffective. One person from the crowd responded: "We are home." Scores were injured between 123rd and 127th Streets and Eighth and Lenox Avenues. At least thirty were arrested.[39]

* Reverend Dukes later told reporters, "If I knew this [full-blown riot] was going to happen, I would not have said anything" at the original rally.

Police clashing with protesters at Seventh Avenue and 126th Street during the 1964 Harlem Riot.
New York World-Telegram and Sun staff photo by Dick De Marsico, Library of Congress, Prints and Photographs Online Catalog, LC-USZ62-136896.

Meanwhile, a handful of city officials and civil rights leaders gathered at the 123rd Street police station. The group decided that Police Commissioner Murphy would write a letter calling for law and order that would be read from Harlem pulpits the next morning, a Sunday. On Sunday afternoon, civil rights leaders rallied again, this time at the Mount Morris Presbyterian Church in central Harlem. James Farmer, CORE's national director, called the riot "New York's night of Birmingham horror," condemned the brutality of police responses toward protesters, and denounced what many saw as Police Commissioner Murphy's self-congratulatory attitude in his remarks on policing the riot. That evening, over a thousand people attended Powell's funeral on Seventh Avenue near 132nd Street. Violence broke out again. Groups

of mainly young African Americans roamed the area and threw bottles and bricks from tenement roofs. The disturbance lasted until early Monday morning but was less widespread than the previous night's activity.[40]

The pattern of calm during the day and rioting at night would last for six days, spreading from Harlem to the Bedford-Stuyvesant neighborhood of Brooklyn.* It was the longest sustained period of unrest in the twentieth century in the city. Members of CORE, the NAACP, and the PLP highlighted the persistent burden of social and economic inequality on the city's black residents, while Mayor Robert Wagner made insensitive calls for law and order among "colored citizens" upon his return home from a European vacation. Though the city's police force was more thoroughly trained and heavily equipped to respond to riots in the 1960s than in previous decades, the response of city officials in 1964 was anemic, especially compared to Mayor La Guardia's more robust efforts in 1935 and 1943. And civil rights groups did not hold back in expressing their disappointment.[41]

Aftermath

Among those arrested during the riots was William Epton, PLP's vice chairman. Late in the rioting, as calm was returning to the streets, he made a speech on a Harlem street corner that was recorded by an undercover cop who had infiltrated the PLP. "If we are going to be free," he exhorted his listeners, "we will not be fully free until we smash this state completely and totally. Destroy and set up a new state of our own choosing and our own liking. And in the process of making that state, we're going to have to kill a lot of these cops, a lot of these judges, and we'll have to go against their army. We'll organize our own militia and our own army." Epton wanted to rally rioters to "create a revolution." He was tried and convicted both of conspiracy to advocate "criminal anarchy" and of actually advocating "criminal anarchy." The trial court had in fact found there was a "lack of evidence

---

* By the 1970s, Bedford-Stuyvesant would become the largest African American neighborhood in New York, eclipsing Harlem.

as to any direct, causal connection between Epton's activities and the Harlem riots of the Summer of 1964" but convicted him anyway because his words—in the view of the court—created a "clear and present danger" that the riots might be rekindled and the state overthrown.* He was the first person since the mid-1920s to be convicted under New York State's criminal anarchy (or criminal syndicalism) law and sentenced to three concurrent one-year sentences—but not before making a forty-minute speech to the court in front of over sixty of his followers, during which he criticized the federal and state governments for scapegoating him and convicting him of dissent.[42]

By contrast, the actual instigator of the riot—off-duty police officer Thomas Gilligan, who had shot and killed James Powell—got off scot-free. In September a grand jury failed to indict Gilligan. Expecting an outraged reaction, District Attorney Frank S. Hogan took the unusual step of summarizing the conflicting evidence when announcing the refusal to indict. This placated few. The *New York Times* urged Commissioner Murphy, a fierce opponent of civil review of police brutality charges, to conduct an internal investigation regarding Gilligan's judgment before returning him to duty. Dissatisfied with the failure to indict, CORE released its own report detailing Gilligan's history of violent episodes, which included shooting another black boy while off duty. CORE's James Farmer proposed several strategies to avoid similar tragedies, including the creation of a civil review board, improved human relations training for officers, and increased recruitment of officers from minority groups.† Partially in response—but also meeting a demand that arose as early as the 1935 riot—Commissioner Murphy appointed a black officer, Lloyd Sealey, as the captain of the 28th Precinct, which had been the primary target of the rioting. Sealey was the

first black commander of a precinct in police department history.[43]

The Harlem Riot of 1964 was to be the first of a long series of urban uprisings across the United States in the 1960s: Rochester, New York, a few days and Philadelphia a month later, Watts in Los Angeles the next year, Cleveland and Omaha in 1966, several cities (most prominently Detroit) in 1967, and more than a hundred in the wake of the assassination of Martin Luther King Jr. in 1968.‡ Harlem seemed to have launched a season of urban insurrection. Scholars seeking to understand the roots of this unrest continually showed—as they had in 1935 and 1947—that, whatever the spark, the root causes were systemic oppression of African Americans (and other minorities) in American cities, including especially New York. This oppression manifested itself in rotten, overpriced housing (and discriminatory housing policies), exclusionary labor markets, and constant police harassment and brutality. In New York researchers found that 41 percent of black respondents in a survey indicated that they understood the rioting in Harlem and Bedford-Stuyvesant as a protest against discrimination and deprivation and argued that only addressing these conditions would make rioting less likely.[44]

Instead, the riots helped accelerate the ongoing disinvestment of capital across the city, a trend that hit minority neighborhoods especially hard. As capital—and much of the white working and middle classes—fled the city, buildings were abandoned, overcrowding (ironically) increased, and neighborhood conditions deteriorated. By the 1970s, with the city bankrupt, whole blocks of Harlem and the Lower East Side and large swaths of the South Bronx and black Brooklyn stood empty, buildings torched for insurance payouts or left to collapse into the street. Lured to Harlem in the

---

* Epton's conviction was upheld on appeal, although the court once again admitted that there was no direct connection between his words and the rioting.

† After extensive campaigning and against concerted opposition from the Patrolmen's Benevolent Association, proponents forced an initiative to create a civilian review board onto the ballot in 1966, but it was decisively defeated (63 percent against) amid fears of a rising crime wave.

‡ While there was some looting in Harlem in the wake of King's assassination, New York City avoided the disturbances that racked so many other cities. Some attribute this to Mayor John Lindsay's decision to quickly go to Harlem to meet with residents, to deploy mass police forces around the city, and to have crews ready to clean up wherever isolated property destruction occurred.

early 1900s to fill overbuilt speculative housing whose developers were about to go belly-up in the 1904–5 recession, working-class black residents have suffered the extremes of deprivation (despite the Harlem Renaissance and important neighborhoods housing the black bourgeoisie) ever since. As geographer Neil Smith summarized in the mid-1990s, "In short, black residents—middle and working-class—who moved into Harlem in the early years of the century largely saved the financial hides of white landlords, speculators and builders who had overdeveloped. In turn, these residents, their children and their children's children were repaid by a bout of concerted disinvestment from Harlem housing that has lasted for nine decades."* The 1964 riot intensified the process.[45]

* As Smith makes clear, this bout of disinvestment paved the way for Harlem's current gentrification.

It also helped launch the rightward turn in crime policing in the United States, as, responding to the 1964 riots and pressured from the Right by Republican presidential nominee Barry Goldwater, President Johnson refashioned the "War on Poverty" into a "war on crime and war on disorder" and engineered the 1968 Safe Streets Act, which opened up the federal funding spigot for local law enforcement. Thus was laid the foundation for President Nixon's "War on Drugs," which followed a few years later and which, in its various iterations, has done so much to eviscerate urban, working-class America.[46]

THE EAST HARLEM ANTIPOLICE RIOT, 1967—
AND THE YOUNG LORDS

Thomas Ryan and Anthony Cinquemani, two white off-duty cops in civilian clothes, were cruising through Spanish Harlem just after midnight on Sunday, July 23, 1967, when they came across a fight between Renaldo Rodriguez and another man. Rodriguez had already slashed the other guy with a knife by the time the cops intervened. According to witnesses, Rodriguez came after Cinquemani, who retreated, then stopped, turned, and shot Rodriguez three times, killing him. Rumors quickly flew around the neighborhood: that Rodriguez had been shot point-blank and that he was unarmed. A crowd formed at the scene—Third Avenue and 111th Street—and soon the New York Police Department sent in its Tactical Patrol Force (TPF), an especially hated unit in minority communities. The TPF officers drew their nightsticks, forcibly clearing the area, while one officer reportedly yelled, "Go home. You didn't lose anything. You just lost another spic." Mayor Lindsay rushed to East Harlem, only to hear one young man declare, "If [the police] want war, we'll give them war. We may go down, but we will take some of them with us." Small skirmishes with the police continued through the early hours before dying down about 6:00 a.m.[1]

The streets remained calm during the daylight hours that Sunday. After sunset, though, crowds returned to the streets, even as Puerto Rican leaders negotiated with the mayor and chief of police to have the TPF removed from Spanish Harlem streets. Around 10:00 p.m. a number of teenagers built a barricade of overflowing trash cans on Third Avenue at 111th Street and lit it on fire. Cops cleared the crowd, but it soon regrouped and marched up Third Avenue toward the 126th Street police station, smashing windows and looting stores as it went. Cops set up barricades along major intersections on Third Avenue but largely stepped back and let the rioters have the run of the street between 111th and 125th Streets. A large contingent of 250 policemen stood guard around the 126th Street station. As the protesters arrived, the cops surged forward, with billy clubs swinging. More than a thousand police officers responded to the scene and, while their commanders sought to restrain them, radiated hatred and anger. The TPF was called back in, angering protesters even more. Skirmishes between police and protesters, along with significant looting, lasted all night (cops themselves were seen breaking store windows, adding to

the mayhem—though they claimed they had done so only because rioters had already significantly damaged the windows). Between 2:00 and 2:30 a.m. police exchanged gunfire with snipers positioned on rooftops at 111th Street.

Monday night, as federal troops were sent into Detroit to quell the much bigger rioting there, tensions in East Harlem remained high. Rumors spread that Mayor Lindsay would visit the neighborhood that night, and when he failed to appear (the police commissioner warned him off, saying the youth on the streets were too drunk to appreciate him coming), the crowds erupted into violence again. Rioting spread south to 103rd Street and across the Harlem River to the heavily Puerto Rican Mott Haven neighborhood in the Bronx. Rioters lit bonfires, smashed windows, overturned and torched cars, and opened fire on the police from rooftops. A forty-four-year-old woman, Emma Haddock, was shot in the head and killed as she watched the rioting from her window on East 103rd Street (her daughter was shot in both legs). Ballistic evidence suggested the shots came from a sniper rather than the police. Earlier in the evening, a twenty-two-year-old Puerto Rican man was killed when police

Police aggression during the East Harlem Riot, 1967.
Getty Images.

unleashed a hail of gunfire aimed at rooftop snipers on East 112th Street. Luis Torres was hit by a .38-caliber bullet (which probably killed him) and fell to the street, breaking his neck.[2]

The next night a big thunderstorm kept large crowds off the streets, but still there were skirmishes. In Mott Haven, police shot and killed a Puerto Rican man who they claimed was threatening another man with a pistol. On Wednesday, East Harlem remained fairly calm, but following a Smokey Robinson concert in Central Park, gangs of black youth—now including teenage girls—roamed Midtown, smashing windows and in one case attacking a young white couple. By then, however, the fury in

Spanish Harlem had largely spent itself—though by the weekend sporadic outbursts of rioting occurred in Bedford-Stuyvesant; a CORE representative attributed them to dissatisfaction with white policing of the neighborhood, as well as ongoing under-investment in it.[3]

In East Harlem, just about all observers agreed, the rioting expressed a generalized dislike and distrust of the police (especially the TPF), even as Mayor Lindsay sought to characterize it as a small "disturbance" perpetrated by a core group of about two hundred youth who had had "too much beer" (a shopkeeper blamed drug addicts; a local priest said of the youth, "There's a sense of fiesta to it"). While Lindsay was

generally sympathetic to the hardships and oppression faced by Puerto Ricans in the city, such comments tended to minimize just how racially charged policing in the Puerto Rican neighborhoods had become. As with African Americans in Harlem, Puerto Ricans in East Harlem were constantly subject to a barrage of casual racist abuse by police officers and routinely called "spics" and "niggers." The cops regarded Puerto Ricans, as one police officer quoted in the *Times* said, as "inherently lazy. Give them something nice and they destroy it."[4]

The Puerto Rican population in New York had grown rapidly in the decades after 1898, when the United States took possession of the island and sugar and coffee

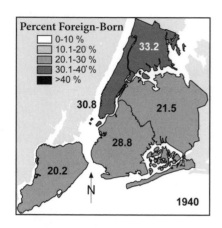

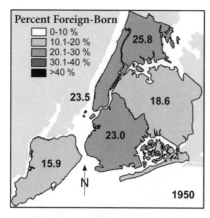

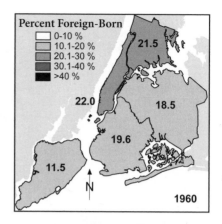

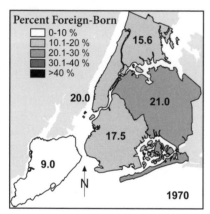

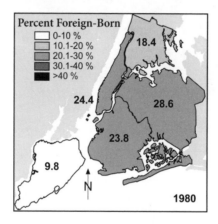

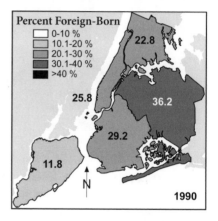

Ethnic Change, 1960–2006.

Cartography: Joe Stoll, Syracuse University Cartography Lab and Map Shop.

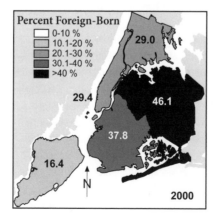

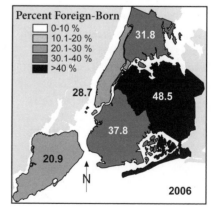

A warming bonfire built by supporters of the Young Lords awaiting arrest for occupying a church at Lexington Avenue and 111th Street, January 6, 1970.
AP Photo / RF.

interests deepened their hold on its economy; immigration to the city spiked again in the wake of the Depression and during the postwar economic boom, with the population exceeding more than six hundred thousand by 1960. The largest number settled in Spanish Harlem—*el barrio*. People were poor; jobs were scarce (unemployment in *el barrio* ran to 40 percent). Conditions, as in other parts of Harlem, were awful. Housing was rundown and filled with rats and cockroaches, and trash was picked up less frequently than in other parts of town. There were few public amenities. And as the deindustrialization of the New York region picked up steam in the 1960s, Puerto Ricans were particularly hard hit. All through the decade, the streets seethed, until the police shooting of Rodriguez sent people over the edge.[5]

In the wake of the riots, Puerto Rican

activists began organizing, taking their lead from the Black Panthers, the League of Revolutionary Black Workers (in Detroit), and international revolutionary liberation movements (Puerto Rican urban activism was crosscut by radical Puerto Rican nationalist struggles). By 1969 New York activists had formed a chapter of the Young Lords, a radical Puerto Rican organization that had begun in Chicago as a street gang in 1959. The New York Young Lords were primarily a youth organization (comprising radical students, ex–gang members, ex-convicts, and so forth) and primarily composed of Nuyoricans—second-generation New Yorkers.[6]

While the Young Lords held some existing neighborhood organizations in contempt for their narrow focus on urban renewal and planning, their earliest work focused primarily on the conditions of the urban environment. Their first main action

was to turn the filthy condition of the streets into a political struggle. Exposing the Department of Sanitation's neglect of Spanish Harlem, in late July 1969 the Lords launched a "garbage offensive," organizing large crews to dispose of neglected garbage bags, clean out empty lots, and sweep the streets. When they asked for more brooms from the sanitation department, they were dismissed. In response, they started hauling uncollected garbage into the streets overnight, forcing the city to respond. Soon they escalated their tactics, lighting the trash (and some cars) on fire, pelting the police with garbage (a "garbage throwing melee," the *Times* called it), and organizing a thousand-person-strong march on the 126th Street police station.

From the streets the Young Lords turned their attention to the rotten housing conditions. As their campaigns expanded (to maternal health, free meal programs, and more), they sought access to the First Spanish Methodist Church on Lexington Avenue and 111th Street but were denied by the pastor. In early December 1969, when members of the Young Lords attempted to address the congregation to make their case, they were beaten by a gang of police officers. The police beating in the church galvanized young activists and many community members, who then, on December 28, occupied the church building, rechristening it La Iglesia de la Gente (the church of the people). The police moved in on January 7, 1970, arresting 105.

But the Young Lords were not done. They then turned their attention to public health, focusing particularly on tuberculosis, which was directly attributable to horrid living conditions. They "ripped off a TB truck," as one activist put it, so that it would be dedicated entirely to their community, not just visit for a couple of hours a week. They tested a thousand people that day. In July 1970 they occupied the Lincoln Hospital in the Bronx for twelve hours to demand better health care.

The Young Lords became increasingly militant. An armed group of them occupied the First Spanish Methodist Church again in October after a Lord had been found hanged in police custody. A year later they fought a pitched battle with police at the Puerto Rican Day parade, injuring nineteen officers (a "score" of Young Lords were injured) in an event that started turning public support against the group. By 1972 the organization had fractured, with some moving toward revolutionary independence movements and others seeking to infiltrate the unions and to jump start a multiethnic communist party in the United States. But in the two years between the garbage offensive in 1969 and the Puerto Rican Day Riot in 1971, the Young Lords managed to galvanize Spanish Harlem and to turn public attention to *el barrio*. More than, say, the New York Police Department's decision to hastily place Spanish-speaking officers in cars patrolling the neighborhood, the Young Lords sparked change, focusing political energy on the urban environmental issues that had, along with racist policing practices, sparked and fueled the 1967 rioting.

"WE WANT THE WORLD AND WE WANT IT NOW"
COLUMBIA UNIVERSITY, 1968

In March 1967, as the United States became ever more entangled in the war in Vietnam and as opposition to the war mounted at home, Bob Feldman, a Students for a Democratic Society (SDS) activist, discovered documents tucked away in a Columbia University library detailing the university's secret arrangement to conduct weapons research for the Institute for Defense Analyses (IDA), a Pentagon think tank. The discovery sparked a good deal of agitation against the war on campus, much of it organized by the SDS, an organization that had grown increasingly radical since its founding in 1962. Simultaneously, Columbia University broke ground on a new gymnasium in Morningside Park, the steep hillside that separated Morningside Heights from Harlem. Not only would the gym destroy city parkland—in rare supply in Harlem—but its design struck many residents of Harlem and many students, especially black student members of the Student Afro-American Society (SAS), as segregationist. Students coming from Morningside Heights would enter the building on an upper floor and have access throughout. A separate entrance down in Harlem opened into a floor of "community space," but community residents would not

have access to the upper floors. Both these issues—Columbia's relationship with the war machine and Columbia's relationship with black Harlem—came to a head in the spring of 1968, sparking a remarkable month and a half of protest, counterprotest, building occupations, police violence, and general upheaval, New York's contribution to an intense year of international student uprising.[1]

On March 27, 1968, more than a hundred SDS members, led by their new chairman, junior Mark Rudd, marched into Low Library, home to President Grayson Kirk's office, with a petition demanding Columbia sever its ties with the IDA. The university had recently banned indoor political demonstrations, and six SDS members were put on disciplinary probation. Organizing on behalf of the IDA Six began immediately. On April 22 the SDS's Mark Rudd and SAS president Cicero Wilson met to plan a coordinated rally the next day to protest the university's war involvements, its disciplining of the IDA Six, and the gymnasium—evidence of Columbia's "Gym Crow" attitudes toward Harlem. (Earlier, the SDS had disrupted the university's memorial service for Martin Luther King Jr., protesting what it saw as Columbia's racist

practices.) Several hundred students, black and white, attended the April 23 rally and then attempted again to march into Low. But they were rebuffed by security guards and a large contingent of counterdemonstrators (conservative students had a large and vocal presence on campus). Instead, they poured into Morningside Park and ripped down the construction fence around the gym site. A police tussle ensued, and one student was arrested. The bulk of the others returned to campus and occupied Hamilton Hall, preventing acting dean Henry Coleman from leaving his office. More students (both for and against the occupation) descended on the building, along with faculty and several deans. The SDS and SAS caucused separately but quickly decided they were on strike and drew up a list of six demands: that probation against the IDA Six be dropped; that charges be dropped against the student arrested at the gym protest; that construction on the gym stop immediately; that the university sever all ties with IDA; that indoor demonstrations once again be allowed; and that all disciplinary actions henceforth be decided by a committee of faculty and students after open hearings. The strikers held the building—and the dean—overnight.

H. Rap Brown meets with the crowd outside occupied Hamilton Hall during the "Gym Crow" and antiwar protests at Columbia University, April 26, 1968. AP Photo.

During the night, however, SAS members decided to ask the white students to leave (Dean Coleman was allowed to go later that day). Many of the black activists were veterans of civil rights struggles and also increasingly influenced by separatist ideologies. Besides desiring to control their own protest, they were worried that the lack of discipline shown by the white students would undermine the occupation, perhaps giving the university an excuse to act violently. The white students left at 5:30 a.m. on April 24 as the SAS renamed Hamilton Hall Malcolm X Liberation College.[2] The white students then entered Low Library, broke into the president's office, and occupied it. That night, architecture students occupied their own building, Avery Hall, and joined the strike. Overnight, graduate students occupied Fayerweather Hall. The campus was in chaos. Many classes were suspended as faculty members met to try to resolve the crisis; black community members massed outside the university gates and marched through campus as pro- and antistrike students jostled in front of the occupied buildings. President Grayson temporized.

At 1:00 a.m. on Friday, April 26, Provost David Truman announced that the police were poised to reclaim the buildings. As a faculty ad hoc group, fearing violence, worked to prevent this, especially radical students from Low and Fayerweather slipped into the Mathematics Building and occupied it. (Nationally prominent SDSer Tom Hayden, over from Newark, where he had been organizing, emerged as a leader of this faction.) Two hours later, instead of calling in the police, the provost announced that construction on the gym had been suspended and that the university would be closed until Monday—the strikers had shut Columbia down. Later that Friday prominent black militants H. Rap Brown and Stokely Carmichael met with the African American students in Hamilton and briefly addressed the crowds outside. As the occupations continued into the weekend, each building developed as its own separate "commune," making relatively autonomous

Uniformed and plainclothed police tackle protesters and clear out occupied halls at Columbia University, April 30, 1968.
AP Photo.

decisions on how to proceed, many by creating intense "participatory democracy" procedures. Collective action was coordinated at "strike central," established in Ferris Booth Hall. As faculty members continued to try to mediate—even as divisions within the faculty itself over the occupation deepened—the Strike Coordinating Committee dug in its heels, soon upping its demands to include the resignation of President Grayson and Provost Truman.

The weekend was a carnival. Faculty members debated and eventually created a cordon around Low Library in an attempt to keep counterprotesters out. Then, members of the Majority Coalition—conservative students—established a ring around the faculty to keep everything out. Strike supporters took to lobbing food over the serried ranks of students and professors to

occupiers perched on the window ledges. Most of the food fell short, showering down on the professors. Radicals from around the city—including City College, NYU, and the New School and progressive redoubts like the Lower East Side—descended on campus. As a huge Central Park antiwar rally ran down that Saturday evening, even more protesters joined their ranks. By early Sunday, an ad hoc faculty committee had drawn up a set of resolutions—ending the university's ties to the IDA, stopping construction of the gym, initiating a new disciplinary process—but the students decided to hold out for total amnesty and on Monday rejected the compromise. Later on Monday night, April 29, President Grayson, yielding to significant pressure from his Board of Trustees, finally decided to call in the police.

At 2:00 a.m. on Tuesday, April 30, a phalanx of one hundred NYPD officers entered Hamilton Hall through an underground tunnel. (Expecting a raid, dozens of students and professors were blocking the doors.) The black students occupying the hall had already decided to go peacefully, to not resist. The students were escorted back through the tunnel, out onto Amsterdam Avenue, and into waiting police buses. Eighty-six were arrested and charged with criminal trespass. Next the cops entered Low, again through a tunnel. Breaking through several barricades, the cops (mostly Tactical Patrol Force officers) were met by ninety-three students determined to passively resist arrest. The students were dragged and shoved out of the occupied office—or kicked and dragged by their hair—and into Low's rotunda, where they were handcuffed and then pushed and dragged onto the waiting buses. Next was Avery. There was no underground entry to the architecture building, so the cops had to enter through the main doors, which were blockaded by a few dozen students. More were massed on the lawns and plazas, protesting the police action. The blockaders were roughly thrown aside (in the description of a reporter sympathetic to the police), and when the occupiers inside offered passive resistance, they were dragged down the marble staircases by their feet or hair. Some were hit with handcuffs; others were kicked.

At Fayerweather, the cops again found a blockade of dozens of professors and students, whom the cops pushed, shoved, and threw aside. Some 130 occupiers walked out peacefully, 70 offered passive resistance and were dragged down staircases, some again beaten with handcuffs and nightsticks. Another 70 fought back, throwing bottles, erasers, and boxes and swearing at the cops; these protesters were met with greater force by the police. In all, 268 people were arrested at Fayerweather. Resistance to arrest in the Mathematics Building was intense at first, but eventually most of the students walked out peacefully on their own.

Then the cops went on a rampage. As one group of police loaded the arrested occupiers onto buses, another—about a hundred strong—pulled out their nightsticks and waded into the crowd watching the arrests, swinging indiscriminately. A smaller troop of twenty chased down fleeing students. Dozens of students and onlookers

were badly beaten, many in the face and head. Nearly ninety protesters and observers were taken to hospitals; thirteen cops were injured. The brutality was intense. Witnesses were outraged, and as word of the police melee grew, rage continued to radiate. While a semiofficial postmortem by the editor of *Columbia College Today* rather laconically noted that the only thing that set Columbia apart from the more than one hundred other protests and riots on American university campuses that spring was that this one got more attention, in reality the brutality of the police set it apart too (even if such brutality was not absent elsewhere).[3]

Inside, the buildings were a mess. While occupiers were responsible for some of the damage—ransacking the president's files, building barricades with desks and chairs, and graffitiing the walls ("Create Two, Three . . . Many Columbias"; "Lenin Won, Fidel Won, WE WILL WIN"; "Che"; "We Want the World and We Want It Now")— there is good evidence that much of the damage was done by rampaging police, a result, like the police beating of students and faculty, later commentators argued, of growing working-class police outrage at the privileged elite youth (and faculty) of the universities.[4] Hamilton Hall—the redoubt of the SAS—remained, throughout the occupation and its abandonment, clean and orderly. After the black students left, it remained as evidence of their steely discipline and impressive logistical organizational skills.

Outside, organizing began immediately for a student general strike and for expand-

ing organizing out into the surrounding neighborhoods. (In Morningside Heights, Columbia had been on a long campaign of buying up buildings and evicting their residents.) The SDS and others established "liberation classes" as faculty resolved to suspend final exams and develop alternative grading systems. On May 17 community members and students took over an apartment house to protest Columbia's expansionism. Three hundred riot-gear-clad police came to arrest them, but the occupiers submitted peacefully in a series of staged arrests. More than half of the 117 arrested were from the community, giving the lie to press reports that the students had no support in the neighborhood. On May 21 students and supporters retook Hamilton Hall and from there organized the erection of fifteen-foot-tall barricades at the campus entrances. When the cops arrived—entering the building again through the underground tunnel—the campus erupted. Small fires were set in Hamilton and Fayerweather Halls. Students ripped up paving bricks and hurled them at the cops. Before the dust settled and the smoke cleared, 38 students, 9 others, and 17 policemen were treated at hospitals for injuries, and 171 rioters were arrested.

The fires were both a tactical mistake— students lost a good deal of faculty support—and the signal of a tactical escalation, a deepening radicalization of some students. Soon Mark Rudd and others would break away from the SDS and help form the more militant (and eventually terrorist) Weatherman, later called the Weather Underground. (Ted Gold, one of the militant

Columbia SDS leaders, was killed two years later as he entered a Weatherman townhouse in Greenwich Village just as a bomb being built by his comrades prematurely exploded.) The student strike sputtered but lasted until a festive "counter commencement" drew together two thousand students and spectators to the center of campus to listen to music and speeches before decamping to Morningside Park for a big party. Not far away, the foundation hole for the "Gym Crow" lay empty. A year later, Columbia University abandoned all plans for the gym—part of a reorientation of campus expansion away from Harlem (and the militancy of black students and community members) and toward Riverside Park to the west. The hole in the ground and the rotting fence around it persisted through the 1980s before being relandscaped into a pond at the end of the decade.

TEACHERS' STRIKE OR ARMAGEDDON?

OCEAN HILL–BROWNSVILLE, 1968

Columbia's "Gym Crow" plans were, perhaps, a keen symbol of how segregationism continued to shape New York's landscape and social geography, maybe nowhere as fatefully as in the schools. Efforts at desegregating the New York City schools over the first two-thirds of the twentieth century were half-hearted at best. Therefore, in the context of growing black nationalism, black community activists, some progressive educators, and many parents in the mid-1960s started agitating instead for "community control" over neighborhood schools. The goal was to create what geographer Bill Bunge (writing about Detroit) called "sympathetic authority" within the schools. Under community control, local school boards, representative of the racial makeup of the neighborhood, and black administrators would assure that school curricula and ideologies aligned with the needs of African American children, introducing ideas and techniques designed to meet the specific needs of, provide role models for, and develop the political consciousness of black schoolchildren.[1]

Beginning in 1967, for reasons of political expediency and because it seemed cheap, Mayor John Lindsay, working with the Ford Foundation (directed by Vietnam War architect McGeorge Bundy), supported community control experiments, starting with (among others) schools in the very poor, predominantly black and Puerto Rican Brooklyn neighborhood of Ocean Hill–Brownsville, where schools had long been struggling. Since local authority was to be an experiment, the city's central school board barred the Ocean Hill–Brownville district from seeking additional external funds; it also refused the local board's request to control its own budget, undermining community control right from the start. Finally, the central administration barred most schools in Ocean Hill–Brownville from participating in the expensive More Effective Schools program, sponsored by the United Federation of Teachers (UFT), driving a wedge between the local school board and the union.

Tensions in Ocean Hill–Brownsville between the newly elected local board and the UFT were already tense. The day the experiment in community control was set to start in September 1967, the UFT called a citywide strike that lasted two weeks. The Ocean Hill–Brownsville board interpreted this strike as undermining local control just as it was getting going and opposed the strike, working hard to keep its schools open (with the assistance of at least some unionized black teachers). As the year got under way, local school board members, together with some parents and civil rights organizations, sparred frequently with the UFT over a variety of issues, each of which involved the question of where power should lie: with the largely African American Community Board or with the majority white unionized teachers. Simultaneously, Bundy and the Ford Foundation, together with Mayor Lindsay, laid out a plan to break up the citywide school district and create thirty to sixty local districts, with boards elected primarily from parents. Fearing that such "balkanization" would undermine the UFT's collective bargaining power, the union vigorously fought any attempt to implement the Ford plan. Ocean Hill–Brownsville was fated to become ground zero in what turned out to be an exceptionally ugly struggle for control of the schools.

Soon after it was established, the new Ocean Hill–Brownsville school board hired Rhody McCoy, an experienced principal with Black Power movement sympathies, as superintendent. The quality of teaching in the district had long been spotty. With teacher tenure making firing incompetent teachers difficult, the central school board's general practice was to continually transfer incompetent teachers from school to school until they landed in a district too politically weak to push them out. Ocean Hill–Brownsville was something of a dumping ground. McCoy's first year was rocky. On the one hand, in the wake of the September strike, a group of experienced principals and assistant principals asked to be transferred out of the district, and the UFT vigorously objected when McCoy and the local board, in an effort to integrate school administration, sought to replace them with people not on the ranked civil service list. On the other hand, McCoy and the board sought in May 1968 to involuntarily transfer a group of nineteen teachers and administrators out of the district, with the board claiming incompetency but the UFT averring that the personnel were being punished for supporting the September strike or otherwise resisting community control.

The New York City superintendent of schools, Bernard Donovan, ordered McCoy to reinstate the teachers and administrators, but he refused. When some of the teachers tried to enter their classrooms, they were blocked by protesting parents and students. Donovan extemporized, ordering the personnel out, then back in again. When the Ocean Hill–Brownsville board refused to reinstate them, two-thirds of the district's 556 teachers struck and remained out for the rest of the school year. McCoy sought to fire or discipline all the striking teachers, which led the UFT, led by Albert Shanker, to claim the conflict was really about the right of teachers to

due process. Shanker played up the racial aspects of the conflict, highlighting images of white teachers being blocked from their jobs by what he portrayed as militant black activists and claiming that the Ford-like decentralization plan then working its way through the state legislature would "mean more of the same," in the words of a full-page ad in the *New York Times* that also implored readers, "Don't let our school system be taken over by local extremists." The state government ended up tabling the decentralization plan but allowed the experiments in community control to continue.[2]

McCoy eventually filed charges against the nineteen teachers and administrators he had sought to transfer out of the district, but over the summer a trial examiner dismissed all the charges and ordered reinstatement. McCoy once again balked while simultaneously hiring 350 new teachers—70 percent white—to replace those who had struck at the end of the previous school year. As the 1968–69 school year got under way, the UFT called a citywide strike, demanding the reinstatement of the nineteen, as well as other concessions related to decentralization. Donovan quickly caved, and teachers returned to work, but again McCoy and the Ocean Hill–Brownsville board refused to rehire the nineteen, with students, parents, and community activists again blockading the schools. The UFT went back out on strike. Donovan and the UFT reached yet another agreement, which the local board once again refused. Out came the teachers again. More than a million students across

the city saw their school year upended, the central city school board dissolved in a shambles, Lindsay seemed powerless, and all the while Shanker escalated tensions—and the union's demands—in an effort to show that the UFT had the power to shut down the schools whenever it wanted to protect members' interests. "In a year that had already seen the Tet offensive in Vietnam, the assassinations of Martin Luther King Jr. and Robert F. Kennedy, the student takeover of buildings at Columbia University, the police riot at the Chicago Democratic convention, and a strong, racist presidential bid by George Wallace," historian Joshua Freeman concludes, "the strike seemed truly apocalyptic."[3]

The strike became especially apocalyptic when—even as the Ocean Hill–Brownsville schools were being kept open by a cadre of older African American teachers and young, largely white recruits (of whom half were Jewish)—the UFT picked up an anti-Semitic flyer that had received some circulation around the district (likely *not* at the hands of any of those directly involved in the community control experiment). The flyer spoke of the "Middle East Murderers of Colored People" and the "So-Called Jewish Liberal Friend" who is "Really Our Enemy" responsible for "*The Serious Educational Retardation of Our Black Children*." The UFT paired the leaflet with a second, fake one (who faked it is in dispute) advocating total community control of the schools, printed out a half-million copies, and distributed them on picket lines, at subway entrances, and in synagogues. "The fear and anger unleashed among New York City's Jews unleashed by Shanker's publicity ploy and the long-term harm it perpetuated," says historian Stephen Brier, "are difficult to overstate." In the estimation of many, Shanker never passed up an opportunity to race-bait and especially to pit Jews against blacks "without regard to the consequences," according to a (Jewish) aid to Mayor Lindsay.[4]

Chief among these consequences was splintering a relatively robust Jewish-black civil rights coalition in the city (which, by the time of the Crown Heights riot in 1991, would be in tatters) and in doing so scuppering any chance for progressive community oversight of schools. The breakaway African-American Teachers Association strongly supported community control and confronted the UFT at every turn, even as many New Left activists were torn between supporting the union and supporting black demands for community control. Black unionists in other industries worked hard to push Shanker toward a settlement, fearing a permanent rift in both the civil rights coalition and the labor movement. Shanker eventually settled, but at the cost of any sense of real community control over the schools—and a deepening racial rift in the city. (One later commentator called the strike "the most racially divisive event in the City's history since the Draft riots.") The legislature's decentralization plan, passed on the heels of the strike, denied the local board the right to hire or fire teachers, restricted involuntary transfers, folded the experimental districts into larger districts, and replaced local, parent-elected boards with ones appointed by borough presidents until new elections could be held.[5]

Like the Gary Plan Riots in 1917 (chapter 10), the 1968 teachers' strike was a battle over both the nature of education—what constitutes proper or progressive education—and where the power to determine that nature resided. More than in 1917, though, the Ocean Hill–Brownsville conflict was defined by the shifting politics of race, and Albert Shanker was not at all averse to raising the specter of anti-Semitism to rally the white working class to his side at a time when many in the city feared the rising tide of the Black Power movement. At the same time, he was able to use the strike to promote the interests of what was essentially a form of craft unionism, ratcheting up the power of a kind of labor aristocracy at the expense of broader class and race solidarities. This is what so many at the time saw as apocalyptic, a moment after which nothing in the city's racial, political, or social landscape would ever again be the same—a sentiment best encapsulated by Woody Allen in his 1973 movie *Sleeper*. When a character awakens two hundred years after being frozen in 1973, he finds that all of civilization has been destroyed. Wondering what happened, he is told, "A man by the name of Albert Shanker got hold of a nuclear warhead."[6]

CHAPTER 13

The CUNY Open Admissions Strike, 1969

JUSTIN SEAN MYERS

Black students at Columbia University were not the only militant university students of color in the city and were far from alone in calling for radical transformation on their campuses. On the morning of February 13, 1969, a crowd of mostly black and brown students gathered outside City College president Buell G. Gallagher's office to listen to his answers to a set of five demands they had delivered a week earlier "while he was away on vacation."[1] The students, organized as the Black and Puerto Rican Student Community (BPRSC), demanded:

1. That a School of Black and Puerto Rican Studies be established;
2. That a separate orientation program for Black and Puerto Rican students be established;
3. That students be given a voice in the administration of the SEEK [Search for Education, Elevation, and Knowledge] program;*
4. [That] [t]he number of minority freshmen class reflect the 40–45 [percent] ratio of Blacks and Puerto Ricans in the total school system;
5. That Black and Puerto Rican history course[s] be compulsory for education majors and that Span-

ish language courses be compulsory for education majors.[2]

The demands were hardly a surprise. They were a revised and focused version of ones drawn up the previous fall by City College members of the W. E. B. Du Bois Club, a mostly black organization affiliated with the Communist Party, and laid out in an advertisement in the *Campus*, the City College paper.†

At 12:45 p.m., about half an hour into Gallagher's response, BPRSC students, accompanied by some white students (mostly from the SDS and the City College Commune), finding that response to be vague and evasive, stormed past the president and occupied the lobby of the administration building on Convent Avenue and 138th Street. Quickly, large signs filled the atrium windows (in part to block photographers), the most prominent reading, "Free Huey, by Order of BPRSC. Malcolm X–Che Guevara University." As administrators left the building (setting up temporary shop in nearby Shepard Hall), students took over the second and third floors and broke into the president's of-

---

* SEEK was a remedial program established by CUNY in 1965 specifically to support Puerto Rican and black students who did not initially meet formal admissions criteria but in whom admissions officers saw significant promise.

† The W. E. B. Du Bois Club demands also asked specifically that SEEK be quadrupled in size; that more new senior colleges be built to accommodate all high school graduates; that stipends be given to students who could not afford to attend college; that community, faculty, and students be given control of CUNY governance; and that "Black, Puerto Rican, and labor history be integrated into the curriculum at all levels."

fice (as well as his liquor cabinet). Like the black occupiers of Columbia's Hamilton Hall nearly a year earlier, BPRSC members asked white student allies to leave. A sign soon went up in the administration building: "Sympathizers. Do Your Own Thing in ANOTHER Building." The white students moved on to Shepard Hall (the architectural heart of the campus) but could not get in. Just before 4:30 p.m., the Puerto Rican and black occupiers gave up the building, leaving without incident through a side door. After a lengthy meeting in a nearby building, the BPRSC reiterated its demands.[3]

So began the CUNY Open Admissions Strike, which rocked City College and other CUNY campuses for the next several months, eventually forcing the restructuring of the entire City University of New York system.

Prying Open the White University

In 1847, following a statewide referendum, City College was established as the Free Academy of the City of New York. With a large gift from Townsend Harris, a wealthy merchant, president of the New York City Board of Education, and later ambassador to Japan, the academy was dedicated to providing free higher education to the sons of immigrants and the poor. Entrance was to be based solely on academic achievement. By the Depression, City College, now coed, had developed a reputation for excellent academics—and the political radicalism of its students.* More than its elite neighbors like Columbia, Yale, and Princeton, City College admitted Jews and first-generation immigrant students—those other than the WASP elite. But, especially given racial inequality in primary and secondary schooling in the city, it remained largely closed to people of color. As post–World War II civil rights struggles intensified, this began to change, slowly.[4]

SEEK—the Search for Education, Elevation, and Knowl-

edge program—was a step, if a small one, toward prying open the white university, and now it—along with the ideal of free, open, supported education—seemed to be imperiled. Before the students rushed past him and into the administration building, President Gallagher had warned that while, through SEEK, CUNY was getting close to admitting students in the racial proportion of those graduating from high school, Governor Nelson Rockefeller's proposed budget cuts to the university would negate the gains. (SEEK was to be cut in half; overall admissions to CUNY were to be cut by 20 percent.) Action shifted north to Albany.† Thirteen thousand students—including five busloads from City College—rallied in front of the state capitol in opposition to Rockefeller's cuts on March 18. But this was unavailing. Not long after the rally, the state legislature passed a budget incorporating most of Rockefeller's cuts. President Gallagher offered his resignation in protest, claiming that with the cuts, he would have to eliminate SEEK, admit no first-year students, cut all evening and summer classes, renege on promises to create black and Puerto Rican studies programs, and eliminate graduate instruction. Twenty-three of twenty-seven department chairs followed Gallagher's lead and resigned their positions. (None of the resignations were accepted.)[5]

SEEK was at the heart of the students'—and Gallagher's—dissatisfaction, even though it was in many ways a token program. In 1968 it enrolled only six hundred (out of twenty thousand) students at City College. There were only three thousand black and Puerto Rican students at the college—15 percent of the total population. Among the twelve thousand day students, African Americans and Puerto Ricans comprised only 12 percent. Among matriculating students, only 7.2 percent were black, and only 3 percent were Puerto Rican. By contrast, African Americans comprised

---

* Women were admitted beginning in 1929.

† All winter, radical students had been active on campus. Though at the end of February, the BPRSC slate, running on a platform of universal free education, had come in second in student elections, it continued intense organizing on campus nonetheless. On March 7, H. Rap Brown spoke to a large crowd in City College's Great Hall.

25.6 percent and Puerto Ricans 5.1 percent of the nonmatriculating population.* For many black and Puerto Rican SEEK students, these numbers were unacceptable, especially for a university built on a hill overlooking central Harlem. City College should reflect the community it was part of, they argued.[6]

Shutting Down the College

Puerto Rican and black students intensified their struggle. On Monday, April 21, 1969, more than a thousand black and Puerto Rican students marched through campus in support of their five demands. The next day more than a hundred BPRSC members chained shut the gates of City College's eight-building South Campus—home to the humanities and social sciences—declaring a "lock-in" and announcing the closing of City College. As students on the North Campus—home to engineering, mathematics, and the physical sciences—continued to go about their business, white student members of the City College Commune (CCC) occupied Bowler Lounge in solidarity. On advice from faculty, President Gallagher announced that City College would be closed the following day, Wednesday, April 23. A faculty meeting would be held that morning at 9:30 to discuss the students' demands. In the meantime, he said, "no police will be called to south campus tonight or tomorrow and no injunctive process will be instigated in this interval."[7]

At the faculty meeting, which lasted until 4:30 p.m., a committee of BPRSC members addressed the faculty and asserted that "this school will stay shut until all of these issues have been resolved. . . . None of these demands are

negotiable. They are fair, just, long overdue and we will not wait any longer." Faculty response was split, with German professor Nathan Susskin warning against "yielding to a minority of terrorists," while Cliff Adelman from the history department contended that "what is truly moral in America today is on the south campus at this moment." As the faculty met, a contingent of fifty white radicals from CCC occupied Klapper Hall, the School of Education, as a symbol of solidarity with the black and Puerto Rican students.† Renaming the building Huey P. Newton Hall, the CCC students stated: "We recognize that we are all niggers, that so long as some people are the victims of oppression, none of us are free."[8]

Sit-ins spread to other campuses in the CUNY system, but at Brooklyn College and Queensborough Community College, the presidents showed less restraint than Gallagher, securing injunctions from the courts and threatening enforcement.‡ At City College, Gallagher and BPRSC students met at the president's home at noon on Thursday to clarify issues. Meanwhile, City College faculty met in another all-day meeting, finally resolving 221–1 to "oppose the employment of force or the resort to injunctive procedures in order to resolve this dispute as long as negotiations are going forward." More narrowly, 115–103, the faculty voted to "deplore the cessation of classes" while urging "against bringing police into campus," fearing a police presence would only intensify student support for the movement and disrupt negotiations. President Gallagher emerged from his meeting with the students to announce that his discussions had been "useful," and, indeed, the college would refrain from seeking injunctions or calling the police as negotiations continued. He declared the entire college closed until Tuesday, angering members of the engineering department, especially students, who vowed to have classes anyway in what they referred to as a "teach-in." One of the engineering students

---

* CUNY defined matriculated students as "those who have met the entrance requirements for the university and have been accepted into a program of study leading to a degree. Matriculated students do not pay tuition." Students "who have not received adequate high school preparation may be admitted as non-matriculates." Such students could earn college credit but were not considered to be advancing toward a degree. They were charged $54 per course in the senior colleges (such as City College) and $45 at the community colleges.

† This move was opposed by members of the SDS who thought occupying a building in a shut-down school was a futile gesture.
‡ At Queensborough, the president summarily fired three faculty members for participating in a sit-in.

asserted that "a small neo-Nazi minority is depriving us of our education."[9]

The next day, defying President Gallagher's closure, seven hundred of the one thousand engineering students scheduled to attend classes did so. While many engineering students expressed their understanding of the reasons for the occupation, they were worried about falling behind and failing their courses. But others were dismissive, arguing that liberal arts students could afford to miss class because their studies involved little or no work. As one student put it, "I can work half an hour a week in liberal arts and pass." Another exclaimed, "We take exams every week. These other kids there in the picket line, they can miss three weeks at school and not lose much."[10]

Faculty divisions sharpened. Forty to fifty professors formed the Black and Puerto Rican Faculty of the City College of the City University and released a statement supporting BPRSC's five demands because they were of "immediate concern to the whole black and Puerto Rican community." The professors were supported by liberal and radical faculty such as Arnold Birnbaum, an assistant professor of sociology who contended that "it is indeed the role of those groups that have been excluded from the system to change and better it." Others, though, were dismissive. Julius A. Elias, the chairman of the philosophy department, said, "I would be in favor of closing a whole lot more if I could only think of some other way of baby-sitting vast numbers of youths who are in our colleges for the wrong reasons." And Louis L. Snyder, a professor of history, expressed himself less concerned with the temporary shutdown of the college than its long-term implications: "The whole fabric of New York City's professional structure—from judges to physicians to engineers owed much to this institution. City College men staff colleges and universities throughout the country. They make up a large portion of the Federal, state and city civil service. To strike down a top institution like C.C.N.Y. would be a kind of blow from which the country would find it difficult to recover." Other faculty members spoke against the methods employed by the students. For example, Samuel L.

Sumberg, chairman of the Department of Germanic and Slavic Languages, argued that "the violent seizure of the college and the exclusion of almost the entire student body, instead of rational discussion, is entirely unjustified."[11]

Campus as Battleground

As students and faculty debated the intent and tactics of the BPRSC and their supporters, the campus remained closed, though reasonably quiet over the weekend.* On Monday, as signs sprouted on the South Campus walls redubbing City College "University of Harlem" and as building occupations spread to Queens College, President Gallagher secured the support of faculty in extending the college's closure as long as negotiations were ongoing.[12] Gallagher's actions seemed to have a calming effect on campus, especially compared to Queens College and (again) Columbia University, where occupations turned violent. Both Queens and Brooklyn Colleges were closed in the wake of the Queens violence; only Hunter College remained open among the CUNY senior colleges.[13]

Then on Friday, May 2, President Gallagher announced that an agreement had been reached with BPRSC. Gallagher was under a deadline. City Controller Mario Procaccino, an alumnus of the college and a candidate for mayor, had secured a court order preventing Gallagher and CUNY chancellor Albert Bowker from keeping the campus closed. Gallagher feared that any forced reopening would lead to violence and would likely draw Harlem in, and he convinced

---

* Perhaps even more than in 1968, in 1969 campuses across the United States erupted in protests, sit-ins, and occupations, many tied to opposition to U.S. involvement in the Vietnam War, many to opening up campuses to black students and other minorities. Simultaneously with the Open Admissions Strike, armed black students took over a building at Cornell, and black students occupied the faculty club at Colgate; turmoil also racked Harvard, Chicago, and innumerable others, including Columbia, where several times in April different groups of students seized buildings. The new administration of Richard Nixon struggled to respond, with Attorney General Richard Kleindienst being quoted as favoring detention camps for protesting students (he later denied he had said this).

CUNY students march at Madison Square Garden as part of the open admissions struggle, 1969. *New York Post* Archives / Getty Images.

Procaccino to refrain from having it enforced at least until Monday. He also said that he would go to jail before he called the police to open the college.

Students had upped their demands and in doing so had paved the way for the agreement. What they wanted now was an open admissions policy: a place at CUNY for every city high school graduate, and, until sufficient facilities were built and faculty hired, admission based on proportion of ethnic groups in the schools. Faculty in the College of Liberal Arts and Sciences quickly endorsed the deal—though, rather than supporting ethnic proportionality, instead supported an ad hoc committee report calling for admissions to be offered to students in three categories: those from underrepresented high schools, those from poverty areas as defined by the state, and "normal" academic admissions. As discussions continued on the details, Representative Adam

Clayton Powell visited the occupying students and urged them to stay strong—and to defy the injunction if necessary.[14]

Negotiations continued, with significant differences arising among students, faculty, and administrators over specific proposals, such as a separate orientation for black and Puerto Rican students and the scope of SEEK. Late Sunday night, the Board of Education ordered City College to reopen the next morning. The board directed the college administration "to take such action as may be necessary to reopen and resume classes" but did not specifically require the use of police or force. Gallagher thus complied and declared the university open, implored the occupying students to leave peacefully, and he issued a statement explaining his decision not to go to jail in defiance of the court order (he had not been required to call in the police). To encourage the protesters, the board resolved to reopen negotiations with the students only after they vacated South Campus.[15]

At 8:00 a.m. on Monday, the university opened the North Campus, which, except for Klapper Hall, was unoccupied. At midday, lawyers for the Board of Education obtained a restraining order from a New York Supreme Court justice banning "disruptive assembly" on the City College campus. Faced with possibly being held in contempt of the state supreme court, the fifty white students occupying Klapper Hall (Huey Newton Hall) left the building, marched around campus chanting "Strike, strike, shut it down!," and joined the black and Puerto Rican students in the still-occupied South Campus.* Along the way, they were hounded by students opposed to the occupation and strike, and several scuffles and fistfights erupted. Division among students across the CUNY system had deepened over the week, and violent confrontations among different factions were becoming common. That evening at 7:30, an assistant city corporation counsel read the restraining order prohibiting disruptive assembly over a megaphone and distributed copies to the occupiers. Two hours later, at 9:40, with a busload of Tactical Patrol Force officers parked nearby "as a precaution," the black and Puerto Rican students, more than two hundred strong, accompanied by the radical white students from Klapper, marched out of the South Campus gates behind students carrying flags and signs reading "University of Harlem." Yelling "Power to the people!" and singing civil rights anthems, they marched down Convent Avenue to 125th and from there into the heart of Harlem before disbanding at Lexington Avenue.[16]

After being closed for two weeks, the entire City College campus opened on Tuesday morning, May 6, but tensions remained. Militant white students—at least two hundred of them—marched through the corridors of buildings shouting "On strike! Shut it down!" and pulled fire alarms. African American women reportedly started a small fire in

the gym. Many faculty members, including forty black and Puerto Rican professors and adjunct teachers, went on strike in support of the open admissions plan, announcing they would not conduct classes until negotiations between the administration and BPRSC resumed. Despite radical white student support for the black and Puerto Rican protesters, confrontations between students took on an increasingly racial cast.† Fistfights broke out between white and black students.[17]

On Wednesday things got ugly. About 9:00 a.m. a female white student was robbed at knife point in a North Campus building by a group of black male and female students. Soon thereafter, black students and white supporters marched through the library imploring students to leave. They moved on to classrooms. But in Wagner Hall on the South Campus, a classroom of white students refused to budge, and a fight broke out. Back on North Campus, a crowd of black students, some apparently with sticks and in one case with a golf club, called engineering students out of Steadman Hall and tried to prevent others from entering. The black students left before the police—called by a professor—arrived. Battles between white and black students broke out around campus. At 10:30 President Gallagher announced the closing of campus.‡ Students poured out of classrooms and converged on the campus gate at 135th Street, where a private Burns Detective Agency guard tried to pull the gate shut while white students struggled to keep it open. The crowd of perhaps three hundred white counterprotesters grew and pushed their way into South Campus, ripping down radical posters and flags. Soon they reached the locked gate at 135th Street and St. Nicholas Terrace, trapping two black girls, who tried to scale the gate and failed. Fifty or sixty black students were massed outside, and as the girls struggled to flee the white crowd, they armed themselves with two-by-fours and tree branches. Twenty-five or so of them scaled

---

* Klapper Hall housed the School of Education. It no longer exists. After the North Academic Building was constructed on the site of Lewisohn Stadium next door, Klapper was torn down to make way for a parking lot.

† This was true also at Queens and Brooklyn Colleges, where battles between students of color and white students were at times fierce.

‡ Gallagher called the situation an "incipient riot, partly fed by persons not associated with the college."

the gate and shouted at the white students to go home (the girls had slipped away, "frightened but unharmed," according to a press account). When most of the white students did not budge, the black students dropped down inside the gate, confronting the white students in a tense standoff. Yelling matches erupted; one devolved into a shoving match, then a fistfight, then an out-and-out brawl that lasted ten minutes before the sound of approaching police sirens led the brawling students to disperse. Seven white students were injured seriously enough to require hospital treatment. The arriving cops cleared the campus. At 12:35 p.m. an administration official read an announcement from President Gallagher: "The College will be open tomorrow with adequate police protection."[18]

On Thursday a heavy police presence did not prevent violence. Few classes were held as roving bands of radical students called students out on strike and competing rallies between BPRSC supporters and counterdemonstrators were held. At midday three hundred radical students met on Convent Avenue in front of Harris and Wingate Halls, urging support for BPRSC's five demands and open admissions. Four hundred counterdemonstrators arrived from their own rally and heckled the supporters. Soon radical students were pelting the counterdemonstrators with eggs; counterdemonstrators responded with rocks and bottles. A phalanx of twenty-five police clad in riot gear arrived, swinging their clubs. The crowds dispersed as black students denounced the police action, which seemed focused on the radical students. The dispersed crowd regrouped—now numbering close to a thousand, radicals and counterdemonstrators alike—and marched toward the South Campus. As one group marched along 138th Street, they confronted a solid line of cops. Within the crowd a fight broke out, and the cops surged forward, seizing black protesters and swinging their clubs wildly. As the crowd broke and ran, the police pursued them up 138th Street. Eight people were arrested, mostly City College students, but also a sixteen-year-old high school student.

As calm was restored, the crowd grew once again, now to

two thousand. Battalions of radical students marched from one South Campus gate to another but found them all locked and guarded by police officers. At 2:30 p.m. a big fire broke out in the Finley Student Center, presumably set by radicals.* Several other smaller fires were also set during the day, and in one instance African Americans and Puerto Ricans torched a giant abstract painting (by two students) hanging in Eisner Hall. The Finley fire severely damaged the Aronow Auditorium and the offices of music professors. Amid the mayhem, negotiations between a team of students and faculty established by the Board of Education and radical students resulted in an agreement to require Spanish-language and black and Puerto Rican history courses for all education majors at City College. A tentative agreement was reached to expand SEEK and to develop a separate orientation program for African American and Puerto Rican students. Negotiations on open admissions were continuing.[19]

Before negotiations could resume, President Gallagher once again tendered his resignation and threw the campus into further turmoil. Gallagher pointed to "the intrusion of politically motivated outside forces" that had "in recent days" made it "impossible to carry on the process of reason and persuasion." He seemed to be referring to Controller Procaccino. "The City of New York and its great college," Gallagher said, "deserve a future which it had been my hope to realize more fully. But when the forces of angry rebellion and stern repression clash, the irrepressible conflict is joined." As a "man of peace," he no longer thought he was the right person to continue leading the college during its time of crisis. He was unsparing: "I will be unfaithful to none of my brothers, black or white." His resignation was imperative, he said, because "instead of serving as a lackey of political expediency and fiscal timidity, I want to be free to fight the battles for freedom and justice and brotherhood." Biology professor Joseph Copeland, who had been one of the faculty members on CUNY's negotiating team, was quickly named

* On Tuesday, May 6, as City College was being opened, several buildings at Brooklyn College were set on fire with Molotov cocktails, and a hundred or so demonstrators blocked firefighters from reaching the last one.

interim president. He expressed himself in sympathy with the demands of the black and Puerto Rican students ("I became even more so during the recent negotiations") while not regarding "illegal action as either proper or efficient." But, he said, "I am convinced this is an issue that cannot be dodged by tokenism or solved by brute power."[20]

Classes resumed on Monday, May 12, and the campus remained quiet in the early part of the week, as it seemed that negotiations would quickly resume (there were ongoing skirmishes at Brooklyn College, leading to arrests). But things quickly broke down when Copeland bucked a faculty senate resolution calling for police to be removed from campus. On Wednesday, as radical white students tore through buildings, setting off fire alarms and breaking windows, the faculty senate approved a plan for a separate black and Puerto Rican studies program. Finally, on Saturday, May 17, the police were withdrawn from campus, and negotiations resumed over the BPRSC demands, amid growing, system-wide support for an open enrollment policy, including among administrators. As CUNY deputy chancellor Seymour Hyman later remarked about his reaction to the growing militancy and violence on the campuses, "The only question in my mind was, How can we save City College? And the only answer was, Hell, let everybody in."[21]

Resolution

On Monday and Tuesday, May 19 and 20, as negotiations continued, classes were suspended at City College in favor of a two-day campus-wide convocation and workshops to discuss the issues. On Wednesday classes resumed as word came that blacks and Puerto Ricans had won a key new demand: that no City College student be given a failing grade for the semester. Students could be given a P (for pass) or a J (for withdrawal), or they could request to be graded on an A–C scale. By Friday a pact had been reached on open admissions: half of City College admissions would be made on the basis of grades. The other half would be admitted from poor neighborhoods and underrepresented high schools

"without regard to grades." Negotiators also agreed that the college would create a new School of Urban and Third World Studies for "the study of the culture and history of Blacks, Puerto Ricans, Latin Americans, and Asians." As historian Allen Ballard concluded, "In short, the students had won their demands."[22]

Almost. The next week the City College faculty senate rejected the deal, opting instead to create a committee to study the feasibility of a black and Puerto Rican studies program and changing the open admissions formula in such a way that it would likely lead to only four hundred more black or Puerto Rican students in addition to those already in SEEK. In November the CUNY Board of Education—the final arbiter—finally weighed in, adopting a system-wide open admissions policy but shifting the formula: students attaining marks equivalent to 80 percent of the school-wide average or who graduated in the top half of their graduating class would be guaranteed a place in a senior college, with preference in choice of schools to higher-ranking students. Under this formula, the chief beneficiaries of the militant black and Puerto Rican student struggle for open admissions were, ironically, white working-class students: the original BPRSC demand for proportional admissions had been lost. The formula also led to a de facto semisegregation of the CUNY system, as white students—who typically attended better high schools—had first call on the places at the more prestigious campuses.*[23]

Despite these consequences, the resolution marked a significant victory for black and Puerto Rican students, though one that came within, and perhaps contributed to, a context of rising racial tensions and increasing divisions between the black and white working classes. The year before, these tensions had come to a head when largely white and Jewish teachers, organized through the United Federation of Teachers, shut down the public school system in the city to protest growing black community control over the schools in the

---

* This result belies sentiments expressed by many conservatives—and some liberals—that the CUNY board's actions were "abetting black racism" and turning City College into an "all-black institution."

Ocean Hill–Brownsville district of Brooklyn. The protests galvanized black and white/Jewish communities against each other amid accusations of racism and anti-Semitism. The fights between black and Puerto Rican (and radical white) students and largely white, often Jewish students during the City College shutdown reflected and intensified these tensions. The Board of Education's open admissions plan sought to ameliorate them by creating a program based less on racial quotas and more on class.*

The immediate effect of the new open admissions policy was the explosive growth of the student body. The 1970 entering class was 75 percent larger than that of the year before, and total university enrollment doubled. By 1974 CUNY's enrollment of 253,327 was 300 percent larger than it was in 1969. Most of the new open admissions students were sent to the community colleges. Despite open admissions rapidly increasing the number of poor and working-class whites in the system, the percentage of students of color rapidly increased. In 1969 three-quarters of all CUNY students were non-Hispanic whites. By 1975 they were half of all students.†

* CUNY had in fact been considering and planning a system-wide open admissions program since the writing of its master plan in 1966. This plan called for a place in the system by 1975 for all New York City high school graduates: the top 25 percent in the senior colleges, the next 40 percent in the community colleges, the next 10 percent in "special schools," and the bottom 25 percent in educational skill centers.
† By 2010 73 percent of CUNY's students were students of color, by far the highest percentage in the United States; 67 percent of students came from households with less than $40,000 in income; 30 percent from households with income of less than $15,000.

Tensions among students hardly dissipated in the wake of the passing of the open admissions policy. The City College protests were part of a remarkable wave of protests on campuses across the United States over race and curricula, the escalating war in Vietnam, university-corporate ties, and expansion into nearby communities. The papers were filled all spring with reports of student unrest, of state and federal investigations into them, of police and National Guard troops—and of an increasingly militant conservative reaction to them that seemed to be pitting working-class whites (including police officers) against minority students, now seen to be beneficiaries of "special rights," and radical white students, who likewise were perceived to be overly privileged and coddled. As the 1960s faded into the 1970s, the tensions that surfaced during the open admissions struggle and similar struggles around the country would occasionally spark into violence, including on the streets of New York.

CHAPTER 14

"Homosexuals Are Revolting"

Stonewall, 1969

ERIN SIODMAK

The Stonewall Inn

Friday, June 27, 1969, late. Or Saturday, June 28, early: it was after midnight. In the back room of the Stonewall Inn on Christopher Street in Greenwich Village, the words "I can't get no satisfaction" burst from the jukebox while men danced with men, women danced with women, and an undercover police officer was beguiled by the charms of a stealth transvestite.* Laws were broken. Two female officers, also undercover, sat at the bar counting gender-appropriate garments.† Overpriced, watered-down drinks were poured into much-used, barely clean glasses. (There was no running water behind the bar, only tubs the glasses could be washed in.) Drinking was not so much the point at this bar, dancing was—and picking someone up. Owned by the Genovese crime family, Stonewall was the only gay bar in New York where dancing was legally permitted. Actually, it was not a bar at all. Legally, it was a private "bottle club," where bottles

were labeled with "members'" names for their private consumption—a ruse, of course. Like an old speakeasy, the front door was kept closed, and potential patrons were first scrutinized by a big doorman before being let in, presumably in part to keep the cops—and agents of the Liquor Control Board—out. Once inside, patrons had to sign in; most put down aliases.[1]

The doorman was not the only way police were kept out. Stonewall's owners, like other Mafia owners of gay bars, paid off the corrupt 6th Precinct cops.‡ Despite payoffs, the police had to occasionally make a show of raiding gay bars. The culture of conservativism and conformity that had descended upon America in the wake of World War II, replete with fears that homosexuality made men Cold War security threats, created an era of repression—repression of the sexual desires of some men and women and, in the other sense of the term, repression by the police. In New York, by 1966, police were arresting more than a hundred men a week for "homosexual solicitation," often in bars that served a gay clientele. Many New Yorkers approved of such actions. The threat of arrest made being gay a risky business, opening up a nice sideline for Mafia bar owners: blackmailing the better-off, perhaps professional, clientele. A virtuous circle

---

* Transgender people at the time referred to themselves as "transvestites" or "queens"; "transsexual" was rarely used, and "transgender" was not used at all. We have retained the historically accurate terms throughout.

† New York State had a law requiring that a person must wear at least three items of clothing appropriate to his or her gender. Men and women could be arrested for wearing gender-inappropriate clothing if they were wearing fewer than three appropriate garments. Stonewall was overwhelmingly a male bar, but lesbians did occasionally visit.

‡ To the tune of about $2,000 a week, according to Martin Duberman.

ensued: huge profits to criminal bar owners from doctoring booze and selling it dear, as well as from preying on their own customers; and payoffs to the cops, who sometimes raided anyway, increasing the vulnerability to patrons and leading to tighter Mafia control over the trade and more opportunities for other forms of graft. Nonetheless, raids were as often as not ritual: bar owners usually kept very little liquor on site (often storing it in cars parked down the block), so if they were raided, they would lose little and could reopen quickly; raids were usually early in the evening, when the bars were less crowded; and the cops often just closed the place down without arresting anyone. Just as often, bartenders, managers, or bouncers would be warned of an impending raid so that dancing could be suspended and untaxed liquor stashed away. Bargoers caught up in the dragnet typically took the raid in their stride, merely having to show their ID before being let back out into the night.[2]

This time, though, things would be different. While there had been rumors of a possible raid, no tipoff had been received, and when nothing happened early in the evening, the Stonewall management let down their guard, though this may have been unwise. Gays in Greenwich Village were already on edge, annoyed by stepped-up raids on bars around the Village, including one at Stonewall the previous Tuesday, as well as increased scrutiny—and the clearing out of trees and bushes—in favorite cruising places. Folks were already beginning to think, "This shit has got to stop." Some of these raids were merely part of the business-as-usual 6th Precinct graft. But others were related to an expanding probe by the New York Police Department's recently reorganized Vice Squad Public Morals Division (headquartered in Manhattan's First Division) investigating Mafia money laundering and financial bonds theft (likely involving Mafia blackmail of homosexual Wall Street workers). The First Division's deputy inspector, Seymour Pine, and his colleagues had increasingly come to see the Stonewall as a key Mafia locale: surveillance had revealed large cars pulling up, disgorging seemingly straight men who rarely stayed at the bar long. Perhaps the bar was a key node in the theft and money-laundering operation? Simultaneously, the Federal Bureau of Alcohol, Tobacco, and Firearms was investigating the pouring of bootlegged or stolen liquor at the inn and in the process uncovered the payoffs to the 6th Precinct.[3]

Raid and Riot

When the cops raided at 1:20 in the morning, it was not the 6th Precinct that took the lead.* It was Inspector Pine's First Division.[4] And it was Pine who stood before the door and announced, "Police! We're taking the place!" The lights went up and the music stopped. The go-go boys dancing in cages on the bar in gold lamé bikinis climbed down and covered up. The bar and dance floors were packed, and not many people knew exactly what was going on. Barring the door behind them, some of the officers met with the four undercover agents who had been inside to determine who the bar employees were and then separated them out from the others.† They were to be arrested for alcohol violations. Other cops separated out the transvestites, many of them teenage "street queens," as they called themselves. Sick of being harassed, many talked back. As was customary, patrons with a legitimate identification and wearing enough "appropriate clothes" were let out one by one onto the sidewalk. It took a long time, and a lot of patrons grew increasingly angry. As they came out onto the street, they found that a crowd had begun to form, attracted by the 6th Precinct foot patrol officers who had rushed to the scene, fearing they were being cut out of the action, and by the growing number of cop cars outside. It was a warm night and a weekend, and the streets were busy. The commotion also attracted a good number

---

* Officers from the 6th Precinct were drafted in at the last minute and mostly played a supporting role. This might be why the undercover cops were able to get inside: coming from outside the precinct, they were not recognized by the bouncers.
† One of the undercover male cops had apparently already arrested a young man. The cop had invited him to dance and insisted they keep on dancing, even though the boy had lost interest.

of teenage queers who hung out or lived in nearby Sheridan Square (known colloquially as Christopher Park) and for whom the Stonewall was sometimes a refuge. Instead of heading home or off to another bar, those who made it out of the bar lingered.

Inside, men in line began refusing to show their IDs. Lesbians, who were lined up along one wall, began complaining loudly of cops feeling them up. Drag queens decided this time that they just might not enter the ladies' room, where women police officers would decide if they were women or not. Pine decided to arrest the lot and called in the paddy wagons.* First to be brought out were Mafia members associated with the club.† The crowd, growing restive and campy in equal measure, erupted in cheers and jeers. Craig Rodwell, a young gay activist who had been attracted by the crowd, shouted "Gay power!" to the startlement of many. Next to be marched toward the paddy wagon were bar employees, to more cheering and jeering—and, tentatively at first, then increasingly campily, a chorus of "We Shall Overcome." Then out came the queens, who waved and smooched at the crowd, which yelled back, "Oh, Lily Law's got you, girl!"

When a cop shoved one of the transvestites being loaded into the wagon, likely Tammy Novak, she swung back with her purse and fists. At the same time—though this is disputed—another cop bashed with his nightstick a lesbian dressed as a man when she complained about her handcuffs being too tight. And, maybe, a gay man was hit.[5] Whatever precipitated it, the whole night came undone. A crowd surged up against the paddy wagon, with some calling for it to be overturned. A number of those in the van, including Tammy, managed to escape before the police handcuffed the rest to the seats and, despite slashed tires, drove off to the station house. As fury deepened, some in the crowd hurried to payphones to call their friends, gay and straight radicals alike, to the scene.‡ Craig Rodwell called the newspapers. Others threw coins at the cops—symbolic of the bribes they received—quickly escalating to cans and bottles. There were still officers and patrons inside Stonewall, and the rumor began to spread that gays inside were being beaten. Anger grew.

As the crowd went berserk, cops hit back. But they were vastly outnumbered and quickly retreated into the Stonewall, grabbing a few members of the crowd as they went, including the well-known (straight) folksinger and veteran lefty Dave Van Ronk, who had joined the crowd from a nearby bar in solidarity with what he quickly sussed out was an important moment in the civil rights struggle. Inside, the cops beat Von Ronk to near unconsciousness, accusing him of having hit a cop, and then arrested him for assault. Finding a firehose, the cops inside the Stonewall opened the door a crack and tried to wash the surging crowd away. The hose's weak stream was met with derisive howls, and the crowd surged toward the inn again.

As at least some bricks from a nearby construction site were added to the barrage being thrown at the Stonewall, street kids from Christopher Park took the lead. One of them, eighteen-year-old Sylvia Rivera, who had been hustling on the street since she was eleven, called that night "one of the greatest moments of my life." She and her friends finally decided they could fight back against those who had been "treating us like shit all these years." Someone pulled up a parking meter, which quickly became a battering ram against the Stonewall's door. Calls of "Gay power!" rang louder. "We want freedom!" "Liberate the bar!"§ The cops inside drew their guns and got ready.

But the cops held their fire. Whenever the door was smashed open, they pushed it shut and tried to strengthen the barricade behind it. Then the guys with the parking meter turned their attention to the boarded-up windows—

---

* Pine had called two paddy wagons, but only one showed up. There is speculation that the other was called back by 6th Precinct officers annoyed at the First Division having trespassed on its turf.

† The Stonewall Inn's actual owners had slipped out a back door at the beginning of the raid.

‡ One of those making a call was Jim Fourratt, who ended up disappointed, but wiser, when none of his radical straight friends rushed to his cause as he had rushed to theirs.

§ Also "We're the pink panthers!"

In the midst of the Stonewall riot.
Photo by *New York Daily News* / Getty Images.

Evidence of police destruction inside the Stonewall Inn after the riots.
Photo by Fred W. McDarrah, Premium Archives / Getty Images.

seemingly much more vulnerable.* As the windows gave way, bricks and quickly assembled (but not very effective) Molotov cocktails sailed in. "My god," Sylvia Rivera remembered thinking, "the revolution is here. The revolution is finally here!" Someone reached through a broken window and sprayed in lighter fluid, tossing a match after it. The fluid caught with a whoosh, but the fire did not take. Inspector Pine and his men were under siege.[6]

Pine had called in the Tactical Patrol Force (TPF), but they were slow in arriving. Apparently, whoever had countermanded the order for a second paddy wagon was also countermanding Pine's calls for help. Finally, after the cops who were barricaded in the Stonewall had been under siege for forty minutes, and as they desperately searched for a way out, the TPF arrived. The force marched up Christopher Street in full riot gear and deployed in a wedge formation. The crowd slowly retreated, allowing those trapped in the Stonewall to make their escape. But the crowd did not break,

and it did not run: it too was a force. Several contingents of rioters peeled off into cross streets, doubled back, and came up *behind* the crack TPF. More bricks were thrown, and garbage cans were set alight. But when the cops about-faced—expecting an onslaught—what they confronted instead was a chorus line of queens, high kicking and singing to the tune of "Ta-ra-ra Boom-de-ay":

> We are the Stonewall girls
> We wear our hair in curls
> We wear no underwear
> We show our pubic hair . . .
> We wear our dungarees
> Above our nelly knees!

Total humiliation. The cops radiated anger and lashed out with their nightsticks, particularly singling out feminine boys and street queens. Finally, just after 3:30 a.m., as the crowd was growing bored with taunting the cops, the TPF succeeded in clearing and calming the streets.

In all, thirteen people were arrested. The interior of the

---

* The owners had long since boarded up the windows to keep cops (and others) from peering in, thereby deterring raids.

Stonewall was destroyed, mostly wrecked by the besieged cops. Innumerable rioters had been injured. Four cops required treatment at area hospitals. The casualty the rioters cherished most was to an Officer Scheu: someone smacked him with a rolled-up newspaper; startled, he fell to the sidewalk and broke his wrist.[7]

One More Time

The rioting had subsided, but the air was electric. Even people who had not seen the rioting or the cops or the damage could feel it. Something had changed. The world had changed. Craig Rodwell's calls to the media worked. Bulletins were broadcast on the radio and TV on Saturday, and while the riot was too late for the Saturday editions, the papers carried the story on Sunday.[8]

Word on the street was more important, though. Crowds gathered all day Saturday, seeking details, swapping information. On the boarded-up door and windows of the Stonewall (which had vowed to reopen that night), painted slogans appeared: "Legalize Gay Bars"; "Support Gay Power"; "They Invaded Our Rights." On the streets couples held hands: boys with boys, boys with men, street queens, lesbians. Blacks and whites showed up, and lots of Puerto Ricans. Christopher Street was now *their* street. By evening they were kissing, out there on the street. Chorus lines formed and reprised "We are the Stonewall girls." The festive crowd swelled into the thousands as the TPF stood by, nightsticks in hand, riot shields poised. Finally, having had enough, the riot cops moved, clubs swinging in an effort to clear the street. Once again, gays and queens slipped into the side streets and came up behind the police line, singing and dancing, enraging the cops. One phalanx of protesters barricaded Christopher Street, stopped cars, and rocked them back and forth until drivers retreated. They soon trapped a taxi. A queen in full drag jumped on the hood and started beating it, terrifying the driver and passengers before several in the crowd, including Rodwell, helped it escape.

The TPF had lost control. Sylvia Rivera watched her friend Marsha P. Johnson climb up a lightpole and drop a heavy bag on a police car windshield, shattering it.* Cops leaped out of the car and beat the nearest person they could find in retaliation. A crowd in Sheridan Square launched a fusillade of bottles, missing the cops but hurting some of those in the crowd. (One witness thought they might have been straight anarchists or police provocateurs.) The crowd on the street radiated anger. New York queers were in open rebellion—a rebellion marked by kicklines as well as street barricades, jeering songs as well as Molotov cocktails, shouts of "Gay power!" as well as hurled stones, handholding, kissing, and posing as well as spitting anger. And it was a rebellion marked by wit: at one point when a squadron of police was forced to turn and run from the angry crowd, the crowd giving chase was soon joyfully chanting "Catch them! Fuck them!" The TPF, assisted by a troop of mounted police, was determined to put the uprising down. By about four in the morning they succeeded, at the cost of a number of bashed heads and the further radicalization of street queens, lesbians, and middle-class gay men alike. On a flyer he produced the following morning, Craig Rodwell predicted that the two nights of rioting would "go down in history."[9]

Before Stonewall

One of the men there on Saturday night, Chris Babick, expressed a common sentiment: "It was an absolutely exhilarating experience to know . . . they had defied authority. And it was . . . like the beginning of a lesbian and gay value system. . . . We were just out. We were in the streets. I mean, can you imagine?" Craig Rodwell said the riot was "a way

---

* The "P." in Marsha's name stood for "Pay It No Mind," which is what she famously told a judge when she was bailing Sylvia out. The judge, who saw a lot of transvestites in his courtroom, had no trouble getting the double entendre and was amused by it. Within a year Rivera and Johnson (a black transvestite who had taught Rivera to survive on the streets) had organized STAR—Street Transvestite (now Transgender) Action Revolutionaries—dedicated to organizing homeless trans youth.

of saying, 'We're tired of hiding, tired of leading two lives, tired of denying our basic identity.'" Stonewall was not the first gay riot in America—three years earlier, gay street kids and drag queens had rioted inside and fought the police outside Compton's cafeteria in San Francisco—but it was the one that seemed to change everything (and not only in New York).*[10]

What did it change? There had always been a gay New York, of course, and at times it could be quite public. Before the Depression, drag shows flourished in the bars and cabarets of the Bowery and Harlem, which, while often catering to straight desires for entertainment, allowed men to meet men and transvestites to be out and open. Public toilets and parks hosted well-known cruising sites. It was not hard to find same-sex dance halls, and in the Bowery or the Tenderloin, gay male, straight female, and transvestite prostitutes could often be found on the street corners. The back rooms of bars hosted gatherings and offered opportunities for sex, as did the city's numerous gay bathhouses. Lesbian bars and salons dotted the landscape.

Queer sex did not always imply a queer sexual identity: identities could be quite fluid, with (particularly working-class) men seeking out other men for sex but not necessarily seeing themselves as gay or effeminate (indeed, gay sex could be a way of asserting masculinity). Some men advertised their same-sex desire by wearing clearly understood "insignia of homosexuality" like bleached hair and red ties. Other men fashioned themselves as queers and fairies (who may or may not have been sexually interested in other men). This was a world constructed more in relation to gender than to sexual activity. Even so, during the 1920s, gay residential enclaves developed in Greenwich Village and Harlem.[11]

And it was a world that was always contested. Cops raided bars—or got paid off by them (or, like Stonewall, both). Gay bashing was all too common. Off and on, city administrations and reform societies launched morality campaigns, vowing to clean up the city and to enforce more decorous sexual mores, reinforcing through its opposition to gay sex and identity a strict heterosexuality defined by a kind of "sexual apartheid" that sequestered women in the home while promoting male virility—a new expression of proper masculinity—in public. Such campaigns were aimed at destroying the fluidity of identity and the polymorphism of sex. Unlike the relatively open 1920s, the Depression years, for all their political radicalism, were simultaneously, in New York, a time when "anti-gay reaction gained force . . . as . . . part of a more general reaction to the cultural experimentation of the Prohibition years and to the disruption of gender arrangements by the Depression. . . . A powerful campaign to render gay men and lesbians invisible—to exclude them from the public sphere—quickly gained momentum." The walls of what we now call "the closet" were being erected.[12]

The doors were pushed shut during the 1950s. The FBI kept a list of known homosexuals, the U.S. Postal Service made note of where queer magazines were sent, and same-sex relationships were understood automatically to be a security threat. In 1952 the American Psychiatric Association defined homosexuality as a mental disorder in its "bible," the *Diagnostic and Statistical Manual.* City police across the country stepped up their street sweeps and barroom raids and set up stings to entrap men in known cruising areas. Throw in the graft, corruption, and organized crime that inevitably tag along with public morality campaigns, and the Stonewall raid was nothing unusual. Gays had been putting up with such repression, as they liked to say, *forever.*[13]

It is not that queers did not push back, did not try to pry the door back open, but it was not easy. In 1950 the Los Angeles communist Harry Hay organized the Mattachine Society to militate on behalf of "sexual deviants."† By 1953

---

* And even earlier, in 1959, police harassment provoked a small riot among queers in Los Angeles.

† Mattachine took its name from a society of medieval French traveling musicians and dancers who performed at festivals and feasts, part of the long tradition of popular overturning—*revolt*—that was so central to the medieval social order. In turn, Mattachine was named after an Italian court jester, Mattaccino.

Barbara Gittings of the Daughters of Bilitis and Randy Wicker of the Mattachine Society picket during the second annual Reminder Day at Independence Hall, Philadelphia, July 4, 1966.
Photo by Kay Tobin, © Manuscripts and Archives Division, The New York Public Library.

to dance formed the Daughters of Bilitis, which advocated lesbian assimilation into larger society—or, rather, for larger society's acceptance of lesbians.* Branches of the two societies, as well as other homophilic groups, spread to other cities. If they proved slow in changing minds, they nonetheless opened up space for meeting and organizing. For many young queers moving to a new city, they were the first port of call.[14]

Spurred on by the civil rights struggle, younger members of these organizations pushed them to emulate black activists' growing militancy, especially after the national Mattachine Society dissolved in 1961, leaving local chapters to their own devices. New York's Daughters of Bilitis and Mattachine, together with the Mattachine Societies from Philadelphia and Washington, D.C., formed East Coast Homophilic Organizations (ECHO), which, under the tutelage of Frank Kameny, soon took to staging annual pickets to protest homosexuals' exclusion from federal employment and the military. Though fairly staid affairs—Kameny pushed for a strategic appearance of conformance, no matter how much he himself cherished nonconformance—the pickets gave gays and lesbians a sense of strength as they demanded what was rightfully theirs. Craig Rodwell soon joined ECHO and by 1964 was pushing it always to go further (he came up with the idea of an annual Fourth of July picket, "a gay holiday," called the Annual Reminder).† He also formed Mattachine Young Adults. And he went on TV to debate antihomosexuals. He drew new members into Mattachine, including Dick Leitsch, who, after winning leadership of the New York branch, stepped up its militancy. Leitsch in turn eventually won new mayor John Lindsay's promise in 1965 to end police entrapment of gays.‡ The next year, Leitsch,

---

* *The Songs of Bilitis* (1894) by French poet Pierre Louÿs is a long, erotic prose poem that relates the life of Bilitis, a fictional companion of Sappho on the island of Lesbos.
† By its second year, 1966, the Annual Reminder had drawn the attention of the federal government's Bureau of Special Services, which carefully reported on it. The FBI tried unsuccessfully to recruit Rodwell to report on homophilic meetings.
‡ The Transit Police, not controlled by the mayor, continued to entrap men.

Mattachine had shifted tactics and become much more an assimilationist society that sought to change minds, to convince the larger society that Mattachine members were just like normal people. Around the same time, a small group of women in San Francisco seeking to create a safe place

Rodwell, and John Timmons decided to stage a sip-in, where they would publicly declare their homosexuality at a bar and demand drinks. Bars in New York could be shut down as "disorderly houses" if they served homosexuals. The first bar the men tried had got wind of the planned protest and was closed. At the second, a Howard Johnson's, they were cheerily served (the bartender made sure the reporters tagging along got a drink too). The same thing happened at the next bar. Finally, they washed up at Julius, a well-known gay hangout. The trio got the bartender to admit he could not legitimately serve them a drink if he knew they were gay and used that as a pretext to file a discrimination complaint with the New York State Liquor Authority. They were backed by the black chairman of the Human Rights Commission, William Booth, who saw little distinction between sex discrimination and racial discrimination. Eventually, a district court ruled that the State Liquor Authority could revoke a bar's license for running a "disorderly house" only if "substantial evidence" of indecent behavior could be provided. Well covered in the papers, the sip-in and its aftermath garnered a good deal of support from prominent straight liberal people.[15]

Police raids continued nonetheless. People dancing in a bar that did not have a cabaret license were subject to arrest, and the bar could lose its liquor license. Men dancing with men or women with women was, by definition, "indecent." So was cross-dressing. Even as homosexuality was gaining some acceptance in the larger society—WBAI hosted a weekly radio discussion devoted to gay issues called *The New Symposium*—and even as gay political organizations around the country were growing increasingly militant, everyday life remained a challenge. Radical college students were expelled from leftist groups because they were homosexual, the *Village Voice* barred the use of the word "gay," and professionals feared exposure and the loss of their jobs, or they faced blackmail. The population of young gays and queens living on the streets swelled; they got by through the hard work of hustling and mutual support—against the violence of gay-bashers, as well as the condescension of some

middle- and upper-class gays (who might anyway be happy to be hustled). Lesbians faced the burdens of their gender, as well as their sexuality.[16]

It was in the midst of all this that Inspector Seymour Pine and the First Division Morals Squad stepped up the campaign against Mafia-owned gay bars, only this time, in the early morning hours of July 28, 1969, to be met by the likes of Sylvia Rivera, ready to say, "Now it's my time. I'm out there being a revolutionary for everyone else and now it's time to do my thing for my own people." Or, as a flyer for the Gay Liberation Front, formed not long after Stonewall, put it, "Do You Think Homosexuals Are Revolting? You Bet Your Sweet Ass We Are!"[17]

After Stonewall

The Wednesday after the weekend of rioting, the *Village Voice* published two stories. One was by reporter Howard Smith, who had been trapped inside Stonewall the first night with the police. The other was Lucian K. Truscott, a young stringer for the paper. He reported on the events of the two nights, and on Sunday he tagged along with Allen Ginsberg as he checked out the Stonewall for the first time.* When Ginsberg came out of the bar and set off through the neighborhood, Truscott continued to tag along. "You know," Ginsberg said, "the guys there were so beautiful—they've lost that wounded look that fags all had 10 years ago." Gay all of a sudden *did* seem beautiful.[18]

But Ginsberg's remarks were all but drowned out by the furor that erupted when Truscott's piece was published. Truscott both admired and belittled "the sudden specter of 'gay power,'" referring to the "forces of faggotry" let loose by the police violence, the limp wrists and primped hair of the rioters, and the scene on Sunday as the "fag follies." People were pissed. Truscott (and to some degree Smith) had ignored the fight many of the rioters had put up, as well as the

---

* As was traditional after a raid, the Stonewall immediately opened up again (it had to borrow furniture from nearby establishments), though it did not do much business on Saturday night.

large presence of many traditionally masculine men. A large crowd formed outside the *Voice*'s office, and someone soon tried to set it on fire.* Angry queers were joined by a growing number of straight radicals looking for a fight with the police. As the night wore on, trash fires were lit, eventually provoking the TPF. The streets exploded again, but this time "the street people were no longer half-serious, half-camping" (as Leitsch put it), and the cops were ready to exact revenge. The fighting was intense, with street queens taking the lead. (The straight radicals seemed more intent on breaking into stores, missing entirely the ones that were most exploitative toward gays.) Dozens of people were injured (including one cop), and five people were arrested. But this time the rioting only lasted an hour or so, not all night. No matter: by now, as Ronnie Di Brienza later wrote, "the word is out. Christopher Street shall be liberated. The fags have had it with oppression."[19]

When the 1969 Annual Reminder was held a few days later on July 4 at Independence Hall in Philadelphia, Kameny tried to keep two women from holding hands, but Rodwell pushed back and got ten couples to defy him. "It was clear things were changing," remarked Lilli Vincenz, who took part. "People who felt oppressed now felt empowered." Bill Weaver changed his picket to read "SMASH SEXUAL FASCISM!" The press lapped it up. Back in New York, Mattachine counseled restraint, but it was clearly overtaken by events. Electric Circus, the hippest nightclub in the city, announced it would gladly welcome gays, and Mattachine worked with it to host a big party a week after the police raid. Mattachine's Randy Wicker made a speech extolling gay power but also criticizing the riots. At that moment, one of Electric Circus's employees, freaked out by all the homosexuals around him, hauled off on the nearest one he could find, starting a brawl that ended the night. It was not going to be an easy struggle.[20]

Three days later Mattachine sponsored a big meeting—

more than a hundred people showed up.† The meeting voted to organize a big demonstration and march to protest police harassment. As planning got under way, Martha Shelley, a Daughter of Bilitis veteran, and others in the room hit on a name: the Gay Liberation Front. The demonstration would be held on the one-month anniversary of the riots and sponsored jointly by the New York chapter of Mattachine and the Daughters of Bilitis. A big ad in the *Voice* urged attendees to wear lavender arm bands. More than five hundred men and women showed up for the 2:00 p.m. rally, gathering at the fountain in Washington Square Park. A big lavender banner was unfurled with two interlinked female symbols on one side and two interlinked male symbols on the other, and lavender arm bands and sashes were passed around. Martha Shelley stood up on the fountain and yelled out to the crowd: "The time has come for us to walk in the sunshine. We don't have to ask permission to do it. Here we are!"‡ She went on, "We will no longer be victimized by straight people who are guilt ridden by sex. We're tired of flashlights and peeping-tom vigilantes. Tired of marriage laws that punish you for lifting your head off the pillow." After more speeches, the crowd set off down 4th Street for Christopher Park (Sheridan Square), but plans to continue on to the 6th Precinct station house were abandoned (to the annoyance of some of the more militant marchers).[21]

The Gay Liberation Front soon consolidated itself around a revolutionary ideology and worked in solidarity with a range of radical Left organizations. Within a few months, members wanting to focus solely on queer issues (and maybe not challenge capitalism) split to form the Gay Activist Alliance, which took to "zapping" politicians and celebrities—ambushing them at public events and forcing them to acknowledge the legitimacy of gay rights. New papers—*Gay*

---

* Gays' grievances against the *Voice* were long-standing, as many found it exceedingly uptight and conservative in matters of sexuality, whatever its reputation for being "alternative."

† One, Bob Kohler, tried to collect money to support the street queens in Christopher Park, but he received little support from the mostly middle-class, mostly white crowd.

‡ Shelley was sounding a theme that would resonate down the years, echoing perhaps most strongly in the 1990s Queer Nation chant: "We're queer, we're here, get used to it!"

Marsha P. Johnson and Sylvia Rivera marching with STAR (Street Transvestites Action Revolutionaries), June 24, 1973.
Photo by Leonard Fink. Courtesy of the LGBT Community Center National History Archive.

Fissures in the movement—between feminists and gay men, women and drag queens, street queens and "respectable" gays, sex workers and professionals in other lines of work, whites and people of color—developed early and deep. Tough street queens like Sylvia Rivera were often pushed aside. Still, the movement shifted the world. The American Psychiatric Association quickly delisted homosexuality as a mental disorder. City governments began—against concerted opposition—writing same-sex protections into civil rights laws. Voters in California refused to pass an initiative that would have kicked homosexual teachers out of the schools. "Gay villages" sprouted everywhere.* When AIDS hit, there was now a history of concerted organizing that could be drawn on to confront the disease and the state that seemed at first content to ignore it or stigmatize it. New militant organizations formed. By the 1990s, bisexuals had fought their way into a place in the struggle, and the old term "queer" was readopted as a badge, an identity, as transgender people joined the struggle. On the twenty-fifth anniversary of Stonewall, more than a million people marched in New York, with, now, Sylvia Rivera holding a place of honor.†[22]

The Stonewall Inn

After the second night of rioting, activists called for a boycott of the Stonewall Inn, declaring it was time to get the Mafia—and the cops—out. In addition to the boycott, the Stonewall faced increased police scrutiny (even as the cops themselves came under fire for corrupt practices) and found it impossible to serve alcohol (elsewhere in the Village and across the city, gay bars continued to be raided). The Stonewall closed within three months. For two decades it hosted various businesses—a bagel shop, a Chinese restaurant—be-

Power and *Come Out!*—were founded. And the first anniversary of the riots, June 28, 1970, was christened Christopher Street Liberation Day and marked by a big rally and march to Central Park (marches were also held in Los Angeles and Chicago), starting the tradition of Gay Pride marches that would soon be picked up worldwide.

---

* These villages included lesbian neighborhoods such as Park Slope and neighborhoods in Northampton, Massachusetts.
† In 1992 the body of Rivera's friend Marsha P. Johnson was found in the Hudson near the Christopher Street Pier. The coroner ruled it a suicide; her friends think she was murdered.

fore a new gay bar, the Stonewall (no "Inn"), opened in the early 1990s in a portion of the building. In June 1999 the U.S. Department of the Interior declared the Stonewall building and surrounding streets a National Historic Landmark, while the inn itself was named a landmark a year later (the city added its imprimatur in 2015). The upper floor of the building was added to the bar at the end of the 1990s, and the Stonewall served as a popular dance venue for a time (despite trouble obtaining a cabaret license that would permit dancing: Greenwich Village's Community Board unan-imously opposed giving the bar a cabaret license in 1997). The bar closed again in 2006 in part because of noise complaints from neighbors in the now hypergentrified Village. It was reopened a few months later by new owners, once again as the Stonewall Inn. Since marriage equality became the law of New York and then all of the United States in 2015, the inn has served as a prime location for gay marriages, perhaps (even as this too is contested by radical queers—the struggle between assimilation and difference has not abated) as good an indication as there is of how the social earthquake the Stonewall Riots helped set off has continued to reverberate.

THE HARD HAT RIOTS, 1970

Early in the morning on Friday, May 8, 1970, students and other antiwar protesters began to gather at the corner of Broad and Wall Streets in Lower Downtown—the very spot Buda had bombed fifty years earlier. Protests had been building on college campuses around the country throughout 1969, and two demonstrations that fall—the October Moratorium and the November Mobilization—had rattled the relatively new Nixon administration. Nixon had promised during his election campaign to wind down the war, but nearly a year into his presidency there was little evidence of this. The president and his advisors thus developed a plan to both disrupt (and infiltrate) antiwar protests and mobilize the broad middle of the populace—the "silent majority," as Nixon famously called it in a November 1969 speech—in support of his Vietnam policies and against students and other radical activists. Instead of withdrawing troops from Southeast Asia, however, Nixon intensified the war, announcing the invasion of Cambodia on April 30, 1970. Campuses erupted in rage, with wave after wave of student strikes. Then on May 4, National Guard soldiers opened fire on protesting students at Kent State, killing four. Twenty percent of all American campuses were

shut down by their students in response. Half of all colleges and universities hosted protests.[1]

The students gathering on Wall Street came mostly from New York University and Hunter College (where classes were suspended), as well as city high schools (classes in the schools had been suspended too). They were there to demand immediate withdrawal from Vietnam and Cambodia, as well as the release of all political prisoners in the United States and the end to military work on American campuses. Finally, they were there to mourn the students killed at Kent State. By midmorning a thousand had gathered, sitting on the street at the intersection and listening to speeches.

A few minutes before noon, about two hundred construction workers wearing overalls and hard hats converged from four directions, directed into position by marshals wearing suits and ties and special identifying badges on their lapels. As the police stood by—or were pushed aside—the construction workers waded into the student protest, swinging flags on poles and lashing out with construction tools and fists. With many Wall Street workers cheering from nearby windows, the students

scattered as workers gave chase, injuring seventy. Witnesses (and victims) said police continued to do nothing, even as the mob of workers ripped down a Red Cross banner from Trinity Church and a flag from the nearby Episcopal church. As more workers—many from the World Trade Center site—joined the melee, the rioters surged to Pace University near City Hall, where they threw rocks at students on the roofs, broke into one of the buildings, trashed the lobby and broke windows, rushed to the roof to grab a peace banner and light it on fire, and beat students. The mob massed again at City Hall and cheered when a mailman in the building ascended to the roof and raised an American flag to full mast. The flag had been lowered to honor the students killed at Kent State. When an aide to the mayor lowered the flag again, the crowd erupted and surged forward over police barricades and across car roofs, striking out at cops and bystanders alike. Afraid the mob could not be contained, Mayor Lindsay (who was at Gracie Mansion uptown) ordered the flag raised again. Workers stopped, sang "The Star Spangled Banner," yelled epithets ("Lindsay's a Red!"), and eventually dispersed.[2]

All through the next week, students

Construction and other workers gather on Wall Street at the outset of what came to be known as the Hard Hat Riots of 1970.
© Henry Gordillo.

remained on strike, and workers paraded and protested, but police—stung by criticism—generally maintained the peace. Students vowed to shut down Wall Street (one protest was organized by East Coast graduate business students with "short hair, modest sideburns, and coats and neckties"), even as construction workers, longshoremen, and an increasing number of white-collar workers held competing rallies, supporting Nixon (and his vice president, Spiro Agnew) and the war and denouncing Mayor Lindsay as "a rat, a Commie rat, a faggot, a leftist, an idiot, a neurotic, an anarchist, and a traitor" (as the *New York Times* summarized the signs observed at the hard hat rallies). A week after the original riot, perhaps as many as five thousand workers gathered in Lower Downtown to rail against the mayor and peace activists. They invaded buildings (including the *Wall Street Journal* offices) and passed out petitions calling for Mayor Lindsay's impeachment. In Midtown, another crowd of two hundred or so construction workers paraded an effigy of Lindsay and occasionally scuffled with bystanders. At both rallies police did little or nothing to restrain the protesters (and arrested no one).[3]

Then on Wednesday, May 20, supporters

of the war held a massive "Honor America, Honor the Flag" rally sponsored and organized by the Building and Construction Trades Council of Greater New York. Between 60,000 and 150,000 people paraded down lower Broadway for more than two hours, hanging the mayor in effigy and waving a sea of American flags in a "show of power that drew cascades of ticker tape in the financial district." More than three thousand cops were deployed to keep the peace. One contingent of "hundreds" of riot-gear-clad police marched at the rear of the parade, giving the impression of enthusiastic participation (a police spokesman said they were an auxiliary contingent detailed to help keep order when the parade broke up, if necessary). The rally and parade were almost entirely peaceful.[4]

The next day the new Coalition for Peace—a student-labor coalition—held a rally of twenty thousand at City Hall (they were taunted by a smaller group of hard-hatted workers) before two contingents of a thousand each began marching north, winding their way through Greenwich Village and then on toward Bryant Park. Police determined to stop them before they reached the park. One group was turned back down Broadway at 40th Street, but the second group, coming up the Avenue of the Americas, tried to push on. The police waded in with batons swinging, injuring nine protesters and arresting several. This proved to be the last day of direct confrontation between the "hard hats" and antiwar protesters.[5]

The week of protests and counterprotests, parades and rallies, student strikes and workers' "shows of power" made visible the deepening divide between an America being remade by antiwar activists, student movements, gay uprisings, and countercultural currents and an America rooted in the desires and sureties of Nixon's silent majority. But as sociologist Penny Lewis has made clear, it is not accurate to say that the riots, protests, and counterprotests somehow represented a split between working-class whites who supported the war and elites, students, and hippies who did not, even if this was the interpretation that the Nixon administration and many in the press immediately sought to advance. On the whole, support for the war was stronger among middle-class and elite Americans than among members of the working class. Coalitions and alliances were far more complex than the simple narrative of hard hat hawks versus hippy doves lets on—and this was evident on the street, where plenty of working people expressed disgust with the war and with the hard hat rioters and their Wall Street cheerleaders. That narrative also suggests a kind of monolithic working-class conservativism that simply cannot be squared with the facts. For example, the first years of the 1970s witnessed the largest and perhaps most militant wave of strikes since the end of World War II, and workers' often left-wing militancy had the effect of drawing students who were seeking to broaden the basis for their own activism and struggles into the labor movement. There is no doubt that deep cleavages in American society were exposed by the Hard Hat Riots and protests, but they did not cleave solely along class—or race—lines. It was not "the white working class" out in Lower Manhattan smashing heads with flagpoles, and it was not just students and hippies on the receiving end (some of those injured were lawyers and Wall Street workers).[6]

Even so, the narrative of a conservative, head-banging, white working class and an increasingly elite counterculture would powerfully affect national politics—and the New York landscape—for years to come.

PEOPLE'S FIREHOUSE #1, 1975–1978

In early February 1976, as New York struggled to emerge from near bankruptcy ("Ford to City: Drop Dead," as the famous headline went), the administrator of the city's Department of Housing and Development, Roger Starr, wondered aloud whether New York should develop a policy of "planned shrinkage" in "slum areas like the South Bronx and Brownsville that are already characterized by large stretches of abandoned and razed buildings and a 'very marked' decline in population." Should the city plan the withdrawal of police and fire services, the closing of public housing and schools, and the creation of inducements to get remaining residents to move to where, as he put it, there was a "continued willingness to live"? Should the city develop a policy to empty out whole neighborhoods and let the land lie fallow "until new land uses present themselves"? Did the population of New York need to "achieve a new configuration," as Starr later asserted? The crisis facing the city was deep and multifaceted, Starr argued, and New York's abandoned neighborhoods and its overstretched infrastructure limited the vitality of what he called the "economic city." The main question for Starr was whether the "political city"—the government, as well as

the polity—had the will to carry out the sort of radical pruning that would be necessary to encourage the vigorous health of the plant as a whole.[1]

Starr had been developing his argument for some time, arguing in a 1966 book that "community" was a fiction, at best. People living together in poor neighborhoods had no bonds, no "kinship," no "web of love and kindness." "American communities," he wrote, "can be disassembled and reconstituted about as readily as freight trains." Given this, he "advocate[d] the continuation of urban renewal, in the course of which we may displace poor people and make room for middle-class people." While he advocated the creation of racially mixed communities and better design for (and more investment in) public housing, he also "urged taking an indeterminate number of children away from the homes of their natural parents or parent, to raise them in new, small, pioneering institutions." Poor and minority neighborhoods in cities were not "communities" but places of pathology.[2]

The arguments about pathology among minority families and the suggestion that perhaps children should be taken from them echoed Daniel Patrick Moynihan's

earlier, deeply racist, but exceedingly influential *The Negro Family: A Case for National Action* (written for the Department of Labor in 1965), which argued that a pathological "culture of poverty" shaped America's slums. As President Richard Nixon's special advisor on urban and social policy, Moynihan followed up his 1965 arguments in 1970 with a specious analysis of fire alarm data (provided by a branch office of the RAND Corporation think tank) that suggested that black pathology in New York had taken the form of a massive wave of arson. "Fires," he argued in a memo to the president, "are in fact a 'leading indicator' of social pathology for a neighborhood. They come first. Crime, and the rest, follows." He thus advocated a policy of "benign neglect": the shifting of resources of poor neighborhoods and their reallocation to middle-class (white) ones. Since arson, crime, and family dysfunction were "pathologies," they were contagious. Young, more middle-class black men would necessarily catch the crime, arson, and dysfunctionality bug from those around them if they lived in the ghettos. Better to let ghetto neighborhoods die. That was the malign reasoning of "benign neglect."[3]

Abandoned New York.
Photo by Manel Armengo,
used by permission of the photographer.

New York's 1975 fiscal crisis provided the opportunity to put Moynihan's "benign neglect" and Starr's "planned shrinkage" into effect, as shrinking city budgets—focused particularly on services like police and fire, on the size and wages of the municipal workforce (at a time when official unemployment reached 12 percent), and on investment in infrastructure that served the poor (like public schools and public housing)—were forced upon the city as a condition of its "rescue" from overwhelming debt. Transit fares were hiked. Tuition was imposed for the first time at CUNY schools, where open admissions had been won only a few years before. Public hospitals were closed. And in poor neighborhoods, firehouses were closed.[4]

During the autumn of 1975, New York laid off nine hundred firefighters, about 10 percent of the total (already significantly reduced from even Depression-era staffing levels), and on November 22 moved to close four firehouses (of twenty-six slated in July to be closed), sparking protests at most of them. One of those set to close on November 22 was Engine Company 212 in Williamsburg, Brooklyn. More than a hundred demonstrators descended on the station at 136 Wythe Avenue and blocked the doors to prevent the engines from being removed and redeployed at other stations (they also prevented the company from responding to several alarms—all false—that last morning). Engine Company 212 served a predominantly Polish Northside

neighborhood bordered by Greenpoint but relatively isolated from other parts of Williamsburg. Residents were scared by what seemed to be an epidemic of fires in poor sections of Brooklyn, the South Bronx, and elsewhere in the city. Firefighters knew well that landlords were torching their buildings to collect insurance. And beginning in 1975, the Housing and Development Administration—Starr's old haunt—stopped sealing abandoned buildings; fires accidently caused by squatters or children or improperly shut down gas and electricity lines became common (saving the city the costs of demolition).[5]

Disinvestment, abandonment, and fire all seemed to be spreading north out of Bedford-Stuyvesant. And area residents had already seen protesters in other parts of Brooklyn (such as the predominantly Hispanic Bushwick) successfully win reprieves for their station houses after blockading the fire engines inside and essentially holding the firefighters hostage. Northside residents were already reasonably well organized following a protracted struggle in 1972 to save housing (for ninety-four families) slated for destruction in order to make way for the expansion of a machinery company. And the firehouse itself served as a significant community center. When the city first announced the closing of Engine Company 212 in July 1975, three hundred people rallied to its defense, winning a reprieve.[6]

Early on November 21, when firefighters sounded the alarm indicating to neighbors that the station would be shut, a crowd quickly formed out front and, like their Bushwick counterparts, held the firemen and engine hostage. A squad of fifty police officers soon arrived and threatened the protesters with arrest. Most would be charged with misdemeanors, but seventeen protesters who had entered the building were threatened with felony kidnapping and larceny charges. The protesters did not budge, though they did let the firemen (but not the engine) out.

After dubbing it People's Firehouse #1, protesters occupied the firehouse for more than a year, sleeping in shifts and holding big community gatherings once a week and big parties on holidays (replete with kielbasa and pierogis, sold for a dollar a plate to support the occupation). Union firefighters supported the occupation, and politicians sometimes appeared in the big hall of the People's Firehouse. From the firehouse, occupiers organized pickets at the home of the fire commissioner and outside mayoral dinners. They held mock funerals for the fire engine. And on April 14, 1976, they climbed en masse onto the Bronx–Queens Expressway and stopped traffic during the morning commute (police surprised many by letting the blockade of the highway happen and continue for some time). Finally, in December 1976 Mayor Abraham Beame announced the reopening of the firehouse, effective the following March. When the reopening proved only to be partial, Northside residents continued protesting, finally winning the complete reestablishment of Engine Company 212 in June 1978. It closed again in 2003, and the firehouse was awarded at auction in 2008 to a community group founded during the 1970s occupation to develop it into a community center.[7]

The People's Firehouse protests were conducted by a largely ethnic Polish population, though African Americans were involved. Like African American neighborhoods, desperately poor ethnic neighborhoods were also targeted for disinvestment—for "planned shrinkage." By New York standards the People's Firehouse struggle was remarkably tame (over its course there were no arrests, and no one was injured, much less killed), perhaps precisely because members of the white, rather than the Latino or black working class, were at its forefront. The struggle was nonetheless indicative of the changing city and the way planners, city officials, and

A meeting during the People's Firehouse occupation.
Photographer unknown.

financiers were laying the groundwork for its phoenix-like rise from the ashes of the 1970s fiscal crisis and the urban maladies that surrounded it. Moynihan in his crudely racist (if liberal) way and Starr in his more racially inclusive (if neoconservative) way were together theorizing how what would soon be identified as "rent gaps"—the deliberate driving down of land rents so that later they might be raised again through gentrification—could be created in the city. The People's Firehouse struggle exposed what planned shrinkage and benign neglect looked like on the ground and showed just how hard working-class people would fight to maintain their communities in the face of the enormous condescension of the city's—and the nation's—elites.[8]

The struggle did not, however, quell the flames of New York.

CHAPTER 15

Burn, Baby, Burn

The 1977 Blackout and Riots

MIGUELINA RODRIGUEZ

Wednesday, July 13, 1977, was sweltering. The city was embarking on a scorching heat wave that would last all week. By evening, big thunderstorms were rolling across Westchester County to the north of the city. At 8:37 p.m. a lightning bolt hit a substation in the town of Buchanan, tripping the circuit breakers. Poor maintenance kept them from resetting themselves. More lightning strikes knocked other transmission lines out of service. In turn, this caused more lines to exceed their limits. Consolidated Edison workers responded by shifting power to other parts of the grid, overloading them. As lines and circuits around the region failed, New York City's power supply grew increasingly isolated. Soon generators within the city were overtaxed. The whole city went dark at 9:36 p.m. Power would not be fully restored for twenty-five hours.[1]

New York Explodes

New York had been through this before. In November 1965 a region-wide blackout darkened the city for thirteen hours. For many, that night turned into a party, though reports of a spike in births in the city nine months later seem to be urban legend. This time would be different. By the time the lights came back on, two people had been killed and more than 400 police officers, 80 firefighters, and 204 civilians had been injured. A thousand fires had been started in a massive arson spree: firefighters responded to 2,780 alarms (compared to an average 1,274) and fought 1,037 fires (compared to a typical 350). Sixteen hundred stores were looted, and 3,776 looters and rioters were arrested. At ten times the number of people arrested during the 1964 Harlem Riot, it was the largest mass arrest in the city's history. The total cost of the blackout (spoiled food, lost wages, and the like), rioting, and looting reached at least $346 million and probably a lot more.[2]

This was no party; it was an explosion. The lights were hardly out before the streets erupted. In some neighborhoods, stores were being looted within ten minutes and in other neighborhoods maybe as fast as five minutes. "It was almost like it came out of the air," a liquor store owner in Bedford-Stuyvesant said. Like the Stonewall rioters eight years earlier, looters in Bushwick found that parking meters made good battering rams. Even so, within twenty minutes someone had driven a car through the metal grate of a sporting goods store there, and soon the store went up in flames. Within half an hour there were disturbances in all five boroughs (though Staten Island got off relatively lightly). Cars, vans, and U-Hauls quickly appeared to haul off TVs, couches, and refrigerators. Sometimes looters showed up in tow trucks and used the winches to pry open roll-down doors and locked gates.[3]

Every poor neighborhood in the city was hit (even as

diners on Manhattan's Upper East Side merely moved out onto the sidewalks, and Broadway shows improvised in the semigloom of flashlights and emergency lighting).* Some were hit hard, but probably none were hit as hard as Brooklyn's Bushwick. When the lights went out, there were only fourteen cops on duty in Bushwick (in a community of more than ninety thousand). All up and down Brooklyn's Broadway, which separates Bushwick from Bedford-Stuyvesant and over which runs an elevated subway that nearly covers the open streetscape, crowds formed and re-formed. Store after store was ransacked, and while everything seemed totally chaotic, at least some of the looters made keen calculations as to what could likely be resold—not just electronic goods (to be sold in better-off neighborhoods) but especially baby food, diapers, and canned food (to be sold in the looters' own neighborhoods). Others went for the guns in sporting goods stores. The cops were largely powerless, and though they made a number of arrests, mostly "they just turned on their sirens and hoped that people would run away," as one looter later put it. The sirens had little effect. Before it was all over, 134 stores along Broadway were looted, and many were also torched. When firefighters arrived and raised their cherrypickers to douse the flames, "the looters went about their business virtually unmolested" down below, as *Time* magazine reported. A working- and middle-class white ethnic district only a decade or so before, Bushwick was now predominantly Hispanic, black, and very poor.† As the night wore on, "the crowds on Broadway . . . seemed to possess a special kind of

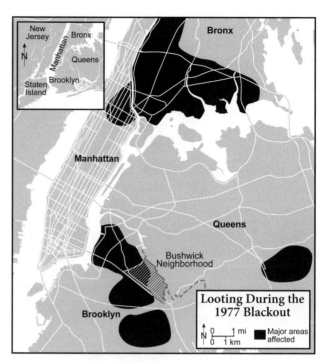

Looting during the 1977 Blackout.
Cartography: Joe Stoll, Syracuse University Cartography Lab and Map Shop.

hysteria," as a postmortem written for the Ford Foundation put it.[4]

As the scale and extent of the rioting, looting, and arson became known (to say nothing of all the other myriad challenges to the functioning of a city of 7.5 million people, almost all without power: blacked-out stoplights, people trapped in elevators and subways, and who knows what else), Police Commissioner Michael Codd called in all hands, but the order was to report to the nearest precinct. Since 1962 New York's finest had been allowed to live outside the city, and many did. Suburban cops who reported (many cops just ignored the call-out) tended to show up in the quiet outer reaches of Queens and the Bronx, where they were joined by growing numbers of cops who had opted to live in the city but tended to locate in the grow-

---

* Looting was not unknown in wealthier sections. At a grocery store in the relatively more prosperous Upper East Side neighborhood of Yorkville, a woman was observed stuffing a bag of ice in her Louis Vuitton handbag as others grabbed sliced pineapples, meats, and soups (on the hottest night of the year).

† In 1950 Bushwick was 100 percent white, with a population of 123,000; in 1960 its 125,000 residents were 89 percent white; by 1970 the population had grown to 138,000, but the white population had dropped to 38 percent. Over the next decade, the population collapsed to 93,000 in 1980, of which only 15 percent were white, 26 percent were black, and 56 percent were of Hispanic origin.

ing white ethnic enclaves on the outskirts (more cops pooled in Staten Island).* When they were eventually reassigned, well into the early morning, they were typically ill equipped (many had shown up in civilian clothes, dressed for hot weather, looking more like "a tennis team" than police ready to put down a riot, according to one police commander in the South Bronx). On the whole, in the worst-hit neighborhoods, the cops remained remarkably passive. This was partly because they were outnumbered. To some degree it was also Daniel Patrick Moynihan's "benign neglect" in action, as cops thought that if folks wanted to destroy their own neighborhoods, the cops should let them. To a degree it was a strike: the police union was in the midst of intense contract negotiations and seething mad about continued cuts (including to support staff, which made it both difficult and time-consuming to process arrestees).† And in part it was pure pragmatism: "If we'd have shot just one person that night, we'd have a war on our hands," one Brooklyn officer later explained. Mostly, though, it was not a riot *against* the cops. The cops were "just pests," according to a Brownsville sergeant: "We were just something to get around so they could get at the goods."5

Cops around the city did open fire, mostly over the heads of threatening crowds. But mostly the defense of businesses was left to their owners or managers, armed with guns, clubs, dogs, and sometimes just flashlights—or to no one at all.‡ (Often, by the time owners got to their stores, it was too late.) And this was not a race riot, as whites and blacks alike took part in the looting. White and black stores alike were

hit. So were places rooted deep in their communities, like the Fort Greene Cooperative Market.6

Mayor Beame called it "a night of terror," but it was not yet over. On Thursday, July 14, as the sun rose over the city, the rioting and looting around the city abated—but not for long, and not on Bushwick's Broadway, where crowds only seemed to grow. Broken glass was everywhere. Dismembered mannequins littered the street. Impromptu street markets arose on the corners. More than twenty fires continued to blaze, even as firefighters were now being pelted by rocks and debris, sometimes thrown from the elevated tracks.§ In Harlem, some who had not participated in looting the night before were now drawn in as looting started up again. "Now we could see what was there and get what we wanted," one teenage girl said. She wanted laundry detergent, baby food, and spinach. Farther south on 110th Street, a middle-aged lady pronounced herself on a shopping expedition, "no money required." In Williamsburg, a tire store was broken open and the new tires taken, four to a man. In University Heights, the Bronx, fifty Pontiacs were stolen from a dealership. Down on East 14th Street in Manhattan, "youths roamed the streets, snatching purses from women," according to the *New York Times*.** Back in Bushwick, looting continued into the late afternoon. A black pharmacist guarded his drugstore, gun in hand, all through the night and into the day. Finally, at 4:00 p.m. he slipped out to get something to eat. When he returned half an hour later, his store was being ransacked, and only when he shot his gun over their heads did the looters disperse. Up in the Bronx, at least some merchants were buoyed by the devastation: they would be collecting insurance for their burned-out stores.7

The power started coming back on in midafternoon—by

---

* About ten thousand officers out of a total force of twenty-five thousand simply failed to heed the call-out. Several thousand others were on sick leave or away on vacation. At the height of the rioting, the force numbered eight thousand; on the second day, it numbered closer to eleven thousand.

† On top of that, there simply was not enough jail space to hold all those arrested. Between slow processing, backlogged courts, and overcrowded jails (or people detained merely by cuffing them to seats in waiting areas), a second crisis unfolded in the wake of the riot, one that this time exposed the devastating effect that cuts were having on the judicial system.

‡ Two looters were shot dead by merchants in the course of the night, one in Fort Greene, the other in Harlem.

§ Bushwick was no stranger to fire. An epidemic of arson—much of it by landlords seeking to push out tenants and claim insurance money—hit the neighborhoods in the first years of the 1970s as the district rapidly shifted from middle- or working-class, ethnic, and white to poor and minority.

** The claim that looters were only after "relatively expensive, highly portable" goods and took the opportunity to grab them, as one academic study by a geographer claimed a few years later, is clearly inaccurate. As one looter told a reporter, "We got Pampers now, baby. Now we got Pampers."

Looting in Bushwick during the 1977 blackout.
Photo © Alon Reininger / Contact Press Images.

which time temperatures were in the midnineties again—but it was slow to reach the poor parts of the city. The last neighborhoods were not lit up until 10:30 p.m. Rioting in Bushwick subsided around 11:00. Finally, New York's most widespread riot—the only time rioting had hit all five boroughs at once—came to an end, but not before the federal Small Business Administration declared the city (and, inexplicably, Westchester County) a disaster area, though President Carter failed to follow suit and grant general disaster status, claiming—accurately—the blackout and looting were not "natural."[8]

Making an Unnatural Disaster

Like the slave revolts and the Great Negro Plot of the eighteenth century, fire seemed to be a tool for expressing outrage and provoking fear, but the 1977 riot was not a plot, and it was not a conspiracy, and it did not seem to be directed

particularly at the property of "masters" (chapter 2). Like rioters in Harlem in 1935, looters across the city saw an opportunity "to seize what rightfully belonged to them but had long been withheld," as a mayor's commission argued then, but this time there had not been the same kind of racist precipitating event, the same sort of heavy-handed policing that sparked rumors and unrest (chapter 12).

It seemed like a spontaneous combustion. Rioting and looting raged—almost immediately—in Harlem and East Harlem, the Lower East Side and the Upper West Side, and up and down Midtown; it exploded in the South Bronx (Morrisania, Mott Haven, Melrose) and even north of the Cross Bronx Expressway along University Avenue, the Grand Concourse, and Webster Avenue up to Fordham; it consumed Brooklyn's Bedford-Stuyvesant, Brownsville, Ocean City, Crown Heights, and Sunset Park and the white redoubts of Flatbush, East Flatbush, Sunset Park, and Coney Island; it flared very briefly in Jackson Heights and caught fire in Jamaica, Queens; and little outbreaks were reported around Staten Island. It seemed totally inexplicable. The best explanation many could come up with right away was that the looters were "animals," "savages," "uncivilized," and merely looking for any excuse to unleash mayhem.[9]

But, in fact, it was an explosion a long time in the making. In Bushwick, according to one of the *New York Times'* editors, before the riot, and after, there was simply "nothing to lose," and, writing ten days after the riots ended, he noted that "today, Bushwick is back to normal. The plight of its citizens was no different than a couple of days before, except that some residents had a little more unexpected food on the table and a few unanticipated articles of clothing. But the unemployed still stand around on street corners or play cards in the shade." Unemployment in Bushwick that summer was 30 percent, and among youth it neared 60 percent, which was also the percentage of residents receiving some form of public aid. By 1972 fire companies in the district were responding to more than six thousand calls a year as neighborhood housing was gutted.* Well before the blackout, torching buildings was "part of the culture," according to a Community Board member. Crime spiked in the 1970s, especially robberies, burglaries, and grand larceny. The blackout just seemed to speed up and make general what was there all along. "It gets dark here every night," according to a local teenager. "Every night stores get broke into, every night people get mugged, every night you get scared on the street. But nobody pays attention until a blackout comes."[10]

What was not being paid attention to extended across the city. In just the three years leading up to the 1976 Bicentennial, New York lost 340,000 jobs. Citywide teenage unemployment among blacks (70 percent) and Hispanics (80 percent) made Bushwick seem reasonably good. The city's near bankruptcy had forced rapid shrinkage of services, planned or not, and the neglect many communities thus suffered was anything but benign. For example, in 1969 New York recognized that Bushwick "urgently need[ed] every type of

community facility and service. . . . Assistance must be provided quickly." Instead, services were cut and disinvestment encouraged. Elsewhere, the northern reaches of the Upper West Side were all but redlined—where big redevelopment projects had not been started and abandoned—leaving a landscape of little more than single-room-occupancy hotels and not nearly enough services for their residents. In the South Bronx, as population hemorrhaged, services were slashed, and the city more or less decided to let it die as remaining residents were abandoned to their fate. Fire companies were pulled out of Brownsville and the Lower East Side, the South Bronx and Harlem, and dozens of other poor neighborhoods besides. The new tuition at CUNY (where most of the students were part of the working class) made college suddenly unaffordable.[11]

Such public disinvestment was met with private real estate schemes that combined active disinvestment with blockbusting strategies and the beginning of rampant speculation (which would take off in the 1980s). In neighborhood after neighborhood, agents perfected the art of fanning the flames of racial resentment and fear, encouraging white residents to sell at a loss, then flipping the homes, selling them at or above market value to incoming minority families, often expecting them to default on their Federal Housing Administration–guaranteed mortgages. As explained by a Bushwick community activist some years later,

> Real Estate Brokers took houses they had bought for cheap panic sale prices, then had them appraised by bribed inspectors, who assigned a high value to them. They were painted to look nice on the outside and sold to minority, first time, unsophisticated buyers, with low down payments and federally insured mortgages. Sometimes the new families were able to hold on for 5 or 10 years, but when major repair problems [arose] or the family's income declined, they had to default. Rather than work things out, it made the broker more money to foreclose quickly, get paid off by FHA insurance, and sell the house to another innocent victim. Families, as well as the neighborhood, paid dearly in this game, as most of

---

* By some estimates, one in every eight buildings in Bushwick was torched each year between 1969 and 1977.

the houses eventually ended up boarded up and uninhabitable.[12]

These blockbusting schemes yielded big profits and a shattered landscape. Perhaps as many as five hundred buildings in Bushwick alone were abandoned through such scams. At the same time, homeownership rates sank from 72 to 30 percent. Most landlords were absentee. The pattern was repeated in working-class neighborhoods around the city.

During the blackout, looters and arsonists around the city seemed indiscriminate, hitting locally owned and minority-owned stores, as well as stores owned by whites, by people from other parts of the metropolitan area, and by corporations. Even so, the majority of stores hit during the rioting were owned by whites who lived outside the neighborhood, mostly in Rockland County, in the outer districts of Queens, or on Long Island. Many of these owners had once been local residents but had joined the white suburban exodus. Of business owners receiving loans from the Small Business Administration, 72 percent went to whites, 15 percent to blacks, and 13 percent to Puerto Ricans. The lack of owners' community connections had been a factor in past riots—nonresident owners of local stores were often understood as "oppressors"—and this was hardly absent this time. As *Newsweek* reported, "One chain supermarket, disliked in the area for its alleged high prices, was picked clean, but another, more popular supermarket nearby went untouched. A particularly large crowd invaded a chic haberdashery, reputed to have an uppity sales staff, and made off with everything but a solitary espadrille. . . . 'A lot of stores in this neighborhood are locally owned,' said Victor Lopez, a teacher in a junior high school. 'They weren't hit as much.'" If the crowds on Bushwick's Broadway "possessed a special kind of hysteria," it might have been because it was a street dominated by suburban shopkeepers. By contrast, in nearby shopping districts on Knickerbocker Avenue and Graham Avenue, where many of the stores were owned by local Puerto Rican residents, damage was comparatively light. Local owners could

more quickly defend their stores, of course, but this is likely not the full explanation.[13]

More than a decade of disinvestment—in jobs, in buildings, in neighborhoods, in social programs, in policing and fire protection, in the welfare of poorer urban residents—a disinvestment that tracked closely the racial geography of the city (if it did not follow it exactly), made conditions ripe for an explosion. The blackout lit a very short fuse. Such disinvestment helps explain why the 1977 blackout was so different from the 1965 one. Then, the social fabric was not quite so frayed.* But not all the rioting and not all the looting can be said to have been determined by such disinvestment. It cannot explain much of the opportunism that clearly marked the night, much less the lady with her Vuitton bag in Yorkville.† Nor can it explain why, often, "there was an element of glee, perhaps of revenge" (as *Time* put it), though perhaps older traditions of rioting can. When the lights went out, norms were suspended. The world was upended. The "Night of Terror" was a fiery, furious, destructive, out-of-control festival.

But Was It a Revolt?

In an anguished editorial published two weeks after the rioting, the *New York Times*, arguing not quite accurately that all the rioting took place in poor, multiply deprived (and nonwhite) neighborhoods, asked, "Could it be that the civility we prize is related unavoidably to prosperity?" Rather than

---

* There were lots of other differences too. The 1965 blackout was far shorter in duration, and it happened on a cool November evening.
† Writing for the Ford Foundation, Robert Curvin (a community organizer) and Bruce Porter (a journalist) drew on interviews and an analysis of arrest data to suggest that the looting evolved in three stages, and each stage involved a different kind of looter. Stage 1 featured people intent on destruction rather than plunder and typically involved alienated youth or ideologically motivated actors. Stage 2 featured more organized criminals seeking loot that could often be resold. Stage 3 was an "open, widespread, and non-systematic taking of goods. At this point plundering becomes the normative, the socially supported thing to do."

answer their own question, the editors commented instead: "If even the prosperous cannot remember to ask that question, more than we think was lost that night."[14]

But plenty of people were asking something like that question and were answering in the negative—looters were nothing more than animals, was the common refrain—setting into motion a "blackout backlash" that helped entrench a growing rightward political shift in the city. "At its best," the journalist Jonathan Mahler later wrote, the backlash admitted that deprivation in "hurting neighborhoods" had to be addressed but that the rioters could not be excused. To do so "was patronizing, paternalistic, racist even. Those who pointed to the misery of life in New York's ghettos to explain the looting weren't just missing its real cause; they were perpetuating it by fostering diminished expectations for the underclass."[15]

Indeed, neither fires (including arson) nor property crimes were at all out of the ordinary in the areas most affected by blackout rioting. What was exceptional, however, was the scale and intensity of the explosion, the involvement of "stable" neighborhood residents who were unlikely to have been involved in routine crime, the almost gleeful destruction and mayhem associated with the looting, and, paradoxically, the visibility and audacity of criminal activity taking place completely in the open that would have typically been committed in secret.* The looting seemed to have "a quality of madness to it," according to psychologist Morton Bard. It was not entirely rational. In some cases, looters stole goods with little monetary value, for example, "cleaning out a store of prayer shawls and bibles." Most strikingly, the torching of buildings and the obstruction of firefighters make any attribution of rationality—if not a kind of inchoate *revenge*—difficult.[16]

Inchoate revenge—a lashing out—is not the same as political revolt, which seemed to set the blackout rioting apart

* And it was not just crime. The magazine *Michael's Thing* reported a big gay outdoor orgy on Weehawken Street, just off Christopher, in the long-since-liberated Greenwich Village.

from the urban uprisings of the 1960s (which included significant looting). Narratives of the time described the blackout rioting as markedly apolitical, an individualistic "free-for-all" of looting and destruction that was much more about taking advantage of an opportunity to acquire material goods than about articulating ideas or demanding change. As *Newsweek* put it, in contrast to the riots of the previous decade, this time it was "apparently not the product of . . . rage against whitey's Establishment." There are few, if any, reports from the time of political arguments or statements being made on the streets. The closest explanation there is beyond mere acquisitiveness and opportunism—and probably the most accurate—is that the night and day of rioting and looting were "a chance to let our frustrations out—a valve."[17]

And it was a valve opened wide. Thousands of residents were angry and frustrated enough to generate an unprecedented rampage of destruction focused on neighborhoods of concentrated poverty and public and private disinvestment but extending well beyond them. There is little doubt that rioters as a whole were deeply dissatisfied with the economic and public circumstances of their lives. Yet, unlike some previous urban uprisings, they did not express this dissatisfaction in the form of a political message or demands made on those who could intervene to make their lives better. In fact, by 1977 such an inchoate uprising may have been the only possibility for revolt. By then, it was not only poor and minority neighborhoods that had been disinvested but, in many ways, the political process itself. President Nixon's "southern strategy"—of which Moynihan's "benign neglect" was an important part—had been successful in ripping apart the Democratic race-class coalition, and the national Democratic Party had rapidly retrenched, embarking on its project of becoming a center-right party. The Black Panthers, Young Lords, Brown Berets, and innumerable Marxist parties had been sundered, through repression, infighting, and strategic errors, leaving few outlets for organized radical politics—and consequently less organizing in the neighborhoods. The high point of urban liberalism, with War on Poverty programs geared directly at community development, sometimes with quite progressive outcomes, had been gutted by Congress and, in New York City, killed off by post–financial crisis policies geared toward saving the banks at the expense of the people. Shrinkage—both planned and unplanned, both geographic and institutional—was accompanied by a vicious ideological assault that positioned poor and minority neighborhoods as a drain, a blight on the city, their residents beset with a moral and psychological pathology, place and people both dying and hardly worth saving.

If the riots were not a "political revolt," in any simple sense of the term, they did have a profound political effect. Whatever the gathering steam of the blackout backlash may have been, the riots focused the eyes of the city, the nation, and the world on conditions in areas deemed by city leaders to be "blighted" and slated for death by disinvestment. Now in view, any continuing neglect of the neighborhoods could not be passed off as benign. People now knew what was up.

Already-devastated neighborhoods were even more devastated when the rioting subsided. Stores stood empty and were often severely damaged. Buildings were burned out. Neighborhoods were burned out. And for a while they continued to burn, right up to the moment in the early 1980s when the big insurance companies decided they would simply stop paying out for claims on tenement buildings. In the year before they stopped paying insurance, thirteen hundred buildings were destroyed by fire in the Bronx. The year they stopped, only twelve were. And on the empty lots there and in Brooklyn, Harlem, and the Lower East Side, neighbors and kids started clearing out rubble and planting gardens, while remaining walls were covered with stunning graffiti murals. If the riots seemed inexplicable in the moment, soon rappers, developing a new art form, started to make sense of them and the urban world that gave rise to them on the streets.

Meanwhile, Mayor Abe Beame was replaced by Ed Koch, who pledged—and followed through on—a $5 billion Ten Year Plan for Housing Rehabilitation, which, in the words of urbanist Marshall Berman, was "an immense success" in beginning to fill back in the landscapes—maybe "anti-landscapes" is the better term—long blanked out by urban renewal and fire.*[18]

Such rehabilitation from the streets and such attention from the government were soon joined by the seemingly new phenomenon of gentrification. Decades of disinvestment, plus a day of arson and looting, rather ironically paved the way for enormous profits to be gained by real estate and development interests. Haltingly at first, but picking up steam over the 1980s, gentrification reversed the course of "planned shrinkage" and turned the benign/malign neglect of the previous years into a new kind of laser-like attention on many of those neighborhoods that had previously been written off. The double irony, of course, was that the poor and working-class residents of these neighborhoods were now faced not with disinvestment but instead with the equally malign force of displacement. If, back in 1976, Roger Starr could promote the removal of as many as *two million* "unproductive" New Yorkers—if he could call for the city government to promote "population transfers" of whole neighborhoods of poor people and people of color right out of the city (we must "stop the Puerto Ricans and rural blacks from living in the city," he wrote)—he could not ever have imagined that the insidious forces of gentrification would be a far more effective tool than his planned shrinkage and the urban rage it helped give rise to ever could be.[19]

---

* Technology historian David Nye defines an "antilandscape" as "a man modified space that once served as infrastructure for collective existence but that has ceased to do so, whether temporarily or long-term. Human beings can inhabit landscapes for generations, even millennia, but they cannot inhabit anti-landscapes. . . . [H]ighly technological societies can create anti-landscapes quickly, even suddenly."

CHAPTER 16

"Die Yuppie Scum"

Homelessness, Gentrification, and the Liberation of Tompkins Square Park, 1988

NEIL SMITH

Another hot, sultry night and another riot. The police riot that erupted on the night of August 6, 1988, in Tompkins Square Park looked a lot like the Tompkins Square Riot of 1874, except for the weather (chapter 7). As then, police truncheons rose and fell; officers charged on horseback; demonstrators scattered for cover; an hours-long struggle ebbed and flowed, sparked and calmed again throughout the neighborhood; and the obligatory investigations were duly convened. This time, however, amid a widespread housing crisis ("immensely successful" as it was, Koch's Ten Year Plan only scratched the surface), the immediate issue was not so much jobs but homes and the right to the city more generally. When a stunned *New York Times* finally covered the riot several days later in a nervously patronizing report, it did so under the headline "Class Struggle Erupts along Avenue B."[1]

Police Riots Happen Here

A demonstration of more than a hundred homeless people, punks, antigentrification activists, students, local residents, and squatters convened in Tompkins Square Park that August evening in opposition to enforcement of a resuscitated nineteenth-century curfew covering city parks. For city authorities, the real target of the curfew was the apparent disorderliness of Tompkins Square Park, which lay in the path of gentrification pulsing in from the west. In the 1980s the park had become home to dozens of the city's burgeoning homeless population, evictees from both the public and the private housing market, as well as a meeting place for squatters, antigentrification activists, kids playing boomboxes, and others attracted by the Lower East Side's traditional acceptance of political radicalism and cultural alterity. By the media and the authorities alike, continuing to reflect the rhetoric of blight, abandonment, and pathology laid down in the 1960s and 1970s, the Lower East Side was treated with suspicion, disgust, and more than a little fear, seen as a place of dirt, dregs, and misfits. Beneath more polite descriptions of the neighborhood as "nontraditional" or "bohemian" lay a more sinister depiction of the Lower East Side as "Indian country, the land of murder and cocaine," raising the specter that on the new frontier (this one urban) the natives were to be wiped out or sent to reservations. The park remained "a holdout, the place for one last stand," suggested one reporter.[2]

Indeed, the park did not exactly operate according to the mores of the city's white upper classes. The basketball and handball courts in the north of the park attracted local teenagers, mainly African American and Puerto Rican, some Caribbean, while the bandshell in the south hosted music, plays, and other performances and offered the only shelter against rain, snow, and wind and a place to store bedding. Elsewhere, Ukrainian men speaking Russian played chess with whoever sat down at one of the stone chess tables and accepted the challenge, homeless men and women shared the benches and walkways with young musicians, young Puerto Rican women pushed kids in strollers, young guys peddled soft drugs along the west side, and fashionably dressed yuppies strode to and from work. Workers on a break tended toward the eastern end of the park. Jamaican Rastafarians hung out as if in mockery beside the 1890s temperance fountain, political activists congregated closer to the bandshell, and hard drug sellers and users gathered on the park's south end—"crack alley." As day became night, punks played boomboxes. The park was scruffy, relaxing, free-flowing, energetic, at times tense, and it had its share of characters, but it was rarely if ever more threatening than any other public space, except when the NYPD, ridiculed by many as the "Bureau of Indian Affairs," arrived on patrol. In fact, with so many "eyes on the street," as Jane Jacobs might have put it, it was a comparatively safe space, which is why homeless people congregated there in the first place.[3]

The police goal that night, then, was to evict this population and, as police and politicians alike put it, "clean up" the park, which had become a focal point of citywide antigentrification politics and organization. The victims of crossed signals or misinformation or both, the posse of police assigned this task had actually barreled into the park the night before in full "where's-the-riot?" mode but, finding no demonstration to target, resorted to surreal face-saving displays, parading on maneuvers in the park's open spaces. Captain MacNamara of the local precinct solemnly explained to Father George Kuhn of St. Brigid's Church, which borders the park (Avenue B and 7th Street), that "we can't afford to lose this one."[4]

The cleansing began in earnest the night after the police misfire. As the small demonstration got under way, a number of chants rang out: "Gentrification is genocide"; "Whose fucking park is it? It's our fucking park"; "Gentrification equals class war"; and (the catchy) "End spatial deconcentration." Through a small makeshift speaker system one demonstrator exhorted the crowd: "Yuppies and real estate magnates have declared war on the people of Tompkins Square Park." But the chant that stuck more than any other, becoming emblematic and gaining international currency, was "Die Yuppie Scum." An acronym for young urban professionals, the term "yuppie" had been coined in the early 1980s to describe the emergence of a new young sector of the budding upper-middle classes; 1984 was deemed by *Newsweek* to be "the Year of the Yuppie."*[5]

Although the new curfew did not officially go into effect until 1:00 a.m., NYPD officers had assembled barricades at all park entrances by 10:00 p.m. Before midnight they moved into the park, and protesters responded with chants of "Hell no, we won't go." As demonstrators were increasingly corralled and obviously outnumbered, and with mounted police joining the park eviction effort, the noisy but peaceful demonstrators reluctantly retreated onto Avenue A. With the park cleared, barricaded, and guarded, the mounted cops now lined up on Avenue A facing the crowd, which had grown to several hundred. An M80 firecracker exploded, and a couple of bottles were thrown at the mounted police, who, after first backing up, suddenly charged down Avenue A, supported by hundreds of riot-shielded, baton-wielding cops on foot. A series of "cossacklike" charges ensued as police, with their badges deliberately turned around to disguise their identities, chased down fleeing protesters and bystanders. According to one eyewitness account:

> The cops seemed bizarrely out of control, levitating with some hatred I didn't understand. They'd taken a relatively small protest and fanned it out over the neighborhood, inflaming hundreds of people who have never gone near the park to begin with. They'd called in a chopper. And they would eventually call 450 officers. . . . The policemen were radiating hysteria. One galloped up to a taxi stopped at a traffic light and screamed, "Get the fuck out of here fuckface . . ." [There were] cavalry charges down East Village streets, a chopper circling overhead, people out for a Sunday paper running in terror down First Avenue.[6]

* "Yuppie" derived from the prior term "Yippie," an acronym for the Youth International Party, coined in 1968 at the height of the 1960s rebellions and itself, of course, deriving from "hippie," which later returned to its roots in cool—though now fully commodified—as "hipster."

Police rioting at Tompkins Square Park, August 1988. Photo by Andrew Lichtenstein, used by permission.

A visiting Chinese student who had been at the earliest demonstrations in Beijing's Tiananmen Square offered a parallel account, later recounted by the poet Allen Ginsberg. "In China, he said, the police were dressed in cloth like everybody else. That was *amazing* because in China it was pushing back and forth, and maybe batons. But here it was people who looked like they were dropped from outer space with these helmets on, dropped in the middle of the street. . . . And just beating people up, passers-by and householders—anyone in their path. Completely alienated and complete aliens."[7]

An appalled local pastor, Father Frank Morales, reported that "there were isolated, insane beatings"—"the police have monopolized violence." In one episode, cops attempted to invade the gentrified Café 7A at the southwest corner of the park. Marina Stoev, manager of the café, had tried to close its doors when the riot started, but several police officers, claiming that fleeing protesters had taken refuge inside, de-

manded entry. Stoev protested, but the police invaded the café anyway, roughed up an employee, and arrested Stoev, who was hauled off in handcuffs. After hours of rioting, the police officers had other, more pressing needs, however. When several police came knocking in search of a toilet the barricaded café employees angrily refused to unlock the doors, relenting only when the café manager was released.

As dawn began to arrive before 5:00 a.m., the police retreated from the area, leaving the park eerily empty. Remaining protesters jubilantly retook the park and quickly appropriated a blue-and-white NYPD sawhorse barrier, which they used as a battering ram against the most hated symbol of gentrification in the neighborhood: the Christadora apartment building. Built as a settlement house in 1928, the outsized sixteen-story Christadora at the corner of Avenue B and 9th Street has its own contentious history but had been empty since the 1970s. The city was unable to offload it until the early 1980s, when the gentrification wave engulfing the neighborhood suddenly made it the object of intense speculation and eventually developer reinvestment. Its renovated condo apartments, including a penthouse advertised for $1.2 million (an unheard-of sum for the Lower East Side at that time), had come onto the market only months earlier. Now, in the emerging Sunday morning sunlight, protesters smashed its glass-and-brass doors with their police barrier and trashed its foyer.[8]

The tally of arrests for the night was only nine people, none on serious criminal charges, but seventy people were injured as a result of the riot, the vast majority at the hands of the police, and in the days that followed, 121 complaints of police violence and other violations were filed with the Civilian Complaint Review Board. Lower East Side video artist Clayton Patterson videotaped the riot, some of it from a perch atop an Avenue A lamppost, in a practice he called the "democratization of surveillance."* The resulting four hours of film, which vividly documented the extent of police brutality perpetrated by the officers with their badges reversed, became a central if contentious exhibit in the aftermath of the riot. Partially on the basis of the evidence of Patterson's video, seventeen officers were cited for "misconduct," and six were eventually indicted, but none were ever convicted. The police commission did admit, however, that some NYPD officers may have been a bit "overenthusiastic."[9]

Despite obvious police culpability, the main response of the media was to intensify its vilification of the area and its denizens, while the president of the Patrolmen's Benevolent Association, Phil Caruso, denied that his officers had instigated the riot, blaming it instead on "social parasites, druggies, skinheads," and "communists." Mayor Edward Koch concurred, adding "anarchists" to the list and describing the park and neighborhood as a "cesspool."[10]

Roots of the Riot

If the Lower East Side was a cesspool, it was because the fiscal crisis of the 1970s had ushered in a set of practices

* In 1988 filming an event was hardly the common practice it later became. Video had not long been easily portable and cheap.

and policies that we now recognize as neoliberalism. These policies had at their heart the dismantling of nearly a half century of liberal urban policy. The effect on cities (as has already been made clear) was dramatic. In New York as elsewhere, disinvestment by property owners and landlords was fueled by postwar suburbanization and intensified after the urban uprising of the 1960s and the rise of the civil rights movement. In the subsequent decade, serious academics debated the possibility of simply abandoning entire central cities, and the signs of such abandonment seemed to be everywhere. Novels like *Last Exit to Brooklyn* by Hubert Selby Jr. and *The Bonfire of the Vanities* by Tom Wolfe and movies like *Fort Apache, the Bronx* and *Escape from New York* made New-York-as-dystopia seem like common sense. In the built landscape of the city, the level of housing abandonment grew to an astonishing forty thousand units lost per year between 1970 and 1978—the making of an antilandscape—and the abandonment was not confined only to housing. Factories and shops were abandoned, schools and firehouses were closed, parks were allowed to fall into disrepair. Some housing was replaced, of course, but still the city lost 321,000 housing units between 1970 and 1981.[11]

Diminished housing availability was compounded by incipient gentrification, since, paradoxically, as capital evacuated parts of the central city, leaving block after block physically decayed and demographically abandoned, it also flowed back in search of selective neighborhoods where land depreciated by disinvestment and abandonment was cheaply available. Many among the poor were increasingly caught between the scissor blades of disinvestment-led abandonment and investment-led eviction, and this, together with the earlier deinstitutionalization of mental health patients without sufficient social support, inevitably multiplied the number of homeless people—evicted from the housing market and social support system alike—on the streets of New York City.[12]

All this was compounded by the city's fiscal crisis—which, among other things, gutted democracy as the city council's authority was usurped first by the unelected Municipal Assistance Corporation and then by the equally un-the pockets of a new generation of rich kids, it also became the homeless capital of the advanced capitalist world. The number of homeless people soared—estimates ranged between seventy thousand and one hundred thousand in the last years of the 1980s, or as much as 1.3 percent of the city's recorded population.[13]

New York's surplus population—surplus, that is, to the productive needs of capital—became more and more visible in public space, especially in the center of the city, where scraping by was marginally easier: panhandling and can and bottle collecting were more lucrative; churches and city shelters offered sporadic refuge; institutional spaces, from libraries to transport hubs to subway tunnels, offered further shelter from the weather; and well-peopled streets and nearby nooks and crannies provided a bit of safety against robbery, attacks, and harassment by police and city residents. Attracted by a large number of vacant buildings, open spaces, less stringent policing, local soup kitchens, and a more accepting population, many homeless people congregated in the Lower East Side. An old working-class neighborhood long dominated by European immigrants and their descendants, heavily German, Ukrainian, Polish, and Russian, many Jewish, the area had long attracted political and cultural rebels; it was a major focus of working-class organization and revolt in the nineteenth century and became the crucible of antiwar, socialist, suffragist, and anarchist organizing around World War I. Emma Goldman, Leon Trotsky (working for the newspaper *Novyi Mir—New World*—on St. Mark's Place), the Yiddish-socialist *Forverts* (published in the now-landmarked Forward Hall on East Broadway), and so many of the radicals who gave labor, socialist, and anarchist politics their heft before World War I called the Lower East Side home. Several decades later, it made room for Beat poets (like Allen Ginsberg) and avant-garde jazz musicians.

Since long before the 1970s, the area's tenements had suffered widespread disinvestment, however, and the post–World War II public housing projects on its eastern edge along the East River were also in increasing disrepair. During the 1950s and 1960s a new group of Puerto Rican immigrants came to the neighborhood, followed later by Chi-

A sign on a squatted building in the Lower East Side in the 1980s.
Photo by Stacy Walsh, Rosenstock / Alamy Stock Photo.

elected Emergency Financial Control Board, both largely run by bankers—and any recovery was delayed by the Federal Reserve–induced recession of 1981–82. But then there was a five-year surge of exuberant economic expansion that saw the stock market reach then-dizzying heights (the Dow Jones Industrial Average peaked at 2,224) before spectacularly crashing on October 19, 1987. The mid-1980s recovery was different from earlier ones, however. It may have given rise to the yuppie down on Wall Street or up on Madison Avenue, but it also gave rise to ever-growing numbers of homeless people. The 1970s fiscal crisis, together with the 1980s recovery, induced "a broad reordering of city life as bankers, financiers and conservative ideologues made an audacious grab for power," as historian Josh Freeman put it. "Normally opaque class relations became shockingly visible." As did class struggle, though less on Avenue B than in the boardrooms of skyscrapers, where city elites engineered a new polarization between rich and poor in place of the comparatively muted differences that had prevailed since World War II. As New York bolstered its position as a global city atop the world's financial system, awash with capital in

nese workers employed by inflowing Chinese capital in an expanding, long-established Chinatown in the Lower East Side's southern reaches. The northern section above Houston Street was optimistically renamed the East Village in the postwar period, a real estate moniker that gained currency only in the late 1970s as the first signs of gentrification appeared on the Lower East Side's western edge.* As the fiscal crisis of the 1970s and the early 1980s recession took hold, the first artists began to set up galleries and residence in the areas, attracted by relatively cheap rents in vacant properties, many on five-year leases. As the decade proceeded, "Lower East Side" became an international brand name in the art industry, connoting the latest in New York cool. Clubs and restaurants—often turning grit into style—as well as squatters and the newly insurgent culturati all gravitated to the area, together with groupies and consumers of the scene. As the trickle of inbound housing capital surged to a flood, especially after 1983, when the city transferred the symbolic but abandoned Christadora settlement house to a developer, the yuppie invasion of the Lower East Side was not far behind.[14]

Redeveloped into a park in the 1880s (following the first Tompkins Square Riot; see chapter 7) and planted out with elms and maple trees, Tompkins Square Park was the scene of periodic riots, police and civilian, and a habitual venue for political movements, organization, and demonstrations well into the next century. It saw action in the 1960s not just around the bandshell, where famous "alternative" music groups performed, but also when the police violently attacked hippies chilling out near Keep Off the Grass signs. Park redesign and reconstruction had long been central tactics in discouraging the political use of the city's public spaces, and Tompkins Square Park was no exception. But park redesign had another purpose too. In the wake of the 1970s economic crisis, the city relinquished any serious effort at new public housing construction, and it is no exaggeration to say that under the Koch mayoralty in the

1980s, gentrification was increasingly *the* housing policy.† To encourage gentrification, the administration sought to rehabilitate and emphasize its long-neglected environmental amenities and embarked on an effort to redesign several Manhattan parks so that they would become magnets to gentrifying capital. First, Union Square on the northern border of the Lower East Side was closed in 1984 for reconstruction in connection with the construction of Zeckendorf Towers, eponymous luxury condominiums built by one of the city's largest developers. Two years later in Washington Square Park to the west, the unearthed nineteenth-century curfew was debuted along with intensified policing in an avowed effort to curtail the drug industry there.‡[15]

Subsequent plans to tackle Tompkins Square Park were rejected by Manhattan Community Board 3 as a patent vehicle for fostering gentrification. Yet as more and more homeless people converged on the park in the late spring of 1988, the board requested greater policing but fell short of calling for a curfew. Citing the expense, the police refused unless the curfew was also included. Waiting until after the board's last meeting before people scattered for the summer, the NYPD summarily announced the curfew in July, but its enforcement was sporadic. A July 20 anticurfew demonstration attracted about three hundred people and several neighborhood bands, and although the police tried to empty the park at midnight, they were outnumbered and forced to retreat. In the end, NYPD used a secret meeting, held the following week with five procurfew members of the fifty-person Community Board, to justify the escalating use of force, which precipitated the riot the following weekend.

---

* Before then the East Village was often called Alphabet City (and still sometimes is) in honor of the alphabet-named north–south avenues (A–D) that spread east of First Avenue.

† Even Koch's Ten Year Plan (see chapter 15) was geared as much toward *regenerating* neighborhoods by making them attractive to wealthier incomers as it was toward developing new forms of housing for the poor. By the 1990s scholars were increasingly showing how *regeneration* was tightly bound to *gentrification* as a "global accumulation strategy."

‡ Perhaps most famously—or infamously—both Central Park and Bryant Park (adjacent to the New York Public Library in Midtown) were all but privatized beginning in 1980, with the latter being closed altogether in 1988 in order to redesign it so that it would be welcoming to corporate events and the corporate lunch crowd alike.

"Tompkins Square Everywhere!"

The NYPD's dawn withdrawal from the park on August 7, 1988, represented more of a victory than even the jubilant protesters could then imagine. They immediately began building a loose coalition of squatters, homeless people, and housing activists; political meetings abounded; and the new chant was raised: "Tompkins Square everywhere!" Increasing numbers of homeless people came to the park, with more than a hundred now living there on any given night. The encampment at the south end grew, while a new one sprang up near the fountain. Although the press still blamed the riot on the protesters, there was nonetheless an irrepressible recognition that the police had resorted to wanton violence, an impression that intensified as clips from Clayton Patterson's "democratization of surveillance" video were picked up by the news media. Within a week the city retreated and lifted the park curfew citywide, and over the next few months, the police, beyond short forays, made no effort to return to the park. For all intents and purposes, Tompkins Square had been liberated. The homeless population, mostly men, mostly African American (though with increasing numbers of Latinos), continued to swell, growing to three hundred or so a night.

On the defensive as coverage made the rounds of national and international news programs, the NYPD conceded that its tactics may have been ill-advised, and several senior officers were reassigned. A court demanded that Patterson relinquish his videotape to the police, but, fearing the tape would be doctored, he refused. Patterson was arrested on a ninety-day contempt sentence and was only released when he provided the video. When the tape was eventually returned it was mysteriously forty-five minutes shorter. The most surreal moment in the aftermath perhaps came when a local news reporter claimed in an exclusive exposé to have discovered the true cause of the riot. Channel 2's Mike Taibbi announced confidently that the riot was secretly orchestrated by a local anarchist performance band, Missing Foundation, headed by Peter Missing. Widely known for its ubiquitous overturned martini glass graffiti, signaling that after the 1987 stock market crash "the party's over," the band was portrayed as promoting dark satanic rituals and unspecified cult activities in the bowels of the neighborhood. Meanwhile, housing activists in squats in many European cities picked up the chant "Tompkins Square everywhere!" *Saturday Night Live*, then in its heyday, picked up on the undercurrents and televised a skit with General George Custer cast as a haughty Mayor Koch.* Custer/Koch appeared in front of a mock western fort, where he welcomed the belligerent local warrior Chief Soaring Eagle with the inquiry: "So how are things down on the Lower East Side?"[16]

December 1988 brought fierce weather, and six homeless people around the city froze to death in a record cold spell, two of them in Tompkins Square Park, where several dozen tents, lean-tos, and other shelters had been erected. On the pretext of saving lives, Parks Commissioner Henry Stern reimposed the park curfew citywide (though Tompkins Square was initially exempted) but did little to open additional warm space for the city's homeless. Over at City Hall, investigating the 121 complaints of police violence, the Civilian Complaint Review Board complained bitterly about hitting a "blue wall of silence," noting that no cops apparently saw anything at the riot. Six junior officers had already been indicted on relatively minor charges (all would be acquitted), and when the review board recommended charges against a further seventeen, the NYPD and the Patrolmen's Benevolent Association (the police union) effectively joined forces to block the charges, diverting them to internal police department review. Meanwhile, the New York Civil Liberties Union director, Norman Siegal, dismissed the review board report as grossly inadequate and a "sham." The city began to offer between $5,000 and $15,000 to people injured by police violence during the riot in order to keep the cases out of court.[17]

* A central motif of selling the Lower East Side to gentrifying incomers is that it *was* the frontier (the meeting point of savagery and civilization, as Frederick Jackson Turner famously defined it) and gentrifiers were the brave pioneers marching west—or east, in this case. As the *Village Voice's* C. Carr wrote, "As the neighborhood slowly, inexorably gentrifies, the park is a hold out, the place for one last metaphorical stand."

In the spring of 1989 the Koch administration began to regroup and opened a new front in the battle over the Lower East Side. Since the riot, not only homeless people but also squatters and political activists had converged on the neighborhood, which now hosted as many as three hundred squatters in more than two dozen previously vacant buildings abandoned by landlords. After a suspicious fire at a squat on East 8th Street, half a block from the park, and amid neighborhood rumors of developer involvement, the city used the pretext of structural instability to attempt to demolish the squat. Squatters vowed to rebuild the burned part of the tenement, but the day after an uneventful May Day, three hundred police in riot gear confronted a two-hundred-person-strong eviction watch protecting the squat and chanting, "No housing, no peace." Sixteen people were arrested and demolition workers moved in, but work was quickly stopped by court order, although not before the fire escape and part of the facade were felled. The wrecking crew returned two days later but was rained upon by the squatters' "secret weapon": bottles of urine stored on the squat's roof. The wrecking crew and police quickly retreated as the squatters (with the help of the priest Frank Morales) lassoed and toppled the demolition scaffolding while other squatters retook the building. The *Voice* covered the episode beneath the memorable headline "Protesters Piss Off Demolition Crew."[18]

With the neighborhood in a state of virtual siege, police reinforcements arrived the next day and held off protesters as workers demolished the building, and the city's focus turned back to the park, where new rules were announced banning tents and other shelters. On July 5, 1989, almost a year after the riot, 250 riot police sealed the park from hundreds of protesters and evicted as many as three hundred homeless people from the park, while crews took knives, sledgehammers, and axes to the tents and shanties, hauling off people's possessions in three garbage trucks. Evicted now both from the park and from the housing market, many homeless people filtered east, reestablishing homes on vacant lots where abandoned buildings once stood, or else

they were taken in by neighborhood squats. But Tompkins Square Park was quickly reoccupied even as the police made occasional desultory forays against individual park residents and structures and staged a larger assault on the one-year commemorative demonstration.[19]

By the fall, Mayor Koch was on his way out, and his replacement, David Dinkins, an erstwhile Social Democrat and the city's first African American mayor, softened the rhetoric of his predecessor but nonetheless promised the park would be "cleaned up." Just weeks before he took office and on the coldest day of the year, December 14, 1989, with temperatures plunging into the single digits, the homeless of Tompkins Square Park—once again reaching three hundred souls—were evicted yet again, as fifteen garbage trucks hauled away as many as a hundred tents and shelters and plenty of other possessions. Among those arrested as they protested the eviction was St. Brigid's Father George Kuhn, who joined with others chanting "New York City, you can't hide, we charge you with genocide" as he was hauled away. Activists predicted that some of the park evictees would inevitably die in the cold, while Parks Commissioner Stern explained that homeless people were evicted from their shelters because "it would be irresponsible to allow the homeless to sleep outdoors." In fact, the city's "help center," established concurrently with the evictions, was no alternative to housing and was ridiculed as "little more than a dispensary for baloney sandwiches."[20]

In January 1990 Mayor Dinkins's administration announced a "reconstruction plan" for the park but did little right away. On May Day the police violently ended the peaceful if raucous "Resist to Exist" concert in the park, causing an open battle that left twenty-eight cops and celebrants injured. Now nearly two years after the initial police riot, a new parks commissioner had to concede that it remained an open question as "to whom the Park belongs." The Parks Department seemed intent on "reclaiming" it. During the summer, the basketball courts were dismantled and rebuilt (and access to them was limited), and the playgrounds were reconditioned, fenced off, and designated for children only. Around the park, city agencies heightened their efforts to evict neighborhood squatters, who were now spearheading the antigentrification efforts. The efforts seemed to have little effect. As summer turned to winter, homeless people began moving back into the park and once again erecting semipermanent shelters.[21]

In what now seemed like a springtime ritual, the police again waded into the park during a 1991 Memorial Day concert and demonstration organized under the banner "Housing Is a Human Right." But this time it was going to be different. The Dinkins administration had earlier announced a $2.3 million redesign and reconstruction plan for the park and decided to end the three-year cat-and-mouse cycle between the homeless people and activists and the police, and so a week later, at 5:00 a.m. on June 3, 1991, the park was finally closed and circled by a heavily guarded eight-foot-high chain-link fence. Dinkins justified the closure by declaring, "The park is a park. It is not a place to live." Pushed

east again, homeless people quickly established or expanded tent cities on vacant lots, settlements soon dubbed "Dinkinsvilles," recalling the hobo camps or Hoovervilles of the Great Depression. As the park was being rebuilt, guards stood at the gates in the fence around the officially closed park, letting in parents with their children or walkers with their dogs but not people who looked homeless. The closing of the park sounded the "death knell" of an occupation that "had come to symbolize the failure of the city to cope with its homeless population," in the words of *Village Voice* reporter Sarah Ferguson.[22]

Gentrification, At Last

Death knell or not, protests continued. Evicted from the park, homeless people and demonstrators gathered routinely at 5:00 p.m. on the steps of St. Brigid's Church, some carrying wire cutters. They would surge toward the fence and

One of the Lower East Side Dinkinsvilles that arose in the wake of the Tompkins Square Park police riot. Photo by Andrew Lichtenstein, used by permission.

Tompkins Square Park as it is being rebuilt for a new class of users.
Photo by Andrew Lichtenstein, used by permission.

turn—sometimes left, sometimes right—to patrol the park perimeter. A large police force, often numbering into the hundreds, would follow them in a ritual that came to be known throughout the neighborhood as the nightly "walk the pig" routine. But everyone knew it was over. The closing of the park symbolized the dénouement of one of the most important antigentrification struggles in the city. A major success for the three years it lasted, it failed for two main reasons. First, as the recession began to bite after 1989, the level of sympathy for homeless people in the city faded. Presaging the revanchism that captured the city in the 1990s under Mayor Rudolph Giuliani, neighborhood residents and others who had previously tolerated or even supported homeless people in the park increasingly grew fed up with the turmoil. Empathy was no substitute for organization. But second, and related, the people in the park, together with neighborhood sympathizers and housing activists, failed to

organize the park and neighborhood sufficiently and especially to expand the struggle throughout the larger city; the loose coalition of squatters, homeless people, and housing activists never gelled.

There were various contributing elements to this failure. By its nature, homelessness makes political organizing notoriously difficult. Likewise, squatters and anarchists involved in the struggle harbored a range of attitudes toward political organizing, from outright rejection in favor of spontaneous revolt, to ambivalence, to a concerted endorsement of organization. At the same time, and crucially, the city's established housing activist organizations, such as the Metropolitan Council on Housing, were more or less oriented toward Democratic Party politics when of course it was Democratic mayors (Koch and Dinkins) who led the assault on the park. Aghast at the prominence of and central role played by squatters and anarchists, these organizations generally remained aloof from the Tompkins Square Park struggle, doing little if anything to build its power.*

The central role played by squatters and anarchists in fact was underlined by the city's strategy after the park's closure. The Dinkins administration and subsequent Giuliani administration took aim at squatters in particular, seeking to turn all vacant, abandoned, or squatted land over to private developers, though the largest Dinkinsville was cleared to build a federally subsidized police fortress at the corner of Avenue C and 8th Street. The assault on squatters and the homeless came to a high point in June 1995, when, incredible as it sounds, Mayor Giuliani sent a half-track armored tank and four hundred riot police toting automatic weapons and deploying tear gas to empty two long-term homesteaded squats at 541 and 545 East 13th Street.[23]

*Meanwhile, old-line Marxist and other revolutionary groups remained impotent.

The struggle over Tompkins Square Park and its three-year liberation combined with economic recession to halt the area's gentrification for more than six years. "Die Yuppie Scum" was a quite effective slogan for keeping gentrifiers at bay, but it was hardly a useful analysis or a useful focus of organizing. When the park reopened in 1994, New York's real estate market was reviving, and Giuliani's revanchist zero tolerance policing campaign chose homeless people and squatters as its first targets. Over the rest of the decade, homeless people were largely cleared from much of Manhattan, banished either out of town or to the outer boroughs. The gentrification of the Lower East Side took off in earnest, and soon even the culturati found themselves priced out of apartments coming onto the market.

BENSONHURST, 1989

One of sixteen-year-old Yusuf Hawkins's friends had seen an ad for a 1982 Pontiac and wanted to check it out. On Wednesday evening, August 23, 1989, Hawkins joined him and two other black friends and headed out from his East New York home to the largely Italian American, working-class neighborhood of Bensonhurst to the southwest. The young men got off the subway, headed down Twentieth Avenue, and walked into an ambush. Between twenty and thirty young white men—in their late teens, mostly—had gathered outside a house on the street with baseball bats and at least one gun. There was to be an eighteenth birthday party at the house that evening for Gina Feliciano. Accounts as to why the guys were there vary. One of them, Keith Mondello, had been close to Feliciano, but they had fallen out. Rumors were that Feliciano was dating black and Hispanic men, and this did not sit well. It may also be that Feliciano had told Mondello and his friends that a gang of African Americans were headed toward the neighborhood to beat Mondello up (this is what many in the neighborhood believed and what Mondello's attorney quickly claimed). The police said that the white gang was looking for Feliciano's new lover and had

staked out her house, expecting him to show up at the party. Whatever the facts, Hawkins and his friends were not necessarily meant to be the target. But Mondello and the gang had been talking each other up. "Let's club the fucking nigger," one witness claims to have heard someone say. "No, let's not club, let's shoot one." "Let's get even with Gina." "Let's show Gina." As the black teens approached the white gang, Hawkins was quickly isolated. "Is it him?" "Is he the one?" Someone in the scrum shot four times. Two bullets hit Hawkins in the chest, and the white boys ran in all directions (witnesses reported seeing guns stashed in a couple of cars). Hawkins's three friends were unharmed. Feliciano ran to a phone and called the police. Neighbors cared for Hawkins while they waited for the police and an ambulance. But by the time Hawkins got to the hospital, he was dead.[1]

Mayor Koch knew immediately he had a serious "racial incident" on his hands. Racist violence was all too common in New York during the 1980s. Three years earlier, just before Christmas of 1986, three African American men whose car had broken down a little way away were chased and beaten by a gang of a dozen white youths on the

streets of Howard Beach, Queens. Rallied by a ringleader who exclaimed, "There's niggers on the boulevard! Let's go fucking kill them!" and shouting "You niggers do not belong here!" the gang chased twenty-three-year-old Michael Griffith onto a highway. Griffith was struck and killed by an oncoming car. A few days after Christmas, antiracist activists, mostly black and led by the Reverend Al Sharpton and NAACP president Benjamin Hooks, marched through Howard Beach, where they were met by a smaller but still significant number of counterdemonstrators, who hurled racist epithets. A force of 250 police was needed to keep the two crowds apart. The incident set the city on edge for months. "This incident," said Mayor Koch the day after Griffith was killed, "can only be talked about as rivaling the kind of lynching party that took place in the Deep South."

Four years before Griffith was killed, a mob of Italian American youth beat and killed thirty-four-year-old Willie Turks, an African American, after he and two colleagues stopped for a bagel in the Brooklyn neighborhood of Gravesend. Though the perpetrators got off with light sentences, and one was charged with civil rights violations, there was little public discussion of "bias crimes," as there would be with the Griffith murder. The concept of bias crimes—crimes that threatened not just an individual but a group—was essentially invented in the intervening years.[2]

For his comments on the Griffith murder, Koch was reviled by some among his base in working-class white neighborhoods and by some sectors of the press, both of which preferred to think the black men had brought on their beating by being in the wrong neighborhood at the wrong time and by the fact that some of them had had past run-ins with the law. In the aftermath of the Hawkins murder, Koch would lose his bid to be reelected mayor. Less than a month after Hawkins was killed, Koch lost out to David Dinkins in the Democratic primary, in part because, while condemning the killing, he spent as much time condemning marches by black and civil rights activists through Bensonhurst. Three days after Hawkins's death, three hundred to four hundred protesters marched through Bensonhurst (again led by Reverend Sharpton) but were met by a jeering white crowd, who held up watermelons and spun basketballs on their fingers in what they thought were derisive gestures, shouted "Niggers go home," and pulled down their pants and told protesters to "kiss my ass." Sharpton, a divisive figure at the time even among African Americans, organized near-daily marches through the neighborhood, which were often met by counterdemonstrations. Some—many in the neighborhood, not a few in the press, a good number around the city—thought Sharpton was inflaming racism, not doing anything to address it. Many

in Bensonhurst felt their neighborhood was being "invaded," especially after some seventy-five hundred marchers showed up for a march to commemorate both Hawkins and Black Panther founder Huey Newton, who had been killed on August 22 in Oakland, California (a march that led to rioting and twenty-three police officers injured). At times over the next several weeks, it seemed as if a race war might break out in the neighborhood; there was certainly one raging in the press. Community meetings in Bensonhurst, called to promote "harmony," erupted into shouting matches as residents blamed politicians for coddling the black protesters. Keith Mondello's mother "shrieked," in the words of a sympathetic Andrew Sullivan, reporting from the scene: "My peace and harmony went out the window on August 24 when they arrested eight Italian boys and told all the Black and Hispanic boys that they had nothing to do with it." The conservative press did its part, consistently arguing that white racism was "understandable," given rising black criminality and drug use—this was, after all the season of presidential candidate (and vice president) George H. W. Bush's infamous "Willie Horton" ad, which used the specter of rampant black criminality to defeat Democratic challenger Michael Dukakis in 1988, something of a culmination of a near decade of vilification of poor African Americans by the political establishment (led by President Reagan's famous invocation of "welfare queens").[3]

The two main defendants were nineteen-year-old Mondello and eighteen-year-old Joseph Fama, both charged with murder.

Fama was suspected of having shot the gun. In a series of closely watched and frequently protested trials (riot cops were present whenever a verdict was announced), Fama was eventually found guilty of second-degree murder (the jury held that the prosecution had not proved he actually shot the gun) and was sentenced to thirty-two years to life in prison. Mondello was acquitted of murder but convicted of rioting, menacing, unlawful imprisonment, discrimination, and criminal possession of a weapon. He was sentenced to five to sixteen years. Police were poised for rioting in East New York in the wake of the acquittal, but the streets remained calm. In Bensonhurst, white counterdemonstrators hurled watermelons at the six hundred or so people who peacefully marched through town.[4]

Another defendant was convicted of unlawful imprisonment, but the judge vacated the felony conviction and sentenced him to community service. Three defendants were acquitted. After a lengthy trial, the final defendant, John Vento, was acquitted of murder but convicted of rioting and sentenced to two and two-thirds to eight years in prison. In the wake of Vento's acquittal for murder, Sharpton organized a protest march in Bensonhurst. As he prepared for it on January 21, 1991, someone rushed up to him and stabbed him in the chest with a steak knife.[5]

Only seven weeks before Yusuf Hawkins was murdered, Spike Lee's *Do the Right Thing* premiered in cinemas around the country. It portrayed one block—in Bedford-Stuyvesant—ripe with racial tensions, which explode into a riot. Lee says the film began as a reflection on the 1986 Howard Beach murder, and innumerable references to the real-life racial tensions and incidents in New York abound. It was also partly inspired by a series of racist attacks in Bensonhurst that predated Hawkins's murder.

It was prescient. "They don't want us here," an Italian American kid says at one point. "We should stay in our neighborhood. Stay in Bensonhurst and the niggers should stay in theirs." Whatever the various motives of the young men in the gang that killed Hawkins, they were clearly trying to keep black people out. The protesters were bent on not only demanding justice for Hawkins but also asserting their right to be on the streets in any neighborhood. The result was an intensification of racial animosity and a hardening of the city's racial geography as the 1980s gave way to the 1990s.

RIOT OR POGROM?
CROWN HEIGHTS, 1991

The population of Crown Heights, Brooklyn, on the east side of Prospect Park and to the west of Brownsville, shifted rapidly around 1970 as its white, mostly Jewish population moved out and black residents, including a large number of Afro-Caribbeans, moved in. But one group of Jews stayed: the fairly large, close-knit community of Orthodox Chabad-Lubavitch Hasidim. Though only comprising 6 or 8 percent of the Crown Heights population and only perhaps 20 percent of the population in the neighborhood where most of them live, the Lubavitchers—the men distinctive with long beards, black wide-brimmed hats, and long black coats—defined Crown Heights, both in the popular imagination of many New Yorkers and on the street, even as Crown Heights became, as sociologist Philip Kasinitz described it, "the center of West Indian culture in the United States." Long led by the seventh Lubavitcher Rebbe, the charismatic Menachem Mendel Schneerson, Chabad-Lubavitch combined a tight-knit insularity with a global messianism. The Rebbe was a powerful figure on the New York stage.[1]

At 8:20 p.m. on Monday, August 19, 1991, the Rebbe was returning to Lubavitch World Headquarters at 707 Eastern Parkway in a three-car motorcade. Heading west on President Street, the lead car—a police car (unmarked, but with lights flashing on the roof)—and Schneerson's car crossed Utica Street on a green light. The third car, driven by Yosef Lifsh (spelled Lifsch in some accounts), had fallen behind. Lifsh sped up to between thirty-five and forty-five miles per hour (well over the speed limit) and crossed Utica either on a yellow or, more likely, a red light and was struck by an oncoming car. Lifsh's vehicle careened onto the sidewalk, pinning two children against the wall and window grate of an apartment building. Seven-year-old Angela Cato was severely injured. Her seven-year-old cousin, Gavin Cato, was hurt even worse. A crowd of neighbors—mostly black—quickly formed. Gavin's father saw it all happen and rushed toward the car to help the children. He was roughly restrained by a cop.[2]

Within a couple of minutes an ambulance from Hatzolah, a volunteer Jewish ambulance service, arrived. Fearing for the safety of Lifsh and his three Lubavitcher passengers, a police officer on the scene instructed the Jewish ambulance crew to take them away. (According to some reports, one of the passengers was earlier whisked to safety by a black man in the crowd.) A city ambulance had just arrived that would look after Angela and Gavin. Gavin was quickly transported to Kings County Hospital but was pronounced dead on arrival. Angela was treated by another Hatzolah crew at the scene but then taken to the hospital by a city ambulance.

Little Gavin and Angela were the children of Guyanese immigrants, and the death of Gavin ignited already tense relations between black—African American and Afro-Caribbean—and Hasidic residents. The crowd gathered at the corner of President and Utica grew as the night wore on, and it grew increasingly angry. Rumors flew—that Lifsh hit the kids on purpose, that he was drunk, that the Lubavitchers in the car were treated before little Gavin and Angela. Relations between blacks and Jews in Crown Heights were already strained. Black residents chafed at the Hasidic street patrols that the Chabad-Lubavitch headquarters had established around its world headquarters and that extended out into the neighborhoods, seeing them as vigilantes. Relations had been especially tense over the previous decade and a half, since 1978, when a large group of Hasidim, men and women, severely beat fifteen-year-old Victor Rhodes, who was black, putting him into a two-month-long coma. The assailants claimed that Rhodes had knocked the yarmulke off one of their number, an account disputed by many. As a result, the Reverend Herbert Daughtry established black counterpatrols, which incensed the Crown Heights Hasidim, as well as many other Jews around the city, who saw the move as distinctly anti-Semitic. By the time the Catos were struck, the memory of Rhodes's beating had not faded, and relations in the neighborhood remained fraught.[3] Black residents of Crown Heights further resented the permanent police guard outside the headquarters and the fact that the Rebbe got a police escort anytime he ventured out.

Soon, shouting matches erupted between blacks and Jews, and as early as 9:07 p.m., 911 received reports of a riot in progress. Black teenagers, incensed at the death of the little boy and angered by the police treatment of his father, threw stones at the cops and at houses. Someone yelled, "The Jews killed the kids!" Anger continued to mount, and soon rocks were hailing down from rooftops. At 10:30 a tow truck peeled Lefsh's car from the wall, revealing the bicycle Gavin had been repairing when he was struck. The crowd grew quiet, and then thirty-seven-year-old Charles Price stepped into the center of it, asking if the crowd felt the pain and then saying (by some accounts), "We can't take this anymore. The Jews get everything they want. They're killing our children. We get no justice, we get no respect."

Price rallied a portion of the crowd to head toward Kingston Avenue (a center of Hasidic settlement) to "get the Jews." Price's crowd ran into Yankel Rosenbaum, a twenty-nine-year-old non-Hasidic Orthodox Jew in the United States from Australia to do a PhD in Jewish studies. At the trial, a black teen recalled Price yelling, "There's one! Get him!" Soon they had him surrounded and were kicking and punching him. As police rushed to the scene, Lemrick Nelson, the sixteen-year-old son of Trinidadian immigrants, stabbed Rosenbaum four times with a pocketknife. Rosenbaum was rushed to Kings County Hospital, where doctors were confident he would pull through. Mayor Dinkins rushed to the hospital to reassure him. But the doctors were wrong. Rosenbaum died three hours later.

Meanwhile, the Rebbe said nothing. He never expressed condolences to the Cato family or offered to meet them. He never apologized to them for the accident. Many in the black community—and well beyond to include innumerable prominent Jewish figures—interpreted this as indifference at best. One of his spokesmen explained Schneerson's silence and seeming lack of interest in the Cato family by saying, "The Rebbe is an international figure. If there is an incident in Washington D.C., should the President get involved with white and black leaders to settle the insurrection?" This statement rather missed the point of the Rebbe's motorcade's culpability and did nothing to quell the fires of rage that ensued for the next two nights.[4]

The next day, Reverend Sharpton and others led a protest march in Crown Heights, drawing several hundred people. Marchers wanted Lifsh arrested. A large group of Lubavitchers gathered in front of the world headquarters. As police tried to keep the two crowds separated, Jews and blacks pelted each other with stones and bottles. Traditional chants by the black marchers—"No justice, no peace" and "Whose streets, our streets"—were supplemented by anti-Semitic ones: "Death to the Jews!" "Back in the ovens!" "Hitler didn't finish the job!" "Heil Hitler!" Lubavitchers returned the taunts. That evening, rioters looted stores on Utica Avenue, making little distinction between those owned by Jews and those owned by blacks. (One rioter later explained they targeted any place that was perceived to perpetuate racial inequality.) On Wednesday black protest marches were again followed by looting and by attacks on pedestrians, reporters, and others. The eight hundred cops on the scene seemed simply unable to control the mobs, giving rise to a widely held sentiment among Jews in Crown Heights, as well as many others, that David Dinkins and his black police commissioner, Lee Brown, were simply allowing black people in the neighborhood to "vent their anger."[5]

The next day, the police presence was beefed up to eighteen hundred, and while there were still protest marches, the violence subsided. Over the course of the rioting, 129 people were arrested (of which only 9 were Hasidim), and injuries to at least 38 civilians and 152 cops were reported.[6]

A grand jury considered indicting Lifsh but decided against it. Lifsh soon returned to his native Israel (with many black leaders saying he got away with murder). Lemrick

Police arrest a man for taking photographs during the Crown Heights Riot, August 21, 1991.
AP Photo / David Burns.

Nelson was tried and acquitted of murder, to the surprise and dismay of many (he was later convicted of federal civil rights charges). Charles Price was eventually convicted of inciting a riot. Dinkins had been elected on the strength of a black-Jewish coalition, but the rioting and perhaps especially the Nelson acquittal (and the mayor's insistence that the people of Crown Heights accept the decision) drove a wedge deeply into that coalition, even as some black and Jewish leaders worked hard to maintain it. Jesse Jackson opined that it was necessary to convict Rosenbaum's killers since his murder and all that surrounded it reached "the heart of black-Jewish relations, a sacred struggle that had shed blood in common graves." Many Jews in New York

remained unplaced, especially after an official New York State report on the rioting and trials of Nelson and Price found Dinkins essentially negligent in his handling of the disturbance (though it did not support the widely held belief that he had let black rioters run wild). Dinkins soon lost the mayoralty to Rudolph Giuliani.[7]

Many Lubavitcher Hasidim, and many other Jews too, understood the rioting to be nothing short of a pogrom. Many black New Yorkers and others saw it quite differently: that whereas the rioting was certainly interlaced with anti-Semitism, it was also a racial struggle, not against Jews as such but against whites understood to be part of an oppressing class. For sociologist Henry Goldschmidt studying the

neighborhood a decade later, it both "was and it wasn't a riot and a pogrom, between Blacks and Whites and Jews and Gentiles, acting on the basis of religion." It was instead an "irreducible multiplicity." For Giuliani, it was an opportunity. A number of Lubavitchers filed a civil lawsuit against Mayor Dinkins, Police Commissioner Brown, and the city. The case dragged on in the courts, well into Giuliani's administration, before the case against Dinkins and Brown was dismissed in 1997. Giuliani took the opportunity to then quickly settle the suit against the city for $1.1 million, apologizing on behalf of the city for his predecessor's "clearly inadequate response." He said not a word about the death of Gavin Cato, which started it all.[8]

THE MILLION COP MARCH, 1998

Central Harlem's population declined rapidly in the 1970s from nearly 160,000 to just over 105,000. The decline slowed but did not stop in the 1980s, with the population sinking below 100,000. Like many poor and nonwhite neighborhoods, parts of Harlem had a wiped-out look, even as some streets retained their stately brownstones and remained the preserve of a black elite. On the whole, it remained poor. Thirty percent of families were on public assistance in 1990, and labor force participation rates were below 60 percent. Official unemployment rates hovered between 20 and 25 percent. For every advertised minimum-wage fast-food job, fourteen applicants showed up. A McDonald's on 125th Street received three hundred applications every month in 1994. Rates of infant mortality, low birth rate, tuberculosis, and HIV/AIDS all exceeded city averages, some by two and three times. Prophesied as early as 1986, gentrification had barely begun making inroads into Harlem a decade later.[1]

When talk turned in 1998 to organizing a Million Youth March to build on the momentum of the successful Million Man March in Washington in 1995 (and later Million Woman March), it found a receptive audience in Harlem. The idea originated in Atlanta, where a Million Youth March was planned for Labor Day. The event there more or less foundered on poor organization and a conservative "black capitalist" and religious ideology. But by then the idea had been picked up in New York by a putatively more militant coalition, and planning began for a Labor Day march and rally in Harlem. The effort, however, was spearheaded by Khalid Muhammad, erstwhile associate of the Nation of Islam's Louis Farrakhan and an inveterate anti-Semite. Farrakhan, himself no stranger to charges of anti-Semitism, had long ago dissociated himself from Muhammad because of the latter's outrageous statements: Jews were "blood suckers" who "deserved Hitler." He declared the Holocaust a hoax and called Jews "hook-nosed, bagel-eating, lox-eating, perpetuating-a-fraud, so-called Jews who just crawled out of the ghettoes."[2]

Many people were ready for a Million Youth March, but many of New York's black activists and elite wanted nothing to do with Muhammad. He returned the favor, doing little to cultivate the extensive network of Harlem civil rights and activist organizations, the churches and politicians, as the march approached. He seemed to be doing even less by way of organizing the detailed work of leasing a stage and toilets, organizing buses and parking for them, assuring medical support, and so forth. He did, however, apply for a permit for the rally, which the Giuliani administration quickly denied. Whatever the myriad motivations of those who might participate, Mayor Giuliani declared it would be nothing more than a "hate march." Such rhetoric goaded even those strongly opposed to Muhammad into action (Congressman Charles Rangel urged Boy Scouts and church choirs to show up in their uniforms and robes to contest the image Muhammad was projecting). Eventually, a court overturned the permit denial; an appeals court narrowed the ruling, saying the march could not take place on Labor Day itself (police resources would be spread too thin) and, after learning that organizers were estimating an attendance of fifty thousand rather than a million, reducing its size from twenty-nine blocks to six blocks and its duration from twelve hours to four hours. A permit was issued for a rally to last from noon to 4:00 p.m. on Saturday, September 5, on Malcolm X Boulevard (Lenox Avenue) between 116th and 122nd Streets. Mayor Giuliani promised vigorous policing.[3]

People took Giuliani at his word. His

election had ushered in a new, aggressive era of policing in the city marked by "zero tolerance," "quality of life" policing that targeted homeless people, "squeegee men," sidewalk peddlers, and the mentally ill and spectacular cases of police violence (such as the beating and sodomizing of Abner Louima and, a few months after the Million Youth March, the police murder of unarmed Amadou Diallo, both black immigrants). Activists called it "Giuliani Time," after a phrase Louima at first claimed Justin Volpe, the cop who beat and raped him, hollered in the midst of his assault (Louima later recanted this). In "Giuliani Time," the old constraints on police conduct were significantly relaxed. "It is fair to say," African American historian Manning Marable commented, "that Giuliani was as widely despised among most Blacks as he was praised and admired by the majority of the city's white electorate."[4]

Actually, "Giuliani Time" began well before he was elected. In September 1992 Giuliani spoke at a big police union rally in front of City Hall. As many as ten thousand cops showed up to protest Mayor Dinkins's putative lack of support for the police force. "He never supports us on anything," said one officer. "A cop shoots someone with a gun who's a drug dealer, and he goes and visits the family." Cops chanted, "No justice, no police" and "The mayor's on crack," carried signs saying "Dinkins, We Know Your True Color—Yellow Bellied" and "Dinkins Must Go," and referred to him as the "washroom attendant." Giuliani egged them on. As he spoke to one contingent of cops, another contingent surged toward City Hall,

jumping up and down on cars as others ran up the steps (meeting no resistance from fellow officers detailed to keep order), while a third contingent invaded the Brooklyn Bridge, stopping all traffic for forty minutes while simultaneously threatening members of the press. When Giuliani was elected, NYPD cops knew they would have a friend in the mayor's office.[5]

Despite intimations that the Million Youth March would be far smaller than the fifty thousand organizers were claiming, the NYPD deployed three thousand officers to the rally, a size of force usually dedicated to crowds of two hundred thousand or more. The police commandeered two of the rally's permitted blocks (116th to 118th Streets), closed the subway stations in the area (both to make it difficult for people to reach the rally and to use the stations as command centers), and, beginning in the early morning, refused to let people into or out of or to cross the rally site (rather inconveniencing shoppers, patients released from a nearby hospital and trying to get home, and the like). Even so, some ten thousand people made their way to the rally, "bring[ing] a festive feel to the streets of Harlem." Speeches were emollient as much as fiery, with anti-white rhetoric toned down and anti-Semitic remarks largely absent (though City College professor Leonard Jeffries, who several years before inflamed sentiment by claiming that Jews were responsible for demeaning depictions of black people in Hollywood films, spoke, as did the Reverend Al Sharpton). The crowd remained peaceful and the spirit festive. Before the rally, Mayor Giuliani even sounded just a little bit conciliatory,

saying that though the permit for the rally expired at 4:00 p.m., police would "allow some flexibility" in allowing it to wind down.[6]

This was not to be. Muhammad finally mounted the stage at 3:55 p.m. to make a short speech. As he did so, a police helicopter swooped low and buzzed the crowd, and hundreds of cops in riot gear surged toward the stage from the two blocks they had commandeered behind it. When Muhammad saw them, he implored his audience to grab police barriers and metal grates, and if the cops came after them, people should grab the cops' guns—"in self-defense." By some (but not all) accounts, he interlaced these statements with his trademark anti-Semitic slurs. At exactly 4:01 p.m., the massed riot police swarmed the stage with raised billy clubs, ripped the cords out of the sound speakers, and knocked them over. Muhammad and one of his aides slipped away. Others on the stage were not so lucky, feeling the blows of the nightsticks. Some in the crowd hurled garbage cans, bottles, and chairs. Others just tried to get away, often with children in tow. The cops unleashed their pepper spray and doused those on the stage and some below. It all only lasted a few minutes, but by the time it was over, twenty-eight people had been injured—sixteen of them cops. Only one person was arrested, however.[7]

Mayor Giuliani, while pronouncing himself pleased with the "admirable restraint" shown by the police, called for Muhammad to be charged with inciting a riot. He explained that raiding the stage was necessary because "this is all about creating a

Police riot at the conclusion of the Million Youth March, September 5, 1998.
AP Photo / Stuart Ramson.

respectful society. The court said they had between 12 and 4; it meant exactly that." "I am very proud of the police," he continued, "in making sure it was over." Black opinion was outraged, perhaps particularly among those who despised Muhammad. *New York Times* columnist Bob Herbert, who had regularly inveighed against Muhammad, wrote,

"Rudolph Giuliani would never, but never, treat an entire neighborhood of white people the way he treated the people in the vicinity of Lenox Avenue on Saturday." State senator (later governor) David Paterson said the cops turned Harlem into a "police state." Congressman Rangel called sending in the riot cops "outrageous." Many people argued that Giuliani's actions would do little more than deliver black youth into the embrace of Muhammad and his brand of black nationalism. Herbert added that

"Mr. Giuliani, by deploying his police as if all black people were a mortal threat, succeeded in intensifying the opposition among blacks toward him and his policy of police overkill. The anti-Giuliani feeling among black people in this city is overwhelming and growing. . . . The Mayor is playing with fire."[8]

Historian Marable later added, "In Harlem folklore, the events of September 5, 1998, will probably be remembered as the 'Million Cop March.'"[9]

GIULIANI'S PLOT

THE COMMUNITY GARDEN STRUGGLE, 1998–2003

Two months after the police violently shut down the Million Youth March, Mayor Rudolph Giuliani sent bulldozers and work crews to Harlem to destroy the Garden of Love. Located on a pretty big lot between 120th and 119th Streets near where St. Nicholas Avenue slashes diagonally across the grid, the Garden of Love had been built up over six years by the kids and teachers at PS 76, which backed onto the other side of 120th Street. Plenty of neighbors got involved too. It was an oasis in the concrete and among the empty lots that pockmarked the neighborhood. Kids planted lawns and saplings, learned to compost, and grew strawberries and mint, flowers and pumpkins. Science classes met there. Teachers and neighbors ate their lunches in the shade of the garden's trees. Within an hour or so, the bulldozers destroyed it all, leaving a pile of rubble. The Giuliani administration said the lot was needed to build affordable housing. Instead, it stood empty for more than a decade (finally, a "mixed-income" apartment house opened on the lot in 2011). The Garden of Love was just one of dozens of community gardens bulldozed in 1998.[1]

The "antilandscape" produced so rapidly through 1970s disinvestment—the

Mary Jones (*left*), the president of the Bedford-Stuyvesant Garden Coalition, meeting with other community garden activists to plan a protest against the planned 1999 auction of 114 gardens by the Giuliani administration.
AP Photo / Suzanne Plunkett.

landscape of burned-out buildings, empty lots, abandoned housing, closed and crumbling schoolhouses and fire stations, and dilapidated parks—was inimical to life, and so it had to be *made* livable by those who lived in it. Across the city, neighbors took over empty lots, clearing out trash and old bricks, hauling in soil, putting up fences, laying down walkways, building casitas or kinetic artworks, hammering together raised beds, planting maple trees

and lettuces and marigolds and apples. Sometimes a family or small group of neighbors would make the new green space their private reserve. Often gardens

A community garden under construction in the 1970s.
Photo by Erika Stone, Archive Photos / Getty Images.

would be understood in essence to belong to the often shifting collective that made and maintained them. Just as often they would be open to the community, an asset made by a few but available to all. Among African Americans, Dominicans, Puerto Ricans, incoming immigrants from Mexico and Central America, China and Laos, they were places where familiar foods (and new ones) could be cultivated. They were spaces for relaxing, for community, and, in many places, for organizing. There was

a specific antiabandonment, antidisplacement, antigentrification politics to much community gardening in the city. On the Lower East Side, Green Guerillas (founded by Liz Christie) would lob balloons of water and seeds over fences and let nature run wild—and then petition the city to get access to the land and tend the garden that resulted. Eventually, in 1978, the city recognized the burgeoning community garden movement and created the Green Thumb Program, run by the Department of Parks. Green Thumb had authority to lease lots to community groups; it provided mulch, soil, and gardening advice; it wrote rules for community access and helped gardeners maintain the security of their plots; it

served as a clearinghouse for gardeners, as well as a conduit into other parts of the bureaucracy. Gardens were increasingly understood as assets to their neighborhoods, grassroots interventions into the antilandscape beyond what the city could hope to do directly. From the beginning of the program, however, the city understood community gardens to be temporary—a good use of land until a "higher and better" use presented itself. Leases could be terminated by the city with thirty-day notice.[2]

The Garden of Love had a lease, but the city let it expire in 1997 (it did not terminate it). By then, the seven hundred or so Green Thumb gardens had been transferred out of the Department of Parks and into the Department of Housing Preservation and Development (HPD), essentially the city's real estate arm. HPD had control of about eleven thousand lots that the city had acquired largely because their owners stopped paying taxes. Under Mayor Giuliani HPD had a mandate to sell—or transfer—as many of these lots as it could to developers. Mayor Giuliani was no fan of the gardens, but he was a big fan of development and a good friend to developers. Instead of rehabilitating tax-delinquent buildings for low- or moderate-income housing, as had been previous policy (hamstrung as it was by budget constraints), the Giuliani administration adopted a policy of selling them (often below market value) to developers to rent or sell at market rate. In 1996 HPD announced that it had slated fifty community gardens for development and began an aggressive program of bulldozing. City officials justified this move by saying that all other possible city-owned sites had already been sold for development: "We've built on all the other available City-owned land first."[3]

Gardeners did not believe it. A study by the Brooklyn borough president, for example, had shown that of 440 vacant properties sold to developers, only 17 were used for housing or other economic activities. More than 60 percent were serving merely as dumping grounds. Around the city, gardens targeted for sale often shared blocks with similar abandoned properties that did not host gardens and that were not slated for sale. The city also continually undermined its own stated reasons for selling off the gardens: to provide low- or moderate-income housing. Late in 1998 it transferred the gardens again, this time to the Department of Citywide Administrative Services (DCAS), which was the department charged with selling off abandoned or surplus property (cars, office furniture, etc.). DCAS quickly put 126 gardens on the block and scheduled an auction for May 1999. Winning bidders would be under no obligation to build housing, much less affordable housing. Indeed, a deputy commissioner at HPD explained that "the Giuliani administration is trying to dispose of property not slated for housing development, economic development and so forth. We are trying to privatize as many city-owned properties as we possibly can." Giuliani later helpfully explained the rationale for these sales: gardeners, he said, seemed to be stuck in the "era of communism . . . but this is a free market economy. Welcome to the era after communism." Apparently, selling the

gardens was just a straight-up ideological assault, especially since their sale would add little to the city's now-burgeoning $2.1 billion budget surplus. As one reporter put it, community gardens seemed to represent to Giuliani the "flower-power/hippie-style '60's liberalism" that he believed was responsible for the city's demise before he came to the rescue.[4]

The reaction was furious. As the threat to the gardens had unfolded over the previous years, gardeners worked hard to construct both local coalitions and a city-wide one called More Gardens! The coalitions created defensive bulldozer alerts and developed mechanisms for exercising political power and articulating the importance of the gardens in the media. Gardeners and supporters took to the streets in protest after protest. DCAS was required to hold a series of preauction hearings, and More Gardens! organized protests at each one. Protesters showed up in costume dressed as insects and sunflowers. In late February they staged a sit-in at City Hall, leading to thirty arrests and forcing "an odd encounter between protesters carrying kazoos and police officers wearing riot gear." (The police put their shields down and took off their helmets before dragging limp-bodied ladybugs and Dr. Seuss characters to waiting paddy wagons.) Other protests were held in Bryant Park (organized with Reclaim the Streets, which was protesting the privatization of public space that Bryant Park represented) and Central Park. Katydids, frogs, flowers, and fairies blocked traffic on Lower East Side streets, leading to sixty-two arrests.[5]

Simultaneously, New York State attorney general Eliot Spitzer filed a lawsuit, seeking to stop the auction. He claimed that the long use of the lots as gardens represented an "existing" use, and thus environmental review and legislative approval were needed before the lots could be sold. The Bronx and Brooklyn borough presidents, together with the Green Guerillas, the NYC Environmental Justice Alliance, and several local Community Boards, also sued to stop the auction both on procedural grounds and because the gardens slated for sale came disproportionately from poor and minority neighborhoods, and thus the sale was discriminatory. Then, the night before the auction, actress Bette Midler's New York Restoration Project and the Trust for Public Land offered to buy the threatened gardens for $4.2 million and preserve them as gardens. At the same time, the State Supreme Court halted the auction because the city had ignored environmental impact laws, forcing the administration's hand. Eventually, Giuliani agreed to the sale of the gardens to the trusts.[6]

But he did not stop bulldozing gardens. On June 29, 1999, crews returned to Harlem and ripped out the sixteen-year-old Harmony Garden on West 122nd Street, the Five Star Garden on West 121st Street (both near the former Garden of Love), and the String Together Garden on West 128th Street (a little more distant). At Harmony Garden, hundreds of protesters showed up and stopped the destruction about halfway through. Gardeners were able to save a few plants, barrels, and garden furniture. Over the course of the day, another four gardens in the neighborhood were destroyed. More gardens were slated for destruction the next day. The *New York Times* reported that the New York City Housing Partnership said it would build 112 units of affordable housing in 41 two- and three-family houses on the sites. It turns out that, in fact, the city had already sold two strips of land within the garden to a fairly notorious New York slumlord and property baron. (Eventually, the Harmony Garden was rebuilt. A three-family townhouse was built at 233 West 121st Street and seems to rent at market rate; the fate of the 128th Street site is unclear.)[7]

Later that summer, gardeners won a preliminary injunction barring the city from selling any of the six hundred other gardens slated for auction, while advocates prepared arguments about the racially disparate impacts of the sell-off. Bulldozing continued. On February 15, 2000, Spitzer won another injunction, barring the city from selling or "physically altering" Green Thumb gardens. But at the very moment Spitzer was winning at the State Supreme Court in Brooklyn, Giuliani sent bulldozers into El Jardin de la Esperanza, a garden that had anchored East 7th Street in the Lower East Side since 1977, when Alicia Torres cleared out a long-vacant lot. Garden defenders knew this was coming. Many

had spent the night in the garden to protect it. Others had chained themselves to cement blocks they had earlier buried in the garden in preparation for this assault. Police in riot gear preceded the backhoes and chain saws, cutting through the chains, arresting thirty-one people, and "scattering dozens of others" (as a reporter put it). Crews moved in and ripped out trees, as well as a giant tripod gardeners had built to stand watch (see chapter 17). They destroyed a large sculpture of a tree frog—a coqui—built to ward off attackers. The gardeners, forced out of their own garden, were charged with trespassing. Vigils and demonstrations were held in front of the now-destroyed and fenced garden for the rest of the month. Early on March 5 a crowd of 150 people ripped down the fence and started planting the garden again. They were met by riot police, and eight people were arrested in a violent clash that sent another eight—seven of them cops—to the hospital. By mid-2000 BFC Inc.—a generous donor to Mayor Giuliani's reelection campaign—was at work building a seventy-nine-unit apartment building, of which fourteen units were required to be "affordable."[8]

The struggle rumbled on after that. The Giuliani administration returned to claiming that garden sales were necessary so that

affordable housing could be built while simultaneously finding ways to sell off forty more—with no proviso that affordable housing be built. Attorney General Spitzer continued to push for injunctions while negotiating with various trusts to take control of the gardens. After Spitzer became governor and Giuliani was replaced by Michael Bloomberg in the mayor's office, the two reached a relatively lasting settlement preserving many of the gardens. Mayor Bloomberg's three terms as mayor (2002–14) would be an era of uneasy truce in the gardens. But, ironically, the election of progressive Bill de Blasio put the gardens back in the developers' sights, as his administration has sought ways—and places—to quickly expand the city's affordable housing stock.

But back then, in the 1990s, Mayor Giuliani's assault on the gardens was part of a much larger ideological assault on the city, its working classes, and its minorities, all of a piece with the aggressive privatization of public spaces, stringent broken windows policing, tolerance—even encouragement—of police violence against protesters and "suspect" people of color, and an all-out assault on homeless people. It was a central plank in making New York into the very archetype of the "revanchist city."[9]

CHAPTER 17

Reclaiming the Streets

New York in the Global Justice Movement, 1999–2004

MALAV KANUGA AND MCNAIR SCOTT

On January 1, 1994, the day the North American Free Trade Agreement took effect, the Zapatistas flared into global view like a blazing light surrounding a world that seemed all but darkened by neoliberal globalization. Activists around the world were mesmerized. Here, finally, was an incandescent challenge to the Washington-led global regime of corporate capitalism. Arriving from the remote and largely "forgotten" mountains of southeastern Mexico, the Zapatista National Liberation Army in Chiapas seemed different from earlier armed guerrilla movements in Latin America. They radiated a real, liberating *joy* in their resistance. Rooted in their indigenous Mayan culture, drawing from liberation theology, and developing a keen Marxian analysis of neoliberal capitalism, the Zapatistas illuminated a new way of doing politics and resistance, both armed and open to the future, that rallied the international Left to engage in openly reinventing the global fight against capitalism. This was an uprising for a post–Cold War world, one for which "official" socialism was no longer an option.* The Zapatista revolution rapidly

became a global inspiration, energizing leftist movements and catalyzing links among local struggles against capitalism, uniting them in a common cause that, by the end of the decade, had come to be known as the Global Justice Movement.

As the rebellion wore on, the Zapatistas convened two Intercontinental Gatherings for Humanity and against Neoliberalism—the first in Chiapas, the second in Spain—through which they hoped both to spread their revolutionary message and cement their hold in Chiapas by assuring a strong global movement of solidarity.† Thousands of people from popular movements around the globe attended, and at the second meeting, a new global network was conceived—and later founded in Geneva at a separate meeting—called the People's Global Action Network against "Free" Trade and the WTO (PGA). Infused with the spirit of Zapatismo, the network dedicated itself to creating a pluralistic political movement that was expansive, "a world where many worlds fit."[1]

The PGA dedicated itself to a "very clear rejection of capitalism, imperialism, and feudalism"; the rejection of "all forms of domination and discrimination"; and "a confrontational attitude," since "transnational capital is the only real policy maker," no matter what sort of popular pressure is put on governments through standard political channels. Thus "direct action and civil disobedience . . . , as well as the construction of local alternatives to global capitalism," were

---

* Not only was the Zapatista revolution the first post–Cold War uprising, it was also the first uprising of the Internet Age. News of the rebellion spread fast through the then-new Net, with reports posted and reposted, shared on Listservs and the like. To a degree, traditional journalism was outflanked. The Zapatistas' specific form of rebellion made a virtue of necessity: they were clearly outgunned by the Mexican army, so they transformed themselves into a civil movement working to create an autonomous, radically democratic form of self-government in Chiapas. The Zapatistas' primary spokesman, Subcomandante Marcos, was adept at circumventing the traditional media and eloquently presenting the Zapatista cause directly to the people of the world.

† From July 27 to August 6, 1996, approximately three thousand people from over forty countries gathered in Chiapas; one year later the meeting in Spain hosted four thousand.

necessary. The PGA also promoted "an organizing philosophy based on decentralization and autonomy." The PGA set about organizing global days of action and other events to coincide with the big meetings of the institutions of global neoliberalism, like the World Trade Organization.* When the WTO's Second Ministerial Conference met in Geneva in May 1998, large marches were held in India (five hundred thousand people), Brazil (fifty thousand), Geneva itself (ten thousand), and another twenty-five cities around the world. New York was not one of them.[2]

A Carnival against Capitalism

The Global Justice Movement came late to New York City. Despite widespread interest in the Zapatista uprising, and despite growing dissatisfaction with the new world order capital was constructing, no organization in New York took the lead in organizing for the first global day of action in 1998. A year later, matters were different. In June 1999 the PGA called for the Global Day of Action against Financial Centers to coincide with the meeting of the Group of Eight (G8) wealthiest nations in Cologne, Germany. Protests were planned in at least forty countries. This time a relatively new organization, Reclaim the Streets / NYC (RTS), decided to take the bull by the horns, holding the Carnival against Capital right in the capital of capital: Wall Street.

RTS's first action had been a rousing success. In October 1998 a few dozen folks gathered at the Cube, a big metal box perched on one corner of a traffic island where Astor Place, Lafayette, and East 8th Street all come together.† They began dancing to heavily amplified Goa trance music broadcast by a pirate radio station set up in a van parked nearby.‡ At a signal, the crowd, a hundred or so strong, ran down Astor to Broadway. A small contingent coming from another direction quickly waded into traffic and threw up a giant tripod, onto which a young man climbed.§ More speakers were set up, and soon the crowd was dancing on Broadway, bringing the Sunday afternoon traffic to a stop. Passersby joined the party, and the crowd in the street grew by a couple of hundred people. When they arrived, the police—in full riot gear—seemed by turns bemused and mystified. Oddly for Giuliani's New York, they let the party rage for a while longer before negotiating a quiet end, though not before making a face-saving show of arresting eleven.[3]

Carnivalesque spectacle soon became RTS's métier—that and confounding the police as to what the group was really up to. A few days after the Broadway street party, RTS activists tipped off the NYPD that they, together with the Lower East Side Collective, would be holding another protest, beginning at the Cube, the next Sunday. Fifty riot-clad cops showed up, supported by a mobile command center and several police vans, ready to haul off arrestees. Instead, they found six or seven activists in formal attire, having tea around a table covered with a white tablecloth, accompanied by a recording of Vivaldi's *Four Seasons*. The cops were stymied, though one was heard telling a pedestrian that the heavy police presence was there "to protect the public from this disturbance." Next, RTS turned to supporting the community garden struggle with street parties and other events. In one, the police arrested nine. RTS members then announced a "massive demonstration" for June 1999 in the long-since-rebuilt Tompkins Square Park. They engaged in extensive planning on a Listserv—one

* The WTO was formed one year after NAFTA went into effect on January 1, 1995. It replaced the General Agreement on Tariffs and Trade, which dated from 1948, and rapidly became a prime architect of the neoliberal global trade regime, which flourished as the Cold War came to an end. It just as rapidly became the focus of activists' ire.
† It is unlikely that RTS activists chose this site because it was central to the Astor Place Riot a century and a half before, but it is true that it remained a passage point between Broadway and Greenwich Village and the Lower East Side (now rebranded as the East Village).
‡ Likely Steal This Radio, a Lower East Side pirate site at 88.7 FM run by squatters and community activists. It was later shut down by the FCC.
§ The use of giant tripods in liberating streets from cars had been pioneered by RTS London, which found them essential to any successful street party: "For opening the street—or rather stopping it being re-closed by the traffic—ribbons and scissors are not enough. A large scaffold tripod structure with a person suspended from the top has been found useful. Practice in your local park."

The Reclaim the Streets / More Gardens! protest with Louis on a tripod.
Photographer unknown.

RTS had begun in London and then spread rapidly across Europe and into Asia in the mid-1990s. Like the Global Justice Movement, RTS arrived relatively late to New York. RTS's New York roots were specifically in the Lower East Side Collective (LESC), an unruly band of mostly younger activists, students, teachers, organizers, and neighborhood residents intent on regaining some of the activist momentum against gentrification lost after the battle for Tompkins Square Park and in the midst of the harsh policing of dissent that marked the Giuliani years. LESC sought to link New York's long history of social justice struggle, especially on the Lower East Side, with new and provocative models for protest and civic engagement. By connecting struggles for fair wages, critiques of consumer culture, and police accountability with celebratory and experimental cultural practices, LESC found effective, as well as fun, means of organizing in radical street performances, block parties, barbecues, and picnics, all of which advanced critical and community consciousness and articulated an alternative to Giuliani's law-and-order administration, the relentless march of gentrification, and the corporate colonization of urban space. LESC involved itself in helping to develop a community labor coalition and a police and prisons project, supporting environmental justice struggles and the community gardens movement, and spawning the New York branch of RTS.[4]

Rooted in neosituationism—an ideology and style of protest that understood the event to be as important as the object of protest—RTS was part of a burgeoning DIY (do-it-yourself) culture in Britain in the 1990s that sought to attack the commodification, branding, corporatization, and alienation of everything and replace it with a lived, self-made world rooted in decommodification and mutual support. In Britain, neosituationist groups learned to turn spectacle into politics, using street theater to expose how forces of capital were dominating every aspect of everyday life. They turned streets, parks, traffic islands, human-made islands in the Thames, even shopping malls into Temporary Autonomous Zones, where life could be lived differently, at least for a time.[5]

that they expected the police would monitor. When the day arrived, instead of a massive protest, the police found groups of twenty dotted around the park, with a twenty-first person visiting each group in succession. The Parks Department had a rule: no gathering of more than twenty people could be held in a park without a permit. The police—again in riot gear—stood around, embarrassed and unsure of what to do. The Parks Department later announced it would stop enforcing the twenty-person limit.

RTS activists revivified old notions of the carnival, explicitly seeking, as RTS/NYC activist Stephen Duncombe put it, to create a world that "is temporarily turned upside down, the fool crowned king and the king made a fool." In doing so, "people glimpse what a different world might look like: a world without priests or kings, or cops or corporations." For RTS, carnival was "not a spectacle seen by the people" but one in which people "live. . . . [E]veryone participates because its very idea embraces all people," the dumbfounded cops, partiers, and passersby alike.[6]

The cops did not stay dumbfounded for long. By the time RTS was organizing its June 18, 1999, Carnival against Capitalism, the police were working hard to infiltrate the organization, and when the day came, they were waiting. The cops confiscated the sound system before it could be set up—in Liberty Plaza Park, later renamed Zuccotti Park—and arrested thirty-seven people. Perhaps more heavily attended by police than by anticapitalist partiers (besides the NYPD, there was a large contingent of federal officers on hand), the Carnival against Capital ended up not being much of a carnival at all, but it did set the stage for further actions.

NO 2 WTO

Already, the People's Global Action Network and others were planning the next big event: a global confrontation with the WTO when it met in Seattle at the end of 1999. The PGA organized an international caravan to visit multiple cities in the United States on the way to Seattle in an effort to educate activists and the public about the WTO and to spread the word about the upcoming protests while trumpeting the rise of an international anticapitalist movement. Their first stop was New York.

Local activists prepared to meet the caravan. Organizers from a dozen organizations (RTS, LESC, Fed-Up Queers, Global Sweatshop Coalition, and the union UNITE, among others) formed the NO 2 WTO NYC coalition. To celebrate the arrival of the PGA caravan, NO 2 WTO planned a teach-in and direct action against the multimillion-dollar public relations firm Burson-Marsteller. B-M was famous—infamous in many people's minds—as one of the world's leading "crisis management" firms, hired to smooth things over for corporate polluters and killers (like Exxon, Philip Morris, and Union Carbide after Bophal) and corrupt governments alike.* Protesters dressed in suits scrawled "perception management" on their foreheads, strapped on paper horse-blinders stenciled with the B-M logo, and dipped their hands in blood-red paint before descending on the B-M headquarters on Park Avenue South and 20th Street. There, they handed out flyers entitled "Burson-Marsteller: Whitewashing Corporate Crime since 1989" and listing a number of B-M's more prominent efforts at "spinning" grievous corporate crimes over the fifty years since.[7]

The Burson-Marsteller demonstration launched a month of actions and teach-ins leading up to the WTO summit in Seattle, peaking in New York on Buy Nothing Day—the day after Thanksgiving. Flyers went up and emails circulated:

> Reclaim the Streets presents an alternative to global capitalism and local commercialism. In solidarity with Seattle Citizen Committee and international November 30th actions.
>
> **A call to action for all:** Revolutionaries, fire breathers, students, dancers, workers, square pegs, activists, oppressed, radicals, liberated, madmen, contented, alternative lifestyles and mal-contents!

The party began at Union Square, where a thousand people—and a large number of riot-clad cops—gathered. Before long, marshals led the crowd down into the subway for an impromptu party as they rode uptown. Out they came into Times Square for an hour of dancing—drawing in startled and bemused shoppers—before heading over to Bryant Park. At every turn, riot cops were waiting for them, preventing the erection of the now-traditional tripods and

---

* Burson-Marsteller admits to only "consulting" with Exxon on its cleanup plan after the *Exxon Valdez* disaster in Alaska; it was a central player in the faux-grassroots and faux-science campaigns that propped up the tobacco industry for so long and that became a template for the corporate campaign against climate change action in the 2000s.

arresting forty-five for the crime of "dancing, rather than shopping." Like the massive "Battle in Seattle" that was to follow, the RTS Buy Nothing Day dance party managed to link substantive issues of daily public life in one city to an already burgeoning international resistance against debt, free market fundamentalism, and the undemocratic policies of neoliberal globalization. No wonder the cops were out in force against the heady and Hydra-headed camp.[8]

Direct Action

In the wake of the Buy Nothing arrests, Reclaim the Streets diversified its tactics, taking its parties from the streets back into the subways and conducting permitless "freak parades" through Lower Manhattan, even as it continued to work within the now-exploding Global Justice Movement. Meanwhile, the PGA caravan left New York in October and wound its way across North America to meet up with West Coast activists busily planning for what would be a historic confrontation with the WTO in Seattle. To better coordinate their actions, a broad array of activists formed the regional Direct Action Network (DAN), which adopted PGA's guiding principles.* DAN based its organizing practices on the notion of prefigurative politics—the belief that the way one organizes has to be consistent with the goals one hopes to achieve. As DAN organized against the unaccountable and undemocratic WTO, it convened in directly democratic and transparent "spokescouncils" and made decisions using directly democratic consensus-forming processes.[9]

On November 30 in Seattle, tens of thousands rallied against the WTO, while a thousand DAN activists locked down the streets, successfully stopping delegates from entering the conference. The police responded with tear gas and pepper spray. Blinded and choking, activists nonetheless held the line. Elsewhere in the city, demonstrators smashed the windows of corporate targets. The ruckus in the streets

shut down the meetings, at least for a time, as TV news spread images of masked militants, smashed windows, and burning trash cans to homes across the United States, introducing many for the first time to the Global Justice Movement (which the media instead dubbed the antiglobalization movement). The next day, the mayor declared a state of emergency, announced a curfew, and created a fifty-block no-protest zone.

To activists in New York the Battle in Seattle looked like a stunning success, and they were receptive when DAN decided to expand its reach and develop the Continental Direct Action Network. CDAN continued to use and further develop anarchist organizing models consisting of broad participation and direct democracy alongside a rejection of hierarchies; feminist-inspired resolve toward personal engagement, garnered through a politics of consensus; and a commitment to invent an effective and decentralized radicalism based on direct action. Structurally, organization would take the form of grassroots associations and networks with varying and flexible aims and tactics joined together through loose "points of unity." Large-scale direct action was to be organized through affinity groups, spokescouncils, and clearinghouses in an attempt to infuse the political experience with a vitality that preserved and amplified the autonomy and self-determination of its varied members. Such directly democratic, transparent, and sometimes naively open organizing structures were created to model and embody the movement's egalitarian ideals.[10]

New York's DAN was founded in February 2000 and drew on existing community groups and radical organizations like More Gardens!, RTS, and the recently formed NO 2 WTO NYC. It met regularly at the CHARAS / El Bohio Community Center on 9th Street between Avenues B and C. An early flyer and eblast read:

> Building on the successes of the World Trade Organization protests in Seattle, a diverse coalition of New York City activist groups are coming together in mutual aid. We are creating a network to support each other's movements and facilitate

---

* Original members of DAN included such groups as the Ruckus Society, Art and Revolution, the Rainforest Action Network, Global Exchange, Seattle's Community Action Network, and members of United Steelworkers.

mass mobilizations on a diversity of issues, beginning with actions on April 16–17 against the World Bank and International Monetary Fund.

This network is just beginning to form, and the energy level is already high—well over 100 people representing dozens of groups attended our most recent meeting. Spread the word: We want YOU to join in making the New York Direct Action Network a powerful vehicle for real social and political change.[11]

Besides individuals and organizations already affiliated with NO 2 WTO, those drawn to the meeting included the Student Liberation Action Movement (SLAM!), members of the United Automobile Workers, former ACT UP members, Radical Cheerleaders, Food Not Bombs, UNITE activists, the Rainforest Action Network, and United Students against Sweatshops. Working within DAN's democratic structures, these organizations sought to discover their underlying commonalities while building a framework for joint action. Much of NYC DAN's effort was spent organizing local struggles while framing them within the larger context of the global movement against capitalism.

NYC DAN's early actions were varied. It walked picket lines and provided media support with striking workers at the Museum of Modern Art who were fighting health care cuts, as well as with International Longshoremen's Association, Local 1814 members who were on strike at the (now-closed) Domino Sugar factory in Williamsburg. And it fought the ongoing privatization and commodification of community space in the Lower East Side, quickly joining the roiling community gardens struggle. DAN and RTS members were central to the attempt to reclaim the Esperanza garden on February 15, 2000. One participant was thrown in the back of a cop car but managed to kick out the window and was pulled free by a friend. In the confusion they made a clear getaway. For those not so lucky, DAN provided legal support afterward.[12]

NYC DAN participated in citywide efforts. On May 1, 2000, NYC DAN organized five hundred people to join the May Day march for labor and immigrant rights. And working with More Gardens! they reclaimed a fenced-in lot on the East River in Brooklyn that the city had promised for a park. Outside the city, NYC DAN members converged at every Global Justice Movement protest on the East Coast. In April 2000 NYC DAN constituents joined thousands of activists in Washington who were seeking to disrupt the annual gathering of the International Monetary Fund and the World Bank, helping to coordinate and secure the barricades used to keep IMF and World Bank members from reaching their conference. In August they converged on the Republican National Convention in Philadelphia. NYC DAN members were among the four hundred protesters arrested as they used lock boxes and their own bodies to disrupt the convention. A New York contingent was also at the Free Trade Agreement of the Americas protests in Quebec City in April 2001, helping to organize the Free Trade Area of the Americas (FTAA) Border Caravan.[13]

But despite this whirlwind of activity, both NYC DAN and the continental DAN dissolved during the summer of 2001.[14]

Another World Is Possible

Even before the terrorist attacks of September 11, 2001, the federal government had begun considering direct action—and RTS street parties!—as a "terrorist threat." The attacks of 9/11 further paralyzed the movement. For some participants, the attack on the World Trade Center and Pentagon, together with the ensuing wars and attacks on civil liberties, changed everything, marking the end—or at least a hiatus—of their radical direct action.[15]

Others, though, tried to press on, most immediately when the World Economic Forum (WEF) decided to move its February 2002 meeting from its traditional home in Davos, Switzerland, to New York City to express solidarity with the stricken metropolis. The WEF had been the target of increasing resistance over the previous years as global justice activists singled out the winter ski-resort meeting of the world's superelite (heads of state, corporate CEOs, anointed members of the commentariat) as one of the key events and places—decidedly undemocratic—where the globalist visions and deceptive policies of the neoliberal order were hammered out. Militant protests had generated bad press for the WEF and cost the local government in Davos millions of dollars for increased security measures. Relocating to New York for 2002, WEF organizers reasoned, would not only show solidarity but also likely result in fewer and tamer protests, if any at all. Unwilling to submit to the 9/11 climate of fear, however, global justice activists in the city immediately began planning to confront the WEF.

Former NYC DAN members regrouped, creating the New York branch of the nascent Another World Is Possible Coalition and calling for an anticapitalist convergence and protest to coincide with the WEF meetings. Another World Is Possible urged activists from around the world to "join us as New Yorkers strike back against corporate terror." They declared with anger and reason that

> for years now, the CEOs of major corporations, hundreds of top international government officials and just plain rich people—from Bill Gates to Bill Clinton—have been meeting every year in Davos, Switzerland. This is where the real rulers of the world give the politicians their marching orders. This is where the schemes that lead to atrocities like GATT and the WTO are actually hatched. And this year, the dining club for the ruling class will be held at the Waldorf Astoria hotel in Midtown Manhattan. . . . This is a provocation. While thousands of New Yorkers are still burying their dead, trying to patch together shattered lives, and desperately trying to see how they can continue to pay insanely high New York City rents after being laid off from their jobs, the richest and most powerful men on earth have decided to come and party on the wreckage—to celebrate, no doubt, the billions of dollars of taxpayer money they've just been handed by their respec-

tive governments and explore new opportunities to profiteer from permanent global warfare. Do they think we have no pride? No self-respect? That we're just going to sit back and let this happen? As our heroic firefighters have shown us, the moratorium on direct action in New York is over.* We are calling for a joyous, creative resistance to the WEF's stifling grey culture of corporate conformity; actions whose diversity of tactics will reflect the rich diversity of our city's communities. We are calling for actions based on principles of non-hierarchy, passionate opposition to patriarchy, white supremacy, and rule-by-elite, and the vision of a world in which no one has to live in fear or daily terror.

Calling for the total abolishment of "states and their wars," Another World Is Possible invited everyone to a "social revolution": "RSVP Waldorf Astoria Hotel New York City January 31–February 4, 2002."[16]

Despite real fears of stringent state repression, Another World members began planning, using the spokescouncil structure developed by DAN, and held open meetings at St. Mark's Church on January 2 and 9, 2002. Among other actions, they planned a march—and sought a permit for it—for February 2. In preparation for the protests, the city poured millions of dollars into security and blocked off the streets around the Waldorf Astoria with dump trucks filled with sand, metal barricades, and a large number of riot-clad cops, as well as horse brigades. Nonetheless, the city issued a march permit. Ten to twenty thousand protesters gathered in two groups at the southeast and southwest corners of Central Park and then marched a circuitous route toward the Waldorf Astoria, near which they were permitted to hold a rally in hastily erected protest pens. Three dozen people

---

* On Friday, November 2, 2001, nearly a thousand firefighters gathered near City Hall to protest Mayor Giuliani's October 31 order reducing the number of firefighters given daily access to the World Trade Center site from sixty-four to twenty-five. After speeches, the firefighters pushed down a barricade and began marching toward the site. When they encountered a wall of police officers, numerous fights broke out. Twelve firefighters (including high-ranking officers) were arrested, and five police officers were injured.

Protesters at the World Economic Forum, February 2002.
ZUMA Press, Inc. / Alamy Stock Photo.

were arrested over the course of the day. That evening, anarchists organized an unpermitted, fast-paced "snake march" that wound through the East Village and the Lower East Side, provoking immediate police pursuit and resulting in an additional handful of arrests.*[17]

While the WEF protest was not as large as many global justice events had been in previous years, it was by many measures a success. Global justice activists demanded and demonstrated their right to speech and assembly; they convened counterconventions that explored and strategized alternatives to neoliberal development; and people traveled from all over the country to be involved. Newspapers reported that at times the Saturday rally seemed almost joyous in demeanor. Even so, as much as anything, the WEF demonstrations were an exercise in regaining lost ground.

Reshaping Resistance

As the Bush administration geared up for war in Iraq, activist energy likewise shifted from contesting corporate-led

* Over the whole weekend, some 150 people were arrested.

capitalist globalization to trying to stop the invasion. RTS, DAN, and Another World Is Possible activists were centrally involved in planning New York's big February 15, 2003, demonstration (see vignette) and other actions. But the fearlessness, the global solidarity, and, perhaps most importantly, the hope and feeling that another world was possible that characterized the Global Justice Movement had largely ebbed. Heightened repressive powers of the state and the subversion of civil liberties that accompanied the War on Terror suppressed direct action and tempered the lofty goals and desire for urgent action of the movement in New York City. Weakened, if not completely deterred, activists continued working locally, but the moment of reciprocal, militant, jubilant, and globally connected organizing that characterized the NYC Global Justice Movement had come to a close.

Some activists returned to reclaiming the streets—this time as part of monthly, rolling Critical Mass bike rides that sought to open up the grid for pedal power and to put cars back in their place—severely testing the limits of new-mayor Michael Bloomberg's desire to promote alternative uses for the streets. Others focused on the increasingly ugly politics of immigration in America, lending support and solidarity to the growing movement for immigrant rights in the middle part of the decade (chapter 18). And yet others began planning for the next big show of "solidarity" in New York: the Republican National Convention to be held in August 2004.

If the moment of global justice organizing had largely passed, the spirit by which it developed had not: modes of organizing and demonstrating—radically democratic, frequently joyous, often seeking to prefigure another world to come—lived on through these movements and others, including the global and national World Social Forum movement, which arose to directly counter the World Economic Forum. Global justice activists reintroduced the notion that a better city could be won through joy, celebration of rebellious communities, and creative protest and resistance. They simultaneously linked the local issues they were struggling over to the global scale, understanding that processes of market liberalization and resistance to it were connected at home and in the world. Furthermore, their practices typified a new orientation to social movements, one that emphasized a robust affirmation of life, an ethos of direct action, and a commitment to building new communities as a fundamental ingredient of "movement building" itself.

In many ways, the commitment to pluralism, openness, and the organizing processes and structures that enshrined these values, along with confrontational and theatrical direct action, defined protest at the turn of the twenty-first century. While its fall was as rapid as its rise, the Global Justice Movement in New York City left a legacy of direct action, as well as a toolkit of tactics, that would continue to prove valuable, perhaps most spectacularly in September 2011, when New York radicals, many of them veterans of the Global Justice Movement, decided to occupy Wall Street (chapter 19).

UNION SQUARE

AFTER SEPTEMBER 11, 2001

Subscribers to the *New York Times* leafing through the paper on the morning of Tuesday, September 11, 2001, would have found an obituary for Roger Starr, the ideologue of New York's "planned shrinkage" in the 1970s. They would also have seen an op-ed piece by the criminologist Bernard Harcourt that was timed to coincide with the mayoral primary election to be held that day, arguing that Giuliani's "broken windows" policing was a failure on its own terms, not just an ongoing assault on New Yorkers' civil liberties. Both were requiems to the city as it had been or, in the second case, for what many hoped it no longer would be: Starr representing the era of "planned shrinkage," Harcourt's piece representing a cri de coeur against the city of aggressive "quality of life" policing that it had become. In the chaos that soon hit, readers would, no doubt, have very quickly forgotten these requiems and maybe even the visions of the city they represented.

The shock of the World Trade Center's destruction and the thousands of lives lost soon gave way to grief, as well as a sense on the part of many that "everything had changed." It also gave rise to the need for many people to gather in public—to share stories, to remember lost friends or family,

to find a new sense of community. Most of Lower Manhattan below 14th Street was closed off, so Union Square became the closest accessible and large public space. Almost instinctively, people gravitated to it, bearing candles and flowers and photos, standing and sitting quietly, communing, "turning it into a shrine and memorial, layered with photos, hand-written messages, schoolchildren's drawings, expressions of sympathy and sorrow from flight attendants who had been spared the luck of the draw."[1]

Union Square had long been a central gathering place in the city. It was the site of America's largest public rally to date when it hosted a huge patriotic rally after Lincoln declared war against the secessionist South. It was the site of New York's first Labor Day rally and parade in 1882. It was a popular gathering place for May Day rallies, for street speakers, for agitation of all types. Then, during World War II, Parks Commissioner Robert Moses closed the square to street speakers and political agitation. With that, Union Square declined, no longer particularly central to the political life of the city. Beginning in 1984, the square was redeveloped as part of the city's campaign to make parks assets into real estate.

Overseen by the Union Square Partnership, the reconstruction of the square did not really "catch on as a public space," according to Marshall Berman, until September 11. "Then, abruptly, it was flooded with candles, flowers, missing person signs, poems and drawings. Some art students unrolled a scroll of paper three feet wide and several hundred feet long. A great assembly of people gathered round the scroll, and wrote radically contradictory messages and meditations. Overnight, Union Square became the city's most exciting public space: a small-town Fourth of July party combined with a 1970s be-in."[2]

In the first days, Union Square was quite quiet. People came to mourn and to reflect, though occasionally heated discussions could be heard—over what really happened, what it meant, what response there should be globally and locally. Soon a new social geography developed in the park. Street kids and homeless people moved into the center; street musicians and activists handing out literature colonized the southern steps; Christians grouped along the east side. Residents and tourists came by the thousands. Many stayed through the night, relighting and replacing candles. A memorial column with a Christmas tree on top, made by two Ukrainian immigrants, became a type of shrine, with candles all around it. Even more candles lit the base of the big equestrian statue of George Washington, his horse soon decorated with brightly colored acrylic peace symbols, while people paraded nearby with American flags. A church from Flushing, Queens, commandeered two flower beds and used donated roses from a canceled flower show to create images of the now-gone World Trade Center towers.[3]

By the weekend, "the park had become an impromptu outdoor festival," as the *New York Times*' architecture critic put it. Union Square was functioning "as urban designs are conceived to do: bring[ing] strangers together on common ground, people who otherwise might never have met, people who would not have bothered to notice one another on the subway or street." Within a week, the square had become a space of debate and proselytizing, but the overriding sentiment was "peace." On the whole, New Yorkers opposed the rush to war, though many, of course, expressed a deep ambivalence about the best way forward. Union Square became a center for those opposed to the Bush administration's newly announced War on Terror and likely plans to attack Afghanistan. Debate flourished. A peace march was planned for Friday, September 21, to begin in the square and work its way north to the armed forces recruiting station in Times Square.[4]

Before it could happen, the city moved. Early Thursday morning, September 20 work crews descended onto the square. Police and city employees pushed home-

less people and street kids out of the center, while other crews dismantled the posters, photographs, "missing" posters, and paintings that festooned the rails and benches. Yet other workers power-washed

Union Square in the aftermath of 9/11 and before the Giuliani administration closed it down and fenced it off.
Photo © Brian Rose, used by permission.

the candle wax and scrubbed Washington's horse clean. Finally, workers erected a fence all the way around the square, closing off its heart, at least temporarily. New York's most vibrant post-9/11 public space and its most important organic shrine, built up over more than a week of mourning, debating, celebrating the city, music making, and street preaching, was destroyed in a single morning.[5]

The city offered shifting rationales for its action. It dismantled the shrine so the makeshift memorials could be preserved (rain was due that afternoon). The homeless had taken over the square, and they needed to be cleaned out. Certainly the presence of homeless people camping in the park rankled the Giuliani administration—during those years, "the city's campaign against the homeless trumped everything," as Berman wrote—but so too, it seems, did the very idea that there could be a *democratic*, popular space in the city, one with its own logic, its own order, its own developing set of customs and mores. Union Square was not an uprising, much less a revolt. But it was an expression of deep democratic currents in the city, currents that ran counter to the Giuliani administration's desire (soon adopted if in a friendlier guise by his successor Michael Bloomberg) to use 9/11 to advance its own, more authoritarian sense of urban order, its own desire to instantiate a narrowly prescribed "quality of life" in the city. The square stood as a sharp rebuke to those "security experts"—officials in the Giuliani administration chief among them—who would assert that the only way to make public space (and the urban landscape more generally) was to harden it, to carefully control access, to increase surveillance, and to eliminate the very possibility of spontaneity. For more than a week after 9/11, Union Square showed what neosituationists (and antiglobalization) activists had long also wanted to show (if in a quite different register): another world was possible.[6]

POPULAR REVOLT IN THE NEW MILLENNIUM

As the new millennium dawned—as the twentieth century bled into the twenty-first—it seemed as if New York was entering another era of intensified unrest. To be sure, with the exception of the short interregnum after World War II and before the 1964 Harlem Riot, popular unrest has never really faded from the scene (as the intense season of revolt that was the 1960s makes so clear). It has always been a part of, and a central shaping force in, New York's urban landscape. Even so, even before the global explosion of anti- or alter-globalization protest around the time of the Battle for Seattle in 1999, a new militancy seemed to be stirring among activists—and the just plain disgruntled.

The Tompkins Square protests and police riot of 1988 was a harbinger of stepped-up antigentrification activism, which perhaps had its fullest flowering in the resistance to Mayor Giuliani's plans to sell off the city's community gardens, even as it continues to this day. The Black Lives Matter movement in New York has its roots in protests against police killings of black men and women in the 1980s and 1990s, as well as in struggling against Giuliani's quality of life / zero tolerance policing policies, which evolved under Mayor Bloomberg into the city's

hyperaggressive stop-and-frisk tactics. By the second decade of the twenty-first century, concerted organizing and protest has forced the administration of Mayor Bill de Blasio to significantly scale back stop-and-frisk practices (partially under court order). In other words, specific urban conditions in New York—most particularly, policies promoting hypergentrification largely at the expense of poor communities of color and the aggressive policing such policies seemed to require to be successful—engendered a surge in activism, protest, and even revolt, as the accompanying map shows.

National policies and global events too have shaped revolt in New York. Many assumed that the terrorist attacks of September 11, 2001, would dampen New Yorkers' zeal for militant organizing and street protest. But that was not to be the case. The temporary memorial at Union Square quickly created a public space of mourning that was at once somber and lively, opening a space for deep, critical reflection and debate when that was precisely what the George W. Bush presidential and Giuliani mayoral administrations did not want, displaying what is best in New York's long tradition of popular resistance

to elite attempts to control the social and political landscape. By February 2002, New Yorkers in large numbers turned out to protest the meeting of the World Economic Forum, which had been moved from Davos, Switzerland, to the city in an act of "solidarity" (but also to escape the culture of militant oppositional protest that had grown up around the meeting's Swiss lair in recent years). Global Justice Movement activists at the New York World Economic Forum meeting and two years later the Republican National Convention reinvented and adapted old modes of carnivalesque protest with the aim of bringing a new joie de vivre into the alter-globalization movement and maybe even turning the world on its head. In between, in the largest coordinated global protest ever, New Yorkers turned out in their hundreds of thousands to try to stop the war against Iraq. And while they failed in that mission, so too did city authorities and police fail to stop the mass demonstration, no matter how hard they tried. Popular revolt, the antiwar protest showed, is an implacable force.

And it is a force that continues to be mobilized: by immigrant activists seeking to secure their place in the city against draconian laws and racist travel bans; by

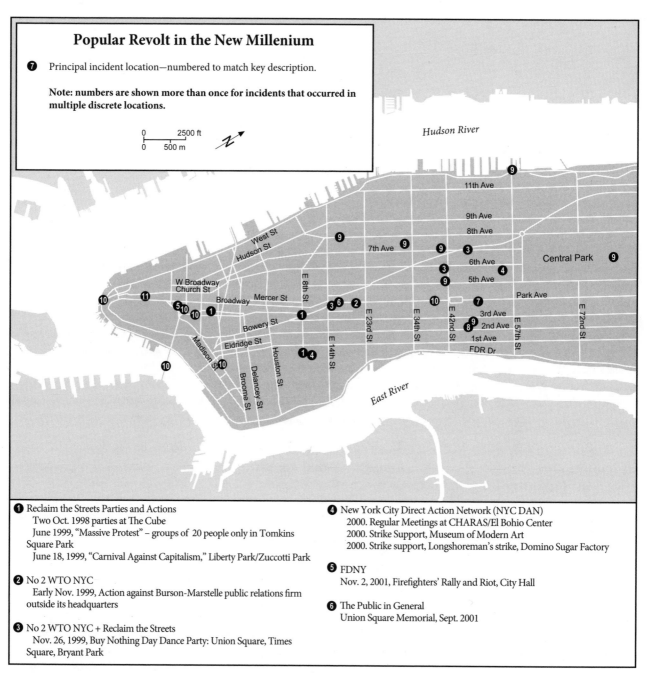

Popular Revolt in the New Millenium

❼ Principal incident location—numbered to match key description.

Note: numbers are shown more than once for incidents that occurred in multiple discrete locations.

Hudson River

East River

Central Park

11th Ave
9th Ave
8th Ave
7th Ave
6th Ave
5th Ave
Park Ave
3rd Ave
2nd Ave
1st Ave
FDR Dr

West St
Hudson St
W Broadway
Church St
Broadway
Mercer St
Bowery St
Eldridge St
Madison St
Delancey St
Broome St
Houston St
E 8th St
E 14th St
E 23rd St
E 34th St
E 42nd St
E 57th St
E 72nd St

❶ **Reclaim the Streets Parties and Actions**
Two Oct. 1998 parties at The Cube
June 1999, "Massive Protest" – groups of 20 people only in Tomkins Square Park
June 18, 1999, "Carnival Against Capitalism," Liberty Park/Zuccotti Park

❷ **No 2 WTO NYC**
Early Nov. 1999, Action against Burson-Marstelle public relations firm outside its headquarters

❸ **No 2 WTO NYC + Reclaim the Streets**
Nov. 26, 1999, Buy Nothing Day Dance Party: Union Square, Times Square, Bryant Park

❹ **New York City Direct Action Network (NYC DAN)**
2000. Regular Meetings at CHARAS/El Bohio Center
2000. Strike Support, Museum of Modern Art
2000. Strike support, Longshoreman's strike, Domino Sugar Factory

❺ **FDNY**
Nov. 2, 2001, Firefighters' Rally and Riot, City Hall

❻ **The Public in General**
Union Square Memorial, Sept. 2001

Popular Revolt in the New Millennium.
Cartography: Joe Stoll, Syracuse University Cartography Lab and Map Shop.

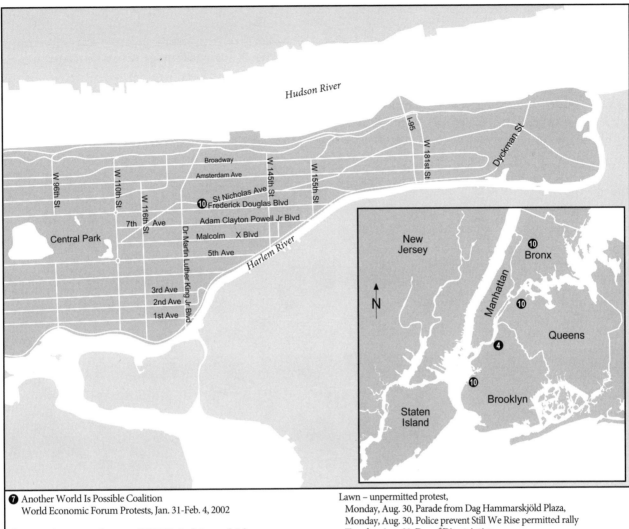

antiracist and antigentrification activists; and by a wide panoply of newly politicized youth as well as old activist hands seeking to expose and expunge the growing local, national, and global economic (and thus social and political) inequality the neoliberal "Washington Consensus," coordinated by New York's Wall Street, has put into place. Perhaps one reason the surge in revolt looks and feels a lot like that which racked the city at the turn of the twentieth century is because the economic and social conditions are not too dissimilar as the city experiences levels of inequality, and outright destitution, not seen since that previous Gilded Age. Perhaps it is also because, like then, when radical workers and others were determined to create a new world out of the shell of the old, now a broad range of activists know that another world is not only possible but necessary.

NO WAR AGAINST IRAQ

A POLICE RIOT AS ACCOMPLISHED AS THE INVASION, 2003

The world had never seen a bigger protest. Simultaneous marches and demonstrations took place in more than six hundred cities on February 15, 2003, to protest the United States' impending invasion of and war against Iraq. Conservative estimates say eight million people took to the streets (some put the total as high as thirty million) worldwide, from Fiji and Tasmania to Norway and Iceland. Scientists at the United States' McMurdo Station in Antarctica joined in. It was a global uprising. There were three million in Rome, a million or so in Barcelona and London. The numbers were smaller in New York City, probably exceeding three hundred thousand (if everyone out in New York and intent on getting to the protest is counted), an impressive showing given the severe jingoism that had taken hold in the nation—and given just how hard the Bloomberg administration and the NYPD worked to keep the protest from happening at all.

On January 22 a coalition of antiwar groups under the name United for Peace and Justice (UFPJ) engaged the New York Civil Liberties Union (NYCLU) to help it secure a permit for a parade and rally on February 15. UFPJ wanted to meet at Dag Hammarskjöld Plaza on East 47th Street

between First and Second Avenues. The plaza is something like a long promenade that leads to the United Nations complex. The location was symbolically important because of how hard the Bush administration was working—fraudulently, as it turned out—to secure the UN's seal of approval for its Iraq adventurism. From the plaza, the throng would march down First Avenue to 42nd Street, head west to Fifth Avenue, and then turn north toward Central Park in order to hold a rally at the park's southern border. The NYCLU understood that significant police coordination would be needed—UFPJ was predicting a turnout of fifty thousand to one hundred thousand. Rather than just apply for a permit, therefore, it contacted the NYPD's Legal Bureau, hoping to negotiate with the police a satisfactory route, police protection, and the like.[1]

Such negotiation had become standard practice for large—and often small—demonstrations in the years since the 1960s upheavals. Policing strategies in North America and Europe shifted beginning in the 1970s from a strategy of "escalating force"—protester militancy being met with ever-increasing police violence—to one of "negotiated management." Under

the negotiated management regime, police and activists—often with lawyers from organizations like the American Civil Liberties Union—would negotiate everything from rally size and parade route to how many people would be arrested, in what way, and for what charge. Long encouraged to do so by the courts, cities developed permit systems as a means of regulating speech and assembly, and it became common for protesters to negotiate the terms of permits before applying for them. But the negotiated management system was fraying. For example, activists in the Battle for Seattle at the World Trade Organization meeting in Seattle in 1999 found that unpermitted protest was far more effective than that which was permitted. The season of anti-globalization protest that followed Seattle cemented this sense in the eyes of many activists (who anyway saw even their permitted activities to be frequently violently dispersed and who also found issued permits so restrictive as to be impossible), including Reclaim the Streets and others who found their post-9/11 footing in time for the February 2002 World Economic Forum meeting, held in New York rather than its usual Davos. From the side of the police, negotiated management was giving way to a "command-and-control" theory of protest policing that sought to assure police authority and police power to dictate the terms of protest at all times—through, for example, the use of protest pens to corral protesters or the creation of temporary barricades (of buses or motorcycle police) that made protesters all but invisible to anyone not in a helicopter, as NYPD did at the World Economic Forum—as well as a new-found enthusiasm for infiltrating and spying on activist groups and engaging in agent provocateur strategies of disruption and discreditization.[2]

The NYCLU requested to meet with the NYPD's Legal Bureau on January 22, 23, 24, and, after a weekend pause, 27 but received no response. On Tuesday, January 28, NYCLU wrote directly to the head of the Legal Bureau, requesting an urgent meeting. That afternoon, the bureau finally responded, saying it could not approve the proposed route because of congestion concerns. The NYCLU told the bureau that it and UFPJ were willing to negotiate an alternative route and asked the NYPD to propose one. On Wednesday, January 29, the NYPD informed the NYCLU that it would not approve any march on any route. The NYCLU informed the city of its intention to file a lawsuit. The city's (not the NYPD's) Law Department asked the NYCLU to hold off while it tried to negotiate a solution. The next day, the parties met. The meeting included the police chief, who commanded Manhattan below 59th Street. The police chief suggested an alternative route (from 14th Street to Dag Hammarskjöld Plaza, mostly along Third Avenue).

Protest organizers did not like the route for various reasons, but the police chief did not have the authority to approve any other. The parties agreed to meet again on Monday, February 3. The city postponed the meeting, saying that Mayor Bloomberg wanted to meet with Police Commissioner Raymond Kelly first and could not do so until that day. City lawyers promised the NYCLU that now that the mayor was involved, "you're going to like our offer." The NYCLU agreed to delay the meeting until the afternoon of February 4. When the meeting happened, city officials reaffirmed the city's unwillingness to permit any march anywhere in the city and instead presented a take-it-or-leave-it offer of a stationary protest on First Avenue north of 49th Street (not in front of the UN). The NYCLU filed suit on behalf of UFPJ.

In court hearings, advocates for UFPJ presented evidence that a number of large marches in front of the UN had been held without incident (including one of at least five hundred thousand people in 1982 marching against nuclear weapons) and that the city regularly allowed large parades to take over streets (as with the annual Saint Patrick's Day parade). The city countered that the extent of the proposed protest march was unknown, that its organizers were likewise unknown to the city (unlike the long-standing organizers of the Saint Patrick's Day parade), that the protest might be unruly, and that it posed a terrorism threat (though the police chief admitted that he had no intelligence along these lines). Under examination, the police chief admitted that the city had denied

every protest march permit application it had received since the fall of 2002. After the hearing, while the judge considered the case, the federal Department of Justice filed a brief with the court, claiming substantive interest in the issue and asking the judge to weigh post-9/11 security concerns heavily in her decision. On Monday, February 10, the judge upheld the NYPD's ban on any and all marches, citing security concerns. She was not willing to second-guess the NYPD, she said. The NYCLU appealed. The United States Court of Appeals for the Second Circuit scheduled a hearing for Wednesday morning. The courtroom was packed. The three-judge panel appeared an hour late, explaining it had been concurring on the matter first and, in an unusual move, that instead of hearing arguments it would ask questions. Questioning lasted for an hour. The judges adjourned, returning fifteen minutes later to announce they were upholding the original decision. They were not willing to doubt the original judge, who had considered the facts of the case, they said.[3]

In the wake of the decision, UFPJ met with NYPD to plan a stationary rally. The police chief refused a request to move the rally from hilly First Avenue (north of 49th Street), which protest organizers had never requested, to flatter Third Avenue. He did allow the protest stage to be moved to the crest of a hill at 51st Street. The chief informed organizers that protest pens would be created in the center of First Avenue, that no people would be allowed to walk up or down the sidewalks on First, and that entry into the pens from side streets

**Aggressive policing at the
February 15, 2003, antiwar rally.**
ZUMA Press, Inc. / Alamy Stock Photo.

would be strictly controlled. Beginning at 52nd Street, gates into the pens would be opened. As the block filled, they would be shut, and new gates would be opened at the next block north. The police would not allow blocks to be designated for certain groups (labor, students, etc.); instead, any affinity groups would have to form elsewhere and walk together to the protest if they wished to stand together. Any such groups would have to use sidewalks only to reach the site, and if they blocked sidewalks while either assembling or walking to the site, they would be dispersed by the police. The NYPD banned portable toilets from the protest, claiming they posed a security threat.

Saturday, February 15, dawned freezing cold. Even so, hundreds of thousands of people started making their way to the pro-test. As they did, they found the police had closed off not only First Avenue but also Second, forcing people farther west to walk up Third. Police engaged in deliberate misdirection, telling people conflicting stories about which access points were open and how to get to them. Despite the announced plan to let people fill the blocks on First Avenue one by one, police instead closed all access to the protest below 60th Street. As cops squeezed people out of Second and blocked cross-street access to First, the sidewalks on Third became jammed, and people spilled into the street. Those people who remained on Second, trapped between barriers, were first boxed in and then faced with a phalanx of mounted officers pushing them south back into Midtown. The mounted cops then swung around and rode over to Third Avenue,

where they were let through a closed gate at 53rd Street and into the center of a large crowd that had essentially been penned there by earlier police actions. The horses pushed into the middle of the throng, breaking it in two, pushing some people north, others south, and wedging them onto the sidewalks on both sides. Riot-clad cops joined in, forcing the crowd away with their batons. As the street was cleared and the sidewalks became jammed, riot cops moved on the packed masses on the eastside sidewalk, forcing them back into the street and then south, away from the protest. Cops yelled at people to "go home." Soon the police closed off Third Avenue at 51st Street and forbade people from heading north—the only way to the demonstration. Police ordered the crowd to disperse to the west (though few heard the command), and soon the cops and horses waded in again, arresting any who did not—or could not—flee. At other intersections, when people sat down to protest police dispersal, the cops lashed out with their batons.

Remarkably, hundreds of thousands made it into the official protest pens anyway, mostly from the north. Southern blocks remained partially unfilled because cops would not let the crowds move south. If demonstrators left a pen—to go to a store for water or coffee or to head along a sidewalk to another pen to meet friends or family—they were typically not allowed back in and ordered out of the neighborhood. By the time the rally was over, more than 350 people had been arrested, largely on minor "disturbing the peace" charges. Those arrested were typically handcuffed and held in unheated police vans for hours without food, water, or access to toilets. Arrestees were not informed of their right to counsel; those who asked for it anyway were threatened with lengthened detention. Many were interrogated about their political affiliations and past protest activities; the police entered the information into the federally sanctioned "Demonstrator Debriefing Form" and later entered it into a computer database.[4]

The NYPD—and thus the Bloomberg administration—had only one goal. If it could not completely prevent an antiwar protest, it would disrupt it, minimize it, and block access to it, effectively barring people from expressing their opposition to the country's march to war. The policing may not have lowered itself to the force's historical standards for disrupting politics it does not like—a full-out police riot—but that's about all that can be said for the NYPD that day.

As for the global antiwar movement, it failed to stop or even slow the invasion of Iraq, which began with heavily hyped "shock-and-awe" tactics on March 20, 2003. Two days later, now that it was too late, the Bloomberg administration permitted UFPJ to stage a big antiwar march from Times Square to Washington Square Park. A quarter of a million people took part.

CONVENTIONAL PROTEST?

UPHEAVAL AT THE REPUBLICAN NATIONAL CONVENTION, 2004

Like the organizers of the World Economic Forum before it, the Republican Party thought it would hold its 2004 Republican National Convention (RNC) in New York City as an act of "solidarity." When New York was announced as the host of the RNC in January 2003, the convention was imagined to be as much a coronation of President George W. Bush as America's "commander in chief" in the War on Terror as it was to be an anointment of the Republicans' presidential candidate for the 2004 election. The Bush administration was busy beating the drums of war at the United Nations, and when the massive global protests on February 15, 2003, failed to deter its plans for the invasion of Iraq, President Bush was riding high. On March 20 U.S. troops invaded, and on May 1 Bush, wearing an air force jumpsuit, landed in a fighter plane on the USS *Abraham Lincoln*, docked in San Diego, to announce that "in the Battle of Iraq, the United States and our allies have prevailed." Standing in front of a giant red, white, and blue banner reading "Mission Accomplished," he actually had a slightly different tale to tell: "Our mission continues. . . . The War on Terror continues, yet it is not endless. We do not know the day of final victory, but we have seen the

turning of the tide." The invasion of Iraq had "shown the world the skill and the might of the American armed forces." Within a few short months, however, it was quite clear that the United States and its allies had *not* prevailed, that the war had become a quagmire, that the invasion had sparked an even more militant guerrilla and "terrorist" response, and that the whole region had been further destabilized. While Bush remained popular with many, by the summer of 2004 he was deeply reviled by many others (many of whom never accepted the legitimacy of his court-ordered victory in the contested 2000 election). It was obvious that, whatever the national and local crackdown on civil liberties and protest, the 2004 RNC would attract vigorous opposition in the streets.[1]

For a generation, political party conventions had been venues for street protest, from the police violence at the 1968 Democratic National Convention (DNC) in Chicago and the 1972 RNC in Miami, to the attempt to corral protesters in specially designated "free speech areas" at the 1984 DNC in San Francisco, to the attempts to deny protest permits in Los Angeles (DNC) and Philadelphia (RNC) in 2000. Events outside the convention hall had been as newswor-

thy as those inside. Activists in New York City—and well beyond—thus began working immediately to ensure that the 2004 RNC would be no different. Police in the city—and also well beyond—likewise immediately went to work to ensure that they would have command and control over the protests at all times. Command-and-control policing—also called the Miami Model—had come to displace the older "negotiated management" system as police increasingly saw it as their duty to solely determine the contours of protest. By 1998, under Mayor Rudolph Giuliani and Police Commissioner Howard Safir, NYPD began implementing a strategy of policing that "utilize[d] large numbers of officers, numerous barricades and protest pens, limited access to demonstration areas, and in extreme cases, the willingness to use force against non-violent demonstrators for minor violations of the law," as the New York Civil Liberties Union (NYCLU) summarized sociologist Alex Vitale's analysis of the practices. That strategy also included the summary denial of permits and a frequent failure to negotiate with protest planners unless forced to do so by a lawsuit (threatened or decided). And it tended to rely on police surveillance and undercover infiltration of activist groups, as well as the use of preemptive arrests. Under Mayor Michael Bloomberg and Police Commissioner Raymond Kelly, command-and-control tactics were refined and frequently deployed, as in the mass demonstration against the Iraq invasion in 2003 (see vignette). By January 2003—while it was simultaneously fighting the Bloomberg administration over the February antiwar protest—the NYCLU, joined by myriad others, was gearing up for a fight for the right to protest outside the RNC.[2]

The increasingly sour wars in Iraq and Afghanistan were not the only issues protesters wanted to highlight during the RNC. Black activists struggling against racism, reproductive rights activists, labor activists, Arab Americans, AIDS activists, the Green Party, to say nothing of various anarchist and direct action groups, all saw the convention as a critical opportunity at a critical juncture in America's history.

As early as June 2003, United for Peace and Justice (UFPJ) applied for a permit to hold a rally of 250,000 on the Great Lawn of Central Park the day before the RNC was to commence. Though concerts had been held on the lawn and other big open spaces in Central Park in the past, including Elton John in 1980, the famous Simon and Garfunkel concert in 1981, Diana Ross in 1982, the New York Philharmonic in 1986, Paul Simon in 1991, and Garth Brooks in 1997 (with the city's own official crowd estimates claiming audiences of between three hundred thousand for Elton John and eight hundred thousand for the Philharmonic), and though Central Park had frequently hosted political protests in the past, the

Parks Department summarily rejected the application, saying the space could not hold 250,000 people and irreparable damage would be done to the Great Lawn.[3]

For the next year, protest groups, the Center for Constitutional Rights, the NYCLU, the Parks Department, the NYPD, and various judges sparred over locations of rallies, routes for parades, and acceptable policing techniques. Decisions by the Parks Department and the NYPD seemed to many to be quite arbitrary—or to be targeted at particular organizations. While UFPJ was banned entirely from Central Park, and the National Council of Arab Americans was barred by a judge from the Great Lawn (citing "security concerns"), the National Organization for Women (NOW) was allowed to hold a large protest on the East Lawn. While some groups were allowed to march right past the Madison Square Garden convention sites, others, like UFPJ again, were told they must march on the West Side highway or other distant routes. By late August 2004, the RNC was shaping up to be one of the most contentious public events in the city in years and potentially one of the most contentious political conventions in a generation. In the end, the NYPD issued twenty-nine permits for parades, rallies with amplified sound, and rallies that would block streets.[4]

Events kicked off on August 26, three days before the official opening of the RNC, with ACT-UP members stripping naked and blocking traffic on Eighth Avenue to protest the Bush administration's AIDS policies; eleven people were arrested (bystanders were split as to whether the greater offense

was blocking traffic or indecent exposure). Down at Union Square, five protesters with the No Police State Coalition were arrested for using a bullhorn without a permit. And up at the Plaza Hotel, a police officer on the roof was injured after he fell through a skylight (he had been warned by protesters that it was cracked). He was trying to prevent protesters from rappelling down the front of the hotel and unfurling a giant anti-Bush banner. Four people were charged with felony assault because of the officer's injuries. Police, the mayor, and the *New York Times* all made it clear that the harsh arrests were a warning to other protesters of their likely treatment at the hands of the police over the coming week.[5]

On Friday, August 27, the monthly Critical Mass bike ride (see vignette) drew five thousand. Police were predicting that fifteen hundred would show up. At first the cops let the ride proceed as others had before it, but as the mass turned onto Seventh Avenue to head toward Madison Square Garden, police stretched orange netting across the road, bringing the procession to a stop. They then proceeded to arrest stalled bicyclists for blocking traffic! Bikes were illegally impounded. Before the night was over, more than 250 riders had been arrested. The use of netting to corral protesters became common during the week of protests, a relatively new tactic in the NYPD's arsenal—despite a judge's earlier ruling that the use of pens and limiting access to protests was unconstitutional and that the NYPD could not use such tactics during the convention.[6]

Saturday was relatively quiet. On Sunday

Police preparing to kettle protesters at the 2004 Republican National Convention.
Photo by Stacy Walsh, Rosenstock / Alamy Stock Photo.

as many as five hundred thousand people marched with UFPJ past Madison Square Garden (following a rally at Union Square sponsored by Not in Our Name), with few incidents. Some of the marchers continued on to Central Park's Great Lawn, but the police did not interfere. Later that night, though, they unrolled their orange netting and trapped and arrested dozens of protesters—and bystanders—at Times Square. On Monday the police decided it was time to aggressively disrupt protests. Thousands of people marched with the Still We Rise Coalition and the NYCLU from Union Square to the officially designated protest site on Eighth Avenue. At the site, stages had been set up just north of 30th Street, and crowds would be allowed to gather there and stretch south as far as 23rd Street. But as the Still We Rise rally got going, cops herded a long line of buses along 30th

Street, pushing protesters south and blocking them off from the stage. Meanwhile, up at Dag Hammarskjöld Plaza, thousands of "unpermitted" protesters were gathering with the intent of marching through Midtown. After tense negotiations, the NYPD allowed the crowd to march down Second Avenue to 23rd Street, over to Eighth Avenue, and up to the official protest stages at 30th Street. As they got near, however, the cops suddenly threw up metal barricades across 29th Street, sowing panic among the marchers. Protesters pushed against the barricades; uniformed police responded with flailing billy clubs. Plainclothes officers on unmarked scooters sped into the crowd, creating even more mayhem.

On Tuesday—a day of direct action and the day before President Bush was due in town—the police commissioner, Raymond Kelly, was happy to take credit for prevent-

ing "anti-Bush" protests. Platoons of police deployed throughout the city, apparently with orders to prevent any unpermitted actions. Hundreds of cops flooded the Financial District to prevent anyone clearly not a banker or trader from entering. As activists with the War Resisters League gathered near the World Trade Center site to march up to the protest site on Eighth Avenue, they managed to negotiate a deal with the police: if they marched only on the sidewalk, did not block traffic, and broke no laws, they could proceed. Off they headed. Police quickly swooped in with mesh netting, surrounded the peaceful—and legal—marchers, and arrested 225 of them. At the Public Library on Fifth Avenue and 42nd Street, a phalanx of officers descended on a small group of protesters unfurling a banner, tackled the two young women holding the banner, and started swinging their clubs wildly into the crowd. "People coming off the subways were thrown to the ground and the steps of the library were left littered with chairs and debris," reported the *Times*. Later that evening as protesters gathered in Herald Square, the cops moved in with metal barricades, sparking a melee. Small skirmishes between police and activists continued the rest of the night. Over a thousand people were arrested.[7]

Most of those arrested were taken to a disused bus depot on the 57th Street pier and held—usually legally too long for the charges leveled—in appalling conditions. They were also illegally fingerprinted. Activists and the NYCLU were convinced the lengthy, illegal detentions were designed to keep activists off the streets for much of the convention and to dissuade others from joining them. On Tuesday, September 1, as thousands languished in detention at the bus depot (most forced to sit and sleep on the oil-stained concrete floor without

access to toilets), labor unions, NOW, and others held largely peaceful rallies without disruption.

The next day, though—Bush's day at the convention—the NYPD resumed its disruptive activities. Deploying techniques similar to those debuted at the February 2003 peace rally, cops used disinformation, as well as menace, to keep many protesters from reaching a large antiwar rally sponsored by the ANSWER Coalition in the designated protest zone on Eighth Avenue. Those who did reach it were penned in by metal barricades. Thousands more gathered at Union Square with the intent of marching to the Eighth Avenue protest site—without a permit. After much negotiation, the NYPD allowed the march, but as it neared the 30th Street protest area marchers were blocked by riot-clad police, preventing further movement. Inside Madison Square Garden, President Bush was nominated for reelection to raucous chants of

"Four More Years." Bush got his four more years, four years that proved decisively that the mission in Iraq—remaking the Middle East in line with neoconservative fantasies—was not at all accomplished.[8]

Some of the lawsuits filed against the NYPD for its handling of protests during the RNC long outlasted the Bush administration and even the official (if not total) withdrawal of troops from Iraq and Afghanistan. While the charges against the War Resisters League marchers were fairly quickly dismissed by the district attorney, charges against many others were not. And it was not until January 2014, almost a decade later, that the city of New York finally settled with most of those wrongfully arrested and detained, paying out more than $18 million. Despite paying out perhaps the largest settlement ever in a mass-arrest case, the city claimed victory, crowing that not *all* its questionable policing tactics had been declared unconstitutional by the courts.[9]

CRITICAL MASS, 2004–2006

The Bloomberg administration spent $460,000 between September 2004 and August 2006 building 15.3 miles of bike lanes in the five boroughs of the city. Over the same period, the city spent $1.32 million policing collective bike rides organized by Critical Mass and arresting numerous participants. The city's Law Department determined such expenses were necessary because Critical Mass was "a danger to the public safety."[1]

Though mass bike rides organized with the aim of opening up the streets of a city for cyclists (as well as to have fun) were organized in several European cities in the 1970s and 1980s, in the United States, mass bike riding as a political movement began with the first Commute Clot ride on Market Street in San Francisco in 1992. By the second ride, Commute Clot had become Critical Mass, a name derived from pedicab designer George Bliss's observation that in China, bicyclists stopped at busy, unregulated intersections and waited until a "critical mass" of riders built up before crossing en masse. It was, in essence, a spontaneous, leaderless, but nonetheless effective and efficient custom. Such was exactly what mass riders hoped to create through their rides. Critical Mass's monthly evening commute-time rides soon grew to hundreds, then thousands of participants. Rides were more happenings and celebrations than they were organized parades, with few goals other than that riders should exercise some control over the streets, vanquish the hegemony of cars, if only for a brief time, and enjoy seeing the city in a new way. Other than a designated starting point and time, rides often started off with no set route and with no designated leaders (though some participants regularly took on the role of "corking" the side streets—blocking cross traffic while the mass rolled through—or peddling at the front of the pack).

In New York, Critical Mass rides had been a monthly feature—if a contentious one—for several years before the Republican National Convention (RNC) came to town in August 2004. Indeed, up until that time Critical Mass rides were something of a "safe space for people to be introduced to cycling as a form of transportation," even though the NYPD had already infiltrated and was spying on Critical Mass activists. But the convention was something of a watershed. As part of the larger convergence of activists that marked the convention (see vignette), many protesters brought not only signs and giant puppets and their bodies but also their bicycles. Time's Up!, an environmental direct action group, had organized the Bike National Convention, a sort of counterfestival of workshops, bike tours, free maintenance clinics, and parties. It was all to kick off with the monthly Friday evening Critical Mass ride on August 27, two days before the RNC was to commence.[2]

The ride was massive—five thousand bicyclists showed up (big rides in the past had been a few hundred; typical rides involved fifty or so bicyclists)—but even so, the police seemed ready to treat it as it had most earlier rides: using scooters to escort and monitor the mass, sometimes racing in front to stop side traffic themselves, occasionally checking more rambunctious riders. When the cops suddenly halted the ride by stretching orange netting across Seventh Avenue, it came as a shock, as did the arrest of more than 260 riders and the impounding of bicycles. Most of those arrested were charged with disorderly conduct (blocking traffic falls under this rubric), which usually results in a citation or bench warrant. This time, though, those arrested were detained on Pier 57 (see preceding vignette), some held for nearly

Police arresting Critical Mass riders and confiscating their bikes during the 2004 Republican National Convention.
Photo by Jason Szenes, epa european pressphoto agency, BV / Alamy Stock Photo.

forty-eight hours. More than three hundred bicycles were impounded, most for three weeks (and some a lot longer), for such offenses as illegal parking, the sort of offense for which car drivers would typically only receive a ticket. One activist was arrested—live on MSNBC as he was being interviewed—for criminal mischief because he had invented a bicycle that also chalk-printed messages on the road. His phone and computer were held for more than a year; his bike was never returned.[3]

The policing was as harsh as it was unprecedented. For the thousands of riders out on a warm Friday evening, it was bewildering. But it was not bewildering to all of them. Time's Up! had for some time been planning to deploy "bike blocs" at many of the RNC protests. Bike blocs were groups of cyclists deployed to take part in major protests, both because as a "bloc" they could form and break up easily, and also quickly escape police "kettling" techniques

(surrounding groups of protesters with mesh netting and essentially imprisoning them), and because they added a festive atmosphere to many events. Such techniques had already attracted the attention of analysts at the RAND Corporation think tank, who had discussed them in a 2001 report entitled "Networks and Netwars," noting the techniques' tactical potential not only for terrorists but also at protests.[4]

Yet, though Critical Mass was clearly aligned with the aims of many of the protests at the RNC, as a social movement its main goal was to use mass rides to call attention to the potential of cycling in the city and of the city for cycling. For whatever reason—and despite an official bike-friendly rhetoric—from the RNC on, the Bloomberg administration was set on disrupting, indeed dismantling, Critical Mass. Its first tactic was harassment. At the September mass ride, the NYPD confiscated the bicycles of forty mass riders, five of

whom were not charged with any offense. The NYPD argued that the Critical Mass ride was an illegal parade and that bikes locked to public property (light standards, parking meters, etc.) were "abandoned" property. Under the city's Administrative Code, it may seize "abandoned" private property that is associated with illegal activity. The NYPD further argued that bikes locked to street furniture or to fences were "pedestrian safety hazard[s]." At the same time, the city sought an injunction against Critical Mass rides, arguing that they necessarily broke a number of vehicular traffic laws and obstructed the free flow of automobile traffic. (Geographer Susan Blickstein does an excellent job of demolishing these arguments, pointing to aspects of the city's own code of regulations that allow bicyclists to behave in the way the police find illegal and citing studies that showed that a typical Critical Mass ride in New York accounted for 0.07 percent of total motor vehicle delays on a typical day.) A judge threw out most of the NYPD's arguments while recognizing that mass rides might pose an obstruction to traffic in some instances.[5]

Next, the NYPD sought an injunction to ban Critical Massers from meeting at Union Square without a permit and to ban Time's Up! from advertising starting times and places for the rides. When it failed to get the injunction, the city amended its regulations to require a permit for any group bike ride of more than fifty riders and that permits be denied for "*any* proposed activity . . . that will substantially or unreasonably interfere with traffic" or that "would be in violation of law, rule, or regulation" in any way. In part, the city justified its actions with the argument that group bike riding was inherently dangerous, an argument a judge accepted in upholding the city's new permit restrictions.[6]

Harassment of riders continued. As one participant reported, "Police have used close-range filming and photographing of bicyclists in Union Square, bike seizures, positioning of police on building rooftops adjacent to Union Square, helicopters, and the prominent display of arrest vans, armored SUVs and other surveillance equipment to deter bicyclists from participating in" Critical Mass rides. The police also continued to impound mass riders' bikes locked to public property and to cite riders for "non-existent traffic violations," extending command-and-control policing tactics from large-scale demonstrations to smaller-scale urban interventions, like typical Critical Mass rides, and even individual bicycling behavior if it was deemed to be politically related to Critical Mass. The result was that Critical Mass changed from a celebration of bicycling and a claim to the right to the streets, to a direct challenge to urban authority.[7]

CHAPTER 18

From Lady Liberty's Fire

The New York City Immigration Protests of 2006

MARNIE BRADY

On December 16, 2005, the U.S. House of Representatives passed H.R. 4437, the Border Protection, Antiterrorism, and Illegal Immigration Control Act, also known as the Sensenbrenner Bill. The act criminalized the provision of housing, health, educational, or social services to undocumented immigrants (in effect, extending border policing into schools, hospitals, housing authorities, and local police departments); changed the crime of entering the United States without papers from a misdemeanor to a felony; and increased penalties for employing undocumented workers. It also required the building of additional fencing along the U.S.-Mexico border. It undermined the rights of asylum seekers. As the Senate took up the bill in early 2006, activists around the country mobilized. Prominent Catholic officials like Cardinal Roger Mahoney of Los Angeles instructed their church workers and laity to ignore the bill if it became law. During March 2006 massive protests were held in Los Angeles, Chicago, and Washington.

New Yorkers jumped into the fray on April 1. More than ten thousand immigrants and their supporters marched across the Brooklyn Bridge to City Hall Park, glimpsing the Statue of Liberty, whose raised torch seemed like a fist raised in solidarity and provocation. Further protests developed over the following week, culminating on April 10, when at least one hundred thousand immigrants from all five bor-

oughs converged on City Hall and, more symbolically, its neighbor, the Jacob J. Javits Federal Building, home to New York's main U.S. Citizenship and Immigration Services office. As momentum against the Sensenbrenner Bill built, activists around the country called for an immigrant strike on May 1—May Day. Dubbed "A Day without Immigrants," the strike was meant to show the centrality of immigrant labor to the American economy—without making a distinction between the documented and undocumented. In New York, thousands of immigrant New Yorkers refused to go to work, took off from school, closed their business, and formed human chains in their neighborhoods. By late afternoon, tens of thousands of people had joined together to march from Union Square, jamming rush-hour traffic throughout the city center in what was one of the largest May Day demonstrations in city history.

While for many the spring immigrant rights protests in New York and across the country seemed spontaneous, they were in fact the result of decades of labor, religious, and community organizing spanning national boundaries. While H.R. 4437 was the trigger for mass action, the protests were part of a much longer struggle for global justice (chapter 17). Many of the protests' organizers and participants brought from their origin countries an explicit critique of imperialism and neoliberalism, which many immigrants connected to their reasons for migration and to their analyses of anti-immigrant legislation. The migrant diaspora in the late twentieth century directly corresponded with the militarization, criminalization, and serial displacement attendant on capitalist globalization. Movements for immigrant rights—in the suburbs of Paris, in Johannesburg, or in New York City—take place at the crossroads of global struggle.[1]

By 2006 New York had come to epitomize the neoliberal contradictions that led many immigrants to leave their countries. Like many of the cities of immigrants' home countries, New York has steadily rolled back state social support (for housing, health care, and the like) while simultaneously seeking to sell itself, its land, its infrastructure, and even its political authority to private enterprise, real estate developers, and multinational corporations. But in New York, multinational corporations in turn use the city as a command-and-control center for their global network of administrative, financial, and industrial operations. These operations are themselves now often located in "free trade zones" in the countries many of New York's immigrants have recently left as they have sought opportunities to supplement family income lost to the ravages of "free trade." The result in New York is a new multiracial, immigrant-heavy working class steadily losing its footing in the city as the captains of finance and the innumerable managers who make the globalized world spin have come to dominate the landscape—and the real estate market. New York's landscape of inequality as it unfolded in the 1990s and 2000s was merely a microcosm of the inequalities likewise unfolding globally.[2]

H.R. 4437 was a response to the insecurities such shifting landscapes unleashed nationally. Promoted as an immigration control measure apposite for a post-9/11 world, the Sensenbrenner Bill seemed poised to work more firmly as a labor-disciplining measure. The bill would create classes of immigrants who were effectively "stateless" and unable to access the normal protections of the law (including especially labor law), since doing so would subject any who aided them to criminal penalties. This was lost on neither immigrants (whether documented or not), nor other laborers, nor organized labor, all of whom took to the streets in impressive numbers. Ironically, a bill designed to push immigrant workers underground led them to become all the more visible.[3]

Immigrant New Yorkers

New York City's protests were the most ethnically diverse actions of all the national immigration protests. Unlike in other locations (e.g., in the southwestern border states with large Mexican populations), no one national-origin group dominates New York. The range of participating groups varies dramatically in languages and in cultural, ethnic, national, and hometown identity networks. Inasmuch as the protests drew from the city's largest immigrant groups from Latin America, the Caribbean, and Asia, they also demonstrated the city's changing working-class base, dramatically altered since 1970. In that year, with the city's deindustrialization continuing apace, the immigrant population registered just 18 percent of the total, the lowest of the century. But over the next thirty years, immigrant numbers increased steadily, reaching a third of the city's population by 2000, radically changing the face of New York's labor force. The Immigration and Naturalization Act of 1965 partly spurred the new wave of immigration (though this was not yet apparent in the 1970 census); the law lifted the nation-based quota system that previously favored Europeans and excluded Asians. In no small measure, postcolonial economic restructuring and related U.S.-backed military interventions in Latin America, Southeast Asia, the Caribbean, and elsewhere further propelled post-1965 immigration to the United States and to New York in particular.[4]

Among the largest groups that moved to New York after 1965 were West Indians, Dominicans, and Asians. Hundreds of thousands of West Indians left newly independent nations as "development" spurred by international capital investments disrupted and undermined local economies;

nearly half of all West Indian emigrants made Brooklyn and Queens their home in the first decades of postcolonial rule. In the 1970s they were joined by a large stream of refugees from the U.S. wars in Southeast Asia, many moving to the northwest Bronx just as the wave of abandonment and arson was peaking, providing some stability in a devastated landscape. And in the 1980s, as "structural adjustment," induced by the International Monetary Fund, disrupted innumerable lives and livelihoods in the Dominican Republic, tens of thousands of Dominicans migrated to New York, many of them settling in Washington Heights, significantly transforming that Manhattan neighborhood. The economic upheavals in Mexico in the 1980s, followed by NAFTA, added to the stream of immigrants, as did China's "March toward the Market" and "Socialism with Chinese Characteristics" in the 1990s and war across parts of Africa in the 2000s.[5]

As the power of financial capital rose and the New York political economy was restructured in the 1980s and 1990s and as wave after wave of gentrification remade neighborhoods, a growing number of urban professionals came to rely on an immigrant workforce—often precariously employed—to serve their cosmopolitan lifestyles. New immigrants worked as domestics, in the back kitchens of restaurants, in the hotels, in the garment factories, as taxi drivers, and as low-wage workers of all kinds. Some post-1965 immigrants, however, also opened small businesses, serving local neighborhoods or larger populations, helping return a vitality to the city lost through the "planned shrinkage" of the 1970s. They created neighborhood organizations that helped remake the city's ethnic geography. The pressures of gentrification, however, have not abated, and by the 2000s many of these ethnic- and community-based groups were fighting for the "right to stay put" in neighborhoods they had brought back from the brink. The 2006 protests brought these diverse groups together, some for the first time, with the challenge of negotiating a common strategy for pushing for their rights globally, nationally, and in the city.

As was the case elsewhere in the country, activists in New York in part framed the April protests in terms of civic and electoral participation and a demonstrated loyalty to the United States.* In New York, a great number of placards at the April 10 rally read, "Today We March! Tomorrow We Vote!"—a reminder, in part, that in the city, approximately 80 percent of the immigrant population has legal papers, and a good number of these people intended to become naturalized citizens.† Even in a city like New York with a high percentage of documented immigrants, tens of thousands of people are undocumented. Central to the protests in New York and across the country, therefore, was a demand for widespread legalization of undocumented immigrants resident in the country—an "amnesty" program. For many, legal status was just compensation for U.S. involvement in the forces—war, structural adjustment, lopsided free trade agreements—that had uprooted them in the first place. For others, it was just compensation for what they had contributed, economically and culturally, to America. Their labor and their presence were indispensable to what America had become.[6]

At the same time, the protests, nationally as well as in New York, also demanded an extension of what can be termed *social* rights: rights to place, dignified work, secure and safe homes free from state violence, and expanded political participation. Here immigrant rights demands dovetailed with similar demands made by antigentrification, anti–police brutality, global justice, antiwar, and anti–Arab discrimination activists over the past decade. The language of immigrant rights organizers overwhelmingly reflected a common view that the interests of workers, families, and people of color were both inseparable and under attack on multiple scales, even as, within the movement, internal debates ensued over the strategies and tactics with which to push the movement forward.

---

* In the earliest marches in California, protesters were urged to keep national flags at home and to repeat to the media that "we are Americans" in hopes of warding off a backlash that many expected (rightly) would soon come.

† This being New York, a fair number of protesters on April 10 ignored the immigrant media and protest organizers' call for an assimilationist framing, opting for a much stronger statement of *immigrant* rights—the right to difference.

¡Presente! Local Organizations Mobilize, April 10, 2006

The "tired," "poor," and "huddled masses" were energized as they marched down Broadway, demanding "Amnesty Now!," locking arms, and, in marked contrast to the largely Hispanic protesters of other cities, waving flags from places as diverse as Burma, Ecuador, and Ireland. The smaller April 1 march had been on a Saturday, but April 10 was a Monday, so many demonstrators had to leave school and work to participate—and they did, by the tens and tens of thousands, gathering in dozens of early afternoon rallies around the city, organized by affinity, neighborhood, political affiliation, or ethnicity, before coming together to march to Federal Plaza.* A Korean contingent gathered in Lippman Plaza in Queens, and Chinatown organizations met in Chatham Square.[7]

One organization from Jackson Heights in Queens, Desis Rising Up and Moving (DRUM), spearheaded a gathering of South Asian immigrants to march from Ground Zero. Founded a year before the World Trade Center attack, DRUM soon became a critical legal service organization, a support network, and an organizing resource for New York's Muslim, Arab, and South Asian families whose loved ones were arrested, detained, and facing deportation after 9/11. In the days following 9/11, some five thousand "September 11 Detainees" had been rounded up in sweeps nationwide, the majority in New York, usually with no evidence publicly presented linking detainees to terrorist activities. Neighborhoods like Jackson Heights and Coney Island, with large numbers of South Asian, Arab, and Muslim immigrants, were especially hard-hit. One young marcher in the DRUM contingent, who had walked out of school that day, spoke to a reporter about how her family had left New York after 9/11 but returned when Canada would not accept them. She feared deportation back to Pakistan, where the Taliban had threatened her father and killed her uncle. She spoke about

Marchers set off down Knickerbocker Avenue, Bushwick, on an April 30, 2006, march for immigrant rights.
Photograph courtesy of Make the Road New York.

Americans who viewed Muslims as terrorists: "They said it was us who did it [attacked the World Trade Center]. We didn't have time to tell them that it wasn't, that these were the same people who were attacking us because of our religion." DRUM organizers Fahd Ahmed and Monami Maulik explained that the continued targeting of Arabs, Muslims, and South Asian New Yorkers after 9/11 "intended to

---

* The strategic use of feeder marches was not new. It was a favorite tactic of labor organizers in the second half of the nineteenth century (e.g., for Labor Day or May Day parades) and had been revived by the global justice and antiwar protesters in recent years.

silence resistance within Muslim communities at the very same moment that our countries and homelands are being invaded or bombed." In defiant response to the immigration raids, government investigations, and persistent suspicion, the protesters who gathered with DRUM streamed into the streets and merged with the march as it made its way to Federal Plaza amid raucous chants of "¡sí se puede!"[8]

Members of the Committee in Solidarity with the People of El Salvador (CISPES) and thousands of rank-and-file union members joined the march after meeting at the Service Employees International Union (SEIU) 32BJ headquarters at the corner of Grand Street and Avenue of the Americas. CISPES had been formed in the 1980s to lend support to the leftist Farabundo Martí National Liberation Front (FMLN) guerrilla army during the Salvadoran civil war. Some of the most active members of SEIU's Justice for Janitors campaigns, which began in the early 1990s, were FMLN leaders in exile, and several became union organizers and leaders who helped to reinvigorate SEIU locals across the country. Many of the CISPES/SEIU marchers linked the immigration struggle to the struggle against neoliberal trade policies in the Americas. Activists affiliated with the CISPES headquarters in New York City encouraged supporters to bring signs to the march reading "Free Trade = Mass Migration & Exploitation."

Latino students who led simultaneous walkouts from their schools earlier in the day gathered in Union Square. Striking New York University graduate students formed part of a solidarity march with mostly Mexican protesters from the Asociación Tepeyac de New York and departed from Washington Square Park. City University of New York students from the Borough of Manhattan Community College, including members of the Haitian Club, Latino Honors Society, Muslim Students Association, Dominican Students Association, International Indian Society, and Hindu Student Council, marched from Chambers and Greenwich Streets. CUNY speakers announced two primary demands: "Full and Complete Amnesty for All Immigrants & Equal Tuition and Full Financial Aid for All Students Regardless of Status." A contingent of Columbia University students joined with CUNY students to march together to City Hall.

Brooklyn Latino-based community organizations, local chapters of Students for a Democratic Society (SDS), United for Peace and Justice (UFPJ)—still a predominant activist force in the city—and the Industrial Workers of the World (IWW) met in Cadman Plaza, Brooklyn, before heading to City Hall over the Brooklyn Bridge. A few days before the march, UFPJ antiwar activists and April 10 march organizers held a joint news conference against both the war in Iraq and new legislative proposals that had developed in response to the Sensenbrenner Bill. One legislative compromise included a Senate bill that would provide legalization measures for some undocumented immigrants and hasten the deportation of others. The press conference speakers averred that this compromise would further escalate homeland security measures that criminalized immigrants by using domestic military bases for indefinite detention of immigrants, heightened border militarization, and allowed individual homeland security agents to expel suspected foreigners immediately. In their joint statement, they explained, "Congress has continued its unabridged efforts to wreak havoc at home, galvanizing fear of so-called external enemies, this time, by targeting immigrants."[9]

At City Hall, the speakers' messages in English, Spanish, Chinese, French, and Korean were amplified up Broadway and out through Foley Square (and Federal Plaza), with views of the stage projected on huge screens positioned all the way to Canal Street in Chinatown. Although several lawmakers reportedly expressed surprise at the numbers of immigrants, many of whom were undocumented, the event preparation and resources (provided in part by local unions) reflected organizers' anticipation of a large turnout. Roger Toussaint, an immigrant from Jamaica and then-president of Local 100 of the New York City Transport Workers Union, was one of the well-known city figures who spoke to the crowd. Earlier that same day, Toussaint had been sentenced to jail time for leading 33,700 (largely immigrant) members out in a three-day transit strike that had crippled the city a few months before. He said: "Everyone here should think long and hard about what is happening in America today. We have a government that creates immigrants by the millions and then mistreats them. . . . If you have tyranny and oppression and famine and poverty around the world, you are going to have immigrants coming to the U.S. No wall is going to stop them. . . . It will just make it easier to arrest and brutalize them." In an interview on the street, Fekkak Mamdough, then codirector of the Restaurant Opportunity Center of New York (ROC-NY), connected anti-immigrant sentiment with U.S. global aggression: "This is related to all the things that's going on all over the world, you know. First going to Iraq fighting other people. Then, second . . . fighting inside our own country." The local Hotel Employees and Restaurant Employees Union (HERE) had founded ROC-NY with immigrant workers formerly employed at the World Trade Center's Windows on the World restaurant. Seventy-three of the restaurant's workers, all immigrants, were killed when the restaurant was destroyed in the 9/11 attacks. The rest were thrown out of work.[10]

Backlash

The backlash against the immigrant uprising in New York and across the country was immediate, and it was led from the top. On April 19, in a coordinated move clearly designed to intimidate, agents from the Department of Homeland Security's (DHS) Immigration and Customs Enforcement (ICE) division arrested hundreds of workers in nationwide workplace raids. In New York, where Mayor Michael Bloomberg spoke publicly and directly against H.R. 4437 and the Mayor's Executive Order 41 prohibited city employees from participating in the enforcement of federal immigrations law, no workplace raids took place. But there were raids on Long Island, in New Jersey, and in Upstate New York. The April 19 raids, together with the continuing campaign of arrests at bus stops, in shopping centers, at day labor sites, in workplaces, and even in homes around the country, put undocumented immigrants in the city on notice that they lived in a sustained state of "deportability."[11]

Since World War II, it has not been uncommon for employers and landlords to call on federal agents to conduct raids when immigrants have organized for improved living or working conditions. Even (or maybe especially) selective enforcement of immigration laws has had the effect of sowing fear throughout immigrant communities, and not just the undocumented.* The postprotest backlash thus spread fear throughout entire immigrant communities, threatening to stifle an entire movement. In New York, as in other cities, the combined effects of three 1996 laws—the Illegal Immigrant Reform and Immigrant Responsibility Act, the Personal Responsibility and Work Opportunity Reconciliation Act ("welfare reform"), and the Anti-terrorism and Effective Death Penalty Act—together with older New York State Rockefeller-era drug laws (and other tools of the "War on Drugs") and newer antiterrorism policing practices authorized by the USA PATRIOT Act, had combined to create a city that for immigrants was a city of threat by interlocking the war on drugs, the war on terror, and welfare controls with immigrant policy. As a result, even legal immigrant green card holders could be arrested in their homes, detained, and deported for minor criminal offenses (even ones for which they had already served a sentence). Also, since 1996, noncitizens associated with groups on the attorney general's terrorist watch list, such as the FMLN, had become deportable. In the first two years after 9/11, the National Security Entry-Exit Registration Program (discontinued in 2003, abolished in 2011) required the interview, registration, and fingerprinting of men resident in the United States from twenty-five predominantly Muslim countries, while mass FBI and ICE sweeps vastly increased the number of men,

---

* In mass deportation movements, such as the large-scale "repatriation" drive in the 1930s or Operation Wetback in 1954, innumerable legally documented residents and even many citizens were swept up.

women, and children who were detained and/or deported. The Sensenbrenner Bill seemed set only to intensify such anti-immigrant practices, and the backlash to the immigrant protests seemed to bode ill.[12]

Deciding Strategy: The May Day Strikes

A sense of foreboding underscored an emerging divide in the immigrant rights movement between those dedicated to persuading national legislators to improve and pass the Senate compromise bill and those calling for more militant protest to demand full legalization and no increased militarization at the border. New York City activists in the latter camp soon picked up on the call by California-based Mexican organizations for a one-day national immigrant workers' strike on May 1—"A Day without Immigrants," also known as "The Great American Boycott." The New York City May 1st Coalition called for a May Day marked by "No School. No Work. No Buying. No Selling." Soon the May Day action was drawing international interest, with activists around the globe calling for a boycott of all U.S. products on May 1. The strike threatened the U.S. economy directly by pulling immigrant labor from the workforce, demonstrating how dependent the American economy is on immigrant workers.[13]

May Day is, of course, an important day in labor and radical history in the United States and globally. Immigrant activists were tapping into a long history of struggle for workers' rights, extending back to 1886 and the first International Workers' Day launched at Union Square. In 2006, May 1 (like April 10 before it) was a Monday, and organizers explicitly drew attention to demonstrators' withdrawal of their labor, reframing the street protests from demonstrating potential electoral power to making an explicit economic threat. The sheer presence of immigrants—at working ports and construction sites; behind street stands, taxi steering wheels, and cash registers in bodegas; in the homes where immigrants worked as domestics; in the office buildings where they were janitors, guards, receptionists, bank tellers,

and computer programmers; and in the hospitals where they were nurses, orderlies, and doctors—would be made visible by their absence.

Ironically, in New York, as in other cities, most of the unions that provided resources and guided the April mobilizations did not lead the protests on International Workers' Day. Instead, immigrant workers themselves, and relatively small community-based organizations and independent workers' centers, mobilized the May 1 actions. Many of these groups were membership based; their grassroots immigrant leaders did not face the same constraints as established labor leaders, with their concerns over collective bargaining agreement provisions, entrenched bureaucracy, or long chains of command for shaping strategy and tactics. Some labor unions were simply opposed to the strike. SEIU, a leader in the newly formed Change to Win federation and central to organizing the April actions, took a strong stance against the nationwide May Day general strike, calling the action premature and in violation of standing union-employer contracts that banned unauthorized strikes.* While not ruling out a boycott, Chung-Wha Hong, executive director of the statewide New York Immigration Coalition, also did not approve of the strike: "What we want to project is a kind of positive message. Not a disruptive one." The Catholic Church's Council of Bishops encouraged immigrant parishioners to go to work. And Mayor Bloomberg, opposed to H.R. 4437, warned against militant action on May 1, saying it would not accomplish anything. The idea of a general strike, Bloomberg thought, was a "little strange."[14]

Despite such opposition, the New York City May 1st Coalition continued calls for a full-day strike, and thousands of students and workers responded. Although no figures esti-

---

* Change to Win was formed in 2005 when SEIU and three other large unions split from the AFL-CIO to create an organization more fully dedicated to labor organizing than the AFL-CIO had become. A primary cause of the split, though, was immigration reform. While the Change to Win unions supported a new guest worker program, major AFL-CIO unions like the Teamsters and the United Food and Commercial Workers International Union did not.

mate the number of people in New York who failed to show up to work at all that day, hundreds of businesses, especially restaurants, bakeries, and delis, closed due to a lack of workers or in solidarity with the protesters. New York City public schools reported that attendance rates were 6 percent below average across the city. The absentee rate in predominantly immigrant neighborhoods such as Bushwick was certainly higher than the city average. Mass walkouts in California had inspired New York City students, as did supportive teachers, such as members of the New York Collective of Radical Educators (NYCORE) who published a guide for how teachers could protect students who organized walkouts for May 1.[15]

The course of action that immigrants took represented the grounded realities and ultimately a tactical compromise among New York City's immigrant rights organizers, including community groups and unions, to support various levels of work stoppage without all declaring a general strike. While many people went on strike the entire day, others waited until 12:16 p.m. to leave school or work to create human chains coordinated in different neighborhoods of all five boroughs. The time was chosen to represent that date, December 16, 2005, when the House of Representatives passed the Sensenbrenner Bill. The lunchtime action allowed many people to leave work legitimately and temporarily, if they were not participating in the full-day strike. The timing also ensured that other New Yorkers would witness the protest while on their own lunch breaks. Zahidi Pirani, director of the New York Civic Participation Project, which brings together labor- and community-based organizations, supported the general strike and reflected on the different ways people participated on May 1: "While many knew the consequences of missing work could possibly lead to losing their jobs, many people participated in the general strike anyway. Others decided that participating in actions during lunch time or late afternoon was more viable. . . . [B]ecause immigrant rights organizers, activists and leaders were conscious of the media's tendency to portray a divided movement, we became very conscious of how we talked about May 1."[16] Pirani and other organizers emphasized the national scope and sophisticated level of coordination carried out by groups across the country to ensure and encourage all forms of mobilization.

Where some organizations and advocates hesitated, however, many immigrants were ready. The first general strike since soon after World War II, the May 1, 2006, strike took place in at least thirty cities across the country in addition to New York, with the greatest numbers of street protesters showing up in Los Angeles. In New York, one of the largest actions with one of the most diverse groups of protesters took place along Thirty-Seventh Avenue between 72nd and 82nd Streets in Jackson Heights, Queens. An estimated ten thousand people formed human chains, with workers of approximately seventy nationalities linking arms. They stopped traffic on the same streets that had previously been emptied by post-9/11 sweeps of homes and businesses, leading to the detention of many mainly Pakistani immigrants. DRUM, one of the most vocal New York nonprofit organizations to publicly support the general strike, had organized with other Queens groups to coordinate the Jackson Heights walkout, apparently to great success.[17]

Along Fordham Road in the Bronx, another large human chain—five thousand people strong—formed, as did a similarly sized one that stretched for ten blocks along St. Nicholas Avenue in the predominantly Dominican and Jewish neighborhood of Washington Heights in northern Manhattan. In Sunset Park, known as Brooklyn's Chinatown and also the home of the city's largest Mexican population, most of the Mexican businesses shut their gates, and thousands of residents joined hands for more than a dozen blocks along Fifth Avenue. One woman at the Sunset Park protest held a sign saying, "I lost my job to be here today." From East Broadway and across Canal Street in Manhattan, Chinese workers, neighbors, parents, and children stood side by side in protest. In Battery Park looking toward the Statue of Liberty, African American and Latino community-based groups created a human chain organized in part by Make

Immigrants march through New York on May Day, 2006.
Photo by Chris Hondros / Getty Images.

the Road New York, an organization led by immigrant youth and workers. In the Garment District at 40th Street and Seventh Avenue, immigrant workers left their job sites and formed human chains along the sidewalks.[18]

After these neighborhood-based protests (and more like them), approximately one hundred thousand people descended on Union Square. With a rally scheduled for 4:00 p.m., the square began filling up in the early afternoon, preparing for a march to Federal Plaza. It wasn't long before demonstrators filled Broadway, all the way from the immigration offices in the Jacob J. Javits Federal Building to Union Square, the birthplace of May Day, halting rush-hour traffic and bringing the city, symbolically at least, to a grinding halt.[19]

Undocumented and Unafraid

Media portraits of the 2006 protests nationwide generally stressed that protesters were appealing to Congress for their own shot at the American Dream, rather missing the point

about how so many of the new immigrants had arrived in the United States precisely because the United States' assertion and protection of at least some versions of the American Dream were deeply complicit in the geopolitical interventions and geoeconomic restructuring that set so many people migrating. Unsurprisingly, the pursuit of a narrow "American Dream" rarely ranks high in immigrants' own explanations for why they have immigrated.[20]

By asserting their right to be in the streets and to make their labor visible—by withholding it—all in the face of a swelling backlash, immigrant rights protesters took over streets and showed themselves to be a mighty force, politically and economically. New York City's immigrant protesters helped create the collective nationwide force that ended up stopping H.R. 4437 as well as the Senate's compromise bill. Both languished in Congress. Immigrant-led organizations in New York City crossed boundaries of language, religion, ethnicity, nationality, and neighborhood to organize protests and grow new capacities for continued resistance in the city. They built upon alliances through which independent workers' centers, in particular, continued to push other organizations—stagnant nonprofits, reluctant unions—to seize the movement momentum and organize with the so-called unorganizable.

In their multitudes, New York City's immigrants demonstrated their dissent in the central symbolic spaces of the city—City Hall, Federal Plaza, Union Square—as well as in the lived spaces of their neighborhoods—Bushwick, Jackson Heights, Washington Heights—and through direct action they created, at least for a time, a different space of citizenship and belonging and, quite possibly, another world existing "beyond the walls and cages" that defined post-9/11 New York and America more broadly.[21] Rather than being silenced by FBI raids targeting Muslims in Queens and by stepped-up ICE enforcement, detention, and deportation, immigrants, especially youth, from across the country have continued the struggles that the movement against the Sensenbrenner Bill sparked. Whenever states and localities move against immigrants, when schooling for undocumented students is threatened, or when ICE once again coordinates workplace raids, undocumented immigrants, with their documented and citizen allies, take to the streets (and campus plazas) despite great risk, answering increased intimidation with proud declarations that they are "Undocumented and Unafraid," the rallying cry for the next wave of escalated protest.

CHAPTER 19

Occupy Wall Street

Finance Capital and Its Discontents, 2011

MANISSA M. MAHARAWAL AND ZOLTÁN GLÜCK

"Are you ready for a Tahrir moment? On Sept 17 flood into lower Manhattan, set up tents, kitchens, peaceful barricades and occupy Wall Street." So read a call from *Adbusters* that made the rounds in July 2011, and sure enough, that September 17, a few thousand protesters eagerly responded, converging in Manhattan's Financial District to "Occupy Wall Street."[1] Many of the places where they had planned to protest, including Wall Street itself, were blocked off by metal barricades and guarded by the police. Undeterred, they marched through the streets of the Financial District and gathered in parks and plazas, holding teach-ins and speak-outs and waving signs with messages like "Democracy Not Corporatization" and "Revoke Corporate Personhood."[2] Later in the afternoon the protesters managed to briefly march on Wall Street but were stopped from proceeding to the New York Stock Exchange by a line of police at William Street in front of an old Greek Revival building that once housed the New York Merchants' Exchange and the headquarters of the National City Bank.* The building is now home to the elite luxury restaurant Cipriani, frequented by Wall Street bankers, with a balcony overlooking Wall Street. Protesters engaged the upscale cocktail drinkers on the balcony in a shouting match. One of the men on the balcony

jeered, "Get a job!" and dumped his drink on the people below, while protesters in turn chanted, "Pay your share!" and ultimately "Jump! Jump! Jump!"

In the late afternoon, those protesters still remaining gathered on the steps of the Museum of the American Indian at Bowling Green (the old U.S. Custom House and the site of the colonial Fort Amsterdam / Fort James / Fort George) to make speeches and listen to performance artist and activist Reverend Billy preach. There, a "tactics team" announced that everyone should move up Broadway to Zuccotti Park, which, through the team's scouting, they knew was open and free of the police barricades that surrounded One Chase Manhattan Plaza (the site originally intended for the occupation). The protesters moved to Zuccotti Park, and the day ended with a General Assembly in which protesters decided to spend the night and indefinitely occupy the park. In the following weeks and months Zuccotti was to become the epicenter of the Occupy Wall Street (OWS) movement, as "Occupy" encampments modeled on the one in Zuccotti sprang up in 1,500 cities around the country and, within a month, some 950 cities in 82 other countries around the globe.

Occupy Wall Street began as a protest against wealth inequality and the obscene power of banks and finance capital within the American political system. It very quickly

---

* It also at one time housed the NYSE and the U.S. Customs House in one of its iterations. The upper floors are now swank condominiums.

became a much broader, more encompassing, global uprising. A commonly recognized symbol of American financial power, Wall Street became a metaphor for everything that was wrong with global capitalism. With its meteoric rise, Occupy in turn became a general symbol for all forms of resistance to global capitalism—the antithesis of Wall Street and a beacon of possibility. In New York, hundreds of working groups—autonomously organized groups of between five and five hundred people—soon began organizing on a variety of political issues under the Occupy Wall Street banner. Many of these groups linked up with ongoing struggles in the city and with existing community groups and organizations, even as they broke new political ground. The occupation in Zuccotti Park itself quickly became a site of radical political experimentation, with Occupiers actively trying to

"prefigure" other possible worlds and modes of social organization (in production and consumption and for solidarity) and decision-making outside of and in opposition to capitalism. In the wake of the 2008 economic crisis and amid rising unemployment, a home foreclosure epidemic, and burgeoning debt across the social spectrum (from student loans to credit card debt and on to medical debt and beyond), Occupy Wall Street issued a clarion call for change. The movement burned hot and bright, radicalized a generation, and brought people into politics who had never before been involved in any form of protest. It burst onto the scene of world politics, exciting millions, but then quickly dissipated, heaving under the weight of its internal contradictions and eventually collapsing under the pressure of coordinated police repression. Though it quickly attained a global character, Occupy Wall Street was also an important chapter in the long local history of revolt and resistance in New York City.

From Zuccotti Park to Liberty Square

Zuccotti Park, at the intersection of Broadway and Cedar, was, for most of its existence, a rather nondescript, mostly concrete, privately owned public space. A couple of blocks north of Wall Street and bounded by Broadway, Trinity Place, and Cedar and Liberty Streets, the park was built in 1968 by U.S. Steel in exchange for a "density bonus" that allowed it to build a fifty-four-floor skyscraper at One Liberty Plaza, creating one of Manhattan's largest office buildings by volume. At the time, such privately owned public spaces (POPS) were relatively new, originally created through a change to the city's zoning code in 1961 that gave real estate developers density bonuses and often higher "air rights" in exchange for the creation of new "public" spaces in the city. Infamously underused and often unwelcoming, there are at least 520 POPS in New York—mostly microparks and corporate pseudolobbies—accounting for over 3.5 million square feet of space in the city. As wave after wave of property speculation and development has washed over the city, critics have lambasted POPS as corporate giveaways. They are also part of a long history of privatizing public, or common, space, stretching right back to the Dutch enclosures of Munsee lands. When protesters descended on Zuccotti Park on the evening of September 17, they stepped right into that history and became, for a time, deeply enmeshed in a struggle for space that has shaped the city.[3]

Zuccotti's owner, Brookfield Properties, was caught flat-footed, unsure at first how to respond, especially since the New York Police Department determined that Occupiers could not be summarily evicted. The terms of the original agreement by which the park was built required it to be open and accessible to the public twenty-four hours a day. Arrests and evictions could only be made if clear evidence of criminal activity was present. Brookfield was thus left, at least at first, able to do little more than fire warning shots across the

Occupy Wall Street bow. "Zuccotti Park," a spokesperson for Brookfield intoned ten days after the occupation began, "is intended for the use and enjoyment of the general public for passive recreation. We are extremely concerned with the conditions that have been created by those currently occupying the park and are actively working with the City of New York to address these conditions and restore the park to its intended purpose."[4]

In the meantime, Occupiers made a show of renaming Zuccotti Park, resurrecting its older name, Liberty Plaza, or, as some inspired by Tahrir Square in Cairo called it, Liberty Square. Badly damaged during the 9/11 destruction of the nearby World Trade Center buildings, the park had been renovated and was renamed after John E. Zuccotti, the chairman of Brookfield Properties. Zuccotti had already had a long career working in the city, at various times chairing the City Planning Commission and the Real Estate Board of New York and serving as Mayor Abraham Beame's deputy mayor during the city's fiscal crisis in the 1970s. Renaming the park Liberty Square symbolically reclaimed a space that had now been physically taken for liberty, protest, and participatory democracy against an otherwise unwelcoming landscape dominated by finance capital.

Occupy Wall Street was not entirely spontaneous, of course. In the month leading up to September 17, there had been a number of General Assemblies in Tompkins Square Park. Tompkins Square was, of course, no innocent choice but was chosen for its long history as a site of social struggle and radical organizing (chapters 7 and 16). The Tompkins Square General Assemblies harked back to the styles of organizing developed in the Global Justice Movement and by the Direct Action Network (chapter 17), relying particularly on consensus and horizontal decision making. Indeed, many veterans from those earlier struggles participated in and helped to shape the nascent Occupy movement. The consensus process and the holding of regular General Assemblies soon became the standard model of governance at Occupy encampments all across the country.

Such horizontal decision making is rarely easy. On September 18, after the first night of occupation, when it was becoming clear that police would not move to clear out the occupation immediately, protesters first attended to the basic tasks of collecting food, making signs, and getting the word out before opening what turned out to be a seven-hour-long General Assembly devoted to deciding what to do next. Over the course of the long meeting, Occupiers hashed out strategy, working diligently until consensus was achieved on points both large and small. The next morning, Monday, September 19, Occupiers marched from the park to Wall Street, disrupting morning commuters with their chants of "We! Are! The 99 percent!" and "Whose streets? Our streets!" These were the first of what would become daily "opening bell protests," which would continue until Occupy Wall Street's second-month anniversary, November 17, when protesters would actually manage to delay the New York Stock Exchange's opening bell by fifteen minutes before they were violently dispersed by the NYPD.

As word of the occupation spread, more and more people showed up. What had begun as a few protesters sleeping in a park soon became a bustling protest encampment. Within three days, a full kitchen was set up, serving three meals a day. The kitchen was soon joined by a medical tent, where volunteer doctors saw walk-in patients; the People's Library, which eventually held over 5,500 books; and information tables, where people could orient themselves and find out about upcoming actions. Liberty Square became a regular meeting place for hundreds of ad hoc working groups, which focused on particular political, practical, or action-oriented issues. On the first day, Occupiers established "a media center on a few uncomfortable tables with a generator and a wifi hotspot." The media center soon became an important hub for the occupation, covered in tarps to keep out the rain and ringed by bicycles rigged up to provide power for the masses of electronics. It seemed to be a place both of exclusivity and of allure. Inside, people edited and uploaded videos, worked on the New York City General Assembly (NYCGA) website, live tweeted, maintained a Facebook page, and dealt with media requests.[5]

Participants at an Occupy Wall Street General Assembly signal their approval.
Photo by Stacy Walsh Rosenstock / Alamy Stock Photo.

Though mutable, a fairly stable geography of occupation soon evolved in Liberty Square. At the so-called front of the park, along the eastern edge at Broadway, people stood holding signs and engaging with passersby, handing out flyers, and answering questions about why they were there. Among the shifting cast of characters along Broadway were

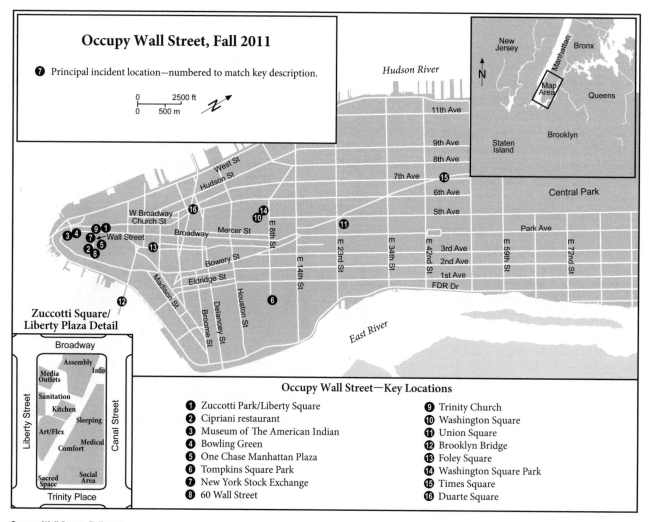

Occupy Wall Street, Fall 2011.

Cartography: Joe Stoll, Syracuse University Cartography Lab and Map Shop. Liberty Plaza redrawn from Jonathan Massey, "Mapping Liberty Plaza," https://placesjournal.org/article/mapping-liberty-plaza/.

some regulars, like the twenty-something South Asian man who danced back and forth, wearing headphones and holding a sign that read "Occupy Everywhere." There was a "welcome" table set up with literature about the occupation, zines on anarchism, and flyers for events and protests.

Across from this row of Occupiers stood a line of NYPD officers, and between these two factions was the hustle and bustle of Broadway, though as the occupation grew, so many people were standing holding signs and so many other people were stopping to take pictures or talk with them that often it was impossible to make it through the crowd.

The northwestern quadrant of the park was covered in hundreds of colorful cardboard signs and placards with political messages. In the southeast, a near-permanent drum circle formed, sometimes with fifteen or more players, other times featuring a lone drummer tapping out a rhythm on a plastic bucket, the sound reverberating off the surrounding buildings. In the northeast was the Tree of Life, a London plane tree that served as a shrine, an altar, a spiritual place within the occupation. People prayed here, had poetry readings, and held "healing circles" after traumatic marches or days. The kitchen was in the center of the park, and next to it was the supplies area, with boxes of blankets and sweaters, hats, gloves, tarps, and so forth. As with the media center, energy bikes powered the kitchen. A gray-water system was built to deal with dirty water. The nightly General Assemblies were held at the northwest corner of the park. They were live streamed and live tweeted, and the notes were posted to the NYCGA website.

Not all events and installations were equally tolerated by the authorities. When a medical tent went up on October 17—a month after the occupation began, it was among the first "permanent" structures—the NYPD threatened to rip it down. Occupiers, joined by the Reverend Jesse Jackson, linked arms and stood their ground until the NYPD backed down. Often sitting in front of the medical tent was a "therapy dog," whose kind eyes and calming presence served as something like a front line for the medics who worked inside. Soon after the medical tent went up, other tents began to proliferate, and the informal division of space in the park became more organized. With hundreds of people sleeping in the park every night and thousands using the site by day, a "town planning" working group emerged, produced a map, and began making proposals for how to better organize the space. (Many of these proposals were met with outrage by those dedicated to a more free-flowing and libertarian vision of anarchism.)

Liberty Square was exhilarating, fascinating, overwhelming, and addictive. People often commented that they had stopped only for a minute but ended up staying for hours. Actions and events happened every day, with marchers leaving from the park and snaking their way across Lower Manhattan, disrupting traffic and daily life in the Financial District. Poetry readings, teach-ins, concerts, and lectures by visiting famous intellectuals and artists became part of the daily rhythm of the occupation. At any given moment, multiple working group meetings were happening at the same time, some held under the "red structure," a sculpture by Mark di Suvero, officially called *Joie de vivre*, on the southeastern edge of the park, others held across the street as the park itself became too crowded to hold meetings inside. Meetings were moved to other spaces throughout the Financial District, many to 60 Wall Street (another POPS), others to benches, plazas, pizza places, and the garden (and graveyard) of Trinity Church on Broadway—any tiny bit of space that could be appropriated and used. In this way, Occupy Wall Street spread across the Financial District.

Liberty Square itself became less functional over time. By late October it had become crowded as more and more people set up tents to sleep in at night and thousands of local sympathizers and tourists flooded the occupation during the day. Other social challenges were more complex. There were rumors (later confirmed) that the NYPD were harassing homeless people around the city and pressuring them to move down to Zuccotti Park; the police were also rumored to be taking people freshly released from jail and dropping them off at the park, telling them that there was free food and other services.* People came to the park with addictions, traumas, and complex needs: people who were hungry, people who had been outcast from society through various forms of exclusion, incarceration, and structural violence. They brought new challenges with them, and this precipitated intense debates. Some people at Liberty Square started to complain that such people were a problem, that they were

---

* In the 1980s police had deployed similar tactics, encouraging homeless people and newly released prisoners to head to Tompkins Square, the site of a large homeless encampment, a place where many activists and social service agencies provided food and services to the homeless, and—not coincidentally—ground zero of antigentrification activism in the city at the time.

freeloading and not working to maintain the occupation, and that the occupation was not about providing services. This infuriated others, who argued that if the occupation could not handle the most marginalized members of society, then how could they talk about taking on wealth inequality and fighting for social justice? These vitriolic debates about inclusion and exclusion intersected with simmering questions about how Occupy was taking on questions of race and racial justice within the movement. Such challenges became ever more palpable in the increasingly claustrophobic park. By November some Occupiers had begun to complain about a "class divide" between the East Side (where the General Assembly was held) and the West Side (where people slept).[6]

The General Assemblies themselves had in fact become large and unwieldy, attended by many who had little stake in the occupation, were there just to watch, or were saboteurs who were paid to disrupt the decision-making process.[7] Many started to complain that it was too chaotic a structure to make day-to-day decisions for the movement. Finally, on October 28, after weeks of negotiation and explanation, the General Assembly approved a new decision-making structure called a "spokes council" for making day-to-day decisions.* This new spokescouncil convened off-site and was structured around the working groups of OWS, each of which participated in the meeting through a designated "spoke" (often a rotating position) that was provisionally empowered to speak for each group. This spokescouncil structure stayed in place long after the encampment itself was violently evicted by the NYPD on November 15, a little under two months after it started.

"All Day, All Week":
An Occupy Timeline, or, Occupying Everywhere

A myriad of events, actions, marches, meetings, confrontations, and struggles happened every day during the occupation—a glorious, contradictory complexity that is im-

possible to summarize. But there were major events and flashpoints—lightning strikes, perhaps—that can be viewed as pivotal, formative moments for Occupy Wall Street, catalyzing and transforming the movement in sometimes unpredictable ways.

SEPTEMBER 22, 2011: TROY DAVIS

On September 22, Troy Davis, an African American man, was executed by the state of Georgia. Convicted of murdering a Savannah police officer in 1989, he and his supporters maintained his innocence until his execution, arguing that the case lacked evidence and contained racial bias. His sentence and subsequent execution became an international symbol of struggles against the death penalty, as well as against racial bias in the criminal justice system, with worldwide calls to stop the execution by numerous human rights groups and commentators, including Pope Benedict XVI and former U.S. president Jimmy Carter. Davis's execution sparked worldwide protests. In New York, protesters marched from Washington Square Park to Union Square, where a vigil and speak-out were held. As the speak-out wound down, protesters spilled into Fifth Avenue, chanting "We are all Troy Davis," "We are all Sean Bell," and "NYPD go to hell!" while marching downtown.† The NYPD attempted to restrict protesters to the sidewalk, using their scooters to aggressively herd them onto the walks and physically shoving them when that failed. The march quickly became one about outrage over the execution of Troy Davis *and* about the right to protest and the ability to express this rage.[8]

Hounded by the NYPD and cut in half by police scooters, the march incurred at least six arrests, all of them fairly violent, with reports of the police grabbing people at random and injuring many. Nonetheless, hundreds of marchers made it down to Liberty Square. The marchers entered the park, and the occupation suddenly swelled with new faces,

---

*Again harking back to the innovations of the Direct Action Network and others in the Global Justice Movement.

† Sean Bell was killed by police officers on November 25, 2006, in Queens. His death prompted widespread protest and outrage over police brutality, use of excessive force, and racism among New York City police.

A protester at a 2012 May Day rally comparing the "pepper spray incident" at Occupy Wall Street with police shootings at Kent State in 1970.
Photo by David Grossman / Alamy Stock Photo.

SEPTEMBER 24: THE PEPPER SPRAY INCIDENT

Saturday, September 24, was the one-week anniversary of the occupation, and a march to Union Square was planned. A few hundred protesters first went to Wall Street, then snaked their way back uptown, chanting "All day! All week! Occupy Wall Street!" and "Wall Street is our street!" At Union Square, the march turned to go back to the Financial District and Liberty Square. But just south of Union Square, marchers were met by a phalanx of police who unfurled large orange nets and began corralling protesters (as well as media, onlookers, and pretty much everyone who happened to be on that stretch of the road), reviving a controversial policing technique used during the global justice and Republican National Convention protests of the previous decade (see chapter 17 and associated vignettes). Once corralled (and unable to move), protesters were arrested for blocking the street and disorderly conduct. The police were not gentle. Film of the event shows cops dragging protesters by their hair, slamming them into the pavement, and, in what became a notorious image, pepper spraying two young female protesters for doing nothing more than asking why they were being arrested. More than eighty protesters were arrested.[11]

The march, the arrests, and the police brutality became media flashpoints, making international headlines and the Sunday cover of the *New York Daily News*. The cop who pepper sprayed the young women was quickly identified through numerous videos and photos as Deputy Inspector Anthony Bologna (known to the Internet as "Tony Baloney"). Less than two days later, the Anonymous Collective posted his address and phone number, as well as those of his relatives, along with this statement: "As we watched your officers kettle innocent women, we observed you barbarically pepper spray wildly into the group of kettled women. We were shocked and disgusted by your behavior. You know who the innocent women were, now they will have the chance to know who you are. Before you commit atrocities against innocent people, think twice. WE ARE WATCH-

many of them much more diverse than the (to that point) mostly white occupation. During that evening's General Assembly, people stepped up to speak about how Occupy Wall Street needed to reach out to marginalized communities in New York City and to take on racism directly.[9]

This moment in the first week of the occupation was significant. The marchers energized the occupation as the two struggles came together, one about systemic economic injustice and the other about systemic racism and disproportionate targeting, imprisonment, and murder of people of color. While some Occupiers commented that they were not sure that Troy Davis's execution had anything to do with Wall Street, others realized that the occupation could be a place where the interweaving of different kinds of oppression could be understood and contested. With the Troy Davis protest, Occupy Wall Street became, for a moment, infused with a concern for racial justice, even as the struggle against racial justice remained a contested terrain as long as the movement lasted.[10]

ING!!! Expect Us!"*[12] The media attention given to this incident galvanized support for the movement, which up until that point had received some international media attention (the *Guardian* had been reporting on the protests since early on) but little local attention. Different media outlets had various ways to explain what the march and protest were about, with some claiming it was about "inequality" (the *Daily News*) and others saying it was "anti-capitalist" (the *Guardian*). Whatever the explanation, Occupy Wall Street was now making national and international news and could no longer be ignored.

OCTOBER 1: BROOKLYN BRIDGE

For the second-week anniversary, Occupiers decided to march from Manhattan to Brooklyn over the Brooklyn Bridge. Around 3:00 p.m. on Saturday, October 1, between one thousand and two thousand marchers set off from Liberty Square and headed toward the bridge. The police presence was large but, at the beginning at least, not overly aggressive. As the march neared the bridge it split, with half the marchers seemingly being led by the cops onto the road while the other half crammed onto the pedestrian walkway overlooking the road.† With marchers less than halfway across the bridge, police came from the Brooklyn side bearing hundreds of pairs of plastic handcuffs. Once again the cops unfurled orange netting and surrounded the marchers, arresting seven hundred of them in the largest single-event arrest in New York City's history.‡ The mass arrests made national and international headlines and served to create publicity for the movement and increase support for it. Soon afterward more and more local Occupy encampments started to appear around the country in solidarity. With every new

---

*The Anonymous Collective is a shadowy network of highly politicized computer hackers.

† In video from the march, a line of cops can be seen at the front, leading the march onto the roadway. What the police were actually doing in that moment has been debated in subsequent court cases about the arrests made that day.

‡ Far more were arrested during the 1977 blackout, but that was over two days and in innumerable locales. See chapter 15.

---

attempt at police repression, it seemed that the movement grew exponentially. Only two weeks old, the Occupy movement now spread like wildfire.[13]

WEEK 2 AND BEYOND: ARTISTS AND ACTIVISTS JOIN THE MOVEMENT

Throughout the first month of the occupation, a number of prominent artists and intellectuals came down to Liberty Square to show their support. Their presence, their impromptu speeches, and their concerts all helped build popular support for Occupy Wall Street and turned the square into one of the most dynamic and exciting cultural, artistic, and intellectual spaces in the city, in addition to its primary role as a hub of political activity. Privately owned, the square was made into a truly public space. Public intellectuals such as Cornel West (September 27), Naomi Klein (October 6), Slavoj Žižek (October 9), Gayatri Spivak (October 15), Judith Butler (October 24), and Angela Davis (October 30) came, spoke to protesters, and gave speeches. Cornel West marched with Occupiers and was twice arrested at protests. Other celebrities and artists such as Susan Sarandon (September 26), Michael Moore (also September 26), Deepak Chopra (who led a meditation on October 3), and Kanye West (October 10) came to show their support (if not always uncontroversially, as some Occupiers thought the celebrities and intellectuals might be there as much to burnish their own credentials as to advance the movement, if not more so). Meanwhile, impromptu concerts were given by Neutral Milk Hotel, Michael Franti (both on October 4), Talib Kweli (October 6), and others. Russell Simmons was a constant presence and daily participant at the occupation from early on. Many of the speeches and lectures given at Liberty Square were soon republished in the movement's nascent publications, the *Occupied Wall Street Journal*, the *Occupy Gazette*, and *Tidal: Occupy Theory*. Hundreds of other intellectuals and artists made appearances around the country (and internationally) or supported the occupation from afar, writing articles and publicly giving voice to the grievances raised by the movement.

OCTOBER 5: LABOR UNIONS JOIN OWS

From the beginning of Occupy, organized labor struggled with how to engage with the movement. In some ways the young movement's insistence on "leaderlessness" and using horizontal decision-making structures confounded the hierarchical union structures. Within Occupy, concerns about labor were also voiced: some accused labor unions of trying to co-opt the movement or of not sharing the same far-left, often anticapitalist and antigovernment message of the movement. But as progressive unions watched Occupy gain popularity, headlines, and support, they chose to back the movement, maintaining that while the two movements were different, they could assist each other. Such solidarity was made visible on an October 5 rally in Foley Square during which several major unions—including the Transport Workers Unions, the Service Employees International Union, the United Federation of Teachers, and the United Automobile Workers—joined forces with Occupy protesters. From Foley Square they marched toward Liberty Square. The mood was jubilant, with dancing in the streets, live music, and the chant "We are unstoppable! Another world is possible!" as well as the now-ubiquitous "We are the 99 percent!" echoing throughout the area. (This time the cops lay low.) The Labor Outreach Committee, which had been one of OWS's most active working groups from early on, now became one of the principal conduits for ongoing coordination between Occupy and the labor movement.

OCTOBER 12–14: EVICTION DEFENSE

On Wednesday, October 12, in what seemed like an intentional attempt to derail a global day of action planned for Saturday, October 15 (called for by the Indignados movement in Spain, which had been one of the inspirations for Occupy), Mayor Michael Bloomberg announced that Brookfield Properties, the company that owned Zuccotti Park, had

The Reverend Billy (Billy Talen) addresses Occupy Wall Street in Zuccotti Park, October 25, 2011.
Reuters / Alamy Stock Photo.

requested the NYPD's help in clearing the park "by the end of the week" for cleaning and to make it "safe" again. In a letter dated October 11 to the police commissioner, Raymond Kelly, Brookfield Properties claimed that "conditions in the park have deteriorated to unsanitary and unsafe conditions." NYPD's assistance was needed in order to "make the park safe for the neighborhood and public." In addition, Brookfield requested continued police assistance after the cleanup to "ensure the safety of those using and enjoying the park." Occupiers immediately interpreted the language of cleanliness and safety as a pretext to evict the protesters.[14]

Aware that this was a tactic to clear the park of the occupation, the Sanitation Committee, which was already working diligently to keep the park clean and sanitary, created a Facebook event called "Operation #WallStreetCleanUp," asking for donations of brooms, mops, and other cleaning equipment and calling on everyone to come to the park and help keep it clean. Throughout the day and night the park was swept, scrubbed, and mopped; trash was gathered up and hauled away; piles of laundry were taken away to be cleaned; passages through the park were cleared; computer equipment and cardboard signs that lined the park were taken to a nearby storage unit; and protesters took to their hands and knees to scrape paint and other detritus off the ground. In conjunction with this cleanup effort, the direct action working group called for thousands of supporters to come to Liberty Square at 4:30 on the morning of October 14 for a "Defense of the Occupation." The call was repeated by MoveOn.org and the Working Families Party, with their extensive email blast lists.

Supporters gathered at the park throughout the night, with most people arriving before 4:30 a.m. ready to defend the park. By early morning some four thousand people had come, filling the park and spilling out onto the adjacent sidewalks and streets. The crowd of supporters was diverse in race and in age, with professionals, hipsters, retirees, and young anarchists all rubbing shoulders in the predawn light rain. Various elected officials also made appearances, as did union members who arrived to show solidarity. It was obvi-

ous by 6:00 a.m. that the NYPD would not be able to clear the park without a major confrontation, likely resulting in thousands of arrests. When the announcement finally came at 6:45 that the police would stand down and the park would not be cleared and cleaned, cheers arose throughout the park, and strangers hugged each other and sang and danced. The mood was jubilant.[15]

City Hall had backed down, the cops had retreated, and the Occupiers had won the battle. Some protesters celebrated by marching to Wall Street to make good on a promise the sanitation working group had earlier made: that after the park was cleaned they would "clean up" Wall Street, "where the real mess was!" Not licking their wounds for long, the police responded with impressive brutality: legal observers were beaten, and one had his leg badly broken from being pinned under a police scooter, protesters were brutalized, and anyone who stepped off the sidewalk was tackled and immediately arrested. But the police violence did not stop most people from feeling that they had vanquished Mayor Bloomberg (whose political power rested squarely in the Financial District) and the NYPD that day.[16]

OCTOBER 15: GLOBAL DAY OF ACTION

The October 15 global day of action (also called a global day of rage) saw protests in more than eighty countries. Hundreds of cities large and small participated, from Miami to Hong Kong, Fairbanks to London, and Berlin to Sydney. Uniting the protests was anger over wealth inequality, the power of large corporations in general, and their ability to corrupt democracy in particular. In New York, dozens of events, rallies, and marches occurred around the city, including occupations of bank lobbies (resulting in mass arrests) and an assembly of over four hundred students in Washington Square Park that launched an enduring citywide coalition of student activists. In the evening, thousands of protesters marched from Liberty Square to Times Square chanting "The banks got bailed out, we got sold out!" Times Square was shut down for hours. The mood was defiant and jubilant as the square's bright news ticker flashed the news

Occupy Wall Street goes worldwide, November 15, 2011.
Photo by Zoltán Glück, used by permission.

"Occupy Wall Street Movement Goes Worldwide" over and over again above the tens of thousands of Occupiers holding impromptu speak-outs, during which people told their stories of why they had joined the movement.[17]

After Times Square a smaller but still significant number of protesters marched to Washington Square Park and held an assembly in the dry fountain in the middle of the park. There, Gayatri Spivak spoke to the assembled protesters, placing Occupy in the context of the Arab Spring and urging the importance of "not settling." After she spoke, a General Assembly was moderated about whether or not to occupy Washington Square Park. As the time of the park's closing neared and more and more cops assembled outside and threatened protesters with arrest if they did not leave, those inside decided not to occupy Washington Square. The cops outside—sheathed in riot gear—watched as people left

the assembly. Though some ran wildly through the streets, with cops sometimes giving chase, most people went home, avoiding police confrontation and feeling triumphant that the day of action had been a major success.

NOVEMBER 15: EVICTION FROM LIBERTY SQUARE

On November 15, 2011, in the middle of the night and without warning, police moved into Liberty Square and violently evicted Occupy Wall Street.* The raid began at 1:00 a.m., when the NYPD threw up arc lights around the plaza, switched them on, and announced that the park was being closed and that everyone had to leave. Most Occupiers were asleep, and they were all caught off guard. Some scrambled to get out of the park before the police raided it, while oth-

---

* This was part of a clearly coordinated move to evict occupations all around the country, if not in all cities, then in many of them.

ers chained themselves together in the middle of the park. Many of those not resisting were forcibly removed anyway by police, who were clad in full riot gear and wielding batons, plastic shields, pepper spray, and tear gas. Occupiers were beaten by police with little restraint.

Outside the park, the Financial District was locked down. Streets for two blocks south and one block east, north, and west of the park were closed completely. Helicopters hovered overhead as between two thousand and three thousand police officers in riot gear guarded metal barricades on every street in the area. Reporters were not allowed in to document the eviction, cameras were confiscated, and subways were prevented from stopping in the neighborhood for hours, limiting access to the district even further. The eviction felt like a military operation. When asked about the middle-of-the-night eviction, Mayor Bloomberg replied that the timing of the raid was set "to reduce the risk of confrontation in the park, and to minimize disruption to the surrounding neighborhood."[18]

When supporters around the city received a message through the OWS text message alert system that the park was being evicted, thousands rushed to the area. But they quickly found they could not get anywhere near the park; with the subway trains not stopping in the Financial District, many were diverted to other neighborhoods. Those who did make it into the area began arriving at the barricades around 1:30 a.m., but, prevented from going any further, most stood around bewildered. Some linked arms and sang, others yelled at the cops, while still others tried to reason with them to let the people through to Liberty Square. As the crowds grew on Broadway, north of the park, the police became uneasy and began pushing, arresting, and trying to disperse the people. The scene was chaotic. Many people decided to stand their ground on Broadway, while a group of three hundred to five hundred protesters decided to march north. People surged through the streets uptown all the way to Houston and some beyond to Astor Place, with cops chasing after them. More than once, a police riot erupted, with sections of the marching people periodically siphoned off and cursed at by the cops, if not simply beaten.[19]

Downtown, south of Liberty Square, protesters sat in the street on Broadway between Thames and Cedar in order to block the garbage trucks trying to enter and leave the area. The trucks had been commissioned to take out the piles of stuff that had been ripped up, smashed, confiscated, and heaped up by the cops. Tents, people's clothes and other belongings, the kitchen, the energy bikes, the objects people had left at the Tree of Life, the thousands of books donated to the library: all of it was cleared out and put into garbage trucks. Nearby, people peered over the barricades to try to see what was happening, but it was almost impossible to see around the wall of cops that ringed the area. Finally, the cops got tired of the blockade on Broadway and marched into the crowd, their plastic shields in front of them, telling everyone to "move back, move back." Worn down by a long night of confrontation, the crowd was eventually pushed back onto the sidewalks, split into two groups, and left to watch the garbage trucks pass by with the detritus of the occupation.

By now the sun had begun to rise and the first early morning commuters had started to arrive, confused by the heavy police presence. The barricades now began to function as quasi checkpoints, as police allowed people who looked like "office workers" to pass by while refusing entry to anyone who looked like a "protester." By 7:30 a.m. the barricades had been pulled back to the block immediately surrounding Zuccotti Park (as it now once again was), and the riot police stood down, replaced by hundreds of police officers in their everyday uniforms. A few dozen protesters remained, standing dejectedly across the street from Zuccotti, watching cleaning crews in neon vests clean the park behind two rows of barricades and protected by the NYPD. Over the course of the night, at least two hundred people were arrested.

Text messages and emails flew around all morning as people called emergency meetings and assemblies and hatched plans. Many of the protesters who had been on the streets all night amassed in Foley Square and opened a General Assembly. Eventually, those who remained decided to march to Durante Square at Canal Street and Avenue of the Americas, about a mile north of Foley Square. When they arrived at Durante Square, they found it surrounded by a newly erected chain link fence and plywood wall, as well as a contingent of police—joined by the cops who had followed the marchers—who stopped anyone from entering.

Meanwhile, a legal battle over the closure of Liberty Square quickly developed as the National Lawyers Guild filed a request for an emergency court order to keep the park open and to let protesters back in—with their tents. Occupy Wall Street won the first round when State Supreme Court Judge Lucy Billings issued a temporary court order reopening the park and ordering the city to allow protesters back in with their tents and to reestablish the encampment. Police refused to comply with the order as the city appealed. Later that day State Supreme Court Judge Michael Stallman reversed the earlier decision, ruling that while the city had to reopen the park and allow protests, protesters could not bring tents or the other paraphernalia of the occupation and could not stay around the clock if doing so interfered with others' use of the park. Later that evening, around 7:00 p.m., people filed back into the park, now eerily empty, and held a General Assembly.[20]

After the Eviction

Nearly all the major Occupy encampments in the United States were evicted in mid-November in a crackdown coordinated by the federal government. In the weeks and months following these evictions, protesters continued to fill the streets of New York and other cities with marches and demonstrations, working groups continued to meet, and major actions were planned. As a banner seen the day after the Liberty Square eviction proclaimed: "You can't evict an idea whose time has come." Two days after the eviction, on November 17, over fifty thousand protesters shut down major areas of New York City, students occupied university buildings, and the movement seemed as strong as it had ever been. By December, Occupy Wall Street had begun planning for a major day of action on May 1, 2012, calling for a general strike. Attempts were made to reoccupy Zuccotti Park and to reclaim other public spaces in New York City, but such attempts were largely unsuccessful and were repeatedly broken up with mass arrests and brutal policing.

As the months wore on, Occupy Wall Street began to fade from public consciousness, with less day-to-day coverage. There was no longer a central space—a vibrant occupation—to capture the media's and the public's attention. Just as importantly, the park had functioned as an open and easy way for new people to get involved. Having a *space* at the heart of the movement was central to its success (as authorities understood well). Now the heart of the movement was less clear, and it was not as easy for outsiders to engage with occupiers or join the movement. "Occupy" increasingly became a semiclosed network of activists.

A number of singular days of action, such as May Day, 2012, and the one-year anniversary of the occupation on September 17, 2012, brought tens of thousands of protesters back onto the streets, momentarily blowing life back into the flagging movement. Perhaps most strikingly, Superstorm Sandy, which caused major damage to New York City on October 29, 2012, catalyzed a recomposition of Occupy as a remarkably successful, mutual aid–based, disaster relief organization. Under the name "Occupy Sandy," activists organized first-responder teams and later distribution/volunteer centers in neighborhoods around the city. Many projects emerged from Occupy Sandy that continue to do long-term political work in affected neighborhoods.

It is in such ongoing projects and in its palpable impact on mainstream political discourse that Occupy Wall Street has had its most enduring effects. While "Occupy Wall Street" might no longer signify a living social movement, its effects remain visible in New York and around the country. Projects that have emerged from OWS include, for example, Strike Debt and the Occupy Student Debt Campaign, which have helped politicize and transform popular conversations about debt in the United States. These organizations are joined by groups such as the Free University that have mobilized against tuition hikes and the privatization of public universities. These movements and conversations found their mainstream echo in 2016 Democratic presidential hopeful Bernie Sanders's vow to make college education

You Can't Evict an Idea, Union Square, March 21, 2012, one of a large number of protests and occupations following the clearing out of Liberty Square. Photo by Zoltán Glück, used by permission.

free and his rival Hillary Clinton's less full-throated calls for lower tuition and increasing student aid.

Other Occupy groups were central in the eventually successful fight against the Keystone XL pipeline, in the fight against gentrification in New York and other cities, and in struggles against evictions and foreclosures. Some of Occupy's other effects have perhaps been more structural and far-reaching, even if these effects are hard to quantify—for example, shifting the conversation about wealth inequality in the United States, which in turn has shifted the electoral landscape (if in clearly contradictory ways). In New York, there is little doubt that Occupy Wall Street helped pave the way for the election of Mayor Bill De Blasio, the most progressive mayor since David Dinkins (De Blasio was an active and vocal supporter of Occupy), while at the national level OWS certainly prepared the ground for the surprising rise

and popular success of Vermont socialist Bernie Sanders in the 2016 Democratic presidential campaign, a campaign in which questions of wealth inequality and the infirmities of the capitalist political economy featured to a degree rarely seen since the Depression.

But perhaps the most important (albeit elusive) impact has been the politically radicalizing effect of the movement on hundreds of thousands of participants across the United States. People who had never previously thought of themselves as "political" have been transformed by the experience of Occupy Wall Street. Indeed, many of them are now seasoned activists. And, of course, we may readily expect that the experiences, lessons, and politicizing moments forged through Occupy Wall Street will remain an active ingredient in each new wave of resistance that breaks over a perennially revolting New York.

Early 2017

DON MITCHELL

This time it does not feel like only a lightning bolt of revolt, only a revealing flash of light. This time it feels like a whole, wild storm is about to break over the city. Ever since New York's native son—and nativist—Donald J. Trump achieved an improbable Electoral College victory in the 2016 presidential election (while losing the popular vote by nearly three million votes), the skies have been darkening. But so too have the electrical charges been building up. Perhaps the only question is what kind of violence is going to rend the city: Will it be a cleansing burst of revolt, the kind of rebellion that reestablishes the city as a place of promise and progressivism? Or will it be the violence of reaction, unleashed by the police and followers of an obviously unstable, irrational, racist, and megalomaniacal president?

The torrent of news and decisions emanating from Washington in the early days of the Trump presidency has been depressing: from the appointment of a cabinet composed almost entirely of self-aggrandizers and people unfit for office; to the immediate global assault on women's health rights; to the weird first-day assault on the pocketbooks of first-time home buyers; to the order starting construction of a wall along the U.S.-Mexico border (launching a full-blown diplomatic crisis); to the hasty, draconian, ill-advised, racist, anti-Muslim executive order signed on January 27, 2017, that temporarily (and, in the case of Syrian refugees, indefinitely) banned visitors, immigrants, and refugees from seven Muslim-majority countries while pointedly excepting visitors and immigrants from Muslim-majority countries where the Trump family has business ties. Yet there are, in fact, reasons for hope, starting with the instant mass protests that erupted at John F. Kennedy International Airport as soon as the Muslim ban was announced (and that were soon followed by protests at airports around the country and world).

Thousands of people descended on the airport to voice their opposition to the Trump administration ban (and the administration more generally), as well as to declare their solidarity with travelers detained at the airport. (In New York and around the country, scores of travelers from the seven countries with perfectly valid visas were detained because they had the bad luck to be on flights to the United States at the moment the executive order was signed; thousands of others were stranded at airports around the world, not allowed to board planes bound for the United States, and sometimes ordered back to the lands they had fled as refugees.) Taxi drivers, organized through the New York Taxi Drivers Alliance, refused to take fares to or from the airport. More and more people descended on the airport, many of them arriving by subway. When New York Police Department barred anyone without a valid plane ticket from boarding the Airtrain that connects the subway with the terminals, Governor Andrew Cuomo (spying a political opportunity) intervened and ordered the cops to stand down. The protests grew and lasted for days.

The airport protests immediately put the Trump administration on the defensive, forcing it to back down on some parts of the ban while "clarifying" others, while surely also stiffening the resolve of judges around the country forced to consider the constitutionality of the ban. It was clear they could not just give Trump a "bye" in his first days in office, offering him a degree of deference sometimes afforded new presidents as they find their feet. The people, in New York and beyond, would not stand for it.

The *New York Times*, hailing the JFK protests, echoed the filmmaker Michael Moore in arguing that they had grown "out of nowhere."[1] Nothing could be further from the truth, of course. The ground for these protests, as we have seen, has been fertilized by nearly four hundred years of struggle, contradictory as that history of struggle has been. More immediately, organizations that had a long history of immigrant rights organizing—like Make the Road New York and the New York Immigrant Coalition—some of which were central to, or grew out of, the immigrant rights protests of 2006, quickly swung into action, mobilizing protesters, deploying lawyers to the airport to assist those detained, and more. The days of protest at the airport that followed were bucked up by large street demonstrations, like the thousands that gathered in Battery Park, not far from old Forts Amsterdam and George and within sight of the Statue of Liberty on January 30 demanding the repeal of the executive order. By then, judges around the country had suspended portions of the order, sometimes within days, as a judge in Seattle stayed it in its entirety, a decision sustained on appeal. By February 16, the Trump administration had more or less abandoned the executive order in its entirety, promising to replace it "soon"—a remarkable and important victory for those opposed to Trump's draconian policies.[2]

Protests on the streets of New York had been an almost daily occurrence since Trump's electoral victory. Beginning election night, crowds formed outside Trump Tower on Fifth Avenue, where the new president-elect was holed up,

and they grew over the next several days, echoing, at least to a degree, the sort of mob action that accompanied political upheaval at the end of the eighteenth and the beginning of the nineteenth century. There was certainly a degree of spontaneity to these protests (as there was in similar outpourings around the country), but, as with the airport protests two months later, it was also the case that activist groups—having honed their organizational skills, their abilities to call out their members on short notice, and their ability to navigate the city's protest-policing bureaucracy over the course of the Giuliani and Bloomberg administrations—had long ago laid the foundation for such seemingly spontaneous uprisings. It took some time before federal and city security forces could establish a cordon around Trump Tower and keep the angry—and dismayed—protesters at bay.[3]

As the New Year dawned and the Trump inauguration grew near, protest continued and even intensified, with near nightly gatherings in Washington Square and other key locales. The night before the inauguration, thousands gathered again in front of Trump Tower to express their dissatisfaction. "The rally," the *New York Times* suggested, "was likely a sign of things to come over the next four years, with Trump-branded buildings in the president-elect's hometown making the perfect backdrop for opponents of his policies."[4] Protests continued around the city on Inauguration Day itself, though all were dwarfed by the much larger protests in Washington, D.C.

Then came the Women's March. The main event was to be in Washington, so in the early days of planning, New York organizers expected the event there to be relatively modest and secured a permit for Dag Hammarskjöld Plaza. But as outrage over the incoming president's unqualified, self-serving, antiwoman cabinet picks grew, as it became clear that he would launch an attack on women's reproductive health rights and subsidized health care as early as his first hours in office, and as outrage continued to smolder over his rank misogyny, it became clear that, as in Washington, New York's Women's March would be huge. Organizers secured serial permits, allowing ranks of eight thousand protesters at a time to gather in the plaza and start off on the march route (New York mayor De Blasio put up little of the resistance to issuing protest permits his two predecessors had shown). On the day of the march some four hundred thousand people showed up in New York (nearly as many as in Washington); and across the nation and around the world, millions participated in the single largest same-day protest since the February 15, 2003, protest against the impending war against Iraq (as with the 2003 antiwar protests, the Women's March was a global event, with sometimes quite sizable protests held in cities around the world).[5]

The streets vibrated with outrage as hundreds of thousands of women, many wearing newly knitted pink "pussy hats" (a reminder of President Trump's recorded boast that he liked to walk up to women as "grab them by the pussy"), were joined by large numbers of men and children in a show of defiant strength. But there was also a joy in numbers and a growing sense of solidarity, as well as a strong commitment to build difference (in race, class, sexuality, and gender) into strength against what is clearly a minority and oppressive government determined to serve only a select, elite, largely Wall Street–bred few while paying lip-service to the disenfranchised white working-class families that provided much of its electoral support. The Women's March in New York and around the world was a remarkable display of resistance, a strong statement that a progressive movement, energized by electoral defeat, was on the rise.

The movement is diverse, attentive, and sometimes surprising. On the day Trump's clearly unqualified but exceedingly rich pick for education secretary, Betsy De Vos (who made her name driving Michigan's public schools into the ground while promoting and protecting private, sometimes for-profit, often ineffectual charter schools), won Senate confirmation when, for the first time in history, the vice president was called on to cast a tie-breaking vote, thousands of high school students walked out of their New York classes (as they did in other cities around the country) and staged a noisy protest of disapproval in Foley Square— that old place of justice that has been so important in New

York's social history.[6] Militancy is no stranger among New York school students, as the Gary Plan Riots, any number of antiwar protests at the end of the 1960s, and the 2006 immigrant rights uprising made clear, but that a relatively low-level cabinet member could draw such animus—could be seen as such a threat—speaks volumes about the perceived extremism of the Trump administration, as well as the number of fronts on which New Yorkers now think they have to fight.

Yet, perhaps inevitably, there was also concern that the movement would not or could not be sustained. Such a sentiment ignores the degree to which organizing already *has been* sustained in New York. Anti-Trump sentiment, and the sense of emergency the Trump administration has instilled in so many, has instead reenergized long-standing organizing efforts among immigrant rights, antipoverty, antiracism, labor, and other activists while drawing into the struggle thousands of heretofore less political people appalled by what they see and now dedicated to building an alternative. New Yorkers repeatedly returned to the streets in the days immediately following the Women's March. For example, a thousand people gathered in Washington Square Park on Wednesday, January 26—the night before Trump signed the executive order banning Muslims—to protest the administration's early actions. Trump earlier in the day had signed one (actually quite toothless but symbolic nonetheless) executive order to build a wall between the United States and Mexico and another one to withhold federal funds from Sanctuary Cities (cities that refuse to cooperate with federal efforts to detain and deport immigrants), and New Yorkers wanted to show their solidarity with immigrants and to stand firm against what they expected would be even more draconian measures to come.[7] When the Muslim ban was signed the next day, New Yorkers were ready. The airport protests did not arise out of nowhere; they very clearly came from somewhere—from years of preparation and a long, long history of revolt.

◻ ◻ ◻

Perhaps such militancy is not very surprising, for, as we have seen, the streets, parks, and neighborhoods of New York have always been the scene of struggle, even as struggles of all kinds have shaped, and continue to shape, the streets, parks, and neighborhoods. During the Depression and again after the financial crisis of 2008, for example, New Yorkers rallied to defend renters against gouging landlords with rent strikes and by blocking evictions. Struggles over class, race, and immigration, over who would benefit from shifts in the social order, to point to another example, flare up over and over again, from the Doctors' Riot in 1788 to the police riots in Tompkins Square Park, to the intense struggles between working-class whites and blacks in Bensonhurst. More generally, at moments of fraught politics—the struggles between parties and factions in colonial New York, for example, or the struggle between the Republican state and democratic city during the mid-nineteenth century, or the economic crises and the War on Terror scares of the late twentieth- and early twenty-first centuries—revolt intensifies and violence proliferates, often in highly repressive ways. This is New York's revolting heritage.

Like any heritage, it is a fraught one. It is most particularly fraught in relation to race. The violence of the Draft Riots might have been exceptional in intensity and duration, but it was hardly exceptional in form. African Americans frighten—at an existential level—white elites (whose fortunes are built on a decidedly *racial* and *racist* capitalism and thus always at risk from the justifiable wrath of the racially oppressed), as well as many plebeian whites who are either tenuous beneficiaries of the racial order or who fear the competition black workers seem to represent. As a result, official and unofficial disciplining violence against black people is a central and continuous part of the city's history—from the hanging of Caesar and Cuffee in the Great Negro Revolt of 1741 through the Tenderloin Riot and on to Bensonhurst. But so is concerted struggle against this racial order and its violence by African Americans, other people of color, and their white allies.

In the twenty-first century, as the racial order has been strained and cracked by the rapidly changing ethnic makeup of the city, by the uneven and partial but very real and still ongoing victories in civil rights struggles in the city and beyond, by the massive economic and political restructuring that has wiped out one social order (rooted in New Deal Keynesianism) and ushered in another (rooted in a by-now dysfunctional neoliberalism), white power has been shored up in many, perhaps increasingly desperate, ways—most prominently in the near sanctioning of police violence and police murder of black people in New York and around the nation, including Eric Garner on Staten Island in July 2014. Garner was strangled by police for attempting to sell loose, untaxed cigarettes in order to get by in an economic system that had no room for him and perhaps just as much for daring to talk back during his arrest. Three weeks later Michael Brown was shot and killed by a police officer in Ferguson, Missouri. Garner and Brown were just two of a long and growing list of black men killed by the police during the second decade of the twenty-first century at what felt like a quickening pace. Rarely have police officers been charged in the killings. If they were, they were typically exonerated by deferential, frequently white-majority juries.

Following the killing two years earlier of black teenager Trevon Martin by a white vigilante in Florida (who was later acquitted of manslaughter), the police killing of Garner and Brown sparked a movement, #BlackLivesMatter, which, as the slaughter of black men—and boys—continued (in Baton Rouge, Baltimore, Cleveland, West Charleston, Charlottesville, Minneapolis, and more), assured through protests and demonstrations, social media organizing, and work in schools and workplaces that police killing, and racist policing more generally, would not fade from public consciousness.[8] In New York, #BlackLivesMatter joined older movements and organizations fighting against the city's "stop and frisk" policing, which targeted people of color. "Stop and frisk" was the descendant of the "quality of life," broken windows policing practices developed by Mayor Giuliani and his police commissioner, Bill Bratton, in the 1980s, and #BlackLivesMatter activists showed how such practices existed on a continuum with—not apart from—police killing of people of color (as the case of Eric Garner made so plain).

Like many contemporary social movements, #BlackLivesMatter is both diffuse and tightly focused. Launched by two queer women on the West Coast and one in New York sharing their anger over police killing of black people, #BlackLivesMatter operates through a network of loosely affiliated chapters that determine many of their own practices and goals, responding to local conditions, linked together through social media. As important as social media is, however, a key aspect of the success of #BlackLivesMatter has been its ability to mobilize large numbers of people of color and their white allies to occupy and hold space, both by making their presence felt and by disrupting the normal flow of business, forcing people to understand that police killing is intolerable.

In New York, #BlackLivesMatter has held weekly demonstrations since its inception, often blocking traffic (e.g., on the Williamsburg Bridge) or interrupting commuters as they seek to transit through Grand Central Station. Sometimes demonstrations have turned confrontational, as when more than a thousand people gathered in Union Square on the evening of July 8, 2016, to protest the police killing—all in one week—of Alton Sterling in Baton Rouge, Philando Castile in Minneapolis, and Delrawn Small in New York. Demonstrators marched from Union Square, up Fifth Avenue, over to the entrances of the Lincoln Tunnel, then back along to Times Square, where they blocked traffic on 42nd Street. Cops rushed the protesters sitting and standing in the street, tackling many and eventually arresting more than forty. The protest march continued nonetheless working its way up to Harlem by the early hours of the morning.[9]

Relations with police were frequently tense, given that the police themselves were the object of protest. They were especially tense after a black man shot and killed two NYPD officers on December 20, 2014 (one Latino, the other Chinese), presumably as "revenge" for the police killing of Eric Garner and Michael Brown, a shooting that sparked a rival Blue Lives Matter movement of retired cops and police supporters that soon allied itself with the Donald Trump presidential campaign. They became even more tense after the NYPD revealed in a September 2016 legal filing that it had infiltrated #BlackLivesMatter-affiliated organizations with undercover agents—as had the police agencies of New York's Metropolitan Transit Authority and the Metro-North commuter rail service—perhaps in violation of the NYPD's own guidelines for protest monitoring.[10] They have also been strained by some police organization support for a growing white-supremacist backlash both in the All Lives Matter and White Lives Matter movements and in the widening space in America for (and semiofficial acceptance of) white nationalist and white supremacist discourse, agitation, and, indeed, policy (e.g., a bill pending before Congress that would make it illegal to use federal funds to conduct spatial research on racial disparities in access to affordable housing).[11]

Despite such surveillance, #BlackLivesMatter has remained militant. In August 2016, for example, Black Lives activists affiliated with #ShutDownCityHallNYC occupied a portion of City Hall Park—the old Common, the site of the Liberty Pole agitation during the Revolution and so much more. They called their encampment Abolition Square and pushed for the total abolition of broken windows policing, reparations for victims of police brutality, the defunding of the NYPD, and the reallocation of its budget to communities of color.[12]

More than two years of continuous organizing, creative demonstrations, and the development of a strong set of social justice initiatives and policies meant that when Trump was elected, #BlackLivesMatter-affiliated activists have been able to mobilize quickly and effectively, allying in New York with activists who cut their teeth on Occupy Wall Street and Occupy Sandy, immigrant rights' organizations, groups affiliated with the Right to the City movement like Picture the Homeless (which, as a homeless-led organization, has done vital work in publicizing how New York's rent and housing crisis is founded on a *constructed* scarcity of housing), and others. #BlackLivesMatter organizers were, like their immigrant rights' counterparts, highly effective in mobilizing people to descend on JFK Airport (and innumerable other airports around the country) when Trump's Muslim ban was announced. And they are preparing to fight the Trump administration on what they imagine will be a wide range of assaults, from a revival of "stop and frisk" and broken windows policing; to assaults on health care; to a concerted attack on the Fight for Fifteen movement, seeking to raise minimum wages across the country; to an assault on public education; to an end to the even minimal efforts the United States has heretofore engaged in to combat climate change, the effects of which will be most strongly felt by marginal communities of color and working-class people.[13]

▫ ▫ ▫

There is no doubt that the storm clouds are gathering, and we are in for a hell of a storm. But it is not "coming out of nowhere." The atmosphere has been charged by the long history of riot, rebellion, uprising, and revolution that today's movements and activists—and today's forces of reaction—are part of and heir to. It is a history that is in no way over. New Yorkers feel like something is about to break—but surely not revolution? Yet if we understand that among the meanings of "revolution" is its definition as "a period or instance of significant change or radical alteration of a particular condition [or] state of affairs," as well as its definition as an "overturning," the way the popular revolts of the eighteenth and nineteenth centuries were an overturning (if temporary) of established orders, then maybe we are in a revolutionary moment.[14] The neoliberal order that has shaped the city since its fiscal crisis in the 1970s is surely now dead, and the wave of right-wing populism that pushed Trump into the presidency is certainly ill-fitting in Gotham. What will emerge now that the old order *is* being overturned is hard to predict.

As the rapid deployment to John F. Kennedy Airport in defense of Muslim, refugee, and immigrant rights—and in favor of our own sanity—showed, however, people are ready to respond. More, they are ready to *resist*, a word that is becoming the sign-off of choice in social media messages (#Resist), emails, and live conversations alike. Even better, on the foundation of generations of organizing, they are ready to *make*—to make not only riots, rebellions, and uprisings (as necessary) but also (if possible) a revolutionary new moment that takes seriously the long history of revolting New York, learns from its contradictions, and—in a lightning flash—illuminates a new world of possibility. Such moments make the city.

ACKNOWLEDGMENTS

Revolting New York began in 2007 in a seminar on urban revolution that Neil Smith taught at the Graduate Center of the City University of New York. Neil and the students in the seminar thought it might be a good idea to write an accessible historical geography of riots and rebellions in New York City, and they got to work. First drafts of many of the chapters included in this volume began as papers for this seminar. Over the next five years, students worked on conceptualizing what such a volume might entail, commented on and edited each other's work, pushed Neil to get serious about finding a publisher, and generally kept the project going (amid their own studies, dissertation writing, and so forth). After Neil died in September 2012, his partner, Deb Cowen, and the students asked Don Mitchell to step in and help bring the project to fruition.

Our first word of thanks has to go to Deb, not only for helping bring us all together but especially for her unflagging support of the project (and also for being a sounding board and shoulder to cry on when things were not going well). Her faith in the project has been of unmeasurable value. We hope she likes what she sees.

At the Grad Center, Don Rowbotham and Alida Rojas at the Advanced Research Collaborative provided a welcoming space, good humor, and lots of intellectual support in the early days of Don Mitchell's involvement. Don R. also donated the use of ARC's conference room when Don M. brought a group of students from Syracuse University to explore revolting New York on the ground. Disguised as a field course, the Syracuse expedition provided a great opportunity to ground truth many of the events and arguments laid out in the book.

The Grad Center's Center for Place, Culture and Politics, led from its founding by Neil and later by David Harvey and Ruth Wilson Gilmore, provided Neil with a vibrant political and intellectual home within which his ideas about urban revolution were nurtured. Everyone who has passed through the center's doors, fellow and visitor alike, has helped shape this book, wittingly or not. If the urban revolution has an intellectual home, it is the Center for Place, Culture and Politics. David and Ruthie were both especially encouraging to Don as he joined the project and worked over many years to bring it to fruition. Cindi Katz was as wonderfully helpful (and critical!) as always.

Much of the book was edited, revised, fact-checked, critiqued, and revised again while Don was a professor in the Department of Geography at Syracuse University. Jamie Winders opened doors, stretched budgets, and made the field course possible, all while proving to be the best department chair anyone could imagine. Not everyone can do that job, and few do it well; Jamie does it extraordinarily well, and she is one major reason this book was ever finished. Margie Johnson is likewise superlative and never once complained—or even looked mildly annoyed (usually just bemused)—when Don showed up with another stack of receipts for images, copyright clearances, books, hotel rooms, meals, drinks (disguised as meals), and all the rest, or just as often when he didn't and she had to get him to cough them up so she could balance the budget. The financial support of the Maxwell School and the central administration of Syracuse University is greatly appreciated. Even more important was the supportive intellectual climate the Department of Geography fostered against all odds in an increasingly hostile university environment. Thanks to Matt, Tod, Tom, Jane, Anne, John, Peng, Jake, Natalie, Bob, Jonnell, Mark, and, more than any of them, Susan. Joe Stoll has done simply a stunning job with the maps. The Social Sciences PhD program threw some excellent researchers our way, especially Nicole Watson, but also Ferdinand Flagstad. Maddy Hamlin, herself a remarkable researcher committed to making a more just city, did a great first copyedit before we sent the manuscript to press while also raising key questions about some of our interpretations. And the students in the spring 2016 Revolting New York class proved invaluable critics and great comrades as we trooped around New York coming to *feel*—not only know and see—how four hundred years of revolt shaped the city.

The Department of Social and Economic Geography at Uppsala University has likewise been a welcoming scholarly environment in which to put the final touches on the book. The Faculty of Social Sciences' financial support as a few last photographs were chased down has been invaluable. A special thanks to those photographers—Manel Armengo, Andrew Lichtenstein, Henry Gordillo, Harvey Wang, and Brian Rose—with whom we had the pleasure of directly working and to the numerous librarians at the New York Public Library, the Library of Congress, the Lesbian and Gay Community Resource Center, and elsewhere who helped us with images.

Nik Heynen and the others involved with the Geographies of Justice and Social Transformation series of the University of Georgia Press have been enthusiastic about this project since Neil and his revolutionary seminarians first started talking about it. At the press itself, Mick Gusinde-Duffy, Jon Davies, Beth Snead, and "the designers" have been immensely supportive and creative and a joy to work with. Mary M. Hill did an extraordinary job copyediting the whole (damn) manuscript, saving us from blunders large and small while improving our writing to boot. Any errors of fact or interpretation, and all infelicities of writing, remain our responsibility alone.

Neil's death hit hard. Whatever his flaws (and of course they were not insignificant), he was a revolutionary figure. He transformed how we understand urban geography even as he dedicated himself to working in and for radical political and community organizations that themselves were trying to revolutionize the urban and geopolitical landscapes. He was loved and respected by activists around New York who, like his academic peers in geography and elsewhere, understood his theories of gentrification, uneven development, geographical scale, and more to be not just incisive new ways of understanding the city (and beyond) but useful tools for chipping away at, and sometimes even overturning, the world that capital and its elites make. *Revolting New York* was a project very dear to Neil's heart. Ever the grounded materialist insistent that we understand the world as it really is, he nonetheless always encouraged us to dive right into the struggle to remake it as it ought to be—and to stay there until we had won, whatever setbacks we might experience along the way. That his insistence was always leavened with wit (sometimes biting!) and an immense joie de vivre (sometimes verging on the manic) only made it all the more powerful. Consider *Revolting New York* to be Neil's last testament, but especially a monument to his *will*.

NOTES

INTRODUCTION. THE LIGHTNING FLASH OF REVOLT

1. Alex Vitale, *City of Disorder: How the Quality of Life Campaign Transformed New York Politics* (New York: New York University Press, 2008); Lisa Keller, *The Triumph of Order: Democracy and Public Space in New York and London* (New York: Columbia University Press, 2009).

2. Raymond Williams, *Keywords: A Vocabulary of Culture and Society* (London: Fontana Press 1976), 329–31.

3. Ibid., 330–31.

4. In general, see Don Mitchell, *The Right to the City: Social Justice and the Fight for Public Space* (New York: Guilford, 2003), chap. 2.

5. For an analysis of how ritualized but now tamed unruliness has resurfaced in the commodified form of rock music, see Greil Marcus, *Lipstick Traces: A Secret History of the Twentieth Century* (Cambridge, Mass.: Harvard University Press, 1989). The classic cultural studies accounts of carnivals, festivals, and ritualized unruliness are Mikhail Bakhtin, *Rabelais and His World* (Bloomington: Indiana University Press, 1984); and Peter Stallybrass and Allon White, *The Politics and Poetics of Transgression* (Ithaca, N.Y.: Cornell University Press, 1986). For specifically geographic takes, see Tim Cresswell, *In Place / Out of Place: Geography, Ideology, and Transgression* (Minneapolis: University of Minnesota Press, 1996); and Don Mitchell, *Cultural Geography: A Critical Introduction* (Oxford: Blackwell, 2000), esp. chap. 6. Guy Debord's analysis of the commodification of dissent in capitalism is always worth reading: *Society of the Spectacle*, trans. Donald Nichelson-Smith (New York: Zone Books, 1994).

6. Mayor's Commission on Conditions in Harlem, *The Negro in Harlem: A Report on Social and Economic Conditions Responsible for the Outbreak of March 19, 1935* (New York: Municipal Archives of New York City, 1936), 5–6.

7. Williams, *Keywords*, 270–74.

8. Williams's context was somewhat but not entirely different. He was interested in charting the long transformation of English culture—modes of thought and ways of life—that unfolded with the democratic and industrial revolutions in Britain. Raymond Williams, *The Long Revolution* (London: Chatto and Windus, 1961).

9. On Manchester and Chicago, see Harold Platt, *Shock Cities: The Environmental Transformation and Reform of Manchester and Chicago* (Chicago: University of Chicago Press, 2005).

10. The classic account of New York's deindustrialization is Robert Fitch, *The Assassination of New York* (New York: Verso, 1993); but see also Jacob Shell, *Transportation and Revolt: Pigeons, Mules, Canals, and the Vanishing Geography of Subversive Mobility* (Cambridge, Mass.: MIT Press, 2015), esp. chap. 4.

11. David Nye, *When the Lights Went Out: A History of Blackouts in America* (Cambridge, Mass.: MIT Press, 2010), 130–32.

12. Rosalyn Deutsche, *Evictions: Art and Spatial Politics* (Cambridge, Mass.: MIT Press, 1996); Neil Smith, *The New Urban Frontier: Gentrification and the Revanchist City* (New York: Routledge, 1996).

13. Henri Lefebvre, *The Production of Space*, trans. Donald Nicholson-Smith (Oxford: Backwell, 1991); Neil Smith, *Uneven Development: Nature, Capital, and the Production of Space*, 3rd ed. (Athens: University of Georgia Press, 2008); David Harvey, *The Limits to Capital* (Chicago: University of Chicago Press, 1982).

14. For just one example of how geographers have shown how social struggle is decisive within a dominant capitalism, see Andrew Herod, *Labor Geographies: Workers and the Landscapes of*

Capitalism (New York: Guilford, 2001). On Robert Moses, see, of course, Robert Caro, *The Power Broker: Robert Moses and the Fall of New York* (New York: Vintage, 1975).

15. Reprinted with a foreword by Pete Hamill and an afterword by Thomas Ruse and James Rogers: Joel Tyler Headley, *The Great Riots of New York, 1712–1873* (New York: Thunder's Mouth Press, 2004).

16. Edwin G. Burrows and Mike Wallace, *Gotham: A History of New York City to 1898* (New York: Oxford University Press, 1999).

CHAPTER 1. THE REVOLT OF THE MUNSEE

1. Edwin G. Burrows and Mike Wallace, *Gotham: A History of New York City to 1898* (New York: Oxford University Press, 1999), 5.

2. Quoted in Eric W. Sanderson, *Mannahatta: A Natural History of New York City* (New York: Abrams, 2009), 24.

3. Richard White, *The Middle Ground: Indians, Empires, and Republics in the Great Lakes Region, 1650–1815* (Cambridge: Cambridge University Press, 1991).

4. Quoted in Paul Andrew Otto, *The Dutch-Munsee Encounter in America: The Struggle for Sovereignty in the Hudson Valley* (New York: Berghahn Books, 2006), 95.

5. Jaap Jacobs, *New Netherland: A Dutch Colony in Seventeenth-Century America* (Boston: Brill, 2005), 113.

6. Quoted in Otto, *Dutch-Munsee Encounter*, 108.

7. Quoted in J. Franklin Jameson, *Narratives of New Netherland, 1609–1664* (New York: Barnes and Noble, 1909), 122.

8. John Romeyn Brodhead, *History of the State of New York, First Period, 1609–1664* (New York: Harper and Brothers, 1853), 276.

9. Ibid., 308.

10. Otto, *Dutch-Munsee Encounter*.

11. Brodhead, *History*, 316.

12. Quoted in Jameson, *Narratives of New Netherland*, 228.

13. Ibid., 229.

14. Brodhead, *History*, 346.

15. Quoted in Allen W. Trelease, *Indian Affairs in Colonial New York: The Seventeenth Century* (Ithaca, N.Y.: Cornell University Press, 1960), 74.

16. Brodhead, *History*, 369.

17. Quoted in Trelease, *Indian Affairs*, 81.

18. Quoted in Otto, *Dutch-Munsee Encounter*, 122.

19. Brodhead, *History*, 347.

20. Ibid., 607.

21. Quoted in Trelease, *Indian Affairs*, 139.

22. Quoted in Jameson, *Narratives of New Netherland*, 459.

23. Ibid., 227.

LEISLER'S REBELLION, 1689–1691

1. Edwin G. Burrows and Mike Wallace, *Gotham: A History of New York City to 1898* (New York: Oxford University Press, 1999), quotation from p. 93. See also Howard McCormick, *Leisler's Rebellion* (New York: Garland Publishing, 1989).

2. See Benjamin Blagge, "A Memoriall of What Had Occurred in Their Mejesties Province of New York since the News of Their Majesties Happy Arivall in England" (1689), in *Empire City: New York through the Ages*, ed. Kenneth T. Jackson and David S. Dunbar (New York: Columbia University Press), 50–53.

3. Burrows and Wallace, *Gotham*, 98–99.

4. Ibid., 100.

5. See Jerome R. Reich, *Leisler's Rebellion: A Study of Democracy in New York, 1664–1710* (Chicago: University of Chicago Press, 1953).

6. Burrows and Wallace, *Gotham*, 101–2; David William Vorhees, "Leisler's Rebellion," in *The Encyclopedia of New York City*, ed. Kenneth T. Jackson, 2nd ed. (New Haven, Conn.: Yale University Press, 2010), 730–31.

THE SLAVE REVOLT, 1712

1. Thomas J. Davis, "Slavery," in *The Encyclopedia of New York City*, ed. Kenneth T. Jackson, 2nd ed. (New Haven, Conn.: Yale University Press, 2010), 1191–92; Edwin G. Burrows and Mike Wallace, *Gotham: A History of New York City to 1898* (New York: Oxford University Press, 1999), 128.

2. T. J. Davis, *A Rumor of Revolt: The "Great Negro Plot" in Colonial New York* (Amherst: University of Massachusetts Press, 1985), 54; Joel Tyler Headley, *The Great Riots of New York, 1712–1873* (New York: Thunder's Mouth Press, 2004), 8; Jill Lepore, *New York Burning: Liberty, Slavery, and Conspiracy in Eighteenth Century Manhattan* (New York: Vintage, 2005), 53.

3. Burrows and Wallace, *Gotham*, 148. Davis, *A Rumor of Revolt*, 55, reports that nineteen (not twenty-three) were executed.

4. Lepore, *New York Burning*, 57–58; Burrows and Wallace,

Gotham, 149; Peter Charles Hoffer, *The Great New York Conspiracy of 1741: Slavery, Crime, and Colonial Law* (Lawrence: University Press of Kansas, 2003), 31.

CHAPTER 2. THE GREAT NEGRO PLOT, 1741

1. T. J. Davis, *A Rumor of Revolt: The "Great Negro Plot" in Colonial New York* (Amherst: University of Massachusetts Press, 1885), 12–14.

2. Peter Charles Hoffer, *The Great New York Conspiracy of 1741: Slavery, Crime, and Colonial Law* (Lawrence: University Press of Kansas, 2003); Jill Lepore, *New York Burning: Liberty, Slavery, and Conspiracy in Eighteenth-Century Manhattan* (New York: Vintage, 2005).

3. Lepore's *New York Burning* provides an appendix listing nearly every accused "plotter," detailing what happened to them (burned, transported, hanged, accused but not arrested, etc.) (247–59); a second appendix arrays these data by slave owner (263–71).

4. Davis, *Rumor of Revolt*, 32.

5. Lepore, *New York Burning*, 154.

6. Peter Linebaugh and Marcus Rediker, *The Many-Headed Hydra: Sailors, Slaves, Commoners, and the Hidden History of the Revolutionary Atlantic* (Boston: Beacon Press, 2000), 187.

7. Lepore, *Burning New York*, 72–77; Hoffer, *Great New York Conspiracy*, 40–42.

8. Linebaugh and Rediker, *Many-Headed Hydra*, 177, 192; Edwin G. Burrows and Mike Wallace, *Gotham: A History of New York City to 1898* (New York: Oxford University Press, 1999), 158.

9. Davis, *Rumor of Revolt*, 27–30; Lepore, *New York Burning*, 15.

10. Lepore, *New York Burning*.

11. Linebaugh and Rediker, *Many-Headed Hydra*, 181–83; Davis, *Rumor of Revolt*, 4–6.

12. Lepore makes this claim at several places in *New York Burning* but tends to drop the line of argument just as soon as she ever raises it.

13. Ibid., 43–46.

14. Davis, *Rumor of Revolt*, 12–21; Lepore, *New York Burning*, 48–50.

15. Davis, *Rumor of Revolt*, 39–41.

16. Ibid., 50–52.

17. Lepore, *New York Burning*, 83–90.

18. Ibid., 102–6; Davis, *Rumor of Revolt*, 94–97.

19. Lepore, *New York Burning*, 110.

20. Ibid., 189–92.

21. Ibid., xviii. The *Journal* was edited and republished in Thomas J. Davis, *The New York Slave Conspiracy* (Boston: Beacon Press, 1971); two selections of the *Journal* are printed in Kenneth T. Jackson and David S. Dunbar, eds., *Empire City: New York through the Centuries* (New York: Columbia University Press, 2002), 65–70.

22. Linebaugh and Rediker, *Many-Headed Hydra*, 178–79.

23. Davis, *Rumor of Revolt*, xii.

24. Lepore, *New York Burning*, offers almost as many motives and explanations as there are pages in her book.

25. Burrows and Wallace, *Gotham*, 164.

26. Linebaugh and Rediker, *Many-Headed Hydra*, 206.

27. Lepore, *New York Burning*, 134–35.

28. Linebaugh and Rediker, *Many-Headed Hydra*, 209–10; Jackson and Dunbar, *Empire City*, reproduce Horsmanden's description (67–68).

CHAPTER 3. THE STAMP ACT REVOLT, 1765

1. Gary B. Nash, *The Unknown American Revolution: The Unruly Birth of Democracy and the Struggle to Create America* (New York: Viking, 2005).

2. C. A. Weslager, *The Stamp Act Congress* (Newark: University of Delaware Press, 1976).

3. Joel Tyler Headley, *The Great Riots of New York, 1712–1873* (New York: Thunder's Mouth Press, 2004), 26; Gary B. Nash, *The Urban Crucible: Social Change, Political Consciousness, and the Origins of the American Revolution* (Cambridge, Mass.: Harvard University Press, 1979), 292–311.

4. Headley, *Great Riots of New York*, 28.

5. Jesse Lemisch, *Jack Tar vs. John Bull: The Role of New York Seamen in Precipitating the Revolution* (New York: Garland Publishing, 1997), 26–27.

6. Paul A. Gilje, *Rioting in America* (Bloomington: Indiana University Press, 1963), 31.

7. Paul A. Gilje, *The Road to Mobocracy: Popular Disorder in New York City, 1763-1784* (Chapel Hill: University of North Carolina Press, 1987). For the broader European context, see George Rudé, *The Crowd in History: A Study of Popular Disturbances in France and England, 1730-1848* (New York: Wiley and Sons, 1964);

John Walter, *Crowds and Popular Politics in Early Modern England* (Manchester: Manchester University Press, 2006).

8. Gilje, *Rioting in America*, 31.

9. Ibid., 22–23.

10. For the American side, see, for example, Gordon Wood, *The Radicalism of the American Revolution* (New York: Vintage, 1993).

11. Eric Foner, *The Story of American Freedom* (New York: W. W. Norton, 1998).

12. Gilje, *Rioting in America*, 21.

13. The following account is based on Edwin G. Burrows and Mike Wallace, *Gotham: A History of New York City to 1898* (New York: Oxford University Press, 1999), 199.

14. Headley, *Great Riots of New York*, 28.

15. Burrows and Wallace, *Gotham*, 203.

16. John Adams, *The Papers of John Adams* (Cambridge, Mass.: Harvard University Press, 2003), 164.

17. Lemisch, *Jack Tar vs. John Bull*.

18. T. J. Davis, *A Rumor of Revolt: The "Great Negro Plot" in Colonial New York* (Amherst: University of Massachusetts Press, 1985).

CHAPTER 4. REVOLUTION

1. Quoted in Edwin G. Burrows and Mike Wallace, *Gotham: A History of New York City to 1898* (New York: Oxford University Press, 1999), 202–3.

2. Alfred Young, *Liberty Tree: Ordinary People and the American Revolution* (New York: New York University Press, 2006), 351; Gary Nash, *The Urban Crucible: Social Change, Political Consciousness, and the Origins of the American Revolution* (Cambridge, Mass.: Harvard University Press, 1979), 363–64; Burrows and Wallace, *Gotham*, 211.

3. Burrows and Wallace, *Gotham*, 203–4.

4. Nash, *Urban Crucible*, 364.

5. For a subtle analysis of how power worked through all these votes, when artisans had to declare their votes publicly before assembled "gentlemen" (the artisans' patrons), see ibid., 365–70.

6. Burrows and Wallace, *Gotham*, 207, 210.

7. On the London upheaval, see E. P. Thompson, *The Making of the English Working Class* (1963; New York: Vintage, 1966), 69–72.

8. Burrows and Wallace, *Gotham*, 211; Young, *Liberty Tree*, 351; Lee Boyer, "Lobster Backs, Liberty Boys, and Laborers in the Streets: New York's Golden Hill and Nassaue Street Riots," *New York Historical Society Quarterly* 57 (1973): 281–308; Peter Line-baugh and Marcus Rediker, *The Many-Headed Hydra: Sailors, Slaves, Commoners, and the Hidden History of the Revolutionary Atlantic* (Boston: Beacon Press, 2000), 231–32.

9. Nash, *The Urban Crucible*, 364; Burrows and Wallace, *Gotham*, 212.

10. Burrows and Wallace, *Gotham*, 213–14.

11. Ibid., 214–15. Linebaugh and Rediker, *Many-Headed Hydra*, 237, position the New York Sons of Liberty as a "counter-revolutionary" force, but this is hard to square with the historical evidence, even if it is the case that their interests did not align with those of rural rebels.

12. American Social History Project, *Who Built America?* (New York: Random House, 1989), 1:134.

13. The first quotation is from ibid., 1:145; the second is from Burrows and Wallace, *Gotham*, 221; and the third is from Nash, *The Urban Crucible*, 372.

14. American Social History Project, *Who Built America?*, 1:145; Burrows and Wallace, *Gotham*, 216.

15. Burrows and Wallace, *Gotham*, 216–18; Nash, *The Urban Crucible*, 369–70.

16. Nash, *The Urban Crucible*, 372–74; Edward Countryman, "Consolidating Power in Revolutionary America: The Case of New York, 1775–1783," *Journal of Interdisciplinary History* 6 (1976): 659; "From the Diary of Pastor Schaukirk," in *Empire City: New York through the Centuries*, ed. Kenneth Jackson and David Dunbar (New York: Columbia University Press, 2002), 86–88.

17. Burrows and Wallace, *Gotham*, 224.

18. Ibid., 226–27.

19. American Social History Project, *Who Built America?*, 1:158–59. For a discussion of Paine's influence in both America and Europe, see Young, *Liberty Tree*, chap. 6; and Thompson, *Making of the English Working Class*.

20. Burrows and Wallace, *Gotham*, 227–29.

21. Ibid., 320–22.

22. See the excerpts from the "Journal of Lieutenant Isaac Bangs," in Jackson and Dunbar, *Empire City*, 89–91.

23. The gruesome fate of the captured is detailed in Kenneth Jackson, "The Forgotten Saga of the Prison Ships," in Jackson and Dunbar, *Empire City*, 94–98; and Edwin Burrows, "Prison Ships," in *The Encyclopedia of New York*, ed. Kenneth T. Jackson, 2nd ed. (New Haven, Conn.: Yale University Press, 2010), 1039–40.

24. Barnet Schecter, *The Battle for New York: The City at the*

Heart of the American Revolution (New York: Walker & Co., 2002).

25. Burrows and Wallace, *Gotham*, 235–41.

26. Schecter, *The Battle for New York*.

27. Burrows and Wallace, *Gotham*, 241–42.

28. Ibid., 245–55.

29. Schecter, *The Battle for New York*; Burrows and Wallace, *Gotham*, 245–56.

30. Burrows and Wallace, *Gotham*, 259–61.

31. Simon Schama, *Rough Crossings: Britain, the Slaves and the American Revolution* (New York: Vintage, 2009).

32. American Social History Project, *Who Built America?*, 1:156; Linebaugh and Rediker, *Many-Headed Hydra*, chap. 7.

33. Burrows and Wallace, *Gotham*, 266–75.

THE DOCTORS' RIOT, 1788

1. Graham Russell Hodges, "Black Revolt in New York City and the Neutral Zone: 1775–83," in *New York in the Age of the Constitution, 1775–1800*, ed. Paul A. Gilje and William Pencak (Rutherford, N.J.: Farleigh Dickinson University Press, 1992), 20–47.

2. Edwin G. Burrows and Mike Wallace, *Gotham: A History of New York City to 1898* (New York: Oxford University Press, 1999), 286.

3. Quoted in Caroline de Costa and Francesca Miller, "The Art of Medicine: American Resurrection and the 1788 New York Doctors' Riot," *Lancet* 377 (January 22, 2011): 292–93; Robert J. Swan, "Prelude and Aftermath of the Doctors' Riot of 1788: A Religious Interpretation of White and Black Reaction to Grave Robbing," *New York History* 81 (2000): 417–56, provides a differently edited version of the letter; see also Steven Robert Wilf, "Anatomy and Punishment in Late Eighteenth-Century New York," *Journal of Social History* 22 (1989): 507–30.

4. William J. Bell Jr., "Doctors' Riot, New York, 1788," *Bulletin of the New York Academy of Medicine* 47 (1971): 1501–3, reprints a contemporaneous letter describing the desecrations.

5. Swan, "Prelude and Aftermath," 441.

6. Joel Tyler Headley, *The Great Riots of New York, 1712–1873* (New York: Thunder's Mouth Press, 2004), 31–39, provides a sensational account that nonetheless totally misses the racial aspects of the riot. A fuller account that also explores just how much is not known about the origins of the riot is Michael Sappol, *A Traffic in Dead Bodies: Anatomy and Embodied Social Identity in Nineteenth-Century America* (Princeton, N.J.: Princeton University Press, 2002), 108.

7. Paul A. Gilje, *The Road to Mobocracy: Popular Disorder in New York City, 1763–1834* (Chapel Hill: University of North Carolina Press, 1987), 81–82.

8. Swan, "Prelude and Aftermath," 419; Wilf, "Anatomy and Punishment," 512.

9. Wilf, "Anatomy and Punishment," 512.

10. Paul A. Gilje, "The Common People and the Constitution: Popular Culture in New York City in the Late Eighteenth Century," in *New York in the Age of the Constitution, 1775–1800*, ed. Paul A. Gilje and William Pencak (Rutherford, N.J.: Farleigh Dickinson University Press, 1992), 48–73, quotation from 64.

11. De Costa and Miller, "The Art of Medicine," 293; Wilf, "Anatomy and Punishment," 507; Swan, "Prelude and Aftermath," 453.

MOBOCRACY, 1792–1799

1. Paul A. Gilje, *The Road to Mobocracy: Popular Disorder in New York City, 1763–1834* (Chapel Hill: University of North Carolina Press, 1987), 83–85; Edwin G. Burrows and Mike Wallace, *Gotham: A History of New York City to 1898* (New York: Oxford University Press, 1999), 309–10.

2. This and the next paragraph rely on Gilje, *The Road to Mobocracy*, 88; Paul A. Gilje, "The Common People and the Constitution: Popular Culture in New York City in the Late Eighteenth Century," in *New York in the Age of the Constitution, 1775–1800*, ed. Paul A. Gilje and William Pencak (Rutherford, N.J.: Farleigh Dickinson University Press, 1992), 48–73, esp. 67–68.

3. Christine Stansell, *City of Women: Sex and Class in New York, 1789–1860* (New York: Columbia University Press, 1986), 23–26.

4. Gilje, *The Road to Mobocracy*, 90–91.

THE ANTI-ABOLITIONIST RIOTS, 1834

1. Paul A. Gilje, *The Road to Mobocracy: Popular Disorder in New York City, 1763–1834* (Chapel Hill: University of North Carolina Press, 1987), 147–53.

2. Edwin G. Burrows and Mike Wallace, *Gotham: A History of New York City to 1898* (New York: Oxford University Press, 1999), 546–55.

3. Ibid., 556.

4. Gilje, *The Road to Mobocracy*, Burrows and Wallace, *Gotham*, and Joel Tyler Headley, *The Great Riots of New York, 1712–1873*

(New York: Thunder's Mouth Press, 2004) all agree on the basic outline of events in 1834. The following is constructed from their accounts.

5. Gilje, *The Road to Mobocracy*, 165–70.

THE FLOUR RIOT, 1837

1. Edwin G. Burrows and Mike Wallace, *Gotham: A History of New York City to 1898* (New York: Oxford University Press, 1999), 603–9; American Social History Project, *Who Built America?* (New York: Pantheon, 1989), 1:332–35.

2. Joel Tyler Headley, *The Great Riots of New York, 1712–1873* (New York: Thunder's Mouth Press, 2004), 65–74.

3. Burrows and Wallace, *Gotham*, 611–13.

CHAPTER 5. THE ASTOR PLACE RIOT, 1849

1. Edwin G. Burrows and Mike Wallace, *Gotham: A History of New York City to 1898* (New York: Oxford University Press, 1999), 762.

2. Edward K. Spann, *The New Metropolis: New York City, 1840–1857* (New York: Columbia University Press, 1981), 474n5.

3. Mark Caldwell, *New York Night: The Mystique and Its History* (New York: Scribner, 2001), 45.

4. Michelle Nevius and James Nevius, *Inside the Apple: A Streetwise History of New York City* (New York: Free Press, 2009), 56–58.

5. "Musical," *New York Herald*, June 9, 1847, 3; Burrows and Wallace, *Gotham*, 486–90. Eric Lott's *Love and Theft: Black Face Minstrelsy and the American Working-Class* (New York: Oxford University Press, 1993) is the standard scholarly account of American blackface minstrelsy, although many of Lott's interpretations remain highly controversial.

6. "Common Council," *New York Herald*, July 2, 1840, 1.

7. George Templeton Strong, *The Diary of George Templeton Strong, Volume 2: The Turbulent Fifties, 1850–1859*, ed. Allan Nevins and Milton Halsey Thomas (New York: Macmillan, 1952), 59.

8. Frances Teague, *Shakespeare and the American Popular Stage* (New York: Cambridge University Press, 2006), 55–56; Burrows and Wallace, *Gotham*, 724, 762; John Kasson, *Rudeness and Civility: Manners in Nineteenth-Century America* (New York: Hill & Wang, 1990), 225; "Pompey's Rambles," in *White's New Book of Plantation Melodies* (Philadelphia: T. B. Peterson & Bros., 1849), 15–16.

9. *New York Herald*, January 30, 1848, 2.

10. Reeve Huston, "Antirent Movement," in *The Encyclopedia of New York State*, ed. Peter Eisenstadt (Syracuse, N.Y.: Syracuse University Press, 2005), 90–92. See also Reeve Huston, *Land and Freedom: Rural Society, Popular Protest, and Party Politics in Antebellum America* (New York: Oxford University Press, 2000); and Charles W. McCurdy, *The Anti-rent Era in New York Law and Politics, 1839–1861* (Chapel Hill: University of North Carolina Press, 2006).

11. Spann, *The New Metropolis*, 233; Burrows and Wallace, *Gotham*, 766–67.

12. Nigel Cliff, *The Shakespeare Riots: Revenge, Drama, and Death in Nineteenth Century America* (New York: Random House, 2007), 65–66, 98, 130–31.

13. Hershel Parker, *The Powell Papers: A Confidence Man Amok among the Anglo-American Literati* (Evanston, Ill.: Northwestern University Press, 2011), 19.

14. *Account of the Terrific and Fatal Riot at the New-York Astor Place Opera* (New York: H. M. Ranney, 1849), 7–8; Allan Nevins, ed., *The Diary of Philip Hone, 1821–1851* (New York: Dodd, Mead and Company, 1927), 2:866.

15. *Account of the Terrific and Fatal Riot*, 12.

16. Tyler Anbinder, "Isaiah Rynders and the Ironies of Popular Democracy in Antebellum New York," in *Contested Democracy: Freedom, Race, and Power in American History*, ed. M. Sinha and P. Von Eschen (New York: Columbia University Press, 2007), 34.

17. Tyler Anbinder, "'Boss' Tweed, Nativist," *Journal of the Early Republic* 15 (1995): 109–16.

18. Cliff, *The Shakespeare Riots*, 197–99.

19. Ibid., 206.

20. This account is from "The Outrageous Assault on Macready," excerpted from the *New York Herald* in the *Boston Herald*, May 9, 1849, 2.

21. Cliff, *The Shakespeare Riots*, 206–7; James W. Cook, "Dancing across the Color Line: A Story of Markets and Mixtures from New York's Five Points," *Common-place* 4, no. 1 (October 2003), http://www.common-place-archives.org/vol-04/no-01/cook/.

22. "The Outrageous Assault on Macready," 2.

23. Cliff, *The Shakespeare Riots*, 210–12.

24. *New York Herald*, May 10, 1849, 2.

25. Anbinder, "Isaiah Rynders," 37.

26. Cliff, *The Shakespeare Riots*, 209–14.

27. Ibid., 215–16.

28. Edward Robb Ellis, *The Epic of New York City: A Narrative History* (New York: Coward and McCann, 1966), 262; Burrows and Wallace, *Gotham*, 763.

29. Burrows and Wallace, *Gotham*, 763; Cliff, *The Shakespeare Riots*, 214.

30. "Riot and Loss of Life," *Charleston Mercury*, May 15, 1849, 2.

31. Ellis, *The Epic of New York City*, 263–64.

32. Richard Moody, *The Astor Place Riot* (Bloomington: Indiana University Press, 1958), 173; Cliff, *The Shakespeare Riots*, 223–24.

33. "The Great Riot in New York," *St. James Magazine* 18 (December–March 1866–67): 415–16; Cliff, *The Shakespeare Riots*, 223–24.

34. Emmons Clark, *History of the Seventh Regiment of New York, vol. 1, 1806–1889* (New York: Seventh Regiment, 1890), 343–45.

35. "Municipal Government," *United States Magazine and Review* 25 (June 1849): 491.

36. Clark, *History of the Seventh Regiment*, 345–46.

37. Burrows and Wallace, *Gotham*, 764.

38. "Additional Particulars of the Terrible Riot . . . ," *New York Herald*, May 12, 1849, 1; Burrows and Wallace, *Gotham*, 764.

39. Burrows and Wallace, *Gotham*, 764.

40. Ibid., 765.

DIVIDED POLICE, DEAD RABBITS, AND THE PANIC OF 1857

1. This vignette is based on Edwin G. Burrows and Mike Wallace, *Gotham: A History of New York City to 1898* (New York: Oxford University Press, 1999), 633–34, 836–51, which is typically excellent. See also Joel Tyler Headley, *The Great Riots of New York, 1712–1873* (New York: Thunder's Mouth Press, 2004), chap. 9.

CHAPTER 6. AMERICA'S DEADLIEST RIOT

1. The *Tribune* is quoted in Edwin G. Burrows and Mike Wallace, *Gotham: A History of New York City to 1898* (New York: Oxford University Press, 1999), 865.

2. Edward K. Spann, *Gotham at War: New York City, 1860–1865* (Wilmington, Del.: Scholarly Resources, 2002), chap. 1; Iver Bernstein, *The New York City Draft Riots: Their Significance for American Society and Politics in the Age of Civil War* (Lincoln: University of Nebraska Press, 1990), pt. 2; Burrows and Wallace, *Gotham*, 864–66.

3. Spann, *Gotham at War*, chap. 2; Burrows and Wallace, *Gotham*, 869–70; Barnet Schecter, *The Devil's Own Work: The Civil War Draft Riots and the Fight to Reconstruct America* (New York: Walker and Company, 2005), 76.

4. Burrows and Wallace, *Gotham*, 872; American Social History Project, *Who Built America?* (New York: Pantheon, 1989), 1:425–26.

5. Spann, *Gotham at War*, chaps. 4 and 5.

6. Burrows and Wallace, *Gotham*, 874–79.

7. Ibid., 883; Kim Hopper, *Reckoning with Homelessness* (Ithaca, N.Y.: Cornell University Press, 2003), chap. 2.

8. Spann, *Gotham at War*, chap. 6; Burrows and Wallace, *Gotham*, 881–82.

9. Spann, *Gotham at War*, 95; Bernstein, *New York City Draft Riots*, 9–10; Schecter, *Devil's Own Work*, chap. 6.

10. Burrows and Wallace, *Gotham*, 884.

11. Spann, *Gotham at War*, 96; American Social History Project, *Who Built America?*, 1:446–47; Bernstein, *New York City Draft Riots*, 11.

12. Burrows and Wallace, *Gotham*, 886–87.

13. Ibid., 888; Schecter, *Devil's Own Work*, 114.

14. Bernstein, *New York City Draft Riots*, 13–14; Schecter, *Devil's Own Work*, 120–21; Spann, *Gotham at War*, 98; Burrows and Wallace, *Gotham*, 888.

15. The following account is pieced together from the sources already cited and from Joel Tyler Headley, *The Great Riots of New York, 1712–1873* (New York: Thunder's Mouth Press, 2004).

16. Something of the ferocity of the attacks can be gleaned from the remembrance of Maritcha Lyons in Kenneth T. Jackson and David S. Dunbar, eds., *Empire City: New York through the Ages* (New York: Columbia University Press, 2002), 265–66. The full typescript of her remembrances is available in the Schomberg Library in Harlem.

17. Iver Bernstein devotes much of *The New York City Draft Riots* to dissecting the specific class and ethnic divisions of the rioters, showing distinct differences in involvement and approach among common laborers, industrial workers, Irish, Germans, and others.

18. Reprinted in Jackson and Dunbar, *Empire City*, 266. Headley, *Great Riots of New York*, 207–11, provides a grisly contemporaneous account of a number of the murders of African Americans.

19. In *The Devil's Own Work*, 219, 251, Barnet Schecter points out that as many as ninety people were killed in just two Wednesday-afternoon battles alone; he suggests that the number of deaths was probably closer to five hundred. Spann, *Gotham at War*, 101, suggests the total was between 120 and 150. Bernstein,

New York City Draft Riots, 5, puts the number at "at least" 105 and suggests that numbers much higher than that are not particularly credible. But in turn, it seems incredible to count only those bodies fully recovered and clearly identified.

20. The *Christian Reporter* is reprinted in Jackson and Dunbar, *Empire City*, 266. See also Burrows and Wallace, *Gotham*, 897; Schecter, *Devil's Own Work*, 265–66.

21. Burrows and Wallace, *Gotham*, 896.

22. Schecter, *Devil's Own Work*, 237–38.

23. Ibid., 303–4.

24. Burrows and Wallace, *Gotham*, chap. 52; Bernstein, *New York City Draft Riots*, 187–88, 195.

THE ORANGE RIOTS, 1871

1. Iver Bernstein, *The New York City Draft Riots: Their Significance for American Society and Politics in the Age of Civil War* (Lincoln: University of Nebraska Press, 1990), chap. 6; Edwin G. Burrows and Mike Wallace, *Gotham: A History of New York City to 1898* (New York: Oxford University Press, 1999), 1002–4; David Harvey, *Paris: Capital of Modernity* (New York: Routledge, 2005).

2. On the Ribbonmen in North America, see Jacob Shell, *Transportation and Revolt: Pigeons, Mules, Canals, and the Vanishing Geography of Subversive Mobility* (Cambridge, Mass.: MIT Press, 2015), 95–101.

3. Burrows and Wallace, *Gotham*, 1004–5.

4. Joel Tyler Headley, *The Great Riots of New York, 1712–1873* (New York: Thunder's Mouth Press), 226–33; Burrows and Wallace, *Gotham*, 1007–8.

5. Burrows and Wallace, *Gotham*, 1008; Bernstein, *New York City Draft Riots*, 232.

6. Burrows and Wallace, *Gotham*, 1009–11.

CHAPTER 7. "A RIOT IS NOW IN PROGRESS IN TOMPKINS SQUARE PARK," 1874

1. Philip S. Foner, *History of the Labor Movement in the United States*, vol. 1: *From Colonial Times to the Founding of the American Federation of Labor* (New York: International Publishers, 1947), 442–43; Tim Cresswell, *The Tramp in America* (London: Reaktion Books, 2001).

2. Iver Bernstein, *The New York City Draft Riots: Their Significance for American Society and Politics in the Age of Civil War* (Lincoln: University of Nebraska Press, 1990), 246–55; Edwin G.

Burrows and Mike Wallace, *Gotham: A History of New York City to 1898* (New York: Oxford University Press, 1999), 1012–13.

3. Cited in Herbert Gutman, "The Tompkins Square 'Riot' in New York City on January 13, 1874: A Re-examination of Its Causes and Aftermath," *Labor History* 6 (1965): 44–70. This chapter draws heavily on Gutman's definitive reconstruction. See also Marilynn S. Johnson, *Street Justice: A History of Police Violence in New York City* (Boston: Beacon Press, 2003).

4. Gutman, "Tompkins Square 'Riot'"; Burrows and Wallace, *Gotham*, 1024–25.

5. Foner, *History of the Labor Movement*, 239–40; Neil Smith, "Tompkins Square Timeline," in *New York City Tableaux: Tompkins Square* (New York: Exit Art, 1990), 14–20.

6. Gutman, "Tompkins Square 'Riot,'" 54–55; Foner, *History of the Labor Movement*, 448.

7. Samuel Gompers, *Seventy Years of Life and Labor* (New York: E. P. Dutton and Co., 1925), 1:93; Burrows and Wallace, *Gotham*, 1025.

8. Gutman, "Tompkins Square 'Riot,'" 61.

9. Burrows and Wallace, *Gotham*, 1026; Gutman, "Tompkins Square 'Riot.'"

10. Swinton's testimony was reprinted as the pamphlet *The Tompkins Square Outrage: Appeal of John Swinton, Addressed to the Legislature . . .* (Albany, 1874); Gutman, "Tompkins Square 'Riot,'" 65.

11. Burrows and Wallace, *Gotham*, 1025–26; Gutman, "Tompkins Square 'Riot,'" 66.

12. Burrows and Wallace, *Gotham*, 1026–27; Foner, *History of the Labor Movement*, 448.

13. *New York Times*, December 12, 1873.

14. American Social History Project, *Who Built America?* (New York: Pantheon, 1989), 1:553–58; Foner, *History of the Labor Movement*; Richard White, *Railroaded: The Transcontinentals and the Making of Modern America* (New York: W. W. Norton, 2011).

15. *Times* quoted in Foner, *History of the Labor Movement*, 470–71; *Tribune* quoted in Burrows and Wallace, *Gotham*, 1036. See also Robert V. Bruce, *1877: Year of Violence* (Chicago: Bobbs-Merrill, 1959), 227–28, 280–81.

16. Burrows and Wallace, *Gotham*, 1036–37; Lisa Keller, *The Triumph of Order: Democracy and Public Space in New York and London* (New York: Columbia University Press, 2009), 190–201.

17. Gompers, *Seventy Years*, 96.

18. Keller, *Triumph of Order*, 180.

CHAPTER 8. A NEW URBAN ORDER

1. Scott Molloy, "Trolley Wars," in *The Encyclopedia of Strikes in American History*, ed. Aaron Brenner, Benjamin Day, and Immanuel Ness (New York: Routledge, 2009), https://login.libezproxy2.syr.edu/login?url=http://search.credoreference.com/content/entry/sharpestrikes/trolley_wars/0?institutionId=499.

2. Edwin G. Burrows and Mike Wallace, *Gotham: A History of New York City to 1898* (New York: Oxford University Press, 1999), 1095–96; *Appleton's Annual Cyclopedia and Register of Important Events of the Year 1887*, n.s. (New York: D. Appleton and Co., 1889), 12:748; Sarah M. Henry, "The Strikers and Their Sympathizers: Brooklyn in the Trolley Strike of 1895," *Labor History* 32 (1991): 329–53, 331.

3. The following account relies particularly on Henry, "Strikers and Their Sympathizers."

4. Lisa Keller, *The Triumph of Order: Democracy and Public Space in New York and London* (New York: Columbia University Press, 2009), 203–5.

5. Burrows and Wallace, *Gotham*, 1194–96.

6. Ibid., 1200–1203; Marilynn S. Johnson, *Street Justice: A History of Police Violence in New York City* (Boston: Beacon, 2003), 56.

CHAPTER 9. "I DID NOTHING WHATEVER TO JUSTIFY THIS BRUTAL ASSAULT UPON ME"

1. *The People v. Arthur J. Harris*, October 29, 1900, transcript and summary of the trial in the New York City Magistrate Court, quoted in Gilbert Osofsky, *Harlem: The Making of a Ghetto*, 2nd ed. (New York: Harper and Row, 1971), 47; see also Osofsky, "Race Riot, 1900: A Study of Ethnic Violence," *Journal of Negro Education* 32 (1963): 16–24; Marilynn S. Johnson, *Street Justice: A History of Police Violence in New York City* (Boston: Beacon Press, 2003), 57–69.

2. *New York Times*, October 26, 1900, 14.

3. Osofsky, "Race Riot, 1900," 16.

4. On the infamous and eventually very wealthy Clubber Williams, see Johnson, *Street Justice*, chap. 1; Edwin G. Burrows and Mike Wallace, *Gotham: A History of New York City to 1898* (New York: Oxford University Press, 1999), 998–99, 1201.

5. Jervis Anderson, *This Was Harlem, 1900–1950* (New York: Farrar, Strauss and Giroux, 1981), 7–8; Paul Lawrence Dunbar, *The Sport of the Gods* (New York: Dodd, Mead and Company, 1902).

6. Timothy Gilfoyle, *City of Eros: New York City, Prostitution, and the Commercialization of Sex, 1790–1920* (New York: W. W. Norton, 1992), 203–10, quotation from 209; Keven J. Mumford, *Interzones: Black/White Sex Districts in Chicago and New York in the Early Twentieth Century* (New York: Columbia University Press, 1997), 16; Thomas Sugrue, *The Origins of the Urban Crisis: Race and Equality in Postwar Detroit* (Princeton, N.J.: Princeton University Press, 1996), 8.

7. The Police Board official report came down on the side of the account in the *Sun*, the *Times*, and the *World*; see Osofsky, "Race Riot, 1900," 20.

8. "Negro Hunt by 10,000 Persons on Broadway," *New York World*, August 16, 1900, 1; "Many Persons Wounded, but One Fatally hurt," *Brooklyn Daily Eagle*, August 16, 1900, 14. See Citizens' Protective League, *The Story of the Riot* (New York: Citizens' Protective League, 1900), which presents a series of affidavits from witnesses and victims attesting to police brutality and mob violence.

9. "Clubbed by Police, Not Protected," *New York World*, August 18, 1900, 2.

10. "Negro Hunt," 2.

11. "Asks Why So Few Whites Are Arrested," *New York World*, August 17, 1900, 2.

12. Johnson, *Street Justice*, 61.

13. Seth M. Scheiner, *Negro Mecca: A History of the Negro in New York City, 1865–1920* (New York: New York University Press, 1965), 126.

14. Osofsky, *Harlem*, 51.

15. The Malby Law is quoted in Evan Friss, "Blacks, Jews, and Civil Rights in New York, 1895–1913," *Journal of American Ethnic History* 24, no. 4 (2005): 70–99, 73; for the 1900 legislation, see Frederick M. Binder and David M. Reimers, *All the Nations under Heaven: An Ethnic and Racial History of New York City* (New York: Columbia University Press, 1995), 110.

16. "Israel Ludlow Injured in Fall of Aeroplane," *New York Times*, April 15, 1906; Johnson, *Street Justice*, 63.

17. "Looking into Race Riots," *New York Times*, September 8, 1900, 7.

18. Letter reprinted in Citizens' Protective League, *Story of the Riot*, inside cover.

19. Quoted in Osofsky, *Harlem*, 50.

20. Quoted in N. G. Gonzalez, "People in Glass Houses, &c.," *World*, August 17, 1900, 2.

21. Anderson, *This Was Harlem*; Osofsky, *Harlem*; Claude McKay, *Harlem: Negro Metropolis* (New York: E. P. Dutton, 1940); Allon Schoener, ed., *Harlem on My Mind: Cultural Capital of Black America, 1900–1968* (New York: Random House, 1968).

THE "POLICE POGROM," 1902

1. This vignette relies on Marilynn S. Johnson, *Street Justice: A History of Police Violence in New York City* (Boston: Beacon Press, 2003), 69–80; see also Leonard Dinnerstein, *Uneasy at Home* (New York: Columbia University Press, 1987).

2. *Jewish Daily Forward*, July 31, August 3, August 13, 1902; Johnson, *Street Justice*, 72.

3. Quoted in Johnson, *Street Justice*, 80.

THE UPRISING OF THE TWENTY THOUSAND, 1909–1911

The epigraph comes from a quote in Françoise Basch, "The Shirtwaist Strike in History and Myth," in *The Diary of a Shirtwaist Striker*, ed. Theresa Serber Malkiel (Ithaca, N.Y.: ILR Press, 1990), 3–77, 29.

1. On the WTUL, see Meredith Tax, *The Rising of the Women: Feminist Solidarity and Class Conflict, 1880–1917* (New York: Monthly Review Press, 1980), chap. 5.

2. Ibid., 208–9.

3. Ibid., 211–14; on striking as violence, see Don Mitchell, *The Right to the City: Social Justice and the Fight for Public Space* (New York: Guilford, 2003), 54–55.

4. *The Souvenir History of the Strike* (New York: Ladies' Waist and Dressmakers' Union, 1910), 12, quoted in Basch, "Shirtwaist Strike," 31.

5. Tax, *Rising of the Women*, 217–18.

6. Ibid., 219–20; Richard A. Greenwald, *The Triangle Fire, the Protocols of Peace, and Industrial Democracy in Progressive Era New York* (Philadelphia: Temple University Press, 2005), 33.

7. Tax, *Rising of the Women*, 226–27.

8. Greenwald, *Triangle Fire*, 47.

9. Quoted in Tax, *Rising of the Women*, 240.

BOMBS AND BOATMEN

1. Sam Roberts, "100 Years Later, Scar Remains from Strike's Fatal Legacy in Manhattan," *New York Times*, July 3, 2014, A17; Thai Jones, *More Powerful Than Dynamite: Radicals, Plutocrats, Progressives, and New York's Year of Anarchy* (New York: Walker and Co., 2012), 236–40.

2. Jacob Shell, *Transportation and Revolt: Pigeons, Mules, Canals, and the Vanishing Geographies of Subversive Mobility* (Cambridge, Mass.: MIT Press, 2015), 140; Beverly Gage, *The Day Wall Street Exploded: A Story of America in Its First Age of Terror* (New York: Oxford University Press, 2009), 104–5.

3. Shell, *Transportation and Revolt*, 129–30.

4. Ibid., 134–35. The journalist Jules Witcover tells a slightly different version of the events around this time in *Sabotage at Black Tom* (Chapel Hill: Algonquin Books, 1989).

5. Witcover, *Sabotage*, 16–17; Shell, *Transportation and Revolt*, 141.

6. Gage, *Day Wall Street Exploded*, 110–13, 115.

7. Mike Davis, *Buda's Bomb: A Brief History of the Car Bomb* (New York: Verso, 2007), 1–3; Gage, *Day Wall Street Exploded*, 1–3.

8. Paul Avrich, *Sacco and Vanzetti: The Anarchist Background* (Princeton, N.J.: Princeton University Press, 1991); Gage, *Day Wall Street Exploded*, 325–26; Shell, *Transportation and Revolt*, 141.

9. Shell, *Transportation and Revolt*, 128.

10. Ibid., 142–48.

"WOMEN IN BREAD RIOT AT DOORS OF CITY HALL," 1917

1. This vignette relies on William Frieburger, "War Prosperity and Hunger: The New York Food Riots of 1917," *Labor History* 25 (1984): 218–39.

2. *New York Times*, February 20, 1917, 1, quoted in ibid., 220.

CHAPTER 10. THE CHILDREN'S CRUSADE

1. "1,000 Pupils in Riot against Gary Plan," *New York Times*, October 17, 1917.

2. Raymond E. Callahan, *Education and the Cult of Efficiency: A Study of the Social Forces That Have Shaped the Administration of Public Schools* (Chicago: University of Chicago Press, 1962), 129.

3. John Dewey, *Schools of Tomorrow* (New York: E. P. Dutton and Company, 1915); David Tyack, *The One Best System: A History of American Urban Education* (Cambridge, Mass.: Harvard University Press, 1974).

4. Ronald D. Cohen and Raymond A. Mohl, *The Paradox of Progressive Education: The Gary Plan and Urban Schooling* (Port Washington, N.Y.: Kennikat Press, 1979), 4, 12.

5. Ibid., 11–12.

6. Randolph S. Bourne, *The Gary Schools* (Boston: Houghton Mifflin, 1916), 14, 17.

7. Cohen and Mohl, *Paradox of Progressive Education*, 37.

8. Diane Ravitch, *The Great School Wars: A History of the New York City Public Schools* (Baltimore, Md.: Johns Hopkins University Press, 1974), 204, 210; Cohen and Mohl, *Paradox of Progressive Education*, 40.

9. "Gary Plan Vicious, Dr. W. M. Hess Says," *New York Times*, October 18, 1915; *New York Times*, November 13, 1915; Ravitch, *Great School Wars*, 204.

10. Quoted in Tyack, *One Best System*, 250–51, citing Selma C. Berrol, *Immigrants at School: New York City, 1898–1914* (New York: Arno Press, 1967).

11. Cohen and Mohl, *Paradox of Progressive Education*, 46–47.

12. Sol Cohen, *Progressives and Urban School Reform: The Public Education Association of New York City, 1895–1954* (New York: Publications Bureau, Teachers College, Columbia University Press, 1963), 1, 89; Cohen and Mohl, *Paradox of Progressive Education*, 42, 49.

13. Cohen and Mohl, *Paradox of Progressive Education*, 50–52.

14. "1,000 Pupils in Riot."

15. "Policemen Stoned by School Children," *New York Times*, October 19, 1917; "Schools Are Stoned as Rioting Spreads," *New York Times*, October 20, 1917.

16. Cohen and Mohl, *Paradox of Progressive Education*, 59; Ravitch, *Great School Wars*, 225; "1,000 Pupils in Riot"; "Hylan Evades Query about Gary System," *New York Times*, October 21, 1917.

17. Cohen and Mohl, *Paradox of Progressive Education*, 59; Dewey quoted in Cohen, *Progressives and Urban School Reform*, 99.

18. Daine Ravitch, *Left Back: A Century of Battles over School Reforms* (New York: New York: Simon and Schuster, 2000), 175; first quotation from Cohen and Mohl, *Paradox of Progressive Education*, 59.

CHAPTER 11. "FIGHT, DON'T STARVE!"

1. Nathan Glazer, *The Social Basis of American Communism* (New York: Harcourt, Brace and World, 1961), 116, 172.

2. Irving Howe and Lewis Coser, *The American Communist Party: A Critical History* (New York: Praeger, 1962), 178–79, 181.

3. Robin D. G. Kelley, *Freedom Dreams: The Black Radical Imagination* (Boston: Beacon Press, 2002), 47–49; Kelley, *Race Rebels: Culture, Politics, and the Black Working Class* (New York: Free Press, 1994), 109; Comintern, "1928 Resolution on the Black National Question in the United States," and "1930 Comintern Resolution on the Black National Question in the United States," both at http://www.marx2mao.com/Other/CR75.html.

4. Victor G. Divinatz, "A Reevaluation of the Trade Union Unity League, 1929–1934," *Science and Society* 71 (2007): 33–58.

5. Ibid., 38–41.

6. Ibid., 47–49.

7. See Judith Stepan-Norris and Maurice Zeitlin, *Left Out: Reds and America's Industrial Unions* (New York: Columbia University Press, 2003).

8. Francis Fox Piven and Richard Cloward, *Poor People's Movements: Why They Succeed, How They Fail* (New York: Vintage Books, 1977), 68.

9. Howe and Coser, *American Communist Party*, 193; *Times* quoted in Piven and Cloward, *Poor People's Movements*, 51; Rick Beard, ed., *On Being Homeless: Historical Perspectives* (New York: Museum of the City of New York, 1987).

10. Robert Fisher, *Let the People Decide: Neighborhood Organizing in America* (New York: Twayne Publishers, 1994), 40–41; Daniel Leab, "'United We Eat': The Creation and Organization of the Unemployed Councils in 1930," in *The Labor History Reader*, ed. D. Leab (Urbana: University of Illinois Press, 1985), 320.

11. Mark Naison, *Communists in Harlem during the Depression* (Urbana: University of Illinois Press, 1983); Piven and Cloward, *Poor People's Movements*, 58.

12. Fisher, *Let the People Decide*, 44; Piven and Cloward, *Poor People's Movements*, 134.

13. Naison, *Communists in Harlem*, 134.

14. Piven and Cloward, *Poor People's Movements*, 66–85.

15. Mark Naison, "From Eviction Resistance to Rent Control: Tenant Activism in the Great Depression," in *The Tenant Movement in New York City, 1904–1984*, ed. R. Lawson (New Brunswick, N.J.: Rutgers University Press, 1986), online version at https://libcom.org/history/chapter-3-eviction-resistance-rent-control-tenant-activism-great-depression.

16. Ibid., 101.

17. This and the next paragraph are based on ibid., 102–10.

18. Ibid., 110–12.

19. Van Gosse, "'To Organize in Every Neighborhood, Every Home': The Gender Politics of American Communists between the Wars," *Radical History Review* 50 (1991): 125–34.

20. Activist quoted in Naison, "From Eviction Resistance," 108; Annelise Orleck, "'We Are That Mythical Thing Called the Public':

Militant Housewives during the Great Depression," *Feminist Studies* 19 (1993): 147–72, 149.

21. Orleck, "'We Are That Mythical Thing,'" 158; Annelise Orleck, *Common Sense and a Little Fire: Women and Working-Class Politics in the United States, 1900–1965* (Chapel Hill: University of North Carolina Press, 1995), 228.

22. Orleck, "'We Are That Mythical Thing,'" 160.

23. Quoted in Naison, *Communists in Harlem*, 149.

24. Quoted in Naison, "From Eviction Resistance."

25. Earl Ofari Hutchinson, *Blacks and Reds: Race and Class in Conflict, 1931–1990* (East Lansing: Michigan State University Press, 1995), 69; Naison, *Communists in Harlem*, 84–88, 104; John A. Wagner, "Harlem (New York) Riot of 1935," in *Encyclopedia of American Race Riots*, ed. Walter C. Rucker and James N. Upton (Westport, Conn.: Greenwood Publishing, 2007), 1:265.

26. Fisher, *Let the People Decide*, 44–46; Kelley, *Freedom Dreams*, 47–51.

27. Hutchinson, *Blacks and Reds*, 63–65; Naison, *Communists in Harlem*, 137.

28. Howe and Coser, *The American Communist Party*, 230.

29. Fisher, *Let the People Decide*, 50; Orleck, *Common Sense*, 241.

30. Stepen-Norris and Zeitlin, *Left Out*, 286–89; Hutchinson, *Blacks and Reds*, 137–55, 179–91.

CHAPTER 12. THE HARLEM RIOTS, 1935, 1943, AND 1964

1. "Rages: Mischief out of Mystery," *Time Magazine*, April 1, 1935; Mayor's Commission on Conditions in Harlem, *The Negro in Harlem: A Report on Social and Economic Conditions Responsible for the Outbreak of March 19, 1935* (New York: Municipal Archives of New York City, 1936); "Complete Riot Report Bared: Report Mayor Hid Complete in This Issue; *Amsterdam News* Is First to Public Harlem Study," *New York Amsterdam News*, July 18, 1936. Generally, see Neil A. Wynn, "Harlem Race Riot, 1935," in *Historical Dictionary of the Roosevelt-Truman Era*, vol. 10 (Lanham, Md.: Rowman and Littlefield, 2008); John A. Wagner, "Harlem (New York) Riot of 1935," in *Encyclopedia of American Race Riots*, ed. Walter C. Rucker and James N. Upton (Westport, Conn.: Greenwood Publishing, 2007), 1:265.

2. "Rages"; Mayor's Commission, *Negro in Harlem*, 2.

3. Mayor's Commission, *Negro in Harlem*, 1–2; Wagner, "Harlem," 266.

4. Mayor's Commission, *Negro in Harlem*, 3–4.

5. "Rages"; Mayor's Commission, *Negro in Harlem*, 1–3, 6–7.

6. "Rages."

7. Ibid.; Mayor's Commission, *Negro in Harlem*, 8–10; Cheryl Lynn Greenberg, *"Or Does It Explode?": Black Harlem in the Great Depression* (New York: Oxford University Press, 1991), 4; Wynn, "Harlem Race Riot," 191.

8. Alain Locke, "Harlem: Dark Weather-Vane," *Survey Graphic* 25, no. 8 (August 1936): 457.

9. "Rages"; Wagner, "Harlem," 266–67.

10. Mayor's Commission, *Negro in Harlem*, chap. 5; "Rages."

11. Mayor's Commission, *Negro in Harlem*, chap. 5.

12. Ibid.

13. Wagner, "Harlem," 265; "Rages"; Greenberg, *"Or Does It Explode?,"* 5.

14. Locke, "Harlem," 457.

15. Mayor's Commission, *Negro in Harlem*, 5; Greenberg, *"Or Does It Explode?"*; Wagner, "Harlem," 265–67.

16. Greenberg, *"Or Does It Explode?,"* 6, 221–22; Wagner, "Harlem," 265–67.

17. "Harlem's Tragedy," *New York Times*, August 3, 1943, 18; Betty Nyangoni, "New York City Riot of 1943," in Rucker and Upton, *Encyclopedia of American Race Riots*, 476–77; Dominic Capeci, *The Harlem Riot of 1943* (Philadelphia: Temple University Press, 1977), 99; Nat Brandt, *Harlem at War: The Black Experience in WWII* (Syracuse, N.Y.: Syracuse University Press, 1996), 183.

18. Greenberg, *"Or Does It Explode?,"* chap. 8; Turner Catledge Washington, "Behind Our Menacing Race Problem: In the Dissensions between Whites and Negroes Lie Deep-Rooted Forces That Grow in Complexity," *New York Times*, August 8, 1943, SM7; Nyangoni, "New York City," 433; Thomas Sugrue, *The Origins of the Urban Crisis* (Princeton, N.J.: Princeton University Press, 1996); Dominic Capeci and Martha Wilkerson, *Layered Violence: The Detroit Rioters of 1943* (Jackson: University Press of Mississippi, 1991).

19. Brandt, *Harlem at War*, 183–84; Nyangoni, "New York City," 478; Capeci, *Harlem Riot*, chap. 6.

20. Brandt, *Harlem at War*, 184–85; Capeci, *Harlem Riot*, chap. 6.

21. Capeci, *Harlem Riot*, 100; Brandt, *Harlem at War*, 184–85; Wynn, "Harlem Race Riot," 191.

22. Gordon Allport and Leo Postman, *The Psychology of Rumor* (New York: Henry Holt and Company, 1947), 193–96; Capeci, *Harlem Riot*, chap. 6; Brandt, *Harlem at War*, 185–86; Nyangoni, "New York City," 476.

23. [James Baldwin], "Harlem Hoodlums," *Newsweek*, August 9, 1943; Nyangoni, "New York City," 476–77; Brandt, *Harlem at War*, 187.

24. [Baldwin], "Harlem Hoodlums"; Brandt, *Harlem at War*, 188, 197, 207; Nyangoni, "New York City," 477.

25. Capeci, *Harlem Riot*, 102–8; Brandt, *Harlem at War*, 195–97, 207; Nyangoni, "New York City," 477; Wynn, "Harlem Race Riot," 191.

26. Washington, "Behind Our Menacing Race Problem"; "Race Bias Denied as Rioting Factor," *New York Times*, August 3, 1943, 11; "Harlem's Tragedy," *New York Times*, August 3, 1943, 18; "No Time for Complacency," *New York Times*, August 4, 1943, 16; Marilynn S. Johnson, *Street Justice: A History of Police Violence in New York City* (Boston: Beacon Press, 2003), 200–201.

27. "Harlem's Tragedy"; "No Time for Complacency"; "Race Bias Denied."

28. "Harlem's Tragedy," 18.

29. "No Time for Complacency"; "Race Bias Denied."

30. Nyangoni, "New York City," 477; Fiorello H. La Guardia, "Announcement of the Formation of the Mayor's Committee on Unity," Municipal Archives of New York City, 1944; Charles E. Hughes, "Mayor's Committee on Unity: Statement of Charles E. Hughes, Jr., Chairman," Municipal Archives of New York City, March 6, 1944; David J. Hogan, ed., *Civil Rights Chronicle: The African-American Struggle for Freedom* (Lincolnwood, Ill.: Publications International, Ltd., 2003); Johnson, *Street Justice*, 202–3.

31. Johnson, *Street Justice*, chap. 6.

32. Ibid., 229–31.

33. Ibid., 231–34.

34. Theodore Jones, "Negro Boy Killed; 300 Harass Police: Teen-Agers Hurl Cans and Bottles after Shooting by Off-Duty Officer," *New York Times*, July 17, 1964, 31.

35. Jones, "Negro Boy Killed."

36. Ibid.

37. Ibid.

38. Shatema A. Threadcraft, "New York City Riot of 1964," in Rucker and Upton, *Encyclopedia of American Race Riots*, 478–79; Paul L. Montgomery and Francis X. Clines, "Thousands Riot in Harlem Area; Scores Are Hurt: Negroes Loot Stores, Taunt Whites—Police Shoot Air to Control Crowd," *New York Times*, July 19, 1964, 1, 54.

39. Montgomery and Clines, "Thousands Riot."

40. Ibid.; R. W. Apple Jr., "Violence Flares Again in Harlem; Restraint Urged: 19 Hurt in New Outbreaks near Scene of the Funeral for Boy Who Was Slain," *New York Times*, July 20, 1964, 1, 16.

41. Apple, "Violence Flares Again"; Threadcraft, "New York City Riot," 479.

42. J. Linn Allen, "Freedom of Speech Seen Also on Trial in Harlem Riot Case," *Baltimore Afro-American*, December 21, 1965, B11; "Epton Gets a Year on Riot Conviction," *Baltimore Afro-American*, February 5, 1966, 12. The Epton case is analyzed in relation to the historical geography of radical free speech in Don Mitchell, "The Liberalization of Free Speech: Or, How Protest in Public Space Is Silenced," *Stanford Agora* 4 (2003), http://agora.stanford.edu/agora/volume4/mitchell.shtml.

43. "Verdict in Harlem," *New York Times*, September 2, 1964; David Halberstram, "Report on Gilligan Assailed by CORE," *New York Times*, September 3, 1964, 1, 19; Johnson, *Street Justice*, 236–37.

44. Joe R. Feagin and Paul B. Sheatsley, "Ghetto Resident Appraisals of a Riot," *Public Opinion Quarterly* 32 (1968): 352–62; Clay Risin, "The Night New York Avoided a Riot," *Morning News*, n.d., http://www.themorningnews.org/article/the-night-new-york-avoided-a-riot.

45. Neil Smith, *The New Urban Frontier: Gentrification and the Revanchist City* (New York: Routledge, 1996), 143.

46. Michael W. Flamm, "The Original Long, Hot Summer: The Legacy of the 1964 Harlem Riot," *New York Times*, July 15, 2014.

THE EAST HARLEM ANTIPOLICE RIOT, 1967—AND THE YOUNG LORDS

1. This and the next paragraph are based on Homer Bigart, "Disorders Erupt in East Harlem; Mob Dispersed: 1,000 Police Rush In to End Melee—Eight Shots Fired on 111th Street," *New York Times*, July 24, 1967; Vincent Cannato, *The Ungovernable City: John Lindsay and His Struggle to Save New York* (New York: Basic Books, 2001), 132–33.

2. Homer Bigart, "2 Killed, 12 Hurt in Violence Here: Disturbance Worse since 1964—Rioters Set Cars Afire and Loot Stores," *New York Times*, July 25, 1967; Bigart, "Looters Invade Midtown; East Harlem Stays Calm," *New York Times*, July 27, 1967; Cannato, *Ungovernable City*, 134–35.

3. Bigart, "Looters Invade Midtown"; Homer Bigart, "Renewed Violence Erupts in 2 Puerto Rican Areas," *New York Times*, July 26, 1967; McCandlish Phillips, "Police in Ghetto to Speak Spanish," *New York Times*, July 29, 1967; "Mayor Hears Angry Pleas in

Brooklyn Ghetto Walk: Negroes Shout Demands," *New York Times*, July 30, 1967.

4. McCandlish Phillips, "Residents of East Harlem Found to Have Ingredients for Violence," *New York Times*, July 27, 1967; Phillips, "Police in Ghetto"; Peter Kihss, "Puerto Rican Story: A Sensitive People Erupt," *New York Times*, July 26, 1967; Deirdre Carmody, "East 96th: Wall between Worlds; Street Reflects Dichotomy of Yorkville-East Harlem," *New York Times*, July 27, 1967.

5. Matthew Gandy, *Concrete and Clay: Reworking Nature in New York City* (Cambridge, Mass.: MIT Press, 2002), 154–62; Phillips, "Residents in East Harlem."

6. This and the next three paragraphs are based on Gandy, *Concrete and Clay*, chap. 4.

"WE WANT THE WORLD AND WE WANT IT NOW"

1. The literature on Columbia is vast. Classic accounts of the Columbia events include Jerry Avorn, ed., *Up against the Ivy Wall: A History of the Columbia Crisis* (New York: Atheneum Press, 1969); Cox Commission, *Crisis at Columbia: Report of the Fact-Finding Commission Appointed to Investigate the Disturbances at Columbia University in April and May, 1968* (New York: Vintage, 1968); James Kunen, *The Strawberry Statement: Notes of a College Revolutionary* (New York: Random House, 1969). An excellent online exhibit from the Columbia University archives can be found at https://exhibitions.cul.columbia.edu/exhibits/show/1968.

2. Stefan M. Bradley, *Harlem vs. Columbia University: Black Student Power in the late 1960s* (Urbana: University of Illinois Press, 2009) provides the fullest account of black student activism and its relation to both the university and the community.

3. George Keller, "Six Weeks That Shook Morningside," *Columbia College Today*, Spring 1969.

4. See Todd Gitlin, *The Sixties: Years of Hope, Days of Rage* (New York: Bantam, 1993), 304; Marilynn S. Johnson, *Street Justice: A History of Police Violence in New York City* (Boston: Beacon, 2003), 264–65.

TEACHERS' STRIKE OR ARMAGEDDON?

1. Most histories of education reform in the United States and many histories of the modern labor movement cover this episode. The standard histories are Martin Mayer, *The Teachers Strike New York, 1968* (New York: Harper and Rowe, 1969); Barbara Carter, *Pickets, Parents, and Power: The Story behind the New York City*

Teachers' Strike (New York: Citation Press, 1971); and Jerald E. Podair, *The Strike That Changed New York: Blacks, Whites, and the Ocean Hill–Brownsville Crisis* (New Haven, Conn.: Yale University Press, 2002). A set of primary documents can be found in Maurice R. Bérubé and Marilyn Gittel, eds., *Confrontation at Ocean Hill–Brownsville* (New York: Praeger, 1969). This vignette relies particularly on the interpretation by Joshua B. Freeman in chap. 13 of *Working Class New York: Life and Labor since World War II* (New York: New Press, 2000). Bill Bunge discusses "sympathetic authority" in relation to schooling in William Bunge et al., "A Report to the Parents of Detroit on School Decentralization," field notes, discussion paper 2, Detroit Geographical Expedition and Institute, 1970, http://freeuniversitynyc.org/files/2012/09/FieldNotesIISchoolDecentralization.pdf.

2. Quoted in Freeman, *Working Class New York*, 221.

3. Ibid., 222–23.

4. Bérubé and Gittel, *Confrontation*, 168; Stephen Brier, "The Ideological and Organizational Origins of the United Federation of Teachers' Opposition to the Community Control Movement in the New York City Public Schools," *Labour / Le Travail* 73 (2014): 179–93, quotation from 181–82. The Lindsay aide Brier quotes was Sid Davidoff; Brier also lays out radical journalist I. F. Stone's similar assessment.

5. Sean Ahearn, review of Podair, *Strike That Changed New York*, *Socialism and Democracy Online*, April 17, 2011, http://sdonline.org/34/the-strike-that-changed-new-york-blacks-whites-and-the-ocean-hill-brownsville-crisis/; Freeman, *Working Class New York*, 226.

6. Freeman, *Working Class New York*, 227.

CHAPTER 13. THE CUNY OPEN ADMISSIONS STRIKE, 1969

1. Peter Kihss, "Building Here Invaded," *New York Times*, February 14, 1969.

2. Conrad Dyer, "Protest and the Politics of Admission: The Impact of the Black and Puerto Rican Student Community (of City College)" (PhD diss., City University of New York, 1990); Allen B. Ballard, *The Education of Black Folk: The Afro-American Struggle for Knowledge in White America* (New York: Harper & Row, 1973), 124; Christopher Gunderson, "The Struggle for CUNY: A History of the CUNY Student Movement, 1969–1999" (New York: William Macauley College, n.d.), 6.

3. Kihss, "Building Here Invaded."

4. Sandra Shoiock Roff, Anthony M. Cucchiara, and Barbara J. Dunlop, *From the Free Academy to CUNY: Illustrating Public Higher Education in NYC, 1847–1997* (New York: Fordham University Press, 2000).

5. Gunderson, "Struggle for CUNY," 6–7.

6. City University of New York, Office of Institutional Research and Assessment, "1967–1968 Data Book," http://cuny.edu/about /administration/offices/ira/ir/data-book/student/1967-1997 .html.

7. Quoted in Murray Schumach, "C.C.N.Y. Shutdown after Blockade by 150 Students," *New York Times*, April 23, 1969.

8. M. A. Farber, "C.C.N.Y. to Close Again, Negroes Agree to Talks," *New York Times*, April 24, 1969.

9. M. A. Farber, "C.C.N.Y. President Orders That Closing Be Continued until Next Tuesday: Gallagher Terms Talks with Dissidents 'Useful,'" *New York Times*, April 25, 1969.

10. Murray Schumach, "700 Engineering Students Ignore C.C.N.Y. Closing," *New York Times*, April 26, 1969.

11. Ibid.; Israel Shenker, "City College Professors Express Their Views on the Campus Shutdown," *New York Times*, April 30, 1969.

12. Edward C. Burks, "C.C.N.Y. to Stay Closed While Talks Continue," *New York Times*, April 29, 1969; David Bird, "Queens Students Occupy Buildings," *New York Times*, April 29, 1969; Bird, "Rebels at Queens College Blockading Main Building," *New York Times*, April 30, 1969.

13. Michael Stern, "Two More Campuses of City U. Closed after Disorders," *New York Times*, May 3, 1969.

14. Thomas F. Brady, "City College Agreement Reached: Settlement Reported by Dr. Gallagher as Court Acts," *New York Times*, May 3, 1969.

15. "C.C.N.Y. Ordered to Reopen Today in Face of Writs," *New York Times*, May 5, 1969; "Statements on Order to Open C.C.N.Y.," *New York Times*, May 5, 1969.

16. Sylvan Fox, "Court Order Ends Blockade by 250 Students," *New York Times*, May 6, 1969.

17. Sylvan Fox, "C.C.N.Y. Open but Tense," *New York Times*, May 7, 1969.

18. Sylvan Fox, "C.C.N.Y. Shut Down, Then Racial Clash Injures 7 Whites," *New York Times*, May 8, 1969; "Dr. Gallagher's Statement," *New York Times*, May 8, 1969; "Seeds of C.C.N.Y. Strife: Frustration on 2 Sides," *New York Times*, May 8, 1969; Thomas A. Johnson, "Whites' Attack at C.C.N.Y. Cited," *New York Times*, May 10, 1969.

19. "One of 5 Demands of C.C.N.Y. Rebels Granted by Board," *New York Times*, May 9, 1969; Emanuel Perlmutter, "100 Students Bar Firemen at Brooklyn College Blaze," *New York Times*, May 7, 1989.

20. Murray Schumacher, "Gallagher Quits; Cites 'Intrusion' in C.C.N.Y. Dispute," *New York Times*, May 10, 1969; "Statement by Gallagher on Resignation," *New York Times*, May 10, 1969; Murray Schumacher, "Copeland Chosen Interim President for City College," *New York Times*, May 11, 1969.

21. "C.C.N.Y. to Resume Its Racial Talks," *New York Times*, May 17, 1969; Francis X. Clines, "Open Enrollment Is Urged for City U.," *New York Times*, May 17, 1969; Murray Schumacher, "Police at C.C.N.Y. Are Withdrawn; Talks Resume," *New York Times*, May 18, 1969; Gunderson, "Struggle for CUNY," 8; David Lavin, Richard Alba, and Richard Silberstein, *Right versus Privilege: The Open Admissions Experiment at City University of New York* (New York: Free Press, 1981), 13.

22. Sylvan Fox, "C.C.N.Y. Reopens and Talks Go On," *New York Times*, May 22, 1969; Murray Schumacher, "Dual Admissions for City College Provided by Pact," *New York Times*, May 24, 1969; Ballard, *Education of Black Folk*, 126.

23. Lavin, Alba, and Silberstein, *Right versus Privilege*, 18; Gunderson, "Struggle for CUNY," 8; Homer Bigart, "C.C.N.Y. Alumni Head Charges Board Is Abetting Black Racism," *New York Times*, November 6, 1969.

CHAPTER 14. "HOMOSEXUALS ARE REVOLTING"

1. The standard histories, which also include the most careful reconstructions of the Stonewall riots, are David Carter, *Stonewall: The Riots That Sparked the Gay Revolution* (New York: St. Martin's Press, 2004); and Martin Duberman, *Stonewall* (New York: Penguin/Plume, 1994). On New York's restrictive dancing laws and how they shape nightlife, see Laam Hae, *The Gentrification of Nightlife and the Right to the City: Regulating the Spaces of Social Dancing in New York* (New York: Routledge, 2012).

2. Carter, *Stonewall*, 82–83; Duberman, *Stonewall*, 187–89.

3. Ronnie Di Brienza, "Stonewall Incident," *East Village Other*, July 9, 1969, 2, quoted in Carter, *Stonewall*, 143, see also 193–95; Duberman, *Stonewall*, 168–69. See also David Bird, "Trees in a

Queens Park Cut Down as Vigilantes Harass Homosexuals," *New York Times*, July 1, 1969.

4. The following account is pieced together primarily from Carter, *Stonewall;* and Duberman, *Stonewall.*

5. The debates about what triggered the riot are rehearsed in Carter, *Stonewall*, 149–252.

6. Rivera is quoted in Leslie Feinberg, "Street Transvestite Action Revolutionaries," *Workers World*, September 24, 2006. *Village Voice* reporter Howard Smith was trapped inside with the cops and published his account a few days later: "Full Moon over the Stonewall," *Village Voice*, July 3, 1969; republished in Tessa Stuart, "Full Moon over the Stonewall: Howard Smith's Account of the Stonewall Riots," *Village Voice*, June 26, 2015, http://www.villagevoice.com/news/full-moon-over-the-stonewall-howard-smiths-account-of-the-stonewall-riots-6704949.

7. Duberman, *Stonewall*, 202; "Four Policemen Hurt in 'Village' Raid: Melee near Sheridan Square Follows Action at Bar," *New York Times*, June 29, 1969.

8. "Four Policemen Hurt"; Dennis Eskow, "3 Cops Hurt as Bar Raid Riles Crowd," *New York Daily News*, June 29, 1969. Duberman, *Stonewall*, 202, says this *Daily News* story was on page 1. That's not true. The page 1 story came later. It was Jerry Lisker, "Homo Nest Raided, Queen Bees Are Stinging Mad," *Daily News*, July 6, 1969.

9. Duberman, *Stonewall*, 203–5; Carter, *Stonewall*, chap. 10; Feinberg, "Street Transvestite Action Revolutionaries."

10. Lillian Faderman and Stuart Timmons, *Gay L.A.: A History of Sexual Outlaws, Power Politics, and Lipstick Lesbians* (New York: Basic Books, 2006).

11. George Chauncey, *Gay New York: Gender, Urban Culture, and the Making of the Gay Male World, 1890–1940* (New York: Basic Books, 1994). Some of the spatial implications of Chauncey's (and others') analysis are laid out in Don Mitchell, *Cultural Geography: A Critical Introduction* (Oxford: Blackwell, 2000), chap. 7.

12. Chauncey, *Gay New York*, 331; see also Michael Brown, *Closet Space: Geographies of Metaphors from the Body to the Globe* (New York: Routledge, 2000).

13. Nicholas Edsall, *Toward Stonewall: Homosexuality and Society in the Modern Western World* (Charlotte: University of Virginia Press, 2003); John D'Emilio, "The Homosexual Menace: The Politics of Sexuality in Cold War America," in *Passion and Power: Sexuality in History*, ed. K. Peiss and C. Simmons (Philadelphia: Temple University Press, 1989), 226–40.

14. Eric Marcus, *Making Gay History* (New York: Harper, 2002); John D'Emilio, *Sexual Politics, Sexual Communities: The Making of a Homosexual Minority in the United States, 1940–1970* (Chicago: University of Chicago Press, 1983).

15. Duberman, *Stonewall*, 102–17; Carter, *Stonewall*, 115–16.

16. Carter, *Stonewall*, 114–25.

17. Marcus, *Making Gay History*, 128; Donn Teal, *The Gay Militants* (New York: St. Martin's Press, 1971), 19.

18. Truscott, "Gay Power"; Smith, "Full Moon."

19. Carter, *Stonewall*, 201–4; Di Brienza, "Stonewall Incident," 2.

20. Carter, *Stonewall*, 213–15.

21. Ibid., 217–18.

22. "About New York; Still Here: Sylvia, Who Survived Stonewall, Time and the River," *New York Times*, May 24, 1995.

THE HARD HAT RIOTS, 1970

1. Penny Lewis, *Hardhats, Hippies, and Hawks: The Vietnam Antiwar Movement as Myth and Memory* (Ithaca, N.Y.: Cornell University Press, 2013), chap. 7; Joshua Freeman, *Working Class New York: Life and Labor since World War II* (New York: New Press, 2000), chap. 14; Linda Charlton, "Some Protests Heckled; Fires Reported at Colleges," *New York Times*, May 9, 1970.

2. Homer Bigart, "War Foes Here Attacked by Construction Workers: City Hall Is Stormed," *New York Times*, May 9, 1970; Martin Arnold, "Police Were Told of Plan," *New York Times*, May 9, 1970; Maurice Carroll, "Police Assailed by Mayor on Laxity at Peace Rally," *New York Times*, May 10, 1970.

3. Homer Bigart, "Thousands in City March to Assail Lindsay on War," *New York Times*, May 16, 1970.

4. Homer Bigart, "Huge City Hall Rally Backs Nixon's Indochina Policies," *New York Times*, May 21, 1970.

5. Homer Bigart, "9 Hurt as Police Disperse Group in Midtown after City Hall Peace Rally," *New York Times*, May 21, 1970.

6. Lewis, *Hardhats, Hippies, and Hawks.*

PEOPLE'S FIREHOUSE #1, 1975–1978

1. Joseph P. Fried, "City's Housing Administrator Proposes 'Planned Shrinkage' of Some Slums," *New York Times*, February 3, 1976; Roger Starr, "Making New York Smaller: The City's Economic Outlook Remains Grim," *New York Times*, November 14, 1975.

2. Roger Starr, *Urban Choices: The City and Its Critics* (Baltimore, Md.: Penguin, 1969), 41–42, 43, 258, quoted in Deborah

Wallace and Roderick Wallace, *A Plague on Your Houses: How New York Was Burned Down and National Public Health Crumbled* (London: Verso, 1998), 24–25. See also Joe Flood, *The Fires: How a Computer Formula Burned Down New York City and Determined the Future of American Cities* (New York: Riverhead Books, 2010); Miriam Greenberg, *Branding New York: How a City in Crisis Was Sold to the World* (New York: Routledge, 2008), 140–44.

3. [Daniel Patrick Moynihan], *The Negro Family: A Case for National Action* (Washington, D.C.: Office of Policy Planning and Research, United States Department of Labor, 1965); "Text of Moynihan Memorandum on the Status of the Negro," *New York Times*, January 30, 1970, 3; Wallace and Wallace, *Plague on Your Houses*, 22.

4. A good brief overview of the fiscal crisis, including how its resolution became a template for "structural adjustment" across the globe, is Joshua Freeman, "If You Can Make It Here: The Resolution of New York City's Fiscal Crisis Became a Template for Neoliberal around the World," *Jacobin* 15/16 (Fall 2014), https://www.jacobinmag.com/2014/10/if-you-can-make-it-here/.

5. Robert E. Thomasson, "City Shuts Down Four Firehouses: 100 Demonstrators Prevent Answering of Last Calls by Brooklyn Company," *New York Times*, November 22, 1975; Ida Susser, *Norman Street: Poverty and Politics in an Urban Neighborhood*, updated ed. (Oxford: Oxford University Press, 2012), 218–25.

6. This and the next paragraphs are based on Susser, *Norman Street*, 225–38.

7. Dena Kleiman, "Reopening of 'People's Firehouse' Is Celebrated," *New York Times*, June 18, 1978; Tara Bahrampour, "Neighborhood Report: Williamsburg; 'The People's Firehouse' Faces Another Fierce Battle of Wills," *New York Times*, April 27, 2003; Michael Wilson, "Developers Picked for 2 Closed Brooklyn Firehouses," *New York Times*, May 3, 2008.

8. On Starr's neoconservativism, see Bruce Lambert, "Roger Starr, New York Planning Official, Author and Editorial Writer, Is Dead at 83," *New York Times*, September 11, 2001; on the rent gap, see Neil Smith, "Toward a Theory of Gentrification: A Back to the City Movement by Capital Not People," *Journal of the American Planning Association* 45 (1979): 538–48; and Smith, *The New Urban Frontier: Gentrification and the Revanchist City* (New York: Routledge, 1996).

CHAPTER 15. BURN, BABY, BURN

1. A vibrant account of the technical and human failures is Jon-athan Mahler, *Ladies and Gentlemen, the Bronx Is Burning: 1977, Baseball, Politics, and the Battle for the Soul of a City* (New York: Picador, 2005), 176–86.

2. Jane Corwin and William Miles, *Impact Assessment of the 1977 New York City Blackout* (Palo Alto, Calif.: Systems Control, Inc., 1978); James Goodman, *Blackout* (New York: North Point, 2005). Much energy was expended in determining Con Edison's culpability for the blackout and ensuing rioting. Besides Corwin and Miles, *Impact Assessment*, see Norman Clapp et al., *New York State Investigation of the New York City Blackout of July 13, 1977* (Albany: The Consultant, 1977).

3. Robert Curvin and Bruce Porter, *Blackout Looting!* (New York: Gardner Press, 1979), 3–4; Mahler, *Ladies and Gentlemen*, 191–192; Goodman, *Blackout*, 38, 47–48.

4. Curvin and Porter, *Blackout Looting!*, 8–9, 27, 30, 41; Mahler, *Ladies and Gentlemen*, 195, 200; "Night of Terror," *Time*, July 25, 1977, 12–26. On demographic change in Bushwick, see John Dereszewski, "Demographic Change in Bushwick in the 1950s–60s," http://www.brooklynhistory.org/upfromflames/uff_path/uff_path_demographic_changes.html.

5. Mahler, *Ladies and Gentlemen*, 197; Goodman, *Blackout*, 60–61; Curvin and Porter, *Blackout Looting!*, 43; Selwyn Raab, "Ravage Continues Far into the Day; Gunfire and Bottles Beset Police," *New York Times*, July 15, 1977.

6. Curvin and Porter, *Blackout Looting!*, 49–51.

7. Raab, "Ravage Continues"; Curvin and Porter, *Blackout Looting!*, 52–53; Goodman, *Blackout*, 84, 86, 96, 100; Ernest Wohlenberg, "The 'Geography of Civility' Revisited: New York Blackout Looting, 1977," *Economic Geography* 58 (1982): 20–28.

8. Robert D. McFadden, "'Disaster' Status Given New York and Westchester to Speed Loans; Services Resume after Blackout," *New York Times*, July 16, 1977; Fred Ferretti, "New York Is Rebuffed by U.S. on Blackout but Gets Local Aid," *New York Times*, July 19, 1977; Mahler, *Ladies and Gentlemen*, 225.

9. Goodman, *Blackout*, provides a broad sampling of arguments from those taking part in the looting (and justifying it as a chance to take what was rightfully theirs) to those—from neighbors to cops to politicians—who saw the rioting as the work of animals.

10. Paul Delaney, "Bushwick: Nothing to Lose," *New York Times*, July 24, 1977; Curvin and Porter, *Blackout Looting!*, 136; Goodman, *Blackout*, 83, 104.

11. Mahler, *Ladies and Gentlemen*, 224; Adam J. Schwartz, "Public Disinvestment: Planned Shrinkage," http://www

.brooklynhistory.org/upfromflames/uff_path/uff_path_shrinkage .html; Deborah Wallace and Roderick Wallace, *A Plague on Your Houses: How New York Was Burned Down and National Public Health Crumbled* (London: Verso, 1998), 40; Curvin and Porter, *Blackout Looting!*, chap. 9.

12. Quoted in Adam Schwartz, "Private Disinvestment: Real Estate Follies," http://www.brooklynhistory.org/upfromflames /uff_path/uff_path_divestment.html.

13. Curvin and Porter, *Blackout Looting!*, 47; Harold Rose, *The Black Ghetto: A Spatial Behavioral Perspective* (New York: McGraw Hill, 1971); Richard Boeth, "The Plunderers," *Newsweek*, July 25, 1977, 23–27; Goodman, *Blackout*, 103.

14. "The Geography of Civility," *New York Times*, July 28, 1977.

15. Mahler, *Ladies and Gentlemen*, 229–30.

16. On the Village orgy, see ibid., 198; for Bard and the prayer shawls, see "Night of Terror."

17. Boeth, "The Plunderers."

18. Marshall Berman, introduction to *New York Calling: From Blackout to Bloomberg*, ed. Marshall Berman and Brian Berger (London: Reaktion Books, 2007), 9–38, quotation from 32; David Nye, *When the Lights Went Out: A History of Blackouts in America* (Cambridge, Mass.: MIT Press, 2010), 131.

19. Miriam Greenberg, *Branding New York: How a City in Crisis Was Sold to the World* (New York: Routledge, 2008), 140–41.

CHAPTER 16. "DIE YUPPIE SCUM"

1. Michael Wines, "Class Struggle Erupts along Avenue B," *New York Times*, August 10, 1988.

2. Jerome Charyn, *War Cries over Avenue C* (New York: Donald I. Fine, 1985), 7; C. Carr, "Night Clubbing: Reports from the Tompkins Square Police Riot," *Village Voice*, August 16, 1988, 17.

3. Neil Smith, "New City, New Frontier: The Lower East Side as Wild, Wild West," in *Variations on a Theme Park*, ed. Michael Sorkin (New York: Hill and Wang, 1992), 61–93. Much of the account that follows draws from this chapter. Jane Jacobs, *The Life and Death of Great American Cities* (New York: Random House, 1961).

4. Retrospectives on the riot include Neil Smith, *The New Urban Frontier: Gentrification and the Revanchist City* (New York: Routledge, 1996), chaps. 1 and 10; Smith, "The Revanchist City—New York's Homeless Wars," *Polygraph* 8 (1996): 44–63; Smith, "After Tompkins Square Park: Degentrification and the Revanchist City," in *Re-presenting the City: Ethnicity Capital, and Culture in the 21st*

Century Metropolis, ed. Anthony King (London: Macmillan, 1996), 93–107. For a longer perspective on the park and riot in the context of the Lower East Side, see Clayton Patterson, Alan Moore, and Joe Flood, *Resistance: A Radical Social and Political History of the Lower East Side* (New York: Seven Stories Books, 2007).

5. Cover, *Newsweek*, December 21, 1984. For an account from the time of yuppies and gentrification, see Joseph Barry and John Derevlany, *Yuppies Invade My House at Dinnertime: A Tale of Brunch, Bombs, and Gentrification in an American City* (Hoboken: Big River Publishing, 1997).

6. Carr, "Night Clubbing"; Sarah Ferguson, "The Boombox Wars," *Village Voice*, August 16, 1988.

7. "A Talk with Allen Ginsberg," *New Common Good*, September 1988, 7.

8. Ferguson, "Boombox Wars"; Leslie Gervitz, "Slam Dancer at NYPD," *Village Voice*, September 6, 1988.

9. Gervitz, "Slam Dancer"; David E. Pitt, "PBA Leader Assails Report on Tompkins Square Melee," *New York Times*, April 21, 1989.

10. Ibid.

11. Peter Marcuse, "Abandonment, Gentrification, and Displacement: The Linkages in New York City," in *Gentrification and the City*, ed. Neil Smith and Peter Williams (Winchester, Mass.: Allen and Unwin, 1986), 158–59; David Nye, *When the Lights Went Out: A History of Blackouts in America* (Cambridge, Mass.: MIT Press, 2010), 131.

12. On the homeless crisis in New York, see (among any number of others) Kim Hopper, *Reckoning with Homelessness* (Ithaca, N.Y.: Cornell University Press, 2003).

13. Bill Tabb, *The Long Default* (New York: Monthly Review Press, 1982); Joshua Freeman, *Working Class New York: Life and Labor since World War II* (New York: New Press, 2000), 256.

14. Walter Robinson and Carlo McCormick, "Slouching toward Avenue D," *Art in America* 72, no. 6 (1984): 134–62; Rosalyn Deutsche and Cara Gendel Ryan, "The Fine Art of Gentrification," *October* 13 (1984): 91–111; Nicolas Moufarrege, "Another Wave, Still More Savagely Than the First: The Lower East Side, 1982," *Arts* 57, no. 1 (1982): 69–73; Anne E. Bowler and Blaine McBurney, "Gentrification and the Avant Garde in New York's East Village: The Good, the Bad, and the Ugly," *Theory and Culture* 8 (1991): 49–77.

15. In general, see Neil Smith, "New Globalism, New Urbanism: Gentrification as Global Urban Strategy," *Antipode* 34 (2002):

334–57; on the privatization of Central Park, see Roy Rosenzweig and Elizabeth Blackmar, *The Park and the People: A History of Central Park* (Ithaca, N.Y.: Cornell University Press, 1992); Cindi Katz, "Whose Nature, Whose Culture? Private Production of Space and the 'Preservation' of Nature," in *Remaking Reality: Nature at the Millennium*, ed. Bruce Braun and Noel Castree (London: Routledge, 1998), 46–63. On Bryant Park, see Sharon Zukin, *The Cultures of Cities* (Oxford: Blackwell, 1995). On Union Square, see Deirdre Carmody, "New Day Is Celebrated for Union Square Park," *New York Times*, April 20, 1984.

16. Smith, "New City, New Frontier," 65; Charyn, *War Cries over Avenue C*, 7; Joel Rose and Catherine Texier, eds., *Between Avenues C & D: New Writing from the Lower East Side Fiction Magazine* (New York: Penguin, 1988), xi; Carr, "Night Clubbing."

17. Pitt, "BPA Leader Assails Report."

18. Sarah Ferguson, "Squatters' Victory? Protesters Piss Off Demolition Crew—for Now," *Village Voice*, May 9, 1989.

19. James C. McKinley Jr., "City Moves to Clean Up Tompkins Sq. after Raid," *New York Times*, July 7, 1989.

20. Bill Weinberg, "Is Gentrification Genocide? Squatters Build an Alternative Vision for the Lower East Side," *Downtown*, February 14, 1990.

21. Smith, "New City, New Frontier," 63.

22. J. Kifner, "New York Closes Park to Homeless," *New York Times*, June 4, 1991; Sarah Ferguson, "The Park Is Gone," *Village Voice*, June 18, 1991; Ferguson, "Should Tompkins Square Be Like Gramercy?," *Village Voice*, June 11, 1991; Smith, *New Urban Frontier*, 608.

23. Marian Axel-Lute, "The Battle for 13th St," Shelterforce Online, May–June 1995, http://www.nhi.org/online/issues/81/squat.html.

BENSONHURST, 1989

1. Ralph Blumenthal, "Black Youth Is Killed by Whites; Brooklyn Attack Is Called Racial," *New York Times*, August 25, 1989. Though scurrilous in many ways, Lorrin Anderson's "Cracks in the Mosaic," *National Review*, June 26, 1990, provides a good sense not just of what happened but especially of the highly racially charged atmosphere of New York at the time.

2. Robert McFadden, "Black Man Dies after Beating by Whites in Queens," *New York Times*, December 21, 1986; Ronald Smothers, "1,200 Protesters of Racial Attack March in Queens," *New York Times*, December 28, 1986; Vicky Monroe, "The Murder of Yusuf Hawkins: Bias Crimes and a Neighborhood on Trial," in *Crimes and Trials of the Century*, ed. Stephen Chermak and Frakie Y. Bailey (Westport, Conn.: Greenwood Publishing, 2007), 2:79–100; J. DeSantis, *For the Color of His Skin: The Murder of Yusuf Hawkins and the Trial of Bensonhurst* (New York: Pharos Books, 1991).

3. Andrew Sullivan, "The Two Faces of Bensonhurst: A Report from the Neighborhood," *New Republic*, July 2, 1980; Anderson, "Cracks in the Mosaic"; Monroe, "Murder of Yusuf Hawkins," 85–86.

4. John Kifner, "Bensonhurst Aftermath; after 2d Bensonhurst Verdict, a March amid Cries for Calm," *New York Times*, May 20, 1990.

5. Sewell Chan, "The Death of Yusuf Hawkins," *New York Times*, City Blog, August 21, 2009.

RIOT OR POGROM?

1. Henry Goldschmidt, *Race and Religion among the Chosen Peoples of Crown Heights* (New Brunswick, N.J.: Rutgers University Press, 2006), 5, 18; Philip Kasinitz, *Caribbean New York: Immigrants and the Politics of New York* (Ithaca, N.Y.: Cornell University Press, 1992), 121. Anna Deavere Smith's one-woman play on the Crown Heights riot is based on extensive interviews with neighborhood residents and some of those active in the riots: *Fires in the Mirror: Crown Heights, Brooklyn, and Other Identities* (New York: Anchor Books, 1993).

2. This and the next paragraph are based on Edward S. Shapiro, *Blacks, Jews, and the Brooklyn Riot* (Lebanon, N.H.: Brandeis University Press / University Press of New England, 2006), 2–5.

3. For a glimpse of how strained the relations were, see Reverend Herbert D. Daughtry Sr., *No Monopoly on Suffering: Blacks and Jews in Crown Heights (and Elsewhere)* (Trenton, N.J.: Africa World Press, 1997). This and the next two paragraphs are based on Goldschmidt, *Race and Religion*, 43–46.

4. Shapiro, *Blacks, Jews*, 9–11.

5. Goldschmidt, *Race and Religion*, 68–69.

6. Shapiro, *Blacks, Jews*, 42–43.

7. Ibid., 115–27.

8. Goldschmidt, *Race and Religion*, 71–74.

THE MILLION COP MARCH, 1998

1. Manning Marable, "Harlem and the Racial Imagination:

Reflections on the Million Youth March," *Souls*, Winter 1999, 6–15; Neil Smith and Richard Schaffer, "The Gentrification of Harlem?," *Annals of the Association of American Geographers* 76 (1986): 347–65.

2. Marable, "Harlem and the Racial Imagination," 11.

3. Abby Goodnough, "Confrontation in Harlem: The Overview," *New York Times*, September 7, 1998.

4. Marable, "Harlem and the Racial Imagination," 12; Neil Smith, "Giuliani Time," *Social Text* 57 (1998): 1–20.

5. James C. McKinley Jr. "Officers Rally and Dinkins Is Their Target," *New York Times*, September 17, 1992.

6. Goodnough, "Confrontation in Harlem"; Dan Barry, "Confrontation in Harlem: The Overview," *New York Times*, September 6, 1998; Marable, "Harlem and the Racial Imagination," 14.

7. Goodnough, "Confrontation in Harlem"; Barry, "Confrontation in Harlem"; Michael O. Allen et al., "Ugly End to Calm Rally: Some Say NYPD Was Overzealous," *New York Daily News*, September 6, 1998.

8. Allen et al., "Ugly End"; Mike Allen, "Confrontation in Harlem: The Mayor," *New York Times*, September 6, 1998; Bob Herbert, "In America; an Insult to Harlem," *New York Times*, September 7, 1998.

9. Marable, "Harlem in the Racial Imagination," 15.

GIULIANI'S PLOT

1. Jodi Wilgoren, "Bulldozers Raze a Garden in Harlem," *New York Times*, November 3, 1998.

2. Histories of community gardening in New York City abound. The place to start is P. L. Wilson and B. Wienberg, eds., *Avant Gardening: Ecological Struggle in the City and the World* (New York: Automedia, 1999); geographic takes include Karen Schmeltzkopf, "Urban Community Gardens and Contested Spaces," *Geographical Review* 85 (1995): 364–81; Schmeltzkopf, "Incommensurability, Land Use, and the Right to Space: Community Gardens in New York City," *Urban Geography* 23 (2002): 323–43; Lynn A. Staeheli, Don Mitchell, and Kristina Gibson, "Conflicting Rights to the City in New York's Community Gardens," *GeoJournal* 58 (2002): 197–205.

3. Schmeltzkopf, "Incommensurability," 328; Staeheli, Mitchell, and Gibson, "Conflicting Rights," 198.

4. Anne Raver, "Auction Plan for Gardens Stirs Tensions," *New York Times*, January 11, 1999; Schmeltzkopf, "Incommensurability," 328. The number of gardens put up for auction varies by source.

5. Dan Barry, "Garden-Lovers Arrested at City Hall Sit-In," *New York Times*, February 25, 1999; Anne Raver, "Hundreds Gather to Protest City's Auction of Garden Lots," *New York Times*, April 11, 1999; David M. Herszenhorn, "Protesters Fight Auctioning of Community Gardens," *New York Times*, May 6, 1999; Lynn Staeheli and Don Mitchell, *The People's Property? Power, Politics, and the Public* (New York: Routledge, 2008), chap. 5.

6. Schmeltzkopf, "Incommensurability," 329–30; Christopher M. Smith and Hilda E. Kurtz, "Community Gardens and the Politics of Scale in New York City," *Geographical Review* 93 (2003): 193–212.

7. Douglas Martin, "Bulldozers Uproot Community Gardens," *New York Times*, June 29, 1999; Project Harmony, http://www .projectharmonynyc.org/extended-chronology.php.

8. C. J. Chivers, "After Uprooting Gardeners, City Razes a Garden," *New York Times*, February 16, 2000; "Death of a Garden," *New York Times*, February 17, 2000; "Crowd Storms Former Garden to Protest Bulldozing by City," *New York Times*, March 6, 2000; Colin Moynihan, "Neighborhood Report: East Village: Construction at Garden Site Shakes Co-op, Members Say," *New York Times*, September 10, 2000; Global Nonviolent Action Database, "New Yorkers Attempt to Prevent Garden Demolition (El Jardin de la Esperanza), 1999–2000," http://nvdatabase .swathmore.edu.

9. Neil Smith, *New Urban Frontier: Gentrification and the Revanchist City* (New York: Routledge, 1996).

CHAPTER 17. RECLAIMING THE STREETS

1. Manuel Callahan, "Zapatismo and Global Struggle: A Revolution to Make a Revolution Possible," in *Confronting Capitalism*, ed. Eddie Yeun, Daniel Burton-Rose, and Geiorge Katsiaficas (New York: Soft Skull Press, 2003), 11–18, esp. 13.

2. See https://www.nadir.org/nadir/initiativ/agp/en/.

3. An insiders account is Stephen Duncombe, "Stepping Off the Sidewalk: Reclaim the Streets / NYC," in *From Act Up to the WTO*, ed. Ron Hayduk and Ben Shepard (London: Verso, 2002), 215–28. RTS London explains how to host a street party at http://rts .gn.apc.org/sortit.htm. Neil Strauss, "Pirate Radio in Touch with the Village Not the F.C.C.," *New York Times*, February 27, 1996.

4. Duncombe, "Stepping Off the Sidewalk."

5. The ur-text of situationism is Guy Debord, *The Society of the Spectacle*, trans. Donald Nicholson-Smith (New York: Zone Books, 1994). An excellent "secret" history of situationism in the twentieth century is Greil Marcus, *Lipstick Traces* (Cambridge, Mass.: Har-

vard University Press, 1989). See Hakim Bey, *TAZ: The Temporary Autonomous Zone, Ontological Anarchy, Poetic Terrorism* (New York: Automedia, 2003); George McKay, ed., *DiY Culture: Party and Protest in Nineties Britain* (London: Verso, 1998); Naomi Klein, *No Logo: Taking Aim at the Brand Bullies* (New York: Picador, 2000).

6. Duncombe, "Stepping Off the Sidewalk," 221–22.

7. Brooke Lehman, "Organizing for the WTO" (master's thesis, Institute for Social Ecology, Plainfield, Vermont, 2000).

8. http://times-up.org/ongoing-demonstrations/reclaim-streets; Katherine E. Finkelstein, "45 Arrested in a Protest against Capitalism," *New York Times*, November 27, 1999.

9. Lehman, *Organizing for the WTO*; Francesca Polletta, *Freedom Is an Endless Meeting: Democracy in American Social Movements* (Chicago: University of Chicago Press, 2002).

10. In general, see David Graeber, *Direct Action: An Ethnography* (Oakland: AK Press, 2009), chap. 7.

11. A copy can be found at http://mailman.lbo-talk. org/2000/2000-February/002499.html.

12. Brooke Lehman, personal communication, May 10, 2008.

13. "Demonstrators Air Grievances; Caravan on Mohawk Land Turns Back until 'No One Is Left Behind,'" *Democracy Now!*, April 20, 2001, www.democracynow.org/2001/4/20/demonstrators _air_grievances_caravan_on_mohawk.

14. Graeber examines why in *Direct Action*.

15. On the "terrorist" designation for Reclaim the Streets and others, see Zack Furness, *One Less Car: Bicycling and the Politics of Automobility* (Philadelphia: Temple University Press, 2010), 8.

16. https://www.nadir.org/nadir/initiativ/agp/free/wef /convergence.htm.

17. The protests were well covered in the press. For one instance, see Dan Barry, "Forum in New York: Protests; at Least 38 Are Arrested, but Rally Remains Peaceful," *New York Times*, February 3, 2002.

UNION SQUARE

1. Michael Sorkin and Sharon Zukin, introduction to *After the World Trade Center: Rethinking New York City*, ed. Michael Sorkin and Sharon Zukin (New York: Routledge, 2002), viii.

2. Marshall Berman, "When Bad Things Happen to Good People," in Sorkin and Zukin, *After the World Trade Center*, 1–21, quotation from 11.

3. Amy Waldman, "After the Attacks: The Memorials; Grief Is Lessened by Sharing and Solace from Strangers," *New York Times*, September 14, 2001; Michael Kimmelman, "In the Square, a Sense of Unity; a Homegrown Memorial Brings Strangers Together," *New York Times*, September 19, 2001; Adina Schecter and Sarah Yahm, "Coming Together in Union Square," *Nation*, September 30, 2001.

4. Kimmelman, "In the Square"; Andrew Jacobs, "Peace Signs amid Calls for War," *New York Times*, September 20, 2001.

5. Andrew Jacobs, "A Nation Challenged: Notebooks; Dismantling a Memorial, Clearing a Camp Site," *New York Times*, September 21, 2001.

6. Berman, "When Bad Things," 11; Schecter and Yahm, "Coming Together"; on securing the public spaces of the city, see D. Barstow, "After the Attacks, Security: Envisioning an Expensive Future in a Brave New World of Fortress New York," *New York Times*, September 16, 2001; and Don Mitchell, *The Right to the City: Social Justice and the Fight for Public Space* (New York: Guilford, 2003), 1–3, 227–28.

NO WAR AGAINST IRAQ

1. Details of the UFPJ/NYCLU efforts at obtaining permits are derived from New York Civil Liberties Union, "Arresting Protest: A Special Report of the New York Civil Liberties Union on New York City's Policies at the February 15, 2003 Antiwar Demonstration in New York City," April 2003, 3–6. This vignette is based largely on this report.

2. For brief overviews, see Donatella Della Porta and Herbert Reiter, eds., *Policing Protest: The Control of Mass Demonstrations in Western Democracies* (Minneapolis: University of Minnesota Press, 1998); Lynn A. Staeheli and Don Mitchell, *The People's Property? Power, Politics, and the Public* (New York: Routledge, 2008), chap. 1; Alex Vitale, "From Negotiated Management to Command and Control: How the New York Police Department Polices Protest," *Policing and Society* 15 (2005): 283–304. On the World Economic Forum protests, see William K. Rashbaum and Al Baker, "A Nation Challenged: The Police; Shrewd Anticipation Helped Avert Trouble," *New York Times*, February 5, 2002.

3. Clyde Haberman, "NYC; Normal, but Not Too Normal," *New York Times*, February 11, 2003; Susan Saulny, "Court Bans Peace March in Manhattan," *New York Times*, February 11, 2003.

4. New York Civil Liberties Union, "Arresting Protest," 7–10; Robert D. McFadden, "Threats and Responses: Overview; from New York to Melbourne, Cries for Peace," *New York Times*, February 16, 2001; Shaila K. Dewan, "Protesters Say City Police Used

Rough Tactics at Rally," *New York Times*, February 19, 2003; Joyce Purnick, "Metro Matters: The Right to Assemble Hits Detours," *New York Times*, February 20, 2003; New York Civil Liberties Union, "Rights and Wrongs at the RNC: A Special Report about Police and Protest at the Republican National Convention," 2005, 2.

CONVENTIONAL PROTEST?

1. A transcript of Bush's speech is available at http://www.cnn.com/2003/US/05/01/bush.transcript/. Apparently, we have yet to reach "the day of final victory."

2. New York Civil Liberties Union, "Rights and Wrongs at the RNC: A Special Report about Police and Protest at the Republican National Convention," 2005, 11; Alex Vitale, "From Negotiated Management to Command and Control: How the New York Police Department Polices Protest," *Policing and Society* 15 (2005): 283–304.

3. By 2008 the city was furiously revising its official crowd estimates in reaction to a series of lawsuits and a large settlement stemming from the denial of permits in 2004. See Jim Dwyer, "Great Lawn: A Bubble of History Bursts," *New York Times*, July 23, 2008.

4. Randal C. Archibald, "Preparing for the Convention: Demonstrations; Days of Protest, Vigils, and Street Theater (Thongs Too)," *New York Times*, August 26, 2004.

5. Diane Cardwell, "Preparing for the Convention: Demonstrations; for Convention, Protests Start Early, as Do Arrests," *New York Times*, August 27, 2004.

6. New York Civil Liberties Union, "Rights and Wrongs"; Randal C. Archibald, "Preparing for the Convention: Protesters; 100 Cyclists Are Arrested as Thousands Ride in Protest," *New York Times*, August 28, 2004.

7. Diane Cardwell and Marc Santora, "At Least 900 Arrested as Protesters Clash with Police," *New York Times*, September 1, 2004; William K. Washbaum and Michael Wilson, "Barricades Help Officers Keep Crowds Corralled," *New York Times*, September 1, 2004.

8. New York Civil Liberties Union, "Rights and Wrongs."

9. Adam Martin, "Illegally Arrested RNC Protesters Finally Getting Paid," *New York Magazine*, January 15, 2014; Colin Campbell, "De Blasio 'Glad' City Agreed to Settle RNC Arrest Suit Lawsuit," *Observer*, January 24, 2015.

CRITICAL MASS, 2004–2006

1. "Judge Dismisses New York's Bid to Force Bike Rally to Get Permit," Associated Press, December 24, 2004; Charles Komanoff and Time's Up! Environmental Organization, "Cost Analysis of Government Expenditures to Suppress Critical Mass Bike Rides," New York, 2006; both quoted in Zack Furness, *One Less Car: Bicycling and the Politics of Automobility* (Philadelphia: Temple University Press, 2010), 2–3.

2. Furness, *One Less Car*, 1; Susan Blickstein, "Automobility and the Politics of Bicycling in New York City," *International Journal of Urban and Regional Research* 34 (2010): 886–905, quotation from 891.

3. Furness, *One Less Car*, 1.

4. Ibid., 104.

5. Blickstein, "Automobility," 894–95.

6. Ibid., 898–99.

7. Ibid., 901–2.

CHAPTER 18. FROM LADY LIBERTY'S FIRE

1. Susanne Jonas, "Reflections on the Great Immigration Battle of 2006 and the Future of the Americas," *Social Justice* 33 (2006): 6–20.

2. David Harvey, "The Urban Process under Capitalism: A Framework for Analysis," *International Journal of Urban and Regional Research* 2 (1978): 101–31; Neil Smith, *The New Urban Frontier: Gentrification and the Revanchist City* (New York: Routledge, 1996).

3. Margaret R. Somers, *Genealogies of Citizenship: Markets, Statelessness, and the Right to Have Rights* (Cambridge: Cambridge University Press, 2008).

4. Nancy Foner, *New Immigrants in New York* (New York: Columbia University Press, 2001); Joshua Freeman, *Working Class New York: Life and Labor since World War II* (New York: New Press, 2000).

5. Foner, *New Immigrants*; Philip Kasinitz, *Caribbean New York: Immigrants and the Politics of New York City* (Ithaca, N.Y.: Cornell University Press, 1992); Eric Tang, "Collateral Damage: Southeast Asian Poverty in the United States," *Social Text* 62 (2000): 55–79.

6. Nina Bernstein, "An Eclectic Crowd Joins a Call for the Rights of Immigrants," *New York Times*, April 11, 2006.

7. Rachel Swarns, "Immigrants Rally in Scores of Cities for Legal Status," *New York Times*, April 11, 2006.

8. Sarah Ferguson, "Marcher: I'm Left with Nothing," *Village Voice Blogs*, April 11, 2006. http://blogs.villagevoice.com /runinscared/archives/2006/04/marcher_im_left.php; Fahd Ahmed and Monami Maulik, "The War Abroad and the War at Home: Immigrant and Black Communities at Stake," *Critical Resistance Magazine* (2008), posted at http://www.drumnation .org/DRUM/Media/Pages/CR_Article.html. More generally, see Lorraine Minnite, "Outside the Circle: The Impact of Post-9/11 Responses on Immigrant Communities in New York," in *Contentious City: The Politics of Recovery in New York City*, ed. John Mollenkopf (New York: Russell Sage Foundation, 2005), 165–204; Immanuel Ness, *Immigrants, Unions, and the New U.S. Labor Market* (Philadelphia: Temple University Press, 2005).

9. United for Peace and Justice, "Fri 4/7, 11 am Press Conference: Immigrants and Anti-war Movements Unite," April 7, 2006 (no longer available online).

10. Bernstein, "An Eclectic Crowd"; Toussant and Mamdough quoted in Amy Goodman, "Immigrant Rights Protests Rock the Country: Up to 2 Million Take to the Streets in the Largest Wave of Demonstrations in U.S. History," *Democracy Now*, April 11, 2006.

11. Nicholas DeGenova, "The Production of Culprits: From Deportability to Detainability in the Aftermath of 'Homeland Security,'" *Citizenship Studies* 11 (2007): 421–48; Paul Vitello, "Path to Deportation Can Start with a Traffic Stop," *New York Times*, April 14, 2006; Terry Frieden and Mike Ahlers, "Hundreds Seized in Immigration Raids," CNN.com, April 19, 2006; Raquel Aldana, "Of Katz and 'Aliens': Privacy Expectations and the Immigration Raids," *UC Davis Law Review* 41 (2008): 1081–1136.

12. National Network for Immigration and Refugee Rights, "Portrait of Injustice: The Impact of Immigration Raids on Families, Workers, and Communities," Oakland, 1998; Arnoldo Garcia and Laura Rivas, "Injustice for All: The Rise of the U.S. Immigration Policing Regime," National Network for Immigrant and Refugee Rights, http://www.nnirr.org/hurricane/Injustice_for_All. pdf; Jonas, "Reflections on the Great Immigration Battle of 2006"; Tram Nguyen, *We Are All Suspects Now: Untold Stories from Immigrant Communities after 9/11* (Boston: Beacon Press, 2005); on earlier immigration sweeps, see Juan Ramón García, *Operation Wetback: The Mass Deportation of Mexican Undocumented Workers in 1954* (Westport, Conn.: Greenwood Press, 1980); Camille Guerin-Gonzales, *Mexican Workers and American Dreams: Immigration, Repatriation and California Farm Labor, 1900–1939*

(New Brunswick, N.J.: Rutgers University Press, 1994); Kelly Lytle Hernández, *Migra: A History of the U.S. Border Patrol* (Berkeley: University of California Press, 2010).

13. See http://www.may1.info/archives/2006-archives/.

14. Vitor Narro, Kent Wong, and Janna Shadduck-Hernández, "Immigrant Uprising: Origins and Future," *New Labor Forum* 16 (2007): 49–56; Darryl Fears and N. C. Aizenman, "Immigrant Groups Split on Boycott," *Washington Post*, April 14, 2006; Leslie Casimir, "City to See Two Worker Rallies," *New York Daily News*, March 30, 2006; Daniela Gerson, "Bloomberg Warns against Strike by illegal Immigrants," *Sun*, April 17, 2006. On the AFL-CIO / Change to Win split, see David Bacon, "Equality or Not," *Truth Out*, March 3, 2006.

15. Michelle O'Donnell, "Thousands Turn Out but Support Is Mixed among New York's Immigrants," *New York Times*, May 2, 2006.

16. Zahida Pirani, "New York City Immigrant Organizing and the Call for Immigrant Rights," *Lines* 5, no. 1–2 (2006).

17. A useful compilation of May 1, 2006, events by location (though one that undercounts events and number of participants in New York City) is Xóchitl Bada, Jonathan Fox, Elvia Zazueta, and Ingrid García, "Immigrant Rights Marches, Spring, 2006," database, Woodrow Wilson Center, cached on Google. On detention of Pakistanis in Jackson Heights, see Nguyen, *We Are All Suspects Now*.

18. O'Donnell, "Thousands Turn Out"; Hugh Son, "Immigrants to Link Hands: Protest Set for Jackson Heights," *New York Daily News*, May 1, 2006.

19. Sarah Ferguson, "A Day without White People," *Village Voice*, April 25, 2006, http://www.villagevoice.com/news/a-day -without-white-people-6428022 (though dated April 25, this article reports on the May Day Union Square rally).

20. Janice Fine, *Workers Centers: Organizing Communities at the Edge of the Dream* (Ithaca, N.Y.: Cornell University Press, 2006).

21. Jenna Loyd, Matt Mitchelson, and Andrew Burridge, eds., *Beyond Walls and Cages: Building Movements of Liberation and Social Justice across Borders* (Athens: University of Georgia Press, 2012).

CHAPTER 19. OCCUPY WALL STREET

1. This chapter is based primarily on the experiences of the authors, who were deeply involved in the Occupy movement.

2. Colin Moynihan, "Wall Street Protest Begins, with Demonstrators Blocked," City Room Blog, *New York Times*, September 17, 2011, http://cityroom.blogs.nytimes.com/2011/09/17/wall-street-protest-begins-with-demonstrators-blocked/?_r=0.

3. Sam Stein, "Sites Speak Louder Than Words: Occupy Wall Street and New York City," *Progressive Planning Magazine* 190 (2012): 2, 7–8. On POPS generally, see Jerold Kayden, *Privately Owned Public Space: The New York City Experience* (New York: Wiley, 2000); Kristen Miller, *Designs on the Public: The Private Lives of New York's Public Spaces* (Minneapolis: University of Minnesota Press, 2007).

4. Ben Fractenberg, "Zuccotti Park Cannot Be Closed to Wall Street Protesters, NYPD Says," DNA Info blog, September 28, 2011, https://www.dnainfo.com/new-york/20110928/downtown/zuccotti-park-cant-be-closed-wall-street-protesters-nypd-says.

5. Nathan Schneider, *Thank You Anarchy!* (Berkeley: University of California Press, 2013), 28.

6. For an empathetic discussion, see Stanley Rogouski, "The Untouchables of Zuccotti Park," *Counterpunch*, November 30, 2011, http://www.counterpunch.org/2011/11/30/the-untouchables-of-zuccotti-park/.

7. "The FBI vs. Occupy: Secret Docs Reveal 'Counter Terrorism' Monitoring of OWS from Its Earliest Days," *Democracy Now!*, December 27, 2012, http://www.democracynow.org/2012/12/27/the_fbi_vs_occupy_secret_docs; Beau Hodai, *Dissent or Terror: How the Nation's Counter Terrorism Apparatus in Partnership with Corporate America Turned on Occupy Wall Street* (n.p.: Center for Media and Democracy / DBA Press, 2013), available as a link in Lisa Graves, "How the Government Targeted Occupy," *In These Times*, May 21, 2013, http://inthesetimes.com/article/15028/how_the_government_targeted_occupy.

8. Kim Severson, "Davis Is Executed," *New York Times*, September 22, 2011; Dominique Zonyee Scott, "In Union Square Tonight, a Protest against the Execution of Troy Davis," *Local East Village*, September 22, 2011, http://eastvillage.thelocal.nytimes.com/2011/09/22/in-union-square-tonight-a-protest-against-the-execution-of-troy-davis/.

9. http://occupywallstreet.org/article/at-least-six-arrested-in-solidarity-march-for-troy/ (site no longer exists).

10. Schneider, *Thank You Anarchy!*, 38–39; Manissa McCleave Maharawal, "So Real It Hurts," in *Dreaming in Public: Building the Occupy Movement*, ed. Amy Schrader Lang and Daniel Lang/Levitsky (Oxford: New Internationalist Publications, 2012), 154–60; Maharawal, "Reflections from the People of Color Caucus at Occupy Wall Street," in *We Are Many: Reflections on Movement Strategy from Occupation to Liberation*, ed. Kate Khatib, Margaret Killjoy, and Mike McGuire (Oakland: AK Press, 2012); Sonny Singh, "Occupying Process and Processing Occupy: Spokes Council Musings by One POC," in Lang and Lang/Levitsky, *Dreaming in Public*, 121–24.

11. Olivia Katrandjian, "Occupy Wall Street Movement Reports 80 Arrested in Today's Protest," ABC News, http://abcnews.go.com/blogs/headlines/2011/09/occupy-wall-street-movement-reports-80-arrested-today-in-protests/.

12. http://anoncentral.tumblr.com/post/10690792721/attention-occupywallstreet-badcop-d)x-target.

13. Lauri Apple, "Lawsuit Filed over Brooklyn Bridge Mass Arrests," *Gawker*, October 5, 2011, http://gawker.com/5846793/lawsuit-filed-over-brooklyn-bridge-mass-arrest; "700 Arrested on Brooklyn Bridge as Occupy Wall Street Enters Third Week, Protest Grows Nationwide," *Democracy Now!*, October 3, 2011, http://www.democracynow.org/2011/10/3/700_arrested_on_brooklyn_bridge_as.

14. "Occupy Wall Street Protesters Believe Zuccotti Park Cleaning a Ploy to End Occupation," *Huffington Post*, October 13, 2011, http://www.huffingtonpost.com/2011/10/13/bloomberg-tells-occupywal_n_1008767.html. For an analysis of the script Brookfield and the city were following—which was pioneered in clearing out homeless encampments—see the 2014 postscript to Don Mitchell, *The Right to the City: Social Justice and the Fight for Public Space* (New York: Guilford, 2014), 238–46.

15. "Occupy Wall Street Protesters Claim Victory in Zuccotti Park Standoff," *Guardian*, October 14, 2011, http://www.theguardian.com/world/2011/oct/14/occupy-wall-street-protesters-zuccotti.

16. Colin Moynihan and Cara Buckley, "Cleanup of Zuccotti Park Is Postponed," City Room Blog, *New York Times*, October 14, 2011, http://cityroom.blogs.nytimes.com/2011/10/14/cleanup-of-zuccotti-park-cancelled/?_r=0.

17. Alan Taylor, "Occupy Wall Street Spreads Worldwide," *Atlantic*, October 17, 2011, http://www.theatlantic.com/photo/2011/10/occupy-wall-street-spreads-worldwide/100171/.

18. Colleen Long and Varena Dobnik, "Zuccotti Park Eviction: Police Arrest 200 Occupy Wall Street Protesters," *Huffington Post*,

November 15, 2011, http://www.huffingtonpost.com/2011/11/15 /zuccotti-park-eviction-p0_n_1094306.html.

19. Astra Taylor, "After the Eviction," *n+1*, November 15, 2011, https://nplusonemag.com/online-only/occupy/after-the-eviction/.

20. "New York Court Upholds Eviction of Occupy Protesters," CNN, November 16, 2011, http://www.cnn.com/2011/11/15/us /new-york-occupy-eviction/index.html.

AFTERWORD. EARLY 2017

1. Eli Rosenberg, "Protest Grows 'out of Nowhere' at Kennedy Airport after Iraqis Are Detained," *New York Times*, January 28, 2017.

2. Peter Baker, "Travelers Stranded and Protests Swell over Trump Order," *New York Times*, January 29, 2017; Niraj Chokshi and Nicholas Fandos, "Demonstrators in the Streets, and Airports, Protest Immigration Order," *New York Times*, January 30, 2017; Nicholas Kulish, Caitlin Dickerson, and Charlie Savage, "Court Temporarily Blocks Trump's Travel Ban, and Airlines Are Told to Allow Passengers," *New York Times*, February 4, 2017; Adam Liptak, "Justice Dept. Drops Travel Ban Case, but Says a New Order Is Coming," *New York Times*, February 17, 2017.

3. Christopher Mele and Annie Correal, "'Not Our President': Protests Spread after Donald Trump's Election," *New York Times*, November 9, 2017; Jonah Enge Bromwich, "Protests of Trump's Election Continue into Third Day," *New York Times*, November 11, 2017.

4. Marc Santora, "Inauguration Protests Held at Trump Tower and Elsewhere," *New York Times*, January 19, 2017.

5. Susan Chira and Yamiche Alcindor, "Defiant Voices Flood U.S. Cities as Women Rally for Rights," *New York Times*, January 21, 2017.

6. Madina Toure, "NYC Students Skip Classes to Protest Trump," *Observer*, February 7, 2017.

7. Liz Robbins, "Even before Trump Acts on Immigration, New Yorkers Protest," *New York Times*, January 26, 2017.

8. Histories of the origins of the #BlackLivesMatter movement abound. Particularly enlightening is the interview with #BlackLivesMatter instigator Patrisse Cullors by Jordan Camp and Christina Heatherton in their *Policing the Planet* (New York: Verso, 2016); see also Kendra Pierre-Louise, "The Women behind Black Lives Matter," *In These Times*, January 22, 2015.

9. Sarah Kaufman, "Black Lives Matter Protesters Clash with Cops in Midtown Manhattan," *NY Patch*, July 8, 2016.

10. George Joseph, "NYPD Sent Undercover Officers to Black Lives Matter Protest, Records Reveal," *Guardian*, September 29, 2016; Vitoria Bekiempis and Thomas Tracy, "Black Lives Matter Says NYPD Spied on Group during Garner Protest," *New York Daily News*, December 8, 2016.

11. S. 103, Local Zoning Decisions Protection Act of 2017, § 3, January 11, 2017.

12. Ben Norton, "Black Lives Matter Activists Launch Abolition Square Encampment, Demanding Reparations, End to Broken Windows Policing," *Salon.com*, August 5, 2016.

13. Benjamin Ellington Patterson, "How the Black Lives Matter Movement Is Mobilizing against Trump," *Mother Jones*, February 7, 2017.

14. "Revolution," in *Shorter Oxford English Dictionary*; Raymond Williams, *Keywords* (London: Fontana, 1976).

CONTRIBUTORS

Marnie Brady holds a PhD in sociology from the Graduate Center of City University of New York and works in digital and experiential teaching and learning at Macaulay Honors College, CUNY, and writing in the social sciences at the NYU Gallatin School of Individualized Studies. Her research examines municipal power in housing and labor confrontations with large-scale financial actors. Brady's dozen years of work in public policy and community organizing included negotiating permits and protest routes for the 2006 immigrant rights mobilizations in Washington, D.C.

Kathleen Dunn is an assistant professor of sociology at Loyola University Chicago whose research focuses on inequality and social justice in the fields of urban sociology, race, class, gender and sexuality, and new labor studies. She is at work on a book based on a multiyear study of criminalization and gentrification within the street-vending industry in New York City.

Zoltán Glück is a PhD candidate in anthropology at the CUNY Graduate Center. His work has been supported by the Social Science Research Council, the Fulbright IIE, the Wenner-Gren Foundation, and the Antipode Foundation. His writing has appeared in *Environment and Planning D: Society and Space*, *Anthropology Now*, and *Anthropological Theory* (forthcoming) and in several edited volumes. Zoltán is also a member of the editorial collective at *Focaal: A Journal of Global and Historical Anthropology*.

Rachel Goffe is a PhD candidate in geography at the Graduate Center of the City University of New York. She was inspired by her experience as a practicing architect to understand the processes through which the built environment changes, becoming engaged with community struggles over the vision for Philadelphia. Her research focuses on how emerging land policy is challenging a long-standing tradition of informal settlements in Jamaica, where she grew up.

Harmony Goldberg is currently the U.S. Movement Education Fellow at the Bertha Foundation, where she is developing political education programs for social movement organizations in the United States. Goldberg received her PhD in cultural anthropology from the City University of New York Graduate Center, where her research focused on organizing among domestic workers in New York City and the development of class politics and labor organizing in the twenty-first century.

Amanda Huron is an assistant professor of interdisciplinary social sciences at the University of the District of Columbia in Washington, D.C. Her research interests include urban geography, the urban commons, affordable housing, and the history of Washington, D.C. Her first book, *Practicing the Urban Commons: Limited-Equity Cooperatives in Washington, D.C.* (2018), examines the challenges of creating and maintaining commons within the capitalist city.

Malav Kanuga is a doctoral candidate in anthropology at the City University of New York and founding editor of Common Notions, an independent publishing and programming house based at the Interference Archive in Brooklyn. His research focuses on space, culture, and power in the making of the Indian metropolis through historical and contemporary struggles around informality and planning. He has taught in various university settings in addition to a range of autonomous education initiatives.

Esteban Kelly is the executive director of the U.S. Federation of Worker Cooperatives and a founding worker-owner in AORTA (Anti-Oppression Resource & Training Alliance), a cooperative whose consulting supports organizations fighting for intersectional social justice and a solidarity economy. Esteban is a mayoral appointee to the Philly Food Policy Advisory Council and recently worked at the New Economy Coalition. His work brings together community organizers, elected officials, and developers to scale workplace democracy and worker-owned cooperative enterprise.

Manissa M. Maharawal is an assistant professor of anthropology at American University in Washington, D.C. Her research looks at political subjectivity, social movements, and urban space. She is the cofounder of the Narratives of Displacement and Resistance oral history project in San Francisco as part of the Anti-Eviction Mapping Project. She has forthcoming articles in *Anthropological Theory* and *Annals of the Association of American Geographers*.

Don Mitchell is professor of cultural geography at Uppsala University, Sweden, and distinguished professor emeritus at Syracuse University in New York. He is the author of *They Saved the Crops: Labor, Landscape, and the Struggle over Industrial Farming in Bracero-Era California* (2012), *The People's Property? Power, Politics and the Public* (2003, with Lynn A. Staeheli), and *The Right to the City: Social Justice and the Fight for Public Space* (2003), among many other works.

Justin Sean Myers is assistant professor of sociology at Marist College. His research utilizes historical and qualitative methods to examine how marginalized communities are organizing against environmental and food inequities. This scholarship has appeared in the journals *Agriculture & Human Values*, *Geoforum*, and *Environmental Sociology* and in the book *Ten Lessons in Introductory Sociology*. He is currently writing a book on the food justice movement for Rutgers University Press entitled *Beyond Access: Food Justice and Urban Agriculture in Brooklyn*.

Brendan P. O'Malley is an assistant professor of history at Newbury College in Brookline, Massachusetts. He studies U.S. immigration history, as well as the history of capitalism, U.S. politics, and New York City. He is currently at work on a book manuscript titled "The Immigrant State: New York and the Origins of Immigration Regulation."

Raymond Pettit is completing his doctorate in anthropology at the CUNY Graduate Center. His research focuses on infrastructure, nature, and place marketing in the history of the Cincinnati riverfront. Past work includes "Predictions and Local History in Cincinnati, 1815–1912" in *Ohio Valley History* (2011). Raymond currently works for ROC United, with previous experience at the Cincinnati Art Museum and Argentine Forensic Anthropology Team.

Miguelina Rodriguez is an urban sociology professor at LaGuardia Community College and holds a PhD from the Edward J. Bloustein School of Planning and Public Policy at Rutgers University. Her interest focuses on gentrification and race, specifically the phenomenon's effect on the second-generation Dominican population in Washington Heights. Outside of academia, Professor Rodriguez and her twin sister, Professor Griselda Rodriguez (CCNY), run a lifestyle platform called @BrujasofBrooklyn, centered on womyn's holistic healing, specifically via womb-wellness.

JenJoy Roybal is an artist, activist, and writer living in Brooklyn. She writes for Arts in Bushwick (*Precarious Constructs: A Dance with the Maelstrom*, 2017); organizes with the Brooklyn Rebels, a citizen action hub; and is part of the review team for the Buckminster Fuller Challenge, a prize program that awards projects trying to solve some of the world's most pressing problems.

Mcnair Scott is a longtime Bushwick resident interested in building movement infrastructure, tactics, and strategies for the long haul. He has been deeply involved with the Direct Action Network, Indymedia, Bluestockings, and riseup.net and has worked with the United Nations in West Africa. He is a founding member of the Mayday Collective, which runs the Mayday community space, bar, and café in Bushwick.

Erin Siodmak received her PhD in sociology from the CUNY Graduate Center. She likes to study art, film, social theory, cities, geography, gender, and a lot more. Her dissertation was on performance and installation art, politics, and development in New York, New Orleans, and Detroit.

Neil Smith (1954–2012) was one of the most influential spatial theorists and radical geographers of his generation. He was the author of *Uneven Development: Nature, Capital, and the Production of Space* (1984/2008), *The New Urban Frontier: Gentrification and the Revanchist City* (1996), *American Empire: Roosevelt's Geographer and the Prelude to Globalization* (2003), and *The End Game of Globalization* (2005), among so much more. At the time of his death he was working on a book on the geography of revolution. *Revolting New York* grew out of a seminar on urban revolution he taught at the Graduate Center of the City University of New York, where he was distinguished professor of geography and anthropology and the founding director of the Center for Place, Culture, and Politics.

Peter Waldman is a teacher, teacher educator, and education scholar. His research interests include critical special education, social model dis/ability studies, addiction and treatment/recovery, and narrative and hermeneutic-phenomenological research methodologies. His book *Educating Desire* (2015) is a first-person narrative account of a meeting of Alcoholics Anonymous and a situated exploration into the lived experience of addiction. He lives in New York City.

Nicole Watson, JD, MA, MS, is a social science analyst at the U.S. Department of Housing and Urban Development's Office of Policy Development and Research. Coming from a multidisciplinary background in law, applied statistics, and the social sciences, her work focuses on the evolving dynamics of housing insecurity and its consequences. Nicole recently coauthored the *Worst Case Housing Needs* (2017) report to Congress.

INDEX

GEOGRAPHIES OF JUSTICE AND SOCIAL TRANSFORMATION